Transportation USA

Transportation USA

FREDERICK J. STEPHENSON, JR.

Department of Marketing and Distribution
University of Georgia

ADDISON-WESLEY PUBLISHING COMPANY

Reading, Massachusetts   Menlo Park, California   Don Mills, Ontario
Wokingham, England   Amsterdam   Sydney   Singapore   Tokyo
Madrid   Bogotá   Santiago   San Juan

Dedicated to:

Sharon, Katie, Jeff, David, Fred, and Ruth Stephenson.

Fred Cronhimer, Frank Smyth, Dr. A. L. Hook, Dr. Donald V. Harper, Dr. Frederick J. Beier, and Rev. Roderick Mc-Donald—all great teachers and friends who significantly influenced my life.

My University of Georgia Transportation students —individuals who have given me so much and who inspired this text.

Sponsoring Editor:	Frank Burns , Jim Heitker
Packaging Service:	Ann Kilbride/Cambridge Design Studio
Production Coordinator:	Marcia Strykowski
Text Designer:	Quadrata, Inc.
Cover Designer:	Marshall Henrichs
Art Consultant:	Joseph Vetere
Illustrator:	Capricorn Design
Manufacturing Supervisor:	Hugh Crawford

Library of Congress Cataloging in Publication Data

Stephenson, Frederick J.
    Transportation USA.

    Bibliography: p.
    Includes index.
    1. Transportation—United States. I. Title.
II. Title: Transportation USA
HE203.S675 1987   380.5'0973   84–24403
ISBN 0–201–07800–7

ABCDEFGHIJ-DO-89876

Preface

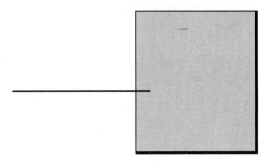

A person who spends more than four years and 3500 hours of time conceptualizing, researching, and writing a text must be motivated by compelling reasons. Mine were rather simple. Although there are many fine principles of transportation texts, no single work satisfied my teaching needs. Teaching is the primary reason I remain in academia, and if there is anything I can do to improve teaching effectiveness, I am willing to make the effort. *Transportation USA* gave me an opportunity to advance my field of study, while it simultaneously allowed me to share my teaching philosophy with other transportation instructors and students.

Consequently, *Transportation USA* was written for the following purposes:

1. To improve transportation management, strategy, and decision making.
2. To provide an interesting, thought-provoking, easy-to-read, easy-to-understand, yet challenging text that helps people to appreciate and improve U.S. transportation.
3. To enhance outstanding teaching and encourage talented, motivated individuals to seek careers in transportation and logistics.
4. To create a comprehensive single book that accurately describes and analyzes all the key elements of U.S. transportation.
5. To develop a valuable reference book particularly useful to transportation practitioners trying to stay current with today's and tomorrow's changing business needs.

Of course, writing a transportation textbook is particularly difficult because of the changing and volatile nature of the industry. While I prepared this book for press, for example, changes occurred within the fields of space exploration and general aviation. Furthermore, recent changes within the airline industry necessitated last-minute revisions in the text.

TEXT ORIENTATION

Transportation USA presents the field of transportation as an environment in which carrier managers, corporate shippers, elected and appointed government officials, and individuals make choices. Management, strategy, and decision making are its primary orientations. It attempts to identify who makes transportation decisions; why they make choices; what decisions they make; what constrains their abilities to formulate strategies, manage, and make correct choices; and how they could make better decisions. The text stresses present and future issues—that is, information and ideas pertinent to today's and tomorrow's transportation decision makers—and practical, rather than merely theoretical, concerns.

TEXT ORGANIZATION

Transportation USA contains five mini-books, which address each of the major transportation modes. The first of these mini-books focuses on railroad transportation (Chapters 5 through 7). The four other mini-books include water transportation (Chapters 8 and 9), pipeline transportation (Chapter 10), highway transportation (Chapters 11 through 13), and air transportation (Chapters 14 through 16).

Modal mini-books integrate information to provide comprehensive understanding and fast referencing. Each mini-book treats a mode as a distinct business environment in which financial, operating, marketing, and human resource strategies are discussed and decisions formulated subject to economic, regulatory, customer, competitive, energy, corporate, safety, labor, technological, and other constraints and considerations. Each mini-book is designed to be a self-contained instructional unit. Cross-references are provided, however, to valuable information contained either in other mini-books or elsewhere in the text.

TEXT CONTENTS

Transportation USA has been designed to be comprehensive. The goal has been to include significant elements of transportation and to provide sufficient details on each transportation component to clarify its role, its strengths and weaknesses, and its changing characteristics. The result is that the text covers the following: corporate, as well as personal, transportation; cargo and passenger transportation; domestic and international transportation; intercity and urban transportation; carriers, users, and government participants in the transportation business; both transportation theory and practice; and economics, finance, marketing, accounting, operations, and personnel management.

More specifically, *Transportation USA* covers all the traditional topics in a principles of transportation text, such as the following: the importance and role of transportation; identification of key industry participants (carriers, users, and government); the five modes (railroad, water, pipeline, highway, and air transportation); transportation economics; economic and noneconomic regulation; deregulation; government transportation policy; promotion and subsidy; urban, intercity, interstate, intrastate, and international transportation; freight and passenger transportation; pricing; transportation history; logistics and traffic management; intermediaries; labor; safety; energy; intermodal transportation; environmental and ecological issues; analytical tools and managerial techniques; and the future of transportation.

Special Features

Transportation USA features the following:

1. A total of 108 tables.
2. More than 50 photographs that were carefully selected to show, better than words can express, many of the technological advancements in U.S. transportation.
3. In total, 194 exhibits and tables.
4. Part introductions that highlight major concepts discussed in the subsequent chapters.
5. Chapter introductions that briefly overview the contents of each chapter.
6. A self-contained three-level outline. Major headings are identifiable by titles shown in the margin in bold capital letters. Secondary headings are also located in the margins with first letters of bold words capitalized. Third-level titles are italicized and begin paragraphs.
7. Marginal notes keyed to major concepts within paragraphs.
8. Thought-provoking chapter summaries.
9. A battery of eight subjective study questions found at the end of each chapter to test students' understanding of text information and examine their ability to think.
10. Extensive references accompanying each chapter.

Reference Tools

Transportation USA also provides readers with an extensive array of reference aids.

1. A 400-word glossary. In addition, key terms defined within the text are italicized.
2. Key words placed in the margins to facilitate quick location of chapter content information.
3. Nearly 1300 citations, including table and figure sources, endnotes, and additional readings. Readings include more than 500 articles and books that are academically oriented. They are also quite current, since 85% were dated 1980 or later.
4. An extensive index.

Appendixes

The text also contains two appendixes that should prove invaluable to anyone seeking current transportation information. Appendix A, "List of Transportation and Logistics Library Sources," contains the titles, descriptions, and names of the publishers of 126 publications that offer transportation information. Appendix B, "List of Transportation and Logistics Organizations," features the names, addresses, and usually the phone numbers of 68 private organizations and 23 governmental units that are involved in transportation and logistics.

INSTRUCTOR'S MANUAL

An instructor's manual is available for classroom teachers. The 20 chapters of the instructor's manual correlate directly with the chapters in the text. Each chapter of the manual contains the following:

1. A detailed explanation of the text chapter's purpose.
2. A three-level chapter outline.
3. Answers to study questions in the text.
4. Five additional essay questions and their answers.
5. A list of 10 multiple choice questions and their answers.

SUITABILITY OF THE TEXT FOR CLASSROOM USE

Transportation USA is an introductory principles of transportation text suitable for the following courses: Principles of Transportation, Transportation Economics, Introduction to Transportation, Domestic Transportation, Principles of Transportation and Logistics, Intercity Transportation, Transportation, and Transportation Management. It is primarily designed for juniors and seniors in business administration or economics, yet it is comprehensive enough for graduate-level courses. Because of its readability and clarity, it is also appropriate for adoption at junior colleges and vocational technical schools and for use in continuing education programs. As a principles text, the book is written primarily for people without any previous transportation education or experience. Nevertheless, because of its comprehensiveness and current nature, it should provide sufficient topical material for instructors and students with prior transportation training and experience.

The text should lend itself well for use in a course that is either the initial course in a program of study that leads to a major or concentration in Transportation and Logistics (Physical Distribution) Management or as a course that is offered in conjunction with one or more logistics electives. *Transportation USA* may precede or follow an introductory logistics course; nevertheless, it has been prepared to minimize the degree of duplication typically found between introductory principles of transportation texts and logistics texts. The content of *Transportation USA* should complement well the content of most logistics texts.

The organization and content of the text provide a high degree of flexibility, enabling instructors to use the book in semester, quarter, or trimester schedules and in courses varying from two- to five-credit hours. In courses of four- or five-credit hours, it is possible to assign and discuss the entire text. In shorter courses, the readability of the text provides the opportunity to assign all 20 chapters for students' reading; however, it is improbable that instructors will be able to discuss the entire text's contents in class. The organization permits instructors to select certain chapters for lecture purposes, while leaving others only for reading.

ACKNOWLEDGMENTS

Initially, I would like to thank all the corporations and organizations and their employees who so graciously answered my inquiries for information and clarifications of issues. In particular, I appreciate all the photos, other exhibit materials, and tables you furnished. A special word of thanks goes to everyone who gave Addison-Wesley permission to use requested information.

In addition, I would like to thank all the reviewers whose suggestions were important to ensure the quality and potential success of the text. These reviewers include the following:

James J. Adams	Professor James Daley
Professor Ogden O. Allsbrook, Jr.	Professor Bob J. Davis
Arnold E. Balk	Professor Gary N. Dicer
Mary C. Berry	Professor Jerry Foster
Dr. Ronald L. Clark	Professor Kevin H. Horn
Professor Thomas A. Corsi	Professor Roger Jerman

John H. Leeper	Howard Peterson
Joseph G. McKeefery	Professor Alan J. Stenger
Dr. Edward A. Morash	James M. Tilley
Professor John Ozment	Professor Ken Williamson

Many individuals at Addison-Wesley are singled out for praise not only for their efforts but also for their extremely positive and helpful attitudes. I am particularly grateful to my sponsoring editors, Frank J. Burns and Cindy M. Johnson. Cindy deserves considerable credit for *Transportation USA*. Her professionalism and sincere enthusiasm for the text were primarily responsible for my decision to sign a contract with Addison-Wesley. I had faith in her ability, and she never let me down. Frank, who assumed the lead editor's role about midway through the writing, proved to be an excellent editor, attentive to my suggestions and questions. I truly appreciate their efforts to produce a quality text. Also, I recognize Jeannie Griffin, the Addison-Wesley sales representative, who was instrumental in my signing on with her employer. Mary Eagleson, Frank's editorial assistant, has been terrific to work with. May I also say a special word of thanks to Mary Berry, my developmental editor, and to the following members of Addison-Wesley's editorial and production team: Mary Clare McEwing, production manager; Marcia Strykowski, production editor; Kathryn Nettles, editorial assistant; Hilary Pierce, editorial assistant.

Many people within the College of Business Administration also have my gratitude for their support and contributions. I appreciated the understanding and encouragement of Fred J. Reynolds, Professor and Head, Department of Marketing and Distribution. I appreciated the positive attitude and excellent typing support provided by Jean M. Abbey, Isabel Barnes, and Nedra Stewart, our office word-processor operators.

I am also grateful to my graduate research assistants, Kathy Faust Bunnell, Kathy Newman Kardoes, Christina Ruddick, Joe Stich, and Steve Richmond, who successively did some of the library research and data collection for me. Kathy Bunnell and Kathy Kardoes did a large portion of the work that led to the creation of Appendix B. I am also deeply indebted to Arnold Balk, Business and Economics Librarian, University of Georgia. Arnold was responsible for the development of Appendix A of the text.

I would also like to thank my colleagues on the faculty of the College of Business Administration—members of the Department of Marketing, as well as individuals in other departments. Hugh Watson, David Kamerschen, and William Shenkel fielded my questions about publishing matters. Charles DeLorme also spent many hours with me discussing textbook strategies. Another individual who deserves thanks is Patti Orr. Without her instructions and assistance, I would still be working on the instructor's manual.

Several other individuals also merit praise. To John and Mary Hebblethwaite and Jemmay McLure, thanks for all the quality manuscript typing you did. I would also like to recognize my attorney, Gregory A. Garcia, for helping me negotiate a good contract with Addison-Wesley. To Dave Clark of

Traffic World, I appreciate all your assistance not only with the book but also with the University of Georgia's Transportation and Logistics Program. Also, I would like to acknowledge the assistance of Ann T. Kilbride, project manager, who supervised the production of this book.

Athens, GA   F.S.
September 30, 1986

Contents

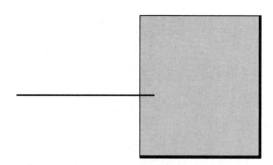

2

3

Railroad Transportation

5 **FREIGHT RAILROAD ECONOMICS AND PRICING**

6   FREIGHT RAILROAD MANAGEMENT ISSUES   143

9   INTERNATIONAL WATER TRANSPORTATION   223

5

Pipeline Transportation

253

10 PIPELINE TRANSPORTATION

255

6

Highway Transportation   **281**

11   INTRODUCTION TO HIGHWAY TRANSPORTATION   283

12   GENERAL COMMODITY TRUCKING   **312**

13   SPECIALIZED TRUCKING   339

16   SPECIALIZED AVIATION SECTORS: INTERNATIONAL AIR TRANSPORTATION AND THE U.S. AIR-CARGO INDUSTRY   435

8

Selective Transportation Issues   463

19   COMPETITION IN THE TRANSPORTATION INDUSTRY: THEORY, PRACTICE, AND STRATEGY   520

9

Future of Transportation   552

20   TRANSPORTATION'S GREATEST CHALLENGES   553

ALTHOUGH TRANSPORTATION IS EXTREMELY IMPORTANT, many people in the United States take it for granted. Part 1 of *Transportation USA* explains why people need to improve their understanding of transportation so that better passenger and cargo choices can be made. Readers are provided with background information that explains an industry in evolution. They are also provided with an overview of the text describing what follows in subsequent chapters. Another function of Part 1 is to define and introduce many of the transportation segments that will be studied in later chapters. Overall, Part 1 establishes the relevance of transportation.

1 Transportation Awareness

The Relevance
of Transportation

1

The United States is a nation on the move. Its people are accustomed to conducting their lives, activities, and travel as they wish, while they engage freely in commerce. Consequently, U.S. citizens regularly make decisions about transportation—the movement of people and cargo—as basic as deciding whether to drive or take a bus to work or as complex as trying to determine the precise moment to fire a rocket to break a manned satellite out of orbit and return it to earth. Thus most people would probably like to improve their skills at making good transportation decisions, since they could then save time, money, or even perhaps lives.

CHANGING TRANSPORTATION ENVIRONMENT

The transportation environment can be confusing, and even the best-intentioned individuals are apt to make less than ideal choices. Most people in the United States have several transportation options to choose from; although this can be viewed as a blessing in one respect, it can also be troublesome. Consider, for example, the person with a 40-lb. package to ship from Boston to Washington, D.C. Many transportation alternatives are available including parcel post, United Parcel Service (UPS), a general freight small shipment trucking company, an intercity bus line, an air freight forwarder or airline, and AMTRAK (the National Railroad Passenger Corporation). Among the numerous factors to be considered are shipment size limitations (i.e., the carrier's willingness to accept the shipment), pick-up and delivery service, liability for loss and damage, and speed requirements. Thus the information collection process can be a frustrating, time-consuming experience.

Unfortunately, transportation decision making will probably not be any easier in the future. The U.S. transportation system, which is still evolving, will face even greater challenges in the future. Since 1973, a myriad of substantive changes in the transportation environment were responsible. To be specific:

deregulation

■ The federal government significantly reduced the economic regulations that controlled modes such as the railroads, trucking companies, bus lines, and airlines. Although *deregulation* is the term often used to describe these changes, in most cases more appropriate terms are *regulatory reform* and *reregulation*—the retention of regulations, but allowing more freedom for the marketplace to work. The term *mode* means one of the five homogeneous groups of carriers in the transportation business, including railroads, water carriers, pipelines, highway carriers, and air carriers.

increased competition

■ Many new firms entered the trucking and airline modes. This new competition, along with the regulatory freedoms, resulted in a great expansion of rate/service transportation offerings. In today's market, far more variety exists in services and prices charged for such services.

fuel prices

■ Fuel prices have increased substantially. In 1972, petroleum could be bought for less than $3 per barrel. By 1981, the price, due primarily to actions by the Organization of Petroleum Exporting Countries (OPEC), had increased to $34 per barrel. Consequently, oil-dependent transportation modes, such as the airline and trucking sectors, saw operating costs escalate dramatically. Although fuel prices declined in the 1981–1986 period, they never returned to the 1972 level.

recession

■ The United States went through the worst *recession* in four decades.

inflation

■ *Inflation* reached one of the highest levels in U.S. history.

government
aid to transportation

■ The federal government's attitude toward providing financial aid to transportation modes changed. Increased user taxes have been levied on automobile and truck operators and, for the first time, waterway user taxes have been imposed on barge operators. As a result, carriers, who are the suppliers of transportation services, and their customers, including passengers and cargo shippers, are being asked to pay a larger share of the transportation bill.

labor/
management
balance of power

■ The federal government took a strong stand against striking transportation unions. For example, in 1981, President Reagan fired striking air traffic controllers. Subsequently their union, the Professional Air Traffic Controllers Organization, was disbanded.

union concessions

■ In unprecedented moves, many airlines demanded that their unions accept pay reductions and increased productivity standards—two moves managers felt were absolutely necessary to survive and to prosper in the more competitive environment.

computers

■ Computers became commonplace tools in the transportation industry.

technological
advances

■ Incredible technological advances in electronics, aeronautics and space (see Fig. 1.1), telecommunications, and robotics, to mention a few, have all affected the way the transportation business is conducted.

FIGURE 1.1.
Astronaut Edwin E. Aldrin, Jr., lunar module pilot, descends steps of lunar module ladder as he prepares to walk on the moon. He had just egressed the *LM*. This picture was taken by Astronaut Neil A. Armstrong, Commander during the Apollo 11 extravehicular activity. (Photo courtesy of the U.S. National Aeronautics and Space Administration)

This dynamic environment has renewed focus on transportation. Carrier owners and managers, for instance, must decide whether to keep their capital in one mode, such as in railroading, aviation, or trucking, or to branch out into other modes or even into nontransportation industries. Certainly the opportunities for diversification have seldom been greater. Increased competition has also given many passengers and cargo shippers far more carrier options to choose from. Thus a pressing need for skilled, intelligent people in the transportation field exists.

TRANSPORTATION SEGMENTS

The transportation field encompasses a number of specialized sectors, such as passenger transportation and cargo transportation, urban versus intercity transportation, and domestic versus international transportation. Because various industry components will be discussed in this text, the following list contains brief, but relevant, definitions.

Segments

- *Passenger transportation* is the movement of human beings, while *cargo transportation* includes everything else carried by any of the five modes.
- *Urban transportation* is the movement between any two points in a met-

ropolitan area or in a particular city; for example, a trip from home to the library.

- *Intercity transportation* is a movement in which the origin is in one city, with the destination in another; for example, a shipment from Providence, Rhode Island, to Boston, Massachusetts.

- *Interstate transportation* refers to a movement where the origin and destination are located in two different states; for example, a shipment from Dallas, Texas, to Phoenix, Arizona.

- *Intrastate transportation* implies a movement between two points in the same state; for example, a trip from Dallas, Texas, to San Antonio, Texas.

- *Domestic transportation* refers to a movement where both the origin and destination are points in the United States or its territories; for example, a movement from Guam to San Francisco, California.

- *International (foreign) transportation* is a movement where either the origin or destination is in the United States or in its territories and the other point is in another country; for example, a trip from Seattle, Washington, to Tokyo. It can also denote a movement between two non-U.S. points, such as from Hong Kong to Tokyo.

- *Intraplanetary space transportation* is a movement in space around Earth, such as a route followed by an orbiting satellite.

- *Interplanetary space transportation* is a movement through space between Earth and other planets; for example, a satellite sent into space to explore the planet Venus.

PARTICIPANTS

Participants in the transportation industry include carriers, users, the government, and other interested parties, such as taxpayers and non-users affected by environmental or other transportation-caused problems.

carriers   Carriers supply transportation services by rail, water, pipeline, highway, or air. Thus the business is stratified by the medium over which or through which transportation vehicles and traffic (passengers or cargo) move. For-hire carriers are transportation companies that are paid fees by users who obtain their services. Another classification is private carriers—in essence, transportation organizations that provide services for their own benefit, such as a manufacturing firm that owns or leases trucks to haul its own products. Examples of the former are Consolidated Freightways, a trucking company that earns income from hauling manufacturers' cargo, and American Airlines, which flies passengers for money. Burlington Industries, in contrast, is the operator of a large private trucking fleet that was created to haul textiles and other products of the same company.

The U.S. transportation system is primarily characterized by carriers owned by private investors seeking to earn profits from their investments—in other words, citizens practicing capitalism. Some exceptions, such as the U.S. Postal Service, AMTRAK, and numerous public transit systems that operate city buses and rapid transit lines, also charge fees, but they are not expected to be profitable. Governmental units have decided that nonprofit carriers are justified by social motives, such as the need for people in remote locations to have mail service and the need to carry nondrivers to work or school.

users　　Individuals, groups, and organizations who use the transportation services provided by carriers are the second major participant in transportation. Every person in the United States—with the possible exception of totally self-sufficient individuals—is a user who relies on the system for passenger and cargo services. Without these customers, carriers would not be needed.

government　　The government is the third major participant in U.S. transportation, and its involvement is extensive. The government's responsibilities include regulating economic matters (e.g., entry into, or exit from, the business, rates, mergers, accounting practices, and services); defining policies that directly or indirectly affect carriers and users; enacting laws and establishing rules regarding such matters as safety, working conditions, pollution controls, and fuel efficiency; promoting and subsidizing various modes; operating ports and airports; defining, collecting, and dispensing taxes; and policing the transportation system to ensure compliance with its rules.

other interested parties　　Among the other interested parties that monitor and help shape transportation policies and actions are environmentalists and ecologists trying to limit the negative consequences of carriers and users, taxpayers trying to tighten controls on public aid to transportation, property owners concerned with the confiscation of private property for the construction of highways or airports, and parents trying to protect their children from drunk drivers.

In reality, many groups with so many conflicting transportation expectations only create confusion, which in turn reinforces the need for increased transportation knowledge. Decisions, strategies, and trade-offs will be made; the challenge is to make the best ones.

ABOUT THIS TEXT

The orientation of this book is management, strategy, and decision making from the perspective of carriers, users, and the government. Although the primary focus is business-related transportation choices—that is, decisions made by carriers and their corporate customers—individuals are not neglected. People make significant decisions such as whether to buy new cars, which mode to take on a vacation trip, and how to haul their furniture and belongings when they move. Another group that makes decisions affecting carriers, users, and concerned citizens, like taxpayers, is government. Consequently, personal transportation management, strategy, and decision making, as well as public transportation management, strategy, and decision making, are also themes of this text. Significant emphasis is placed on the present and the future—the relevant timeframes for decision making.

Objectives

Transportation USA has the following objectives:

1. To teach the principles of transportation, providing students with a comprehensive understanding of important concepts, terminology, and issues pertinent to the industry.
2. To inform readers of significant changes that have dramatically altered the way the transportation industry functions, and in particular, to help readers comprehend the impact of the changing regulatory environment (deregulation), fluctuating fuel prices, the recession, and inflation on carriers and their customers.
3. To use transportation as a learning laboratory in which to define, demonstrate, and test functional business theories, concepts, and practices (e.g., financial ratio analysis, market segmentation and targeting, pricing theory, and human resource management methods)—information learned in accounting, finance, marketing, economics, and management courses.
4. To teach students how to be better business managers and leaders.
5. To encourage students to pursue careers in transportation and logistics.

Transportation Segment Coverage

Transportation USA attempts to portray the U.S. transportation system as it truly exists today and as it might look in the future. A determined effort was made to present the proper mix between the cargo (freight) and passenger transportation sectors. Primarily, the text is concerned with interstate transportation; however, a second goal was to ensure that no important segment of the industry is neglected. Where appropriate, intrastate, international, and urban transportation will be discussed. In addition, the intraplanetary and interplanetary space transportation segments will be covered, because, for more than 25 years, the United States has been a world leader in space exploration. Now, with the commercial launching of satellites as part of the Space Shuttle program, for-hire transportation has entered a new era (see Fig. 1.2). The United States has also been actively involved in interplanetary space transportation with vehicles like the Voyager 2 that have explored Jupiter and other planets. The focus of transportation is broadening rapidly, and this textbook will attempt to explain these developments.

Questions To Be Answered

Questions intended to be answered by the text are as follows:

1. Who participates in U.S. transportation?
2. What are the participants' roles, objectives, strengths, weaknesses, and concerns?
3. What decisions do the participants make?
4. Why do they do what they do? What constrains the participants' abilities to formulate strategies, manage, and make decisions?
5. How could participants make better decisions?

FIGURE 1.2.
Carrying the first commercial satellite payload in the history of the STS program and the first four-person crew in a single launch in the history of space flight, Columbia lifts away from Launch Pad 39A on schedule at 7:19 A.M. on November 11, 1982—Cape Kennedy Space Center, Florida. This flight began STS-5, the first operational flight for the Space Shuttle system. (Photo courtesy of the U.S. National Aeronautics and Space Administration)

Text Organization and Features

Transportation USA contains 20 chapters that move in topical coverage from the general to the specific. The initial four chapters contain general subject matter. After the first chapter, which discusses the relevance of transportation, the next three chapters cover the general characteristics and decision-making concerns of the industry's major participants—carriers, shippers, and the government. In the next 12 chapters, a modal sequence covers railroad transportation (Chapters 5–7), water transportation (Chapters 8–9), pipeline transportation (Chapter 10), highway transportation (Chapters 11–13), and air transportation (Chapters 14–16). The purpose of using this modal arrangement is to present information in a more integrated way. While many similarities exist between modes, there are also many differences. By presenting information modally, the text will better simulate what a manager in the railroad industry, for example, must handle in making corporate decisions. Readers will become familiar with what carriers do, what carrier customers want, why carriers operate as they do, how the decision-making process works, how that process is changing, and what it takes to be successful in the changing competitive environment.

The next three chapters are concerned with strategy and decision making, and the last chapter addresses the system's future. Chapter 17 focuses on transportation decisions made by individuals, especially automobile own-ership and use choices. Chapter 18 examines public sector transit manage-ment, strategy, and decision making—government involvement in, and oper-ation of, urban mass transportation systems. Chapter 19 discusses competition in the transportation industry: theory, practice, and strategy. The greatest transportation challenges in the United States are examined in Chapter 20.

Several tools have been incorporated into *Transportation USA* to aid the student's learning experience. With the transportation system being restruc-tured so rapidly, it is impossible to publish an entirely current textbook. To stay up-to-date, students must tune their senses to more current information sources. Therefore readers are challenged to use the chapter endnotes and additional references in both Appendix A (*List of Transportation and Logistics Library Sources*) and Appendix B (*List of Transportation and Logistics Organ-izations*), which can provide valuable supplemental information.

MEETING NATIONAL PRIORITIES

An appropriate beginning for addressing the relevance of transportation is by verifying its contributions to the achievement of national priorities. Trans-portation is considered crucially important to the nation; therefore the U.S. federal government seldom permits a prolonged interruption in any part of this business. Two fairly recent situations illustrate the government's impa-tience with striking transportation workers. In the first case, President Reagan responded swiftly to a 1981 national strike by the Professional Air Traffic Controllers Organization (PATCO), ordering striking workers to return to work or be fired. When they did not return to their work, 11,000 transportation employees lost their jobs.[1] One year later, Congress passed and President Re-agan signed a resolution calling for an end to a strike by the Brotherhood of Locomotive Engineers that was affecting most of the nation's railroads.[2] At stake in each case was the commerce of the nation; and, in the former in-stance, there was the additional concern about the safety of air passengers.

Transportation cannot be isolated and treated independently by public officials. Perhaps the most difficult task U.S. senators and representatives have is trying to satisfy the important needs of their constituents while simulta-neously protecting the good of the nation. Transportation policies are impor-tant to users and carriers; however, they may be just as important or even more crucial to the accomplishment of other national priorities.

Transportation's National Benefits

Washington's task is to try to balance economic, social, energy, environmental, and security priorities with every tool available. One such tool is transpor-tation, which provides the following national benefits.

▪ It is the nation's link with domestic and world resources, such as energy supplies and other raw materials.

- It is vital to the national defense, providing the logistics to support combat forces.
- It is important in the nation's communications network from its role in carrying the mail to the launching of communications satellites.
- It is the answer to the mobility needs of transit independents (i.e., people able to perform their own urban transportation) and transit dependents (e.g., the handicapped, the aged, and the young who must rely on for-hire urban transportation).
- It provides the means for U.S. people to get to schools to obtain their educations.
- It creates an immeasurably large impact by taking people places where they gain exposure to the arts, see the lifestyles and interests of other people in different geographic settings, and lessen their biased attitudes.
- It saves thousands of lives annually by creating ways to deliver critically needed blood, organs, and medicines to patients all over the country and by speeding the transportation of the sick to medical facilities.
- It helps the entire democratic system to function by allowing diplomacy to occur in all corners of the world.

From a national perspective, then, transportation is to a great extent the cement that holds this geographically dispersed country together. It is not a typical business, and it is not treated as one by the government.

TRANSPORTATION'S ECONOMIC CONTRIBUTIONS

Transportation makes significant contributions to the U.S. economy. One leading indicator is that an estimated $713.2 billion was spent on passenger and freight transportation in 1984. This amount represented 19.47% of the gross national product of $3.663 trillion.[3]

Employment

highway employment

In a nation concerned about jobs, transportation plays a vital role. Approximately 2 million U.S. citizens work for railroads, airlines, and trucking companies carrying cargo and passengers, while millions more work in related industries. A good illustration is U.S. highway transportation direct and indirect employment. As indicated in Table 1.1, in 1982 more than 5 million citizens earned their livings through employment in trucking and trucking terminals, working in the intercity bus industry, operating taxicabs, or running school buses. Others worked in equipment manufacturing, the tire industry, wholesale and retail trades, the petroleum industry, road construction, vehicle repair, and other industries working to place and keep trucks, buses, and cars on the road. Actually, many others not listed in Table 1.1 are also tied to the transportation business, such as workers in the insurance, glass, steel, and electrical sectors of the economy. In all, the entire transportation

TABLE 1.1. U.S. highway direct and indirect employment (May 1982)	
Category	**Employees**
Trucking and trucking terminals	1,120,000
Intercity buses	36,600
Taxicabs	46,200
School buses	109,100
Motor vehicle and equipment manufacturing	717,000
Tires, innertube manufacturers	102,900
New and used car dealers	732,000
Auto and home supply stores	275,200
Gasoline service stations	552,300
Motor vehicles and automotive equipment wholesalers	414,500
Automotive repair shops	361,000
Highway and street construction	236,100
State and local government highway employees	607,000[a]
TOTAL	5,309,900

[a]Estimate derived from Transportation Association of America figures for 1981.

Sources:
1. U.S., Department of Labor, Bureau of Labor Statistics, *Employment and Earnings, August 1982* (Washington, D.C.: Government Printing Office, 1982), Table B-2.
2. *Transportation Facts and Trends,* 17th ed. (Washington, D.C.: TAA, August 1982), p. 24.

industry provides work for approximately 10 million people and 10% of the nation's civilian (nonmilitary) work force.[4]

City Growth

Transportation is a key determinant in the prosperity of states and cities. Why is a city located where it is? Usually there is a connection to transportation: New York City, San Francisco, and Boston started as seaports, New Orleans and St. Louis developed as important river communities, Kansas City and Omaha were important railroad towns (see Fig. 1.3). It may not always be clear what came first—transportation or the people who demanded good transportation—but a definite link exists between the growth and prosperity of cities and transportation availability.

Atlanta example Atlanta is a good illustration of this link. Founded as the last stop on a railroad, Atlanta has grown to become a leading metropolitan center. One key factor is Atlanta's geographic location, because it is almost midway between Miami and Chicago and it is also well positioned for traffic from Texas and Louisiana to the Northeast. Growth, however, is tied more precisely to several transportation developments. Atlanta's Hartsfield International Airport, for example, is the second busiest airport in the country in terms of passengers processed; it is also the single largest private (nonmilitary) site employer

FIGURE 1.3.
Locations of major U.S. transportation centers.

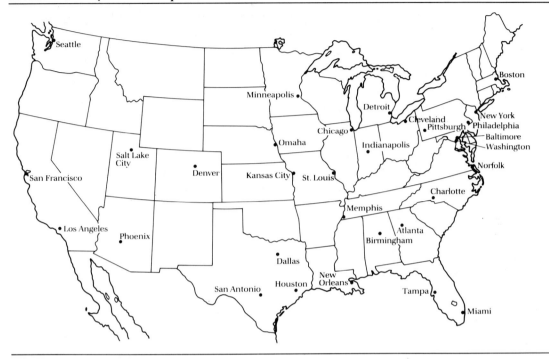

in Georgia with more than 24,000 workers, and its payroll contributes more than $2 billion annually to the economy. Atlanta is not accidentally a major convention center, either. Hotels, restaurants, and shops depend on air, high-way, and rail service to move people to and from the metropolitan area. Similarly, Atlanta is a regional and national distribution center, as well as a major railroad, trucking, and air cargo hub. It is also the headquarters for Colonial Pipeline Company, the largest refined oil products pipeline in the United States. Without transportation, Atlanta could not be the city it is today.

Tourism

Across the country lies the beautiful city of San Francisco. For many who have been there, it is hard to picture San Francisco without its famed cable cars (Fig. 1.4). Both the city and the federal government jointly supported extensive renovation of this national historic landmark. It is difficult to measure what part cable cars play in San Francisco's $1.2 billion annual tourist business or in the morale of the city's people; however, few would question that cable cars are important economic and social contributors to the region.[5]

FIGURE 1.4.
San Francisco cable car. (Fred Stephenson photo)

Transportation is the source of tourism in any area, and tourism is vital to the economic well-being of many places. In 1982, tourism brought in $72.9 billion to the states of California ($24.6 billion), Florida ($14.6 billion), Texas ($13.7 billion), New York ($12.9 billion), and New Jersey ($7.1 billion)—the five leading states in domestic travel expenditures for all trips.[6]

leading states in tourism

Land Values

Land values are also affected by transportation. Rapid escalations in land prices often occur on property adjacent to parts of the interstate highway system or near subway stations. Why, however, is land farther from the city's central business district (CBD) typically less expensive than land near the CBD? First, rural areas do not have as many business opportunities as do those nearer the CBD. Secondly, rural, remote locations necessitate longer trips to the business center. Trade-offs exist between lower rural land costs and higher transportation expenses—more time and greater dollars expended for commuting.

Tax Transfers

A relatively unique feature of the U.S. economic system is the emphasis on capitalism and the operation of businesses under private control and for profit. Consequently, when transportation firms have income, they usually pay corporate income taxes, social security, and other taxes. In 1977, the last year the information was published, total transportation taxes contributed 14% of all federal, and 23% of all state, taxes collected in the United States.[7] Since a portion of these aggregate tax collections is spent on nontransportation programs, such as education, health and welfare, and police and fire protection, transportation contributes directly to outside social programs.

BUSINESSES NEED TRANSPORTATION

Businesses need transportation to sell their goods and services at competitive prices, to create production and marketing opportunities, to locate plants and distribution centers advantageously, and to transact business. One important equation in business is the following:

$$\text{SELLING PRICE} = \text{PRODUCTION COSTS} + \text{TRANSPORTATION} \\ \text{COSTS} + \text{PROFIT MARGIN}$$

Low transportation costs enable sellers to reduce prices or expand selling efforts to reach more distant markets. The money saved can then be either passed directly on to consumers or spent on transportation to haul goods more miles. As the U.S. interest in exporting increases, these benefits will become even more important.[8]

Production and Marketing

For goods to be produced and marketed, inventories must be moved and stored. Raw materials and parts are purchased and shipped to warehouses, from which they are eventually transferred to plants for processing into finished goods. A company's products are then distributed through marketing channels—that is, all those units, such as wholesalers, retailers, and customers, which act as an infrastructure to distribute goods from producer to consumer. Between each inventory location—whether it is a supplier's warehouse, a public warehouse, a manufacturing plant, a wholesaler's facility, or a retail location—transportation is relied on to move products efficiently. For clarity, a *public warehouse* is a facility where shippers can pay a warehouse operator to store their inventories (stock) and where inventories of several customers are typically held and eventually distributed.

Location Decisions

The profitability of businesses is often closely correlated to the proper location of facilities. Although many variables are considered in making site selections, a *Fortune* study of 577 corporations ranked "efficient transportation facilities for materials and products" tied with "productivity of workers" as the two most important factors in locating mainland U.S. plants.[9] A bad choice for the location of a warehouse, for example, can result in inadequate consumer services, stockouts (i.e., situations in which the number of units of an ordered item exceeds the number of units available in inventory), and noncompetitive prices due to high transportation costs. All of these factors can drive firms out of business.

Transacting Business

Firms also need efficient passenger transportation to transact business. Millions of workers are engaged in selling, and of these, many are traveling salespeople whose incomes are dependent on automobile and air transportation: for instance, sales representatives in the apparel industry who drive an average of 38,500 miles per year.[10] Corporate executives also need efficient passenger transportation to make distant sales presentations and to manage field operations. Therefore, for marketing and control purposes, businesspeople must be able to react to crises and not waste valuable time riding in transportation vehicles.

RELEVANCE TO CONSUMER PRODUCTS AND SERVICES

Geographic Specialization and Mass Production

Consumers in the United States not only expect a wide variety of reasonably priced products, but also depend on others to supply their wants and needs. Geographic specialization and mass (large-scale) production are two key factors. The former encourages regions and workers to do what they do best, because goods not produced locally nevertheless can be brought in for consumption by low-cost transportation. Mass production, by comparison, encourages long production runs and creates economies of scale through the reduction in long-run average costs as the size of the company increases. These factors, in turn, enable producers to cut prices and open new markets to a wider variety of goods. Without efficient transportation to move vast quantities of raw materials, components, and finished products over great distances and at affordable rates, mass production would be only a theory.

It is interesting to note which regions in the United States specialize in what products. California is a center for wine production and produce (fruits and vegetables); Texas is known for oil; Wisconsin is the U.S. dairy capital; and North Carolina is the country's leading furniture-producing state. In short, a country with poor transportation would have great difficulty specializing and mass producing its products. Without this capability, individuals would have to spend a far greater amount of time producing a wide variety of locally needed products.

Because transportation efficiently moves goods produced in widely dispersed areas, New York consumers enjoy oranges from both California and Florida and give minimal thought to the question of how California orange producers are able to compete against Florida growers in the New York market. How can California producers cover the additional 1500-mile trip distances and compete on an equal footing with Florida growers? The answer, in part, is that freight rates from California are low enough to permit market entry. As indicated in the equation given earlier in the chapter, a reduction in transportation costs can help producers lower their selling prices and reach more distant markets.

Service and Energy Sectors

Transportation is also important to the service sector comprised of businesses and institutions not primarily engaged in the production of products. Some places specialize in medicine, education, and finance. Boston is a good example. To move patients, students, and clients to and from this center of health care, learning, and commerce, efficient transportation is essential.

Energy is another primary concern in the United States. To run cars, heat homes, and generate the electricity needed for appliances and lights, oil, coal, and gas are needed. The country depends on the railroad, pipeline, water carrier, and trucking industries to deliver energy raw materials. When OPEC jolted the U.S. public and started the United States on a push toward energy self-sufficiency, new discoveries of oil, gas, and coal followed. The real question, however, is whether newly discovered or previously located energy fields can be developed and the resources marketed, given monumental transportation problems. Alaska, for example, has huge coal and gas reserves, but can these energy supplies be brought to market at affordable, competitive prices?

LIFE WITHOUT TRANSPORTATION

Picture life without transportation; consider how people's lives would change if their environments extended no farther than as far as they could walk. People spend most of their time near home, so transportation offers an escape route when a change of scenery is needed. Most people in the United States can fly to most parts of the country within 24 hours; thus air transportation links individuals with distant relatives and vacation spots.

Dietary Changes

Consider also the foods eaten in the United States. It is not unusual for a Rhode Islander to consume a breakfast of orange juice from Florida, coffee from South America, toast from North Dakota wheat, milk from Vermont, salt from Texas, pepper from Java, sugar from Louisiana, hash brown potatoes from Maine or Idaho, jellies from grapes grown in California, and sausage from Iowa. It is possible that only the eggs are locally produced. If people could eat only what they could grow, catch, shoot, or buy from local suppliers, their diets would change considerably. Levels of nutrition would probably be lowered as well.

Vacation Changes

Now imagine the impact on vacation plans. Vacations are functions primarily of time and money. It takes time to make money, but with money yet little time to travel, trips by surface modes like highway transportation are sometimes impossible. Herein lies the advantage of air travel, because it provides the flexibility to travel great distances in a matter of hours. Without it, people would be forced to stay closer to home.

Sports Changes

Consider also the repercussions on sports. List the opponents any college football team would play without transportation. What allows the Boston Celtics, Atlanta Hawks, Seattle SuperSonics, and Los Angeles Lakers to play each other? Without transportation, sports would not exist at the competitive levels known today.

Lifestyle Changes

Finally, without transportation, lifestyles would change dramatically. Remove cars, small trucks, and motorcycles from the environment, and a total relocation of work, educational, and medical centers must occur. People would lose the opportunities to live more than a few miles from work. The finest internationally recognized universities would probably become regional institutions. Superb medical centers, such as the Mayo Clinic in Rochester, Minnesota, just could not exist as they do now, for they would be virtually inaccessible to most patients. From a freight perspective, the goods people have grown accustomed to—such as fresh meat and produce, cut flowers, and household appliances—would be curtailed by such problems as perishability or higher prices. Furthermore, the elimination of recreational transportation vehicles (e.g., boats) and access to the playgrounds where people enjoy them would result in dramatic shifts not just in leisure time habits, but also in the economic sectors that create these opportunities.

UNITED STATES THRIVES ON MOBILITY

The United States has an insatiable demand for mobility, and its citizens pride themselves on barrier-free travel. As noted in Table 1.2, U.S. citizens owned more than 124 million cars in 1981, and on a per capita basis in 1980, possessed nearly 3 times as many cars as in Japan and almost 19 times as many as in the USSR. Nearly 148 million citizens—representing 65% of the total U.S. population—were licensed motorists in 1981.

TABLE 1.2. Automobile statistics

Item	Value
Automobiles registered in the United States (1981)	124,336,000
U.S. population (1980)	226,505,000
Automobiles per person (1980)	
United States	0.56
Japan	0.20
USSR	0.03
U.S. licensed motorists (1981)	147,968,000

Source: Derived from Motor Vehicle Manufacturers Association of the United States, *MVMA Motor Vehicle Facts and Figures '82* (Detroit, Mich., 1982), pp. 21, 32–33, 58.

time and place utility

Efficient transportation creates time utility; in essence, it produces benefits when people and cargo reach destinations when it is necessary they be there. Likewise, transportation creates place utility by delivering people and cargo to the locations where they are needed. People who have been late to important meetings because an aircraft departure was delayed can appreciate the value of reliable air service. Those people who have gone to Miami while their luggage has gone to Kansas City also see its merits.

U.S. TRANSPORTATION SYSTEM

The U.S. transportation system is one of the most advanced, comprehensive networks in the world. Singled out for particular recognition are the oil and natural gas pipeline industries for both extensive route systems and sophisticated technology (see Table 1.3). Moreover, the U.S. airline system is perhaps the best one on Earth. By no means does this imply that the U.S. transportation system could not be improved; indeed, much work is needed.

modal split

Tables 1.4 and 1.5 present estimates of modal split market share data for passenger and cargo traffic. These estimates refer to the percentage of the market controlled by each mode. The first table shows the dominance of the automobile; and, among the for-hire carriers, the central role of the airline industry. In the cargo sector, water carrier traffic and railroad traffic represent the greatest ton-mile shares. Traffic data usually use the ton-mile or passenger-mile unit as a common measure. Each represents the unit multiplied by distance: thus, 500 ton-miles could reflect 1 ton moved 500 miles; 250 tons moved 2 miles; or any product of tons multiplied by the miles they move. In addition, 500 passenger-miles could mean 5 passengers moved 100 miles, 1 passenger moved 500 miles, and so forth. Since private carrier and nonregulated firms have no requirement for reporting traffic data, these charts should be used only to obtain a rough approximation of market shares. Nevertheless, each mode plays a necessary role regardless of market share results.

TABLE 1.3. U.S. transportation modal route mileages

Mode	Miles
Rail-passenger	23,356[a]
Rail-freight	151,998[b]
Domestic water	25,777
Pipelines-petroleum	237,643[c]
Pipelines-gas	1,064,200[d]
Highways	3,866,000[e]
Airways	372,953[f]

[a]1984

[b]Class I railroads only, 1984. Excludes parallel track and yard track.

[c]Petroleum and other liquid products, 1981.

[d]Includes distribution mains, transmission pipelines, and field and gathering lines, 1981.

[e]Federal, state, and local highways and roads, 1982.

[f]1983.

Sources:

1. Association of American Railroads, *Railroad Facts 1985 Edition* (Washington, D.C.: Association of American Railroads, August 1985), pp. 42, 61.
2. The American Waterways Operators, Inc., *Waterways of the United States* (Arlington, Va.: AWO, 1981).
3. Frank A. Smith, Senior Associate, *Transportation in America*, 3d ed. (Washington, D.C.: Transportation Policy Associates, March 1985), p. 21.
4. *Gas Data Book* (Arlington, Va.: American Gas Association, 1982), p. 7.
5. U.S., Department of Commerce, Bureau of the Census, *Statistical Abstract of the United States 1985*, 105th ed. (Washington, D.C.: U.S. Government Printing Office, 1984), p. 591.
6. U.S., Department of Transportation, Federal Aviation Administration, *FAA Statistical Handbook of Aviation Calendar Year 1983* (Washington, D.C.: U.S. Government Printing Office, December 1984), p. 35.

TABLE 1.4. U.S. domestic intercity passenger travel by mode (1984)

Mode	Passenger-Miles (in billions)	Percent
Private carriage		
Auto	1,436.8	82.7%
Air	13.0	0.7%
Total private	1,449.8	83.4%
For-hire		
Air	249.7	14.4%
Bus	27.1	1.5%
Rail	11.5	0.7%
Total for-hire	288.3	16.6%
TOTAL	1,738.1	100.0%

Source: Frank A. Smith, Senior Associate, *Transportation in America*, 3d ed., *July 1985 Supplement* (Washington, D.C.: Transportation Policy Associates, July 1985), p. 8. (Adapted with permission.)

TABLE 1.5. U.S. domestic intercity freight traffic by mode (1984)

Mode	Ton-Miles (in billions)	Percent
Railroads	922	29.1
Trucking	602	19.0
Oil pipelines	567	17.9
Water carriers[a]	1,069	33.8
Air carriers	7	0.2
TOTAL	3,167	100.0

[a]Includes domestic ocean traffic (i.e., shipments moving on the high seas).

Sources:
1. Association of American Railroads, *Railroad Facts 1985 Edition* (Washington, D.C.: AAR, August 1985), p. 9.
2. Frank A. Smith, Senior Associate, *Transportation in America*, 3d ed., *July 1985 Supplement* (Washington, D.C.: Transportation Policy Associates, July 1985), p. 6. (Adapted with permission.)

Air cargo represents less than 1% of the ton-mile traffic, for example, but no substitute exists for air transportation if packages need to reach destinations hundreds of miles away in a few hours.

A CONTROVERSIAL BUSINESS

Pollution

As beneficial as it may be, transportation is also quite controversial: for instance, the industry is a source of national problems such as pollution, deaths, and injuries. Many city dwellers endure air pollution caused to a considerable extent by highway vehicle exhaust emissions. Moreover, when tankers go down at sea, oil pollution coats beaches, interrupts fishing, and kills fowl. Noise pollution likewise disrupts sleep and lifestyles. These byproducts of transportation are facts of life, yet that does not mean the public must tolerate excesses. In fact, it does not; for example, the last decade witnessed considerable public pressure to tighten pollution controls.

Highway Accidents

The dichotomy of the automobile is that, although people in the United States enjoy driving cars, highway accidents represent one of the largest killers this nation has ever known. Statistics indicate that in 1979, for example, there were an estimated 7,330,000 police-reported accidents involving 12,800,000 vehicles and 19,466,000 people. As a result, there were 51,083 highway fatalities, 271,000 serious (severe or critical) injuries, and 4,026,000 total injuries. Most of these tragedies were passenger-car related.[11] Many factors contribute to these problems, ranging from alcohol to human errors to vehicle deficiencies; however, what is troubling is the result. One pressing U.S. problem is to minimize such accidents and their consequences.

Hazardous Goods Movements

Consider also, that daily the freight transportation system is asked to move hazardous materials, such as chemicals, poisonous gases, acids, radioactive materials, and explosives. This is not likely to cease as long as the end products of such cargoes—plastics, paint, cancer-controlling drugs, and fuels—are in demand.

Accidents while transporting such materials are costly, threatening, and sometimes fatal. To minimize these risks, the railroad industry and its shippers have taken measures in recent years to curb tank car dangers by modifying car couplers and adding protective shields to tank cars. Still, as the Livingston, Louisiana, derailment on September 28, 1982, clearly revealed, the problem has not been eliminated. In that accident, tank cars carrying vinyl chloride ruptured and burned, forcing the evacuation of 3000 residents for more than a week.[12]

Resource Utilization

Transportation's use of scarce natural resources such as oil is also criticized. The record shows that transportation was responsible for 62.7% of all the petroleum consumed in the United States in 1983. Fuel for highway vehicles amounted to 2.747 billion barrels, or the equivalent of 49.4% of the 5.559 billion barrels consumed domestically in 1983.[13] Similarly, transportation consumed 71% of the rubber, 23% of the steel, and 23% of the cement used in the United States. The criticism is not of consumption per se, but of the inefficiency of the consumption. Too many modes have excess capacity problems. Consider automobiles. Far too many cars travel the roads bearing only one occupant. As compared to the typical car's capacity of approximately five people, this causes a tremendous waste of fuel. Competition, regulation, and consumer preferences may dictate excess capacity, yet the depletion of limited resources, for whatever reasons, is the important outcome.

Land Usage Shifts

Transportation can force changes in land use, thereby frustrating citizens. Desirable residential locations may become highly undesirable living places due to increased aircraft, railroad, or highway traffic noise. Highways also disrupt society by splitting farms and neighborhoods. Although transportation system improvements may help passenger and freight efficiency, these changes may decrease residential and farming values, forcing unwanted relocations. Even though land values may soar because the land is highly desired for other uses, the money may be no consolation to families forced to leave lifestyles, friends, and memories.

SUMMARY

The U.S. transportation system contributes more than $700 billion annually to the economy. It is vitally important to the nation's defense, mobility, and the achievement of societal priorities. Equally important is its impact on the individual citizen, because transportation is the means to obtain an education, go to work, reach medical aid, return home, and travel to places for rest and relaxation. U.S. lifestyles could not be what they are today without transportation.

Because everyone is so dependent on efficient transportation and distribution, individuals must make wise transportation decisions. This task is not becoming any easier, for changes in the external environment, such as regulatory reform, the recession, inflation, and energy price shifts, have made this sector more confusing. Carriers are experimenting with newfound freedoms to alter rates and services. In turn, users have more choices and opportunities, but also perhaps more risks. Thus, to satisfy needs and manage time and money better, people need to be more knowledgeable of transportation. Public officials, in particular, must take a greater interest in this sector if they want the transportation system to continue to function efficiently.

STUDY QUESTIONS

1. What types of changes in the 1970s and 1980s have made the transportation decision-making environment more complex?

2. What national benefits does transportation provide?

3. How can efficient transportation services enable businesses to sell their goods in more distant markets?

4. Discuss how transportation is involved with the hauling and consumption of petroleum.

5. How does efficient transportation affect the lifestyles of U.S. citizens?

6. In what ways is the government a participant in U.S. transportation?

7. How does Atlanta exemplify the importance of transportation to city growth?

8. How does efficient transportation encourage geographic specialization and mass production?

ENDNOTES

1. Joann S. Lublin, "Reagan Threatens Air Controllers with Dismissal if Strike Continues," *Wall Street Journal,* 4 August 1981, p. 3.

2. Association of American Railroads, "Congress Halts BLE Strike," *Rail News Update,* 23 September 1981, p. 1.

3. Frank A. Smith, Senior Associate, *Transportation in America,* 3d ed., *July 1985 Supplement* (Washington, D.C.: Transportation Policy Associates, July 1985), p. 2.

4. Frank A. Smith, Senior Associate, *Transportation in America,* 3d ed. (Washington, D.C.:

Transportation Policy Associates, March 1985), p. 18.

5. Laurel Sorenson, "Will San Francisco Dissolve into the Fog Without Cable Cars?" *Wall Street Journal,* 16 July 1982, p. 2.

6. Telephone conversation with Susan Zimmer, Travel Industry Association of America, 15 October 1984.

7. Transportation Association of America, *Transportation Facts & Trends,* 16th ed. (Washington, D.C.: Transportation Association of America, July 1980), p. 27.

8. For an excellent discussion of pricing to accommodate transportation, see Donald V. Harper, *Transportation in America: Users, Carriers, Government* (Englewood Cliffs, N.J.: Prentice-Hall, 1982), pp. 46–67.

9. The *Fortune* study of "Facility Location Decisions," as cited in American Trucking Associations, Inc., *Research Review,* no. 202, 15 September 1978, p. 1.

10. Bureau of Wholesale Sales Representatives, Position Paper in regard to *The Need to Increase Commission Rates Paid to Manufacturers' Representatives in the Apparel Industry: 1981 Update,* prepared by Frederick J. Stephenson, 1 November 1981, p. 4.

11. National Highway Traffic Safety Administration, *Report on Traffic Accidents and Injuries for 1979* (Washington, D.C.: U.S. Department of Transportation, 1980), pp. 7, 9, 16, 33.

12. "ICG Rail Cleanup Crews Clearing Derailment Site; NTSB Probe Underway," *Traffic World,* 18 October 1982, p. 19.

13. Smith, *Transportation in America,* p. 25.

ADDITIONAL READINGS

Altschiller, Donald, ed. *Transportation in America.* New York: H.G. Wilson Co., 1982.

Bowersox, Donald J.; Calabro, Pat J.; and Wagenheim, George D. *Introduction to Transportation.* New York: Macmillan Publishing Co., 1981, Chapters 1 and 2.

Coyle, John J.; Bardi, Edward J.; and Cavinato, Joseph L. *Transportation.* St. Paul, Minn.: West Publishing Co., 1982, Chapters 1 and 2.

Fair, Marvin L., and Williams, Ernest W., Jr. *Transportation and Logistics.* Plano, Tex.: Business Publications, 1981, Chapters 1, 2, and 3.

"The Great American Transportation Mess." *U.S. News and World Report,* 31 August 1981, pp. 18–21.

Harper, Donald V. *Transportation in America: Users, Carriers, Government.* 2d ed. Englewood Cliffs, N.J.: Prentice-Hall, 1982, Chapters 1, 2, and 3.

Lieb, Robert C. *Transportation: The Domestic System.* 2d ed. Reston, Va.: Reston Publishing Co., 1981, Chapter 1.

Locklin, D. Phillip. *Economics of Transportation.* 7th ed. Homewood, Ill.: Richard D. Irwin, 1972, Chapters 1 and 2.

Morgenthaler, Eric. "Uphill Task: U.S. West Has Energy, But Poor Transport Is a Bar to Development." *Wall Street Journal,* 7 June 1982, p. 1.

Owen, Wilfred. *The Accessible City.* Washington, D.C.: The Brookings Institution, 1972, Chapter 5, "Combining Transportation and Community Development," pp. 114–135.

———. *Strategy for Mobility.* Washington, D.C.: The Brookings Institution, 1964, Chapter 3, "Transport Requirements for Development," pp. 44–85.

Pegrum, Dudley F. *Transportation Economics and Public Policy.* 3d ed. Homewood, Ill.: Richard D. Irwin, 1973, Chapters 1, 2, and 3.

Poulton, M. C. "The Relationship Between Transport and the Viability of Central and Inner Urban Areas." *Journal of Transport Economics and Policy* 14, no. 3 (September 1980):249–265.

Sampson, Roy J.; Farris, Martin T.; and Shrock, David L. *Domestic Transportation: Practice, Theory, and Policy.* 5th ed. Boston: Houghton Mifflin Co., 1985, Chapters 1, 2, and 3.

Wood, Donald F., and Johnson, James C. *Contemporary Transportation,* Tulsa, Okla.: Petroleum Publishing Co., 1980, Chapter 1.

PART 2 PRESENTS detailed information on three groups of participants who share major transportation responsibilities: carriers, shippers, and government. Chapter 2, which examines carrier management and strategy, defines the role of suppliers of transportation services (carriers) in transportation and stresses the need for carrier managers to become more skilled businesspeople to compete successfully in a dynamic, less-regulated environment. Profitability tools and strategies are also emphasized.

Transportation management, strategy, and decision making from a corporate cargo shipper perspective are covered in Chapter 3. It provides a broad overview of logistics in an attempt to introduce important theories, concepts, and shipper responsibilities and concerns. It also examines traffic management—the primary link between the fields of logistics and transportation. Chapter 3 complements Chapter 17, which addresses transportation management, strategy, and decision making from a personal, and primarily a passenger, perspective.

Chapter 4, entitled "Government Participation in U.S. Transportation," reveals that various levels of government are deeply involved in transportation decision making for a variety of reasons. This chapter establishes a foundation for understanding how the government is involved in U.S. transportation and what regulatory reform of transportation means. Similar to Chapters 2 and 3, Chapter 4 presents broad, but necessary, background information that should facilitate the learning of information in subsequent chapters.

2 Major Transportation Participants: Carriers, Users, and Government

Carrier Management and Strategy

2

Similar to the insurance, banking, and communications industries, transportation is a service-based industry in which carriers provide transportation services for passengers and cargo shippers. Like managers in any industry, carrier managers are responsible for planning, organizing, staffing, analyzing, and controlling their firms' activities. In other words, they manage people and capital assets. They do this in specialized industries called railroad, water, pipeline, highway, and air transportation—that is, within one of the five modes of transportation. Regardless of mode, though, carrier management decision making is concerned with four functional areas: operations, marketing, finance, and human resource management.

Two different views of the carrier manager prevail. In one viewpoint, the carrier manager is perceived as a transportation specialist first, and as a businessperson second. As a specialist, the individual has considerable knowledge of the particular working mode. Such a manager may be called a railroad man, a trucker, and so on. In the second viewpoint, less importance is assigned to the need for modal expertise and more stress is placed on the person's general abilities to manage people and capital, regardless of the industrial setting. Adherents to this view assume that gifted managers can produce in any business setting; given a short time, they can learn the idiosyncrasies of any marketplace. This chapter will adopt the second viewpoint, while in no way attempting to minimize the need for modal expertise. Accordingly, the focus of this chapter is on developing astute businesspeople who can make excellent decisions in the carrier management field. Topics to be discussed will be carrier management objectives, carrier management strategy, decision-making limitations, operations, marketing, finance, and human resource management. The chapter concludes with reviews of financial ratio analysis as a way to measure carrier performance and the characteristics of successful carrier management.

CARRIER MANAGEMENT OBJECTIVES

What are the objectives of carrier management? While the answer may seem obvious, it is surprising how many managers in transportation never seem quite sure of the answer. Consider the leaders of a trucking company who seem interested in handling any type of cargo regardless of the commodity characteristics or shipment sizes, or airline managers trying to decide if they want to haul documents (courier pack services), small packages, or plane loads of live animals. Transportation managers need to focus on their goals, for to do otherwise might lead to failure in any and all marketplaces. Also, they must decide whether they are in business to operate transportation equipment or if the operation of equipment is the means to more important ends. Explicit purposes could be profits, traffic growth as measured in ton-miles or passenger-miles carried, sales as measured in operating revenues, market share, returns on investment, or other defined objectives.

profit and other goals In the U.S. economic climate of capitalism, transportation managers, whether they are employed by for-hire or private carriers, primarily strive to improve the net worth of their companies (i.e., wealth of their owners as measured by assets less liabilities). The achievement of profits, however, depends on correctly accomplishing two tasks: interpreting customer needs for services and properly setting prices to cover costs incurred in delivering those services. Again, these tasks require that carrier managers devise intelligent strategies and make astute choices.

corporate risk Miscalculations of market potential, mismanagement of labor and capital, and misjudgment of the competition can cause a firm to fail as it succumbs to either short-term cash inadequacies (e.g., a company's inability to meet payroll or other payables due within 30 days) or long-term financial bankruptcies (i.e., sustained unprofitability). The U.S. enterprise system assumes that financial rewards and the consequences of failure should be sufficient motivation to help transportation managers make wise choices.

CARRIER MANAGEMENT STRATEGY

yield strategy Different strategies could enable individuals to achieve carrier management success. Some people have done well following a revenue-oriented strategy. Emphasis is placed on pricing services at levels high enough to provide a comfortable profit margin between revenues and costs. Another term for this technique is yield strategy. *Yields* are revenues per unit of output sold, such as cents per ton-mile or cents per passenger-mile. Two companies that have used the yield strategy quite successfully are Roadway Express and Delta Air Lines. Although both are high-cost carriers, they have been able to find market niches and provide quality services, which their customers in turn have been willing to pay higher average yields for. These carriers and their strategies will be discussed further in Chapter 12 (Roadway) and Chapter 15 (Delta).

cost control strategy

A second management strategy that can work well in improving carrier profitability is cost controls. The objective is to improve the competitive position of the firm by minimizing expenses. If successful, managers practicing this tactic are able to sell services at more favorable prices since some cost savings can be redistributed to consumers. One well-known and historically successful user of the cost control strategy is Northwest Airlines. (As will be explained in Chapter 15, the management of Northwest practiced rigorous cost controls long before the strategy was adopted by many other U.S. airlines.)

productivity strategy

low-interest strategy

Two other strategies that can be used effectively to enhance carrier earnings are productivity tactics and the avoidance of high interest payments. United Parcel Service (UPS) is a leading example of a carrier with high costs and low yields but good profitability due to high productivity. Each employee is expected to produce outstanding results, such as the number of packages delivered per driver per day. (UPS specifics will be provided in Chapter 12.) Examples of carriers who have minimized debt and high-interest payments are Northwest Airlines and Roadway Express. Chapter 15 will present the risks associated with borrowing too much money during a period of inflation.

Carrier management success in earning acceptable levels of profits in the current highly dynamic transportation environment will depend in no small measure on people's abilities to use one or more of the above four fundamental strategies—yields, cost controls, productivity, and the avoidance of high interest payments.

DECISION-MAKING LIMITATIONS

Today's transportation companies consist of owners, boards of directors, managers, and labor. Senior carrier managers (e.g., corporate presidents) answer to the boards of directors, who in turn answer to the owners. Likewise, junior managers answer to middle and senior managers. Accordingly, there is no guarantee that managers at any level have the freedom to make all the choices they would like. Many times it is easier to conceptualize ideas than to have them approved.

managing problems

Even if managers do gain approval for suggestions, they then must implement them, analyze the feedback, and if necessary, modify the plan or activities. In essence, managers must accept risks; they must be willing to try new ideas and make decisions. Furthermore, they must be prepared to handle changes beyond their control, such as the changing economy, technological advancements, competitors' initiatives, revised federal policies and regulations, and shifts in energy prices or supplies. These factors are all part of the transportation business, and while some people are uncomfortable with these pressures, others thrive on the challenge.

OPERATIONS

One major carrier management decision-making area is operations, which is responsible for the physical movement of passengers and cargo. In other words, operations is the wherewithal of the business; it is to the transportation industry what manufacturing is to a product-based business. Operating departments produce something that can be sold, namely, services. The task of operating personnel, such as drivers and terminal dock workers, is to see not only that marketing promises (e.g., delivery by noon tomorrow, extra care in handling, or notice on arrival at the carrier's terminal) are fulfilled, but also that services are performed in a manner that minimizes carrier costs.

Types of Transportation Movements

A simple understanding of operations can be obtained from Fig. 2.1, which shows an uninterrupted bulk load movement from an origin to a single destination. It indicates that the carrier must pick up the goods at one place, carry the goods over long-distance routes (linehaul), and deliver the cargo at the specified destination. One example is a 40,000-lb. truckload of apples moving from an orchard in one state to a grocery store in another state. Another example is a unit coal train movement in which a group of coal cars travel in nonstop service from a mine to an electric power generating plant. A picture of a unit coal train is shown in Fig. 2.2.

bulk load movement

Many transportation operations acquire added complexities. If, for example, a single consumer cannot use an entire bulk load, subsequent transportation movements are necessary. To continue the apple illustration, a single grocery store probably could not sell all 40,000 lbs. of apples before they begin to spoil. Thus a distribution center (warehouse) would perform a breakbulk operation dividing the apple shipment into smaller portions (boxes) for subsequent distribution to individual supermarkets (Fig. 2.3). At the supermarket

breakbulk operation

FIGURE 2.1.
Point-to-point bulk load movement.

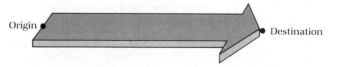

Origin ●   ● Destination

FIGURE 2.2.
Burlington Northern Railroad unit train approaches a low sulfur coal mine near Gillette, Wyoming, where it will take on an 11,000-ton load. (Photo courtesy of Burlington Northern Railroad)

level, boxes of apples would again be broken down into even smaller units (e.g., 5-lb. bags) and moved again, but this time by private automobiles hauling groceries home for consumption.

intermodal movement   A third example of a transportation movement is the illustration of how corn might be shipped from an Iowa farm to an end user in Georgia, a farmer purchasing grain for animal feed (Fig. 2.4). After corn has been harvested, the Iowa farmer's immediate need is to truck the grain to the nearest rural ele-

FIGURE 2.3.
Bulk load movement with subsequent distribution after breakbulk operation.

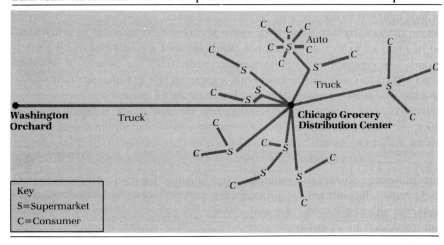

FIGURE 2.4.
Bulk corn movement: Iowa farm to Georgia farm.

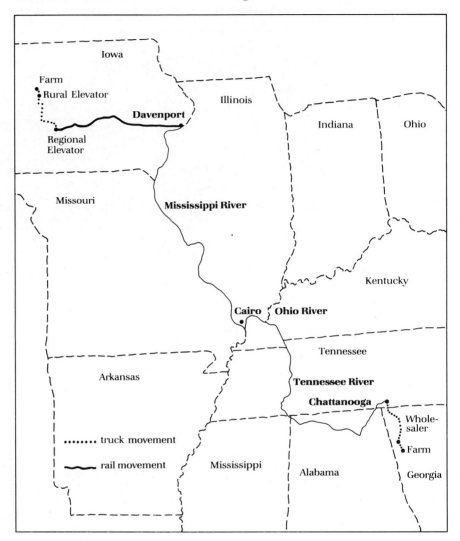

vator for storage and protection from rain and other elements (Fig. 2.5). At a future date, the corn is moved by truck to a regional elevator. Eventually the corn is loaded onto a rail car and dispatched to a Mississippi River port. Once the barge is loaded (Fig. 2.6), the corn then journeys south to Cairo, Illinois, then upstream on the Ohio River and subsequently on the Tennessee River. At Chattanooga, the corn is transported by truck to a regional wholesaler, who ultimately delivers the corn by truck to the farmer in Georgia.

FIGURE 2.5.
Rural grain elevator. (Fred Stephenson photo)

This example combined four distinct truck moves, one rail shipment, and one barge journey to form a door-to-door intermodal (more than one mode) movement during a period of months, and quite possibly years, depending on the time in storage at the rural and regional elevators. Some hauls were iso-

FIGURE 2.6.
A 1300-ft conveyor connects Port Cargill's 15-million bushel elevator to the loading dock. Here a barge is loaded with 50,000 bushels of soybeans. (Photo courtesy of Cargo Carriers, Inc.)

lated (e.g., the movement from farm to the rural elevator), and others were planned and coordinated (e.g., the rail-barge-truck intermodal movement from the regional elevator to the wholesaler). In all, seven channel members were involved in a logistics network that made six pick-ups and six deliveries in moving the corn to market.

Activities of Operating Personnel

Figures 2.1, 2.3, and 2.4 show that the activities of operating personnel include the pick-up of full vehicle loads, the collection (consolidation) of smaller loads into larger loads (e.g., a barge can hold 15 rail car loads), the linehauling of bulk load shipments for great distances, delivery of bulk loads to distribution centers, breakbulk operations, and ultimately the delivery of shipments to consumers. Basic to operations, then, are routes, schedules, fleets (equipment), and sorting facilities such as the Union Pacific System's Bailey Yard at North Platte, Nebraska. In essence, operating personnel collect, sort, haul, sort again, and deliver. They might also bypass some of these activities with door-to-door (point-to-point) services.

Although the illustrations are freight examples, they easily could have been drawn to demonstrate similar aspects of the passenger trade. Consider the commercial airline industry. This industry uses distant flights of high-capacity aircraft dependent on cars, buses, and feeder aircraft delivering passengers to, and taking others from, collection and sorting facilities called airports.

Operating Decisions and Responsibilities

Operating decisions and responsibilities differ substantially among carriers. For instance, companies concentrating on point-to-point bulk movements are able to minimize terminal activities. Consequently, they avoid consolidating loads and breakbulk operations, which require considerable time and result in high labor costs. Other firms, like general commodity less-than-truckload (LTL) trucking companies and air freight airlines, are involved in small ship-ment traffic. While their costs per hundred pounds are high, yields are sim-ilarly larger. Thus whether to concentrate on bulk or small shipment loads is a decision of carrier management.

bulk versus small shipments

Another important decision is whether a carrier will provide scheduled or charter (or contract) operations. Scheduled operations imply adherence to predetermined, announced departure times, whereas charter service and con-tract carriage are demand-activated (i.e., unscheduled services that honor the customized needs of users). In contract carriage operations, vehicles usually move only when vehicles are satisfactorily full. Many ships and planes are engaged in charter operations, and such arrangements often imply either sin-gletrip or roundtrip commitments. Contract carriage usually means longer term agreements (in railroading, a 20-year contract is not unusual); however, other contracts, such as in trucking, may be for periods as short as 90 days. Actually, charter and contract services are so similar that at times they are

scheduled versus charter or contract services

indistinguishable. Rail and truck modes tend to call demand-activated transportation *contract carriage,* although airlines, water carriers, and bus companies prefer *charter* transportation. More important to remember is that both contract and charter services concentrate on full vehicle loads or charging users as if vehicles were full.

people versus cargo

backhaul decisions

Whether carriers primarily or exclusively haul either people or cargo also has an operating impact. People almost always return home (book roundtrip routings), whereas cargo rarely if ever returns to its origin point. Consequently, a high level of passenger backhaul (return) traffic is always available, which, with attractive services and marketing, should produce roundtrip revenues. On the one hand, cargo can be a more difficult sector, since backhaul traffic is a potential problem, which forces management to make a decision whether to search for backhaul traffic or to return empty vehicles to the origin point as fast as possible. Truckers hauling wheat, for instance, might try to find a load of fertilizer to return to the farming districts or decide to return as fast as possible to the origin elevator for another load of grain. The problem with the second strategy is that the front-haul revenues must cover the costs of deadhead (empty) movements. Excess, unused, capacity is a serious problem in cargo transportation, which forces higher shipper prices. On the other hand, passengers tend to be more demanding of operating personnel than are cargo customers. If passengers are dissatisfied, they can voice their displeasure immediately. Thus pros and cons of operating in each sector exist.

nature of cargo

The nature of the cargo also affects carrier operating decisions. If carriers move live animals, for example, fixed needs exist for feeding and watering. But if they move sand, almost nothing can physically damage the cargo. By comparison, great care must be taken shipping glass, flowers, ice cream, and so forth. Again, managers must satisfy diverse operating requirements.

linehaul operations

Operating activities can usually be divided into two areas—linehaul operations and terminal management. Managers handling *linehaul operations* are concerned with *rights-of-way* (the paths over which transportation vehicles move), *traffic lanes* (routes linking each origin and destination: e.g., New York to Tulsa), equipment, fuel and power, and operating crews, among other variables. In short, their job is to ensure that goods and people move securely, safely, and efficiently between origin and destination cities. To accomplish this goal, considerable time and money must be invested in terminals, rights-of-way structures like bridges and tunnels, and dependable equipment like trucks and airplanes. These expenditures represent fixed costs, which eventually must be recovered from carrier customers. Providing good services, good engineering, maintenance to keep the system in good operating order, and properly working communications—all require technological equipment. Consequently, in today's dynamic transportation environment, operating personnel are expected to be aware of technological advancements. Furthermore, they must constantly monitor their terminals, rights-of-way, and maintenance shops to spot potential deficiencies.

terminal operations

The primary responsibilities of terminal managers are the collection and dispersing of passengers and cargo. Intramodal and intermodal transfers of equipment or traffic are also part of their tasks. Thus the terminal manager's job is to build larger loads expeditiously for efficient linehaul operations; efficiently control vehicular and cargo movements at consolidation or breakbulk points; and stay in direct contact with linehaul personnel, the marketing staff, and often customers. In addition, terminal managers are often held accountable for cargo loss and damage problems. Therefore they must focus their attention on cargo control measures, such as recordkeeping to monitor traffic passing through the terminal. Two important types of records are *manifests* (i.e., lists of shipments in a vehicle) and *bills of lading* (i.e., documents that act as shipping contracts, receipts, and evidence of cargo ownership and that provide operating personnel with important shipping instructions).

Operating Strategies

make or buy decisions

Operating managers thus face many challenges and have the opportunity to choose from among many available working strategies. The firm must decide, for example, whether it should attempt to operate the total door-to-door system or rely on other carriers or intermediaries, such as brokers or freight forwarders, to feed it traffic. Trucking companies must likewise decide whether it is desirable to give traffic to other truck lines, which would then deliver the shipments to customers. This process, called *interlining*, happens in trucking and other transportation sectors any time two or more carriers are involved in through services whereby passengers or cargo are transferred between two or more carriers. In another case, railroads must decide whether to depend on shippers' agents to feed them TOFC/COFC piggyback trailers (trailers-on-flat-cars or containers-on-flat-cars) or to pick up that traffic directly using their own railroad personnel. By relying on others, carriers lessen their responsibilities by allowing other firms to do the sales soliciting, but the trade-off is the loss of direct control. The carrier no longer has direct contact with the customer, and if the shippers' agent makes a mistake, the carrier is limited in its ability to correct the problem.

Major airlines must determine whether they can rely on smaller airlines to feed them passengers for subsequent long-haul movements or whether they (the long-haul carriers) should absorb the added costs and fly their own planes into the smaller airports. By doing the latter, they will probably retain the passenger for the long-haul segment. But choosing the former strategy might mean the passenger interlines with a competitive long-haul carrier. A final illustration is the decision air freight forwarders must make about whether they should rely on scheduled airlines for cargo space or operate their own aircraft to guarantee sufficient space. All these examples address the matters of control, maintaining direct contact with customers, the management of costs, delivery of promised services, and the equitable division of revenues among interlining carriers. The overriding question in any case is how much to depend on others.

productivity or service decision

Carriers must further decide if their objective is building cost-efficient loads or providing regular services regardless of demand fluctuations. For example, should a trucking company hold cargo for another day because the present traffic volume to a particular point is too low, or should it dispatch the vehicle today with considerable excess capacity? In other words, a firm must decide when and under what circumstances its operating personnel should deviate from normal service standards.

maintenance or
replacement decision

Another issue, the choice between maintaining old equipment or replacing these assets with new technology, is particularly important because of high energy prices and escalating labor costs. However, the advantages of more fuel-efficient or productive vehicles must be traded off with the potential of high equipment prices, expensive interest payments, and other negative consequences such as problems disposing of present equipment.

loss and damage
claims versus
prevention decision

Carriers must also balance the need for reducing loss and damage (L&D) payments against the cost of L&D prevention. Shippers expect cargo to arrive at destination in the same condition that the goods were tendered to the carriers. When problems are caused by theft, breakage, and so forth, customers initiate claims against carriers to recover financial losses. The resulting payments can annually cost a carrier millions of dollars. Firms can reduce L&D costs by tightening security and control procedures; at some point, however, the costs of prevention can exceed the costs of paying claims. For example, it might be necessary to reduce the speed of cargo handling to reduce breakage, but this would cut productivity. Insisting on better packaging would possibly raise shipper costs and hurt sales.

MARKETING

Marketing, the second functional decision-making area of carrier management, is undergoing radical change. Stimulating these modifications is regulatory reform, which has given transportation marketing managers considerable freedom to broaden their rate/service offerings. Entry freedom enables carriers to serve a wider variety of customers, and pricing freedom gives managers another tool with which to attract business. Consequently, transportation is changing from a field that stressed personal selling to a full-fledged total marketing enterprise. Carrier personnel are becoming far more attentive in listening to shipper and passenger desires and needs. In addition, they are

marketing concept

practicing the marketing concept by researching what consumers expect in services and rates and responding accordingly. Too often in the past, the operating personnel created a new service, and only then did the company attempt to sell the idea to the public. Although this practice still continues to a great extent, more and more firms are scanning current and potential cus-

market segmentation
and targeting

tomers to segment the public into market targets (i.e., segments with high potential). This effort can determine more realistic appraisals of demand and potential sales profitability.

Marketing Mix Strategies

Marketing is not the same as sales; in fact, marketing includes sales as a subset. For years, manufacturers of products have developed strategic plans called *marketing mixes* combining "the four P's": product, price, promotion, and place. The same idea can be applied in modified form to carrier marketing. The only variations are to substitute the term "services" for "products," and to substitute "origin-destination network" for "place."

service
Carriers do not supply products; they provide and sell services. Nevertheless, the concept of services has many meanings. Reliability, speed, frequency of departures, destination and arrival times, pick-up and delivery service, convenience, ease of obtaining reservations or cargo space, loss and damage records, and in-transit passenger meal and drink services are just a few of the customers' interpretations of service. Most important, in carrier marketing the users should determine the service standards. Setting improper goals is a common carrier malady, for if firms misread the needs of the market, they can become bankrupt achieving meaningless objectives.

price
One component of good marketing is pricing services at attractive levels to stimulate traffic, revenues, and profit margins. Carrier prices are influenced by costs, the degree of available competing services, the level of customer demand, and external factors such as regulations, which restrict pricing freedoms, and a recessionary economic climate. An important strategic issue is the inclusive or exclusive nature of the price—that is, what services are covered by the charge and what other charges will have to be paid. Whereas rates almost always cover linehaul costs, they may or may not fund pick-up or delivery services, loading or unloading of the vehicle, added packaging costs necessary to protect goods from damage, or the need for additional insurance. Carriers must be careful to establish rates that generate profits and to avoid rates that produce profitless traffic movements. Increasing sales revenues is not meaningful in a capitalistic environment unless those sales produce sufficient earnings. One risk of surrendering pricing decision-making power to sales personnel is that the latter tend to become more motivated with market share and traffic volumes than with corporate profitability. This risk intensifies when salespeople are rewarded on the basis of units sold.

promotion
Promotion, the third factor in strategic marketing plans, is the collection of all activities designed to finalize a sale—in the case of transportation, to use the carrier's services. Included, then, are advertising, sales, and promotional devices like pamphlets or give-aways such as pads or pens with the corporate logo on them. Considerable emphasis is placed on direct selling efforts, particularly in the cargo sector—an understandable practice since carriers must answer questions about customized, complex shippers' needs.

Sales management is charged with the responsibility of staffing, training, organizing, directing, and controlling the sales force, which includes inside and field sales personnel who bridge the gap between customers and carrier operating personnel. As their names imply, inside sales personnel stay close to the phone arranging business transactions from the office, whereas field sales personnel go to customer locations. Many carriers rely heavily on company salespeople to accomplish this task, but there are notable exceptions. Most airline passenger tickets, for example, are sold by independent travel agents. Also, many international water carriers depend on ship agencies. These agencies are shore-based organizations that solicit cargo on behalf of the ship operator and handle the needs of a ship in port, such as arranging for bunkering (fuel), supplies, and stevedore gangs.

Carrier promotional strategies are diverse and changing. Considerable differences exist across the modes and even within the modes, such as in the choice of whether to emphasize promotion (e.g., free trip coupons) or advertising and in the selection of advertising media (e.g., television, radio, magazines). One noteworthy trend is the increased emphasis on corporate sales accounts. Rather than restricting sales calls to local plants and other customers such as retail establishments, carrier marketing personnel are soliciting business from corporate executives such as vice-presidents of logistics. The goal is to attract large volumes of traffic by having corporate decision makers specify which carriers are to be used at the local plant and warehouse levels.

origin-destination network

Marketing managers today are giving more of their time to a reassessment of the fourth marketing mix function—the *origin-destination network*. Carriers are reexamining the cities and routes they serve, the specific origin-destination lanes over which vehicles move passengers and cargo, directional traffic flows (e.g., west-bound versus east-bound business), and passenger and cargo targets. As noted by the expansion of some carriers' routes and the contraction of other networks, profit concerns are now becoming far more relevant in marketing decisions.

Transportation Marketing Today

Transportation marketing is undergoing a rationalization and maturing process, and as a result, responsibilities and ways of conducting business are changing. Decision-making powers traditionally vested in traffic—essentially, pricing—and sales personnel are being transferred to people more concerned with the achievement of corporate profitability. The days when salespeople seemed more interested in the success of the sales department and operating people seemed myopically tuned to running equipment without regard to company earnings are quickly coming to a close.

FINANCE

Financial management is another area of growing importance to the transportation industry. Responsibilities include profits, costs, investments, and control of the firm's cash and other assets. Typically involved would be officers and managers such as the treasurer and controller, as well as people involved in accounting and management information systems, namely, computers and the people who run them. In addition, financial management can include a planning and analysis group—that is, a team of individuals trying to prepare plans for the future success of the firm.

Costs

fixed and
variable costs To succeed, of course, carriers must cover the costs of doing business. In broad terms, expenses can be segregated into fixed and variable costs. Fixed costs do not vary with the level of traffic (output): Mortgage payments, interest expenses, the president's salary, and property taxes are examples of fixed costs. Variable costs, on the contrary, occur only by producing units of volume. Some examples are fuel, hourly wages, and maintenance expenses as a function of use.

Other items fall under both cost categories; telephone service, for instance, contains both a fixed monthly charge and variable long-distance call fees. Some people would also argue that an airplane flight is essentially a fixed cost, too, because crew and fuel costs will not vary much whether the plane is full or empty. The decision to fly the aircraft locks the company into these charges. On the other hand, the costs of providing a meal for a passenger or paying a commission to the travel agent who booked a passenger on a flight are variable costs.

cost recovery needs Carriers must recover variable costs on each movement. If they cannot accomplish this objective, they are better off not hauling the traffic, for they are losing money. In fact, firms thought to be operating below variable costs are often accused of predatory pricing; it is assumed that their prices are aimed at driving out the competition. In the long run, however, firms must recover fixed costs as well if they are to avoid bankruptcy.

modal cost
differences Differences exist, however, in the levels of fixed and variable costs for the respective modes. Some modes, such as pipelines and railroads, have proportionately higher shares of fixed costs than do highway, water, and air carrier modes. This occurs because they provide their own rights-of-way, while the other modes benefit from publicly provided rights-of-way. Note, too, how various cost structures affect carrier pricing and competitiveness. Also, some modes are more sensitive to inflation such as those with large, unionized work forces, those that require more petroleum products, and those that rely on heavy debt financing and must pay interest payments.

managing costs To manage costs, accountants and controllers approve budgets that establish predetermined spending targets. Then they create reports to compare results to these budgetary limits and determine trouble spots as well as superior performance. Quite popular today is the profit center concept, which holds a subunit of the company accountable for its managerial decisions. However, management should be careful not to design a reward system that encourages self-interests. The objective is not to encourage sales personnel to increase revenues at any cost, but rather to increase sales that result in greater company profits or other corporate objectives.

Financial Strategies

Increased profitability and growth in sales, traffic, and market share are possible through internal improvements, by expansion of the present business, and through mergers and acquisitions (combinations with other firms either in or out of transportation).

Internal Improvements.   The first strategy, internal improvements, includes productivity betterments and cost control measures. Both can enhance a company's financial posture. The carrier manager's challenge is to try to achieve more with the present routes, equipment, and facilities, without adding to the company's assets. In the case of a scheduled combination airline, for instance United Airlines or Northwest Airlines, which hauls passengers and cargo on the same flight, increased productivity is possible in many ways. The carrier can board more passengers or increase its mail and freight volumes per flight, thereby filling excess capacity. It can fly each airplane more hours per day, redesign its aircraft to hold more seats per flight, or fly planes at greater speeds, thereby having them available more quickly for added flights. The airline can streamline ground handling activities, minimize deadhead mileage (i.e., do less empty shuttling of aircraft from airports where they are not needed), and motivate labor to handle more baggage per worker.

productivity strategy

Likewise, a carrier can increase profits by reducing fixed and variable costs through measures such as the removal of excess personnel, routes, and equipment; subcontracting work to non-unionized labor; and finding fuel suppliers who have lower prices than what the carrier has been paying. Carriers with lower unit costs can reduce prices to stimulate demand or keep prices the same while benefitting from greater profit margins.

cost strategy

Expansion of the Present Business.   A second financial strategy calls for expansion of the present asset base. The process of deciding which projects to fund has been termed *capital budgeting.* The goal is to achieve acceptable profits from newly invested capital. In the transportation industry, capital budgeting implies the expansion of the service network and marketing activities to reach more origin and destination points, more customers, and more traffic. This practice usually involves fleet and route additions. Other investments, however, could be made for facilities, computers, communications equipment, and traffic handling equipment such as fork lifts.

capital budgeting

Financial managers charged with capital budgeting responsibilities have many duties; for instance, they need to specify minimum acceptable return levels, such as a 15% after-tax return on equity. Another task is to determine sources of capital. Specifically, they need to know how much cash can be made available from internal funds, new issues of preferred or common stock (equity), and debt (borrowing). A third challenge is to select projects while remembering that requests for funds usually exceed available cash. Ever present is the concern for opportunity costs—that is, alternative investment opportunities that will be bypassed in favor of the chosen projects. Consequently, carrier managers resort to quantitative methods to help them choose wisely.

Normally, the technique used to make capital budgeting decisions is *present value analysis.* This method accounts for the fact that many assets have different years of service (e.g., one may last 5 years, while another, 20 years).

*present
value analysis*

Inflation is also considered. Recognizing that a dollar received at a future date is not worth as much as a dollar in hand today, the technique translates all cash inflows into present value money terms. A simple illustration will provide the basic methodology.

Suppose Gentex Trucking Company is considering the purchase of $20,000,000 in new truck tractors, which will be depreciated on a straight-line basis for five years, at the end of which the equipment will be sold for a salvage value of $4,000,000. Company forecasters have estimated that the vehicles will produce $8,000,000 in annual cash savings in each of the five years of use; however, the company requires an 18% after-tax return on invested capital (income divided by funded debt after one year and equity). Should the equipment purchase be approved?

As Table 2.1 shows, the project would create an estimated annual after-tax income of $2,592,000 in the book account. More important for computational purposes, however, is the projected $5,792,000 in annual cash inflows (cash available for emergency spending purposes) shown at the bottom of the cash flow account. Another way to compute annual cash inflows, also called *cash throw,* is by adding after-tax income to depreciation (see the book ac-

---

TABLE 2.1. Gentex Trucking Company present value analysis

	Book Account	Cash Flow Account
Annual cash savings	$8,000,000	$8,000,000
Depreciation $\left(\dfrac{\$20,000,000 - \$4,000,000}{5 \text{ years}}\right)$	3,200,000	
Additional pretax income	4,800,000	
Federal corporate income tax	2,208,000	2,208,000
Added income after tax	$2,592,000	$5,792,000

$20,000,000 (initial cash outflow)

				$4,000,000 (salvage value)
$5,792,000	$5,792,000	$5,792,000	$5,792,000	$5,792,000

(annual cash inflows)

Computation of the present value of the cash inflows:

PV of $5,792,000 @ 18% @ Yr 1 = $5,792,000 (0.8475) =	$4,909,000
Yr 2 = $5,792,000 (0.7182) =	4,160,000
Yr 3 = $5,792,000 (0.6086) =	3,525,000
Yr 4 = $5,792,000 (0.5158) =	2,988,000
Yr 5 = $5,792,000 (0.4371) =	2,532,000
PV of $4,000,000 @ 18% @ Yr 5 = $4,000,000 (0.4371) =	1,748,000
	$19,862,000

count). *Depreciation* is simply a way of retaining earnings in a firm to set aside resources for the eventual day when obsolete or worn out assets must be replaced. As Table 2.1 indicates, cash inflows will come from five annual equal returns of $5,792,000, plus one injection of $4,000,000 after sale of the truck tractors at the end of the fifth year. Since the company demands an 18% return on invested capital, $5,792,000 at the end of year one is worth only $4,909,000 today. Viewed another way, if $4,909,000 is invested at 18%, it would be worth $5,792,000 at the end of year one ($4,909,000 × 1.18). Thus a cash inflow of $5,792,000 at the end of year two is worth only $4,160,000 today, and so forth for each of the other cash injections.

decision rule
    According to the decision rule, an investment achieves the minimum acceptable return on investment if the present value of the cash inflows either equals or exceeds the present value of the cash outflows. Since the present value of all the cash inflows is $19,862,000 and the present value of the cash outflows is $20,000,000, the investment falls short of the required 18% return level. Unless management is willing to lower its expected return on capital, the purchase should be rejected. The above illustration does not imply that trucking companies universally expect 18% after-tax returns on capital. Instead, this example merely illustrates the methodology and interprets the results. Given the array of computer programs and inexpensive hand-held calculators available today with present value capabilities, present value techniques probably should be incorporated into the capital budgeting process.

fleet
equipment decisions
    Financial managers are constantly being asked to make fleet equipment decisions. Some of the many questions needing answers are whether present equipment should be maintained or replaced and whether new equipment should be purchased or leased. Other issues are whether carriers should rely on shipper-owned equipment or company vehicles, and whether carriers should place some of the equipment burden on interlining carriers or intermediaries. Again, these decisions should be made according to company plans as well as needs. It is one matter to want to control the entire fleet and another to find the capital to do so. Moreover, the availability of funds for equipment purchases does not necessarily mean that is the best place for company money to be spent. Decisions should be based on careful analysis of the impact of these choices on costs, revenues, profits, and growth expectations. If the choice is to expand or modify the fleet, decision makers should consider various needs, such as cost savings, operating efficiencies, reduced maintenance, reliability, satisfying customer desires, productivity, fuel efficiency, and improved employee morale. It is difficult to do any job right without the right tools and motivated workers.

Mergers and Acquisitions.   Financial strategy also extends to mergers and acquisitions, since growth can be achieved by combining two or more firms under common ownership (*merger*) or by purchasing control of another business enterprise (*acquisition*). For many years, trucking companies have

intramodal
combinations
been growing by obtaining other trucking firms, *intramodal combinations,*

intermodal
combinations

diversification and
holding companies

and the same trend has been seen in railroading, water carriage, and aviation. An emerging trend is toward *intermodal ownership,* that is, the merging of two or more transport firms of different modal interests or the acquisition of one mode by another. Diversification, the control of a nontransportation company by a carrier or vice versa, is also occurring. Frequently, today's carriers announce the formation of holding companies. These organizations are usually created for tax and other financial reasons, and they control a number of subsidiary transportation and nontransportation businesses.

Although growth can be attained by expanding the traffic and sales volumes of the present organization, mergers and acquisitions often produce the most dramatic one-year growth trends. Corporate gains in revenues, traffic, and profits can result from improved marketing, operations, and management, or they may simply reflect mergers and acquisitions. While many mergers and acquisitions are excellent decisions, some turn out to be major corporate mistakes that deplete profits and cause bankruptcies.[1] Mergers and acquisitions can require considerable expenditures of time and money; therefore they should be decided on carefully.

Computers and Management Information Systems

The complexities of modern-day carrier management have created increased demands for computers; software and programmers; and accurate data recording, reporting, and analysis. Computers provide the data base for the airline industry's reservation systems. They are the means by which current carrier pricing information is retrieved by trucking employees and quoted to potential customers, and they are used to pinpoint the location of an air freight shipment. They are also used to analyze complex routing problems, help man-

FIGURE 2.7.
Seaboard System Railroad computer console equipment. (Photo courtesy of Seaboard System Railroad, which is now called CSX Transportation, Inc.)

agers decide which pieces of equipment need to be replaced, and facilitate the preparation of budgets and payrolls. As shown in Fig. 2.7, computers and management information systems are employed by railroads as well as by all other modes of transportation to improve and expedite decision making.

HUMAN RESOURCE MANAGEMENT

A company, of course, is built from a foundation of people—owners, managers, laborers, and customers. Machines exist to help people run their businesses. Thus, although it is possible to find successful carriers who rely on a capital-based strategy (i.e., they either prefer or have to substitute machines for people), most well-managed firms have built their accomplishments primarily on the contributions of individuals.

importance

The process of recruiting, hiring, training, assigning, motivating, and managing people is called human resource management, which is not the exclusive domain of Personnel Department specialists, but rather the responsibility of every individual in a firm who supervises anyone else. It is an important, challenging part of carrier management. Employee costs represent the highest single cost category for most modes, labor-management relations in the field have not been ideal, and productivity and cost gains depend to a great extent on improved labor-management cooperation. Consequently, survival of some carriers often depends on better human resource management.

Managers' Responses to Labor Demands

carrier responses

For many carriers, rising labor costs are a serious problem. Workers believe they have the right to share in the profitable results of their labors; however, a balance must be struck between employee demands and the risks of company noncompetitiveness, operating losses, and bankruptcies that can and do occur in part from excessive wage and benefit packages. Carriers respond to labor demands with demands for increased productivity to spread costs over more units of output. Failing to achieve this objective, management frequently reduces employment and substitutes machines for people. This is management's prerogative, just as it is labor's right to seek wage and benefit increases or shorter work weeks. Nevertheless, management is paid to motivate workers toward greater output. However, not every manager is particularly effective in this endeavor, nor are all laborers doing their best to improve their employers' profits.

leadership

Contrary to popular opinion, managers are not necessarily natural, or even well-trained, leaders. Leadership means accomplishing things through people. Note that this does not say that leaders do the job themselves, since guiding others is the objective. Consequently, senior managers must be careful in hiring middle managers and junior managers who are not only technically

motivating workers

skilled professionals but who are also gifted at motivating labor. Money alone, however, is not sufficient to guarantee sustained worker performance. Most carrier employees, like their managers, want to believe what they do is important, that their work makes a meaningful contribution to the company, and that they have the respect of their fellow workers and bosses. It is management's responsibility to capitalize on these motivational factors. Table 2.2 lists suggestions that can help carrier managers improve worker motivation. Although they are all commonsensical ideas that work, it is surprising how many managers do not practice them.

Management Errors

Labor productivity begins with smart management and a recognition that most workers want to help. Progressive companies have recognized the need to hire skilled, people-oriented managers who will listen and observe and know how to use reward and punishment effectively. Managers are often too quick to find fault with labor; in fact, many problems are caused by management. Sometimes supervisors blame employees for careless work habits that management actually causes. For example, dock workers may be accused of damaging goods, although the problem may in fact be due to management's insis-

---

TABLE 2.2. Ways to improve worker motivation

1. Clearly define what is expected of workers and how their work makes a difference to the company.
2. Delegate responsibilities; most people want to play a valuable role.
3. Spot check workers; do not constantly be looking over their shoulders.
4. Praise in public and criticize in private; put favorable comments in writing.
5. Avoid favoritism real or perceived; be fair.
6. Do not stay at a desk; be visible and concerned.
7. Take advice; listen to workers.
8. Reward people for innovative ideas.
9. Provide progress reports and be conscientious about performance evaluations.
10. Work hard setting the pace and the example.
11. Give credit where credit is due; do not steal workers' ideas.
12. Be consistent.
13. Do not try to be all things to all people.
14. Do not criticize bosses in the presence of employees.
15. Provide social events that cut across organizational barriers; learn to know workers outside the office setting.
16. Have empathy.
17. If employees must work late, give them as much advance warning as possible; remember, work is not their only priority.
18. Be a little humble; no one is perfect.
19. Have a sense of humor.
20. Be professional; the manager's attitude will set the tone for workers' attitudes.

tence that workers meet unreasonable productivity standards. In order to comply, workers repress their own good judgment and literally throw goods across the dock. In some cases managers also ask workers to take unreasonable risks, but those workers who fear injury and thus refuse to take these risks are labeled "lazy." At other times, workers do exactly what is asked of them even though they know the results will be detrimental to the company. When they try to tell the manager this, they are told to work, and not to think. Managers therefore need to make wiser labor decisions.

PERFORMANCE: FINANCIAL RATIO ANALYSIS

One important aspect of carrier management is judging performance. How does a manager know whether the firm is doing well or poorly? Unless this situation becomes apparent, strategy changes are almost random, speculative exercises. To fill this need, the transportation industry uses ratio analysis—essentially a process that computes figures, which can then be compared against norms. In other words, a company needs to be able to compare its results (performance) against corporate goals (internal standards), modal industry standards, modal industry leaders' standards, other modes' standards, and even nontransportation industry performance criteria. What needs to be measured, among other factors, is capital productivity (output per unit of fixed assets), labor productivity, and financial achievement.

liquidity
solvency

profitability

Carriers have concentrated on three areas of financial ratio analysis: *liquidity,* the company's ability to meet current obligations due in less than one year; *solvency,* sometimes called *leverage* or *debt service,* but basically the company's ability to repay principal and interest on long-term loans; and *profitability,* the determination of income levels of the firm. Table 2.3 shows the income statement and balance sheet of the Bullet Transportation Company, which will be used to illustrate these financial ratios.

Liquidity Measures

Two common measures of liquidity are *working capital* and the *current ratio,* which are computed as follows:

working capital

(a) *working capital* = current assets $(-)$ current liabilities

$$= \$1,548,000 - \$531,000$$

$$= \$1,017,000$$

current ratio

(b) *current ratio* $= \dfrac{\text{current assets}}{\text{current liabilities}}$

$$= \frac{\$1,548,000}{\$531,000}$$

$$= 2.92:1$$

TABLE 2.3. Bullet Transportation Company income statement and balance sheet (in thousands)

Income Statement (in thousands)	
Gross operating revenues	$7,000
Total operating expenses	6,625
Net carrier operating income	375
Interest expense	102
Net income before taxes	273
Income taxes	125
Net income after taxes	$148

Balance Sheet (in thousands)		
Assets		
Cash	$815	
Receivables (net)	520	
Materials and supplies	213	
Total current assets		$1,548
Carrier operating property	$3,350	
Reserve for depreciation	1,427	
Carrier operating property net		1,923
Other assets		10
Total assets		$3,481
Liabilities and equity		
Accounts payable	$385	
Taxes payable	53	
Funded debt due within one year	93	
Total current liabilities		$531
Funded debt due after one year		809
Common stock	$1,700	
Preferred stock	250	
Retained earnings	191	
Total stockholders' equity		$2,141
Total liabilities and stockholders' equity		$3,481

meaning

Both ratios indicate that Bullet has considerably more cash available than it requires to meet its short-term needs. In fact, it may have too much cash available, indicating that Bullet might want to consider investing its surplus funds.

Solvency Ratios

debt-to-equity

One commonly used solvency ratio is funded debt-to-equity, often simply called the *debt-to-equity ratio.*

$$debt\text{-}to\text{-}equity\ ratio = \frac{\begin{array}{c}\text{funded debt due within one year }(+)\\ \text{funded debt due after one year}\end{array}}{\text{total stockholders' equity}}$$

$$= \frac{\$93,000 + \$809,000}{\$2,141,000}$$

$$= 0.42{:}1$$

meaning *Highly leveraged carriers* are firms that rely on borrowed funds out of necessity or by design. To use other people's money to make money for them (i.e., to borrow at one interest rate and hope for returns at higher levels), they must realize that debt obligations take precedence over stockholders' equity claims in the event the company experiences bankruptcy problems. Bullet has a low debt-to-equity ratio (0.42:1), implying that the carrier is relatively secure from creditor (debt holder) claims on the firm's assets. Some carriers (oil pipelines) have ratios exceeding 9:1, but leverage of this magnitude is possible and recommended only under unusual circumstances. (More will be said about this situation in Chapters 10 and 15.) Usually in transportation, debt-to-equity ratios exceeding 2:1 cause concern.

Profitability Ratios

Profitability ratios represent the third group of financial measures. Some of the most common types are the five shown below.

pretax income-to-gross revenues (a) *pretax income-to-gross revenues* $= \dfrac{\text{net income before taxes}}{\text{gross operating revenues}}$

$$= \frac{\$273,000}{\$7,000,000}$$

$$= 0.039{:}1$$

meaning This ratio says that Bullet has 3.9¢ available from each dollar of sales for the purpose of paying taxes and for the dispersal of profits.

after-tax income-to-equity (b) *after-tax income-to-equity* $= \dfrac{\text{net income after taxes}}{\text{total stockholders' equity}}$

$$= \frac{\$148,000}{\$2,141,000}$$

$$= 0.069{:}1$$

meaning   On this basis, owners had earnings of 6.9% on their equity.

after-tax
income-to-total
capital

(c) *after-tax income-to-total capital* $= \dfrac{\text{net income after taxes}}{\substack{\text{funded debt due after one year } (+) \\ \text{total stockholders' equity}}}$

$$= \dfrac{\$148,000}{\$809,000 \; + \; \$2,141,000}$$

$$= 0.050{:}1$$

meaning   This ratio, which reflects investment as a consequence of debt and equity, shows that Bullet had a return of 5%.

operating ratio

(d) *operating ratio* $= \dfrac{\text{total operating expenses before interest and taxes}}{\text{gross operating revenues}}$

$$= \dfrac{\$6,625,000}{\$7,000,000}$$

$$= 0.946{:}1$$

meaning   Operating ratios, which are frequently used in transportation and extensively used in trucking, reveal how much it costs to deliver a dollar's worth of sales. In Bullet's case, the figure is 94.6¢.

expense ratio

(e) *expense ratio* $= \dfrac{\text{total operating expenses } (+) \text{ interest expense}}{\text{gross operating revenues}}$

$$= \dfrac{\$6,625,000 \; + \; \$102,000}{\$7,000,000}$$

$$= 0.961{:}1$$

meaning   The expense ratio is a modification of the operating ratio. It adds in interest to other operating expenses, which can be important for a fair portrayal of a leveraged company, particularly during periods of high interest rates.

SUCCESSFUL CARRIER MANAGEMENT

What distinguishes outstanding carrier management from mediocre and poor management? Many factors, such as those listed in Table 2.4, are self-explanatory and are included to give students some goals to strive for.

TABLE 2.4. Characteristics of successful carrier management

What separates outstanding carriers from the rest? Success seems to be correlated to the following:

- Having good leadership.
- Hiring and retaining dedicated, industrious employees.
- Having a labor force that has confidence in its managers and company owners.
- Having a management group that respects its workers.
- Maintaining strong communication links between operating, marketing, finance, and human resource people.
- Having good luck and good timing, i.e., obtaining some breaks along the way.
- Making one's own breaks by forcing the action rather than simply reacting to change.
- Being alert, searching for changes in the external environment, and anticipating threats and opportunities.
- Having a firm that stands for something, has people with purpose and pride, and works daily to maintain its reputation.
- Doing the small things like saving some here, improving services a little there, finding small productivity gains, and doing what was promised to customers and employees.
- Concentrating on profits rather than sales, traffic, market share, or other incidental goals but not being so bottom-line oriented that people are treated as capital assets.
- Hiring and retaining managers willing and encouraged to take risks (but not foolish ones), to try new approaches, to bury the phrase "We can't," and to be innovative.
- Being willing to absorb short-term losses in order to reap the greater rewards of long-term strategic objectives.
- Combining common sense with sophisticated techniques to finish the job properly.
- Having patience and not being overreactive to present problems.
- Having the courage and intelligence to know when on the wrong path and sufficient humility to admit it and change direction.
- Understanding that if some mistakes are not tolerated, there will be few new ideas.
- Being socially and ethically responsible.

SUMMARY

Carrier managers are being pressed to make smarter transportation decisions. The changing regulatory environment has broadened the scope of decision making and has added to its complexity. Strategies have to be planned. Choices have to be made. What will probably determine the survival or failure of railroads, trucking companies, and firms in other modes is the ingenuity of people to devise ways to earn and sustain adequate profits.

No simple blueprint exists for achieving this objective, but there is ample evidence that managers of successful transportation firms concentrate on at least one of four key corporate strategies: yields, cost controls, productivity, and the avoidance of high-interest payments. These tactics are not unique to transportation. They are practiced in virtually all for-profit business sectors. But there has been a change—in essence, the transportation industry has increased its desire to apply these profit-oriented strategies.

Carrier managers must place greater emphasis on company objectives, while they change policies that falsely encourage selfish, myopic thinking. Instead of operating personnel focusing on running vehicles, they must see how critically important operating activities are to the success of satisfying shipper and passenger needs. No longer can carriers afford for sales personnel to strive simply for revenues, traffic, or market share goals. Marketing managers must ensure that everyone understands that all these activities mean little unless services are sold profitably.

Carrier management must refine its decision-making methods. Present value analysis can improve capital budgeting decisions, while financial ratio analysis can warn firms of liquidity, solvency, and profitability problems. Computers can analyze complex cost and revenue issues.

Finally, management and labor must start viewing each other as partners rather than adversaries, and together build their corporate futures. A compelling need exists for improved human resource management and mutual trust.

STUDY QUESTIONS

1. How can a carrier decision to improve services decrease company productivity?

2. Define the term "intermodal movement" and then give an example of one.

3. How are scheduled carrier operations different from charter carrier operations?

4. Sales is not the same as marketing. Explain the prior statement, and then define how carriers can use this knowledge to improve company profitability.

5. Explain what is meant by the make or buy decision as it applies to carrier management.

6. Explain how a breakbulk operation works and why carrier movements involving breakbulk operations are usually more costly than point-to-point bulk load movements.

7. How can an effective yield strategy overcome high carrier costs and lead to increased profitability?

8. What are the differences between liquidity, solvency, and profitability ratios?

ENDNOTES

1. Anne B. Fisher, "The Decade's Worst Mergers," *Fortune*, 30 April 1984, pp. 262–263.

ADDITIONAL READINGS

Cavinato, Joseph L. *Finance for Transportation and Logistics Managers*. Washington, D.C.: Traffic Service Corporation, 1977.
——; Novoshielski, Paul; and Stenger, Alan J. "A Decision Model for Freight Rate Retrieval and Payment System Selection." *Transportation Journal* 21, no. 2 (Winter 1981):5–15.

Cook, James. "A Railroad and Proud of It." *Forbes*, 1 October 1979, pp. 81–82.
Coyle, John J.; Bardi, Edward J.; and Cavinato, Joseph L. *Transportation*. St. Paul, Minn.: West Publishing Co., 1982, Chapters 21 and 22.
Coyle, Michael P., and Lanconi, Richard A. "A Comparison of Two Methods for Measuring Motor

Carrier Market Potential." *Transportation Journal* 22, no. 1 (Fall 1982):63–74.

Cunningham, Lawrence F., and Wood, Wallace R. "Diversification in Major U.S. Airlines." *Transportation Journal* 22, no. 3 (Spring 1983):47–63.

Daley, James M. "Holding Companies, Common Carriers, and Public Policy." *Transportation Journal* 19 (Winter 1979):67–73.

———, ed. *Marketing Motor Transportation: Concepts and Applications.* Washington, D.C.: American Trucking Associations, 1981.

Davis, Grant M.; Farris, Martin T.; and Holder, Jack J., Jr. *Management of Transportation Carriers.* New York: Praeger Publishers, 1975.

"Delta: The World's Most Profitable Airline." *Business Week,* 31 August 1981, pp. 68–72.

Fair, Marvin L., and Williams, Ernest W. *Transportation and Logistics.* Rev. ed. Plano, Tex.: Business Publications, 1981, Chapters 15, 20, and 22.

"Federal Express Rides the Small-Package Boom." *Business Week,* 31 March 1980, p. 108.

Gbur, Jonathan; Lieb, Robert C.; and Wiseman, Frederick. "Railroad Employee Attitudes: A Case Study." *Transportation Journal* 19 (Fall 1979):62–70.

Glaskowsky, Nicholas A.; Ledford, Manfred H.; and Sugrue, Paul K. "Operating Economies of Scale in the U.S. Longhaul Common Carrier, Motor Freight Industry." *Transportation Journal* 22, no. 1 (Fall 1982):27–41.

Harper, Donald V. *Transportation: Users, Carriers, Government.* 2d ed. Englewood Cliffs, N.J.: Prentice-Hall, 1982, Chapter 15.

Imperatore, Arthur E. "On the Importance of People." *The (Delta Nu Alpha) Alphian,* Summer 1983, pp. 7–9.

Kinnunen, Raymond M., and Janell, Paul A. "Man-

agement Control in the Railroad Industry." *Transportation Journal* 22, no. 1 (Fall 1982):4–10.

Kotler, Philip. *Principles of Marketing.* 2d ed. Englewood Cliffs, N.J.: Prentice-Hall, 1983.

Langley, C. John. "Strategic Management in Transportation and Physical Distribution." *Transportation Journal* 22, no. 3 (Spring 1983):71–78.

Lieb, Robert C. "Intermodal Ownership: The Perspective of Railroad Chief Executives." *Transportation Journal* 21, no. 3 (Spring 1982):70–75.

Malone, Frank. "C & NW: New Dimensions in Managing Freight Car Maintenance." *Railway Age,* 31 March 1980, pp. 44–46.

National Council of Physical Distribution Management. *Transportation Strategies for the Eighties.* Oak Brook, Ill.: NCPDM, 1982.

Quinn, Francis J. "Effective Vehicle Selection Begins with the 'Specs'." *Traffic Management,* July 1979, pp. 30–32.

Sampson, Roy J.; Farris, Martin T.; and Shrock, David L. *Domestic Transportation: Practice, Theory, and Policy.* 5th ed. Boston: Houghton Mifflin Co., 1985, Chapters 18, and 25.

Shrock, David L., and Stutts, Mary Ann. "A Comparative Analysis of Carrier Print Advertising." *Transportation Journal* 21, no. 1 (Fall 1981):77–87.

"Tiger International: Is Its Grand Transportation Plan More Than a Dream?" *Business Week,* 27 April 1981, pp. 90–91.

Truskie, Stanley D. "The Driving Force of Successful Organizations." *Business Horizons,* May–June 1984, pp. 43–48.

Wright, Norman B. "Productivity: Winners and Losers: Six Conditions That Separate Them." *Business Quarterly,* Spring 1984, pp. 19–20.

Logistics and
Traffic Management

3

To the cargo shipper, transportation is a means to an end, the device that enables goods to move from places where they are not needed to points where they are needed. Just as carriers need users (shippers and passengers), users are equally dependent on carriers, and they expect carriers to perform their tasks efficiently. If transportation companies are successful, raw materials and finished goods will move to distant markets; the whole marketing channel, comprised of suppliers, production facilities, wholesale establishments, retail outlets, and consumers, becomes workable. Equally significant to users is the ability of an efficient transportation system to carry the mail and other documents such as blueprints, reports, manuscripts, contracts, and check payments.

Collectively, users are the second major group of participants in the transportation industry. (The first group is carriers.) Users have considerable stake in the ability of carriers to provide various services at low costs. Since there is no guarantee that performance will match expectations, shippers and passengers are compelled to know the limits and opportunities of the transportation system and to choose wisely from the alternatives available. They also often want to improve the system.

Chapter 3 will provide an overview of transportation management and decision making from a user perspective. Because most corporate transportation decisions involve cargo shipments, this chapter will focus on that area and, specifically, on logistics and traffic management. Although businesses usually book employees on airline flights and often provide company automobiles for executives and salespeople, the bulk of the passenger transportation sector encompasses personal (noncorporate) decision making, which will be covered extensively in Chapter 17. For now, the discussion concentrates on the concepts, responsibilities, concerns, and strategies of managers who ship and control inventories of raw materials, parts, and finished products.

LOGISTICS

Many definitions of logistics are available, including the following:

> Logistics (or physical distribution, as it is often called) deals with the *coordination* of the physical movement aspects of a firm's operations such that a *flow* of raw materials, parts, and finished goods is achieved in such a way that *total costs* are minimized for the *levels of service* desired.[1]

Logistics System

Figure 3.1, which presents a simplified diagram of the logistics system, shows a continuous movement of inventories from origin locations through an inbound warehouse, a production facility, and a distribution warehouse to the ultimate consumers. Consider the production of an automobile. The manufacturer could purchase steel (raw material), bolts (parts), or components (radios and transmissions); ship these items to consolidating warehouses and subassembly locations; and eventually send all the needed materials to a single location, where the autos leave the production line ready to drive.

automobile example

Until a company has completed its finished product, the logistical efforts are collectively grouped under the title of *materials management*. Thereafter,

materials management

FIGURE 3.1.
Logistics system.

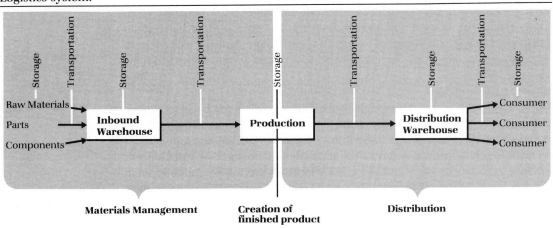

Materials Management   Creation of finished product   Distribution

distribution

logistics

the movement of finished products through the marketing channel of whole-salers and retailers to consumers is frequently called *distribution*. Logistics includes both materials management and distribution activities (i.e., all re-sponsibilities for moving and storing the company's inventories from every origin point to all destination points).

Aspects of Logistics

In the definition of logistics previously given, note that four terms are em-phasized: *coordination, flow, total costs,* and *levels of service.* Although all four are important, some have priority.

Levels of Service.   The normal starting point is the concept of service. Before any other objectives are addressed, someone should establish what the firm is trying to accomplish. With sales so dependent on service, the market-ing manager or marketing staff should specify the quality of logistical support necessary or desirable to consummate the sales transaction. As noted in Chapter 2, the customer will ultimately decide meaningful service standards; never-theless, it is the marketer's job to find out what the customer wants. Mar-keting, however, is not the only group interested in services. Production man-agers, concerned with materials management, should also define their needs for inbound materials.

just-in-time example

A good illustration is production managers who practice the just-in-time approach to production and inventory control management. *Just-in-time methods* emphasize reduced order quantities, frequent and reliable delivery schedules, reduced and highly reliable *replenishment lead times* (i.e., the com-bination of the supplier's manufacturing lead time and transportation time from origin to destination), and consistently high product quality levels for purchased materials (essentially, zero defects).[2] Key corporate objectives are reduced inventory costs and improved quality of the firm's own finished prod-ucts. Consequently, for the just-in-time approach to work as planned, pro-duction managers are usually dependent on daily, or twice daily, deliveries of small quantity shipments of materials and parts. Thus production managers will specify frequent, highly reliable transportation movements. Likewise, sup-pliers must provide quality parts and materials and dependable production schedules, since failure of inbound supplies to arrive on time would most likely shut down the production line.

Total Costs.   In any case, someone should state the service level objec-tive. Then the logistics manager reviews the request and determines if the service standard is achievable, and if so, whether the service can be delivered at reasonable cost. In other words, just because a Boston candy manufacturer wants to sell chocolate in southern California does not mean the firm should. If the cost is too great, causing the candy price to rise above the competition's prices, or if the price could not be raised due to market pressures and losses would thus result, the marketing manager needs to be so advised. However, if the desired level of service is achievable, the logistics manager should define the alternatives that can meet the standard and favor the one that minimizes total logistical costs. The essence of this total cost concept is best illustrated by Fig. 3.2.

FIGURE 3.2.
Graph of total cost concept.

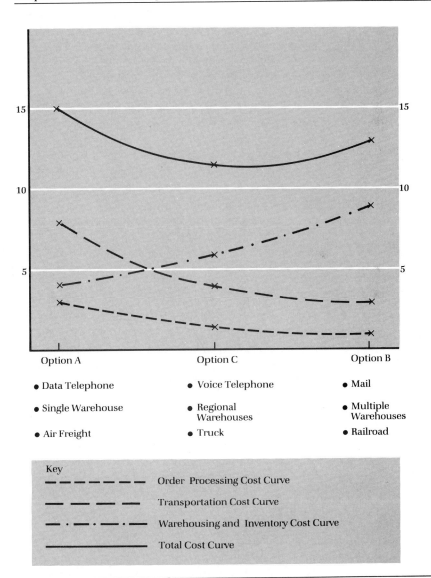

total cost illustration

Assume, for example, that a logistics manager has studied a request for selling portable, battery-powered television sets to the national market. The sets are produced in a single plant in Kansas City. Marketing has told the logistics manager that the service standard requires having the sets available in retail stores within two days of the date of the customer's order. The logistics manager has found that this goal can be accomplished in at least three ways. Under option *A*, the backup stock of TV's would be kept at a single warehouse location in Kansas City. When a set is needed, the local distributor would send a *data telephone message*—that is, nonvoice electronic transmission sent over the telephone network—to the Kansas City facility, which would then ship the TV by air freight to the market area for local truck delivery. Under option *B*, the TV manufacturer would establish 25 market distribution centers, warehouses located in the major retail markets, which would stock inventories of the TV sets. Periodically, each market distribution center would send a replenishment order by mail to Kansas City for more sets. The Kansas City plant would then ship the TV sets by rail to the market location for subsequent truck delivery to retailers. In a third workable alternative, option *C*, the firm could establish eight regional distribution centers that would order resupplies from Kansas City by voice telephone and use truck transportation to and from each regional warehouse. If all three options would satisfy the service requirement, which alternative should be selected?

total cost analysis

Referring to Fig. 3.2, the logistics manager must estimate the total logistical costs under each option. The total cost concept is the idea that logistical decisions should favor the option that minimizes the sum of all logistical costs and not be based on cost reductions in one area alone, such as lower transportation charges. In this simplified case, the manager would determine the total costs based on three particular expense items: order processing, warehousing and inventory, and transportation costs. Option *A* has an ordering cost of 3 units, a warehouse and inventory charge of 4 units, and a transportation expense of 8 units for a total cost of 15 units. Similarly, option *B* has a total cost of 13 units (1 + 3 + 9), and option *C* tallies 11.5 units (1.5 + 4 + 6). By definition, if these were the only three alternatives capable of meeting the specified service level, option *C* should be chosen. Option *C* is chosen, even though option *A* has the lowest warehousing and inventory costs (4 units) and option *B* has the lowest order processing and transportation costs (1 unit and 3 units, respectively). The choice of either option *A* or *B* would unnecessarily increase total costs.

This example should not be misinterpreted by assuming the cost relationships are absolute; for instance, air freight charges can be lower than truck costs. It demonstrates, however, that logistics managers should not overly stress the low-cost option on a particular variable (e.g., transportation), but rather concentrate on the lowest sum of the parts. Option *C* did not contain the lowest unit cost on any of the three cost curves, but it did minimize total logistical costs.

How can logistics managers be certain they have investigated all the options, and how can they be sure a better choice is not available? Because they may never know the answers, the logistics manager must decide how much effort to invest in the search for an optimal solution. In the age-old problem of knowing when to end the search for more information and make a decision, experience and intelligence pay off.

Flow.   The remaining two key aspects of logistics are flow and coordination. Flow usually means avoiding or minimizing plant interruptions, slowdowns, and shutdowns, as well as lost sales caused by poor planning or unexpected environmental consequences, such as a severe storm that paralyzes transportation services. The logistics system operates similarly to a highway: Its users assume that vehicles will move with normal rates of speed; therefore they allocate sufficient time to move something somewhere. Occasionally, passengers are delayed and frustrated by unexpected events such as road construction, traffic congestion, accidents that can block traffic lanes, or mechanical failures like a broken water pump. The same or similar interruptions can interfere with cargo movements, such as what happened when a lock wall collapsed in 1985 in the Welland Canal, blocking shipping for three weeks. Imagine the pressures on a logistics manager whose auto plant is running out of a part, but whose resupply is delayed by a blizzard that has stopped air and road traffic. It is unimportant that the weather is at fault, since the problem requires a solution before the assembly line must be halted and thousands of dollars are wasted. While this is an extreme case, it clarifies the fine line a logistics manager walks between having too much inventory available, which would waste the firm's investment capital, and not enough, which can interrupt production or result in lost sales from being out of stock. Thus logistics managers must constantly look for potential problems and develop contingency plans.

Coordination.   Coordination stresses the need for good working relationships and communications within the logistics organization; between logistics and other units of the firm, such as with marketing, production, or finance; and between logistics people and carriers, parts and materials suppliers, and consultants. The logistics manager must know what the firm and its customers need before attempting to meet those needs. Simultaneously, production, marketing, and customer groups need to know where goods are located and when they are expected to be at destination. Coordination requires talking, listening, and cooperating.

Logistics Activities

Firms that produce and sell products engage in a wide assortment of logistics activities, including procurement, inventory control, plant and warehouse location, production scheduling, warehousing, materials handling, order processing, protective packaging, and traffic management. Considerable debate pertains to the organization of logistical activities, such as deciding which managers should have responsibilities for what functions. However, little debate exists concerning the question of whether these activities are essential. If a firm produces goods, these functions must be performed. The following paragraphs will discuss the responsibilities and concerns of managers of these logistics activities.

procurement

Procurement is the sum of the responsibilities involved in locating and purchasing raw materials, parts, and components needed for production and consumption. These are usually the responsibilities of purchasing agents who order from independent supply sources. Procurement can also encompass ordering materials from other units of the parent company. Corporate transportation managers would like procurement managers to order in large quantities to take advantage of volume discount rates. Unfortunately, rates may be the lowest priority of a purchasing agent under pressure to obtain a product quickly (e.g., in situations where production managers use the just-in-time inventory control approach).

inventory control

Inventory control is the management of raw materials, parts, components, and finished products. Inventory control managers determine what items to place in which storage locations and in which amounts. They also determine *reorder points* (i.e., the signal when to initiate stock replenishment orders), while noting the trade-offs between holding too much or too little stock. As noted previously, holding too much inventory unnecessarily ties up the firm's capital, but holding too little can result in stockouts, lost sales, high transport cost emergency shipments, and costly production problems.

Inventory carrying costs—the costs of capital, property taxes, cargo insurance, product deterioration, obsolescence, and damage or loss resulting from holding goods—and *inventory ordering costs*—clerical costs, supplies, order transmission charges, and overhead costs associated with processing a shipment order—can be quite expensive. For example, inventory carrying costs can be as high as 40% of the average value of the goods in stock each year.[3] Therefore, inventory control is now attracting attention, because the potential savings can be significant.[4]

plant and warehouse location

Plant and warehouse location is another key logistics activity. Similar to the case of a retail store doomed by a poor location before it sees its first customer, poor site selection for production and storage facilities can place a firm in a losing situation. As Chapter 1 noted, the availability of efficient transportation facilities is a primary determinant in location decisions. Firms should ask what modes serve the location and with what services, whether there are risks that such services will end or be changed (e.g., rail service might end due to line abandonment), and whether the site is located where the firm can take advantage of rate-saving peculiarities. The latter refers to situations such as locating a plant or warehouse just inside a state boundary to take advantage of lower rates offered by an exempt carrier. *Exempt* means the carrier is free from economic regulation. An example is locating a grain elevator in Superior, Wisconsin, because trucking movements of corn and soybeans from Minnesota origins would be exempt from federal rate regulations. If the elevator had been located two miles to the west in Duluth, Minnesota, the rates would be regulated under intrastate (Minnesota) trucking rules. At times, considerable rate savings can be obtained on exempt shipments of agricultural goods. (More will be said about exempt trucking in Chapter 13.) Sometimes, however, the decision to locate across the river, or even across the street, can make a huge difference in corporate logistics costs. Therefore logistics managers, having learned not to assume too much, research location decisions thoroughly.

production scheduling

Production scheduling refers to the process of deciding which plants will produce what items in which quantities and at what points in time. From a production and transportation perspective, what is desirable is uninterrupted runs of large amounts of individual items to avoid costly changeovers in production equipment and processes and to take advantage of the volume transportation rate savings possible on both the inbound and outbound traffic. Logistics managers do not run the production equipment but merely determine the most efficient schedule for use of the facilities, given the need to balance costs against needed customer services.

warehousing

Warehousing includes all questions relevant to the facilities and equipment used for holding inventory. Responsibilities include the design of the building (e.g., the choice between a single story or multiple-level building; ceiling heights; the need for specialized areas for stock needing cooling, heat, humidity, or security; and the layout of racks, bins, or other inventory location equipment); balancing the various needs for receiving, shelving, locating, order processing, and shipping goods; and deciding what cargo handling schemes are desirable. Efficient warehouses are carefully designed and cautiously coordinated to satisfy inventory control, transportation, and materials handling needs.

materials handling

Materials handling is the management and control of all the equipment designed to aid warehouse workers in moving inventories within a single facility or between adjacent or nearby buildings. Equipment includes fork lifts, conveyors, elevators, pallet transporters, towlines, and automated storage and retrieval systems, as well as basic accessories like pallets and strapping (see Table 3.1). Materials handling equipment differs from transportation equipment because the latter moves goods greater distances. Materials handling equipment is also frequently used to load or unload transportation equipment, such as truck trailers and railroad box cars.

order processing

Order processing encompasses all activities from the moment someone initiates a request for inventory through the receipt of the goods by the order initiator. Included, then, are filling out the order form, transmittal of the order, receipt of the order at the warehouse, location of the stock and retrieval of the same, packaging, transportation of the items, receipt of the items at the order point, notification of availability of the goods, and pick-up or delivery. A good illustration is the process a consumer experiences at a Sears, J. C. Penney, or other catalog order facility when goods must be ordered from another location.

Order processing decisions interface with other logistics activities. If, for example, a decision is made to collect daily orders and batch mail them weekly to the resupply warehouse (i.e., send the orders out only once per week), an unnecessary burden may be placed on transportation to expedite shipments

TABLE 3.1. Examples of materials handling equipment and accessories

Fork lift:	A specialized truck capable of horizontal movement but mainly used for lifting stock vertically to reach elevated storage locations. Used in positioning and retrieving pallets.
Conveyor:	A fixed-path device using belts, wheels, rollers, or other items to move cargo from one location to another by gravity or power.
Elevator:	A vertical lift device used to move freight from one floor in a building to another.
Pallet transporter:	A piece of equipment designed to lift a pallet minimally off the floor and then to allow the moving of the pallet horizontally. Equipment can be either motorized or nonmotorized.
Towline:	A continuously moving, in-floor or overhead conveyor system to which carts can be attached to haul goods through a warehouse.
Automated storage & retrieval system:	A sophisticated, often computer-controlled piece of equipment, which can route itself to a storage location, pick up (or deposit) inventory, and return to the starting point in some cases without any human involvement.
Pallet:	A platform, usually made of wood, on which inventory is stacked to build unit loads for faster cargo handling.
Strapping:	Tape made of nylon, steel, plastic, or other materials and used to hold cargo securely in place.

to meet customer service deadlines. The result, which usually is a higher cost in transportation services, could have been avoided by sending in the orders on a daily basis. In some cases, that measure would have saved almost a week in time, enabling the use of a slower mode of transportation at a lower shipping rate.

protective packaging

Protective packaging is another logistics responsibility area, but it is not to be confused with "promotional" packaging. Marketers, recognizing that consumer buying can be influenced by the colors, touch, or uniqueness of the container, design packages to sell goods. Logisticians, in contrast, are concerned with the following: (1) enabling the goods to arrive at their destination in the same condition they were in at the origin point, (2) being in compliance with required transportation packaging specifications (e.g., some items must be shipped in metal containers), and (3) controlling packaging costs and transportation charges. Therefore marketing and logistics objectives often conflict. For instance, a 3-ft-high, long-stemmed collector's item wine bottle is a marketer's dream but a logistics manager's nightmare, since the latter's task is to protect the item from breakage but not spend unnecessary money doing so. The logistics manager might also advise the marketing staff when their packaging initiatives are creating cost problems. This problem could lead to product price increases to cover added packaging costs, package design changes, or deletion of the item from the list of company product line items.

traffic management

Traffic management, a most important subset of logistics because it often accounts for more than 25% of total logistics costs, is responsible for most transportation decisions in the firm. Traffic management therefore deserves considerable analysis. Thus much of the remainder of Chapter 3 focuses on the activities, concerns, and strategies of the traffic manager.

TRAFFIC MANAGEMENT

Traffic managers provide advice and make decisions regarding inbound and outbound transportation matters. Choices can be as broad as deciding between using for-hire or private transportation or as precise as specifying the carrier and the exact routing for a particular shipment. In essence, the traffic manager must be a diversified individual who is comfortable handling operating, paperwork, financial, and regulatory matters, as well as be a capable manager who can control labor and capital.

Overview

Traffic managers must understand the meaning of the logistics concept and how their area of responsibility can help to achieve logistics and corporate objectives. Minimizing transportation costs is not enough, because the result can often be suboptimal for the firm. Errors in judgment can increase logistics costs, reduce services, hurt sales, shut down plants, and ultimately lower profits. Therefore senior management must clarify the tasks they expect the traffic manager and staff to accomplish and match the reward system to the production of these desired goals. If the traffic manager can help the company by choosing a higher cost mode of transportation, he or she should not be penalized for doing something in the company's best interests. In fact, a traffic manager whose particular budget is sacrificed for the good of the firm should be rewarded. Likewise, if marketing alters its promotional packaging, necessitating more protective packaging, reducing the number of units that can be placed in a vehicle, and increasing transportation costs, management should realize that the cause of the transportation cost increase was not traffic management, but marketing. Although it is difficult to assign benefits and costs to those responsible, that is exactly what should be done.

Mode and Carrier Selection

Two of the traffic manager's major responsibilities are making mode and carrier selections. Mode selection requires choosing among the rail, water, pipeline, highway, and air alternatives. Rarely, however, does the traffic manager have all the modal options available. The specialized nature of the cargo, the characteristics of the mode, and the nonavailability of service at origin or destination often eliminate some modes from consideration. Also, selecting the carrier—or in the case of traffic that is to be interlined, carriers—requires careful deliberation. Ultimately, mode and carrier choices usually revert back to service and rate considerations.

Service Variables.   Service variables include all the benefits that could be derived from transportation. Traffic managers must decide which of these variables are essential or desirable for each shipment. The variables described in the following paragraphs are not the only ones, but they do provide an idea of the types of concerns traffic managers must handle in choosing modes and carriers.

accessibility

Accessibility refers to the traffic manager's ability to place a shipment on a mode or carrier. Key factors are the length, width, and height of the object to be shipped: Can it fit within the vehicle's length, width, height, or cubic limitations, and if it will fit, can it be loaded through the vehicle's door or other access point? Similarly, although an object might have a small cubic measurement, it might weigh too much for safe haulage. Aircraft, for example, cannot exceed their maximum allowable take-off weights. Sometimes carriers also refuse to haul small shipments that exceed the maximum weight or length and girth (the shortest distance around a package). The latter limits are typical among small parcel carriers trying to move cargo manually, for drivers must be able to pick up and carry packages by hand. An example is United Parcel Service, which, as of April 1986, would not accept a package larger than 70 lbs. or 108 in. of length and girth for interstate transport.

Sometimes the vehicle and shipment sizes match, but a shipper does not desire to have that much commodity delivered at one time to one location. A traffic manager at a brewery, for example, might consider shipping barley by water transportation because of low rates. However, because a barge load is so large, the entire quantity of barley might not be used before some spoilage occurred. Similarly, many traffic managers do not use rail transportation because the quantity they need to ship is too small for the size of the available cars. Other shippers are denied access to carriers because space is not available when they need it. Still others cannot get the shipment to the carrier's terminal because there is no pick-up service, or they cannot get it delivered because the carrier does not serve the destination point.

Specialized equipment may also be required. Oversized cargo—too wide, too heavy, too long, or too high—is often moved by uniquely designed trucks. In another case, to ship long telephone poles, it is often necessary to use three rail cars with the poles loaded on the middle flat car and permitted to swing freely over empty flat cars located before and after the loaded car. This accommodates curvatures in the track; if they tried to use a single longer car, the center part of the car would tend to extend too far over adjacent track on sharp curves. Specialized transportation equipment and packaging are also needed for cargo that spoils, shrinks, rusts, breaks, freezes, cracks, changes color, boils, absorbs odors, wilts, melts, punctures, scratches, or expands. Likewise, highly pilferable cargo or classified documents cannot be treated casually. If cargo needs are specialized, shippers usually supply their own customized vehicles.

reliability

Moreover, reliability is often an important consideration. Does a carrier perform as promised, and do goods leave and arrive as scheduled? If cargo arrives late, sales can be lost, yet if goods arrive early, firms can face increased warehousing and inventory carrying costs and related problems. Traffic managers often emphasize consistency and hesitate to use firms that deviate significantly from schedules. Smart traffic managers watch carrier performance records and notice signs indicating that carriers are neglecting maintenance of their equipment, because they do not want to be victimized by service breakdowns. With so many carriers unionized, the possibility of labor strikes is another threat to reliability. Nevertheless, the alert traffic manager can predict carrier shutdowns or service cutbacks fairly accurately and find transportation alternatives to help survive the crises. One option some traffic managers exercise is to rely on non-unionized firms to avoid the strike threat.

speed

Speed is another factor in making mode and carrier decisions. How time-sensitive is the shipment? If cargo must be someplace quickly—such as in the case of emergency shipments of late orders, the transportation of living organs, or the movement of contract bids trying to meet deadlines—speed can be the dominant selection variable. For example, something in Washington, D.C., needed in Portland, Oregon, in 24 hours, must go by air.

control and liability

Tracing and control are important to the traffic manager who is concerned that a shipment arrives where it is expected to be in time and in good condition. Traffic managers need to be able to locate shipments and obtain shipment status information—a process called tracing. Thus accuracy and timeliness are important information considerations. As the traffic management field becomes increasingly sophisticated, carriers often grant shippers direct access to their computers for shipment status updates. Loss and damage can also be important: Traffic managers want to know what a carrier's loss and damage record shows. For some shipments, the avoidance of damage, theft, or loss caused by the separation of documentation from cargo takes precedence over all other considerations. In fact, a traffic manager with such a shipment is likely to be far less concerned with the ease of filing and collecting on a liability claim against the carrier than in finding a carrier whose probability of loss and damage is minimal. Avoidance of the claim is the objective in this case. If a claim has to be filed, it is already too late.[5]

flexibility

Flexibility is another service variable closely related to reliability and speed. Which carriers can meet extraordinary shipper needs? Which try hardest to help the traffic manager succeed? Which are inflexible due to legal, operating, or attitude obstructions? Which will expedite (rush) a shipment? How rigid are carriers in scheduling pick-ups and deliveries? Will they come when a shipper requests service or only at their convenience? These questions need to be answered before a carrier can be selected.

Rate Variables.   Rate variables can be as important in mode and carrier selection as are service variables. Carrier fees and hidden charges can affect significantly the goal of minimizing total costs. Consequently, when choosing modes and carriers, traffic managers must consider all costs incurred; otherwise, fair comparison of competing alternatives cannot be made.

transportation rate   The transportation rate is usually clearly defined as a charge per unit weight per distance (e.g., $8.50 per 100 lbs. between Cleveland and Pittsburgh), but the traffic manager should question what that rate covers and add on any supplemental costs before making comparisons to other carriers' price quotations. For example, there may be charges for pick-up and delivery services, or there may be charges for positioning equipment, such as an empty truck trailer left at a warehouse dock. Who is required to load and unload the equipment is another consideration. What are the demurrage and detention rules

demurrage and detention   and charges? *Demurrage* is a charge levied by a railroad for holding equipment beyond an acceptable loading or unloading time, and *detention* is the word truckers use for this procedure. One might provide days of *free time,* which is time provided at no charge for loading or unloading, whereas another might provide only hours of free time. In addition, since demurrage or detention charges can be much higher for one mode than another, differences should be noted.

packaging and dunnage   Other costs to consider are packaging and dunnage, such as wood or other materials used to prevent cargo's shifting in the vehicle. Some modes and carriers require more extensive, and more expensive, protective packaging and dunnage than do others. Traffic managers need to appraise these costs against carrier loss and damage risks.

cargo insurance   The traffic manager must ask if the shipment is fully covered against loss and damage, and if not, must the shipper, or should the shipper, purchase cargo insurance? What are the costs of insurance, or the costs of delayed, lost, or damaged goods in terms of missed sales, reduced profits, lost good will,

clerical costs   and bad word-of-mouth advertising? Other concerns are the clerical costs of documentation, claims processing expenses, and differences in credit and payment terms between modes and carriers.

In short, to compare transportation alternatives, estimates of the total transportation costs are required. Who would buy a new car, for example, without inquiring if the price included the delivery charge, dealer prep, accessories, and sales tax? The traffic manager must know what the firm is receiving for its money.

Cost-cutting Strategies

Skilled traffic managers are constantly on the alert for ways to reduce transportation charges. Some of the more recognized ways to achieve this objective are as follows:

- Shipping larger quantities to take advantage of volume rate discounts (lower rates per 100 lbs.).

- Taking advantage of low backhaul rates, where carriers are trying to fill unused capacity.

- Shipping concentrated items like frozen orange juice to reduce the amount of cargo weight to be shipped. Why ship water, for instance, when it can be added at the consumption point?

- Shipping in off-peak periods when the carrier is anxious to fill idle equipment.

- Working with packaging specialists to redesign containers that permit more units to be loaded in a transport vehicle.

- Shipping items disassembled; for example, bicycle parts in compact boxes versus set-up (assembled) bicycles.

- Offering multiple shipments to a carrier at one time, a move that increases carrier productivity, cuts unit transport costs, and can lead to rate reductions.

Quite often, traffic managers will negotiate with carriers to try to reduce rates. Remember, of course, that carriers need shippers as much as shippers need carriers. Realistically though, carriers tend to work harder to keep or acquire big shipper accounts, and traffic managers with the decision-making power to provide extensive business usually have more negotiating leverage than do small volume shippers. By working together to reduce each other's cost burdens, both carriers and shippers benefit. As noted in Chapter 2, carriers are constantly searching for ways to increase productivity. Moreover, traffic managers should seize available opportunities and suggest additional ways to cut carrier costs or increase productivity.

Other Traffic Management Responsibilities

After the mode and carrier have been selected, the traffic manager places an order with the carrier for specific services. In other words, the traffic manager must define the nature of the shipment, determine when the carrier's transportation equipment can be expected to arrive at the facility, and plan the transfer of the goods to the jurisdiction of the carrier. Traffic managers must also make decisions about the need for expediting shipments and how to monitor shipments in transit. Simply calling carriers to ask if everything is okay is not sufficient. In fact, service standards must be clearly defined, shipment information should be compared to these standards, discrepancies should be noted, and corrective action should be taken. Since traffic managers usually do not have time to monitor each shipment being hauled, they use spot audits—sudden reviews of carrier services—and sampling—planned, random or nonrandom checks of carrier services. An example of the latter might be a review of every tenth shipment according to bill of lading number.

Rate Determination and Auditing.   Traffic managers devote a large portion of their time to paperwork. Much of that time is spent monitoring rate information, such as determining rates and auditing charges. In addition to reviewing the accuracy of the invoice to protect against overcharges, traffic managers should look for clerical errors that could result in duplicate pay-ments: for example, a carrier might inadvertently send two bills for the same service. Some traffic managers examine high-cost shipments or sample paid bills to check for errors. Others hire outside consultants. If the latter find no overcharges, there is usually no fee; if they find excessive rates, they normally collect a percentage of the overcharge amount, often 50%.

Funds Management.   The processing of freight bills can be a tedious undertaking; however, it should be done carefully. Recent changes have left credit terms to the discretion of some modes and carriers. By shopping for favorable credit terms and practicing better funds management (i.e., firms try to collect quickly sums due the company and delay payments owed by the firm to other businesses so that cash can be accumulated for short-term in-vestments), traffic managers can improve corporate profitability.

Documentation.   One time-consuming, yet necessary part, of traffic management is documentation. Each shipment requires a bill of lading and a freight bill (invoice), and other records such as claims documents might be necessary. The purposes of freight documentation are control, billing, and recordkeeping.

The *bill of lading,* perhaps the most important document in transporta-tion, is a contract between a shipper and a carrier or carriers that prescribes the conditions of the agreement for shipping a particular commodity. It also serves as a receipt for the goods by verifying which party assumed respon-sibility for the shipment at each point, thereby serving as evidence in liability proceedings. In addition, the bill of lading is evidence of title; it identifies the owner or indicates how ownership is to be maintained or transferred during transit.

bills of lading: purposes and types

Bills of lading exist in all modes of transportation, but they are called dif-ferent names by the different modes. Rail, truck, and water modes call the document a *bill of lading.* Air carriers use the term *airbill,* whereas pipelines call it a *tender of shipment.* Nonetheless, each document essentially covers the same information. Government property and livestock move on special-ized bills called government bills of lading (GBLs) and livestock contracts, re-spectively. The bulk of the traffic, nevertheless, is domestic commercial cargo. If commercial cargo is being sent to another country, an export bill is used. If ownership of domestic commercial cargo is not subject to change during transit, a straight bill of lading is used. Otherwise, goods move on an order bill of lading, which permits a change of title.

bill of lading preparation

Bills of lading today are preprinted multicopy documents designed to min-imize clerical costs. For-hire carriers usually provide the blank bills of lading; shippers are usually responsible for filling them out. Copies of the bill of lading are distributed to a number of parties for their particular needs: some go to shippers, and others are distributed to carrier groups such as accounting and billing personnel.

bill of lading information and its value

Figure 3.3 shows a straight bill of lading that defines the consignor (the originator, Sam Brown, John Doe Company), the pick-up point (112 Elm Street, Athens, Georgia), and the time and date of pick-up (2 P.M., July 20, 1985). Also indicated is the name of the carrier (AZQ Motor Freight Lines) and the carrier representative (John Smith). The consignee (destination recipient) is revealed to be the XYZ Company (6021 Woodland Drive, Charlotte, N.C., 23201). Note that five packages are being shipped, which is important for recognizing an

FIGURE 3.3.
Sample bill of lading. (Form reprinted with permission and compliments of Moore Business Forms, Inc.)

SPEEDISET ● MOORE BUSINESS FORMS, INC., A

DRIVER PLEASE NOTE ▶ IF SINGLE SHIPMENT 500 LBS OR LESS—CHECK BOX BELOW

SHIPPER PLEASE NOTE ▶ FREIGHT CHARGES ARE PREPAID ON THIS BILL OF LADING UNLESS MARKED COLLECT

STRAIGHT BILL OF LADING
ORIGINAL-NOT NEGOTIABLE

AZQ MOTOR FREIGHT LINES

SHIPPER NO 12345

CARRIER NO.

FORM OP 297 11/81
SINGLE SHIPMENT PICKUP ☐

DATE 07 20 85

TO: (CONSIGNEE)		FROM: (SHIPPER)	
XYZ Company		John Doe Co	
STREET 6021 Woodland Dr		STREET 112 Elm St	
CITY, STATE Charlotte, N.C.	ZIP CODE 23201	CITY, STATE Athens, Ga	ZIP CODE 30601

ROUTE:

VEHICLE NO:

BILL TO:

NUMBER SHIPPING UNITS	HM	KIND OF PACKAGING, DESCRIPTION OF ARTICLES, SPECIAL MARKS AND EXCEPTIONS	WEIGHT (SUBJECT TO CORRECTION)	RATE	CHARGES (FOR CARRIER USE ONLY)
5		cases shoes noi	560		

REMIT C.O.D.
TO
ADDRESS

COD AMT: $

C.O.D. FEE
PREPAID ☐ $
COLLECT ☐

NOTE—Where the rate is dependent on value, shippers are required to state specifically in writing the agreed or declared value of the property.
The agreed or declared value of the property is hereby specifically stated by the shipper to be not exceeding.
$ ______ per ______

Subject to Section 7 of the conditions, if this shipment is to be delivered to the consignee without recourse on the shipper the shipper shall sign the following statement:
The carrier shall not make delivery of this shipment without payment of freight and all other lawful charges. Sam Brown
(Signature of Shipper)

TOTAL CHARGES $

FREIGHT CHARGES:
FREIGHT PREPAID except when box at right is checked
Check box if charges are to be collect ☑

RECEIVED, subject to the classifications and tariffs in effect on the date of the issue of this Bill of Lading, the property described above in apparent good order, except as noted (contents and condition of contents of packages unknown), marked, consigned, and destined as indicated above which said carrier agrees to carry to its usual place of delivery at said destination, if on its route, otherwise to deliver to another carrier on the route to said destination. It is mutually agreed as to each carrier of all or any of said property over all or any portion of said route to destination and as to each party at any time interested in all or any of said property, that every service to be performed hereunder shall be subject to all the bill of lading terms and conditions in the governing classification on the date of shipment.
Shipper hereby certifies that he is familiar with all the bill of lading terms and conditions in the governing classification and the said terms and conditions are hereby agreed to by the shipper and accepted for himself and his assigns.

This is to certify that the above named materials are properly classified, described, packaged, marked, and labeled and are in proper condition for transportation, according to the applicable regulations of the D.O.T.

carrier
AZQ MOTOR FREIGHT LINES

SHIPPER John Doe Co	PER John Smith		
PER Sam Brown	DATE 7-20-85	TIME 2:00 P.M.	PIECES 5

EQUAL OPPORTUNITY CONDITION: This contract contains the provisions of Sec. 202 of Executive Order 11246, Paragraph 1 through 7.

* fictitious data and names

overage or shortage. John Smith signed for five pieces; therefore the shipper has proof that five pieces were given to the carrier. If six pieces arrive at the XYZ Company, an additional package was added by mistake (an overage); but if four arrive, there is a shortage. In the center of the form, the weight is shown as 560 lbs. Moreover, the article is described as cases shoes NOI (not otherwise indexed), meaning that no precise description exists in the freight classification to match the shipped item. Freight classification refers to a book that, among other purposes, lists items by name and description. The bill of lading reflects distance (as determined by origin and destination information), weight (560 lbs.), and description of the shipped commodity. All influence carrier rates. (More will be said on using freight classifications to determine rates in Chapter 5.)

freight claims

Claims and Liability.   One frustrating, yet consequential, aspect of traffic management is the freight claims process. Whatever the mode, there is always a chance that goods will be damaged, stolen, or lost (i.e., they cannot be located for whatever reason). When such events happen, traffic managers must decide whether to initiate claims in an attempt to recover monetary damages. Claims are also filed for recovery of *overcharges*—the difference between the price paid and the legal maximum rate. Traffic managers do not automatically initiate claim action, because they must first weigh the costs of preparing and following up on claims against the potential payoff. The high cost in time and money of locating and/or assembling as many as 12 documents, which may be required as accompanying evidence, may be too much to make filing the claim worthwhile. Consequently, many claims are never filed.

liability

As previously noted, traffic managers should be knowledgeable about the liability provisions of a mode or carrier before using it. They need to determine the dollar limitation of the carrier's coverage, since some carrier protection is minimal. For instance, air cargo liability is often limited to 50¢ per pound or $50, whichever is greater. Some traffic managers also need to be concerned about consequential damages. These are costs related not to physical loss or damage to the item shipped but to external consequences, such as missing a contract bidding deadline because the envelope carrying the bid was temporarily lost or delayed in transit. For example, consider the case of a 2-lb. air shipment that contains a contract proposal that cost $50,000 to develop and offers the potential of $100,000 in profits. If the package was delayed, the bid deadline was missed, and the contract was awarded to another party, how much can the shipper expect to receive from the carrier? The answer is not clear. Shippers must determine the need for added insurance to protect themselves against inadequate carrier liability coverage. In addition, they must know how much time they have available to file the claim before eligibility for carrier compensation expires.

legal
forms of carriage

Of the four legal forms of carriage (common, contract, exempt, and private carriage), common carriage usually offers the greatest liability protection. *Common carriers* are for-hire transportation companies that are required to

common
carrier duties

practice four duties: to charge reasonable rates, to avoid undue or unjust discrimination, to serve the public, and to deliver. The duty to charge reasonable rates means that rates should not be so high as to harm carrier customers nor so low as to hurt other carriers unfairly. Common carriers are not prohibited from discriminating, per se, but they are not blatantly allowed to treat people, places, and shipments unfairly. For example, students and senior citizens regularly receive discount fares that businesspeople do not realize, and volume shippers receive cargo discounts that small shippers do not receive. The former action is justified on social grounds; the latter is legitimatized by economic reasons (i.e., cost economies). Common carriers are expected to serve all customers who request their services provided they have the equipment and operating authority (legal right) to haul the commodities in question. Obviously, a carrier with vans could not be expected to haul liquid in bulk. The fourth duty, to deliver, means that the carrier is expected to deliver the shipment to the right person, with reasonable dispatch (i.e., close to the time it normally takes to complete the job), and in the same condition as it was received from the shipper.[6]

contract, exempt,
and private carriage

Contract carriers are far less constrained by legal obligations than are common carriers. In fact, these for-hire carriers are limited only by the terms specified in agreements (contracts) signed with the users they serve. By definition, exempt carriers are free from economic regulations, so they, like contract carriers, negotiate liability terms with their customers. The fourth legal class, private carriers, are also exempt from economic regulation. Since they haul goods for their owners, liability is an in-house matter of deciding how much insurance to carry.

common
carrier liability

The duty to deliver is the legal basis for common carrier liability. The purpose of this duty is to insist that carriers be accountable for the property entrusted to their care. Even common carriers, however, are not liable under certain mitigating circumstances, such as loss and damage caused by an act of God.[7] This loss refers to a totally unavoidable situation, such as a vehicle's being caught in a tornado or flash flood. Therefore traffic managers must thoroughly investigate and understand the conditions of liability and prepare for contingencies. Often they will discover they need to buy additional insurance or, in more extreme cases, change carriers.

Advising Others.   Traffic managers are expected to advise others in their firms about transportation matters and to take active roles in changing the transport system to help their companies. Not only do they work closely with the remaining logistics staff, such as purchasing agents, warehousing people, and inventory control personnel, but they also interface with marketing and production managers who need their expertise and assistance.

Traffic managers must work carefully with carriers to establish relationships that lead to mutual benefits for both. When traffic managers are dissatisfied or see opportunities for service improvements or rate reductions, they should seek carrier changes. Moreover, when carriers need shipper assistance to win government approval of rate reductions or expanded operating authority—actions that could help shippers—traffic managers should volunteer to testify in support of the carriers' initiatives.

professional participation Memberships in professional associations, such as the National Industrial Transportation League, Council of Logistics Management, Delta Nu Alpha, and the American Society of Transportation and Logistics, provide traffic managers with opportunities to share knowledge and learn new approaches to common problems. (Appendix B contains details on these and other associations.) Traffic managers should also take a more active role in helping to shape government policies, laws, and rules affecting transportation. For example, if Congress holds hearings on further economic regulatory revisions of a mode such as trucking or railroading, traffic managers might ask to be allowed to testify to make their views known to elected officials.

PRIVATE TRUCKING

One important logistics decision facing a firm today is the choice between using for-hire or private carriage. Many firms, by necessity or choice, obtain their own specialized transport equipment such as private rail cars or barges. However, the heaviest involvement in private transportation is in trucking, where there are an estimated 150,000 private fleets.[8]

local versus intercity operations Since private trucking operations are exempt from federal economic regulation and thus their reporting requirements are minimal, estimating their traffic and financial impact on the transportation system as a whole is difficult. Nevertheless, private sector involvement in local delivery operations is extensive. Consider, for example, the number of bread and beverage trucks that service any particular city. The activity level is also significant in terms of the intercity market. What distinguishes local private trucking from intercity private trucking is the nature of the equipment. Local operations tend to require small vehicles designed for easy cargo handling, maneuverability, and efficiency at making numerous stops. Intercity private trucking is highly oriented toward 18-wheel tractor-trailer rigs and the truckload sector featuring full vehicles moving door-to-door from origin to destination.

reasons for private trucking Firms engage in private trucking primarily because they perceive either rate or service advantages, or both. If suitable for-hire services are not available, private trucking may be the only alternative. In many cases, however, initiators simply believe private trucking accomplishes the task better or more economically than for-hire trucking does, although they may not be correct. As in the case of for-hire carriage, success in private trucking depends on productive use of equipment and cost efficiencies. In contrast to for-hire carriers, however, private truck operators tend to have far fewer sources of traffic available. By definition, they are supposed to exist to haul the goods of their parent companies. Consequently, backhaul traffic might be hard to find, and private truck operators might experience seasonal traffic downturns. Both of these situations could result in poor equipment utilization, excess capacity, and high unit costs.

private trucking
regulatory changes

Regardless, the private trucking sector is growing, due to relatively low start-up costs; for example, used trucking equipment is almost always available at reasonable prices. Furthermore, deregulation reduced the backhaul risks. Private truckers have been granted intercorporate hauling rights, which have expanded interstate freedoms to carry the goods on a for-hire basis for other 100% owned subsidiaries or affiliates of their parent companies, a right denied prior to the Motor Carrier Act of 1980.[9] They can also apply for, and be granted, federal common carrier and contract carrier authority for hauling goods for fees. An important case relevant to the latter was the 1978 Toto decision of the Interstate Commerce Commission, which allowed the Toto Purchasing and Supply Company, a private truck operator, to move backhaul traffic under specific circumstances on a for-hire basis.[10]

Advantages of private trucking to a firm include the following:

advantages of
private trucking

1. *Flexibility.* Equipment can be used as needed without depending on the for-hire carrier's schedule or other constraints.

2. *Control.* Control is the power to take actions to align performance with standards. With private trucking, the shipper can adjust operations and correct employee deficiencies without using an intermediary. With for-hire carriage, a shipper can only request an improvement or try to find another carrier, but with private carriage, management can directly influence the needed response.

3. *Speed.* Schedules can be changed, routes can be realigned, stops can be added or subtracted, and partial loads can be dispatched immediately. While each of these moves might raise unit transportation costs, the shipper using private trucking has the right to enact them if necessary to send something to a destination in a hurry.

4. *Reduced packaging and less loss and damage.* Since private truck operators should know their products better than for-hire carriers do, they should be able to load their vehicles more properly to lower damage risks. Through a reward and punishment system, firms using private carriage can encourage dock workers and drivers to exert more care with the cargo. Finally, they should be able to control the shipments better from origin to destination to minimize lost and delayed cargo problems.

5. *Lower transportation costs.* A private carrier can often operate transportation equipment at lower costs than for-hire carriers can. Even if costs are equal, however, private carriage may be attractive, since for-hire rates sometimes exceed by a wide margin the actual costs of carrying the item. When the situation exists, the market is encouraging private trucking.

disadvantages
of private trucking

Naturally, there are some disadvantages to private trucking. The firm may not have the capital to invest in private trucking equipment. It may either lack the managerial talent necessary to make the project succeed or fear that such a move would encourage organized labor initiatives. In addition, the firm may not know if for-hire rate-service offerings will substantially improve; if they do, the advantages of private trucking will be lessened. Often, the firm faces the potential of uncertain backhaul traffic, or it may not want to accept new paperwork responsibilities. For example, driver log books must carefully verify that truck drivers comply with federal safety requirements that they not drive more than 10 hours in a day followed by 8 consecutive off-duty hours, more than 60 hours in a consecutive 7-day period, and more than 70 hours in a consecutive 8-day period.

Private truck fleets are also required to pay state fuel taxes for fuel consumed by vehicles operating on each state's highways. Furthermore, private carriers must concern themselves with liability not just on the cargo, but also on possible damage to the equipment, its operators, and other people's property. Worse, private carrier operators run the risk of injury or death to innocent bystanders. Finally, private carriers assume the risks of a changing environment. For instance, if fuel costs rise rapidly or if demand for the firm's products declines, the firm must deal with truck-related problems. As in most decision areas, private trucking involves risks as well as opportunities.

Leasing

The risk side of private trucking is lessened by truck leasing. Companies like Ryder System Incorporated, Rollins Leasing Corporation, and Gelco Corporation have grown rapidly, building their businesses on the assumption that firms might become involved in private trucking if the financial risks were lessened. They offer full service leasing or its derivatives. Full service leasing permits a shipper to obtain a fleet of trucks with minimum upfront capital; to avoid maintenance responsibilities; to bypass the need to obtain skilled truck managers, since their duties can be assigned to the equipment supplier in some cases; and to reduce the risks by enabling the lessor (shipper) to exit from private trucking more easily if plans do not materialize.

benefits and costs

Leasing can provide answers to many problems such as obtaining back-up trucks for ones that break down due to mechanical failures, lowering fuel costs through bulk fuel purchases, and meeting a one-way trip need. Of course, shippers pay for each service received; thus, during an extended period of time, leased equipment could cost more than a privately owned and managed fleet. Still, leasing is an option that has attracted many shippers to the private transport sector who would not have switched otherwise.

single source leasing

Since April 6, 1984, private carriers have also been able to engage in single source leasing. On that date, the U.S. Supreme Court refused to review a lower court ruling that upheld a 1982 Interstate Commerce Commission policy statement.[11] The effect was to allow private carriers to lease equipment and drivers from owner–operators. By using single source leasing, private carriers are quickly able to increase fleet capacity at minimum cost and risk. Leases could be as short as 30 days. Once contracts are signed, lessees (the private carriers) have exclusive domain and control over the transportation service conducted by it with the leased equipment during the term of the lease. Since lessors provide equipment, capital costs are minimum. Furthermore, lessees need not be concerned with collective bargaining since drivers are contract employees. In short, single source leasing combines the advantages of control, flexibility, and cost savings. ICC decisions in June 1986 further expanded single source leasing opportunities. More will be said about these changes in Chapter 11.

GROWING INTEREST IN LOGISTICS

Logistics and traffic management are gaining influence and support. In the past, producers seemed to consider shipping and warehousing to be relatively insignificant activities. Much of the problem was that management directed its attention to other concerns, such as manufacturing and marketing, in seeking ways to tap the growth potential of the firm. Eventually, as these areas were refined, new avenues were investigated as sources of improved profit-

profitability potential ability. In the 1950s, logistics emerged as one possibility.

What really increased the logistics momentum was intensified competi-
competition tion, not only among producers trying to outdo one another, but also among
and other reasons transport companies. Emphasis on the marketing concept, which stressed the need to satisfy customer needs, made firms search for ways to improve services. Likewise, changes in the economy; the evolution in computer technology, which enabled logistics managers to obtain answers in seconds that used to take months; dramatic technological developments in transportation equipment and materials handling machines; and regulatory reform—all have combined to encourage corporate users to examine logistics. Together, these factors have increased the demand for qualified logistics managers and created expanded opportunities for professionals in this field.

SUMMARY

Just as carriers need customers to exist, the sellers of products cannot prosper without transportation services. Production and marketing depend on transportation.

In today's changing environment, the logistics manager has emerged to coordinate the movement and storage of raw materials, parts, and finished goods inventories. Under this person's control is the transportation specialist, often called the *traffic manager.* The logistics manager, on the one hand, must have the ability to merge numerous logistical activities, such as purchasing, warehousing, inventory control, packaging, and traffic management, while remembering the increasing importance of serving the firm's customers at the lowest total logistical costs. The traffic manager, on the other hand, is responsible for selecting modes and carriers according to the needs of the firm to meet various rate and service requirements. In this capacity, the traffic manager must master diverse activities, including negotiating rates and services with carriers, understanding and preparing documentation, filing claims, and possibly managing a private transportation operation.

Logistics and traffic management have become more important in recent years as firms have recognized the potential of these areas to improve overall corporate profitability. The evolution of computers and software programs, advancing technology, and regulatory reform have created many new opportunities for logistics-oriented firms and their managers. Consequently, management decision making and strategic planning are becoming more sophisticated.

STUDY QUESTIONS

1. Explain how the "just-in-time" approach to production and inventory control changes logistics needs and costs.

2. Why are transportation savings not necessarily in the best interests of the manufacturing firm?

3. What three purposes does a bill of lading serve?

4. How can a slow order transmittal process impact negatively on transportation costs and service?

5. Why do traffic managers often not file freight claims when there are shipment loss and damage problems?

6. How might private carriage improve the amount of control and flexibility a traffic manager has over transportation services?

7. What is the difference between a consignee and a consignor?

8. Among the service variables shippers use to select modes and carriers are speed and reliability. Differentiate between the two.

ENDNOTES

1. Based on a definition provided by Donald V. Harper in his class at the University of Minnesota, Fall 1970.

2. Chan K. Hahn; Peter A. Pinto; and Daniel J. Bragg, " 'Just-in-Time' Production and Purchasing," *Journal of Purchasing and Materials Management* (Fall 1983):5–6. For other sources on just-in-time and kanban, see (a) George C. Jackson, "Just-in-Time Production: Implications for Logistics Managers," *Journal of Business Logistics* 4, no. 2 (1983):1–19; (b) Richard J. Schonberger and Abdolhossein Ansari, " 'Just-in-Time' Purchasing Can Improve Quality," *Journal of Purchasing and Materials Management* (Spring 1984):2–7; and (c) Craig R. Waters, "Why Everybody's Talking about 'Just-in-Time,' " *Inc,* March 1984, pp. 77–78.

3. Ronald H. Ballou, *Basic Business Logistics* (Englewood Cliffs, N.J.: Prentice-Hall, 1978), p. 262, citing research by Bernard J. LaLonde and Douglas M. Lambert, entitled "A Methodology for Determining Inventory Carrying Costs: Two Case Studies." *Supplement in Proceedings of the Fifth Annual Transportation and Logistics Educators Conference,* edited by James F. Robeson and John R. Grabner (Chicago, 12 October 1975).

4. Vivian Brownstein, "The War on Inventories Is Real This Time," *Fortune,* 11 June 1984, pp. 20–24.

5. Frederick J. Stephenson and John W. Vann, "Air Cargo Liability Deregulation: Shippers' Perspective," *Transportation Journal* 20, no. 3 (Spring 1981):48–58.

6. Donald V. Harper, *Transportation in America: Users, Carriers, Government,* 2d ed. Englewood Cliffs, N.J.: Prentice-Hall, 1982. See pp. 123–126 and 509–511 for more information on common carrier duties.

7. Ibid., pp. 126–128.

8. Jean V. Strickland, "Private Carriage Boosted by Deregulation," *Distribution,* September 1980, p. 30, citing the estimate of William H. Borghesani, special counsel to the Private Carrier Conference of the American Trucking Associations.

9. 94 *Statutes at Large* 793.

10. *Toto Purchasing & Supply Co., Inc.,* 128 Motor Carrier Cases 873 (1978).

11. Ex Parte MC-122, Sub. 2, *Lease of Equipment and Drivers to Private Carriers,* ICC policy statement served 17 February 1982; and David J. Airozo, "Supreme Court Ruling Upholds ICC's 'Single Source' Leasing Policy," *Traffic World,* 9 April 1985, pp. 23–24.

ADDITIONAL READINGS

Allen, Mary K., and Emmelhainz, Margaret A. "Decision Support Systems: An Innovative Aid to Managers." *Journal of Business Logistics* 5, no. 2 (1984):128–142.

Ballou, Ronald H. *Business Logistics Management.* Englewood Cliffs, N.J.: Prentice-Hall, 1973.

Barrett, Colin. "Negotiating with Carriers: Meeting Motor Carriers Head-On." *Distribution,* May 1982, pp. 54–55.

———. "Negotiating with Carriers: Meeting Motor Carriers Head-On (Part Two)." *Distribution,* June 1982, p. 53.

Beier, Frederick J. "Off-Peak Freight Rates: Effects on Shippers and Carriers." *Traffic Quarterly* 33, no. 1 (January 1979):117–138.

Blanding, Warren. *Blanding's Practical Physical Distribution.* Washington, D.C.: Traffic Service Corporation, 1978.

Bloom, Gordon F. "Industry Co-operation: Key to Productivity in Physical Distribution." *International Journal of Physical Distribution and Materials Management* 13, no. 7 (1983):5–16.

Bruning, Edward R., and Lynagh, Peter M. "Carrier Evaluation in Physical Distribution Management." *Journal of Business Logistics* 5, no. 2 (1984):30–47.

"Business Gets a Grip on Inventories," *Business Week,* 14 May 1984, pp. 38–39.

Carter, Phillip L., and Narasimhan, Ram. "Decision Support Systems in Operations Management." *Journal of Business Logistics* 5, no. 1 (1984):126–147.

Cavinato, Joseph L.; Novoshielski, Paul; and Stenger, Alan J. "A Decision Model for Freight Rate Retrieval and Payment System Selection." *Transportation Journal* 21, no. 2 (Winter 1981):5–15.

Colbert, Ronald N. "Who's Liable for What in Piggyback?" *Handling and Shipping Management,* August 1984, pp. 57–58.

Coyle, John J., and Bardi, Edward J. *The Management of Business Logistics.* 2d ed. St. Paul, Minn.: West Publishing, 1980.

Dadzie, Kofi Q., and Johnston, Wesley J. "Skill Requirements in Physical Distribution Career-Path Development." *Journal of Business Logistics* 5, no. 2 (1984):65–84.

Fair, Marvin L., and Williams, Ernest W., Jr. *Transportation and Logistics.* Rev. ed. Plano, Tex.: Business Publications, 1981.

Feldman, Joan M. "Liability: Are Shippers Paying Too High a Price for Low Rates?" *Handling and Shipping Management,* June 1984, pp. 45–46.

Foster, Thomas A. "Negotiating with Carriers: Railroads." *Distribution,* November 1982, p. 40.

———. "Negotiating with Carriers: Railroads (Part Two)." *Distribution,* January 1983, pp. 54–57.

Friedman, Walter F. *Distribution Packaging.* Huntington, N.Y.: R. E. Krieger Publishing Co., 1977.

Johnson, James C., and Wood, Donald F. *Contemporary Physical Distribution & Logistics.* 2d ed. Tulsa, Okla.: Penn Well Books, 1982.

Kaminski, Peter F., and Rink, David R. "Industrial Transportation Management in a Systems Perspective." *Transportation Journal* 21, no. 1 (Fall 1981):67–75.

LaLonde, Bernard J. "A Reconfiguration of Logistics Systems in the 80s: Strategies and Challenges." *Journal of Business Logistics* 4, no. 1 (1983):1–11.

Lambert, Douglas M., and Stock, James R. *Strategic Physical Distribution Management.* Homewood, Ill.: Richard D. Irwin, 1982.

Langley, C. John, Jr. "Strategic Management in Transportation and Physical Distribution." *Transportation Journal* 22, no. 3 (Spring 1983):71–78.

———, and Wood, Wallace R. "Managerial Perspectives on the Transportation Equipment Leasing Decision." *Transportation Journal* 18, no. 3 (Spring 1979):36–48.

Mellios, George G. "Logistics Management: What, Why, How." *Journal of Business Logistics* 5, no. 2 (1984):106–122.

Muskin, Jerold B. "The Physical Distribution Infrastructure." *Transportation Quarterly* 37, no. 1 (January 1983):115–133.

National Council of Physical Distribution Management. *Measuring Productivity in Physical Distribution: a $40 Billion Dollar Goldmine.* Chicago: NCPDM, 1978.

Nishi, Masao, and Gallagher, Patrick. "A New Focus for Transportation Management: Contribution." *Journal of Business Logistics* 5, no. 2 (1984):19–29.

Shapiro, Roy D. "Get Leverage from Logistics." *Harvard Business Review* (May–June 1984):119–126.

Smykay, Edward W. *Physical Distribution Management.* 3d ed. New York: Macmillan Publishing Co., 1973.

Taff, Charles A. *Management of Physical Distribution and Transportation.* 6th ed. Homewood, Ill.: Richard D. Irwin, 1978.

Tersine, Richard. *Principles of Inventory and Materials Management.* 2d ed. New York: North Holland, 1982.

Voorhees, Roy Dale; Allen, Benjamin J.; and Pinne-kamp, Dale J. "An Examination and Analysis of the 'Invisible' Full-Service Truck Leasing Industry." *Transportation Journal* 22, no. 3 (Spring 1983):64–70.

Waller, Alan G. "Computer Systems for Distribution Planning." *International Journal of Physical Distribution and Materials Management* 13, no. 7 (1983):48–59.

Government Participation in U.S. Transportation

What separates transportation from most industries is extensive government involvement in the decision-making process. In most cases, neither carriers nor transport users are totally free to manage their business affairs. At the federal, state, and local levels of government, public officials share the decision-making responsibilities with transportation firms and their customers.

FORMS OF GOVERNMENT INVOLVEMENT

operation of
transportation
systems

In what ways is the public sector involved in transportation? First, the government manages, controls, or significantly influences the operation of several transportation systems. At the federal level, examples are the U.S. Postal Service; the National Railroad Passenger Corporation (AMTRAK); the Washington Metro mass transit system; vehicles of the National Park Service; V.I.P. limousine, helicopter, and aircraft services; and extensive activities within the Department of Defense, such as the Military Airlift Command. At the state level, the Alaska Railroad is owned by the state of Alaska, ports are usually controlled and operated by state agencies, and government-owned fleets of automobiles and trucks are commonplace occurrences. Cities, towns, and other local governmental units operate school bus fleets, transit systems, and public vehicles such as police cars. Local government also builds, maintains, and manages roads and airports.

Government is likewise a procurer of for-hire transportation services. In

79

procurer of
transportation
services

fact, the biggest single customer of the for-hire transportation sector is the federal government, which spends billions of dollars annually to move U.S. civil service workers, military personnel, and huge volumes of cargo.

procurer of
transportation
equipment

A third aspect of government involvement in transportation is procurement of transportation equipment. The U.S. government purchases ships for the National Defense Reserve Fleet; ships, aircraft, and trucks for the military forces; and space vehicles for the National Aeronautics and Space Administration.

regulator, promoter,
and policymaker

chapter
content and purpose

The government is best known for its roles in regulating the transportation modes, providing promotion and subsidy (P&S) aid, and establishing policies for this industry. These important functions are the focus of Chapter 4. Specifically, the discussion will include details on both the regulation and the deregulation of transportation, a description of promotion and subsidy programs, and an explanation of the transportation responsibilities of the executive branch of government. Thereafter, an evaluation of the government's role in transportation will be presented, followed by a review of the process of changing federal transportation policies and regulations. Most important, Chapter 4 provides the basis for understanding the specific modal issues that will be discussed in the remainder of the text.

GOVERNMENT REGULATION OF TRANSPORTATION

Origin of Transportation Law

common law

The emergence of transportation law can be traced to English common law and the need to protect the rights of shippers and passengers. Common law refers to legal findings long accepted as correct and whose origins derive from decisions by judges rather than from written statutes. The latter refers to laws enacted by legislatures, namely, bills passed by Congress and signed by the President. The former gravitated toward common principles and precedent; in other words, a decision in question would be based on previous decisions made in similar cases in the past. From common law developed the concept of *common carrier.* As noted in the previous chapter, the latter is a firm that holds itself out to serve the general public. In return for this privilege, it is obligated by the government to perform certain duties such as to charge reasonable rates and deliver the goods. From the early days of U.S. transportation, an attitude has prevailed that public officials need to treat the transportation business differently from most other industries. Since it affects the public interest, government involvement is often necessary.

statutory law

In the late 1800s, the public recognized the need for a more structured set of regulatory guidelines and began applying statutory law to the transportation sector. Many common law principles became the bases for legislation. First came the state-enacted Granger Laws (1871–1874). Then commenced a long list of federal transportation laws starting with the Act to Regulate Commerce in 1887. (The Granger Laws and the Act to Regulate Commerce will be discussed in Chapter 5.)

Forms and Causes of Regulation

economic and
noneconomic
regulation

For more than 90 years, transportation has been one of the most regulated sectors of the economy, and this regulation has assumed two forms. *Economic regulation* encompasses rules governing the entry of new firms into a particular mode, the expansion of operating authority of established carriers, services, the abandonment or shrinkage of operations, exit from the transportation business, rates, mergers, and accounting and financial practices. The second type of regulation is called *noneconomic regulation.* Its domain is safety, environmental protection, vehicle registration taxes, and other limits such as smoking rules on aircraft, automobile seat belt requirements, and aircraft noise abatement regulations. Nonetheless, what separates transportation from most other industries is economic regulation.

monopolistic
controls

Transportation economic regulation emerged to correct both carrier monopolistic abuses and competitive problems. The origin of the former is traced to the late nineteenth century. At the time, railroads were accused of charging excessive rates, discriminating against shippers, and engaging in unfair practices aimed at driving competitors from the marketplace. Government officials responded with maximum rate rules (price ceilings) and penalties aimed at stopping unfair practices. By the 1930s, another problem emerged: The trucking industry, burdened with excessive competition, asked for and received entry regulations to limit the number of competitors and minimum rate rules, floor prices that curb rate wars. Thus the motivation for economic regulation can be too little competition and monopolistic abuses or too much competition and competitive excesses.

control of
excessive
competition

reasons for
government
involvement

Contrary to what one might expect, the federal government was a reluctant participant in transportation affairs. Before acting, the government usually received a clear mandate from the public to become involved. In the monopolistic regulation case, shippers did most of the beckoning. Established carriers, however, led the chorus for competitive controls. Similar to the federal sector, states also took an active role in transport decision making, control, and enforcement. Essentially, government had found the private sector incompetent to police itself.

Thus transportation decision making occurs not in a free-market atmosphere, but rather under the watchful eye of bureaucrats. Of course, government participation in transportation is not totally opposed by businesses. The regulated business setting also has its advantages. For example, it simplifies management tasks by providing step-by-step requirements. Also, it can protect established carriers from new competition. However, innovative managers are often frustrated with government prohibitions and procedures.

Federal Economic Regulatory Commissions

ICC, FMC,
FERC, and CAB

Responsibility for the federal economic regulation of interstate transportation modes was delegated by Congress to independent agencies called commissions and boards, which act as extended arms of the legislative branch. Since laws are written in general terms, experts capable of interpreting questions of law and deciding on individual transportation cases are required. Burdened with heavy workloads, neither the Congress nor the courts seemed interested in this duty. Consequently, the commission form of regulatory administration originated in 1887 with the creation of the Interstate Commerce Commission (ICC). Currently, there are three commissions—the Interstate Commerce Commission (ICC), the Federal Maritime Commission (FMC), and the Federal Energy Regulatory Commission (FERC). The Civil Aeronautics Board (CAB), until January 1, 1985, was a fourth independent economic regulatory agency, but the Airline Deregulation Act of 1978 (92 *Statutes at Large* 1705) eliminated it. Likewise, the Federal Power Commission, which used to regulate interstate natural gas pipelines, was eliminated with the creation of the FERC.

Power and Status of Commissions.   Commissions are charged with directing the business of the transportation modes as governed by the U.S. statutes and the U.S. Constitution. History has shown commissions to have been given considerable administrative powers to influence and even dictate private sector business choices. Consequently, a singular decision, such as the granting or denial of a proposal to reduce transportation rates, has been known to affect significantly modal market share distributions. A pertinent example is the ICC's 1965 decision in the *Ingot Molds* case.[1] The railroads proposed a rate on ingot mold stools that was above their variable costs but below their *fully distributed costs*—variable costs plus a fair share of their total annual fixed costs. However, the ICC ruled that the rate could not be set that low because it was below the fully distributed costs of the bargeline competitors, who, in the Commission's opinion, had the inherent advantage.[2] Therefore the railroads were prohibited from implementing a marketing strategy they thought necessary to attract the ingot mold stool business.

Many signs indicate a change in the status of the commission form of regulation. Most obvious was the demise of the CAB. In addition, a Congressional mandate reduced ICC membership from 11 to 7 people effective January 1, 1983,[3] and the ICC's budget and staff were reduced. In short, once tightly controlled carriers, such as airlines, trucking companies, and railroads, now have less need for federal overseers because of regulatory reform measures.

As noted in Table 4.1, the ICC is primarily concerned with railroad and highway transportation. The FMC's concern is water transportation on the high seas, and the FERC rules on oil and gas pipeline issues. Tradition can play as much a role in deciding modal jurisdictional matters as does logic, as noted by the location of coal slurry pipelines under the ICC. It would seem today that the FERC would be a more appropriate home, given pipeline and energy responsibilities, but this is not the case. Details on how each commission's decisions and powers affect railroad, water carrier, pipeline, and highway carrier management personnel will follow in the modal chapters (Chapters 5–13).

Structure of Commissions.   From the beginning, Congress has placed considerable emphasis on keeping the commissions independent of the three

Margin notes:

responsibilities

power of commissions

lessening of commission influence

modal jurisdictions

independence

TABLE 4.1. Jurisdictions of the federal transportation regulatory commissions

Interstate Commerce Commission (ICC)	Federal Maritime Commission (FMC)	Federal Energy Regulatory Commission (FERC)
Railroads	International water transportation	Oil pipelines
Trucking	Domestic water carriage on the high seas	Natural gas pipelines
Bus lines		
Coal slurry pipelines		
Surface freight forwarders[a]		
Domestic water carriers[b]		
Brokers[c]		

[a]Intermediaries who collect and consolidate small shipments to common destinations and tender the consolidations primarily to railroads and truckers.

[b]Mainly inland waterway (river and canal), Great Lakes, and coastal operators.

[c]Intermediaries who try to match companies desiring traffic with shippers needing trucking services.

branches of government, namely, the executive, legislative, and judicial branches. Considering the controversial nature of the decisions that were to be made by these agencies, the intent was to minimize undue influence. The ICC, CAB, and FMC were clearly organized as independent agencies. The FERC, on the other hand, although labeled an independent agency, is housed in the Department of Energy, a unit of the executive branch.

ties to the legislative branch

Each federal transportation economic regulatory agency has close ties to all three branches. The Legislature has the power to create or disband commissions, approve budgets, and pass bills defining transportation regulations and policies. Moreover, the Senate must approve commission appointments before members can serve on these agencies. Of equal importance, the president has the power to nominate commission members, to select the chairperson of each agency, to recommend transportation policy, to influence commission budgets, and to institute investigations into commission matters.

ties to the executive branch

ties to the judicial branch

The judicial branch is also involved, because it must enforce commission decisions and review these decisions when it deems that the commissions overstepped their Congressional or Constitutional authority or misinterpreted the intent of the federal statutes. Administrative decisions by commissions, such as what rate to allow a carrier to charge, are not decided by the courts, because the commissions are supposedly competent and responsible enough to make judgments without establishing a long appeals process, which would add to the court's workload. Collectively, then, commissions are not really independent. They are tied to each of the three governmental branches but hopefully not obligated so excessively to any one branch that it can unduly prejudice commission decisions. In this setting, they perform quasi-legislative, quasi-judicial functions.

State Regulatory Role

Intrastate economic regulatory matters usually fall within the jurisdiction of state regulatory bodies. These agencies include the Public Service Commission, the Public Utilities Commission, and the Railroad Commission. These agencies are similar to federal economic regulatory commissions because they handle such matters as entry, expansion, services, exit, abandonment, rates, mergers, and other controls for carriers serving points within a state's borders.

federal and state commission differences

In other ways, however, state and federal regulatory bodies differ. Typically, a single commission at the state level regulates all the modes rather than having several bodies with distinct jurisdictions. State agencies also tend to regulate public utilities such as electric, gas, and telephone companies. Not only is this different from the federal level, but also state agencies typically dedicate more of their time to nontransportation matters than to regulating the modes. Another distinction is that state regulatory bodies are often charged with policing and enforcement duties. At the federal level, this is usually the responsibility of other organizations, such as the Federal Aviation Administration, the Coast Guard, or other U.S. Department of Transportation agencies or local units of government.

Commerce Clause and Conflicting State–Federal Policies

conflicting state rules

Finally, bordering states, or states and the federal government, occasionally disagree on the nature of the transportation regulations to be administered. For instance, one state may have strict trucking regulations and another has deregulation. Conflicting rules necessitate efforts by both federal and state officials to resolve disputes and coordinate differences. Although the Commerce Clause of the U.S. Constitution (Article 1, Section 8, Clause 3) delegates the power to regulate interstate commerce to the federal government, state commissioners perceive a need to help local constituencies. Thus issues like railroad line abandonment are not readily welcomed by state officials. Small towns resent the loss of rail service because it may negatively affect community economic growth and cause transportation rates to increase, or people may lose jobs. State regulations, designed to protect intrastate transport interests, can diminish the profitability of interstate carriers. For example, state-imposed maximum rate regulations often force carrier prices down to low levels on intrastate shipments. Because conflicts have been difficult to resolve, the federal government has been increasingly assuming more power over intrastate transportation matters.

increasing federal role

Regulatory Reform Movement

One sweeping change to occur in transportation is the regulatory reform movement, or as many call it, deregulation. Starting in 1977, with the deregulation of the domestic air-cargo business, Congress has passed, and two successive presidents (President Carter and President Reagan) have signed, bills

TABLE 4.2. Chronology of regulatory reform of transportation

Date of Enactment	Title	Source
Nov. 9, 1977	Federal Aviation Act of 1958—Insurance Risks (i.e., Air Cargo Deregulation Act)	91 *Statutes at Large* 1284
Oct. 24, 1978	Airline Deregulation Act of 1978	92 *Statutes at Large* 1705
Feb. 15, 1980	International Air Transportation Competition Act of 1979	94 *Statutes at Large* 35
July 1, 1980	Motor Carrier Act of 1980	94 *Statutes at Large* 793
Oct. 14, 1980	Staggers Rail Act of 1980	94 *Statutes at Large* 1895
Oct. 15, 1980	Household Goods Transportation Act of 1980	94 *Statutes at Large* 2011
Sept. 20, 1982	Bus Regulatory Reform Act of 1982	96 *Statutes at Large* 1102
March 20, 1984	Shipping Act of 1984	98 *Statutes at Large* 67

to lessen government controls on the airline, trucking, railroad, and other transportation industries (see Table 4.2). No evidence suggests, however, that the process has been completed, as noted by the more recent enactment of the Shipping Act of 1984 and legislation introduced in 1985 to further deregulate truckers, freight forwarders, brokers, and domestic water carriers.[4]

Early Victories: Airline Sector.   Given considerable credit for initiating the regulatory reform movement is a small group of economists who, starting in the 1960s, proposed that increased competition would decrease air fares, or at least curtail future price increases. Soon they were joined by Congressional supporters like Senator Edward M. Kennedy and key Carter administration personnel in a more unified effort to deregulate the airline industry. An off-shoot of the movement was the Congressional decision in 1977 to deregulate the air-cargo business. Proponents argued that this action would provide a test case to preview the implications of less regulation of the airline business.

Examining the air, trucking, and railroad sectors, some conclusions can be drawn about the causes of the deregulation movement. Consider the airline case, for example: Airline fares had been rising rapidly in the wake of escalating labor, fuel, aircraft, and interest costs (see Table 4.3). In testimony before the Senate Committee on Commerce, Science, and Transportation, Senator Edward M. Kennedy stated in 1977 that there was an emerging consensus among legislators, executive branch officials, consumer groups, airline regulators, economists, and many in the business community that rigid federal economic regulation of the airlines tended to increase prices, foster ineffi-

reasons for airline deregulation

TABLE 4.3. Airline, trucking, and railroad federal regulatory reform goals

Airlines	Trucking	Railroads
Reduce fares	Reduce rates	
Stimulate demand		
		Strengthen competitive position against other modes
Improve profits		Improve profits
Provide access to private capital		Provide access to private capital
Stimulate aircraft industry		
Stimulate airline employment		
Create operating efficiencies	Create operating efficiencies	Create operating efficiencies
Hold down labor costs		
		Shrink industry to a more efficient size
Maintain safety		Improve safety
Reduce regulatory costs/delays	Reduce regulatory costs/delays	Reduce regulatory costs/delays

ciency, and perpetuate excessive government control, bureaucracy, and red tape.[5] It was believed that this trend would continue unabated unless the government removed its stringent barriers to entry that effectively had shut the door for 40 years on low-cost carriers wanting the right to operate aircraft in the domestic markets.

At the same time, airline traffic growth had reached a plateau. Increased competition and pricing freedom, Senator Kennedy argued, would stimulate discount air fares, which in turn would stimulate primary demand (untapped potential).[6] Lower prices would provide opportunities for millions of citizens to fly who had not been able to afford to do so in the past. More passengers, in turn, would mean fewer empty seats, greater operating efficiencies, and increased profits.[7] With profits on the upswing, the airlines would once again find the private capital necessary to replace a rapidly aging fleet. These efforts would further stimulate an ailing U.S. aircraft industry and also increase employment in the airline and aircraft manufacturing sectors. Side benefits would derive from greater pressure on high-cost carriers to develop greater operating efficiencies and to fight harder to hold down labor costs. If firms did not succeed in these cost control/productivity endeavors, they would eventually be nonprice competitive with the lower cost entrants.[8] A final goal was to maintain safety, and new aircraft would help.

The Airline Deregulation Act of 1978 removed a substantial hurdle in the debate concerning regulatory reform of not only the airline industry but also of the trucking and railroad industries as well. No longer was deregulation an unacceptable concept. Washington was ready to accept changes in the regulatory environment of other modes besides aviation.

Trucking and Railroad Deregulation.   Deregulation of the trucking and railroad sectors was motivated by logic both similar to and different from that motivating airline deregulation. As in the airline case, tight entry rules had accelerated trucking cost increases, as service competition prevailed. Trucking deregulation assumed that increased competition would reduce trucking rates. However, unlike the airline situation, where industry profits were unstable and often poor, trucking deregulation backers submitted that profits were too healthy in this sector. They pointed out that freight rates would not likely decline or even be held in check unless low-cost firms had the opportunity to market their services. A. Daniel O'Neal, former Chairman of the Interstate Commerce Commission, testified in 1979 that he believed relaxed entry rules would improve trucking services, lower rates, and provide more innovative pricing techniques.[9] If government would give low-cost operators and more efficient carriers the opportunity to seek the traffic, competition would force high-cost trucking companies to become more productive and control costs better. Less regulation would reduce the costs and time involved in filing applications for entry. Note the absence of the goals of stimulating demand, improving profits, providing access to private capital, and so on, which had motivated airline deregulation. Truck deregulation was primarily an anti-inflation and pro-consumer measure, rather than a pro-carrier measure, but some people concluded that it was only an anti-big carrier and anti-union measure.

reasons for trucking regulatory reform

Unlike the trucking and air modes, railroad deregulation did not focus on lowering prices. It was primarily backed by people like John Sullivan, Federal Railroad Administrator, as a necessary strategy to improve rail industry profits.[10] Pro-deregulators seemed convinced that the nation's freight railroad industry needed to be saved and modernized, a process that would be accomplished either by giving private companies more freedom to adjust to the marketplace through regulatory reform or by increasing taxpayer support. Of these two options, regulatory reform seemed to be the more attractive solution.

reasons for railroad deregulation

The goals of railroad regulatory reform, then, were to strengthen the freight railroad competitive position versus other modes and to improve carrier profits as a result. These objectives would supposedly be accomplished by allowing the industry to shrink to a more efficient size, by encouraging the industry to improve its operating efficiencies, and by giving the sector more pricing and service flexibility. If successful, improved profits would be reinvested to modernize rights-of-way and equipment, which would help accomplish the goal of improved rail safety. Furthermore, deregulation would reduce regulatory costs and delays.

Momentum is the key idea in regulatory reform. Strict regulation was

momentum established

evident from 1887 until the late 1970s. After the railroads were regulated by the federal government in 1887, oil pipelines were regulated in 1906, and the trucking industry was regulated in 1935. Aviation was regulated next in 1938, and domestic water transportation regulation followed in 1940. After the precedent had been set, the competition was soon guided by similar rules. Thus deregulation may someday be recorded in history as the single most consequential event of the modern transportation era. As with regulation, after deregulation of one mode occurred, its momentum carried the other modes. The regulatory tradition was broken.

PROMOTION AND SUBSIDY

The U.S. transportation industry is a highly promoted, highly subsidized system. Government aid distinguishes transportation from most other business sectors of the economy. By definition, *subsidies* are grants or other financial aid that are not repaid, whereas *promotion,* a broader term, includes subsidies as well as other sources of assistance. Forms of promotion (see Table 4.4) include low-interest loans, guaranteed loans, and advantageous tax programs, as well as other types of transportation promotion and subsidy (P&S).

Types of Government Aid

Promotion and subsidy programs exist at the federal, state, and local government levels. As noted in Table 4.5, federal expenditures for transportation facilities and services for 1984 included $2.867 billion for airways, $0.891 billion for airports, $15.244 billion for highways, $1.148 billion for rivers and harbors, $2.291 billion for railroads, and $3.096 billion for mass transportation.

state and local aid

Table 4.5 also reveals the significance of state and local aid to transportation. During 1984, nearly $35 billion of the $39.549 billion state and local total was spent on highways. In addition, $3.200 billion was contributed to airports, and $1.480 was spent on river and harbor projects. Furthermore, recent increases in fuel taxes at both the federal and state level will result in higher public highway expenditures in the future.

aggregate P&S payments and user taxes

Collectively, public expenditures for transportation promotion and subsidy at all levels of government, across all modes, and throughout U.S. history exceed $600 billion. However, in just one year, 1984, transportation contributed an estimated $713.2 billion to the nation's $3.663 trillion gross national product.[11] Some would argue that the more than $600 billion in aid has therefore not been too high a price to pay for the contributions this industry has delivered, particularly when most of it was repaid through *user taxes*. These taxes are levied against people or modes who directly benefit from a transportation system: for example, a fuel tax paid by an automobile driver using the highways. Although the government spends money to construct trans-

---

TABLE 4.4. Selected types of transportation promotion and subsidy

Type of Promotion and Subsidy	Definition
Aid to transportation equipment manufacturers:	Usually loans to help troubled companies eliminate cash flow problems, e.g., loans to Chrysler.
Capital grants:	Subsidies in the form of free land, equipment, or facilities or cash to acquire the same items.
Eminent domain:	The power to obtain property rights-of-way either through buying property or acquiring easements despite land-owner opposition.
Exemption from or reduction of property taxes:	Favorable rulings by local authorities on property tax assessments of transportation companies.
Forgiveness of debt interest or principle:	Rulings in which the government decides a carrier cannot or should not have to meet borrowing responsibilities.
Funding of labor guarantees:	Government payments to transportation workers who lose jobs where they had been guaranteed employment, e.g., job separation (severance) payments to Conrail workers who had lifetime job guarantees.
Government guaranteed loans:	Government-backed loans reducing risks to private lenders and subsequently lowering interest rates.
Government loans:	Taxpayer-provided direct loans at low interest rates.
Maintenance, repair:	Assistance for right-of-way (such as roads, waterways, and airport runways) modifications.
Navigation aids:	Government-provided safety equipment, such as channel markers, street signs, and runway lights.
Operating subsidies:	Grants to cover deficits between operating revenues and operating costs.
Operation and control of rights-of-way:	Essentially, traffic control such as the functions performed by federal air traffic controllers, the Army Corps of Engineers, the Coast Guard, and highway patrollers.
Research and development:	Funding of private studies or conducting of government research aiding transportation.
Retirement aid:	Aid to finance the unfunded cost of transportation worker retirement programs.
Weather advice:	Safety information provided at government expense to aircraft, water, and other vehicle operators.
Technical assistance:	Planning, design, construction, and other forms of government-provided technical advice.

portation rights-of-way such as highways, user taxes help to offset public capital outlays.

Promotion and Subsidy Goals

Government provides transportation promotion and subsidy for many reasons. Capital requirements, such as for highway construction, are so high that reliance on private funding sources (e.g., carrier capital) would have meant

TABLE 4.5. 1984 federal and state/local government expenditures for transportation facilities and services (billions of dollars)

Recipient	Federal Expenditure	State/Local Expenditure	Total Expenditure
Airways	$2.867	——	$2.867
Airports	0.891	$3.200	4.091
Highways	15.244	34.869	50.113
Rivers and harbors	1.148	1.480	2.628
Rail (AMTRAK)	2.291	——	2.291
Mass transportation	3.096	——[a]	3.096
TOTALS	$25.537	$39.549	$65.086

[a]State and local governments contribute a sizeable amount of aid to mass transportation, but figures were not available.

Source: Frank A. Smith, Senior Associate, *Transportation in America,* 3d ed. (Washington, D.C.: Transportation Policy Associates, March 1985), p. 16. (Adapted with permission.)

long delays or perhaps, in some cases, no rights-of-way construction at all. Promotion and subsidy accelerate modal development: for instance, government aid for airport and airway development encouraged airline progress. A correlated goal of promotion and subsidy is improved transportation safety. Without question, P&S support has helped significantly to improve airline safety and to convince initial airline passengers that their flights would be safe experiences.

Other goals also exist for P&S. In the 1850–1880 period, the federal government provided financial support to the railroads to encourage the construction of lines from the Mississippi River to the Pacific Ocean. Here, the primary objective was not transportation, but rather the desire to develop the western frontier. Aid was also given to help save carriers from financial collapse, save workers' jobs, and prevent transportation users from losing badly needed services. For instance, the U.S. government came to the rescue of the bankrupt Penn Central Railroad in the early 1970s and, by creating Conrail, saved both railroad jobs and rail customer services in the Northeast United States. In essence, government promotion and subsidy have been provided because of the importance of transportation to the people of the United States.

Policy Changes in Promotion and Subsidy

Traditionally, government has chosen to help sectors in which the public interest is involved, such as education, health, and welfare. Therefore transportation is not an isolated, favored sector. However, history has shown P&S not to be the panacea some thought it would be for troubled transportation modes or carriers. Furthermore, the Reagan Administration, stating that Washington was excessively involved in matters that should be handled by the private business sector, has attempted to lessen the federal role in P&S transportation funding.

Reagan policy and logic

President Reagan endorsed the following measures: increases in waterway user taxes; elimination of construction differential subsidies, which subsidized the construction costs of merchant ships built in U.S. shipyards; increases in highway user taxes; decreases in transit operating subsidies; the government sale of Conrail to the private business sector; and increases in local funding of port projects. Increases in private, state, and local funding of transportation systems would aid the presidential effort to shrink the federal tax burden and force closer scrutiny of individual projects. If direct beneficiaries, such as carriers and transportation users, or local taxpayers had to pay for transportation capital projects, they would make wiser transportation decisions. As noted in the case of increased fuel taxes, President Reagan was successful in implementing some of his programs despite strong opposition from members of Congress who rose to defend established P&S programs.

TRANSPORTATION RESPONSIBILITIES OF THE EXECUTIVE BRANCH

All three branches of the federal government play a role in transportation; however, the responsibilities of the executive branch are by far the most encompassing. As noted in Fig. 4.1, many cabinet departments have transportation policy, P&S, safety, and operating responsibilities. The Departments of Transportation (DOT) and Defense (DOD), however, are the two executive departments most heavily involved in transportation matters.

Department of Transportation

The principal advisor to the president on transporation matters is the Secretary of Transportation. Created as an executive department by an act of Congress on October 15, 1966 (80 *Statutes at Large* 931:49 *United States Code* 1651), the DOT became operational in April 1967. Its main concerns are policy, safety, and promotion of the various modes. The organization of the Federal Department of Transportation is delineated in Fig. 4.2.

UMTA and MARAD

At its inception, the DOT was flawed by the absence of the Urban Mass Transportation Administration (UMTA) and the Federal Maritime Administration (MARAD). The former was then a part of the Department of Housing and Urban Development and was moved to the DOT in 1968. MARAD was a part of the Department of Commerce from 1950 to 1981, when it was also placed under DOT. These additions have helped facilitate DOT's role of coordinating the programs of the various transportation modes. Figure 4.2 introduces the broad scope of the DOT's responsibilities, which are further discussed in later chapters.

FIGURE 4.1.
Transportation responsibilities of the executive branch.

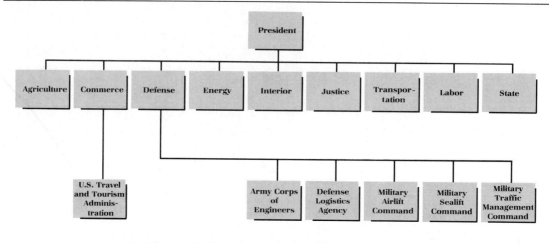

OFFICE/ORGANIZATION	RESPONSIBILITIES
President	Appoints members and chairs of the Interstate Commerce Commission, the Federal Maritime Commission, and the Federal Energy Regulatory Commission.
	Rules on matters of international air policy.
	Recommends transportation policy.
	Authorizes transportation studies and reviews.
Agriculture	Develops transportation policies for agriculture and rural development.
	Represents agricultural interests before transportation economic regulatory bodies.
Commerce	
U.S. Travel and Tourism Administration:	Established in 1981, this organization advises on tourism policy; charged with using the contributions of the tourism and recreation industries to promote economic prosperity, full employment, and the international trade balance.
	Attempts to eliminate unnecessary trade barriers to the U.S. tourism industry.
	Collects, analyzes, and disseminates tourism data.
	(By encouraging trade and tourism, encourages transportation use.)
Defense	
Army Corps of Engineers:	Plans, constructs, maintains, operates, and improves river, harbor, and port facilities.
Defense Logistics Agency:	Procures and manages supplies in support of the military services, other DOD components, federal civil agencies, and others as authorized.
	Requires and uses transportation services.
Military Airlift Command (Air Force):	Provides air transportation for personnel and cargo for all military services on a worldwide basis.
Military Sealift Command (Navy):	Provides ocean transportation services by government-owned or commercial vessels for personnel and cargo of all components of the DOD and as authorized for other federal agencies.

FIGURE 4.1. *(Cont.)*

OFFICE/ORGANIZATION	RESPONSIBILITIES
Military Traffic Management Command (Army):	Directs military traffic management, land transportation, and common-user ocean terminal service within the United States, excluding Alaska and Hawaii.
	Directs the worldwide traffic management of DOD household goods moving and storage.
	Administers DOD activities pertaining to highways for national defense.
Energy	Develops and manages the national energy plan.
	Manages long-term research and development of energy technology.
	Houses the FERC to regulate oil and natural gas pipeline transportation.
Interior	
National Park Service:	Operates transportation services within more than 350 units of the National Park System.
Justice	Represents the commissions (ICC, FMC, and FERC) in court.
Labor	Fosters, promotes, and develops the welfare of wage earners of the U.S.
	Improves working conditions of transportation employees.
	Administers the Occupational Safety and Health (OSHA) program.
	Provides labor-management collective bargaining assistance.
	Ensures that transportation labor protective clauses are adhered to.
	Collects and disseminates labor statistics, including transportation labor data.
State	Develops policy in respect to international aviation and maritime transportation.
Transportation	Has primary responsibility for transportation matters (see Fig. 4.2 for details).

Source: U.S. General Services Administration, *U.S. Government Manual 1982–83* (Washington, D.C.: National Archives and Records Service, July 1982).

Department of Defense

The U.S. Department of Defense manages the complex task of supporting the needs of about 2 million active duty and 2.5 million reserve duty military personnel and about 1 million civilian employees.[12] The DOD, through its various units—the Defense Logistics Agency (DLA), Military Airlift Command (MAC), Military Sealift Command (MSC), and Military Traffic Management Command (MTMC)—is responsible for the travel of personnel and their personal property, such as furniture and automobiles, as well as the supplying of weaponry and support needs. Transportation services are accomplished through using military transportation equipment and facilities, as well as through contracts

FIGURE 4.2.
U.S. Department of Transportation organization and responsibilities.

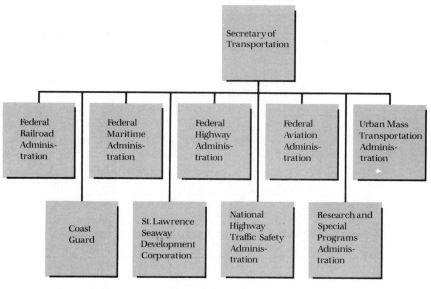

OFFICE/ORGANIZATION	RESPONSIBILITIES
Secretary of Transportation	Assures the coordinated, effective administration of the transportation programs of the federal government.
	Develops national transportation policies and programs conducive to the provision of fast, safe, efficient, and convenient transportation at the lowest cost consistent with these goals.
Federal Railroad Administration	Administers and enforces rail safety programs.
	Administers rail financial aid programs.
	Conducts R&D programs.
Federal Maritime Administration	Promotes the U.S. merchant marine, including administration of subsidy programs.
	Organizes and directs emergency merchant ship operations.
	Maintains the National Defense Reserve Fleet.
	Operates the U.S. Merchant Marine Academy.
Federal Highway Administration	Administers the federal-aid highway program.
	Administers federal highway safety programs, such as construction to remove roadside obstacles.
	Exercises jurisdiction over the safety of commercial motor carriers (trucking).
	Inspects facilities, vehicles, and driver qualifications.
	Implements programs governing the highway movements of hazardous materials, cargo security, and noise abatement.
Federal Aviation Administration	Enforces aviation safety programs, including inspections of facilities and aircraft and pilot certification.
	Promotes civil aviation, including airports, airways, and R&D.
	Manages the air space through the air traffic control function.
Urban Mass Transportation Administration	Promotes public mass transit through capital grant and operating subsidy programs, planning and technical assistance, and funding of R&D and demonstration projects.

OFFICE/ORGANIZATION	RESPONSIBILITIES
Coast Guard	Operates under DOT, except in time of war or when the President directs it to operate under the Navy.
	Conducts search and rescue operations by air and water.
	Removes hazards to navigation and manages aid to navigation.
	Enforces maritime law on or under the high seas and in U.S. waters.
	Administers and enforces safety standards for commercial vessels, boating safety, and port security and safety.
	Investigates marine accidents.
	Implements marine environmental policy.
St. Lawrence Seaway Development Corporation	Develops, operates, and maintains that part of the Seaway between Montreal and Lake Erie within the territorial limits of the United States.
	Enforces Seaway safety.
	Joins the Canadian government in assessing and collecting Seaway-user tolls.
National Highway Traffic Safety Administration	Implements motor vehicle safety programs and issues standards for safety.
	Ensures compliance with safety standards.
	Helps fund state and local safety programs.
	Works with the Environmental Protection Agency and the Department of Energy to set auto fuel standards.
Research & Special Programs Administration	Serves as DOT's research, analysis, and technical development arm to run programs with emphasis on safety, cargo security, and funded R&D.

Source: U.S. General Services Administration, *U.S. Government Manual 1982–83* (Washington, D.C.: National Archives and Records Service, July 1982).

with private sector for-hire carriers. Another key DOD unit, the Army Corps of Engineers, essentially a civil engineering organization, is involved in water navigation projects for military and civilian purposes. Specifically, this unit plans, constructs, maintains, and improves river, harbor, and port facilities.

EVALUATION OF THE GOVERNMENT'S ROLE IN TRANSPORTATION

Government involvement in transportation is highly controversial; in fact, almost every phase of government participation has sometimes been criticized for mismanagement, excessive interference, biased administration, or poor decision making. In evaluating the government's role in transportation, let us start with the issue of public sector transportation management.

Management of Transportation Systems

deficits

A popular criticism is that the public sector does not manage transportation systems as efficiently as the private sector does. Critics contend that people need to look for proof no further than the records of the U.S. Postal Service, AMTRAK, mass transit systems, or the U.S. rail system, which was run by the government during World War I. These records, which show that public systems almost always need taxpayer support or frequent rate increases to cover operating deficits, reveal that most bureaucrats are not efficient financial managers.

burden of restoring worn out systems

Singled out for blame is the political environment that constantly impairs the decision-making process. While true in many respects, this criticism is too simple. Governments rarely take over profitable private sector transportation systems. By necessity, worn-out systems, such as the nation's rail passenger system, which AMTRAK was designated to restore, require accelerated funding to return them to acceptable service standards. Still, it could be argued that once services are better, operating costs escalate. The problem is the tendency of public officials to avoid difficult decisions, such as cost-cutting or price-increasing actions. Too often, public officials are unwilling to make choices unpopular with voting constituencies whom they depend on to keep them in public office.

trouble making decisions: politics

conflicting performance standards

Nevertheless, it is important to differentiate between manager problems and public system problems. Private sector managers work for owners who tend to evaluate performance by profitability measures. The public sector has different evaluation criteria. In fact, it is rarely, if ever, charged with making a profit. Consequently, there is no clear measure of performance, nor even one evaluator who is the judge. In an environment where success is measured by one group on the basis of improved services; by another, on protecting the interests of labor; by a third, on maintaining low consumer prices; by a fourth that wants taxes reduced, and so forth—the public sector manager is frequently caught in a no-win situation of conflicting guidelines. In such a setting, it is understandable why public management is criticized. People work for too many bosses, and too many constituencies expect their programs to be protected. In many ways, being an efficient public sector manager is far more difficult than being a senior executive in the private sector.

Federal Economic Commissions

expertise

The federal economic regulatory commission form of transportation regulation is also hotly debated. In fact, the expertise and experience of the membership, the "independence" of these commissions, and the soundness and legality of their actions are all subject to criticism. Consider the expertise issue. Before 1970, 34 of the 77 ICC-appointed commissioners served 10 or more years. Since 1970, however, only 5 of 17 members stayed at least three years.[13] How can expertise be built with that kind of turnover rate? Is an ICC appointment merely a springboard to a political or carrier management career? The rebuttal to these concerns is that the regulatory environment is changing so rapidly that experience is not particularly beneficial; in fact, it could be a handicap if commissioners are too entrenched in precedent and not flexible enough to follow the changing mandates of Congress.

transportation
experience

Another criticism of the federal economic commissions is that nominees rarely have much transportation experience. Typically, appointees are experienced in legal matters, and many are lawyers. However, do commissioners have enough transportation knowledge to appreciate fully the implications of their decisions? In the past, government officials have avoided appointing experienced carrier and shipper executives to the commissions, because of fear that these people would favor the sectors from which they came. The alternative, however, is often inexperienced appointees.

independence

A related issue is the criticism that the appointment process is used to "stack the deck," in essence, to staff a commission with people who agree with the president's philosophy. Critics complain that recent presidents nominated pro-deregulators to the Civil Aeronautics Board and Interstate Commerce Commission. Although the law limits the number of Republicans and Democrats on a commission, deregulators can be found in either party. The argument is that the appointment process biases the voting of the commissions and thus negates the goal of commission independence.

Senate approval
of nominees

Of course, this activity occurs because a president wants a commission that agrees with the administration's viewpoint. Still, the U.S. Senate has the power to reject a presidential nominee, but rarely does it do so. In general, nominees are prescreened to ensure that the Senate will support the president's nominations. Often, too, senators agree with the president's ideas on deregulation or regulation, and thus party lines are not a particular obstacle to commission appointments. Still, some critics might argue that the Senate rubberstamps nominees so regularly that senators are either playing politics or not giving serious enough attention to the importance of the commission appointments.

Aside from the previous complaints, commission actions also raise the public's ire. A frequent suggestion is that both the CAB and ICC tended to exceed their statutory powers with de facto deregulation of the air and truck modes. *De facto deregulation* is the lessening of economic regulation by commissions who take great liberty in interpreting their powers and who make liberal decisions. The ICC, furthermore, has been accused of not complying with the law.[14] Specific complaints are that the ICC has been taking virtually no action against trucking companies that practice allegedly predatory pricing, which is pricing below variable costs, or to screen applicants for entry into the trucking industry to ensure that new firms are prepared to serve the public in a responsible manner. Perhaps a shrinking ICC staff cannot handle the workload. However, whether duties are being neglected because of the workload or on purpose, a legitimate question is raised: Why are legal duties not being complied with?

rebuttal

Regulatory commissions have been assigned the difficult task of making controversial decisions. They too are affected by deregulatory changes that are sweeping away years of precedent-setting judgments. Like court judges, no matter what they decide, they are likely to make some, and often many, individuals unhappy. Furthermore, administering regulations at a time when the commissions themselves are threatened with elimination or other major reorganizations can be difficult. A case in point was Senator Robert Packwood's proposal in 1983 to consolidate the regulatory commissions into fewer agencies.[15] The only certainty is that, as long as transportation commissions exist, they will be controversial.

Promotion and Subsidy

Many people are also unhappy with promotion and subsidy programs. Those who believe they are not receiving their share want more government transportation assistance. Meanwhile, some of the recipients want increased aid; at the least, they do not want to see programs cut. Even within the public sector, the federal government seems bent on shifting more of the financial aid burden to the state and local levels. What are the specific complaints?

distorts the marketplace

1. P&S allocations favor selected modes at the expense of others (see Table 4.5). When government backs one mode, its carriers can improve their services or lower their costs and make market share gains: for example, a carrier who can charge rates below true costs and assign deficits to taxpayers. If that carrier had to charge its customers the full cost of service, competitors' prices would seem more attractive. In other words, P&S distorts a free-market customer's determination of which mode does what best.

biases transportation development

2. P&S can bias the direction of transportation development. The United States has an automobile-airline passenger orientation, whereas Europe has a much more advanced mass transit/passenger train structure—a fact highly correlated to the selection of the modal beneficiaries of government P&S dollars.

results in low-priority projects

3. The availability of federal P&S transportation dollars has strengthened recipient regions at the expense of nonrecipient locations. A local area is often compelled to propose questionable projects to retrieve a fair share of the tax dollars sent to Washington by that region's taxpayers. How many of these projects would be approved if total funding was a local responsibility? In other words, P&S encourages low-priority projects.

creates excess capacity

4. It is difficult for elected officials to choose projects to be funded from those to be rejected. Because rejections upset constituents, considerable political pressure is placed on public officials, which in turn raises spending levels and often results in unnecessary duplication. Thus excess capacity is a product of P&S policy.

protects inefficiency and causes inflation

5. P&S is a crutch that protects inefficient operations. It also weakens management's ability to negotiate with labor unions, which are led to believe their jobs are secure. Fundamentally, it removes the threat of firm failure, which, although painful, forces workers to be realistic in their contract demands.

rebuttal

Collectively then, P&S is criticized as a disruptive force in the marketplace and as a waste of taxpayer dollars. To a great extent, the arguments have substance. However, the positive consequences of transportation P&S should also be recognized. The idea of ending government aid programs may be appealing, but the needs of the transportation industry do not disappear. Someone must pay to keep the U.S. transportation system modernized, or the nation will pay the price for letting it deteriorate.

"Let the users (carriers, passengers, and shippers) pay" is a popular platform today, but is this a totally fair objective? Instead of narrowly limiting the cost burden to these direct beneficiaries, government officials need to reflect on all the indirect beneficiaries of transportation aid and incorporate these people into the taxing picture. When a port is improved, as in the case of the deepening of the channel to allow larger vessels to serve the area, who else gains besides carriers and shippers? National defense might be strengthened since larger military ships could also use the port; farmers or miners hundreds of miles removed from the port might now be able to sell grain and coal in the international markets; the local and national economies are strengthened; and if more people are employed due to rising export trade, local retail businesses experience increased sales. Perhaps too much emphasis is placed on making carriers and transportation users pay the full costs of transportation facilities, since few sectors of the economy escape transportation's benefits.

Many projects backed by government aid are called transportation projects, but their primary purpose is not to aid passengers and shippers. Often, transportation P&S programs are simply the means to other objectives. A waterway dam project, for instance, creates jobs for construction workers, demands huge supplies of steel and concrete, attracts new industries to the region when completed, raises land values, and stimulates the local economy. Pursuing this logic, it can be argued that given transportation's historic and annual contributions to the economy, transportation P&S has been one of the best investments this country has ever made. Certainly, some excesses and questionable public decisions exist, but where would the United States be without the P&S programs? On the other hand, it can be argued that public officials should try to receive the most return from each tax dollar invested.

Federal Policy

mass of
conflicting policy

A fourth area of criticism regarding the government's role in transportation is federal policymaking. The National Transportation Policy Study Commission (NTPSC) found that 64 federal agencies implemented approximately 1000 policies affecting transportation.[16] According to Ernest W. Williams, Jr., who reviewed the NTPSC's findings, federal transport policymaking is ad hoc, filled with inconsistencies, and characterized by conflicts and overlaps in agency jurisdictions.[17]

no true national
transportation policy

Ironically, despite all these policies, the United States has no true national transportation policy. The closest facsimile is the amended section 10101 of the Interstate Commerce Act (see Table 4.6). However, the Interstate Commerce Act has no jurisdiction over air or maritime transportation; Section 10101 (Table 4.6) excludes these modes. What the United States has is a set of separate policies for railroads [49 *United States Code Annotated* Section 10101(a)], air transportation [49 *United States Code* (U.S.C.) Section 1302(a)],

---

TABLE 4.6. U.S. transportation policy

(a) Except where policy has an impact on rail carriers, in which case the principles of section 10101a of this title shall govern, to ensure the development, coordination, and preservation of a transportation system that meets the transportation needs of the United States, including the United States Postal Service and national defense, it is the policy of the United States Government to provide for the impartial regulation of the modes of transportation subject to this subtitle, and—

  (1) in regulating those modes—

    (A) to recognize and preserve the inherent advantage of each mode of transportation;

    (B) to promote safe, adequate, economical, and efficient transportation;

    (C) to encourage sound economic conditions in transportation, including sound economic conditions among carriers;

    (D) to encourage the establishment and maintenance of reasonable rates for transportation, without unreasonable discrimination or unfair or destructive competitive practices;

    (E) to cooperate with each State and the officials of each State on transportation matters; and

    (F) to encourage fair wages and working conditions in the transportation industry.

  (2) in regulating transportation by motor carrier, to promote competitive and efficient transportation services in order to

    (A) meet the needs of shippers receivers, passengers, and consumers;

    (B) allow a variety of quality and price options to meet changing market demands and the diverse requirements of the shipping and traveling public;

    (C) allow the most productive use of equipment and energy resources;

    (D) enable efficient and well-managed carriers to earn adequate profits, attract capital, and maintain fair wage and working conditions;

    (E) provide and maintain service to small communities and small shippers and intrastate bus services;

    (F) provide and maintain commuter bus operations;

    (G) improve and maintain a sound, safe, and competitive privately owned motor carrier system;

    (H) promote greater participation by minorities in the motor carrier system; and

    (I) promote intermodal transportation; and

  (3) in regulating transportation by motor carrier of passengers

    (A) to cooperate with the States on transportation matters for the purpose of encouraging the States to exercise intrastate regulatory jurisdiction in accordance with the objectives of this subtitle;

    (B) to provide Federal procedures which ensure that intrastate regulation is exercised in accordance with this subtitle; and

    (C) to ensure that Federal reform initiatives enacted by the Bus Regulatory Reform Act of 1982 are not nullified by State regulatory actions.

Source: 49 *United States Code Annotated* Section 10101.

air cargo service [49 U.S.C. Section 1302(b)], and maritime transportation (46 U.S.C. Section 1101).

Students of National Transportation Policy (NTP) are baffled about how the United States expects to maximize the benefits of the national transportation system or, for that matter, coordinate the various modes without a singular guiding policy. The presence of many parochial interest policies is the cause of considerable frustration. No matter how hard federal decision makers try to do all things for all people, the task is impossible. Each move to assign more weight to a particular national priority tends to conflict directly with another policy requirement. Consider the following illustrations:

examples of conflicting policies and the impacts

- To reduce fuel consumption, the executive branch in the 1970s backed the 55 mph maximum highway speed limit. This action inadvertently forced over-the-road trucking costs to rise, because operations had been built around 10-hour driving days at higher average speeds. Truck drivers, paid on a per-mile basis, demanded higher payments per mile to compensate for fewer miles driven, and their demands were answered.

- Washington required auto manufacturers to increase the fuel efficiency of new automobiles. One result was lighter weight cars, which increased the probabilities of serious injuries or deaths to occupants involved in accidents. (Specifics will be provided in Chapter 17.)

- The federal government instituted requirements that mass transit buses be redesigned to better serve the handicapped. When this need was met through such measures as requiring that bus floors be lowered and that buses kneel so that the door side of the bus could be hydraulically lowered, bus operators incurred increased capital and operating costs. This in turn put pressure on managers to either raise transit fares or seek increased subsidies.

- A labor dispute between the federal government and the Professional Air Traffic Controllers Organization resulted in President Reagan's decision to fire strikers. A consequence was a significant reduction in flight operations at major airports, which in turn affected airline traffic, revenues, and profits.

- When the Soviet Union invaded Afghanistan, the federal government embargoed (denied export of) grain and other shipments to the Soviet Union. This action, in turn, reduced domestic water and rail grain shipments to New Orleans and other ports and hurt carrier profits.

consequences of federal policy changes

This list is only a sampling of the consequences of federal policy. Many changes in federal policy—whether direct or indirect transportation changes—affect not only the carriers, but also the achievement of other policy objectives. People can hardly expect the hindered parties to take kindly to these measures. A good example is the reaction to deregulation.

criticism of deregulation

Deregulation policies are blamed for carrier bankruptcies, unemployment, reduced small-town services, and numerous other problems affecting the various modes and their customers. Carriers shudder at the potential consequences of transportation legislative actions, for they realize the disruptive power of changing the regulatory rules. How, they ask, can the government expect private investors to build public-interest businesses when the regulatory foundation is so unstable? What is to stop government from reversing itself again in the near future?

rebuttal on
deregulation

Deregulation supporters would offer the following rebuttals. First, dereg-ulation policy is a convenient scapegoat for numerous problems that affected the transportation industry in the late 1970s and early 1980s. If deregulation had not occurred, would the recession and inflation not have happened any-way? Without question, deregulation caused much business turbulence, but people should not forget the other problems of the period (e.g., the recession, inflation, and rising fuel prices) nor fail to examine the benefits of deregulation (e.g., freedom to price and expand a carrier's territory). Carriers should not build businesses around assumptions of regulatory protection. Although it is true that many carriers, formerly protected by entry regulations, were hurt by greater competition, many of these firms failed to control costs sufficiently during the highly regulated days. Perhaps in recent years high costs hurt them more than deregulation.

discussion

What, then, do these comments evaluating the government's role in trans-portation indicate? First, just the fact that bureaucrats are making transpor-tation decisions antagonizes free-market thinkers. Secondly, by their nature, decisions help some people and hurt others. Thirdly, it is difficult for carriers to predict and manage changing governmental guidelines. Fourthly, many pub-lic decisions seem to contradict directly other government policy objectives and, in the process, whipsaw the transportation modes between the various program objectives.

rebuttal

Nevertheless, people need to acknowledge the positive effects of govern-ment involvement. All things considered, the U.S. transportation system is a sound, if imperfect, system and the envy of many around the world. Govern-ment employees helped make it that way. When the private sector neglected its duties or needed help, the government accepted these responsibilities. When tough, unpopular decisions had to be made, they were. Also, who would debate the positive impact of government aid in advancing transportation technology? Where would the U.S. aviation system, for example, be without federal aid? Like the other two major participants in transportation, carriers and transportation users, government has accepted its decision-making re-sponsibilities. People can criticize the results, but they could just as logically praise the record of achievement.

PROCESS OF FEDERAL CHANGE

need to
become involved

As verified by the events of the last 10 years, carriers and users need to be-come actively involved in transportation policy and legislative matters. Gov-ernmental changes have been known to affect instrumentally the profitability of transportation firms, and, as previously noted, many transportation com-panies have shaped their businesses around the regulations and loopholes in the same rules. It is not sound strategy to await change complacently or as-sume blindly it will not happen. Too many carriers and users have already learned the hard way that change is inevitable. At the same time, it makes no sense for firms who are frustrated by the present legal environment to do nothing to correct the system's shortcomings; in fact, these people should fight for what they believe in.

Legislative Strategy

What can be done to create constructive governmental change? Actually, several avenues are available, but they can be grouped into legislative and political strategies. The former requires that interested parties express their views to existing governmental organizations and, in particular, to individuals in positions to cause change. Testimony before commissions of state or federal legislative bodies gives people direct access to decision makers. Letters to elected officials or statements for publication as parts of government records provide another way to express views. Other options are to write letters to the editor of a newspaper or magazine or to join professional associations to state views through a larger constituency.

Political Strategy

The second strategy, and one that is gaining popularity both inside and outside transportation, is the political tactic of backing candidates who share specific beliefs. Basic to this approach is exercising the right to vote in federal, state, and local elections. Opinions can also be expressed to officials charged with appointing or approving government transportation decision makers, such as nominees for the ICC. In fact, people have the right to suggest the nominees themselves. Without question, it is helpful to a constituency to have people sitting in judgment who share its philosophy. There is a proliferation of political action committees (PACs) because citizens and companies have seen a need to pool votes and campaign dollars to help elect people who share their goals. Lobbying (i.e., trying to influence legislators), while unacceptable to many, is nevertheless a highly practiced strategy that answers the needs of those who feel their individual pleas will not be answered.

Therefore, individuals who do their homework, deal with facts and not hysteria, and take the initiative to speak their minds can have a surprisingly positive impact. At the least, they are heard, which is not the case for people who do nothing.

Legislative Change Process

Legislative battles are fought between those wishing to effect change and those wanting to protect the status quo. Initiators of statutory change should remember the realities of how difficult the process can be. As one piece of evidence, in a typical two-year Congress, more than 20,000 bills are introduced in the House of Representatives alone. Of these, only about 5% of all bills introduced become law. Few are major, controversial pieces of legislation, such as the airline, trucking, and railroad deregulation bills.

*use of
staff personnel*

The public expects each senator and House member to understand fully the tens of thousands of pages of legal documents and statements presented for review. However, legislators obviously do not have the time to study personally all this material on such diverse topics as defense, abortion, human rights, and so forth. For this reason, senators and representatives appoint staffs to monitor and advise them on these specialized topics. Usually it is a good strategy for someone desiring to effect legislation to realize this and work closely with staff specialists. Nevertheless, what is typically required to enact legislation successfully is careful advance planning, persistent lobbying, and patience.

How a Bill Becomes Law: The Case of Airline Deregulation. How does a transportation bill become a law? One way to explain the process is by tracing the legislative history of the Airline Deregulation Act of 1978, a measure that involved two Congresses, four years of congressional debate, and five separate sets of hearings. The process saw no less than 18 different bills introduced in Washington. Figure 4.3 is provided to clarify the discussion.

*drafting and
introducing the bill*

The initial step is the introduction of a bill. Usually, bills are prepared by members of Congress or their staffs, but private parties or federal agencies often become heavily involved in drafting legislation as well.

*referral to
committee*

*referral to
subcommittee*

Once prepared, each bill is introduced in one of the two chambers, in essence, in the Senate or the House. Eventually, however, a bill must pass both chambers. One strategy is to introduce similar or identical bills in both chambers simultaneously, as was done by Ford's administration in late 1975 with S. 2551 and H.R. 10261. Likewise, in early 1976, other dual bills, such as the Kennedy and Civil Aeronautics Board bills, were introduced calling for changes in the domestic airline sector. Once introduced, these 1975 and 1976 bills were referred to committees, which then referred the bills to subcommittees. The Senate bills were given to the Subcommittee on Aviation of the Committee on Commerce. In the House, the Subcommittee on Aviation, a component of the Committee on Public Works and Transportation, received the House measures.

hearings

Subcommittees are created so that selected members of Congress can specialize in certain areas of legislation. Members are expected to become the experts on whom the Senate and House memberships can rely for legislative guidance. One important responsibility of a subcommittee is to hold hearings—forums at which various sides can express their views on controversial matters. The right to testify before a subcommittee of Congress, however, is not guaranteed to everyone. Normally, a person must forward to the subcommittee staff a prepared statement for review prior to receiving an acknowledgment stating whether the subcommittee will honor the request to speak. Often, however, the subcommittee solicits testimony from individuals; in essence, it asks them to testify. In addition, those desiring to do so can submit prepared statements for inclusion in the record (published hearings). Then, after completion of the hearing, the subcommittee offers its recommendations to the full committee on the bill(s) before it. This is the second of the subcom-

*subcommittee
reports*

FIGURE 4.3.
Airline Deregulation Act of 1978: Legislative history.

94th CONGRESS

Introduced in Senate   *Introduced in House*

  S. 2551 Ford Administration Bill, 10/22/75   *H.R. 10261* Ford Administration Bill, 10/21/75

  S. 3364 Kennedy Bill, 5/2/76   *H.R. 13742* Kennedy Bill, 5/12/76

  S. 3536 Civil Aeronautics Board Bill, 6/8/76   *H.R. 14330* Civil Aeronautics Board Bill,
                                                 6/11/76

|

Referred to Committee on Commerce   *Referred to Committee on Public Works
         and Transportation*

|

Referred to Subcommittee on Aviation   *Referred to Subcommittee on Aviation*
  hearings in April and June, 1976   hearings in May–July, 1976

|

Introduced in Senate

  S. 3830 Cannon Bill, 9/20/76

Bills die; end of 94th Congress

95th CONGRESS

Introduced in Senate

  S. 292 Pearson–Baker Bill, 1/18/77

  S. 689 Kennedy–Cannon Bill, 2/10/77

|

*Referred to Committee on Commerce, Science
and Transportation**

|

Referred to Subcommittee on Aviation
  hearings in March–April, 1977

                              Introduced in House

                                H.R. 8812 Anderson et al. Bill, 8/5/77

                                                 |

                              *Referred to Committee on Public Works
                                 and Transportation*

                                                 |

                              Referred to Subcommittee on Aviation
                                   hearings in April, June, July, August,
                                   October, 1977

                                                 |

                              Introduced in House

                                        H.R. 9297 Levitas Bill, 9/26/77

                                        H.R. 9588 Crane Bill, 10/17/77

*New name of Commerce Committee

(continued)

FIGURE 4.3. *(Cont.)*

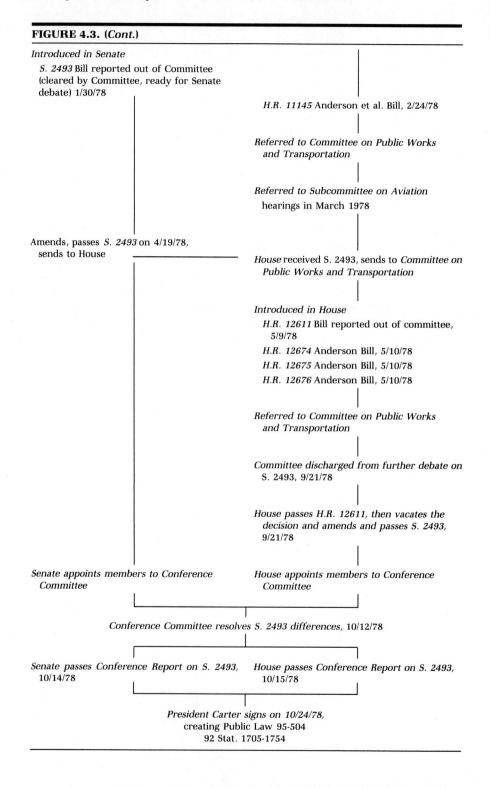

Introduced in Senate

S. 2493 Bill reported out of Committee (cleared by Committee, ready for Senate debate) 1/30/78

H.R. 11145 Anderson et al. Bill, 2/24/78

Referred to Committee on Public Works and Transportation

Referred to Subcommittee on Aviation hearings in March 1978

Amends, passes *S. 2493* on 4/19/78, sends to House

House received S. 2493, sends to *Committee on Public Works and Transportation*

Introduced in House

H.R. 12611 Bill reported out of committee, 5/9/78

H.R. 12674 Anderson Bill, 5/10/78

H.R. 12675 Anderson Bill, 5/10/78

H.R. 12676 Anderson Bill, 5/10/78

Referred to Committee on Public Works and Transportation

Committee discharged from further debate on S. 2493, 9/21/78

House passes H.R. 12611, then vacates the decision and amends and passes S. 2493, 9/21/78

Senate appoints members to Conference Committee

House appoints members to Conference Committee

Conference Committee resolves S. 2493 differences, 10/12/78

Senate passes Conference Report on S. 2493, 10/14/78

House passes Conference Report on S. 2493, 10/15/78

President Carter signs on 10/24/78, creating Public Law 95-504 92 Stat. 1705-1754

mittee's principal duties. As noted in Fig. 4.3, the outcome of the Senate hearings in 1976 was the creation of S. 3830, sponsored by Senator Howard Cannon. However, nothing came of S. 3830 or any other Senate or House bill, as the 94th Congress ended.

bills die: end of Congress

At the commencement of the 95th Congress, the Senate went back to work with the introduction of two new bills, S. 292 and S. 689, which were then sent to the Subcommittee on Aviation. Again, hearings were held on the deregulation issue. Meanwhile, no action was occurring in the House; in fact, the first House bill was not introduced until August. As noted, this led to more House hearings and additional bills.

95th Congress bill introduction and hearings

Perhaps the first big break in the debate happened in January 1978, when the Senate Committee reported out (cleared) S. 2493, a new bill that evolved from the hearings and the subsequent markup (amendment) sessions. House activities included more bill introductions and further hearings. On April 19, 1978, S. 2493 cleared the Senate and was sent to the House for consideration. For five more months the House continued its review. Then on September 21, 1978, the House passed an amended S. 2493. Because of differences in the Senate and House versions of S. 2493, and because only one bill can be forwarded to the president, a conference committee, comprised of Senate and House members, was created to resolve differences, which it did successfully on October 12th. Then the revised bill returned to both chambers, where each passed the measure. Subsequently, President Carter signed S. 2493 into law on October 24, 1978.

S. 2493 reported out of committee

conference committee

subsequent action

Obstacles to Change

Legislation can be stopped by several obstacles, such as inadequate time to complete the process prior to expiration of a two-year Congress. A bill may clear one chamber, only to be stymied in the other; or if the president decides to veto a bill approved by both Houses, two-thirds approval in both chambers is necessary to override that veto. With so many potential roadblocks along the way, it is understandable why controversial transportation legislation often requires strong perseverance, as well as resources. Nevertheless, many parties did successfully enact strong regulatory measures decades ago, and backers of recent acts to lessen regulation were not intimidated.

Why Legislate?

In light of these obstacles, why legislate in the first place? Would it not be easier to try to implement change through de facto efforts at the regulatory commission level? In the days before the Airline Deregulation Act of 1978, for example, Civil Aeronautics Board Chairman Alfred Kahn and the members of the CAB had liberally interpreted the Board's authority and substantially lessened aviation regulation. But these de facto actions were not satisfactory, because legislation is more permanent. Unlike a commission—whose membership and, more important, whose decisions can be reversed by future appointees—an act has more precise language and is less subject to sudden reversals. A law, although it can reverse the established business climate, is far more enduring and less threatening.

SUMMARY

Contrary to what might be expected, the transportation business is not a free enterprise decision-making environment. From the broad formation of corporate guidelines to the creation of precise parameters defining exact operating procedures to the financing of capital assets, the private sector is closely linked to the desires of public officials at all levels of government. Although there are exceptions, the public sector significantly influences the way private businesspeople conduct their corporate transportation affairs.

In the 1880s a reluctant government was drawn into the transportation business by a disgruntled public that demanded the control of railroad monopolistic abuses. In the 1930s the federal government was asked to intervene by established trucking companies who sought help against excessive competition. At the urging of various constituencies, government likewise assumed a promotion and subsidy role in the transportation field. History also records a growing list of government policies to guide the transportation business. Each added level of involvement increases the chorus of criticisms attacking bureaucratic interference in the private domain. The record, however, shows many benefits, as well as costs, from government participation in transportation matters.

The last 10 years eventually may be recorded as the most controversial, yet consequential, decade in U.S. transportation history. Deregulation is primarily responsible, for it suddenly engulfed the transportation industry, increased competition, allowed more freedom for carrier marketing and operating initiatives, and returned more of the decision making to private-sector businesspeople. (The next chapter examines how carriers and their customers are responding to this radically different environment.)

STUDY QUESTIONS

1. Does transportation decision making occur in a free-market atmosphere in the United States? Explain why or why not.

2. In what ways is the government involved in U.S. transportation?

3. How were the regulatory reform goals for the airline industry similar to or different from the deregulation goals for trucking?

4. Why does the government provide transportation promotion and subsidy?

5. How has transportation P&S policy changed under Reagan's administration?

6. What are the transportation responsibilities of the Federal Railroad Administration?

7. Does the United States have a national transportation policy? Explain your answer.

8. Why is it difficult to appraise the impact of transportation deregulation?

ENDNOTES

1. 326 I.C.C. 77 (1965).

2. For more information on this case, see (a) Dudley F. Pegrum, *Transportation Economics and Public Policy,* 3d ed. (Homewood, Ill.: Richard D. Irwin, 1973), pp. 308–309; and (b) Donald V. Harper, *Transportation in America: Users, Carriers, Government,* 2d ed. (Englewood Cliffs, N.J.: Prentice-Hall, 1982), pp. 610–611.

3. Association of American Railroads, "Congress Sets 'Lame-Duck' Stint," *Rail News Update,* 7 October 1982, p. 1.

4. "Action on Truck Decontrol Bill Appears Unlikely by Year's End," *Traffic World,* 23 September 1985, pp. 72–77.

5. U.S., Congress, Senate, Subcommittee on Aviation, Committee on Commerce, Science, and Transportation, Senate Bills 292 (*Commercial Aviation Regulatory Reform Act of 1977*) and 689 (*Air Transportation Regulatory Reform Act of 1977*), *Hearings,* 95th Cong., 1st sess., 1977, p. 97.

6. Ibid., pp. 102–112.

7. For an explanation of the need for improved profits, see (a) Senator Howard Cannon's opening statement, ibid., p. 2; and (b) the testimony of Frederick J. Stephenson and James F. Molloy, ibid., p. 318.

8. Stephenson and Molloy testimony, ibid.

9. U.S., Congress, Senate, Committee on Commerce, Science, and Transportation, *Economic Regulation of the Trucking Industry, Hearings,* 96th Cong., 1st sess., 1979, p. 31.

10. U.S., Congress, Senate, Subcommittee on Surface Transportation, Committee on Commerce, Science, and Transportation, Senate Bill 796 (*Railroad Deregulation Act of 1979*), *Hearings,* 96th Cong., 1st sess., 1979, prepared statement, pp. 69–71.

11. Frank A. Smith, Senior Associate, *Transportation in America,* 3d ed., *July 1985 Supplement* (Washington, D.C.: Transportation Policy Associates, July 1985), p. 2.

12. U.S., General Services Administration, *U.S. Government Manual 1982–83* (Washington, D.C.: National Archives and Records Service, July 1982), p. 157.

13. Robert D. Hershey, Jr., "Bulletin Boards Hint at the End of the I.C.C.," *The New York Times,* 12 July 1983, p. A18.

14. "ICC Accused of Failing Adequately to Implement 1980 Laws on Trucking," *Traffic World,* 6 December 1982, pp. 57–58.

15. Association of American Railroads, "Agency Consolidation Bill Introduced by Packwood," *Rail News Update,* 9 February 1983, p. 3.

16. National Transportation Policy Study Commission, *National Transportation Policies Through the Year 2000 (Final Report)* (Washington, D.C.: U.S. Government Printing Office, 25 June 1979), p. 43.

17. Ernest W. Williams, Jr., " The National Transportation Policy Study Commission and Its Final Report: A Review," *Transportation Journal* 19, no. 3 (Spring 1980):7.

ADDITIONAL READINGS

Arnould, R. J., and Grabowski, H. "Auto Safety Regulation: An Analysis of Market Failure." *The Bell Journal of Economics* 12, no. 1 (Spring 1981):27–48.

Basedow, Jurgen. "Common Carriers—Continuity and Disintegration in U.S. Transportation Law." *Transportation Law Journal* 13, no. 1 (1983):1–42.

Bess, David H., and Farris, Martin T. "U.S. Maritime Policy: A Time for Reassessment." *Transportation Journal* 21, no. 4 (Summer 1982):4–14.

Boaten, Henry O. "States Participation in Railroading and the Impending Demise of the Local Rail Assistance Program." *Transportation Quarterly* 37, no. 3 (July 1983):325–336.

Chapman, R. Stanley. "Battered Airline Industry Unwilling to Return to Regulatory System." *Traffic World,* 7 June 1982, pp. 20–21.

Cunningham, Lawrence F.; Singer, Marc G.; and Williamson, Kenneth C. "Scheduled Passenger Air Service to Small Communities: A Role for State and Local Governments." *Transportation Journal* 21, no. 4 (Summer 1982):25–34.

"Deregulating America." *Business Week,* 28 November 1983, pp. 80–83.

Due, John F. "Government versus Private Financing

of the Railroad Industry." *Transportation Journal* 21, no. 3 (Spring 1982):16–21.

Enis, Charles, and Morash, Edward A. "The Economic Losses from the Devaluation of Motor Carrier Operating Rights." *ICC Practitioners' Journal* 50, no. 5 (July–August 1983):542–555.

Fair, Marvin L., and Williams, Ernest W., Jr. *Transportation and Logistics.* Rev. ed. Plano, Tex.: Business Publications, 1981, Chapters 19, 23, and 24.

Farris, Martin T. "The Multiple Meanings and Goals of Deregulation: A Commentary." *Transportation Journal* 21, no. 2 (Winter 1981):44–50.

Fielding, Gordon J. "Transportation for the Handicapped: The Politics of Full Accessibility." *Transportation Quarterly* 36, no. 2 (April 1982):269–282.

Harper, Donald V. "Consequences of Reform of Federal Economic Regulation of the Motor Trucking Industry." *Transportation Journal* 21, no. 4 (Summer 1982):35–58.

——. *Transportation in America: Users, Carriers, Government.* 2d ed. Englewood Cliffs, N.J.: Prentice-Hall, 1982, Chapters 16, 19 and 20.

Hazard, John L. "Government Railroading." *Transportation Journal* 19, no. 3 (Spring 1980):38–50.

McGillivray, Robert G. "Should the Intercity Bus Industry Be Subsidized?" *Traffic Quarterly* 33, no. 1 (January 1979):99–115.

Pucher, John. "Effects of Subsidies on Transit Costs." *Transportation Quarterly* 36, no. 4 (October 1982):549–562.

Ross, Myron H. "Kalamazoo Taxis: The Case of Regulatory Overkill." *Transportation Quarterly* 35, no. 4 (October 1981):609–622.

Smerk, George M. "Update on Federal Mass Transportation Policy: The Surface Transportation Act of 1978." *Transportation Journal* 18, no. 3 (Spring 1979):16–35.

Stephenson, Frederick J., and Balk, Arnold E. "Fast Track Legislation—Public/Private Sector Roles in Harbor and Channel Deepening Projects." *ICC Practitioners' Journal* 50, no. 3 (March–April 1983):310–321.

Stephenson, Frederick J., and Beier, Frederick J. "The Effects of Airline Deregulation on Air Service to Small Communities." *Transportation Journal* 20, no. 4 (Summer 1981):54–62.

Stock, James R. "Regulations, Regulators, and Regulatory Issues: A Motor Carrier Perspective." *Transportation Journal* 18, no. 3 (Spring 1979):65–73.

Talley, Wayne Kenneth. *Introduction to Transportation.* Cincinnati: South-Western Publishing, 1983, Chapters 3 and 4.

Williams, Ernest W., Jr. "A Critique of the Staggers Rail Act of 1980." *Transportation Journal* 21, no. 3 (Spring 1982):5–15.

PART 3, "RAILROAD TRANSPORTATION," is the first of five mini-books that describe and analyze the following five modes of transportation: railroad transportation, water transportation, pipeline transportation, highway transportation, and air transportation. From the base of introductory material presented in Parts 1 and 2, Part 3 now presents two chapters (Chapters 5 and 6) on freight railroad transportation, the primary business of this mode, and a third chapter (Chapter 7) on U.S. intercity passenger train transportation.

Chapter 5 focuses on economic issues in the reregulated freight railroad industry. Topics covered include ownership, entry, route expansion, exit, abandonment, and merger and acquisition decisions and strategies. This chapter integrates federal economic regulations, ICC decisions, and court decisions into the context of freight railroad choices. In addition, it analyzes railroad costs, revenues, and earnings. Pricing theories pertinent to railroads and other modes, as well as railroad pricing practices, are explained.

Freight railroad operating, marketing, labor, and safety issues are discussed in Chapter 6. Providing practical information about managing freight railroads is a major objective. What commodities railroads carry and in what quantities, how changing technology is affecting railroad transportation, and what role intermediaries play in today's business are a few of the questions Chapter 6 attempts to answer.

Because Chapter 7 is concerned with the past, present, and future of intercity passenger trains in the United States, it is treated as a separate subject, distinct from freight railroad transportation. The text describes and analyzes AMTRAK and examines high-speed passenger train alternatives, both existing and futuristic, such as Japanese Shinkansen, French TGV, and magnetic levitation trains. Chapter 7 defines what was, what is, and what might be in passenger train service in the United States.

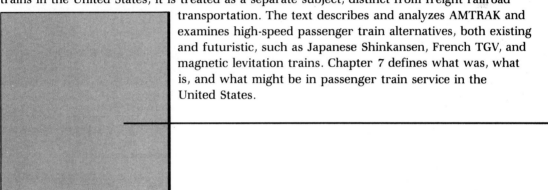

3 Railroad Transportation

5

Freight Railroad Economics and Pricing

Today's freight railroad industry is undergoing enormous changes. For nearly 100 years, the industry was rigidly regulated by the Interstate Commerce Commission. Most major decisions, such as expansion of services, abandonment of unprofitable branch lines, mergers and acquisitions, and adjustment of rates, called for prior ICC permission. Now, regulatory reform has returned considerable decision-making power to carrier management. Primarily because of the Staggers Rail Act of 1980 and liberal actions by the ICC, the future of the freight railroad industry now resides with the men and women who run the railroads and with their abilities to function decisively and efficiently in a dynamic marketplace.

Chapter 5, which focuses on freight railroad economics and pricing, discusses the railroad industry's background, railroad ownership decisions, entry and route expansion decisions, exit decisions, and merger and acquisition decisions. The chapter concludes with an examination of freight railroad finances and a review of pricing theory and practice. In addition to defining and explaining many of the important decisions made by railroad owners and managers, this chapter also specifies the terms and conditions of current federal economic regulations affecting freight railroad decisions.

INDUSTRY BACKGROUND

Railroading in the United States is predominantly a freight-hauling business. In 1984, cargo traffic accounted for more than 97% of the railroad industry's operating revenues. The remaining sales came from AMTRAK's intercity passenger operations, a subject discussed in Chapter 7. Freight railroading is a 24-hours-per-day, 365-days-per-year business, which has operated that way for more than 100 years.

History

Early U.S. railroads served limited purposes. Most cities emerged as ports in need of raw materials and agricultural goods for consumption and export, and railroads filled that need. This pattern of feeding the ports was eventually altered by the Baltimore and Ohio Railroad (B&O). Chartered in 1827, the B&O created a rail system connecting the Atlantic Ocean and the Ohio River, proving that railroads could haul traffic across the mountains at a price competitive with water transportation rates via New York's Erie Canal. This action also established railroads as a year-round transport mode, something water transportation could not guarantee under the threat of winter icing problems.[1] From this humble beginning, the railroad industry expanded until in 1984 it originated 1.429 billion tons of cargo.[2]

Regulated Industry

In the late 1800s, state and federal governments concluded that the railroad industry (1) was crucially important to U.S. citizens and (2) could not be trusted to self-police its own activities and simultaneously protect the public interest. The result was state and federally imposed economic regulations.

Granger Laws

Efforts to regulate railroads began at the state level. Farmers, distraught with agricultural problems, protested high and excessively discriminatory railroad freight rates on agricultural products and supplies. Consequently, Illinois, Iowa, Minnesota, and Wisconsin passed separate state laws between 1871 and 1874, mainly regulating railroad maximum rate levels. Called the *Granger Laws,* they refer to the primary organization that supported economic regulation at the time, namely, the National Grange of the Patrons of Husbandry, an organization of farmers.[3]

Act to Regulate Commerce

More than a decade passed before the federal government in 1887 enacted the Act to Regulate Commerce, which is now officially called the Interstate Commerce Act. Since 1874, Congress had been considering regulating railroads. Railroads had been accused by taxpayers and railroad investors of financial malpractices such as stock market manipulation and appropriating company assets for personal use. Complaints were also voiced by shippers protesting excessive freight rates and rebates—a form of personal discrimination in which favored shippers received kickbacks, that is, refunds of a portion of the paid freight bills.

Wabash Case

Finally, in the *Wabash Case* of 1886,[4] the U.S. Supreme Court ruled that Illinois could not regulate railroad rates beyond its borders because such regulation violated the Commerce Clause of the Constitution (Article 1, Section 8, Clause 3). To effect economic regulation of interstate railroad transportation, federal action was necessary. Thus Congress passed the Act to Regulate Commerce, an anti-monopoly, anti-malpractice law that established the Interstate Commerce Commission to oversee railroad business affairs.[5]

amendments to
the Interstate
Commerce Act

Since 1887, Congress has enacted many laws amending the Interstate Commerce Act's railroad regulatory provisions. The Hepburn Act of 1906, for instance, gave the ICC power to prescribe maximum rates and made the ICC's decisions binding on carriers. Previously, in order to enforce its orders, the ICC had to seek court action. Another important statute was the Transportation Act of 1920, which gave the ICC power to prescribe minimum rates. A third illustration is the Railroad Revitalization and Regulatory Reform Act of 1976, called the 4R Act, which established new and expedited procedures for railroad mergers.

Staggers
Rail Act of 1980

However, no other statute amended the Interstate Commerce Act and changed railroad economic regulation as dramatically as did the Staggers Rail Act of 1980. The Staggers Act reregulated the freight railroad industry but did not totally deregulate the business. Although it considerably lessened rate regulation, it did not end it. Similarly, the Staggers Rail Act made it easier for railroads to abandon track or finalize railroad mergers and acquisitions, but it did not end the need for carriers to obtain the ICC's approval to accomplish either objective. Today's freight railroads are still governed by the provisions of the Interstate Commerce Act (49 *United States Code Subtitle* IV) and the ICC's railroad economic rules, located in 49 *Code of Federal Regulations* 1000. However, the regulations and rules have been significantly reduced. Since the late 1970s, the executive branch of government, the Congress, and the ICC have been encouraging railroad managers to assume greater decision-making responsibility.

Promotion and Subsidy

As indicated in the following list, freight railroads have benefitted from government promotion and subsidy.

land grants

1. Approximately 70 railroads in the West and South during the mid-1800s received a total of 130.4 million acres of land. By selling the land, railroad companies raised money for system development.[6]

loan guarantees

2. The Transportation Act of 1958 provided for guaranteed loans not to exceed $500 million dollars so that troubled railroads could acquire necessary funds for roadbed, facility, and equipment needs.[7]

Northeastern
railroad crisis

3. The bankruptcy of the Penn Central Railroad in 1970 and six other Northeastern railroads (the Boston and Maine, the Central of New Jersey, the Erie Lackawanna, the Reading, the Lehigh Valley, and the Ann Arbor) caused Congress at that time to worry about the severe negative consequences to the Northeast and the rest of the country if these railroads ceased operating. Northeastern railroads had been severely weakened by many factors, including the relocation of manufacturing firms from the Northeast to the Southeast, Southcentral, and Southwest regions; changes

in the commodity mix, since fewer items from New England were produced in sufficient volumes to fill large rail cars; and heavy intermodal
competition from trucking. In response, Congress enacted the Regional
Rail Reorganization Act of 1973, called the 3R Act, which created the
United States Railway Association (USRA) to plan the restructuring of the
bankrupt Northeastern railroad network. The 3R Act also gave USRA authority to guarantee loans up to $1.5 billion to aid system restructuring.
In addition, federal grants totaling $558 million were provided to subsi-
dize branch lines (lightly used track) not included in USRA's final system
plan, for protecting railroad labor affected by the Northeastern restructuring, and for upgrading rail passenger service in the Northeast corridor—principally, the route from Boston to Washington, D.C. The 3R Act
created the Consolidated Rail Corporation, Conrail, to operate the company that survived the restructuring of the bankrupt lines.

3R Act of 1973

The Railroad Revitalization and Regulatory Reform Act of 1976, called the
4R Act, provided $6.4 billion in railroad aid. Much of these funds were for
troubled Northeastern railroads. The USRA was authorized to purchase $2.1
billion in Conrail securities so that Conrail could modernize, rehabilitate, and
maintain equipment. Portions of the remaining funds were provided for
Northeast corridor rail passenger improvements ($1.6 billion in grants),
for railroad branch line service continuance assistance ($360 million), and for
commuter rail service subsidies ($125 million).[8]

4R Act

Although the above illustrations do not represent the entire scope of railroad promotion and subsidy assistance, they do show that public aid has been
an integral factor in railroading. Promotion and subsidy affect costs, pricing,
and the competitive capabilities of the railroad industry. Furthermore, public
aid has been provided to expedite the development of rail services, improve
railroad safety, strengthen national security, and satisfy political needs.

*relevance
of public aid*

RAILROAD OWNERSHIP DECISIONS

Most railroads in the United States are owned and operated by private citizens
who are trying to earn money from their investments. Unlike railroads in most
other countries, U.S. railroads are privately held, not publicly controlled by
the government. Of course, there are exceptions, such as the Alaska Railroad,
built in 1923 and administered by the federal government for 61 years until
it was sold and transferred to the state of Alaska in 1985.[9]

Another exception occurred during World War I when the federal government assumed control and operated the U.S. railroad system from December 28, 1917, until March 1, 1920, when the government again returned operation of the railroads to the private sector.[10] A third exception is ownership
of railroads by states, or by public authorities that states help to create. In
the latter case, the typical process is for public agencies to use public financial
assistance to acquire lines and subsequently sign contracts with designated

*exceptions
to private ownership*

operators to manage the acquired railroad properties.[11] A final exception is Conrail.

Conrail

Conrail, which began operations on April 1, 1976, was created from six previous railroad systems: the Penn Central, the Central of New Jersey, the Erie Lackawanna, the Lehigh Valley, the Lehigh and Hudson River, and the Reading. From the beginning of government ownership, taxpayer costs were high. Conrail had cumulative operating losses of $1.5 billion from 1976 through 1980. In addition, billions of dollars were spent from 1976–1984 to repair and modernize track and vehicles and to make payments to workers whose jobs were eliminated. In total, taxpayers had invested $7 billion in Conrail by 1984.[12]

NERSA

In 1981, Congress enacted the Northeast Rail Service Act (NERSA), which served an ultimatum to Conrail's management and labor. By October 1, 1983, Conrail had to convince the federal government that it could become, and stay, profitable or the Secretary of Transportation had the authority to sell it piece by piece. The emphatic message was that if management and labor wanted to keep their jobs, they would have to make some sacrifices to help Conrail become more efficient.

Conrail's profitability and why

Conrail turned its first profit in 1981, when it posted net income of $39 million. In consecutive years thereafter, Conrail increased net income to $174 million in 1982, $313 million in 1983, and $500 million in 1984.[13] Not only did Conrail meet NERSA's demands to pass the test enabling the railroad to be sold in its entirety, but suddenly Conrail became an attractive acquisition property. Aided significantly by provisions contained in NERSA, Conrail had cut its work force from 90,000 to 38,000 employees, gained wage and productivity concessions from labor, cut its route system by 15% by eliminating unprofitable branch lines, and transferred costly commuter railroad passenger services to other operators. According to Conrail's Robert H. Platt, Executive Vice-president–Finance and Administration, success also came from the Staggers Rail Act of 1980, which lifted antiquated and burdensome regulation and allowed Conrail the opportunity to earn adequate profits.[14]

By 1984, Conrail had cash reserves of nearly $800 million, total assets of $5.7 billion,[15] and a modern, efficient railroad system. The almost certain probability that the government would cancel Conrail's $7 billion public debt to whomever acquired the railroad also encouraged private investor interest.

interested Conrail buyers

In 1984, 10 bids were received for Conrail; each exceeded $1 billion. Bidders included other railroads (the Norfolk Southern Corporation and Guilford Transportation Industries, a company that owned the Maine Central and was acquiring the Boston and Maine and the Delaware and Hudson railroads) and Conrail's employees. Nontransportation bidders included, among others, the Allegheny Corporation, Citicorp, and an investor group headed by J. W. Marriott, Jr.[16] On February 8, 1985, the U.S. Department of Transportation selected Norfolk Southern as its candidate to buy Conrail. However, Congress was charged with the ultimate responsibility of deciding the ownership issue.

ENTRY AND ROUTE EXPANSION DECISIONS

Since 1920, entry into the for-hire railroad business has been regulated by the federal government. Today, anyone interested in constructing, extending, acquiring, or operating railroad lines in the United States must obtain a certificate of public convenience and necessity. Unless the applicant obtains a Designated Operator Certificate under Section 304 of the 3R Act or a Modified Certificate under 49 *Code of Federal Regulations* 1120.21, for short-line railroad authority,[17] requirements must be met under 49 *United States Code* 10901. If the ICC is satisfied that the present or future public convenience and necessity require or permit the construction or acquisition (or both) and operation, then the applicant can enter the business or extend an existing route system.

Entry Activities

construction of new lines

Few new freight railroads have been started, but there have been successful efforts to build new branch lines and to acquire lines or routes formerly operated either in whole or in part by other railroads. In 1973, for example, Burlington Northern received an ICC certificate to construct a 94-mile line into the coal-rich Powder River Basin in Wyoming.[18] To facilitate such expansionary efforts, the Staggers Rail Act, Section 221, makes it difficult for competitive rail lines to block either construction or extension initiatives by refusing to allow the developing railroad to cross existing track.

acquisition of abandoned lines

The creation of Conrail and the bankruptcies of two large carriers—the Chicago, Rock Island & Pacific Railroad Company (the Rock Island) and the Chicago, Milwaukee, St. Paul & Pacific Railroad (the Milwaukee Road)—as well as several recent railroad mergers and acquisitions that created a handful of large railroads, and relaxed abandonment rules—all have produced two notable effects. Large railroads have been selectively buying choice sections of available track to add to their existing networks, and many new short-line railroads have been started to operate over abandoned rights-of-way. A *short-line railroad* is a small company with track mileage ranging from one mile to several hundred miles; however, the average system size is 28 miles.[19]

major railroad line purchases

Examples of major railroad trackage acquisitions are (1) Southern Pacific Transportation Company's purchase from the Rock Island of the 1000-mile Tucumcari line, which runs from Tucumcari, New Mexico, through Kansas City to St. Louis, and (2) the Chicago and North Western Transportation Company's purchase from the Rock Island of the Spine Line, a 770-mile route from Minneapolis/St. Paul to Kansas City.[20]

short-line activities

Growth in the number of short lines is evident by increased membership in the American Short Line Railroad Association (266 in 1984 versus 215 in 1971).[21] Entry activity stems from the ability of citizens to acquire at favorable prices unwanted branch lines. Because most short lines are non-unionized, low overhead operations, they are better able to earn profits than the larger, previous route owners. Major carriers abandoned these lines because of profitability problems or redundancy (i.e., they owned parallel lines performing the same task, so these lines were not needed).

Legal Forms of Carriage

common carriers

private carriage

U.S. freight railroads are either common carriers or private carriers. The former must possess a certificate, offer for-hire services to the public, and comply with the four duties of common carriers that were defined in Chapter 3—(1) to serve, (2) to deliver, (3) to charge reasonable rates, and (4) to avoid undue or unjust discrimination. Private railroads exist totally to serve the shipping needs of their owners: for example, a railroad owned and operated by a steel-producing company.

Two other legal forms of railroad carriage are contract and exempt transportation. Prior to 1976, for-hire railroads were prohibited from these sectors. Now, common carriers have the right to sell contract and exempt freight services subject to the Interstate Commerce Act. Although railroads are not classified as contract carriers, per se, they also do not apply for authority to become contract carriers as is the case in trucking. However, the laws allow common carrier railroads to sign contracts with specific shippers. Contracts

contract carriage

define rates, commodities, traffic volumes, the duration of the contract, and special contract service features. Unlike common carriage with its emphasis on serving everyone without discrimination, contract carriage excludes everyone from rail services, except the shippers signing the contract. Although full disclosure of contract rates is reported to the ICC, this information is not available to the general public as in the case of published common carrier rates.[22] Contract carriage therefore produces the likelihood of discrimination between large and small shippers and even between two large shippers, for one customer may pay a lower price than the second one does for identical services. Prices are set by shipper/carrier negotiations.

exempt carriage

Similarly, railroads are not legally classified as exempt carriers, but they can engage in exempt services, which are operations free from ICC regulation. Prior to 1976, there were no exemptions; however, Section 207 of the 4R Act gave the ICC the right to exempt railroad activities from regulation if it determined such regulations were not necessary in the public interest. The Staggers Rail Act of 1980 amended the 4R Act provision enabling the ICC to grant exemptions when regulation is not necessary to fulfill the National Transportation Policy and when regulation is of limited scope or is not needed to protect users of railroad services from abuses of market power.

fresh fruits, vegetables, and other foods

Types of Railroad Exemptions.   In 1979, the ICC used the 4R Act provisions to exempt rail haulage of fresh fruits and vegetables.[23] In 1980, several other agricultural and food commodities were exempted such as peanuts, sweet potatoes, and fresh fish.[24] Subsequently, the ICC, on March 4, 1983, further expanded the list of federally exempt agricultural products.[25]

Still regulated, however, were grains, soybeans, and sunflower seeds, which represent a large portion of the ton-mile traffic.

piggyback services

Section 10505(f) of the Interstate Commerce Act led to the exemption in 1981 of all railroad and truck service provided in railroad-owned equipment in trailer-on-flat-car (TOFC) and container-on-flat-car (COFC) service (Fig. 5.1). Exemptions applied to rail-truck piggyback operations, as well as to operations involving ocean carriers.[26] On September 20, 1984, the ICC further deregulated piggyback traffic by exempting from regulation freight hauled by independent (nonrailroad-owned) motor carriers, as long as some part of the movement was by rail. The 1984 ruling freed all remaining piggyback traffic from rate regulations.[27]

box car traffic

Two other ICC decisions made on March 3, 1983—to exempt rates on all box car traffic and to exempt from economic regulation coal shipped by rail for export[28]—were later reversed by the U.S. Court of Appeals for the District of Columbia. In its box car decision served on June 27, 1984, the U.S. Court of Appeals overturned the ICC's exemption insofar as it pertained to joint rates on box car traffic. A *joint rate* is a price for a movement by two or more carriers. The court said the ICC failed to consider adequately the potential of large railroads to appropriate profits, which deservedly belonged to small railroads with whom they would be interlining box cars. Nevertheless, single line box car rates remained exempt from regulation.[29] On September 18, 1984, the Appeals Court overturned the ICC's export coal rates exemption and remanded the case to the ICC for any further proceedings that may be appropriate. The Appeals Court stated that the ICC's earlier decision ignored the necessary market protection Congress meant to guarantee to shippers.[30]

FIGURE 5.1.
Santa Fe Railway's ten-pack unit piggyback train near Victorville, California, en route to Chicago. (Photo courtesy of Santa Fe Railway)

EXIT DECISIONS

Since 1916, when the U.S. railroad system peaked at 254,037 route miles, railroad management has been trying to shrink its track system. The goal has been economic efficiency. By reducing excess capacity and deleting unprofitable branch lines, railroads hope to improve earnings. However, shippers are hurt by abandonments, for they lose railroad services. Consequently, Congress has regulated railroad exit decisions since 1920 to try to prevent undue hardship on railroad customers. Abandonment or discontinuance of service requires a certificate of public convenience and necessity from the Interstate Commerce Commission. Prior to 1980, if railroad management decided to abandon a piece of track, it had to be patient, because obtaining ICC approval often took years. Still, between 1920 and September 30, 1980, railroads abandoned 78,896 miles of track;[31] therefore, although the task may have been tedious, it was not impossible.

faster ICC decisions today

Section 402 of the Staggers Act has helped railroad management by significantly shortening the government's abandonment review and decision process. Today, ICC abandonment cases are almost always decided within 345 days of the filing of the application and as quickly as 75 days after filing in nonprotested cases.

Conrail abandonment

Carrier interest in rail line abandonment has been particularly acute in the Northeast, where the U.S. Department of Transportation recommended in 1974 that 25% of the region's track-miles be discontinued.[32] Expedited abandonment rules under the Northeast Rail Service Act of 1981 allowed Conrail to abandon more than 2000 miles of unprofitable lines. However, as previously noted, efforts by large railroads to reduce trackage does not necessarily mean that railroad services end, for other operators, such as large railroads and short lines, have been buying rail properties. Conrail, for instance, sold 600 miles of line to 33 new and existing short lines.[33]

exit by merger or acquisition or liquidation

In the broader sense, exit implies that owners wish totally to leave the railroad industry. Usually, they achieve this objective through a merger or acquisition, but rail service continues under the new ownership. Occasionally, firms go bankrupt and wish to cease railroad operations and liquidate assets. In the Penn Central case, for example, the bankrupt carrier was kept in business from June 21, 1970, the day it filed Chapter 77 bankruptcy papers, until it became part of Conrail on April 1, 1976. Even when Penn Central trustees in 1972 announced that they intended to cease all rail operations, the federal government refused to let the railroad exit from the industry. However, when the Rock Island, on March 17, 1977, filed for bankruptcy under Section 77 of the Bankruptcy Act, the reaction was different. In June 1980, after federal loan guarantees failed, the bankruptcy court ordered the Rock Island liquidated. What was once a 7600-mile railroad, stretching from Minnesota and Chicago to New Mexico, Texas, and Louisiana, was sold or abandoned. On June 1, 1984, the Rock Island ceased to exist.

MERGER AND ACQUISITION DECISIONS

Presently, a key decision area for railroad managers is mergers and acquisitions, and one strategy for achieving corporate growth is combining one firm with another. The record shows not only considerable past interest in intramodal railroad mergers and acquisitions, but also, since 1980, growing interest in intermodal combinations and diversification.

Intramodal Combinations

Intramodal combinations occur when two or more railroads merge or one railroad acquires control of one or more other railroads. There are two kinds of combinations—side-by-side (parallel) and end-to-end (connecting) mergers or acquisitions. In the side-by-side type, carrier route networks combine to serve common origin and destination points; therefore the proposed combination partners compete against one another. Side-by-side combinations are controversial because they lessen competition. For example, the 1968 side-by-side merger of the Penn Central joined two railroads—the Pennsylvania Railroad and the New York Central Railroad—which had previously competed against each other for New York–Chicago traffic. Today, most merger or acquisition proposals are end-to-end combinations. Rather than competing directly with one another, proposed railroad partners primarily connect routes only at common points. For example, the CSX merger of 1980 joined a Northeastern railroad, the Chessie System, with a Southeastern company called the Seaboard System Railroad.

side-by-side and end-to-end combinations

Since 1920, the ICC has had the power to approve or disapprove intramodal railroad combinations. At times, the regulatory procedure for obtaining ICC approval has been excessively slow and burdensome. In one particularly trying case, it took nine years from the date of filing the initial application to the date the merger of the Great Northern, Northern Pacific, and Burlington & Quincy Railroads into the Burlington Northern Railroad Company was finalized (February 17, 1961 to March 2, 1970).[34]

ICC's powers and past delays

Congress, sensitive to complaints of ICC delays, included provisions within the 4R Act of 1976 to expedite government decision-making procedures. The 4R Act required the ICC to conclude evidentiary proceedings in 24 months and render its decision within 180 days after ending the proceedings unless Congress granted an extension. Subsequently, the Staggers Rail Act of 1980 contained provisions that permitted combinations not involving two or more Class I (Class "one") railroads to be decided in as little as 150 days. Combinations of two or more Class I railroads (the industry's largest firms, each having annual sales of at least $87.3 million in 1984) are the ICC's main concern because of the potential consequences the consolidation might have in lessening competition.[35]

expedited ICC decisions

In deciding consolidation cases among two or more Class I carriers, the ICC must consider the effect an inclusion or exclusion of other railroads not party to the application would have both on the public interest and on the

ICC's consolidation criteria

total fixed charges resulting from the proposed combination. It must also consider whether the approval of the application would result in an adverse effect on competition among rail carriers in the affected region or on the interests of railroad employees involved. A consolidation found consistent with the public interest is to be approved by the ICC.

Reasons for Intramodal Consolidations.   According to Grimm and Harris, the 4R Act of 1976, together with two reports issued separately in 1978 by the U.S. Department of Transportation and the ICC, accelerated railroad consolidation efforts. The combination of expedited application processing offered by the 4R Act and a changing government attitude found in the latter reports that advocated railroad combinations as a partial solution to railroad industry financial problems, motivated carrier owners to consider mergers or acquisitions of other railroads.[36] Nevertheless, these factors only facilitated combinations, because the actual objectives were reduced costs, increased productivity, improved services, and greater profitability.

consolidation goals   Carriers forming side-by-side mergers or acquisitions hope to reduce or eliminate duplicate track, freight yards, and personnel. Another goal is increased productivity such as derived from combining traffic to form one longer train from two former competing trains. End-to-end consolidations are intended to improve services through single carrier service over more direct routes and bypassing costly switching delays. Better services are seen as ways to attract higher traffic levels and to increase yields. In addition, either type of consolidation should offer greater pools of cars, which can be positioned as needed around the unified network, and a larger supply of cash to meet business needs. Important considerations are economies of scale and density.

economies of scale and density   The definition of economies of scale is long-run average (unit) costs, which decline as the size of the firm increases—that is, the larger the firm, the lower the cost per unit of output. In economies of density, short-run unit costs decline as the utilization of fixed capacities increases—that is, greater traffic volumes lead to reduced short-run unit costs.

Both Keeler in 1974 and Harris in 1977 found significant economies of density in the freight railroad industry,[37] but Griliches (1972) and Keeler (1974) did not find increasing economies of scale.[38] This discrepancy implies that the objective of consolidating is to increase traffic to reduce excess capacity.

Examples of Recent Major Railroad Combinations.   The following highlight significant recent mergers and acquisitions in the railroad industry.

Burlington Northern Railroad Company   ■ The St. Louis–San Francisco Railway Company (Frisco) merged into Burlington Northern Railroad, effective March 1980. With 28,000 route miles connecting the Northwest, Midwest, and Gulf Coast, the Burlington Northern operates the longest rail network in the country.

CSX Corp.   ■ In September 1980, CSX Corporation was approved, consolidating the Chessie System and the Seaboard System Railroad. This consolidation produced a 27,000-mile system—the second largest in the United States—linking 22 states from Ontario, Canada, to the Gulf of Mexico and from the East Coast to Chicago and St. Louis.

Norfolk Southern Corp.

■ Another major eastern consolidation occurred on March 25, 1982, when Norfolk and Western Railway merged with the Southern Railway System to form an 18,000-mile rail network as part of the Norfolk Southern Corporation, a new holding company. Serving an area from Kansas City to Buffalo, Norfolk, New Orleans, and Jacksonville, Florida, the Norfolk Southern railroad subsidiaries compete directly with the larger CSX Corporation.

Union Pacific System

■ The ICC approved the merger of the Union Pacific Railroad and Missouri Pacific Railroad and acquisition of the Western Pacific Railroad on September 13, 1982. The action created the Union Pacific System, the third longest railroad in the United States at 22,000 miles. Union Pacific System serves 21 states in the western half of the United States.

proposed combinations

■ In 1986 two proposed combinations were also significant because of their sizes: (1) As previously mentioned, the Norfolk Southern's bid to acquire Conrail and (2) the proposed merger of the Atchison, Topeka, and Santa Fe Railway Company (Santa Fe) and the Southern Pacific Transportation Company. Santa Fe Southern Pacific Transportation Corporation, a holding company formed on December 23, 1983, filed an application with the ICC on March 23, 1985, to merge the Sante Fe and Southern Pacific railroads to form the third largest railroad in the United States, a 25,600-mile system stretching from the Pacific Coast to Chicago, Kansas City, and New Orleans. Like the Norfolk Southern-Conrail combination, the Santa Fe-Southern Pacific merger met with considerable resistance because of its side-by-side characteristics. Opponents argued that each combination would substantially lessen competition. However, officers of the Santa Fe Southern Pacific Corporation, because of recent ICC approvals of major railroad combinations, expected their merger would be accepted. Thus they were stunned by the announcement on July 24, 1986, that the ICC had rejected the merger by a 4–1 vote. The company must now divest one of the railroads or possibly submit a revised merger plan.

Intermodal Combinations

Railroad Control of Trucking Companies.   One controversial freight railroad issue is the federal government's growing permissiveness toward railroad ownership of other modes of transportation, after decades of prohibitive restrictions against such combinations. This problem particularly applies to railroad control of motor carriers (trucking) and water carriers. In January

special circumstances doctrine

1983 the ICC decided in *Ex Parte* MC-156 to abolish the "special circumstances doctrine," a policy that since 1935 had discouraged railroad ownership of motor carriers. Previously, railroads were not prevented from owning motor carriers; however, the Motor Carrier Act of 1935 restricted the services of railroad-owned carriers to providing supplemental services to their railroad operations. Essentially, railroad-owned motor carriers provided pick-up and delivery services in conjunction with rail linehaul service, but there were two exceptions. Under grandfather rights provisions, railroad-owned motor carriers that had provided unrestricted, nonsupplemental, services prior to the

1935 Act could continue to do so. Aside from grandfather rights, the only other way to avoid the restriction on truck operations was for the railroad to convince the ICC that special circumstances showed that unrestricted trucking authority was required to fulfill a compelling public need for service that was not being offered by independent, nonrail affiliated, motor carriers.[39] These regulations were intended to protect established motor carriers from competition.

expanded
trucking rights

The ICC's decision in *Ex Parte* MC-156 gave railroads two trucking opportunities: (1) to expand the operating scope of established railroad trucking affiliates beyond the supplemental rail service role and (2) to allow railroads to establish new trucking companies with broad operating rights. In September 1983, the Denver and Rio Grande Western Railroad was the first railroad to receive ICC motor carrier authority not restricted to rail-related movements. It asked for, and received, 48-state general commodities authority.[40]

In another controversial decision (*Ex Parte* MC-438), the ICC ended requirements that, before a railroad could acquire an established motor carrier, it first demonstrated the acquisition would be consistent with the public interest, would enable the rail carrier to use motor carrier transportation to public advantage in its operations, and would not unreasonably restrain competition.[41] The key word is *established*. Trucking firms see a railroad's ability to purchase an existing trucking company as a much greater competitive threat than having to contend with a new trucking company started by a railroad. One of the first tests of this new ICC policy was Norfolk Southern Corporation's 1984 bid to acquire North American Van Lines, Inc., a large trucking company with 1983 revenues of $560 million.[42] In April 1985 the ICC unanimously approved the acquisition, and in that same year, the purchase was consummated.[43]

trucking
decisions
by railroads

Unless the courts overturn the ICC's decisions to eliminate the special circumstances doctrine, railroad managers now have the choice of becoming unrestricted truck operators. Two strategies are likely to be followed. Railroads can acquire trucking companies and primarily operate them as they were, that is, as firms competing mainly with other trucking companies. A more probable tactic, however, is to purchase trucking companies and use them to extend railroad services to points beyond the end of their tracks. Trucking services and TOFC/COFC operations are the most expeditious way for railroads to expand geographic market coverage and establish coast-to-coast route networks.

Railroad Control of Water Carriers.   When the ICC decided on September 7, 1984, to allow CSX Corporation to control American Commercial Lines, Inc., it reversed a long-standing policy obstructing railroad ownership of barge lines. In 1983, CSX Corporation acquired Texas Gas Resources Corporation, an energy and shipbuilding company and parent to American Commercial Line, Inc. (ACL), which in turn owned American Commercial Barge Line Company. Water carrier interests argued the barge line acquisition violated provisions of the Panama Canal Act of 1912, which contains specific language prohibiting railroads from gaining control of water carriers. These same

Panama
Canal Act of 1912

opponents contended that the rail-barge merger would result in predatory pricing and the diminution of the barge market. However, the ICC found joint rail-barge ownership by CSX Corporation would not diminish competition and would not violate the Panama Canal Act of 1912. Thus the first major rail-barge merger in U.S. history was permitted. The ICC, to lessen merger fears, called for annual ICC oversight proceedings for five years or longer.[44] Thus another choice—whether to acquire potentially competitive barge lines—has been presented to rail management.

Railroad Control of Pipelines and Air Transportation Companies.   Railroads have also spread their realm of control to pipeline and aviation sectors. To cite some examples, both CSX Corporation and Burlington Northern Inc. control natural gas pipelines. CSX Corporation obtained its pipeline as a result of the Texas Gas Resources Corporation acquisition of 1983. Burlington Northern Inc. added its pipeline through the acquisition of El Paso Company, a big oil and gas producer, in 1983. In another development, Norfolk Southern Corporation received permission from the Civil Aeronautics Board to acquire control of Piedmont Airlines. As of May 1984, it owned 17.6% of Piedmont Aviation's stock. (Piedmont Aviation is the parent of Piedmont Airlines.) On the contrary, several railroads have divested themselves of pipeline and aviation companies. In May 1982, Burlington Northern Inc. sold Burlington Northern Air Freight, a large air freight forwarding company, and the Union Pacific Corporation in 1983 agreed to sell its natural gas pipeline subsidiary, Mississippi River Transmission Corporation.

Diversification

During the early 1980s, railroad companies diversified rapidly into nontransportation business activities. Many invested capital in energy, such as coal, oil, and gas, as well as in real estate opportunities. Others ventured into new frontiers. The Santa Fe Southern Pacific Corporation and Norfolk Southern Corporation, for instance, announced joint plans to lay 8000 miles of fiber-optics lines and sell communications capacity to telecommunications carriers.[45] Both railroad owners and managers are redefining their business interests, and they are no longer narrowly focusing on railroad endeavors. Because investments are being made where profit potential can be maximized, money is often spent outside of railroading, as well as outside of transportation.

FREIGHT RAILROAD FINANCES

Turning now to railroad finances, let us focus on the costs, revenues, and earnings of Class I carriers, the industry's largest carriers. Although the ICC regulates smaller carriers, its primary concern is Class I carriers, for they dominate the railroad industry. In 1984, the 25 Class I railroads accounted for more than 95% of the industry's freight.[46]

Costs

fixed and variable costs

Compared to trucking companies and water carriers, railroads have high fixed costs. Unlike highway and water carriers, railroads own, operate, and maintain their rights-of-way; the public does not provide them. This situation has resulted in significant industry assets. In 1984, Class I carriers had net investments of $45.4 billion.[47] Nevertheless, variable costs account for 65% to 79% of total railroad costs.[48] Although annual fixed costs are high, variable costs dominate railroad cost structures.

labor costs

Table 5.1 breaks down Class I carrier expenses for 1984. It shows labor costs for wages, health and welfare and pensions, and payroll taxes to be the industry's dominant expense item, accounting for 50.58% of total industry costs. Between 1972 and 1984, Class I freight railroad management reduced employment from 526,061 to 323,030 (a decrease of 38.6%); however, annual compensation per employee, including wages and benefits excluding payroll taxes and retirement costs, increased 178.9% during the same period from $12,213 to $34,064.[49] Labor costs are primarily variable expenses. Other significant expense categories in 1984 were fuel and power (electricity) for locomotives (10.33%) and depreciation (7.04%).

fuel and power costs

From 1976 through 1984, fuel and power costs more than doubled from $1.3 billion to $2.78 billion. Mainly, the change is indicative of inflated petroleum prices. Still, because railroad transportation is relatively fuel-efficient, Class I carriers were not burdened as much by rising fuel prices as were motor carriers and airlines. Railroad management also helped its cause by adopting measures that increased fuel productivity. In the last decade, revenue ton-miles per gallon improved 30%. Also helping the situation was the

TABLE 5.1. Class I total railroad expenses (1984)

Expense Items	(in Millions)	Percent
Labor costs	$13,613	50.58%
Fuel and power for locomotives	2,780	10.33
Depreciation	1,896	7.04
Deferred taxes	930	3.45
Loss and damage, injuries, and insurance	840	3.12
Income taxes on ordinary income	255	.95
All other expenses[a]	6,602	24.53
TOTAL	$26,916	100.00%

[a]Includes other materials and supplies and miscellaneous, equipment and joint facility rents, current taxes (other than payroll taxes and income taxes) and retirement charges, and rent for/income from leased roads and equipment.

Source: Association of American Railroads, *Railroad Facts 1985 Edition* (Washington, D.C.: AAR, August 1985), p. 11. (Adapted with permission.)

decline in fuel prices per gallon that began in 1982. In 1984, the average price per gallon for Class I carriers had fallen to 82.59¢ from a level of 101.22¢ in 1981.[50]

cost trends

Carrier cost trends show a reduction in total costs per ton-mile from a 1981 level of 3.22¢ to 2.92¢ in 1984 (a 9.3% decrease). Between 1981 and 1984, Class I carriers trimmed total expenses and taxes from $29.398 billion to $26.916 billion, a decrease of $2.482 billion. Lower fuel prices contributed to a reduction in fuel and power costs for locomotives from a 1981 level of $3.835 billion to a 1984 figure of $2.780 billion. Labor costs during the same period fell from $13.995 billion to $13.613 billion, primarily reflecting a reduction in employees. Another $82 million was achieved in reduced expenses for loss and damage, injuries, and insurance payments.[51]

Revenues

In 1984, freight revenues of the Class I railroads totalled $28.5 billion, a decline of 1.4% from 1981 freight revenues of $28.9 billion. The 1984 average yield per ton-mile was 3.09¢, a figure 2.8% below the 1981 level of 3.18¢.[52] Thus the recession and changing market conditions caused lower average railroad prices.

Earnings

During 1984, Class I railroads earned $2.537 billion in net railway operating income, i.e., operating revenues minus total expenses and taxes. This figure, which compared quite favorably to 1981 net railway operating income of $1.336 billion, was primarily due to cost reductions. As previously stated, yields declined from 1981 to 1984. A contributing factor was a slight increase in traffic. In 1984, the railroads hauled 921.5 billion ton-miles, whereas in 1981, a total of 910.2 billion ton-miles was moved. Due to the railroad industry's high net investment ($45.4 billion), its 1984 rate of return on net investment (ROI) was only 5.71%,[53] which compares favorably to the 1983 ROI of 4.29%.

Low returns are closely correlated to the railroad industry's capital structure. As previously noted, railroads own their rights-of-way. They also have a high level of equity in their capital structure (63% equity and 37% debt in 1983).[54] Consequently, returns on equity tend to be low. For example, the industry's 1984 after-tax return on equity was 9.75%.[55] To achieve higher returns on investment or on equity, railroads need to increase income levels.

low return impact

Because of low returns, which have been an industry problem for decades, it has been difficult to attract investment capital at reasonable cost to modernize and improve rights-of-way and rolling stock or vehicles. In 1978, the U.S. Department of Transportation concluded that the railroad industry needed investments of $42.5 billion between 1976 and 1986 to maintain and improve its system.[56] During the years 1977 through 1984, Class I carriers, primarily due to improved income, made capital expenditures of $23.3 billion for roadways, structures (bridges, tunnels), and equipment.[57] Unfortunately, at the present average annual rate of $2.9 billion, private sector investments will fall short of the DOT spending target by $13.4 billion. If the required investment is to be accomplished, sources besides internally generated cash will probably be necessary.

Super Railroad System Statistics

This section concludes with a brief review of several financial statistics from the so-called super railroads. First, according to 1984 operating revenues, CSX Corporation was the largest railroad at $4.848 billion, followed by Burlington Northern ($4.440 billion), Union Pacific System ($3.863 billion), Norfolk Southern ($3.510 billion), Conrail ($3.322 billion), Southern Pacific ($2.625 billion, but this includes revenues of its subsidiary, the St. Louis Southwestern), and the Santa Fe ($2.305 billion). Burlington Northern was the leader in operating income at $947 million, followed by Norfolk Southern at $717 million, CSX Corporation at $580 million, Conrail at $450 million, Union Pacific at $365 million, Santa Fe at $135 million, and the Southern Pacific at $58 million. As measured by operating ratios, the most efficient systems were Burlington Northern (78.68%), Norfolk Southern (79.58%), and Conrail (86.45%).[58]

PRICING THEORY AND PRACTICE

Railroad pricing has transitioned from being a rigorously regulated activity to a point where more than two-thirds of all interstate freight railroad rates are set independently of the Interstate Commerce Commission. In the concluding pages of Chapter 5, we will examine transportation pricing theories, transportation price determinants, railroad rate regulation and deregulation, railroad rate-making, railroad pricing practices, and computer pricing advances.

Transportation Pricing Theories

Freight railroad managers, like managers in other modes, use two basic pricing theories in determining the rate for moving a particular shipment: (1) *cost of service pricing*, which is also called cost-based pricing or fully distributed cost pricing, and (2) *value of service pricing*, which is also known as differentiated pricing. Figure 5.2 illustrates the distinction between these two theories.

Cost of Service Pricing. Cost of service (C of S) pricing means that freight rates should be based on the total of the variable costs of that particular shipment; a proportionate, fair share of the firm's fixed costs; and a reasonable profit margin. As shown in Fig. 5.2, variable costs of 60¢, a fixed cost assessment of 20¢, and a profit of 10¢ equal a price of 90¢.

FIGURE 5.2.
Theories of transportation pricing.

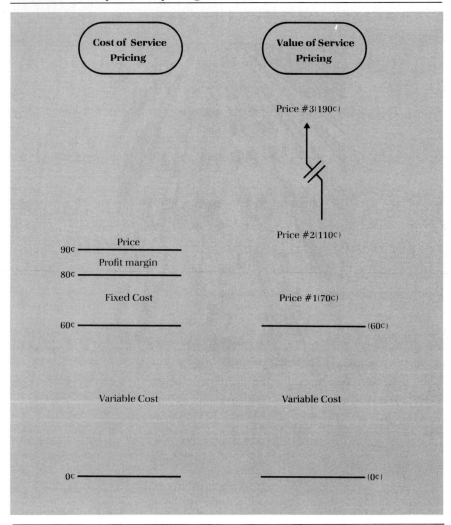

Value of Service Pricing. Value of service (V of S) pricing sets rates according to what the traffic will bear. V of S pricing is similar to C of S pricing in only one way: Variable costs must be covered, or the carrier automatically loses money on that shipment, would be better off not accepting the freight, and can be accused of predatory pricing. The actual V of S price, however, theoretically can be set at any level above variable costs or the floor price: For example, the price might be 70¢, 110¢, or 190¢. Obviously, there is a maximum price, called the ceiling price, above which a carrier attracts no volume. A carrier pricing at the maximum is also likely to alienate customers.

How, then, does a manager decide the price to charge, given the example showing choices of 70¢, 110¢, or 190¢? V of S theory says that the actual charge should be the rate that would maximize contributions to fixed costs when forecasted traffic demand is considered at each possible price. If each shipment is priced accordingly, total fixed costs are covered and additional contributions to fixed costs become income. Table 5.2 assumes that low prices will stimulate demand. As noted, the 70¢/cwt rate creates the highest revenues ($2,100), but the lowest contribution to fixed costs ($300). In this case, the price (190¢) and the 130¢ margin per unit above variable costs (190¢ minus 60¢) more than compensate for the smaller demand. Often, however, prices just above variable costs produce huge levels of demand and greater fixed-cost contributions. If so, the lower price is more appealing from the carrier's perspective.

motivation for V of S

Several economic factors motivate carriers to use value of service pricing: for instance, high fixed costs that must be covered, excess capacity and the need for more traffic to increase utilization, and many different market segments or differentiated products. Since railroads have all three characteristics, they are particularly well suited for V of S pricing; furthermore, they usually follow this theory, rather than the cost of service theory.

discrimination

In essence, value of service pricing discriminates, because different prices are often charged to different customers for similar commodities moving between the same two points. Remember, discrimination is not prohibited unless it is undue or unjust. As Chapter 3 discussed, competitive, economic, and social factors frequently justify transportation discrimination.

legality

Value of service pricing, despite its tendency to anger both shippers who pay more than fully distributed costs and intermodal competitors who are unhappy with railroad rates below fully distributed costs, is a legitimately accepted pricing theory. The 4R Act of 1976 stated that the ICC could no longer declare that railroad rates equal to or above variable costs were unjust or unreasonably low. That act also established that no rate was to be judged too high in determining the rate's reasonableness unless the ICC determined that the carrier had market dominance. Market dominance was later defined by the ICC to mean a situation in which a freight railroad has an effective monopoly. Since 1981, the ICC has considered indirect, as well as direct, competition in determining whether a railroad has market dominance. By this

market dominance

TABLE 5.2. Computation of maximum contributions to fixed costs

Possible Rate (rate per cwt) (A)	Forecasted Demand (B)	Total Revenues (A) × (B) = (C)	Total Variable Costs (@ 60¢ per Unit) (B) × (60¢) = (D)	Fixed Cost Contribution (C) − (D) = (E)
190¢	400	$760.00	$240	$520
110¢	1000	$1100.00	600	500
70¢	3000	$2100.00	1800	300

FIGURE 5.3.
Indirect railroad competition.

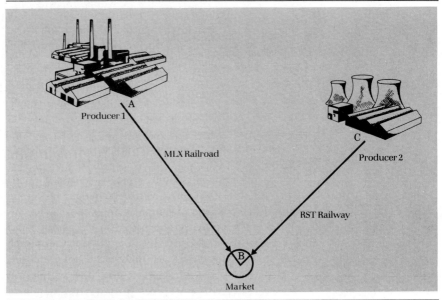

criterion, even though the MLX railroad is the only carrier capable of serving market *B* from point *A* (see Fig. 5.3), it may not have monopoly powers if, for example, the producer at point *A* endures effective competition from another producer at point *C* who also sells in market *B*. Such indirect competition, according to the ICC, limits the ability of a railroad to raise prices indiscriminately because the effect may be to reduce sales in market *B* of producer *A*'s products. The Staggers Rail Act of 1980 further legitimized value of service pricing by allowing freight railroads to reduce rates more easily to meet motor and water carrier competition. As long as a railroad rate contributes to the *going concern value,* which is defined as a rate equal to or above variable costs, it is reasonable.

going concern value

Transportation Price Determinants

In reality, many factors influence rates. Carrier marketing and traffic personnel should incorporate in their pricing strategies demand considerations, the ability and willingness of shippers to pay the new rate, competitors' services and prices, and costs.

derived demand

Transportation is, for the most part, a derived-demand business, because the demand for transportation services is based on the need for goods or other services. For example, residents in Nevada wanting dairy products create a demand for transportation to deliver cheese and milk to the market; in other words, without the demand for products, there is no demand for transportation service to haul traffic. Furthermore, transportation demand is sensitive to changes in the economy. During the recent recession, shippers lowered production levels and reduced inventories. Price increases during economic downturns must be implemented with care. Carriers face the dual threats that shippers will not be able to pay higher rates and will possibly shut down production facilities or that other carriers, either within railroading or in the form of intermodal competitors, will offer lower prices and capture the shipper's business.

shippers' ability to pay

In 1929, railroads controlled a 75% market share of the country's intercity ton-miles. However, intermodal competition eroded that share over the years. Oil pipelines emerged, particularly since World War II, as formidable competitors for the oil traffic once hauled by railroads. Trucking also made great inroads, increasing its share of the total freight market from 3% in 1939 to 19% in 1984 (refer to Table 1.5). Finally, water carriers, competing for the same bulk commodities that rails wanted to carry, proved to be tough foes. The emergence of intermodal competition pressured the railroads to keep rates low. Depressed yields were primarily responsible for unsatisfactory industry earnings.

intermodal competition

Transportation firms in this country rarely have total pricing freedom. A railroad may perceive itself to be in a market dominant situation, but intermodal competition limits price increases. Railroads are not alone; other modes face the same market constraints. In the dynamic transportation environment, price changes by one carrier spur competitor initiatives or shipper actions. If one carrier cuts rates, others likely follow. If one carrier raises rates and competitors do not, the first may lose traffic.

Pricing would be much easier if a railroad knew exactly how much a shipment would cost. Unfortunately, costs can be difficult to calculate. A freight car might be added to a train one day at practically no marginal cost, whereas the next day it might require the addition of another locomotive, because that one car added just enough weight to make the present horsepower insufficient. Railroad car costs can vary tremendously, according to the routing, number of carriers involved in hauling a shipment, number of yards a car passes through, terrain, and weather conditions. Establishing accurate rail car movement costs is challenging, given the massive number of commodities, origin and destination pairs, routes, and traffic volumes railroads work with.

costs

Railroad Rate Regulation and Deregulation

Today, because of the Staggers Rail Act of 1980, nearly two-thirds of all freight railroad rates are free from ICC maximum rate regulations. Unless a railroad has market dominance, and then only if the rate exceeds 190% of variable costs, the ICC cannot suspend or investigate rate changes. This revenue to variable cost threshold, which was established by the Staggers Rail Act of 1980, gives railroad managers the opportunity to increase prices quickly. In addition, railroads are also allowed to lower prices to variable cost levels with-

maximum and minimum rates

out ICC approval. Thus the ICC's power to set maximum and minimum rates has been significantly lessened.

revenue adequacy

Conscious of poor railroad returns on investment and significant needs for capital expenditures, the ICC in 1983 set a 17.7% composite cost of capital as a standard by which to determine the amount of pricing flexibility it should give railroads. At the time, the ICC determined the cost of railroad debt was 14% and the cost of equity capital was 19.8%.[59] Section 10701a(b)(3) of Title 49 *U.S. Code* provides that "In determining whether a rate established by a rail carrier is reasonable for purposes of this section, the Commission shall recognize the policy of this title that rail carriers shall earn adequate revenues, as established by the Commission under section 10704(a)(2) of this title." Thus rate increases by individual carriers are acceptable if such railroads are not earning sufficient revenues to match what they have to pay to attract outside capital.

Contract Rates.   Contract rates represent another form of freight pricing freedom. Prior to 1976, for-hire railroads were not allowed to sign contracts with shippers but were restricted to common carrier services. Section 206 of the 4R Act of 1976 altered this long-standing restriction making contract rates lawful upon individual approval of the ICC. In November 1978 the ICC issued a policy statement (*Ex Parte* 358F) declaring that railroad contract rates no longer were unlawful per se and that the ICC would encourage their use. However, little contract activity resulted as verified by the filing of only 80 contracts during the two-year November 1978 through October 1980 period.[60]

Staggers Act Impact

The source of a boom in contract rate activity was Section 208 of the Staggers Rail Act of 1980 (now Section 10713 of the Interstate Commerce Act), which directed the ICC to approve rail contracts unless the ICC found them to be in violation of the Interstate Commerce Act. The Staggers Act shifted the burden to the ICC to deny contracts—something that has rarely happened. During the six-year period from November 1978 through February 1984, a total of 13,000 rail contracts were filed with the ICC. During the last eight months of that period, an average of 603 contracts per month was filed.[61]

contract specifics

Railroad contracts have been signed by railroads and shippers to haul practically all types of commodities. Their duration is as brief as 30 days or as long as 39 years; most, however, cover periods of one year or less. As to their importance, the ICC surveyed 11 Class I carriers, and the respondents reported that contracts constituted an average of 26.5% of total revenues and 24.3% of total tonnage. Railroads praised the ability of contracts to lock in traffic and guarantee volumes, the confidentiality of contracts, and contract pricing flexibility.[62] Only the ICC has access to contract rate terms that allow carriers to negotiate different prices with different shippers. Furthermore, since the ICC has permitted contracts to become effective on the date of filing, prices can be established quickly. Shippers cite rate concessions, rate stability, and service/equipment guarantees as some of the benefits they derive from railroad contracts.

exemptions and pricing freedoms

A final major form of rate freedom was created through previously defined exemptions on fresh fruits and vegetables, piggyback service, and single line box car traffic. Railroad traffic qualifying under these exemptions faces no federal pricing restrictions. What carriers charge is entirely at the discretion of management.

goals of rate deregulation

In reviewing the behind-the-scenes debates that preceded the above forms of railroad deregulation, it becomes apparent that the motivation for pricing freedom was a perceived need to improve rail revenues in order to restore, maintain, and improve physical facilities, while achieving financial stability of the national rail system. Other goals were to foster independent carrier pricing and curtail the activities of rate bureaus and collective ratemaking. These terms and changes are next defined as part of a discussion on the changing ratemaking process.

Railroad Ratemaking

past procedures for changing rates

Nearly all railroads belong to one or more rate bureaus, which are carrier organizations whose member railroads hear, discuss, and vote on their rail rate proposals. The process is called *collective ratemaking*. Also, bureaus publish tariffs; in essence, they act as rate publishing organizations. To raise or lower its prices, prior to the Staggers Rail Act of 1980, a railroad would bring the matter before the rate bureau. For the most part, requests were for rate reductions, often instigated by shippers who either promised increased traffic or threatened to give freight to other carriers if they did not receive what they wanted. The bureau would meet, hear the pros and cons of the rate proposal, discuss, and vote to accept or reject the rate change. The public was not privy to the discussion and vote of the bureau members. Bureau-approved rate changes were filed with the ICC, which could then approve, suspend, and/or investigate the matter. In most cases, the ICC approved, without debate, rates sanctioned by a rate bureau.

independent action

If a bureau rejected a proposed rate change, however, the proponent railroad could terminate the rate request or use the right of independent action, guaranteed under the Reed-Bulwinkle Act of 1948, to file the rate change with the ICC. Realistically though, carriers seldom defied a bureau's wishes, fearing this would disrupt the positive working relationship with other bureau-member railroads that interlined traffic with them.

general rate increases

In fact, most rate increase proposals before 1980 were handled somewhat differently. Whereas carriers liked to have their names attached to rate reductions, most railroads tried to avoid the negative publicity associated with requests for price increases. A solution was the *general rate increase*, an across-the-board percentage markup of prices on almost all rail commodities.

General rate changes included national or regional increases, and ICC approval was necessary.

evaluation
of bureaus Bureaus have been criticized as ratemaking cartels free to discuss rates of their members. Such activities are strictly forbidden by antitrust statutes in most industries. However, railroading and, as will be discussed later, trucking, intercity bus carriers, and inland waterway barge lines have antitrust immunity, so collective ratemaking is legal. Bureaus have also been widely praised by shippers, as well as carriers, for performing useful functions such as helping to control rate discrimination, lessening rate instability, and facilitating *joint line service*—that is, interline service between two or more railroads.[63]

Staggers Act changes Nevertheless, the Staggers Rail Act of 1980 significantly reduced the powers of railroad rate bureaus prohibiting the discussion of, and voting on, single-line (local) rail rates by bureaus. Secondly, since January 1, 1984, no carrier can participate in the discussion of a joint rate unless the railroad actually participates in the routing. Finally, rail general rate increases were eliminated on January 1, 1984. These actions, plus the rate freedoms discussed earlier in the chapter, will probably transfer much of the rate decision making from rate bureaus to individual carriers. As a result, prices will more closely reflect marketplace conditions, and the primary role of rail rate bureaus will be that of rate publishing organizations.

Railroad Pricing Practices

Railroad pricing is complex. Since railroads can carry many types of shipments between any two cities of any size in the United States, numerous prices are possible. To simplify the problem of having to quote so many rates, the railroad industry began to classify freight, combining commodities with similar transportation characteristics, such as value and weight density. In 1952 this Uniform
Freight Classification information was incorporated in the Uniform Freight Classification, a book containing rules, ratings, and regulations, which were applicable to railroad traffic throughout the United States. A rating is a number that combines a group of commodities into a homogeneous class for pricing purposes. It is not to be confused with *rate,* which is a price in dollars and/or cents, and which common carriers publish in a book called a *tariff.* Rules and regulations found in the Uniform Freight Classification concern such matters as shipper packaging requirements and the handling of dangerous commodities. For every item moved by rail, there is a *class rate*—a price found by using the information in the Classification and the class tariff.

class rates If a shipper wants to determine the class rate, the item must first be located by name in the Classification. Finding an item is not always easy. In fact, the problem is similar to trying to look for an item in the Yellow Pages of a telephone book. "Wine," for example, may be listed under the larger heading "alcoholic beverages."

The following is an example of an item found in the Classification.

Item	Article (Item Description)	Less Carload Rating (LCL)	Carload Minimum	Carload Rating (CL)
16480	Ironing boards, folding, wooden, in metal cabinets, in boxes or crates	85	24,000	55

example   Item 16480 shows an LCL rating of 85 and a CL rating of 55, as well as a carload minimum of 24,000 lbs. If the shipper gives the railroad at least 24,000 lbs. of ironing boards or is willing to pay for 24,000 lbs., even if that weight is not actually shipped, then the class 55 rating applies. If not, the shipment has a class 85 rating. The difference is important, for the higher the class rating, the higher the price per 100 lbs. Carload minimums are designed to encourage shippers to offer more weight per shipment. Volume shipments enable carriers to increase productivity, and shippers receive volume rate discounts.

Once the shipper knows the above information, the next step is to enter the tariffs to find the *rate basis number*—a figure that reflects the distance between origin and destination—before being able to determine a class rate. Class rates tend to be closely tied to weight and distance.[64]

In reality, less than 10% of all items move under railroad class rates. Many of the remaining shipments are hauled at prices set by contract terms or negotiated with shippers under various railroad exemptions, while others move under exception and commodity rates. Since contract and exempt traffic were discussed, let us now focus on exception and commodity rates.

exception and commodity rates   As the name implies, exception rates deviate from class rates and represent discounts implemented because of unusual competitive needs and/or to retain or attract traffic volume. More important, because they produce even higher traffic levels, are commodity rates—special rates on specific commodities moving between specific points and often applicable only in one direction. Typically, this is a high-volume discount aimed at traffic like grain (e.g., wheat or corn).

applicable rate   Railroads, as common carriers, are required by law to charge customers the lowest applicable rate. Therefore shippers must search for exception and commodity rates, because of their potential savings.

Computer Pricing Advances

Computer technology is rapidly changing railroad pricing. After the 1981 deregulation of piggyback traffic, Conrail's piggyback rate system evolved from just a few freight all-kinds rates, which are insensitive to the types of commodities being shipped in a container or trailer, to more than 30,000 individual rates tailored to specific markets and customers. Conrail's response was to computerize piggyback rates and the billing system.[65] Another illustration of how computer science affects railroads is the National Railroad Ratemaking and Information Retrieval System (NRRIRS). Developed by DSI*Rail in cooperation with U.S. freight railroads, NRRIRS is a computer system that enables participating railroads to accomplish pricing, joint rate negotiation, reporting on rate docket (a case awaiting action) status, and retrieval of rate information. The system offers carriers the benefits of simpler, faster ratemaking; faster rate retrievals; easier documentation; and sophisticated computer communications. Benefits to shippers are faster rate quotes, easier publication of rates, and single sources for joint rates.[66]

SUMMARY

The freight railroad industry has just emerged from the worst recession in 50 years not in worse shape, but in the best financial condition it has experienced in decades. Despite sluggish traffic, railroad dollar profits and returns on investment and equity improved considerably. Taking advantage of liberalized economic regulations, freight railroads abandoned uneconomical branch lines, raised or lowered prices to match market conditions, and seized market opportunities.

Today's freight railroads have reinvested billions of dollars of earnings in improved rights-of-way and equipment, and these expenditures are paying off in improved services. Railroad owners and managers have also formed huge new rail systems through intramodal mergers and acquisitions, and they have expanded their control to other sectors of the economy through intermodal combinations and diversification. Apparently, railroad deregulation goals are being realized, for freight railroads are proving their ability to compete in a dynamic marketplace. Still, much needs to be done to control costs, increase productivity, and maintain the industry's positive momentum. After many years of pleading for more private sector decision-making power, railroads have it. The question now is whether carriers can continue to make the most of this freedom from government controls.

STUDY QUESTIONS

1. Explain the difference between an end-to-end merger and a side-by-side merger. Why is there usually more opposition to a side-by-side merger?

2. Discuss the impact of the Staggers Rail Act of 1980 on the railroads and their customers.

3. Railroad mergers have frequently been proffered as a mechanism for addressing the problems of the industry. Under what circumstances could mergers be successful in improving rail transportation in the United States? In general, how successful have railroad mergers been in this regard?

4. What changes made Conrail profitable?

5. How do exemptions help freight railroads to compete better in the marketplace?

6. What is responsible for the increase in short-line railroads in the United States?

7. Explain this statement: "Railroads are a high fixed cost industry, but variable costs outweigh fixed expenses."

8. What do market dominance and revenue adequacy have to do with a railroad's ability to raise prices?

ENDNOTES

1. John H. Armstrong, *The Railroad—What It Is, What It Does* (Omaha, Nebr.: Simmons-Boardman Publishing Corp., 1978), pp. 7–8.

2. Association of American Railroads, *Railroad Facts 1985 Edition* (Washington, D.C.: AAR, August 1985), p. 28 (hereafter cited as *Railroad Facts 1985*).

3. For a more in-depth review of early economic regulation of railroads, see Donald V. Harper, *Transportation in America: Users, Carriers, Government*, 2d ed. (Englewood Cliffs, N.J.: Prentice-Hall, 1982), p. 460.

4. *Wabash, St. Louis, and Pacific Railway* v. *Illinois*, 118 U.S. 557.

5. Harper, *Transportation*, pp. 457–462.

6. Frank N. Wilner, *Competitive Equity: The Freight Railroads' Stake* (Washington, D.C.: Association of American Railroads, February 1981).

7. D. Phillip Locklin, *Economics of Transportation*, 7th ed. (Homewood, Ill.: Richard D. Irwin, 1972), p. 271.

8. 90 *Statutes at Large* 31.

9. (a) Association of American Railroads, "Alaska Railroad Value Set at $22.3 Million," *Rail News Update*, 5 October 1983, p. 4; (b) Association of American Railroads, "Alaska Railroad Transfer Requirements Are Met," *Rail News Update*, 25 July 1984, p. 2; and (c) for background, see Bill Richards and Eugene Carlson, "Debate over Future of Alaska Railroad Involves Coal, Cash," *Wall Street Journal*, 20 September 1983, p. 1.

10. Walker D. Hines, *War History of American Railroads* (New Haven, Conn.: Yale University Press, 1928), as cited by D. Phillip Locklin, *Economics of Transportation*, 7th ed. (Homewood, Ill.: Richard D. Irwin, 1972), p. 238.

11. See (a) John D. Heffner, "Shortline Railroads," *Traffic World*, 31 January 1983, p. 68; and (b) Bill Richards, "Keeping Track: Worried States Enter the Railroad Business to Save Branch Lines," *Wall Street Journal*, 22 September 1983, p. 1.

12. "And the Name of Conrail's New Owner is . . . ," *Business Week*, 2 July 1984, p. 31.

13. (a) Testimony by Robert H. Platt, Executive Vice-president–Finance and Administration, Consolidated Rail Corporation, before Senator Arlen Specter, Hearing at Harrisburg, Pa., 24 October 1984, p. 1, copy of which was enclosed in a letter from L. Stanley Crane, Chairman and Chief Executive Officer, Conrail to Conrail shippers, dated 5 November 1984; and (b) *Carrier Reports Annual 1984* 25, no. 4 (Old Saybrook, Conn.: Carrier Reports, April 1985), p. 34.

14. Ibid., Platt testimony, p. 1.

15. Ibid., p. 2.

16. Richard Koenig and Daniel Machalaba, "Conrail Attracts 10 Bids Offering $1 Billion or More," *Wall Street Journal*, 20 June 1984, p. 2.

17. Heffner, "Shortline Railroads," p. 70.

18. "Burlington Northern's Fight to Repel Invaders," *Business Week*, 3 November 1980, p. 121.

19. Stephen J. Morgan, "Short-line Railroads Growing Nationwide," *Washington Business*, 29 October 1984, p. 19.

20. DeMaris A. Berry, "Rock Island Fades into History as Nine-year Reorganization Ends," *Traffic World*, 30 April 1984, p. 22.

21. Morgan, "Short-line Railroads," p. 19.

22. "ICC Favors Confidentiality of Rail Charges in Final Contract Rules," *Traffic World*, 8 November 1982, pp. 7–8.

23. Interstate Commerce Commission, *Ex Parte 346 Sub. 1, Rail General Exemption Authority—Fresh Fruits and Vegetables*, decided 21 March, 1979.

24. Interstate Commerce Commission, *Ex Parte 346, Sub. 2, Rail General Exemption Authority—Miscellaneous Commodities*, 45 *Federal Register 20484 (1980)*.

25. Association of American Railroads, "ICC Votes to Deregulate Export Coal, Boxcar Rates," *Rail News Update*, 9 March 1983, p. 4.

26. Interstate Commerce Commission, *Ex Parte 230, Sub. 5, Improvement of TOFC/COFC Regulation*, 45 *Federal Register 79123 (1980)*.

27. Association of American Railroads, "ICC Votes to Extend Exemption for Piggyback," *Rail News Update*, 3 October 1984, p. 3.

28. Association of American Railroads, "ICC Votes," p. 4.

29. "Appeals Court Ruling Further Complicates Box Car Deregulation," *Traffic World,* 2 July 1984, p. 7.

30. Association of American Railroads, "Appeals Court Overturns ICC Export Court Ruling," *Rail News Update,* 19 September 1984, p. 4.

31. Interstate Commerce Commission, *Annual Report, 1980* (Washington, D.C.: U.S. Government Printing Office, 1980), p. 112.

32. "D.O.T. Report Asks 25% Cut in Northeast Track," *UTU News,* 9 February 1974, p. 1.

33. Eric D. Lindeman, "Conrail Sale Process Is Criticized by Crane at Short Line Conference," *Traffic World,* 29 October 1984, p. 17.

34. Paul W. Cherington, "Note on Railroad Mergers," (Boston, Mass.: Harvard Business School, 1973), order number 9-373-143, p. 12.

35. Association of American Railroads, *Railroad Facts 1985,* p. 2. As of 1 January 1982, the ICC started adjusting the Class I threshold for inflation by restating current revenues in 1978 constant dollars.

36. Curtis M. Grimm and Robert G. Harris, "Structural Economics of the U.S. Rail Freight Industry: Concepts, Evidence, and Merger Policy Implications," *Transportation Research,* 17A, no. 4 (1983):271.

37. (a) Theodore E. Keeler, "Railroad Costs, Returns to Scale, and Excess Capacity," *Review of Economics and Statistics* 56, no. 1 (May 1974):207; and (b) Robert G. Harris, "Economics of Traffic Density in the Rail Freight Industry," *Bell Journal of Economics* (Autumn 1977):561.

38. (a) Grimm and Harris, "Structural Economics," p. 277, citing Zvi Griliches, "Cost Allocation in Railroad Regulation," *Bell Journal of Economics,* 7, no. 2 (1972); and (b) Keeler, "Railroad Costs," p. 207.

39. "Court Refuses ATA Plea for Review of ICC Policy on Rail–Truck Authority," *Traffic World,* 30 January 1984, p. 7.

40. "Bulk Haulers Protest D&RGW Trucking Bid," *Traffic World,* 13 February 1984, p. 57.

41. "Norfolk Southern Asks ICC Approval of North American Purchase Proposal," *Traffic World,* 27 August 1984, p. 51.

42. Ibid.

43. "ICC Approves Plan of Norfolk Southern to Buy Motor Carrier," *Wall Street Journal,* 18 April 1985, p. 41.

44. For background on this case, see (a) John A. LoDico, "ICC Allows CSX and ACL to Create Nation's First Rail-Barge Company," *Traffic World,* 30 July 1984, pp. 31–33; and (b) "CSX-ACBL Decision Issued as Merger Plans Advance; WTA Quickly Files Appeal," *Traffic World,* 17 September 1984, pp. 40–41.

45. "Santa Fe, Norfolk Plan Fiber-Optics System Along Rights of Way," *Wall Street Journal,* 14 September 1984, p. 22.

46. *Railroad Facts 1985,* p. 2.

47. Ibid., p. 9.

48. Frank N. Wilner, "Railroad Pricing: Should Market Forces or Some Yet to be Devised Harvard Computer Program Prevail?" A speech before the Railroad Pricing and URCS Costing Seminar, University of Wisconsin, Madison, 14 July 1982, p. 11.

49. *Railroad Facts 1985,* p. 56.

50. Ibid., pp. 6, 60.

51. (a) Ibid., p. 11; and (b) Association of American Railroads, *Yearbook of Railroad Facts 1982 Edition* (Washington, D.C.: AAR, September 1982), p. 11 (hereafter cited as *Railroad Facts 1982*).

52. *Railroad Facts, 1985,* pp. 13, 30.

53. Ibid., p. 18.

54. Association of American Railroads, "ICC Sets 17.7 Percent as Rail Cost of Capital," *Rail News Update,* 24 August 1983, p. 4 (hereafter cited as "ICC Sets 17.7 Percent").

55. *Railroad Facts 1985,* p. 21.

56. Federal Railroad Administration, *A Prospectus for Change in the Freight Railroad Industry, a Preliminary Report of the Secretary of Transportation* (Washington, D.C.: FRA 1978), p. 3.

57. *Railroad Facts 1985,* p. 55.

58. *Carrier Reports Annual 1984* 25, no. 4 (Old Saybrook, Conn.: Carrier Reports, April 1985):34–35.

59. "ICC Sets 17.7 Percent," p. 4.

60. "Staggers Act—Contract Rates," Information released by ICC Contract Advisory Service on 30 June 1983, as cited in Bob J. Davis and C. K. Walter, *Contract Railroad Rates* (Macomb, Ill.: Western Illinois University Center for Economic Research, 1984), p. 26.

61. Interstate Commerce Commission, *Report on Railroad Contract Rates Authorized by Section 208 of the Staggers Rail Act of 1980* (Washington, D.C.: ICC, 1984), p. 8.

62. For an excellent review of the ICC's study shown

in endnote 61 above, see "ICC Survey of Rail-Shipper Contracts Shows Fast Growth, Mutual Benefits," *Traffic World,* 26 March 1984, pp. 10–17.

63. Garland Chow, "Motor Carrier Rate Bureaus: Shippers' vs. Carriers' Views," *Journal of Purchasing and Materials Management* (Spring 1980):22.

64. John J. Coyle and Edward J. Bardi, *The Management of Business Logistics,* 2d ed. (St. Paul,

Minn.: West Publishing, 1980). For examples of how to use classification information in computing class rates, see Chapter 8.

65. Public Affairs Department, Consolidated Rail Corp., "Computerized Rate Systems Mean Faster Response for Our Customers," *Conrail Update,* no. 31 (n.d.), pp. 1–3.

66. Eric D. Lindeman, "DSI*Rail System Brings Accuracy, Speed to Rail Rate Negotiations," *Traffic World,* 1 October 1984, pp. 27–28.

ADDITIONAL READINGS

Altrogge, Phyllis D. "Railroad Contracts and Competitive Conditions." *Transportation Journal* 21, no. 2 (Winter 1981):37–43.

Blackwell, Richard B. "Pitfalls in Rail Contract Rate Escalation." *ICC Practitioners' Journal* (July–August 1982):486–502.

Carr, Ronald G. "Railroad–Shipper Contracts under Section 208 of the Staggers Rail Act of 1980: An Antitrust Perspective." *ICC Practitioners' Journal* (November–December, 1982):29–41.

Caves, Douglas W.; Christensen, Laurits R.; and Swanson, Joseph A. "The High Cost of Regulating U.S. Railroads." *Regulation* (January–February 1981):41–44.

Coyle, John J.; Bardi, Edward J.; and Cavinato, Joseph L. *Transportation.* St. Paul, Minn.: West Publishing, 1982. For a thorough review of the 4R Act of 1976, see pp. 332–334, and for the specific provisions of the Staggers Rail Act of 1980, see pp. 353–359.

Due, John F. "New Railroad Companies Formed to Take Over Abandoned or Spun-off Lines." *Transportation Journal* 24, no. 1 (Fall 1984):30–50.

Dunbar, Roger L. M., and Sarnat, Marshall. "Measuring Industrial Stagnation: The Case of the U.S. Railroads." *Journal of Industrial Economics* 28, no. 3 (March 1980):255–268.

Fisher, Peter S. "Alternative Institutional Structures for State and Local Government Ownership of Railroads." *The Logistics and Transportation Review* 18, no. 3 (1982):235–254.

Gand, Heino. " 'Bottom Line' Business Standards Versus Public Service Obligations: The Case of the German Federal Railway." *Transportation Research* 18A, no. 2 (March 1984):151–161.

Graham, Kenneth. "Rail-based Holding Companies: A View of Some Indicators of Strategy, Management Change, and Financial Performance." *Transportation Journal* 19, no. 4 (Summer 1980):73–77.

Harper, Donald V. *Transportation in America: Users, Carriers, Government.* 2d ed. Englewood Cliffs, N.J.: Prentice-Hall, 1982. Chapter 8, "Theory of Transportation Pricing," Chapter 9, "Transportation Pricing in Practice," and Chapter 21, "Government Economic Regulation of Railroad Transportation."

Hazard, John L. "Government Railroading." *Transportation Journal* 19, no. 3 (Spring 1980):38–50.

Horn, Kevin H. "Deregulation of Produce Traffic: Will the Railways Be Able to Produce?" *Transportation Journal* 19, no. 1 (Fall 1979):5–18.

——. "Pricing of Rail Intermodal Service: A Case Study of Institutional Myopia." *Transportation Journal* 20, no. 4 (Summer 1981):63–77.

Langdon, Jervis (Jr.). "The Struggle for Viability—First by Penn Central; Then by Conrail." *ICC Practitioners' Journal* (May–June 1982):374–394.

Levin, R. C. "Railroad Rates, Profitability, and Welfare under Deregulation." *Bell Journal of Economics* 12, no. 1 (Spring 1981):1–26.

Levine, Harvey A.; Eby, Clifford C.; Rockey, Craig F.; and Dale, John L. *Small Railroads.* Washington, D.C.: Association of American Railroads, 1982.

Lieb, Robert C. "Intermodal Ownership: The Perspective of Railroad Chief Executives." *Transportation Journal* 21, no. 3 (Spring 1982):70–75.

McCaffrey, R. Lawrence, Jr., and Gilbertson, Peter A. *Starting A Short Line.* United States: McCaffrey and Lawrence, 1983.

Oman, Gary A., and Walker, Larry D. "Reactivating Profitable Segments of a Bankrupt Railroad." *The Logistics and Transportation Review* 17, no. 4 (1981):387–401.

Roberts, Merril J. "Railroad Maximum Rate and Discrimination Control." *Transportation Journal* 22, no. 3 (Spring 1983):23–33.

Thuong, Le T. "Lessons for Amtrak and Conrail from Railroads in the United Kingdom and France."

Transportation Quarterly 36, no. 3 (July 1982):391–406.

Warren, William R. "The Unit Train and the Development of Low Sulfur Coal Resources in the Western Interior Region." *Transportation Journal* 18, no. 4 (Summer 1979):53–63.

Wilner, Frank N. "History and Evolution of Railroad Land Grants." *ICC Practitioners' Journal* (September–October 1981):687–699.

Wilson, George W. "Regulation, Public Policy, and Efficient Provision of Freight Transportation." *Transportation Journal* 15, no. 1 (Fall 1975):5–20.

Freight Railroad Management Issues

6

Like all industries, the freight railroad business is exposed to its own set of opportunities and risks. Success or failure of individual carriers depends on management's ability to understand key issues and make wise decisions. This chapter concentrates on operating, marketing, labor, and safety issues—four decision areas of considerable relevance to freight railroads.

OPERATING ISSUES

Almost everyone knows that trains are locomotives and cars linked into long units that roll on steel wheels over steel rails. Few, however, seem to understand some common elements of railroading, such as who owns the rights-of-way, who can use the tracks, why cars in a train show different company logos, who is the boss of a train crew, or even why trains traditionally have had cabooses. This section explains the basics of *freight railroad operations*—the area of carrier management responsible for the physical movement of cargo.

Operating Organizations and Functions

Freight railroad operations are important to corporate success. Operating departments usually employ about half of all railroad workers, and they also have traditionally been the source from which senior company executives have been drawn.

143

FIGURE 6.1.

Freight railroad operating functions.

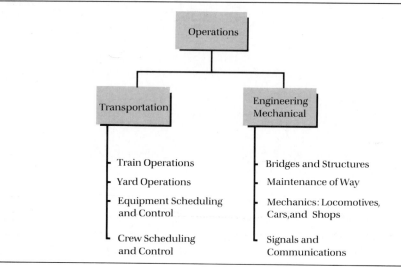

Operating activities can be collectively divided into transportation functions and engineering/mechanical duties (Fig 6.1). Transportation managers are responsible for train operations, yard operations, equipment scheduling and control, and crew scheduling and control. Engineering/mechanical managers supervise the construction of bridges and structures, maintaining the rights-of-way (the roadbed), and all mechanical functions, such as repairing and servicing locomotives and railroad cars and operating the shops. They also handle all signal and communications responsibilities.

Routes

The main components of railroading are routes, yards, and vehicles. First, railroads own their rights-of-way, which means the tracks and roadbed over which trains operate. This situation is different from trucking and water transportation, where roads and waterways are publicly owned. Consequently, the use of rail trackage is restricted to the owner railroad unless the owner has signed a trackage agreement with other railroads allowing them to operate trains over the tracks for a fee or shared costs. Jointly owned tracks, where two or more railroads share costs, are also common occurrences. Why, then, can freight trains be seen hauling cars belonging to numerous railroads? The answer is interlining, a long-standing operating practice whereby cars of one railroad are passed on to connecting carriers all the way to destination.

standard gauge track   U.S. railroads can interline because of standardization. Couplers that hook cars together, brakes, and tracks match defined standards. Rails, for instance, are 4 ft $8\frac{1}{2}$ in. apart as measured from the inside of one rail to the inside of the second. Without standard gauge, at the junction of two railroads, cars would have to be emptied and then the cargo would have to be reloaded onto the second railroad's cars, as is the normal practice when trucking companies interline freight. The origin of standard gauge track can be traced to President Abraham Lincoln, who signed an act in 1863 fixing the gauge at 4 ft $8\frac{1}{2}$ in. on the Pacific Railroad. In 1897 the American Railway Association, predecessor of the Association of American Railroads, officially accepted this measure as the standard for the nation.

shipper sidings

Although railroads own their rights-of-way, to use the system, shippers usually need rail sidings. These sidings are railroad spurs or tracks that link plants and warehouses to the railroad network and permit rail car loading or unloading at the shipper's facility. Usually they are owned by rail shippers or consignees. The use of trucking equipment in conjunction with piggyback rail service is one way to eliminate the necessity for siding.

miles of railroad lines and tracks

types of railroads

Class I railroads owned 151,998 miles of railroad lines in 1984 and 255,748 miles of tracks including multiple (parallel) main tracks, yard tracks, and sidings.[1] Approximately 96,000 miles of the railroad lines (63%) were owned by just four linehaul railroad companies (Burlington Northern Railroad, CSX Corporation, Union Pacific System, and Norfolk Southern Corporation). A *linehaul railroad* is a company that hauls freight over long distances. Class I railroads are linehaul carriers. Short-line railroads, however, typically are either *bridge lines* (i.e., those that connect two or more other railroads), *originating* and/or *terminating railroads* (i.e., those that pick up loaded rail cars at a shipper's dock and feed them to linehaul railroads or reverse the process delivering cars that come from linehaul railroads), or *terminal* and *switching companies*, which tend to serve metropolitan areas transferring cars between connecting railroads and providing car pick-up and delivery services to shippers. Short-line railroads usually own few miles of track, as noted in Chapter 5.

linehaul operations

Linehaul operations, because they constitute the longer haul movements between cities, generate most of the industry's revenues. Because of their importance, linehaul routes therefore tend to be the best maintained parts of the route system, since approximately 67% of railroad ton-miles are derived from less than 20% of the route mileage.[2] Because only 33% of the traffic derives from more than 80% of the system, railroads tend to abandon the weaker network links. Revenues from these lines are often too minimal to support capital investments.

mainlines and branch lines

Rail lines are divided into mainlines and branch lines based on track usage criteria such as annual tons or cars rolling over a section of track. Branch lines may carry only a few cars each day. By comparison, the busiest tracks, called "A mainlines," might move in excess of 20 million gross tons of cargo and equipment weight per year. Over these mainlines and branch lines, most trains operate in both directions over a single pair of rails. For two trains to pass each other, one must pull off on a siding, a short section of parallel track, and wait for the other to clear the area.

Railroad transportation managers make decisions that strive to balance

transportation decisions

economic efficiencies with service needs. Types of choices include setting train schedules, choosing train routings, determining which trains go on sidings to let others pass, establishing the need for interlining, and deciding which yards trains will enter for car sorting and other purposes. Rising train crew costs and fuel expenditures have encouraged transportation managers to seek improved train productivity. Thus, between 1973 and 1984, the average number of cars per freight train increased from 66.6 to 71.5 (7.4%), the average tons of freight per train load improved from 1844 to 2543 (37.9%), and revenue ton-miles per gallon of fuel increased from 210 to 275 (31.0%). One factor influencing these outcomes was an improvement in the average number of tons carried per car from a 1973 level of 56.7 to 68.2 (20.3%), a phenomenon made possible in part by management's decision to purchase larger rail cars.[3] Productivity also increased through the use of *unit trains*—that is, dedicated sets of locomotives and cars typically hauling one commodity from one origin to one destination and bypassing freight yards. Unit trains improve average train speeds, enabling each car to haul more carloads in a year (see photos, Figs. 2.2 and 5.1).

computers and Centralized Traffic Control

To facilitate train operations and improve safety, linehaul railroads have been installing Centralized Traffic Control (CTC) systems, which have computers that permit an individual operator to control switches and signals many miles away. Computers automatically figure and execute "meets" and "passes" allowing approaching trains operating on a single pair of rails to pass one another safely. CTC increases the capacity of a single pair of mainline rails by 60%.[4]

Railroad safety and efficiency are also primary responsibilities of engineering personnel within the operating department. These individuals design, construct, and maintain bridges, tunnels, and rights-of-way.

track structure

The typical track structure includes steel rails fastened to wooden crossties buried in crushed rock, called ballast, which in turn rests on subgrade dirt. After years of using rail in pieces 39-ft long, most railroads now lay 1500-ft sections of continuous welded rail. These sections are subsequently welded together while on the roadbed to provide a smoother ride with less wear and tear on equipment and tracks. Crossties act as buffers between rail and ballast and hold the tracks in place. Although some carriers now use concrete crossties, wood is the norm. Ballast materials must resist wear, be able to interlock to hold ties in place, and drain well. Failure to do the latter can result in fouling the roadbed with dirt and losing some of the ballast's load-spreading properties. In addition, when soggy ballast freezes, it causes higher rail stress.

Yards

Freight yards, which comprise the second major component of railroading, serve the dual functions of sorting and repairing cars. Figure 6.2 is a view from inside the control tower of Norfolk Southern Corporation's computerized classification yard in Sheffield, Alabama. Modern classification yards like the Sheffield facility use computers to classify cars (i.e., take apart incoming

FIGURE 6.2.

Highly computerized freight classification yard, Sheffield, Alabama—One of Norfolk Southern's two highly computerized Southern Railway classification yards shows the yard conductor, Paul Rice, what is happening and what to expect. Rice observes the operation of cars being classified on the top television screen, while the second screen provides him with information on the next 10 cars to be classified. The freight classification yard's computer is tied to the Management Information Services computer in Atlanta, as is the newer freight classification yard, also most highly computerized, at Linwood, N.C. It is known as Spencer Yard. The Sheffield yard can handle as many as 2400 cars a day, while Spencer can handle slightly more. Computer-fed information that reaches the yard hours before the cars arrive can tell the operators where the cars are coming from and to what area they are to be forwarded. This information increases efficiency, while easing recordkeeping chores. (Photo courtesy of Norfolk Southern Corporation)

trains and put together outgoing trains). Prior to a train's arrival at the Sheffield yard, Norfolk Southern's Management Information Services computer center in Atlanta sends information and instructions for classifying the train to one of the control computers in Sheffield. When the incoming train reaches Sheffield, cars are moved over a hump—a small hill where freight cars are uncoupled at the crest—and then they roll at computer-controlled speeds through computer-controlled switches onto computer-assigned tracks (see Fig. 6.3).

classifying cars

A master retarder (shown in Fig. 6.3 between the first and second tank cars) and group retarders (not shown) clamp onto a car's wheels to maintain slow speeds. These retarders minimize damage to cargo when a car recouples with other cars on the classification tracks (Fig. 6.2). Groups of cars, coupled on one of the Sheffield yard's 32 classification tracks, form what is termed a *block*. At the appropriate time, several blocks of cars going to common destinations are pulled to the adjacent forwarding yard and coupled together and to locomotives and usually to a caboose. Today, some cabooses have been elim-

FIGURE 6.3.
Humping cars by computer—Southern Railway's highly automated classification hump yard at Sheffield, Alabama, has a computer housed in its tower, shown here behind one of the entering tank cars it controls automatically. This car, followed by other tank cars, was retarded (slowed) automatically as the others following it will be. The car in the foreground is just coming off the master retarder. (Photo courtesy of Norfolk Southern Corporation)

inated for economic reasons. Then, the entire outgoing train is dispatched to another classification yard.

comparison to truck terminal functions

Modern computerized yards can classify up to 5000 cars per 24-hour day. Their functions are similar to those of breakbulk trucking terminals, such as receiving, sorting, consolidating, and shipping, but with one exception: Railroads process cars, while trucking companies tend to sort shipments. The cargo in railroad cars is not removed from one car and placed in another vehicle.[5]

A second major function performed at freight yards is car maintenance and repair. Yards contain repair shops, tools, materials, and personnel capable of correcting both minor and more serious car repair problems. Regardless of who owns a mechanically deficient or dangerous car, industry practice is for the car to be repaired immediately. All railroads do this service for each other and subsequently bill the car owner for repair costs.

Vehicles

locomotives

Vehicles—locomotives and cars—comprise a third major component of railroading. At the close of 1984, Class I railroads had 24,506 locomotives in service, and all except 63 of these locomotives were diesel-electric units. Diesel-electric locomotives burn diesel fuel for power and electrical generation for onboard systems. The remaining locomotives included 61 electric units, which are locomotives powered by externally generated electricity, and 2 steam locomotives.[6] Rail locomotives are purchased primarily from two U.S. producers, General Motors and General Electric, with two needs in mind—horsepower and tractive force (i.e., the ability to pull cars from resting positions). Different types of locomotives are purchased for different tasks, such as road (linehaul) or switching duties. Larger locomotives (2400–3600 horsepower) are preferred for linehaul services; 600–1500 horsepower units perform most yard-switching functions. A new road locomotive costs more than $1 million.

elimination of roundhouses

A relatively unique feature of locomotives is their ability to run as fast in reverse as in forward gears. This capability, together with the linking of locomotives usually into sets of three units with the first and third units facing in opposite directions, virtually eliminated the need for roundhouses. Previously, roundhouses were needed to turn locomotives around at destination to face the opposite direction. Now, locomotive engineers merely walk to the opposite end of the set of three units and operate trains from the cab of the last locomotive.

locomotive technology

Locomotive technology is focusing primarily on ways to reduce fuel costs. General Motors Corporation's Electric-Motive Division in 1984 unveiled its SD-60 locomotive, which is supposed to be 14% more fuel efficient than the previous 50 series model. General Electric Company's Dash 8 locomotive has been found to be 17% more fuel efficient than GE units produced in 1978.[7] Preliminary work has also been done on the development of new generation coal-fired steam locomotives that would be more powerful and have longer service lives than today's diesel-electric locomotives. It is anticipated that steam locomotives could operate at 70 mph for a range of 15 hours and 1000 miles at full throttle without exposing ash (soot) to the atmosphere. In other words, they would meet comparable diesel-electric capabilities. Norfolk Southern has expressed an interest in coal-burning development.[8] However, reduced petroleum prices have lessened the incentive for coal-fired locomotive development.

numbers and types of cars

Cars.   The 1,486,282 freight cars in service in the U.S. railroad industry at the end of 1984, as can be seen in Table 6.1, include various types. *Box cars* had the highest frequency, although the 308,252 figure was 86,923 below the 1981 level. Box cars, however, are rapidly becoming less attractive equipment investments. Just about any commodity that can be hauled in a box car can also be hauled in a truck, and it is difficult for box cars to compete with trucks on either a price or service basis. Railroads have been marketing piggyback, not box car, services, as the best way to compete for the general commodity (packaged freight) traffic, and piggyback uses railroad flat cars.

hoppers, gondolas, and cabooses

Hoppers are vehicles loaded from the top and unloaded from the bottom. Covered hoppers carry primarily grain protected from the weather by permanent car tops with hatches; open hoppers have no covers and carry coal and other minerals insensitive to weather. *Gondolas,* which are rail cars with

TABLE 6.1. Freight car statistics (1984)

Type	Total	Ownership		
		Class I railroads	Other railroads	Car companies and shippers
Box cars	308,252	245,154	47,778	15,320
Covered hoppers	302,522	159,686	11,415	131,421
Flat cars	142,046	85,191	4,697	52,158
Refrigerated cars	58,619	45,866	3,412	9,341
Gondolas	163,663	122,555	9,817	31,291
Hoppers	303,339	269,430	10,452	23,457
Tank cars	182,661	1,695	66	180,900
Others	25,180	18,594	3,372	3,214
	1,486,282	948,171	91,009	447,102

Source: Association of American Railroads, *Railroad Facts 1985 Edition* (Washington, D.C.: AAR, August 1985), p. 47. (Adapted with permission.)

a flat platform and sides 3 ft to 5 ft high, carry heavy items needing top loading. *Cabooses* are not included in the freight car totals, because they primarily serve as offices for train conductors. Conductors, not engineers, are in charge of trains.

car ownership   Table 6.1 further reveals that 948,171 of the freight cars were owned by Class I railroads, 91,009 belonged to non-Class I railroads, and 447,102 were the property of car companies and shippers. An example of a car company is Trailer Train Company of Chicago, an owner of more than 50,000 piggyback flat cars. Fruit Growers Express Company, an owner of refrigerated cars, is another example.

shipper-owned cars   Shippers own large numbers of tank cars and covered hopper cars. Why they buy them, rather than rely on railroad-owned cars, often is to ensure that they have specialized vehicles available when they need them. Car demand can fluctuate considerably from month to month. When grain is ready for harvest, for example, shippers must have cars available to move crops to market.

demurrage   The owners of railroad cars desire productive use of their vehicles. The system of payments called demurrage and per diem aims at improving car efficiency. Railroad customers are responsible for loading and unloading of cars delivered to their facilities, and normally they have only one or two days of free time—periods not subject to charges—to take care of their loading/unloading responsibilities. Beyond this free time, *demurrage*, a freight car charge levied on shippers who hold cars beyond an acceptable loading or unloading time, is assessed.

per diem   In *per diem*, a second form of car rent, the fee is levied on railroads who use cars owned by other railroads. For example, Conrail would pay per diem on an Illinois Central Gulf Railroad car it was using. Per diem encourages user railroads to return cars to their owners or produce income, per diem, for car owners who cannot use their own cars while they are in some other carrier's control.

excess capacity In 1984, Class I railroads generated 26.4 billion freight car-miles (A *car-mile* is the movement of a car one mile), but only 57.0% of those car-miles was made by loaded cars.[9] Freight railroads have a serious excess capacity problem. Too many cars are being deadheaded or returned empty to their owners to minimize per diem payments. One logical answer is to reduce car supply, which railroads have been doing since 1929 by eliminating 1,124,380 cars (43%).[10] Simultaneously, they have been able to accommodate rising traffic demand levels by increasing average car capacities from 46.3 tons to 83.3 tons. For instance, new cars added to the fleet in 1983 had an average capacity of 96 tons.[11] Still, reducing capacity has been difficult because of public demands that railroads, as common carriers, have equipment available when needed.

Nevertheless, the recent formation of super railroads should help the excess capacity problem by allowing railroads to reduce the number of cars they own of a particular type, yet still retain a large enough corporate pool of vehicles that can be dispatched quickly to high demand locations. Furthermore, there will be less interlining, since individual carrier systems cover much broader geographic regions, and less need to return empty cars to their owners to avoid per diem payments. Thus railroads will be using their own cars more frequently.

Illustration of Car Movement

To show some of the realities of railroad operations, this section documents an actual movement of a shipper-owned, loaded car from Harrisburg, Pennsylvania, to Fresno, California. Table 6.2 lists the trip particulars, and Fig. 6.4 maps the actual route followed. According to the car's owner, the illustrated trip was representative of car movements between Harrisburg and Fresno.

four interlining railroads As noted in Table 6.2 and Fig. 6.4, four railroads participated in the cross-country routing. Conrail moved the car 890 miles from Harrisburg through Pittsburgh and Indianapolis to East St. Louis, Illinois. At this point, the car was delivered to the Alton & Southern Railway Company (A&S), a terminal and switching company connecting 13 railroads in the metropolitan St. Louis area. The A&S transported the car four miles from the Conway East Yard to the St. Louis Southwestern Railway Company (SLSW) yard. From that point the SLSW hauled the car southwestward through Arkansas to Corsicana, Texas, where the Southern Pacific's (SP) tracks officially begin. Subsequently, the SP routing passed through such cities as San Antonio, El Paso, Tucson, Yuma, and W. Colton (east of the Los Angeles metropolitan area), then northerly through Bakersfield to Fresno.

trip distance and time The entire trip was 3615 miles in length and took 225 hours (9 days, 9 hours) from the time the car departed the Enola yard near Harrisburg to the Fresno yard. Actual door-to-door time from the consignor's dock to the consignee's siding was longer. Typically, it takes 1–2 days for transfers from the shipper's siding to the originating yard and an equal time at destination for

TABLE 6.2. Trip events: loaded car movement Harrisburg, Pennsylvania to Fresno, California (1982)

Railroad Name	Closest City	Action	Date	Hour	Road Hours	Delay Hours
Conrail (CR)	Harrisburg, Pa.	departed	10/15	7 A.M.	—	—
CR	Altoona, Pa.	arrived	10/15	12 A.M.	5	—
CR	Altoona, Pa.	departed	10/15	1 P.M.	—	1
CR	Pittsburgh, Pa.	arrived	10/15	9 P.M.	8	—
CR	Pittsburgh, Pa.	departed	10/16	3 P.M.	—	18
CR	Marion, Ohio	passing	10/16	9 P.M.	6	—
CR	Indianapolis, Ind.	arrived	10/17	2 A.M.	5	—
CR	Indianapolis, Ind.	departed	10/17	3 A.M.	—	1
Alton & Southern	East St. Louis, Ill.	junction de-livered[a]	10/17	11 A.M.	8	—
St. Louis South-western (SLSW)	East St. Louis, Ill.	junction re-ceived[a]	10/18	3 A.M.	—	16
SLSW	Pine Bluff, Ark.	arrived	10/18	8 P.M.	17	—
SLSW	Pine Bluff, Ark.	departed	10/20	8 A.M.	—	36
Southern Pacific (SP)	Corsicana, Tex.	passing	10/21	n/a	—	—
SP	San Antonio, Tex.	passing	10/21	11 A.M.	27	—
SP	El Paso, Tex.	passing	10/22	8 A.M.	21	—
SP	Yuma, Ariz.	passing	10/23	n/a	—	—
SP	West Colton, Calif.	passing	10/23	10 A.M.	26	—
SP	Bakersfield, Calif.	arrived	10/23	7 P.M.	9	—
SP	Bakersfield, Calif.	departed	10/24	10 A.M.	—	15
SP	Fresno, Calif.	arrived	10/24	4 P.M.	6	—
				TOTAL ROAD HOURS	138	—
				TOTAL DELAY HOURS	—	87
				TOTAL TRIP HOURS	225	

[a]Place where one railroad transfers a car to another.

Source: Records from a company that wishes, for competitive reasons, to remain anonymous. (Adapted with permission.)

transfers from the yard to the consignee's facility. As noted in Table 6.2, the road time (i.e., linehaul time) was 138 hours. Delays added another 87 hours; in other words, 39% of the time, the car was basically stationary. Collectively, average trip speed was 16 mph; excluding delay hours, road speed averaged 26 mph.

train speed

circuitry

This example reveals some basic characteristics of railroading. First, rail routings can be quite circuitous; for instance, the highway distance from Harrisburg to Fresno is 2735 miles. Circuitry may be due to shipper routing instructions on the bill of lading. Quite often, however, it is caused by natural barriers like mountains, operating authority limitations (a railroad cannot go

FIGURE 6.4.
Route map of loaded car movement from Harrisburg, Pennsylvania, to Fresno, California.

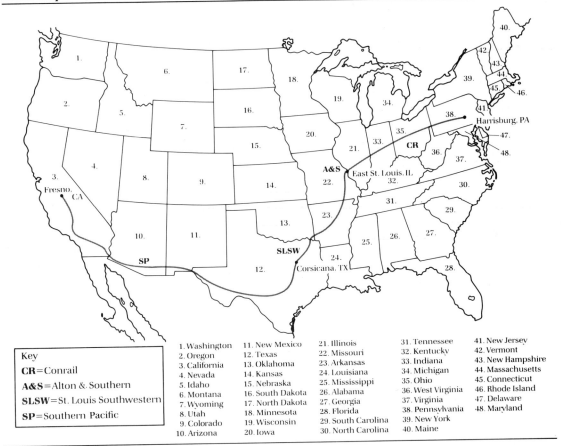

Key
CR=Conrail
A&S=Alton & Southern
SLSW=St. Louis Southwestern
SP=Southern Pacific

1. Washington	11. New Mexico	21. Illinois	31. Tennessee	41. New Jersey
2. Oregon	12. Texas	22. Arkansas	32. Kentucky	42. Vermont
3. California	13. Oklahoma	23. Arkansas	33. Indiana	43. New Hampshire
4. Nevada	14. Kansas	24. Louisiana	34. Michigan	44. Massachusetts
5. Idaho	15. Nebraska	25. Mississippi	35. Ohio	45. Connecticut
6. Montana	16. South Dakota	26. Alabama	36. West Virginia	46. Rhode Island
7. Wyoming	17. North Dakota	27. Georgia	37. Virginia	47. Delaware
8. Utah	18. Minnesota	28. Florida	38. Pennsylvania	48. Maryland
9. Colorado	19. Wisconsin	29. South Carolina	39. New York	
10. Arizona	20. Iowa	30. North Carolina	40. Maine	

where its tracks do not go), operating choices (e.g., an operating decision to classify cars at a certain yard can cause cars to be routed extra miles to get them there), and regulations. (The Federal Railroad Administration can prescribe routings for hazardous materials.) Since extra car-miles cost money, railroads won't usually make money if costs are for a 3615-mile trip and rates are set at a level low enough to compete with a railroad competitor or trucker traveling only 3000 miles.

A second conclusion is that train speeds are slow, which may not be a critical decision factor for a shipper, but it might be. Customers might either change carriers or abandon the rail mode entirely. Speed certainly has been a factor in the growth of trucking, a mode that even over long hauls is frequently faster than rail. Railroads, then, must strive for greater train speeds to improve their marketability and their productivity. If railroads could keep

slow speeds

loaded cars moving, they would need fewer cars to handle the same number of ton-miles. Car delays need to be reduced to improve train speeds.

common
control advantages Finally, the St. Louis Southwestern is a subsidiary of Southern Pacific. Common control permits preblocking of cars—grouping cars at one yard for a distant yard—and run-through trains—trains that pass by, not through, yards or junction points between interlining railroads. Both reduce yard delays.

MARKETING ISSUES

Until the 1980s, railroads lagged far behind most business sectors in marketing sophistication. Previously, marketing primarily consisted of traffic departments setting prices and sales departments making sales calls to prospective and regular customers. Then, the marketing concept meant little, and sizeable deficiencies existed in the areas of market research, promotion, and coordinated marketing mix plans. Now, this situation has changed. Markets are being better researched, segmented, and targeted; furthermore, marketing management is being given more decision-making power to determine customer needs and to obtain operating department assistance in meeting shippers' service expectations.

Traffic Statistics

During 1984, Class I railroads originated 1.429 billion tons and hauled 921.5 billion ton-miles of freight traffic. The tonnage figure was 10.5% greater than the 1983 level (1.293 billion), but 4.9% below the 1979 figure (1.502 billion tons). The 1984 ton-mile figure set an all-time traffic record and was 11.3% higher than the 828.3 billion ton-miles carried in 1983.[12] Traffic growth reflects a stronger U.S. economy and heavy coal traffic as shippers stockpiled coal in anticipation of a fall strike by coal miners.

revenue carloadings Table 6.3 shows trends in revenue carloadings by commodity group. During 1984, the largest percentages in carload gains were as follows: a 16.8% increase in crushed stone, gravel, and sand; a 16.5% rise in motor vehicles and equipment, primarily new automobiles and parts; and a 15.0% improvement in waste and scrap materials. The most noteworthy increase came in coal, with an additional 709,000 carloadings—a 13.6% increase. Table 6.3 vividly shows that railroads have almost totally removed themselves from LCL traffic, since 1984 LCL carloadings amounted to only 11,000, which is not even $\frac{1}{10}$ of 1% of the industry carload total. Freight railroading is clearly a carload business.

leading commodities Railroad marketing today is directed at key commodities, and as depicted in Table 6.4, for good reason. Coal, by far, is the leading commodity both in terms of tons originated (566,647,000 tons and 39.7% of the total) and revenues ($6.965 billion and 23.3% of all revenues). Farm products, nonmetallic minerals, and chemicals and allied products are also important traffic gen-

TABLE 6.3. Revenue carloadings by major commodity groups (1983 and 1984)

Commodity Group	Carloadings (in thousands)		Percentage Change
	1983	1984	
Coal	5,210	5,919	13.6%
Grain	1,379	1,417	2.8
Chemicals and allied products	1,199	1,272	6.1
Motor vehicles and equipment	867	1,010	16.5
Metallic ores	823	850	3.4
Pulp, paper, and allied products	777	763	(1.8)
Primary forest products	738	697	(5.5)
Food and kindred products	610	560	(8.2)
Grain mill products	592	548	(7.5)
Nonmetallic minerals	589	608	3.9
Stone, clay, and glass products	531	560	5.6
Crushed stone, gravel, and sand	503	588	16.8
Forwarder and shipper association traffic	433	386	(10.9)
Metals and products	433	475	9.7
Waste and scrap materials	420	483	15.0
Lumber and wood products, except furniture	367	373	1.8
Coke	261	265	1.2
Petroleum products	239	248	3.6
Other farm products	207	209	0.8
All other carloads	2,625	3,005	14.4
LCL traffic	13	11	(13.9)
TOTAL LOADED CARS	18,815	20,249	7.6%

Source: Association of American Railroads, *Railroad Facts 1985 Edition* (Washington, D.C.: AAR, August 1985), p. 25. (Adapted with permission.)

erators. In terms of revenues, the leading commodities in 1984, after coal, were chemicals and allied products (11.3%), transportation equipment (9.6%), and farm products (8.3%). Transportation equipment, while responsible for only 1.8% of the tonnage, contributed an impressive 9.6% of the revenues, which reflects high yields. The opposite case is metallic ores, a low-yielding freight with 6.0% of the tonnage, but only 1.9% of the industry's revenues.

Marketing Organizations

Because of the traffic and revenue potential of the key commodities shown in Table 6.4, many railroads have reorganized their marketing departments to cater to the needs of specialized customer groups. Burlington Northern Railroad Company, for instance, in 1982 listed marketing positions of Senior

TABLE 6.4. Tons originated and revenues, Class I railroads, by commodity (1984)

Commodity	Tons Originated		Revenues	
	Tons (in thousands)	Percentage of total	($ millions)	Percentage of total
Coal	566,647	39.7%	$6,965	23.3%
Farm products	151,128	10.6	2,483	8.3
Nonmetallic minerals	108,188	7.6	997	3.3
Chemicals and allied products	107,424	7.5	3,360	11.3
Metallic ores	85,503	6.0	567	1.9
Food and kindred products	72,058	5.0	2,309	7.7
Lumber and wood products	69,823	4.9	1,611	5.4
Stone, clay, and glass products	44,745	3.2	1,024	3.4
Pulp, paper, and allied products	37,654	2.7	1,762	5.9
Primary metal products	36,130	2.5	955	3.2
Petroleum and coal products	35,301	2.4	913	3.1
Waste and scrap materials	28,803	2.0	496	1.7
Transportation equipment	26,134	1.8	2,859	9.6
Subtotal	1,369,538	95.9%	$26,301	88.1%
All others	59,850	4.1	3,565	11.9
TOTAL	1,429,388	100.0%	$29,866	100.0%

Source: Association of American Railroads, *Railroad Facts 1985 Edition* (Washington, D.C.: AAR, August 1985), p. 28. (Adapted with permission.)

Assistant Vice-president, Marketing–Grain; Senior Assistant Vice-president, Marketing–Forest Products; Senior Assistant Vice-president, Marketing–Intermodal; and Senior Assistant Vice-president, Marketing–Food and Manufactured Products. Organizational structures, such as the Burlington Northern's, help decision makers recognize when customers need service and price adjustments.

Coal

Coal, at the Burlington Northern, is so important that it has been assigned its own department—the Coal and Taconite Business Unit—to coordinate equipment and service planning, pricing, and economics and research.[13] Coal is also important at the CSX Corporation, Norfolk and Southern, and Conrail. Railroads are well suited for hauling high volumes of coal over great distances. In 1983, approximately 63% of all the coal produced in the United States (i.e., 494 million tons of the total of nearly 780 million tons) was moved by railroads. When oil prices were escalating, railroads saw an excellent opportunity for coal traffic, revenue, and income growth, especially since coal could be substituted for oil in generating electricity. Furthermore, the United States had huge coal reserves, and the railroads were in the primary position to haul coal to market. Therefore railroads invested billions buying open hopper cars and locomotives and improving rights-of-way to carry coal to markets.

traffic trends

Although railroad coal demand has increased from 1977, a substantial coal boom has not materialized. The railroad industry loaded 1,206,000 more cars with coal in 1984 (5,919,000) than in 1977 (4,713,000); however, as previously explained, much of the 13.6% increase in coal carloadings during 1984 versus 1983 was the result of stockpiling. Coal shipments declined in the first half of 1985 as shippers reduced coal inventories. Even though industry analysts forecast continued increases in U.S. coal production,[14] coal traffic growth projections have moderated.

market segments

The coal market can be segmented into domestic and export markets and by product-end use. In 1983, more than 700 million tons of the 780 million tons produced in the United States were sold domestically.[15] The export market was estimated that year at 74 million tons, which was far below the 1981 record of 110 million.[16] Coal is also segmented by end use—steam coal, burned to generate steam used in creating electricity as well as industrial process heat, and metallurgical coal, a higher quality coal used to make coke, an ingredient in steel production. Railroads serve all the above market segments; however, the primary market target is electric utility plants, purchasers of 624 million tons—80% of total coal production—in 1983.[17]

reasons for coal trends

The recession and declining oil prices negatively affected domestic coal production and railroad coal traffic. The recession resulted in a reduction in industrial output, which caused a decline in the need for electricity. Lowered oil prices also made coal less attractive since coal was no longer needed as a substitute for fuel oil. U.S. coal exports, moreover, were reduced because of a worldwide recession; heavy competition from other exporting nations like South Africa, Australia, and Poland; and a strong dollar, which had the relative effect of raising U.S. coal prices compared to other export coal prices. Escalating railroad freight rates made possible by pricing freedoms under the Staggers Rail Act of 1980 were likewise blamed for coal demand problems. The main complaint of shippers was that railroads were abusing captive coal customers, who were served by only one railroad operating the entire route from mine mouth to coal customer or port.[18]

railroad coal prices

Railroads have strongly denied price gouging, and U.S. Labor Department statistics show that, on average, railroad coal rates increased only 28% from 1980–1984. Under the Staggers Act, railroads were permitted automatic recovery of cost increases—26% by the ICC's estimate—and additional increases of 18% during the four years.[19] On this basis, average increases appear to be reasonable. However, the issue is not average rate increases, but captive shipper price hikes. Some railroad coal prices rose far more than 28%.

coal traffic concerns

Railroads do not want to lose coal traffic nor do they want to lose their ability to change prices to meet dynamic market conditions. They know they need coal traffic to be profitable, because it is their primary revenue source. However, shippers will probably push for more regulation if railroads continue to raise rates too rapidly. All these pressures certainly increase the risks of further railroad coal transportation investments and temper optimism about surging railroad coal traffic in the years ahead. The market is attractive but not golden.

Piggyback Services

traffic growth

Another part of the railroad business—piggyback service—has been given considerable marketing emphasis since 1980, and the results have been impressive traffic gains. In 1980, revenue cars loaded in piggyback service totaled 1,687,121. This figure increased to 1,752,479 in 1981 (+3.9%), to 1,920,377 in 1982 (+9.6%), to 2,347,530 in 1983 (+22.2%), and to 2,688,949 in 1984 (+14.5%). Piggyback traffic, with 13.3% of 1984 total industry carloadings, was second to coal in importance.[20]

reasons for piggyback growth

Recent piggyback traffic gains are attributed to aggressive marketing, improved services, low prices, and box car traffic diversion. Conrail is a good example of a railroad that has boldly and successfully pursued intermodal business. In 1983, Conrail, which hauled 16% of all the piggyback traffic in the United States, obtained about $430 million in revenues in the process. In 1984, 83% of Conrail's piggyback traffic was running on dedicated (piggyback only) trains, and management had such confidence in the reliability of its services that new customers were guaranteed delivery as promised or they would receive their money back.[21]

low prices

Another factor contributing to traffic growth was low railroad rates. According to W. C. McCormack, Seaboard System's Vice-president of Marketing and Planning, 1983 prices per piggyback trailer were just about equal to 1980 prices as a result of intense competition.[22] Primarily, the source of that competition was highway truckload carriers. Moreover, James W. Down of Temple Barker & Sloane warned railroads of the possibility that intermodal growth came from traffic that used to move in box cars. Mr. Down said that the trucking market had yet to be really penetrated.[23]

profitability problems and necessary actions

More important, piggyback traffic is producing marginal profits and low returns on investment. Although yields are unacceptable, railroads fear price increases would divert traffic to highway carriers. Accordingly, railroad management says piggyback's future resides in management's ability to reduce costs and improve productivity. Specifically, management says labor costs must be lowered and/or worker productivity raised,[24] and operating efficiencies must improve. Regarding the latter, traffic flows must be better balanced to correct backhaul deficiencies and reduce unit costs. In the deregulated environment, the future of piggyback services resides primarily with the railroads. They must become better competitors on a service and price basis. Since yields are likely to be depressed by truck competition, cost controls and productivity gains seem essential. In addition, services must continue to improve in terms of reliability and speed.

decision to wholesale or retail

Third Party Issues.   An important decision is whether railroads should wholesale or retail piggyback services. Wholesaling implies that railroads rely on surface freight forwarders, shippers' agents, and brokers—third parties—

to retail piggyback services to shippers and consignees, while railroads concentrate on linehaul flat car operations. If railroads fully retail piggyback services, they work directly with customers and obviate the need for intermediaries. Although the choice to retail intermodal services can increase railroad control and profitability, the risks are high. Third parties are routinely supplying railroads with more than 50% of their intermodal business, and in the Santa Fe's case, 80% of the traffic.[25] Third parties are primarily responsible for the past growth in piggyback carloadings. Trying to bypass third parties is risky, for intermediaries will continue to solicit freight and give their business to other railroad competitors.

role of shippers' agents

Let us look at two important groups of third parties to describe better their roles in the transportation market. *Shippers' agents,* who are also called *marriage brokers, consolidators,* or *agents,* began operations functioning as companies that would find a second trailer to accompany a first trailer being loaded on a flat car for a particular destination. Railroad piggyback rates were assigned to the flat car and not to a trailer. Hence, if the railroad rate was $500 per flat car, the charge for a single trailer was $500. Shippers' agents, by loading two trailers per car, could charge a shipper a trailer price of, for instance, $275. In effect, the shippers' agent purchased the flat car service for $500, sold space for $550, and had a profit margin of $50. By greatly reducing charges to shippers with a single trailerload, shippers' agents made intermodal services far more attractive to users. At the same time, they increased railroad traffic.

shippers' associations

Today's shippers' agents can provide door-to-door pricing, single invoice billing, cargo insurance, pick-up and delivery service, and expedited claims handling. Many own their own trailers, trucklines, and distribution and warehousing facilities, and they also perform consolidating—building their own trailerloads of less-than-truckload, small shipment, traffic. Deregulation now enables shippers' agents to negotiate with railroads for volume flat car discounts; no longer must they pay the fixed, flat car rate. Finally, some are signing agreements to become exclusive agents for particular railroads. But then they transition into a grey area between being shippers' agents and carriers' agents (The question is: To whom are they primarily responsible—shippers or carriers?), they are assigned territorial rights, and the railroads pay them guaranteed percentages of the gross revenues.[26] Shippers' agents are not to be confused with *shippers' associations,* which are intermediaries that pool small shipments of their members and tender consolidated shipments to carriers with the goal of gaining rate reductions from larger shipments. Shippers' associations use piggyback services, as well as railroad box car and trucking services.

surface freight forwarders

Surface freight forwarders are important transportation intermediaries that use piggyback services. They act between shippers and carriers, collecting smaller shipments and consolidating them into trailer, container, or box car loads. How forwarders make profits is a function of spreads—differences in rates charged to shippers for small shipments and the volume discount prices paid to rail, motor, and water carriers. Recently, the federal government decided to allow freight forwarders to enter into contracts with railroads and water carriers and to use motor contract carriage [49 *United States Code* 10703(a)(4)(E)]. This decision further enhanced the rail business derived from the forwarder group.

direct customers

Piggyback traffic is not limited to third party sources. Railroads engage in business with private trucking companies, steamship (ocean transport) lines, and for-hire motor carriers. (Steamship-related intermodal services are explained in Chapter 9 under the section, "Bridge Services.") One substantial user of piggyback services is United Parcel Service (UPS), the largest trucking company in the United States. (A discussion of UPS is found in Chapter 12.)

Technological Developments.   Piggyback equipment is changing.

larger
trailer decisions

Truck operators are now allowed to use 48-ft-long by 102-in.-wide trailers, an increase beyond the previous limits of 45 ft and 96 in. Railroad managers, as a result, must decide whether to purchase larger trailers and replace smaller trailers in an attempt to increase trucking productivity; for years, in fact, railroads have owned and supplied many shippers with truck trailers for intermodal transportation purposes. They must also realize that they cannot place two 48-ft trailers end-to-end on an 89-ft-long flat car, and industry restrictions do not allow longer cars. Therefore railroad operating equipment needs to be modified. One action they are taking is to cut superstructures from excess 50-ft box cars and convert them to flat cars, which can haul one 48-ft trailer.

advanced
designed cars

Intense pricing competition from over-the-highway trucking companies has also forced railroads to develop and deploy new technological intermodal equipment to try to reduce operating costs. Several of these innovations are described next.

RoadRailer

Figures 6.5 and 6.6 show RoadRailer equipment. RoadRailer is a highway trailer with two sets of wheels—rubber-tired wheels for highway transportation and a moveable set of flanged wheels for railroad track operations (Fig. 6.5). RoadRailer equipment obviates the need for rail flat cars because trailers are coupled together and pulled behind locomotives (Fig. 6.6). RoadRailer equipment, in Conrail service for 18 months between Buffalo and New York City, operated 16,000,000 unit (trailer) miles free from accidents and without one bad order set-out on route (a unit breakdown). Conrail said it was mechanically and operationally superb equipment. RoadRailer equipment improves fuel efficiency by 50% over standard piggyback equipment, and it reduces overall operating costs by 15% on short hauls, and 19% to 21% on hauls of 2000 miles.[27]

Ten-pack
Fuel-Foiler car

Santa Fe management had a leading role in developing a lightweight, articulated (permanently linked) flat car, called the *Ten-pack Fuel-Foiler* (Fig. 6.7). In regular service since June 1978, these 10-trailer cars logged 415,000 miles of excellent performance in the first two years of Chicago–Los Angeles service.[28] Lawrence Cena, Santa Fe's President and Chief Executive Officer, however, in 1984 said that he expected containers will eventually replace trailers in piggyback service because they reduce the costs of hauling around bogies (chassis and wheel assemblies).[29] Santa Fe, under Mr. Cena's leadership, also

A-Stack container

developed a stackable container, called the A-Stack, which has the capability

FIGURE 6.5.
RoadRailer vehicles are equipped with both rubber tires and steel railroad wheels for dual operation on highways or railroad tracks. Trailers are driven over the rails, at which time the steel wheel assemblies are lowered onto the rails. In the process, the rubber tires are lifted off the ground. (Photo courtesy of the RoadRailer Corporation)

FIGURE 6.6.
RoadRailer train. (Photo courtesy of the RoadRailer Corporation)

FIGURE 6.7.
Ten-pack Fuel-Foiler at Corwith Yard, Chicago. Each car can haul ten trailers or containers. The four ten-pack cars shown in the photo are coupled together to make up the train. (Photo courtesy of Santa Fe Railway)

of handling bulk commodities or packaged goods (Fig. 6.8). These containers, too, can be hauled on modified Ten-pack Fuel-Foiler cars.

double-stack car

Another example of stackable container equipment is the articulated double-stack car used by Southern Pacific (Fig. 6.9). As pictured, the car is a series of low platforms joined by trucks—two-axle wheel assemblies located between platforms. Containers have not been modified from conventional designs. When double-stacked, the height of the top container approximates the height of a trilevel auto-rack car. This height can present some clearance problems.

delays in
implementation

Despite vivid evidence that innovative equipment is quite capable of improving operating costs, it is not rapidly being placed in service. RoadRailer is an excellent example of the problem, for it could not make money in the Buffalo–New York traffic lane. Although RoadRailer service reduced costs compared to conventional piggyback service, it could not compete cost-wise with truckers pulling twin 48-ft trailers over the New York State Thruway. High railroad labor costs were blamed for the termination of Conrail's RoadRailer service.[30]

FIGURE 6.8.
Santa Fe's unique Fuel-Foiler containers ride close to the rail, achieving a low center of gravity compared to conventional containers. When double-stacked, two containers soar more than 19 ft above the rail. The prototype can handle either bulk commodities or packaged goods and can readily be adapted for liquids. They would be stacked aboard the rail car when empty or lightly loaded, and they can be stacked six high aboard ship or in staging areas. (Photo courtesy of Santa Fe Railway)

FIGURE 6.9.
Southern Pacific double-stack container cars. (Photo courtesy of Southern Pacific Transportation Company)

LABOR ISSUES

In the more deregulated environment, railroad modal share and corporate profitability will be closely correlated to costs per ton-mile. With wages, benefits, pensions, and payroll taxes responsible for more than 50% of total industry expenses (see Chapter 5), management cannot be expected to save much money unless it cuts labor costs or significantly improves productivity—necessary tactics in markets where intermodal competition will not allow steady yield increases.

Labor Strategies and Results

For years, railroad management has attempted to improve labor economics, and it has achieved a measure of success by substituting capital for labor. Already discussed in Chapters 5 and 6 were the purchase of larger cars and more powerful locomotives, the running of longer trains, the installation of computers and Centralized Traffic Control systems, and a 38.6% reduction in the labor force between 1972 and 1984. These and other changes have increased by 81.6% the annual number of ton-miles per worker from the 1972 level of 1,476,532 to a 1984 level of 2,681,598.[31] However, counterbalancing these productivity gains were a 178.9% rise in compensation costs per worker (see Chapter 5) and growing labor fears about job security. Unfortunately, management has made minimal progress in reducing labor costs and improving labor cooperation; thus, from its frustration, it has tried to circumvent the problem by replacing workers with machines. Attrition through not replacing retired, resigned, or deceased employees has been used extensively, as opposed to layoffs (furloughs). Railroads have improved their overall cost structures, as verified in Chapter 5, but not by enough if they expect to sell piggyback services profitably during either the short- or long-term.

Railroad Unions and Crafts

Rail workers are organized into 13 major unions, which represent one or more crafts (classes) of employees. These unions are listed in Table 6.5. Craft unionism creates several problems for management. Because there are so many unions with whom to negotiate, the bargaining process seldom ends. In addition, the picket lines of any one union usually are honored and not crossed by other labor unions. Crafts are also protective of their jurisdictional rights (job responsibilities) and will defend them not only against management, but also against other unions. Likewise, unions fight to retain arbitraries, which are special forms of treatment. For example, a major cause of the 1982 national strike was the Brotherhood of Locomotive Engineers' (BLE's) insistence that its members retain the right to strike to maintain the highest wages of any operating personnel.[32] Finally, a negotiating union expects equal or better treatment than the unions received that had previously signed agreements

```
TABLE 6.5.  Major railroad unions
```

- United Transportation Union (UTU)
- Brotherhood of Railway & Airline Clerks (BRAC)
- Brotherhood of Locomotive Engineers (BLE)
- Brotherhood of Maintenance of Way Employees
- International Association of Railway Carmen
- International Association of Machinists
- Brotherhood of Railway Signalmen
- International Brotherhood of Electrical Workers
- International Brotherhood of Firemen & Oilers
- Railroad Yardmasters of America
- International Association of Sheetmetal Workers
- American Train Dispatchers Association
- International Brotherhood of Boilermakers & Blacksmiths

with railroad management. Consequently, management's demands for labor concessions are usually met with stiff labor opposition.

Labor Negotiations

Railroad labor relations are governed not by the Taft–Hartley Act but by the Railway Labor Act. Railroads bargain nationally with the independent craft unions, and management is represented by the National Railway Labor Conference, a team of railroad industry officials. Surprisingly, rail contracts do not expire; agreements remain in force until labor or management asks for changes. When this request for change occurs, the parties negotiate. If an impass is reached, either party may request the involvement of the National Mediation Board, but the latter's powers are limited. Consequently, Congress and the president frequently become involved in settling rail strikes.[33]

Management Goals

Railroad management persists in trying to achieve the following labor goals:

- To reduce train crew sizes from the standard four-person crews (engineer, conductor, and two brakemen) to three (engineer, conductor, and brakeman) and sometimes even to two (engineer and conductor–brakeman). These are called crew consist changes.
- To change the basis for operating crew pay from the system that equates a full day's pay with 100 miles of train service to an hourly wage rate system. The present payment plan dates to 1880, when 100 miles was a full day's work. Today, trains are often capable of going 100 miles in $2\frac{1}{2}$ hours.
- To eliminate work rules that impede productivity and other efficiencies. The requirement that road (linehaul) crews transfer train control to yard

crews who switch cars in terminal areas is an example of a craft jurisdictional issue.

■ To eliminate many of the arbitraries that provide extra pay for questionable purposes. "Lonesome" payments provided to some engineers operating without firemen is one illustration.[34]

labor cooperation
and progress

Some progress toward these objectives has been made. The United Transportation Union (UTU) agreed to increase the basic miles in through-freight
service to 108 miles from 100 miles and has worked with the Union Pacific,
Missouri Pacific, Milwaukee Road, and Conrail to establish agreements to operate some trains of nearly 70 cars with three-person crews. Conrail was also
successful in 1979 in consolidating 43 separate UTU contracts into one
contract[35] and recently negotiated major wage concessions from 15 of its 16
unions.[36] Consolidating contracts has the potential to lessen strike interruptions. Normally, however, labor concessions arrive only after management has
guaranteed that compensation would not be reduced. The noted exceptions
are the Milwaukee Road and Conrail cases, where the threat of carrier demise
gave management the leverage needed to gain labor's cooperation.[37]

Florida East Coast Railway

One thought-provoking case in rail labor–management relations is the Florida
East Coast Railway (FEC) case. In 1963, the FEC accepted a strike, rather than
submit to union demands, and undertook to operate the railroad with super-
visory personnel. In a bitter labor dispute—one that witnessed more than 400
separate acts of sabotage and vandalism and more than 20 court challenges
that lasted until 1979—management succeeded. The result is one of the most
productive, modern, and profitable railroads in the country. In the process,
the 100-mile pay rule was replaced by 8-hour days, and time and a half after
8 hours; the FEC eliminated restrictions concerning road crews running in
and out of terminals; it gained the flexibility to use road and yard train crews
interchangeably; it negated crew-consist minimums, assigning workers as services required; and it created a single seniority date for all train and engine
employees, so that qualified personnel can switch jobs from one traditional
craft to another.[38] Accordingly, the FEC is envied by many carriers in the
business. It is still unionized, but it has secured many of the labor changes
others still desire.

strike risks

Why don't the other railroads take similar steps? Overall, it is not practical. First, who would relish a violent strike, which is certainly a possibility?
It is painful for management to look across a picket line, even a peaceful one,
at its workers, many of whom it respects and counts on. Secondly, the FEC
was near bankruptcy and desperate, whereas most carriers are not, because
they have other options. Thirdly, the FEC was small and somewhat isolated,
while most railroads could expect far greater competitive and political pressures to settle a strike. A final argument is that the railroad industry prefers
not to disrupt the status quo. Since all carriers face an equal labor burden,

they are on an equal competitive footing with other railroads.[39] Whatever the rationalization, the cost of success for a long strike solution would be high, whereas the cost of failure could be bankruptcy. Still, management may inevitably decide to risk a strike to become more productive and cost efficient.[40] As a contingency plan, management has been training its supervisors to operate its railroad systems and equipment.

SAFETY ISSUES

Every year from 1978 through 1983, railroad accidents, fatalities, and injuries declined; however, safety continues to be a mutual concern of management, labor, government, and the general public. During 1983, there were 42,264 railroad-related accidents and 3731 train accidents, which resulted in 1045 fatalities and 34,469 injuries.[41] The September 28, 1982, derailment of an Illinois Central Gulf train carrying hazardous materials in Livingston, Louisiana; three Burlington Northern train accidents in 1984 that claimed 10 lives; and a series of AMTRAK accidents in 1984—all provide evidence that much work still needs to be done to reduce safety hazards.[42] Particular concerns are rail-highway grade crossings, hazardous materials movements, and alcohol and drug use by railway crew members.

Grade Crossings

The leading cause of railroad-related deaths is accidents at rail-highway grade crossings, where in 1983, a total of 553 people died in 6819 accidents. For some time the federal government has been trying to reduce the dangers at the country's 400,000 crossings, and by the end of fiscal year 1986, approximately $2 billion will have been spent by federal taxpayers to make grade crossings safer. Nevertheless, as long as railroad tracks and roads cross and people continue to go around or under railroad crossing gates or try to beat freight trains through crossings, accidents and fatalities will occur. Efforts to improve safety are helping, however, as noted by a 48% reduction in grade crossing fatalities between 1978 and 1983.[43]

Hazardous Materials Movements

U.S. railroads each year transport more than 1 million carloads, about 80 million tons, and approximately 70% of all hazardous materials, excluding petroleum, in the United States; nevertheless, their safety record is comparatively good. Fewer than 10% of hazardous materials transportation incidents are railroad incidents, although hazardous materials carried include acids, chemicals, explosives, and other dangerous commodities. What concerns safety advocates, however, is the constant threat of a serious accident that could cause many people to die: for example, the rupturing of a car containing poisonous gases. Consequently, prevention of accidents is a major safety focus of both the railroad industry and the U.S. Department of Transportation. The Association of American Railroad's Hazardous Materials Bureau, comprising recognized experts in the field, serves all modes of transportation by acting as a central agency for the collection, analysis, and dissemination of information about hazardous materials. Association of American Railroad and Department of Transportation hazardous materials regulations (49 *Code of Federal Regulations* 171) cover loading, operating practices, equipment specifications, inspection of cars carrying hazardous materials, and procedures to be followed in the event of an accident.[44]

Alcohol and Drug Use

Recent publicity has focused on alcohol and drug use by railway crew members. For example, a 1978 study sanctioned by the Federal Railroad Administration (FRA) concluded that an estimated 23% of the operating employees of the seven unidentified surveyed railroads could, at that time, have been called problem drinkers.[45] This is an important, yet troublesome, finding, particularly considering the accident and hazardous goods problems previously discussed. The FRA estimated that about 30% of railroad accidents involved human error.[46]

FRA proposed rules   Because alcohol and drug use was implicated in 48 train accidents claiming 37 lives and causing more than $34 million in property damage in the last 10 years,[47] the U.S. Department of Transportation established new safety rules that prohibit railroad employees from reporting to work impaired by alcohol or drugs and using or possessing such substances while at work. The rules, which fully took effect on March 1, 1986 (although most took effect on November 1, 1985), mandate drug and alcohol testing for employees involved in major accidents, authorize toxicological testing of employees when there is reason to suspect impairment, require preemployment drug screening, require improved accident reporting by railroads, and require railroads to establish incentives for employees with alcohol or drug problems to seek help voluntarily.[48]

SUMMARY

Freight railroads were optimistic in the early 1980s that they could strengthen their market position and profitability, because of railroad deregulation and the prospects for a substantial increase in coal traffic. Thus railroads attempted to improve operating efficiencies and services in order to attract freight traffic, reduce costs, and improve productivity.

Among their operating achievements, railroads have modernized rights-of-way and yards, have improved services by doing less interlining and using more direct routings, and have improved car and train efficiencies by developing computer systems that increase the speed and accuracy of decision making. Marketing departments and activities have also been adjusted to improve services to important customer groups. Still, that early optimism has been tempered by a deep recession, disappointing coal traffic, increasing complaints about railroad rate increases, and the marginal profitability of piggyback services.

The future prosperity of freight railroads is probably linked to costs, which will determine how competitively railroads can price their services. Costs will also influence any future government decisions on whether to restore railroad economic pricing regulations. Shippers expect railroads to operate efficiently, and they will oppose price increases to cover cost excesses. To reduce costs significantly, railroads must continue to push for labor concessions, particularly for changes in archaic work rules that restrict productivity. Intermodal competition, particularly from non-unionized truckers, will suppress railroad yields, but in the absence of competition, if shippers experience rapid railroad price increases, they may demand stronger maximum rate rules.

Thus, although railroads have made progress in recent years, they must still strive for further operating and marketing improvements and substantive labor cost reductions and/or productivity gains. Furthermore, railroad safety must continue to receive considerable attention, particularly in resolving what appears to be a serious alcohol and drug abuse problem.

STUDY QUESTIONS

1. Explain why piggyback services are only marginally profitable despite exceptional traffic growth in the 1980s.

2. What is the primary safety concern regarding railroad carriage of hazardous materials? Explain how the railroad industry and the U.S. Department of Transportation try to minimize this risk.

3. Why don't railroads substantially reduce the sizes of their car fleets to lessen excess capacity problems?

4. How have railroad marketing organizations changed in recent years to better serve customers' needs?

5. Why are average railroad door-to-door train speeds usually slow, and how could railroads improve train speeds?

6. What roles do computers play in classifying freight cars?

7. Discuss how RoadRailer equipment works, how well it has performed, and what is retarding more use of this equipment.

8. According to Table 6.4, what five commodities represented the highest yielding railroad freight in 1984 in terms of dollars per ton?

ENDNOTES

1. Association of American Railroads, *Railroad Facts 1985 Edition* (Washington, D.C.: AAR, August 1985), p. 42 (hereafter cited as *Railroad Facts 1985*).

2. John H. Armstrong, *The Railroad—What It Is, What It Does* (Omaha, Nebr.: Simmons-Boardman Publishing, 1978), p. 165.

3. *Railroad Facts 1985,* pp. 35–37, 40.

4. Association of American Railroads, "Computerized Railroads: The Wave of the Present," A news release, 20 October 1983, p. 4.

5. (a) Ibid., p. 3; and (b) Southern Railway System, "Sheffield Yard: Southern's New Computerized Car Handler," a publicity release (n.d.) of the Southern Railway System, pp. 2, 5.

6. *Railroad Facts 1985,* p. 44.

7. Association of American Railroads, "Fuel-efficient Engines Unveiled at Rail Expo," *Rail News Update,* 3 October 1984, p. 2.

8. Association of American Railroads, "NS Chief Discusses Coal-burning Engine," *Rail News Update,* 5 September 1984, p. 2.

9. *Railroad Facts 1985,* p. 34.

10. Ibid., p. 46.

11. Association of American Railroads, *Railroad Facts 1984 Edition* (Washington, D.C.: AAR, October 1984), p. 48.

12. *Railroad Facts 1985,* pp. 27, 29.

13. *The Official Railway Guide: North American Freight Service Edition* (New York: National Railway Publication, July/August 1982), p. 68.

14. Association of American Railroads, "Coal and the Railroads—1984," (Washington, D.C.: AAR, Office of Information and Public Affairs, 30 August 1984), p. 4.

15. "A Banner Year Coal Finds Hard to Believe," *Business Week,* 2 July 1984, p. 32.

16. "U.S. Rail Rates for Coal Raise Tempers Abroad," *Business Week,* 21 November 1983, p. 43.

17. "A Banner Year," p. 32.

18. "U.S. Rail Rates," pp. 43–44.

19. Daniel Campbell and John Bradley, "Assault on Rail Deregulation Gains Steam," *Wall Street Journal,* 4 October 1984, p. 32.

20. *Railroad Facts 1985,* p. 26.

21. (a) Don Byrne, "Seaboard Exploring Agency Facts for Third Party Intermodal Use," *Traffic World,* 4 June 1984, p. 16; and (b) Conrail, "The Impact of Intermodal Growth on the Future of Railroads," *Conrail Update,* no. 32 (n.d.), p. 6.

22. "Piggyback Potentials and Problems Are Probed at Atlanta Conference," *Traffic World,* 23 April 1984, pp. 25–26.

23. Byrne, "Seaboard Exploring," p. 16.

24. Don Byrne, "Piggyback Seen as Rails' Future But Not with Current Work Rules," *Traffic World,* 27 August 1984, p. 18.

25. Byrne, "Seaboard Exploring," p. 15.

26. Ibid.

27. Byrne, "Piggyback," pp. 18–19.

28. Gus Welty, "Intermodal: Evolution and Revolution," *Railway Age,* 28 July 1980, p. 27.

29. Byrne, "Seaboard Exploring," p. 15.

30. Byrne, "Piggyback," pp. 18–19.

31. Computed from *Railroad Facts 1985,* pp. 29, 56.

32. "Carriers, Unions Wrap Up Negotiations," *Railway Age,* 11 October 1982, p. 8.

33. For an excellent review of this subject, see Douglas M. McCabe, "The Railroad Industry's Labor Relations Environment: Implications for Railroad Managers," *ICC Practitioners' Journal* (September–October 1982):593–608.

34. Standard and Poor's *Industry Surveys,* 2 (October 1982):R 34–35.

35. "Conrail, UTU Sign Pact Covering Crew Consist, Wages, Fringe Benefits," *Traffic World,* 25 September 1978, pp. 81–82.

36. Robert Snowdon Jones, "Crane Now Has Conrail on a Profitable Track," *The Atlanta Constitution,* 9 March 1983, p. 1–D.

37. (a) "Rail President Calls Union Contracts 'Deadweight' at NRIA Fall Meeting," *Traffic World,* 11 October 1982, p. 26; (b) "USRA's April 1 Report on Conrail Will Attack Obsolete Work Rules," *Traffic World,* 23 March 1981, pp. 20–21; and (c) Association of American Railroads, "AAR Chief Cites Rails as 'Growth Industry,'" *Rail News Update,* 7 October 1982, p. 2.

38. Luther S. Miller, "The Great Railroads' Florida East Coast: 'We Dared to be Different,'" *Railway Age,* 26 November 1979, pp. 26–30.

39. *Industry Surveys,* p. 33.

40. Don Byrne, "Railroad Management Seeking Showdown on Work Rules in This Year's Talks," *Traffic World,* 13 August 1984, pp. 20–21.

41. Association of American Railroads, "Rail Accident Statistics Hit New Lows," *Rail News Update,* 22 February 1984, p. 1.

42. See (a) "Findings on Derailment Released by NTSB; ICG Hits Conclusions," *Traffic World,* 27 June 1983, pp. 29–30; and (b) "Burlington Northern Railroad Is Subject of U.S. Safety Audit; 11 Died This Year," *Wall Street Journal,* 17 August 1984, p. 25.

43. (a) Association of American Railroads, "Rail Accident Statistics," p. 1; and (b) Association of American Railroads, "Railroad Safety Record Continues to Improve," a news release of the Of-

fice of Public Affairs, 4 January 1984, pp. 9–12 and App. A (hereafter cited as "Railroad Safety Record").

44. "Railroad Safety Record," pp. 1, 5, 6.

45. Bill Paul, "Danger Signal: Alcohol and Drug Use by Railway Crewmen Poses Threat to Safety," *Wall Street Journal,* 16 August 1983, p. 16.

46. Eric D. Lindeman, "Conrail Sale Process Is Crit-

icized by Crane at Short Line Conference," *Traffic World,* 29 October 1984, p. 19.

47. Association of American Railroads, "Education Sessions Set on Alcohol–Drug Rules," *Rail News Update,* 4 September 1985, p. 2.

48. Association of American Railroads, "DOT Sets Up Rail Drug, Alcohol Rules," *Rail News Update,* 7 August 1985, p. 1.

ADDITIONAL READINGS

Beier, Frederick J. "The Viability of Consolidated TOFC Terminals." *Transportation Quarterly* 36, no. 2 (April 1982):317–329.

——, and Frick, Stephen W. "The Limits of Piggyback: Light at the End of the Tunnel." *Transportation Journal* 17, no. 1 (Winter 1978):12–18.

Brown, Terence A. "Shippers' Associations: Operations, Trends, and Comparative Prices." *Transportation Journal* 21, no. 1 (Fall 1981):54–66.

"Burlington Northern's Fight to Repel Invaders." *Business Week,* 3 November 1980, p. 119.

Campbell, Thomas C., and Dalton, Amy. "Coal Exports: A Problem in Energy and Transportation." *Transportation Journal* 22, no. 3 (Spring 1983):34–46.

Cobert, Ronald N., Esq. "Who's Liable for What in Piggyback?" *Handling and Shipping Management,* August 1984, pp. 57–58.

Duncan, Thomas W. "Intermodal: Truckers Rethink Linehaul Operations." *Fleet Owner,* February 1983, pp. 53–55.

Felton, John Richard, and Cowen, Janna. "Economic Implications of a Freight Car Rental Market for Shippers of Agricultural Products." *Traffic Quarterly* 34, no. 3 (July 1980):473–488.

Gallagher, Patrick. "The Appeal of Shipper Co-Ops." *Handling and Shipping Management,* September 1982, pp. 74–78.

Henjum, Scott E. "Is the Road Finally Clear for Intermodal?" *Fleet Owner,* February 1983, pp. 48–53.

Keeler, Theodore E. *Railroads, Freight, and Public*

Policy. Washington, D.C.: The Brooking's Institution, 1983.

Kinnunen, Raymond M., and Janell, Paul A. "Management Control in the Railroad Industry." *Transportation Journal* 22, no. 1 (Fall 1982):4–10.

Koot, Ronald S., and Tyworth, John E. "The Determinants of Railroad Track Maintenance Expenditures: A Statistical Analysis." *Transportation Journal* 21, no. 1 (Fall 1981):24–43.

Lieb, Robert C.; Wiseman, Frederick; and Gbur, Jonathan. "Railroad Employee Attitudes: A Case Study." *Transportation Journal* 19, no. 1 (Fall 1979):62–70.

Middleton, William D. "Southern's Spencer Yard: 'It's Just a Beautiful Operation.' " *Railway Age,* 11 October 1982, pp. 14–18.

Overbey, Daniel L. *Railroads, the Free Enterprise Alternative.* Westport, Conn.: Quorum Books, 1982.

Stephenson, Frederick J., and Balk, Arnold E. "Fast Track Legislation—Public/Private Sector Roles in Harbor and Channel Deepening Projects." *ICC Practitioners' Journal* 50, no. 3 (March–April 1983):310–321.

Tyworth, John E., and Reinschmidt, Albert J. "Role of Safety and Train Speed in Track Maintenance Spending Decisions: A Case Analysis." *Traffic Quarterly* 35, no. 1 (January 1981):43–67.

Welty, Gus. "Intermodal Innovation: Still Coming on Strong." *Railway Age,* 30 March 1981, pp. 34–36.

Wyckoff, D. Daryl. *Railroad Management.* Lexington, Mass.: Lexington Books, 1976.

U.S. Intercity Passenger Train Transportation

7

Passenger train service in the United States is provided by the National Railroad Passenger Corporation (AMTRAK), the Alaska Railroad, tourist railroads, and commuter railroads. AMTRAK is a federally owned railroad, which in 1984 operated approximately 250 passenger trains per day serving 500 communities linked by a national route network of 23,356 miles.[1] AMTRAK is the only railroad providing regularly scheduled long-haul passenger train service in the lower 48 states in direct competition with airlines and interstate bus companies. On October 30, 1983, it also began operating Auto Train overnight automobile and passenger service between Lorton, Virginia, and Sanford, Florida. The only other railroad offering intercity passenger services in direct competition with for-hire airlines is the Alaska Railroad. Owned by the state of Alaska, it operates both freight and passenger service over a route connecting Anchorage and Fairbanks.

Other forms of passenger railroads operated in the United States are tourist railroads and commuter railroads. Tourist railroads tend to be short-line carriers operating in picturesque locations and catering to sightseers. Many, like the Durango and Silverton Narrow Gauge Railroad in Colorado, operate steam locomotives, appealing to railroad historians and hobbyists, as well as anyone wishing to see spectacular scenery. Commuter railroads either shuttle people in and out of a city or link two nearby cities. Their primary function is to move people, on a daily basis, from home to work and then home again. Examples include train service to the Boston suburbs, and trains hauling Philadelphia citizens to jobs in New York City, or vice versa. (More will be said about commuter railroads in Chapters 17 and 18.) For now, however, our focus is on intercity passenger train services provided by AMTRAK and the future of U.S. intercity passenger trains.

AMTRAK

Foreign rail systems differ significantly from those in the United States. Abroad, systems are known more for their passenger lines, which operate internationally praised high-speed trains like Japan's Shinkansen Bullet trains, France's TGV ("très grande vitesse," or very great speed), and Italy's Settebello, than for their freight operations. In fact, little is heard or printed about the foreign freight railroad business. In the United States it is just the opposite, but this was not always true. For instance, more than 20,000 passenger trains used to operate daily in the United States. To understand how popular trains once were, compare the 20,000 train figure to the approximately 15,000 daily flights flown by U.S. airlines today. In 1944, railroads captured 75.7% of the for-hire revenue passenger-mile market, but in 1984, their market share was only 4.0%.[2] Obviously, something went wrong.

demise of U.S. rail passenger service

The demise of U.S. rail passenger service began in 1926—according to ICC records, the last year the railroads made money on passengers under nonwartime conditions.[3] The development of attractive airline and automobile alternatives after World War II, in large part due to substantial government promotion and subsidy, encouraged many railroad passengers to switch modes. Declining traffic and profits then encouraged many railroads to reduce train frequency and try to abandon money-losing passenger routes. When abandonment requests were denied or delayed by federal or state officials, many carriers chose not to reinvest in passenger services, and more passengers, frustrated with deteriorating services, departed railroads for airlines and automobile transportation.[4] Only during the 1942–1945 war years, when automobiles were not built for civilian use, was there a resurgence in railroad modal share. With the war's end and the sudden availability of air and automobile transportation, consumers quickly left the railroads, and many never boarded passenger trains again.

Transportation Act of 1958

After World War II, U.S. railroads, which at the time engaged in both freight and passenger operations, experienced reduced earnings. To help alleviate capital deficiencies (shortfalls in reinvested capital), Congress enacted and President Dwight D. Eisenhower signed the Transportation Act of 1958. This law provided that the ICC could guarantee up to $500 million in public or private loans to railroads to finance capital expenditures for road and equipment or for maintenance work. Secondly, it significantly weakened state powers to prevent train discontinuances. In August 1958, there were 1448 daily intercity passenger trains in operation; by 1970, primarily due to the 1958 Act, only 300 remained.[5] Many of the railroads obligated by the ICC to continue operating those 300 trains had allowed services to slip drastically. Trains frequently failed to run on schedule, because speeds were slow due to roadbed problems, and equipment, for the most part, was old and worn out.

AMTRAK's Origin

RPSA's goals

In this depressing environment, the federal government passed the Rail Passenger Service Act of 1970 (RPSA) (PL 91-518) in order to turn the deteriorating intercity rail passenger situation around. Section 101 of the RPSA declared the intentions of Congress as follows:

> The Congress finds that modern, efficient, intercity railroad passenger service is a necessary part of a balanced transportation system; that the public convenience and necessity require the continuance and improvement of such service to provide fast and comfortable transportation between crowded urban areas and in other areas of the country; that rail passenger service can help to end the congestion on our highways and the overcrowding of airways and airports; that the traveler in America should to the maximum extent feasible have freedom to choose the mode of travel most convenient to his needs.

other RPSA provisions

Other RPSA provisions required that the federal government create a quasi-public corporation (later called AMTRAK) to own, manage, operate, or contract for the operation of a national system of intercity passenger trains. AMTRAK was to arrest the decline in railroad passenger traffic and become a profit-generating business; however, in 1978, after several years of financial losses, this last requirement was dropped.[6] A quasi-public corporation combines private and public sector control. To accomplish these tasks, interim federal financial aid was to be provided, railroads previously operating passenger trains were to be relieved of their unwanted passenger operations, and the route system was to be reduced to a basic core network. Section 306 of the RPSA gave AMTRAK management considerable freedom in rate, abandonment, and service matters. Another provision [Section 401 (c)] virtually made AMTRAK a monopoly by forbidding competition on AMTRAK's routes without AMTRAK's approval.

operations begin

On May 1, 1971, AMTRAK began operations. Of the 300 trains operating prior to that date, AMTRAK retained 186 in its national network. Railroads that previously had operated passenger trains were given the choice of transferring passenger service to AMTRAK or continuing their operations; all but three railroads transferred services to AMTRAK. The Southern; Denver & Rio Grande Western; and the Chicago, Rock Island & Pacific—all opted at the time to continue operating 10 passenger trains.[7] Eventually, they too decided to remove themselves from the passenger business, and with the transfer of passenger services from the Denver & Rio Grande Western to AMTRAK on April 24, 1983, the era of private sector long-haul passenger train services was brought to a close. All left the market because of continuing operating losses; for instance, the Denver & Rio Grande Western lost $3 million in 1982.[8]

AMTRAK's task

AMTRAK's managers faced many obstacles. A route system had to be defined that not only met the goals of the RPSA, but was also politically acceptable. Contracts had to be negotiated with each railroad that would operate AMTRAK services over its tracks. In addition, terminals and equipment had to be selected and improved. Last but not least, a disenchanted public had to be convinced to try rail services again. In short, AMTRAK was expected (1) to operate an enterprise in extensive disrepair, (2) to do so without having full control of most employees, who would still be direct employees of the freight railroads over whose tracks AMTRAK trains would operate, (3) to try to eliminate parts of the route system for efficiency reasons without angering members of Congress who wanted to retain services in their home states, and (4) to earn a profit. The task was enormous.

AMTRAK's Report Card

Although AMTRAK has made progress in many areas, profits never materialized. AMTRAK succeeded in rebuilding a core national rail passenger network (see Fig. 7.1), stopping the demise of passenger traffic, and giving U.S. intercity travelers an attractive railroad alternative.

fleet modernization

Compared to the antiquated fleet AMTRAK operated in 1972 (the average ages of cars and locomotives were 22.0 and 22.3 years, respectively), AMTRAK today has modern, attractive, and efficient equipment. By 1983, AMTRAK had completed a 10-year program to refurbish old equipment and had purchased hundreds of new cars. AMTRAK's active fleet of passenger rolling stock consisted of 1394 coach, sleeping, dining, and lounge cars; 110 self-propelled cars; 64 electric locomotives; and 214 diesel locomotives. Included in the fleet were 284 double-decker Superliner cars used on long-distance routes (Fig. 7.2) and 640 new short-haul Amfleet cars (Fig. 7.3). Examples of AMTRAK's new diesel locomotives are pictured in Figs. 7.2 and 7.4, while an AEM-7 electric locomotive is shown in Fig. 7.3.

ride quality improvements

Except for 712 miles of rights-of-way owned by AMTRAK and primarily located in the Northeast corridor between Boston and Washington, D.C., AMTRAK trains operate on rights-of-way owned by U.S. freight railroads. Therefore AMTRAK passengers have been direct beneficiaries of some of the $23.3 billion spent between 1977 and 1984 by freight railroads for improvements of their roadways, structures, and equipment (Chapter 5). Furthermore, in 1985 a $2.5 billion improvement project was scheduled to be completed upgrading the 456-mile Northeast corridor (NEC). Both efforts have made AMTRAK passenger rides smoother, quieter, and faster. NEC improvements allow AMTRAK to raise train speeds to a maximum of 120 mph and reduce running time between Washington and New York to $2\frac{1}{2}$ hours.[9]

improved services

AMTRAK successfully completed, or is in the process of completing, several other initiatives. Stations have been modernized, and AMTRAK has placed in operation one of the most technologically advanced computerized reservations systems in the travel industry. AMTRAK has also improved its marketing efforts by more aggressively advertising its services and by offering some unique travel opportunities. For example, in 1985, AMTRAK patrons were permitted to leave trains at scenic locations, pay for convenient tours

FIGURE 7.1.
AMTRAK's National Rail System.

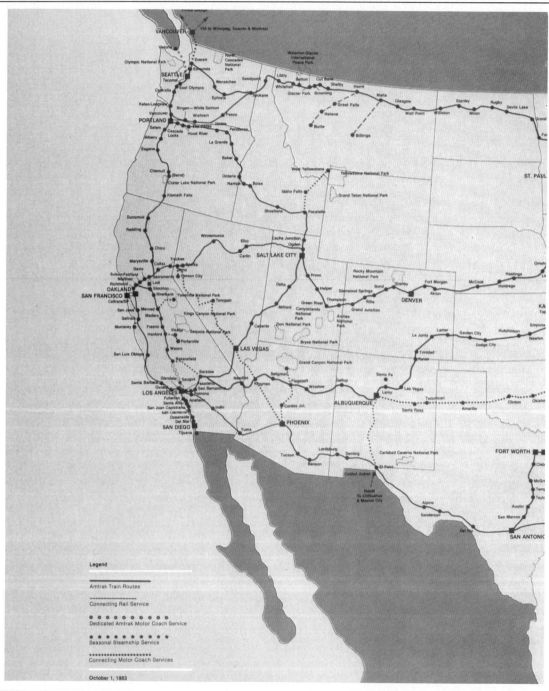

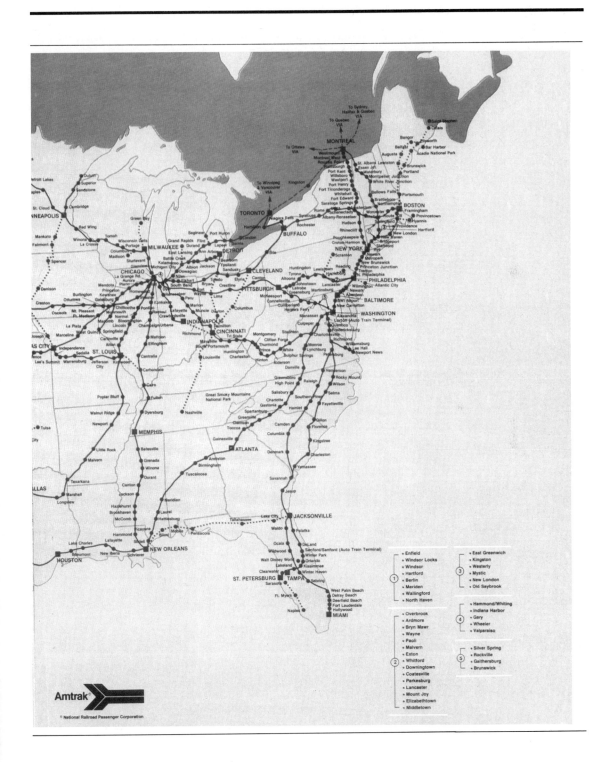

FIGURE 7.2.
AMTRAK's Superliner-equipped *Empire Builder* making its way across the high plains.

FIGURE 7.3.
A consist of four Amfleet cars, pulled by one of AMTRAK's latest AEM-7 electric locomotives, stops at the newly opened Baltimore Washington International (BWI) Airport station. Connecting buses take passengers directly from the station to BWI's main terminal building.

FIGURE 7.4.
Headed by a P30CH diesel locomotive, an AMTRAK Superliner-equipped train prepares to leave a station on its way along one of the many western routes the new bi-level equipment will operate. The latest in American rail passenger transportation, the Superliner fleet will set a new standard for luxury and reliability in rail travel.

to places like the Grand Canyon, and board the next day's trains toward their ultimate destinations. Trips by AMTRAK can be comfortable, enjoyable experiences, particularly if passengers avail themselves of sleeper accommodations. Bedrooms for two to four people and roomettes for an individual provide private accommodations with sinks and toilet facilities, reading lights, attendant call systems, and individual climate controls at moderate costs above coach fares.

traffic trends

In 1984 AMTRAK hauled 19.5 million passengers an average trip distance of 227 miles for a total of 4.427 billion revenue passenger-miles (RPMs). Passenger and RPM figures were improvements over 1983, when 18.9 million passengers and 4.227 billion RPMs were recorded, but were still below 1980 levels of 20.8 million and 4.503 billion, respectively.[10] AMTRAK traffic, like freight railroad traffic, suffered during the recession. Since AMTRAK's 1984 RPMs represented only 1.5% of the for-hire market total of 286.5 billion RPMs, AMTRAK is a minor market factor compared to commercial airlines, which had an estimated 86.5% of the for-hire RPMs.[11]

Subsidy Controversy

During 1984, AMTRAK had operating revenues of $658,661,000; operating expenses of $1,399,867,000; and a net railway operating loss of $890,078,000.[12] Through 1984, taxpayers had spent nearly $10 billion meeting AMTRAK's capital and operating financial needs.[13] AMTRAK's opponents decry these high taxpayer subsidies, which support more than 50% of each passenger's service costs. In 1981, for example, Drew Lewis, then Secretary of Transportation, singled out the Washington, D.C., to Cincinnati route, which at the time was so unprofitable that Lewis said it would have been cheaper for the federal government to give each AMTRAK rider a free airline coach ticket in that market.[14] In general, the opposition wants to know why, if AMTRAK services are so beneficial, its patrons are not willing to pay prices high enough to cover the full costs of service.

subsidy rebuttal

Subsidy is a sensitive issue. AMTRAK officials object to the singling out of intercity rail passenger transportation for criticism. They argue that urban transit riders in general, as well as airline and bus passengers, do not actually cover the full costs of their seats. Air passenger tickets do not provide for the full costs of the air traffic control system or the weather service used by the airlines. Bus passengers benefit from roads built and maintained for the most part by nonbus users. Nonetheless, the high amount of AMTRAK subsidy per revenue seat-mile has been a steady source of criticism almost since AMTRAK started services. Under pressure from Congress, AMTRAK during the early 1980s raised fares and cut costs by substituting airline-type meals for full dining car services. It also signed more favorable union contracts under the terms of which train and engine crews on the Northeast corridor are now paid on an hourly pay basis rather than by the 100-mile rule (Chapter 6).[15]

demands on
AMTRAK
management

However, it is difficult to make sizeable cuts in AMTRAK's costs. Politicians not only oppose route reductions or less frequent train services that affect their constituents, but they also press for additional routes. Consequently, management is whipsawed between demands for increased services and reduced operating deficits. Clearly, a strong grassroots lobby wants the United States to have a good intercity passenger train system.[16] Nevertheless, mounting pressures to cut the federal budget deficit increase the likelihood of continued controls on AMTRAK's financial losses.

AMTRAK's Problems

AMTRAK faces a number of unresolved problems such as the following.

- AMTRAK's labor costs are still too high, at approximately 60% of total expenses. AMTRAK has little control over train crew costs and productivity outside the Northeast corridor, because freight railroads sign the union contracts and bill AMTRAK for the costs. AMTRAK needs to control and pay directly all its workers.

- The AMTRAK route system is incomplete. A passenger can easily travel from Phoenix to Los Angeles but another, wishing to go by train from Albuquerque to Phoenix, would have to travel via Los Angeles (see Fig. 7.1). Connecting links are needed; however, they would probably increase deficits.

- Train frequency is inadequate. Passengers traveling by air who miss a flight usually can catch another within a few hours. With AMTRAK, they may wait a day.

- The scenery can be beautiful, provided the trains arrive during daylight. Given infrequent long-haul service, this is not always possible.
- Train speeds can be slow. Express trains would help, but that means fewer stops at many of the smaller cities AMTRAK serves. This is a difficult choice, since eliminating stops would affect local ridership and be politically unpopular.

FUTURE OF U.S. INTERCITY PASSENGER TRAINS

The United States has a modern, comfortable intercity train system. Like its world contemporaries, it is highly subsidized. Unlike its contemporaries, it generally lacks speed (the average door-to-door system speed is about 50 mph) and a solid reputation. The U.S. system can do the job, but not nearly as well as it might. One basic problem is that AMTRAK is trying to serve a huge country without hurting any one area by the absence of service. To help everyone, it has had to sacrifice optimality, in the form of the most advanced technology available, in those markets where train passenger service has proven in other parts of the world to be a profitably viable option—the short-haul, densely populated corridors. Instead of concentrating investment dollars in markets with the most potential, the federal government elected to follow the more politically acceptable solution by operating a system serving 44 states. In no market is AMTRAK a smashing success based on traffic and profits. The vast majority of the traveling public prefers other modes.

passenger trains at a crossroad

Passenger trains in the United States are at a crossroad. The alternative routes are to recognize AMTRAK as a residual carrier unacceptable to the vast majority of U.S. citizens, to reduce the AMTRAK system to lessen annual deficits by focusing on short-haul corridors, or to try to improve train services vastly to satisfy consumers. A basic question is whether intercity travelers find train service in general unappealing or AMTRAK services in particular unappealing. If it is the latter, one strategy is to improve vastly the product-offering—not everywhere, but rather in selected, densely populated corridors.

prospects for advanced train technology

Many people increasingly appear to favor the development of advanced passenger train systems. In September 1982, the Subcommittee on Transportation, Aviation, and Materials of the U.S. House Committee on Science and Technology released a report concluding that high-speed train systems could, in some cases, be cost effective, energy efficient, and potentially profitable for the United States; in addition, it listed 20 regional corridors as likely locations for profitable service.[17] The Federal Railroad Administration has awarded grants for feasibility studies of high-speed rail systems between Miami, Orlando, and Tampa, and in the Las Vegas–Los Angeles, Philadelphia–Pittsburgh, Montreal–New York City, and Chicago–Detroit corridors.[18] Faster and more frequent train service was unlikely, according to a report by the Office of Technology Assessment, a special body created by Congress, which concluded that any U.S. corridor with totally new high-speed rail service would have difficulty generating adequate revenues to pay entirely for operating and capital costs.[19] Another setback occurred in November 1984 when the American High Speed Rail Corporation announced it was dropping plans to build a $3.1 billion, Los Angeles–San Diego high-speed rail line because it could not attract investment capital.[20]

High-Speed Train Technology

High-speed enthusiasts must overcome several obstacles before new train services will be developed in the United States. An important decision is the choice of technology to use in service, such as the Japanese Shinkansen (Bullet) trains, the French (Société National de Chemins de Fer—SNCF) TGV trains (Fig. 7.5), or still being developed magnetic levitation, called *maglev,* trains.

JNR
Shinkansen
Bullet Trains

Conventional Rail Technology.   Japanese Shinkansen ("new trunk line") trains are the most widely praised high-speed passenger trains in the world. Since the Tokaido Shinkansen started service between Tokyo and Osaka in October 1964, Bullet trains have carried more than 2 billion passengers at speeds up to 160 mph (about 260 km/hr) without a single passenger fatality— a remarkable record. Running at 12–15 minute intervals in each direction, Shinkansen trains have approximately 1400 seats, use six-person crews, operate with conventional steel-wheel on steel-rail technology, and generate operating revenues at 169% of operating costs on the 668-mile main route between Tokyo and Hakata, yet fares are about one-half the price of airline tickets. Door-to-door trip speeds, including stops, are about 102 mph (165 km/hr); furthermore, on-time reliability is outstanding. Shinkansen's electrically powered locomotives and cars operate on exclusive guideways. There are no

FIGURE 7.5.
French National Railways TGV train. (Photo courtesy of F. F. Nouvion, Paris, France)

grade crossings; only Shinkansen passenger trains use the rights-of-way, for safety and speed reasons.[21]

French TGV Trains

French TGV trains (Fig. 7.5) did not begin regularly scheduled service until September 27, 1981, but quickly they have earned an outstanding reputation for speed and reliability. Operating primarily between Paris and Lyon, TGV trains have reached test speeds of 235 mph (380 km/hr), but in regular service, they cruise at up to 162 mph (260 km/hr). Not only the world's fastest conventional trains in commercial service, they are also quite popular, filling an average of 70% of their seats. French Transport Minister Charles Fiterman in 1983 projected that TGV trains would earn a 15% return on capital investment by 1985, after interest and amortization charges had been paid off.[22] TGV trains are powered by electric traction motors with electricity supplied by overhead catenary, power cable (touching pantographs located on the tops of cars).[23]

Magnetic Levitation Trains. Possibly the future of high-speed trains resides not in conventional rail systems but in magnetic levitation, maglev, vehicles. For more than a decade, Japanese and West German engineers have been developing equipment and guideways that could eventually carry passengers in trains at 250 mph (400 km/hr) or more. Already a Japanese National Railways (JNR) test vehicle has surpassed 321 mph (517 km/hr).[24] Both countries hope to market maglev as the successor to Bullet train, TGV, and other forms of conventional rail technology. They note that rail technology has a practical speed ceiling, thus, if vehicles are needed to exceed 200 mph, conventional rail technology must be bypassed. Maglev has that potential.

JNR maglev technology

Japanese National Railways (JNR) has been developing maglev technology since 1969, ultimately intending to construct a line in the Tokyo–Osaka corridor and deploy 16-car trains carrying about 1400 passengers at speeds of up to 310 mph (500 km/hr) or more. In the early 1980s, JNR researchers developed the MLU001, a three-vehicle train, which in August 1983 reached a speed of 249 mph (400 km/hr) in tests on the U-shaped Miyazaki Test Track (Fig. 7.6).

MLU001 levitation, guidance, and propulsion

JNR maglev technology works as follows: When one of the magnets aboard an MLU001 vehicle approaches and passes over a coil laid on the bottom of the U-shaped guideway (Fig. 7.6), electric current is induced in the coil, and it becomes an electromagnet whose polarity is the same as that of the magnet aboard the vehicle. The repulsive force of these two magnets, as well as others running the length of the train, of the same polarity levitates the vehicle (i.e., lifts it off the guideway and suspends it in air up to 4 in. above the coils in the bottom of the guideway). When the vehicle deviates toward either the left or right guideway wall, a current circulates in the coils located along the sides of the guideway for propulsion and guidance. The interaction of forces between this circulating current and the onboard superconducting magnet brings the vehicle back to the center of the guideway. (These coils can be seen in Fig. 7.6.) Propulsion is caused by the interaction of onboard magnets and magnetic coils on the sides of the guideway. Each magnet on the vehicle is pulled

FIGURE 7.6.
Front view of the Japanese National Railways MLU001 maglev train in the U-shaped Miyazaki Test Track. (Photo courtesy of Railway Technical Research Institute, Japanese National Railways)

toward a guideway coil of different polarity immediately ahead of it and repulsed by a coil of the same polarity immediately behind it.[25]

    In the 1970s, the federal government in West Germany sponsored the creation of a consortium to develop maglev trains. TR06, the latest Transrapid vehicle, is a full-sized, 200-passenger, high-speed system (Fig. 7.7) that was scheduled for testing at speeds up to 250 mph (400 km/hr). Transrapid is being marketed in the United States by the Budd Company.

West German Transrapid maglev technology

    West German maglev technology differs from JNR maglev technology by using vehicles that wrap around a T-shaped guideway. Instead of using a repulsive force, like JNR's system, to lift the vehicle off the guideway, West German technology uses electromagnetic attractive levitation. Figure 7.8 explains how vehicles are levitated. The TR06 maglev vehicle glides about $\frac{3}{8}$ in. above the guideway.[26]

TR06 levitation

    Maglev technology offers the following advantages compared to conventional rail systems:

maglev advantages

1. Higher speeds.
2. Electrical propulsion without friction.
3. Electrical braking without friction.
4. Lateral guidance without friction.
5. Not dependent on oil, since it is powered by electricity.
6. Ability to climb grades up to 10 degrees, whereas most rail systems do not climb grades of more than $3\frac{1}{2}$ degrees.

FIGURE 7.7.
Transrapid TR06 maglev train seen on its elevated T-shaped guideway system.
(Photo courtesy of The Budd Company)

7. Low noise, only from aerodynamics.

8. Environmentally clean; no exhaust emissions discharged into the air by the vehicles.

U.S. maglev potential

The Budd Company has been studying the feasibility of placing maglev trains in service between Las Vegas and Los Angeles, connecting Milwaukee with Chicago's O'Hare Airport, and in the Miami–Orlando–Tampa corridor. A sign that maglev interest is increasing is that three other U.S. companies (American Mag-Lev, Inc. of Pitman, New Jersey; Guideway International, Inc. of Wadsworth, Ohio; and United States Research Laboratories, Inc. of Lynwood, California) in addition to the Budd Company, submitted maglev plans for the Miami–Orlando–Tampa route.[27]

U.S. Barriers To High-speed Development

Although high-speed trains, whether of the conventional rail design (Shinkansen, TGV, or other steel-wheel on steel-rail systems) or of the new maglev technology, seem to have much to offer the U.S. traveling public, many barriers separate plans from actual construction and operation of any one of these systems. The major barrier is funding. After its costly experiences with AMTRAK, the federal government is an unlikely candidate to fund a multi-billion-dollar passenger train system, particularly if it would serve a restricted geographic area like Florida or any other single state. Neither do local taxpayers relish the idea of promoting and possibly subsidizing high-speed trains.

FIGURE 7.8.

Principle of electromagnetic attractive levitation. Levitation magnets (*A*) are attracted to stators located on the underside of the guideway at (*B*), lifting the vehicle bogie and passenger cabin off the guideway pads (*C*) and suspending the vehicle in air (*D*). (This is not a scale drawing; spacing is exaggerated to explain the principle of electromagnetic levitation.)

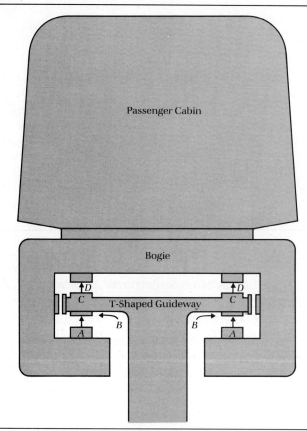

Florida officials, for instance, insist any new system be built with private-sector funds.[28] As previously verified by the decision of the American High Speed Rail Corporation to end its plans for Bullet train service between Los Angeles and San Diego, investment capital will be difficult to raise.

profit concerns   Although in Japan and France high-speed trains may make profits, their citizens are positively conditioned to intercity trains, have fewer automobiles per capita than in the United States, and have extensive public transit systems to move them to and from train stations. Furthermore, foreign trains do not have to contend with an extensive, deregulated airline industry offering some exceptionally low ticket prices. For high-speed trains to earn profits, U.S. citizen modal preferences for automobiles and airplanes will need to change. Although high-speed trains might prove to be popular in the United States, who will risk billions of dollars to build the first system to test the market? Investors are waiting for others to make the first commitment.

SUMMARY

Intercity passenger train transportation is to the U.S. railroad industry what air freight is to air transportation—a small, yet to its customers, important sector of the mode's business. Passenger train service is at a crossroad. AMTRAK provides U.S. citizens with a national route network and trains that are comfortable if, by world class standards, relatively slow and infrequently scheduled. Services are not so attractive, however, that passengers are willing to pay the full costs of service. AMTRAK is a highly subsidized public transportation company, which probably won't make a profit.

People returning from Europe and Japan who have experienced French TGV and Japanese Shinkansen trains ask why the United States cannot duplicate the superb services of these high-speed trains. Momentum is building to construct and operate similar trains in the United States in selective, densely populated short-haul corridors like Miami–Orlando–Tampa, Los Angeles–Las Vegas, and Milwaukee–Chicago. Seeing these services actually materialize is another matter. Is AMTRAK the final U.S. passenger train choice, or is this country about to embark on an era of advanced passenger train development? Should U.S. investors risk their fortunes to build and operate high-speed conventional steel-wheel on steel-rail passenger systems? Should they increase those risks and elect to operate faster, yet unproven, maglev trains? Has the vast majority of the U.S. population written off passenger train service, or is it simply waiting for bold new technology? Unfortunately, investment capital will have to be risked first, before U.S. citizens will receive a chance to answer whether passenger trains can be profitable.

STUDY QUESTIONS

1. How successful has AMTRAK been in achieving the goals of the Rail Passenger Service Act of 1970?

2. What were the consequences of the government's decision to establish a national railroad passenger system, rather than allowing AMTRAK to serve only the routes with the most potential to earn profits?

3. What are the problems associated with running AMTRAK trains over tracks owned by freight railroads?

4. Compare AMTRAK and Japanese National Railway Shinkansen services, equipment, and operating results.

5. Explain the basic technological differences between high-speed conventional rail passenger systems and maglev systems.

6. What is responsible for the increased interest in high-speed ground transportation (HSGT), in essence, high-speed intercity passenger trains, in this country?

7. What is delaying the construction of high-speed passenger train systems in the United States?

8. How do you believe airlines would respond to plans to develop high-speed trains in corridors they serve, and why do you draw these conclusions?

ENDNOTES

1. Association of American Railroads, *Railroad Facts 1985 Edition* (Washington, D.C.: AAR, August 1985), p. 61 (hereafter cited as *Railroad Facts 1985*).

2. Ibid., p. 32.

3. Edwin P. Patton, Jr., "A Plan to Save the Passenger Train," *Business Horizons*, February 1969, p. 7.

4. "Amtrak to Benefit Railroads," *Magazine of Wall Street*, 22 May 1971, p. 9.

5. "Corporation Created to Operate Rail Passenger System," *Congressional Quarterly Almanac* 26 (1970):806.

6. Francis P. Mulvey, "AMTRAK: A Cost-effectiveness Analysis," *Transportation Research* 13A (1979):330.

7. "Amtrak: The Need for a Hard Sell," *Business Week*, 8 May 1971, p. 19.

8. "Grand Old Rio Grande Zephyr Makes Last Run Today," *The Atlanta Journal and Constitution*, 24 April 1983, p. 9-A.

9. Ernest Holsendolph, "Amtrak Chief Says Railway Is Coming of Age," *New York Times*, 20 February 1983, p. 28.

10. (a) *Railroad Facts 1985*, p. 61; and (b) Association of American Railroads, *Yearbook of Railroad Facts 1981 Edition* (Washington, D.C.: AAR, June 1981), p. 62.

11. *Railroad Facts 1985*, p. 32.

12. Ibid., p. 61.

13. Derived from (a) "The Great American Transportation Mess," *U.S. News & World Report*, 31 August 1981, p. 20; (b) *Railroad Facts 1985*, p. 61; and (c) Association of American Railroads, *Railroad Facts 1984 Edition* (Washington, D.C.: AAR, October 1984), p. 61.

14. Albert R. Karr, "Derailed Cutbacks: As Congress Comes to Rescue, Amtrak Envisions the Best Passenger-Train Service in Its History," *Wall Street Journal*, 25 June 1981, p. 50.

15. Association of American Railroads, "Clayton Pledged To Improve Amtrak Service, Revenues," *Rail News Update*, 29 June 1983, p. 3.

16. (a) Albert R. Karr, "Anguish over Amtrak: Proposal to Cut Passenger-Train Network Irks Citizenry in Places Like Minot, North Dakota," *Wall Street Journal*, 21 December 1978, p. 38; and (b) "Constituents Used Right Track; Congress Keeps Amtrak Chugging," *Atlanta Constitution*, 2 July 1981, p. 35–A.

17. For a synopsis, see Al Senia, "Back on Track," *Iron Age*, 25 March 1983, pp. 17–19.

18. Association of American Railroads, "High-Speed Rail Grant Awarded to Las Vegas," *Rail News Update*, 11 January 1983, p. 4.

19. "High-Speed Rail Questioned," *Engineering News Record*, 19 January 1984, p. 20, citing the unspecified Office of Technology Assessment report.

20. "California Company Drops Plans to Build a High-Speed Train," *Wall Street Journal*, 16 November 1984, p. 52.

21. Information supplied by Japanese National Railways and the author's personal experiences using Shinkansen trains.

22. David Fairlamb, "France's New High-Tech Train," *Dun's Business Month*, January 1984, p. 57.

23. Information supplied by French National Railways.

24. Information supplied by Japanese National Railways. For more information on this vehicle, see William D. Middleton, "Japan's Maglev Train Hits New Speed Record," *International Railway Journal*, February 1980, p. 37.

25. Information supplied by Japanese National Railways.

26. Information supplied by the Budd Company.

27. "High-Speed Train Plans Are Submitted to Florida," *Engineering News Record*, 12 January 1984, p. 35.

28. Ibid., p. 35.

ADDITIONAL READINGS

Atherton, David L.; Campbell, T. I.; Eastham, A. R.; Fitzpatrick, C.; Hayes, W. F.; and VanDalen, K. "Design Study of the Guideway for the Canadian High Speed Magnetically Levitated Vehicle System." *Journal of Advanced Transportation* 16, no. 1 (Spring 1982):25–58.

Borchet, Jürgen, and Parnitzke, R. A. "The Vehicle of the Emsland Transrapid Test Facility (TVE)." *Journal of Advanced Transportation* 17, no. 1 (Spring 1983):57–71.

Caywood, James A. "A Candid View of the Northeast Corridor Improvement Project." *Traffic Quarterly* 34, no. 1 (January 1980):45–59.

Chambliss, Anthony G. "Advanced Passenger Rail System in the U.S.: A Question of Success Transfer." *Proceedings—Twenty-fourth Meeting of the Transportation Research Forum,* vol. 24, no. 1. Oxford, Ind.: Richard B. Cross Company, 1983, pp. 166–172.

Chambron, Etienne, and LeBoeuf, Michel. "The TGV Atlantique." *French Railway Review* 1, no. 4 (1983):371–381.

del Cid, Lisandro, and Eastham, Tony R. "MAGLEV—A Status Overview." A paper presented at the Twenty-fifth Anniversary Meeting of the Transportation Research Forum, Arlington, Va., November 1983.

"French Flyer Challenges Airlines." *International Railway Journal,* September 1981, p. 14.

Gaede, Peter Jürgen. "Project Design of a MAGLEV System with Shortstator Linear Motor Propulsion." *Journal of Advanced Transportation* 17, no. 1 (Spring 1983):49–56.

Johnson, James C. "Lessons from Amtrak and Conrail." *ICC Practitioners' Journal* (March–April 1982):247–256.

Kyotani, Yoshihiro, and Tanaka, Hisashi. "High-Speed MAGLEV Development in Japan." A paper presented at the Twenty-fifth Anniversary Meeting of the Transportation Research Forum, Arlington, Va., November 1983.

Laithwaite, E. R., ed. *Transport Without Wheels.* Boulder, Colo.: Westview Press, 1977.

Lukasiewicz, J. "The Future of Railway Electrification and Passenger Operations in North America." *Proceedings—Twenty-third Annual Meeting of the Transportation Research Forum,* vol. 23, no. 1. Oxford, Ind.: Richard B. Cross Company, 1982, pp. 62–79.

McGrath, Anne. "Railroaded: Will High-Speed Passenger Trains Ever Be Economically or Technologically Feasible for the U.S.?" *Forbes,* 12 March 1984, pp. 172–173.

Read, Robert L. "High-Speed Intercity Rail for North America: The Technology—the Issues." *Journal of Advanced Transportation* 15, no. 1 (Spring 1981):61–81.

Rhodes, R. G., and Mulhall, B. E. *Magnetic Levitation for Rail Transport.* New York: Oxford University Press, 1981.

Scott, David, and Free, John. "MAGLEV: How They're Getting Trains Off The Ground." *Popular Science,* December 1973, p. 94.

"TGVs In, TEEs Out." *Modern Railways,* February 1983, pp. 88–92.

Thuong, Le T. "Government Railroading, Japanese Style." *Transportation Journal* 22, no. 2 (Winter 1982):21–31.

Topolnicki, Denise M. "Five Top Trains." *Money,* April 1982, p. 76.

U.S., Congress, Office of Technology Assessment. *U.S. Passenger Rail Technologies.* Washington, D.C.: Office of Technology Assessment, December 1983.

Warren, William D. "Changes in American Intercity Rail Transportation: 1950–1980." *Transportation Quarterly* 36, no. 1 (January 1982):145–160.

Weimer, George A. "Bullet or Maglev? Who's on the Right Track?" *Iron Age,* 12 May 1982, p. 59.

PART 4, THE SECOND MODAL MINI-BOOK, addresses domestic and international water transportation. Chapter 8 describes and analyzes each of the three major segments of domestic water transportation—the domestic oceans trade, the Great Lakes trade, and the inland waterways trade. Differences between water transportation segments and freight railroad transportation are exposed. Also reviewed are water carrier economics and pricing, government regulations, and promotion and subsidy. Industry problems, causes, and decisions are also discussed. Primarily the orientation is cargo transportation.

Chapter 9 is entirely concerned with international water transportation, the means by which most U.S. exports and imports are transported. It describes the U.S. maritime industry and defines federal maritime policy, regulations, and promotion and subsidy programs and benefits. Chapter 9 also segments the shipping industry into three distinct areas—the general cargo, tanker, and dry bulk trades. Among other topics covered are carrier registry decisions; the emergence of superships; the roles of shore support facilities and organizations; the linkage between energy supplies, demand, and prices and shipping; controversial port issues; and ocean passenger transportation.

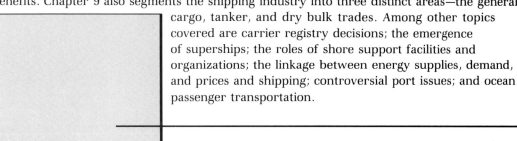

4 Water Transportation

Domestic Water Transportation

8

The United States is rich in water resources suitable for commerce. With the Atlantic Ocean on the east, the Pacific Ocean to the west, the Gulf of Mexico to the south, the Great Lakes to the north, and thousands of miles of navigable rivers and canals, practically all of the states have access to waterborne trade (see Fig. 8.1).

Water transportation is an integrated, interdependent business in which carriers, customers, ports, and shipyards all play a part. It is a commercial freight business with some for-hire passenger traffic; it is involved in international as well as domestic trade; and its oceans, Great Lakes, and inland waterways offer divergent services. Water transportation is also an intermodal business, since most cargo originates not at ports, but at inland points requiring rail, truck, or pipeline delivery to marine terminals. At destination ports, the reverse need arises. In other cases, water transportation segments feed one another. Consider, for example, midwestern wheat for export: Grown on farms in states like North and South Dakota, wheat is hauled by trucks from farms to local grain elevators. Subsequently, railroads or trucks move much of that wheat to river terminals; river barges move the goods to Gulf of Mexico ports like New Orleans; and ships take it across the seas to foreign markets.

Chapter 8 focuses on domestic water transportation, including the industry's background, the domestic oceans trade, the Great Lakes domestic trade, the inland waterways trade, water transportation economics and pricing, concerns of water carriers of freight, and the passenger sector.

193

FIGURE 8.1.
Waterways of the United States. (Reprinted with the permission of The American Waterway Operators, Inc.)

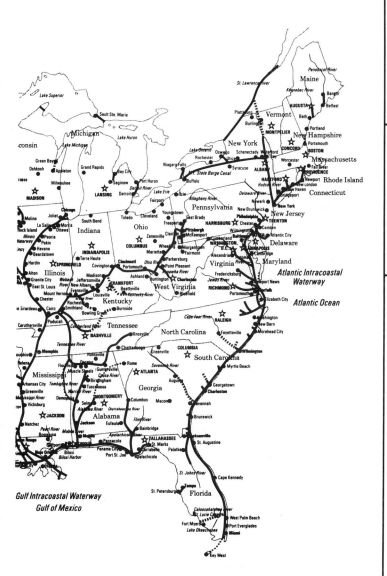

Waterways of the United States

CONTROLLING DEPTHS

▪▪▪▪▪▪▪▪▪▪ 9 FEET OR MORE

▪▪▪▪▪▪▪▪▪▪ UNDER 9 FEET

●●●●●●●● AUTHORIZED EXTENSIONS

PUBLISHED 1981 BY
THE AMERICAN WATERWAYS OPERATORS, INC.
1600 WILSON BOULEVARD ▪ SUITE 1000
ARLINGTON, VA. 22209

Compiled from Information Supplied by
CORPS OF ENGINEERS, U.S. ARMY

NAVIGABLE LENGTHS AND DEPTHS [1] OF UNITED STATES WATERWAY ROUTES

GROUP	LENGTH IN MILES OF WATERWAYS					
	UNDER 6 FT.	6 TO 9 FT.	9 TO 12 FT.	12 TO 14 FT.	14 FT. AND OVER	TOTAL
Atlantic Coast Waterways (exclusive of Atlantic Intracoastal Waterway from Norfolk, Va. to Key West, Fla.), but including New York State Barge Canal System	1,426	1,241	584	938	1,581	5,768
	1,487	1,445	589	965	1,544	6,030
Atlantic Intracoastal Waterway from Norfolk, Va. to Key West, Fla.	—	65	65	1,104	—	1,234
	—	160	65	1,104	—	1,329
Gulf Coast Waterways (exclusive of Gulf Intracoastal Waterway from St. Marks River, Fla., to Mexican Border)	2,055	647	1,135	79	378	4,292
	2,174	812	2,095	269	388	5,738
Gulf Intracoastal Waterway from St. Marks River, Fla., to Mexican Border (including Port Allen-Morgan City Alternate Route)	—	—	—	1,137	—	1,137
	—	—	—	1,180	—	1,180
Mississippi River System	2,020	969	4,957	740	268	8,954
	4,365	1,457	5,062	755	268	11,907
Pacific Coast Waterways	597	498	237	26	2,367	3,825
	700	515	237	27	825	2,554
Great Lakes	45	89	—	8	348	490
	100	148	14	8	369	639
All Other Waterways (exclusive of Alaska)	76	7	—	1	7	91
	76	7	—	1	7	91
GRAND TOTAL	6,352	3,516	6,976	4,033	4,666	25,543
	8,935	4,544	8,062	4,309	3,368	29,218

[1] The mileages shown in this table in bold type represent the lengths of all navigable channels of the United States including those improved by the Federal Government, other agencies, and those which have not been improved but are usable for commercial navigation.
The mileages shown in this table in light type represent the lengths authorized for improvement by the Congress of the United States in legislation known as Rivers and Harbors Acts.
The sources for these tabulations are publications of the Corps of Engineers, United States Army.

INDUSTRY BACKGROUND

Definitions

The U.S. Department of Transportation defines *domestic waterborne commerce* as all movements of commercial and military cargos in commercial vessels within and between the three trade areas called the domestic oceans, Great Lakes, and inland waterways. Excluded are military cargos moving in Department of Defense vessels.[1]

domestic
oceans trade

Domestic oceans trade is subdivided into three trade sectors: noncontiguous, coastwise, and intercoastal. *Noncontiguous* includes trade between the U.S. mainland (the contiguous 48 states) and Alaska, Hawaii, Puerto Rico, the Virgin Islands, and the trust territories (e.g., Wake Island, Guam, and Midway Island). Examples of noncontiguous movements are shipments between San Francisco and Honolulu and between ports linking Hawaii and Alaska. *Coastwise* includes trade within the Atlantic, Gulf of Mexico, and Pacific coasts, as well as trade between the Great Lakes, Atlantic, and Gulf of Mexico coasts. Thus movements from San Diego to Portland, Oregon; Chicago to New York City; and Mobile, Alabama, to Philadelphia are called coastwise movements for statistical purposes. *Intercoastal* includes trade in interstate commerce of the United States by way of the Panama Canal: for example, Los Angeles to New York City.[2]

Great Lakes
domestic trade

Great Lakes domestic trade includes shipments within the territorial limits of the United States on Lakes Superior, Michigan, Huron, Erie, and Ontario (Fig. 8.1). Examples are movements from Duluth, Minnesota, to Toledo, Ohio, and from Buffalo, New York, to Milwaukee, Wisconsin.

inland
waterways trade

Inland waterways trade includes shipments on the Atlantic and Gulf intracoastal waterways, coastal rivers and constructed canals—such as the Tennessee-Tombigbee Waterway in Alabama and Mississippi, Mississippi River System, and Pacific coast waterways (Fig. 8.1). Examples of inland waterways movements are journeys from Pasco, Washington, to Portland, Oregon; Pittsburgh to St. Louis; and Buffalo, New York, to New York City via the New York State Barge Canal and Hudson River.

Traffic

intermodal
comparisons

During 1982, domestic water carriers hauled 970 million short tons, representing 19% of the U.S. total of 5012 million tons hauled by all modes (Table 8.1), and 978 billion ton-miles accounting for 34.5% of the U.S. total. Statistics indicate that domestic water transportation carried more ton-miles than did any other mode, thereby revealing the mode's importance to U.S. commerce. The much larger ton-mile percentage figure is explained by the long-haul nature of the business: For instance, the average movement by waterways is 1008 miles, compared to railroad shipments averaging about 560 miles.

trade area statistics

Table 8.2 shows that inland waterways generated the most tonnage in 1982—568.2 million tons representing 59% of the mode's total. However, while inland waterways movements averaged 438 miles in 1982 and Great Lakes

TABLE 8.1. Intercity freight tonnage by mode (1982) (millions of short tons)[a]

Mode	Tons (in millions)	Percent
Domestic Waterborne	970	19%
Rail	1351	27
Truck	1791	36
Pipeline	897	18
Air	3	0
TOTAL	5012	100%

[a]2000 lbs.

Source: U.S. Department of Transportation, Maritime Administration, *Domestic Waterborne Trade of the United States 1978–1982* (Washington, D.C.: U.S. Government Printing Office, 1984), p. 25.

movements averaged 494 miles, domestic ocean shipments, on average, traveled 2034 miles. Consequently, domestic oceans traffic comprised 71.4% of industry ton-miles, versus 24.5% for inland waterways and 4.1% for Great Lakes traffic.[3] Primarily responsible were long-haul movements of Alaskan oil to the contiguous United States.

principal commodities hauled

The principal commodities hauled in domestic waterborne commerce in 1982 were petroleum and petroleum products, representing 45% of all tons carried by the mode; coal and lignite, sometimes called brown coal (16%); grain and soybeans (7%); sand, gravel, and crushed rock (5%); and iron ore and concentrates (4%) (Table 8.3). Water transportation, like railroad transportation, is primarily a bulk-hauling business. A comparison of Table 8.3 to Table 6.4 also reveals a high degree of intermodal competition between water carriers and railroads for coal, grain/farm products, iron ore/metallic ores, and other commodities.

The domestic water transportation industry operates 24 hours a day, 365 days a year, barring shutdowns due to the elements. For example, parts of the system are immobilized by ice from December to March, while fog, floods, droughts, and damaged locks can occasionally restrain commerce.

TABLE 8.2. U.S. domestic waterborne commerce by trade area (1982) (millions of short tons)[a]

Trade Area	Tons (in millions)	Percent
Domestic oceans	324.9	33%
Great Lakes	77.0	8
Inland waterways	568.2	59
TOTAL	970.1	100%

[a]2000 lbs.

Source: U.S. Department of Transportation, Maritime Administration, *Domestic Waterborne Trade of the United States 1978–1982* (Washington, D.C.: U.S. Government Printing Office, 1984), p. 27.

TABLE 8.3. Principal commodities carried in domestic waterborne commerce (1982) (millions of short tons)[a]

Commodity	Tons (in millions)	Percent
Petroleum and petroleum products		
Crude petroleum	178.409	18%
Residual fuel	113.351	12
Gasoline	75.096	8
Distillate fuel	62.105	6
Jet fuel	13.078	1
SUBTOTAL	442.039	45%
Coal and lignite	157.684	16
Grain and soybeans	71.494	7
Sand, gravel, and crushed rock	46.980	5
Iron ore and concentrates	37.119	4
Waste and scrap	22.176	2
Basic chemicals	18.801	2
Limestone flux and calcareous stone	16.823	2
All other	156.989	17
TOTAL	970.105	100%

[a]2000 lbs.

Source: U.S. Department of Transportation, Maritime Administration, *Domestic Waterborne Trade of the United States 1978–1982* (Washington, D.C.: U.S. Government Printing Office, 1984), p. 30.

Economic and Noneconomic Regulation

Little economic regulation applies to domestic waterborne commerce. U.S. Army Corps of Engineers' data indicate that 2.8% of the ton-miles moved in the domestic oceans trade, 6.2% of the ton-miles hauled on the inland waterways, and 0.1% of the Great Lakes ton-miles were regulated by the federal government in 1982. By comparison, 65.7% of the domestic oceans ton-miles, 85.3% of the inland waterways ton-miles, and 80.0% of the Great Lakes ton-miles were exempt, for-hire traffic. Private, not-for-hire, carriage represented 31.5%, 8.5%, and 19.9% for the three trade sectors, respectively.[4] For-hire water carriers, in general, have greater freedom to make business decisions than do railroads today.

operator constraints

To qualify as a carrier authorized to operate in domestic waterborne commerce, one must be a U.S. citizen, or, if a corporation, association, or partnership, at least 75% of the controlling interest must be owned by U.S. citizens. In addition, the president or other chief executive officer and the chairperson of the board of a corporation must be U.S. citizens.

other constraints

A domestic water carrier's vessels must be U.S. constructed and crewed with U.S. citizens. If the firm is a regulated common carrier, which offers scheduled service at published rates, it must file a schedule or tariff of rates, charges, and conditions of carriage with the federal regulatory agency that

ICC and
FMC jurisdictions

has economic regulatory jurisdiction. Carriers engaging solely in the inland waterways or Great Lakes trades are governed by the Interstate Commerce Commission. The same agency regulates domestic oceans traffic that moves between ports in the contiguous United States. Furthermore, the ICC has jurisdiction over domestic water common carriers offering service at joint trucking/water or joint rail/water rates between points in the contiguous United States and points in Alaska and Hawaii. Jurisdiction over domestic oceans traffic between the contiguous 48 states and Alaska, Hawaii, Guam, Puerto Rico, and the U.S. Virgin Islands and between noncontiguous points resides with the Federal Maritime Commission.[5]

regulated carriage

To operate, an ICC water transportation common carrier requires a certificate of public convenience and necessity (*U.S. Code Annotated* 10922). Contract interstate water carriage under a charter, lease, or other agreement requires a permit (*U.S. Code Annotated* 10923). Dual operations as both a common and contract carrier are discouraged but possible (49 *U.S. Code Annotated* 10930). Also, on a few occasions, private water carriers, in the business of hauling goods for their companies, have been granted common or contract authority, which allows them to solicit freight to reduce deadheading and to generate revenues to offset return voyage operating costs.[6]

exempt carriage

Cargo movements are regulated unless they qualify for exempt status. Many forms of exempt traffic, in essence, shipments exempt from economic regulation, are listed in 49 *U.S. Code Annotated* 10542. Most important are exemptions of for-hire dry bulk commodities without wrappers or containers e.g., corn, sand, coal, or cement and liquid cargos in bulk in tank vessels, e.g., oil or liquid sulphur. In addition, contract carriers can request traffic exemptions to be able to compete better with rail, pipeline, or motor carriage. Of course, all private carriage is exempt. Because most water traffic is petroleum, products of mines, and products of farms, few commodities fail to qualify for exempt status. Moreover, rules permit the mixing of regulated and unregulated traffic in a single vessel.

noneconomic
regulation

All domestic water carriers are subject to noneconomic regulations such as safety and navigation rules, listed in 33 *Code of Federal Regulations* (CFR) and 29 CFR, and water pollution provisions (40 CFR and 46 CFR). The U.S. Coast Guard has primary responsibility for policing domestic waterways, since water transportation can be dangerous to carrier crew members and innocent bystanders. Because many of the commodities carried, such as oil and chemicals, could cause injuries, deaths, or serious environmental and ecological problems if spilled, extreme care must be exercised. Regulations are designed to lessen accident risks.

Promotion and Subsidy

federal
waterway policy

Another characteristic of water transportation is the substantial involvement of federal, state, and local governments in promoting and subsidizing water carriage. Federal waterway policy has attempted to develop commerce, hydroelectric energy, recreation, and flood control; create jobs, increase purchasing power, and develop industry and resources; and provide low transportation rates. To help accomplish these objectives, billions of dollars have been spent to pay for the costs of planning, designing, constructing, operating, and maintaining navigable waterways. Today, most of these tasks fall on the U.S. Army Corps of Engineers, the Federal Maritime Administration, and the U.S. Coast Guard—organizations whose responsibilities were defined in Chapter 4, Figs. 4.1 and 4.2. Thus domestic water transportation differs significantly from railroad transportation, because the latter's rights-of-way are usually owned and maintained by private corporations. Anyone can use the waterways, but carriers own the vessels. In addition, land-based marine terminals, where vessels take on and discharge cargo, and port facilities, a collection of terminals, are provided by local public and private investment.

no tolls and exceptions

Prior to 1980, water carriers used the domestic waterways free of charge. No user taxes were collected from those who benefited from the waterway system, except on the Panama Canal and the St. Lawrence Seaway—two waterways that serve international traffic. Seaway tolls were collected to pay for borrowed principal, used to construct the Seaway, and interest. In recent years, however, the U.S. government cancelled the interest payment obligation.[7] User taxes remain today on the Seaway, but they are primarily collected to defray operating expenses. The U.S. government is in the process of totally transferring ownership of the Panama Canal to the government of Panama, which intends to continue collecting fees from vessels using the canal.

Ports and Shipyards

No water commerce would exist without supporting shore-based facilities, including ports and shipyards. Ports develop because shippers need water transportation or because public officials see ports as the link to their area's industrial development. Local governments often create port authorities that sell revenue bonds to finance the acquisition of ports, their development, or both. Port fees levied on users are then collected to retire the debt. Other sources of capital are states and private investors. In 1982, there were 219 ports in the United States,[8] as well as 26 major deep-sea shipyards and more than 300 small- and medium-sized shipyards that build and repair vessels used in both domestic and foreign commerce.

DOMESTIC OCEANS TRADE

The domestic oceans trade is predominantly a long-haul oil transportation business. During 1982, more than 84% of the tonnage was petroleum and petroleum products.[9]

Alaskan Oil

The source of 89.8 million tons of crude oil, 50.5% of the 177.762 million tons of noncontiguous traffic (Table 8.4), 27.6% of the total of 324.947 million tons of domestic oceans commerce (Table 8.4), and 9.3% of the 970.1 million

TABLE 8.4. U.S. domestic oceans trade by trade sector (1982) (millions of short tons)[a]

Trade Sector	Tons (in millions)	Percent
Noncontiguous	177.762	54.7%
Coastwise	141.871	43.7
Intercoastal	5.314	1.6
TOTAL	324.947	100.0%

[a]2000 lbs.

Source: U.S. Department of Transportation, Maritime Administration, *Domestic Waterborne Trade of the United States 1978–1982* (Washington, D.C.: U.S. Government Printing Office, 1984), p. 41.

TAPS

tons hauled in domestic waterborne commerce in 1982 (Table 8.2) was Alaskan oil.[10] Alaskan oil, in turn, can be traced to the opening of the Trans Alaska Pipeline System (TAPS) on June 20, 1977 (Fig. 8.2) and to tanker movements originating from the pipeline's southern terminus at Valdez, Alaska (Fig. 8.3). The opening of TAPS did more to alter domestic cargo traffic than did any other single event in U.S. history, because the waterborne tonnage it created was substantial.

distribution of Alaskan oil

Federal law requires that Alaskan oil be used domestically. Since Alaska lacks refining capacity, as well as substantial intrastate demand, during 1982, 42% of the crude oil tonnage was shipped to Panama destined primarily for

FIGURE 8.2.
Finned radiators frame a mountain peak and a section of insulated above-ground pipe on the Trans Alaska Pipeline. The radiators improve heat transference between the atmosphere and the 2-in. diameter heat pipes to which they are attached. The heat pipes maintain soil stability in ice-rich permafrost areas by drawing heat from the ground. (Photo courtesy of the Alyeska Pipeline Service Company)

FIGURE 8.3.
ARCO JUNEAU, a 120,000-DWT ARCO Marine, Inc. tanker, loads the first barrel of crude oil from the Trans Alaska Pipeline at Valdez in 1977. (Atlantic Richfield Photo, 1984)

U.S. Gulf of Mexico ports, another 37% went to California, and 13% was hauled to Northwest Pacific ports, such as in Washington. The remainder of the oil was distributed to other places such as Puerto Rico and Hawaii.[11] By 1982, Alaskan oil was supplying 17% of U.S. crude oil needs.[12]

port of Valdez   Crude oil has made Valdez the largest port in the United States for domestic tonnage (Table 8.5). Valdez handled 90,164,663 tons in 1982, of which

TABLE 8.5. Top ten U.S. ports, domestic commerce only (1982) (short tons)[a]

Port	Tons Shipped	Tons Received	Total Tons
Valdez	89,961,569	203,094	90,164,663
Puerto Armuelles	30,165,527	37,914,993	68,080,520
New York	30,209,864	32,809,083	63,018,947
Christiansted	17,010,086	6,143,931	23,154,017
Tampa	4,357,251	15,633,972	19,991,223
Long Beach	1,001,355	17,100,447	18,101,802
Houston	9,524,899	8,257,061	17,781,960
Los Angeles	5,034,878	10,562,040	15,596,918
Carquinez Strait	4,888,231	9,312,676	14,200,907
Baton Rouge	6,889,293	7,011,452	13,900,745

[a]2000 lbs.

Source: U.S. Department of Transportation, Maritime Administration, *Domestic Waterborne Trade of the United States 1978–1982* (Washington, D.C.: U.S. Government Printing Office, 1984), p. 70.

89,961,569 tons (99.8%) took the form of outbound shipments. Thus the Valdez trade is extremely one-directional, since tankers generate revenues almost entirely on the front hauls, from Alaska moving south. After oil has been unloaded at destination, vessels deadhead to Valdez. As shown in Table 8.5, Valdez handled nearly 50% more domestic tonnage than New York. Puerto Armuelles (Panama) and Christiansted (the Virgin Islands) also are busy oil ports, but they primarily receive oil from one tanker and transfer it to another transportation vehicle for eventual delivery to contiguous U.S. markets.

Ocean Vessels

Ocean vessels are constrained by significant wave action, harbor depths, the sizes of harbor turning basins, and lock sizes. For example, the largest cargo vessels using the Panama Canal cannot exceed 950 ft in length, 106 ft in beam (width), and 36 ft of draft. A longer or wider vessel cannot use it, and if a vessel lightens its load to meet draft requirements (*draft* measures the extent that a vessel can be loaded before its keel risks striking bottom or the vessel becomes dangerously low in the water), it loses efficiency. Consequently, most vessels are purchased to accommodate these constraints, or their owners realize they cannot use some waterway passages. In the Alaskan case, the oil industry avoided the problem of tankers being too large for the Panama Canal by convincing U.S. investors to build a pipeline across the Isthmus of Panama. For trips requiring thousands of miles, smaller tankers typically are not used, because they are less cost efficient than supertankers (large oil-carrying ships).

self-propelled vessels
tugboats

Most ocean-going vessels are self-propelled ships with high, pointed bows to cut through waves. Large vessels move under their own power until they are well into the confines of a port, where tugboats then secure lines to the vessels and maneuver them to terminals (Fig. 8.4). Ocean-going tugs are often involved in the long-haul transportation of barges—nonself-propelled vessels. A line is secured between the tugboat and the barge, then the tugboat pulls the barge to destination: For example, Trailer Marine Transport Corporation's roll-on/roll-off barge provides service between Jacksonville, Florida, and San Juan, Puerto Rico. In this service, a tugboat pulls a triple-deck barge measuring 580 ft by 105 ft and capable of carrying 376 truck trailers measuring 40–45 ft.[13] *Roll-on/roll-off* refers to the way trailers are loaded on the barge by driving them on and parking them; then at destination they are driven off the barge.

GREAT LAKES DOMESTIC TRADE

The Great Lakes comprise one of the largest fresh water masses in the world (see Fig. 8.5). In fact, Lake Superior, with its 383-mile length, 160-mile width, 31,200 square miles of surface, and 1332-ft depth, is the largest single body of fresh water on Earth.[14]

FIGURE 8.4.
Tugboats working a ship and barges in the port of Savannah, Georgia. In the foreground are two tractor-trailers being driven over a ramp that has been lowered by a roll-on/roll-off ship. (Photo courtesy of Georgia Ports Authority)

Geography and History

By one account, 1798 marked the beginning of commercial water transportation activities on the Great Lakes.[15] Although movements on individual lakes and between Lake Michigan and Lake Huron via the Straits of Mackinac were possible before that time, the full potential of the lakes could not be realized until natural barriers were eliminated. It was virtually impossible to traverse the St. Marys River connecting Lake Superior and Lake Huron or the St. Clair and Detroit Rivers linking Lake Huron and Lake Erie. The Niagara River and Niagara Falls also posed an impossible constraint between Lake Erie and Lake Ontario. Thus initiating a system of dams, locks, and channels permitted vessels of deeper draft to move freely between all the lakes. Locks permitted vessels to be raised or lowered from one elevation to another.

Great Lakes–
St. Lawrence Seaway

In 1797 and 1798, the first locks were established at Sault Ste. Marie, joining Lake Superior to Lake Huron. Later, the remainder of the lakes were linked by individual efforts of the United States and Canada. Finally, the completion of the Great Lakes–St. Lawrence Seaway in 1959 created a 2342-mile international waterway stretching from Duluth, Minnesota, to the Atlantic Ocean. Vessels drawing up to 27 ft of water can now descend from Lake Superior's 602-ft elevation to sea level (Fig. 8.5). In the process, they pass through the Sault (pronounced "Soo") locks and the St. Marys River channel; cross Lake Huron; navigate the St. Clair River, Lake St. Clair, and the Detroit River; cross Lake Erie; bypass Niagara Falls via the Welland Canal; cross Lake Ontario; follow the 182-mile Lake Ontario to Montreal channel on the St. Lawrence River; and move the remaining 1000 miles on the lock-free St. Lawrence.[16]

FIGURE 8.5.
St. Lawrence–Great Lakes Waterway. (Reprinted with permission from The Saint Lawrence Seaway Development Corporation)

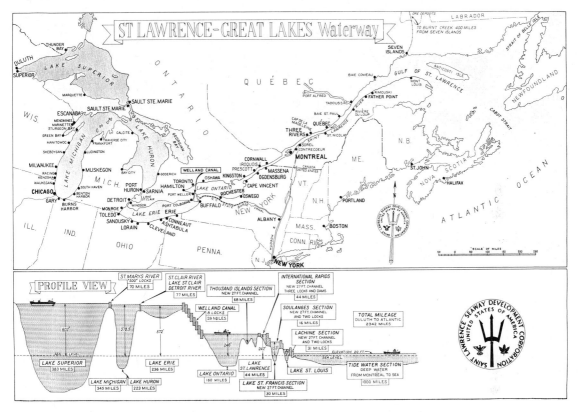

The Great Lakes–St. Lawrence Seaway developed as a joint Canadian–U.S. effort; Canada is the major partner, holding a 73% interest in the system. The project resulted in the creation of the 112-mile international section just east of Lake Ontario; improvements at the Sault locks, which were totally U.S. financed and controlled, and Welland locks, which were Canadian financed; and improvements in the connecting channels between Lake Huron and Lake Erie—a U.S. effort—and in the St. Lawrence channel southwest of Montreal— a Canadian effort. To be precise, the Seaway consists of the Welland Canal and the international portion east of Lake Ontario: in essence, the only two portions where tolls are collected.[17] However, many call the entire 2342 miles, the *Great Lakes–St. Lawrence Seaway.*

joint Canadian–U.S. venture

Traffic

As previously stated, the Great Lakes–St. Lawrence Seaway is an international waterway. During 1982, 127 million tons of traffic, divided into 61% U.S. domestic commerce, 32% trans-lakes tonnage, and 7% other foreign traffic, moved on the Great Lakes– St. Lawrence System.[18] *Trans-lakes trade* is traffic between U.S. Great Lakes ports and Canadian ports extending from the Great Lakes to the St. Lawrence Seaway. Other foreign traffic is commerce involving U.S. Great Lakes ports and all other foreign nations, as well as Canadian ports outside the Great Lakes–St. Lawrence Seaway.

leading commodities

Dry cargo accounted for 96% of domestic Great Lakes tonnage in 1982.[19] Leading commodities, as shown in Table 8.6, were iron ore and concentrates (i.e., taconite, the product of a process that increases the iron content in low grade iron ore leaving marble-sized concentrated pellets) (47%), coal and lignite (24%), and limestone (16%)—the three key raw materials needed to make steel. The principal job of Great Lakes water carriers has been to keep most U.S. blast furnaces operating. Table 8.6 shows that Great Lakes petroleum movements are limited (3% of the total tonnage); what moves is almost exclusively refined oil products (residual fuel oil, distillate fuel oil, and gasoline). Also, little grain traffic is hauled in the domestic Great Lakes trade.

Great Lakes Fleet

The U.S. flag Great Lakes fleet, which includes only vessels registered in the United States, contained 695 vessels in 1982. However, most tonnage moved in a smaller fleet of about 130 ships called *lakers* or *bulkers.* These vessels primarily carry ore from Lake Superior ports like Duluth and Superior to

TABLE 8.6. Principal commodities carried in the U.S. Great Lakes domestic trade (1979 and 1982)

Commodity	1979		1982	
	Short tons[a]	Percent	Short tons[a]	Percent
Iron ore and concentrates	78,523,000	52%	36,421,000	47%
Limestone	25,543,000	17	12,626,000	16
Coal and lignite	24,756,000	16	18,398,000	24
Building cement	3,452,000	2	2,196,000	3
Sand, gravel, and crushed stone	3,406,000	2	522,000	1
Residual fuel oil	2,338,000	2	811,000	1
Distillate fuel oil	1,723,000	1	667,000	1
Wheat	1,364,000	1	1,471,000	2
Nonmetallic minerals[b]	1,299,000	1	659,000	1
Gasoline	1,261,000	1	696,000	1
All other commodities	7,544,000	5	2,526,000	3
TOTAL	151,209,000	100%	76,994,000	100%

[a]2000 lbs.

[b]The 1979 figure, but not the 1982 figure, included gypsum (crude and plasters).

Source: U.S. Department of Transportation, Maritime Adminstration, *Domestic Waterborne Trade of the United States 1978–1982* (Washington, D.C.: U.S. Government Printing Office, 1984), p. 109.

lower lake ports such as East Chicago, Detroit, and Cleveland, often to return only with a load of ballast—nonrevenue-producing freight loaded merely to provide ship stability. These unique ships are basically flat-bottomed and flat-sided (i.e., shaped to use the maximum cubic capacity of the locks and channels they traverse) and self-propelled.

superlakers

New ore boats are different from older vessels. With the passage of the Merchant Marine Act of 1970, which declared the Great Lakes the fourth official U.S. seacoast, ship owners on the Great Lakes became eligible for federal aid for the first time. Among the benefits available were tax deferrals and tax incentives, ship construction loan guarantees, and direct ship operating and construction subsidies. The outcome has been the construction and introduction of huge lakers 1000 ft long, with a beam of 105 ft, and drawing up to 25.75 ft of water. Most important, these superlakers are capable of hauling about 60,000 tons of cargo. Two items make these vessels unusual. First, they are landlocked. Although they can pass through the Sault locks, they are too long to traverse the Welland Canal. Secondly, they tend to be self-unloaders and can off-load cargo without aid from shore-based equipment.

Carrier Problems and Causes

Carrier management decisions to concentrate on serving steel customers have proven costly in the 1980s. As long as U.S. steel demand was high and U.S. mines had plenty of high-quality iron ore, the laker fleet stayed busy and prosperous. Since 1979, however, Great Lakes tonnage has declined, as Table 8.6 verifies; thus, from the 1979 level of 151,209,000 tons, total tonnage in 1982 had dropped 49% to 76,994,000 tons.

problem causes

Most of this tonnage decline was caused by a depression in the iron ore mining industry. In turn, this depression was due to increased market competition from iron ore exporters like Brazil, which has abundant supplies of high-quality ore, and a strong U.S. dollar, which allowed U.S. steel manufacturers to buy imported ore at favorable prices. Simultaneously, a strong dollar raised the relative prices of U.S. steel exports, discouraging U.S. steel production and demand for iron ore. Another cause of the problem was the high cost of U.S. iron ore mining and taconite processing. Additional factors were increased competition from foreign steel exporters who increased their sales in the United States, changes in U.S. steel production methods, such as the increased use of more recycled steel to produce new steel, and efforts by automobile manufacturers to use less steel to reduce vehicle weight in new automobiles. All these variables contributed to a severe reduction in U.S. iron ore and concentrate production and shipments.[20]

illustration of derived demand

What happened to Great Lakes traffic is a classic illustration of the negative consequences transportation firms face in derived-demand situations. The steel mills reduced demand for iron ore; between 1979 and 1982, Great Lakes carriers hauled 54% less iron ore and concentrate; and when the ore stopped moving, there was an abrupt 51% reduction in limestone tonnage, and a 26% decline in coal and lignite. Consequently, approximately 50% of the

Great Lakes bulk-cargo vessels were taken out of service,[21] because the traffic was no longer available for transportation.

Future of the Great Lakes Trade

As for the future, Great Lakes carriers will find it difficult to return to former iron ore and concentrate traffic levels. If they are unsuccessful, vessels are so specialized that limits exist on what other commodities the lakers might carry even if carriers and the Great Lakes shipping industry could stimulate primary demand among other nonsteel-related commodities. It is quite possible one major decision carrier managers will have to make in the future is how to dispose of excess shipping capacity.

INLAND WATERWAYS TRADE

In addition to the domestic oceans and Great Lakes trade routes, the United States has 25,777 miles of navigable inland waterways, capable of handling commerce, in the lower 48 states, plus hundreds of other miles in Alaska. How much commerce a waterway can handle depends on many factors, but clearly a key limitation is vessel draft. To load more cargo than the waterway can safely accommodate would foolishly risk grounding or sinking a vessel. Many waterways are by nature sufficiently deep to support vessels drawing 30 ft or more of water. As vessels progress inland from the sea, however, surface elevations rise and rivers become shallow. Hence, people must build locks and dams and construct canals to carry loads efficiently and safely. Consequently, about 16,000 miles of U.S. rivers and canals can handle vessels drawing up to 9 ft.

Geographic Features

Mississippi River System

The heart of this extensive river and channel system is the Mississippi River and its tributaries, which include, among others, the Ohio, the Illinois, the Tennessee, the Missouri, and the Arkansas Rivers. In total, the Mississippi River System contains more than 5000 miles of 9-ft channels and more than 100 locks. Shipments can be moved from the Gulf Coast as far as Tulsa, Oklahoma; Minneapolis; Pittsburgh; Knoxville, Tennessee; and Chicago. Shipments to and from Chicago are possible because of canals that join the Illinois River and Lake Michigan.

coastal waterways

Many short rivers are on the East and Gulf Coasts, and there are also intracoastal waterways. As differentiated from navigable coastal rivers like the James in Virginia and the Hudson in New York, the Atlantic and Gulf Intracoastal Waterways are artificial canals that hug the coasts, slicing to the inside of coastal islands to enable vessels to avoid high winds and heavy seas.

Pacific waterways

Because of the mountainous terrain and absence of many rivers in the West, few navigable inland waterways are available. Two exceptions are (1) the Columbia and Snake Rivers, providing a route from the Pacific Ocean to Lewiston, Idaho, and (2) the Sacramento River in California. To the north, Alaska's waterways are primarily natural; therefore many cannot handle vessels exceeding 6 ft of draft. Collectively, all these rivers and canals are simply referred to as *inland waterways*.

Locks and Dams

Today's inland waterways are extremely dependent on locks and dams. Because of locks and dams, a city such as Knoxville, lying 889 ft above sea level, has water transportation available to New Orleans and the Gulf of Mexico. Without them, Knoxville's shippers would have to rely on other modes of transportation.

how a lock operates

Figure 8.6 shows how a lock operates. First, a vessel wishes to go either from a higher water level, called a *pool*, to a lower one, or vice versa. A *lock*,

FIGURE 8.6.
Drawing and explanation of how a lock works. (Photo courtesy of U.S. Army Corps of Engineers)

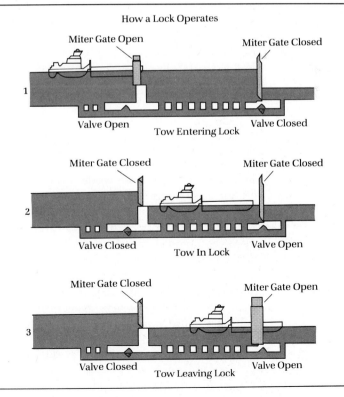

How a Lock Operates

which is part of a dam, contains two gates that open toward the upstream pool, but both gates never open at the same time. For a vessel to go downstream, both gates are closed and a filling valve opens, raising the water level in the lock chamber to the height of the upper pool. With the lower gate shut, the upper gate is opened, permitting the vessel to access the chamber. Once the vessel is in the lock, the upper gate is closed. The drain valve is then opened, allowing gravity to empty the lock until the water level in the lock equals the lower pool level. Naturally, the vessel descends with the dropping water level in the lock. With the upper gate closed, the lower gate is opened, and the vessel exits the lock.

lock capacities

Since standardized lock and vessel sizes create the most efficient system, the Army Corps of Engineers usually builds locks of a standard 110-ft width (i.e., wide enough to hold three barges, each 35 ft wide, side-by-side). Lock length is determined by traffic projections on each part of the system. Locks just north of St. Louis, for example, are usually 1200-ft long, whereas locks on the less-traveled upper Mississippi River in Minnesota are typically 600-ft long. A 1200-ft long by 110-ft wide lock can accommodate 15 barges—that is, three rows of five barges (each barge is the standard 195 ft by 35 ft), with space for the towboat behind the barges. A 600-ft by 110-ft lock can handle six barges—two rows of three barges side-by-side, plus towboat—or eight barges if one barge is positioned on each side of the towboat.

two-directional traffic flows

Although busier sections of the inland waterways often have a dam and two parallel locks, at many locations there is only one lock. For efficiency, however, once a tow—that is, the combination of barges and towboat secured together in an integrated unit to act as a single vessel—going downstream exits a lock, a vessel going upstream, if available, enters the same lock to be lifted to the higher pool elevation. Dual locks are not one-directional, because they are supposed to increase lock capacity.

Traffic

As revealed in Table 8.2, inland waterways in 1982 carried 568 million tons representing 59% of all domestic water traffic. Of this total, 341 million tons were dry cargo, and 227 million tons were liquid commodities. The leading commodities shipped, based on tonnage figures, were petroleum and coal products (27.1%), coal (24.0%), farm products (12.7%), nonmetallic minerals such as sand, gravel, limestone, and rock salt (9.5%), crude petroleum (6.6%), and chemicals and allied products (5.7%).[22]

regional trade

Inland waterways traffic is characterized primarily by regional trade; most shipments never leave the region from which they originate. The regions in the inland waterways system include the Northeast (New York State Barge Canal and points from Maine to Northern New Jersey), Atlantic Inland Waterways (Philadelphia and Southern New Jersey to Key West, Florida), Gulf Inland Waterways (St. Marks, Florida, to Brownsville, Texas), and Lower Mississippi (New Orleans to the Ohio River/Mississippi River junction). Others are the Upper Mississippi (St. Louis to Minneapolis), Ohio and Tributaries (Ohio River/

Mississippi River junction to Pittsburgh), California area (Los Angeles, Sacramento, and San Francisco areas), Pacific Northwest (Portland, Oregon; Seattle; and Walla Walla, Washington, areas), and Great Lakes. Only two regions ship out more of their tonnages to other regions than they deliver to ports in their home regions. Of the Great Lakes cargo, 100% leaves the region mainly for Upper Mississippi and Lower Mississippi points. Likewise, 72% of the tonnage originated in the Upper Mississippi ventures to ports in other regions, particularly to the Lower Mississippi region.[23] For the most part, the inland waterways trade is short-haul oriented since most shipments travel under 300 miles.

regional
commodity
differences

Regional differences are evident in the types of commodities shipped. The Ohio River and Tributaries region, which shipped more tonnage than did any other region in 1982 (140 million tons), is primarily in the dry bulk trade, since 90.1% of its total tonnage is dry bulk. Coal, which dominates shipments in this region, accounted for 96 million tons or 69% of the region's total traffic in 1982. In comparison, the Gulf Inland Waterways, the second busiest region with 105 million tons in 1982, primarily ships petroleum and coal products, crude petroleum, and chemicals and allied products—mostly liquids requiring tank, not dry, barges. The above-listed commodities represented 70% of regional tonnage in 1982. The Upper Mississippi, in 1982, shipped the third most tonnage (86 million), of which 51% (44 million tons) were farm products. The region's primary business is hauling wheat, corn, and soybeans.[24]

imbalanced
shipments
and receipts

Shipments and receipts on the inland waterways can be divergent and out of balance. The Upper Mississippi shipped 60 million tons to Lower Mississippi ports in 1982, yet received only 5 million tons back from that region. Barges may come back loaded to the Upper Mississippi, but only a small percentage of these loaded barges originates in the Lower Mississippi.

Equipment

One major difference between the inland waterways and both the domestic oceans and Great Lakes trade sectors is in the choice of equipment. Inland waterways primarily use shallow draft, nonself-propelled vessels, that is, barges. Power is supplied by towboats, which push the barges rather than pull them. Pushing achieves greater control, which is needed on rivers and canals where there can be little maneuvering space and tough currents.

fleet size

towboat size
decisions

Approximately 1800 companies operate the inland waterways fleet, which consists of almost 30,000 barges and almost 5000 powered vessels.[25] Towboat sizes are matched to traffic projections and lock capacity (size). If locks are small, so are the towboats. An objective is to have adequate power to push upstream the maximum number of barges that will fit through the smallest lock in a particular region of the river, and without double locking (i.e., without splitting a tow into two groups of barges to pass through the lock). Obviously, this is a slow and expensive procedure. Therefore, where 600-ft-long locks exist, small towboats powered enough to push six or eight barges are commonly purchased for service. Where 1200-ft locks are available, larger towboats capable of pushing 15 barges are the norm.

largest
towboat and tows

Once the last lock is cleared, towboats up to 10,500 horsepower can be used efficiently. Since a standard-sized barge can handle up to 1500 tons of cargo before reaching a draft of 9 ft, on the Mississippi River south of St. Louis, 50,000 tons of cargo moving in a single tow are relatively common occurrences. In fact, the largest tow ever recorded was a 72-barge movement by the towboat M/V Miss Kae-D, owned by Flowers Transportation, Inc. From bow to stern, the tow was 1700 ft long.

barge
capacity limitation

How much tonnage can be loaded on a barge is a function of barge capacity, cargo density, and waterway operating conditions. Many petroleum and chemical barges are longer than the 195-ft standard; thus they can haul more than 1500 tons. Light density commodities tend to *cube-out*—that is, use all the space before reaching the maximum weight-hauling capacity of the vehicle. For example, 1500 tons of sawdust cannot be loaded in a standard 195-ft-long barge. Changing waterway conditions can also alter load limits. During a drought, for instance, channels may be too shallow to allow barges drawing 9 ft; thus they are light-loaded (i.e., tonnage is reduced per barge). Safety is the paramount deciding factor.

equipment
shapes and costs

Neither inland barges nor towboats have pointed bows as tugboats do (compare Fig. 8.7 to Fig. 8.4). A barge has a rectangular shape to make lashing together easier and for more cubic capacity. Towboats, which are squared off and have bumpers at the bow to facilitate pushing, rely on the angular bows of the front row of barges in the tow to reduce water resistance. A new *covered hopper barge* (i.e., a dry bulk barge with hatch covers used for hauling grain) costs about $300,000, while tank barges can cost more than $500,000.

FIGURE 8.7.
Small towboat used in fleeting operations. (Reprinted with permission of The American Waterways Operators, Inc.)

Towboat prices are approximately $5 million for a 5600 horsepower model, and more than $10 million for a 10,000 horsepower vessel. A depression in inland waterways traffic in the early 1980s that idled about 25% of the barge fleet made it possible, however, for carriers to obtain used equipment at significantly lower costs.

trip speeds and distances

Movement along the inland waterways is slow. Towboats average about 10–12 mph downstream and 4–6 mph upstream. Fog, double locking, lock congestion, fleeting delays, and other constraints can slow operations. Furthermore, rivers are not straight, and some resemble ribbon candy. Thus waterway routes usually are circuitous, adding many miles to a journey.

Illustration of Barge Operations

Tracing a barge as it journeys on the inland waterways will clarify how the system functions. Assume, for example, that a grain company desires to ship a barge load of corn from Minneapolis to New Orleans (see Fig. 8.1). First, where will an empty dry hopper barge come from? Many arrive in Minneapolis loaded with coal mined in Illinois, shipped down either the Illinois River or Ohio River, and then brought north on the Mississippi River to Minneapolis. Coal is then unloaded, and the barge is picked up at the coal terminal, cleaned, and positioned at a grain-loading facility. Each port has operators who perform this type of service. Once the barge is loaded, lightweight hatch covers are closed to protect the grain from water damage. When enough loaded barges are assembled, an integrated tow is formed, or, in other words, the barges and towboat are lashed together, and the long journey of about 1700 miles to New Orleans begins. During the trip, the barge will be lowered 840 ft to sea level.

integrated tow

First, the barge movement takes the grain through 26 locks between Minneapolis and St. Louis, approximately 669 miles down river. Since most of the Upper Mississippi locks are 600-ft long, the tow is likely to be as small as six barges. Along the way, some barges are cut out (dropped off) at local terminals, and other barges are added. At river junctions such as at Grafton, Illinois, where the Illinois River flows into the Mississippi River, at St. Louis, just south of the Missouri River's mouth, or at Cairo, Illinois, where the Ohio River comes in, smaller towboats frequently are dispatched (Fig. 8.7); and then fleeting operations begin. Barges are separated, collected for common destinations, and then reattached to towboats. At this stage, much activity occurs; for instance, at St. Louis, about 82% of the port movement is in fleeting operations.[26] Surprisingly, barges are often simply secured to trees during this sorting and shuttling process.

fleeting

At St. Louis, our grain barge becomes part of a large tow, which is pushed the remaining 1021 miles to New Orleans. Once emptied at destination, the barge would probably head north to either the Ohio or Illinois River systems, but its destination will depend on supply and demand. Furthermore, *deadheading* (i.e., moving empty barges) to Upper Mississippi River ports also would not be unusual.

deadheading

WATER TRANSPORTATION ECONOMICS AND PRICING

The economics of the domestic water carrier industry are considerably different from those in railroad transportation. Because water carriers do not own and maintain their rights-of-way, fixed costs tend to be quite low. Variable costs consequently approach 85% of water carrier expenditures. Of course, some variation exists between market sectors, such as between the domestic

costs   oceans trade, which uses more expensive vessels and larger crews, and the inland waterways. One interesting distinction between water and rail modes is the dollar allocation to labor. More than 50% of the railroad industry's costs are labor related, whereas in the nonlabor intensive domestic waterborne trade, labor accounts for only about 20% of expenses. On the other hand, port charges, fleeting, and fuel represent more than 35% of water carrier costs.

In general, domestic water transportation is a low-cost business per ton-

revenues   mile. Low average rates (i.e., less than 2¢ per ton-mile) reflect the combination of low costs and promotion and subsidy benefits not needing full recovery from the rate structure. During 1982, regulated and exempt U.S. domestic waterborne freight charges were estimated to have been $6.9 billion.[27] Compared with railroad, trucking, or airline industry revenues, water transportation figures are small. Firms also tend to be small. For example, no towboat operator appears to have sales exceeding $200 million, whereas individual railroads often exceed $1 billion in annual revenues.

As previously noted, the 1980s have been difficult for Great Lakes car-

inland waterways   riers. Likewise, inland waterways operators have been struggling with de-
problems and causes   pressed traffic, prices, and profits. Between 1979 and 1982, for example, inland waterways tonnage declined 8.7% from 622,444,000 tons in 1979 to 568,164,000 tons in 1982.[28] Traffic reductions were a reflection of a depressed U.S. economy and problems with U.S. exports in coal and grain, which are commodities that water carriers haul to ports for export. Export problems in turn can be traced, if not totally, then at least partially, to a strong U.S. dollar and increased competition from low-cost and low-priced foreign suppliers of coal and grain. Because of decreased barge traffic demand and excess barge supply, inland waterways equipment was taken out of service, more than 20% of the work force was laid off, yields fell, and profits tumbled.

Water Transport Pricing

To gain a better understanding of water transport pricing, consider the inland waterways trade. The Waterways Freight Bureau is an ICC-sanctioned rate bureau that acts on rate proposals of regulated common carrier barge lines; in essence, it performs functions similar to those of railroad rate bureaus, discussed previously in Chapter 5.

Pricing of exempt for-hire water carriers, however, is another matter. In

exempt   a strong economy, much for-hire barge traffic moves under negotiated long-
pricing: agreements   term agreements between shippers and carriers. However, during the

volatility

1981–1982 recession, long-term agreements were seen as risky. Therefore spot market (short-term) agreements were more prevalent. How volatile this market became is exemplified by barge rental rates as low as $5 per barge per day versus the normal rate of about $150. Carriers were practically giving the equipment away to avoid fleeting and insurance charges on idle equipment.[29]

grain barge pricing: Merchants Exchange

One significant aspect of barge pricing involves the Merchants Exchange of St. Louis and grain shipped to New Orleans for subsequent export. Since 1978, grain company members of the Exchange have been able to bid for and buy barge capacity from towing companies who are also Exchange members. For instance, a grain company could agree to pay a certain amount for a specific number of grain barges moving from any point on the Illinois River to New Orleans. The accepted price would cover all transportation costs for the barge and towboat, as well as fleeting, insurance, and other carrier expenses. It is a locked-in price that will not change, even if carrier costs change between the bid date and the movement. For clarity, however, the price does not include the purchase price of the grain. When the market was strong in 1979, about 4000 barge trips—representing about 10% of the grain barge market—were sold through the Exchange.[30]

CONCERNS OF WATER CARRIERS OF FREIGHT

Water carriers of freight have several key concerns. Because they are part of a derived-demand business, they are hurt by economic downturns. In addition, federal trade policies leave water carriers vulnerable to dramatic traffic losses: For example, the 1979 U.S. embargo against Soviet trade that resulted from the conflict in Afghanistan eliminated millions of tons of grain traffic that would have moved on the inland waterways. Ice is another problem in the northern states. From December 15 to April 1, many miles of waterways cannot be navigated. Carriers also live with the constant risk that a damaged lock or dam will totally stop traffic for weeks on end. On October 14, 1985, for example, the collapse of a lock wall on the Welland Canal tied up 126 ships

waterway congestion

above and below the lock for three weeks.[31] Another major source of frustration is bottlenecks in the waterways system. When lock capacity is too small, extreme delays can result. For instance, congestion at Lock and Dam Number 26, a small lock on the Mississippi River near Alton, Illinois, caused towing

waterway improvements

delays of $2\frac{1}{2}$ days in either direction in 1980.[32] Consequently, lock and dam improvements are high on carrier priority lists.

Waterway Funding

user taxes

Waterway funding for system improvements or route extensions is a relevant issue today because of its potential impact on water carrier service, efficiency, and economics. Money is required for modernization, repair, maintenance, and operation of the waterways system. But who should pay for waterway projects? Should taxpayers, users, or both be responsible for system improvements? If the federal government reverses its policy assumed in 1824 of taxpayer developed, improved, maintained, and operated waterways, carriers will have to include these additional costs in their rates. This rate increase is the ultimate fear in the industry, for it would divert traffic to other modes.

the controversy

The concept of subsidized waterways has received considerable national attention in recent years. Railroads, which lobby extensively against waterway subsidies, claim that water carrier competitors receive an unfair rate advantage. As an illustration, when water interests pushed for twin 1200-ft locks and a new dam at Lock and Dam Number 26, railroads protested, arguing that this was the beginning of a multi-billion dollar modernization program that would involve many locks and dams. Another major controversy focused attention on funding for the Tennessee–Tombigbee Waterway, a 234-mile waterway, which was completed and opened for service in 1985 at a cost of $1.9 billion.[33] The Tennessee–Tombigbee Waterway, which connects the Tennessee River in northeastern Mississippi with the Tombigbee in Alabama (Fig. 8.8), was entirely taxpayer financed.

Lock and Dam Number 26

Tenn–Tom

pork barrel criticisms

Critics often call waterways, like the Tenn–Tom, *pork barrel projects,* implying that they are financed by government appropriations for the benefit of the constituents of only a limited number of legislators. They also argue that such projects have questionable value and would probably not be completed if users or local taxpayers, rather than federal taxpayers, had to finance

FIGURE 8.8.
Tennessee–Tombigbee Waterway. (Photo courtesy of U.S. Army Corps of Engineers)

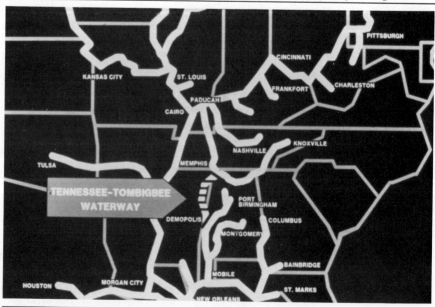

them. Historically, the U.S. Army Corps of Engineers has been responsible for conducting cost-benefit studies to establish economic justification for federal funding of waterway projects. Federal taxpayers in states not located near the new waterways ask why their income taxes are being spent on projects that give them few, if any, benefits. Furthermore, critics question whether these waterways will ever reach projected traffic levels and fulfill Corps of Engineers' cost-benefit expectations. Thus, while the need for waterway improvements continues, water transportation interests are experiencing demands for fiscal changes.

new lock and
start of user charges

In 1978 for example, Congress, under mounting pressure to reduce waterway congestion at Lock and Dam Number 26, authorized the construction of a new dam and single 1200-ft lock at Alton. Simultaneously, it imposed commercial user taxes for the first time on the inland waterways. This action resulted in fuel charges, which started at 4¢ per gallon in 1980, but which were gradually increased to 10¢ per gallon in 1985.

threat

Furthermore, the Reagan Administration might push for substantially higher waterway user fees. According to the U.S. Department of Transportation, the tax levels established in 1978 are not equivalent to the 47¢ per gallon necessary for a full cost recovery.[34] In 1984 the Reagan Administration indicated it would continue to press for less federal assistance for waterway projects and increased user taxes. Partially motivating the administration was the desire to reduce the federal budget deficit.[35]

AWO responses

The American Waterways Operators, Inc. (AWO), the trade association of inland water carriers, opposes greater taxes and questions their justification. The AWO argues that private boaters, regional and nonlocal businesspeople, the military, cities protected from floods, and many others share the benefits of waterway projects. In addition, other modes, and not just water transportation, benefit from subsidies. The AWO has stated that singling out commercial water carriers and their customers to shoulder the entire waterway financial burden would be unfair.[36] Nevertheless, water carriers are increasingly realizing that future waterway construction projects will be financed through strict cost-sharing formulas. Thus users or states and local governments, along with federal taxpayers, will be expected to help finance capital costs. Consequently, water carrier costs should be expected to increase as waterway modernization occurs.

Intermodal Competition

Inland waterway carriers, already weakened by the events of the early 1980s (i.e., the recession, user taxes, and reductions in traffic destined for export markets), face increased intermodal competition primarily from railroads. Water carriers must contend with financially stronger railroads (Chapters 5 and 6). Another fear is intermodal ownership of water carriers by railroads. As explained in Chapter 5, CSX Corporation acquired American Commercial Barge Line, and other railroads may attempt similar rail/water combinations. Although it is not clear how railroads will use barge lines to further their business objectives, water carriers see intermodal ownership efforts by rail-roads as a threat to their own competitiveness. Water carriers cannot afford to lose more traffic or reduce yields to retain tonnage. Past problems and future risks imply that water carriers must find ways to cut costs and improve productivity.

PASSENGER SECTOR

private boating
Passenger transportation is a small, yet important, sector of the domestic for-hire water trade. In dollar expenditures, private boating is the center of the passenger business. In 1981, for example, U.S. citizens owned 12.5 million boats; furthermore, sales of boats, motors, and accessories in 1981 totalled $3.63 billion.[37] In addition, a commercial, for-hire segment also exists.

fishing
Commercial boating can be divided into fishing and passenger-hauling components. Along the coasts, many people pay charterboat operators to take them sport fishing. Furthermore, many people work in the commercial fishing business catching fish, lobster, shrimp, and other seafood, as well as digging clams, quahogs, and oysters.

ferries
The largest sector of the for-hire passenger business is the ferry trade. Several areas of the country operate ferryboats carrying walk-on passengers, as well as people and their vehicles. New York's Staten Island Ferry is the largest operator, carrying more than 18 million passengers and 60,000 vehicles per year. Washington State Ferries operating on Puget Sound in the Seattle area and the Golden Gate Ferry in San Francisco are also large, busy systems.[38] Many of these ferries, but not all, are part of urban transportation systems. Likewise, many ferries are ridden for sightseeing to places like Martha's Vineyard off the Massachusetts coast, Catalina Island off the California shore, and Mackinac Island in the Great Lakes. Most ferry companies are small, and several are subsidized.

equipment
Ferry equipment is usually diesel or gas turbine self-propelled vessels; however, high-speed hydrofoils and hovercraft are gradually being introduced. The former have planing devices (blades) that act like waterskis to lift the hull above the water, which minimizes water resistance and improves speed. Hovercraft are air-cushion vehicles that lift the vessels above the water by blowing air under the hull. Both can attain speeds greater than 40 mph.

cruise lines
Other sectors of the for-hire passenger business include cruise lines and working vessels. Cruise lines operate along the coasts. For example, American Cruise Lines provides services along the Atlantic coast and intracoastal waterways. Also, there has been a resurgence in schooner (sail-powered) cruises in recent years. Called windjammers, they sail between scenic ports along the Maine coast and in other locations. Inland, the Delta Queen Steamboat Company, operates paddlewheel riverboat passenger vessels on the Ohio and Mississippi Rivers. Finally, quite a few work boats service islands and offshore facilities like oil drilling rigs. They deliver freight and mail, as well as carry passengers.

work boats

water
safety and taxes

Two concerns of water passenger interests are safety and taxes. Congress has expressed a desire to tax recreational boat users to offset the costs of services provided by the Coast Guard, which is responsible for water safety.[39] In a precedent-setting event, the Recreational Boating Safety and Facilities Act of 1980 established a motorboat fuel tax, the funds of which are used for docks, moorage, and safety programs. As in the freight sector, user taxes are a sensitive issue.

SUMMARY

Domestic water transportation is comprised of cargo and passenger industries. The former is a complex, diversified industry comprised of three trade areas—the domestic oceans trade, the Great Lakes domestic trade, and the inland waterways trade. The passenger sector is predominantly a recreational industry oriented around power boats and sail boats used for private, personal, and leisure activities.

Domestic water transportation moves more ton-miles than does any other mode, which reveals its importance to the United States. Each trade sector is unique and generally noncompetitive with other waterborne trade segments. Domestic oceans carriers predominantly move crude petroleum in self-propelled oil tankers; Great Lakes carriers primarily haul iron ore and concentrates, coal and lignite, and limestone—dry-bulk commodities transported in lakers and in support of the steel industry; and inland waterways carriers are barge lines transporting refined petroleum and coal liquids, coal, and farm products.

Two of these trade areas—the Great Lakes and inland waterways trades—have been experiencing substantial traffic and financial problems during the 1980s. In the Great Lakes case, demand for taconite has dropped significantly since 1979, causing Great Lakes carriers to idle many ships in their fleets. A depressed U.S. economy, problems with U.S. coal exports, and excess barge capacity resulted in reduced tonnages, rates, and profits among inland waterways carriers. Managers in both trade areas are seeking ways to rebuild their depressed industries. In this threatening environment, managers must refine business tactics to cut costs, increase productivity, and improve marketing efforts and yields.

STUDY QUESTIONS

1. How important is domestic waterborne commerce to the United States?
2. What factors dictate the dimensions of vessels operating on the U.S. inland waterways system?
3. What makes the domestic oceans trade, Great Lakes trade, and inland waterways trade areas unique and basically noncompetitive with each other?
4. How is fleeting both similar and dissimilar to classifying railroad cars?

5. How has Alaskan oil altered U.S. domestic cargo traffic and domestic waterborne commerce?

6. Why will it be difficult for Great Lakes carriers to rebuild their iron ore and taconite traffic to 1979 levels?

7. What role does passenger transportation play in domestic water transportation?

8. From a shipper perspective, what are the advantages and disadvantages of using for-hire inland waterways carriage?

ENDNOTES

1. U.S., Department of Transportation, Maritime Administration, *Domestic Waterborne Trade of the United States 1978–1982* (Washington, D.C.: U.S. Government Printing Office, 1984), p. 7 (hereafter cited as *Domestic Waterborne Trade*).

2. Ibid.

3. U.S., Department of the Army, Corps of Engineers, *Waterborne Commerce of the United States, Calendar Year 1982, Part 5, National Summaries* (Fort Belvoir, Va.: U.S. Army Corps of Engineers, 1984), pp. 89–90. The data base for this report deviates somewhat from the one used in the Maritime Administration report in *Domestic Waterborne Trade* (endnote 1) in how it defines the trade areas and by excluding some noncontiguous traffic. However, the Corps' report offers the best estimators of ton-miles and trip distances, and therefore the Corps' figures were used.

4. Ibid., p. 89.

5. *Domestic Waterborne Trade*, pp. 2, 4.

6. For example, see *Ohio Barge Line, Inc., Control,* vol. 250, Interstate Commerce Commission Reports, decided 28 October 1941.

7. Association of American Railroads, "Congress Sets 'Lame-Duck' Stint," *Rail News Update,* 7 October 1982, p. 1.

8. *Domestic Waterborne Trade*, pp. 70–75.

9. Ibid., p. 33.

10. U.S., Department of the Army, Corps of Engineers, *Waterborne Commerce of the United States, Calendar Year 1982, Part 4, Waterways and Harbors: Pacific Coast, Alaska, and Hawaii* (Fort Belvoir, Va.: U.S. Army Corps of Engineers, 1984), p. 82.

11. Derived from (a) ibid., p. 82; and (b) *Domestic Waterborne Trade*, p. 53

12. Jay Matthews, "Five Years Later, Alaskan Pipeline a Wild Success," reprinted from *The Washington Post* in *The Atlanta Journal and Constitution,* 29 August 1982, p. 21A.

13. Trailer Marine Transport Corporation advertisement, *Traffic World,* 10 December 1984, back cover.

14. Jacques Lesstrang, *Cargo Carriers of the Great Lakes* (New York: American Legacy Press, 1977), p. 90.

15. Gennifer Sussman, *The St. Lawrence Seaway* (Montreal: C. D. Howe Research Institute, 1978), p. 5.

16. Ibid.

17. Ibid., p. 66.

18. *Domestic Waterborne Trade*, pp. 7, 107.

19. Ibid., p. 108.

20. (a) Patrick Houston, Zachary Schiller, Sandra D. Atchison, Mark Crawford, James R. Norman, and Jeffrey Ryser, "The Death of Mining," *Business Week,* 17 December 1984, pp. 64–68; and (b) Bill Richards, "Pocket of Poverty: Minnesota Iron Range Is Hurt and Despairing as More Plants Close," *Wall Street Journal,* 26 November 1984, p. 1.

21. Paul Ingrassia, "Master Pilot: Steering an Ore Boat on the Great Lakes Is a Demanding Job," *Wall Street Journal,* 24 October 1983, p. 1.

22. Derived from *Domestic Waterborne Trade*, pp. 232, 235, 239, 242, 245, 248, 250, 252, 255.

23. Ibid., pp. 228–229.

24. Ibid., pp. 239, 245, 248.

25. The American Waterways Operators, Inc., *Big Load Afloat: Economics,* vol. 2 (Arlington, Va.: American Waterways Operators, 1982), p. 4.

26. W. G. Twyman, "Overview of Regional Fleeting and Intermodal Implications," *National Studies of Commodity Flow,* Transportation Research Record 825 (Washington, D.C.: Transportation Research Board, 1981), p. 13.

27. *Domestic Waterborne Trade*, p. 39.

28. Ibid., p. 27.

29. Robert J. Kursar, "Barge Interests Hold Little Hope for Increased Traffic in New York," *Traffic World,* 3 January 1983, p. 9.

30. Information provided by Jay Vroom of the Merchants Exchange of St. Louis, 3 March 1983.

31. John Urquhart, "Ships to Sail again over Troubled Waterway," *Wall Street Journal,* 6 November 1985, p. 6.

32. Jack K. Lambert, "Wish List for the 80s," Remarks before the American Society of Traffic and Transportation, 14 August 1980, Minneapolis, Minn., p. 5.

33. John LoDico, "Historic Tenn-Tom Waterway Opens Amid Cautious Forecasts for Growth," *Traffic World,* 10 June 1985, p. 23.

34. "Inland Waterway User Taxes and Charges," *The Journal of Commerce,* 22 February 1982, p. 6c.

35. John LoDico, "Inland Waterways Interests Begin Push to Revitalize Barge Industry," *Traffic World,* 1 October 1983, pp. 25–26.

36. Position of the American Waterways Operators, Inc., Arlington, Va., February 1983. A position paper (no title), numbered PS 382-2.5M.

37. Standard and Poor's *Industry Surveys* 1 (October 1982):L29.

38. Roger P. Roess, "Role of Waterborne Transportation in Urban Transit," *Transportation of Coal, Grain, and Passengers by Rail and Waterways,* Transportation Research Record 824 (Washington, D.C.: Transportation Research Board, 1981), pp. 33–34.

39. Even Kossoff, "Torrent of Protest Likely if Boat Tax Gets Approval," *The Atlanta Journal and Constitution,* 10 May 1981, p. 11–C.

ADDITIONAL READINGS

Allman, William P. "Determining Barge and Towboat Requirements for Simple Waterway Movements." *Transportation Journal* 22, no. 1 (Fall 1982):75–78.

The American Waterways Operators, Inc. *Annual Report 1981–1982 of the American Waterways Operators, Inc.* Arlington, Va., 1982.

——. *Big Load Afloat: The History of the Barge and Towing Industry,* vol. 1. Arlington, Va.: The American Waterways Operators, Inc., 1981.

Babcock, Michael, and German, Wade. "Forecast of Water Carrier Demand to 1985." *Transportation Research Forum—Proceedings of the Twenty-fourth Annual Meeting.* Oxford, Ind.: Richard B. Cross Company, 1983, pp. 249–257.

Baldwin, Peter; Lane, L. Lee; and McNamara, Thomas M. "Congestion and Congestion Tolls on the Inland Waterways." *Transportation Research Forum—Proceedings of the Twenty-fourth Annual Meeting.* Oxford, Ind.: Richard B. Cross Company, 1983, pp. 758–766.

"The Barge and Towing Industry—A Statistical Profile." Arlington, Va.: The American Waterways Operators, Inc., 1981.

Bronzini, Michael S. "Analytical Model of Operations at Inland River Ports and Terminals." *Transportation Research Forum—Proceedings of the Twenty-third Annual Meeting.* Oxford, Ind.: Richard B. Cross Company, 1982, pp. 490–498.

Burdg, Henry B., and Daley, James M. "An Assessment of Shippers' Perceptions in the Modal Selection of Shallow-Draft Waterway Transportation." *Transportation Research Forum—Proceedings of the Twenty-fourth Annual Meeting.* Oxford, Ind.: Richard B. Cross Company, 1983, pp. 751–757.

Burns, John J.; Goicoechea, Ambrose; Sharp, Francis M.; and Sweeney, Don. "A Transportation Model for Economic Policy Analysis of National Inland Waterways Navigation." *Transportation Research Forum—Proceedings of the Twenty-fourth Annual Meeting.* Oxford, Ind.: Richard B. Cross Company, 1983, pp. 767–778.

Camino, Mark M.; Mattzie, Donald E.; and Syskowski, David F. "Development of Inland Waterway and Competing Overland Rate Matrices." *Transportation Research Forum—Proceedings of the Twenty-first Annual Meeting.* Oxford, Ind.: Richard B. Cross Company, 1980, pp. 288–297.

Carroll, Joseph L. "Tennessee–Tombigbee Waterway Revisited." *Transportation Journal* 22, no. 2 (Winter 82):5–20.

——, and Rao, Kant. "Financing the Inland Waterway System: A Role for the States?" *Transportation Research Forum—Proceedings of the Twenty-fourth Annual Meeting.* Oxford, Ind.: Richard B. Cross Company, 1983, pp. 173–182.

Casavant, Ken L. "Impacts of User Fees and Dam Development on Energy Consumption in Transporting Pacific Northwest Wheat." *Transportation Research Forum—Proceedings of the Twenty-second Annual Meeting.* Oxford, Ind.: Richard B. Cross Company, 1981, pp. 441–447.

Cook, Peter D.; McGaw, David C.; and Roark, Philip.

"Water Flow, Light Loading, and Transport Cost on the Missouri, the Apalachicola, and the Alabama Rivers." *Transportation Research Forum—Proceedings of the Twenty-first Annual Meeting.* Oxford, Ind.: Richard B. Cross Company, 1980, pp. 311–318.

Crew, James, and Horn, Kevin H. "The Impact of Inland Waterway Lock Congestion upon Barge Shippers." *Transportation Research Forum—Proceedings of the Twenty-fourth Annual Meeting.* Oxford, Ind.: Richard B. Cross Company, 1983, pp. 779–787.

——. "The Impact of Rail Rates or Costs upon Waterway Project Planning: An Uncertain Future." *Transportation Research Forum—Proceedings of the Twenty-second Annual Meeting.* Oxford, Ind.: Richard B. Cross Company, 1981, pp. 432–440.

Hong, J. T., and Ploh, C. R. "Rate Filing Policies for Inland Water Transportation: An Experimental Approach." *The Bell Journal of Economics* 13, no. 1 (Spring 1982):1–19.

Isley, Edwin Kirby. "Inland Waterway User Charges: Policy Objectives, Criteria and Performance." *Transportation Research Forum—Proceedings of the Twenty-first Annual Meeting.* Oxford, Ind.: Richard B. Cross Company, 1980, pp. 328–332.

Liba, Carl J. "Definition of the Inland Waterways Hinterland." *Transportation Research Forum—Proceedings of the Twenty-third Annual Meeting.* Oxford, Ind.: Richard B. Cross Company, 1982, pp. 153–161.

Vanderlust, Henry W. "Great Lakes Ports & General Cargo Export Traffic: A Current Assessment." *Transportation Research Forum—Proceedings of Twenty-second Annual Meeting.* Oxford, Ind.: Richard B. Cross Company, 1981, pp. 96–101.

Vroom, Jay J. "Success in St. Louis: Barge Freight Trading on the Floor of Merchants Exchange." *American Shipper,* June 1980, p. 50.

Wolfe, K. Eric. "An Evaluation of Inland Waterway Tax Collection Mechanisms." *Transportation Research Forum—Proceedings of the Twenty-second Annual Meeting.* Oxford, Ind.: Richard B. Cross Company, 1981, pp. 423–431.

International
Water Transportation

Since the first explorers reached the shores of what was to become the United States of America, international water, or as many call it, *merchant marine,* transportation has been significant to this nation. During times of war, merchant marine vessels operate on the high seas hauling supplies and weapons for combat forces. Free of war, ocean-going vessels carry U.S. exports to world markets and return laden with petroleum, automobiles, electronic equipment, and other imports. The U.S. maritime industry provides international water transportation services and is thus a link that helps minimize the separation of nations; it brings the world to the doorsteps of U.S. citizens.

Because of oceans, only two modes—air and water transportation—enable U.S. citizens and commerce to reach Europe, Asia, and Africa. Prior to the 1920s, ocean shipping was the only choice. It was then that trans-Atlantic air transportation was first shown to be possible. At that time the world was served not only by thousands of cargo ships, but also by great ocean-going passenger liners that crossed the North Atlantic and other key routes carrying international travelers. The advent of aviation and, in particular, long-range jet aircraft, however, virtually eliminated the demand for passenger liner service. International cargo traffic, however, remained primarily with water carriers. During 1984, U.S. exports and imports totalled $217.9 billion and $325.7 billion, respectively.[1] It is estimated that more than 95% of U.S. foreign trade, including both exports and imports, is transported by water carriers.[2]

This chapter will provide background on the U.S. maritime industry; segment the shipping industry into three markets—the general cargo, tanker, and dry bulk trades—and provide specifics on each; explain the roles of shore

223

support facilities and organizations; review several important port developments; and review ocean passenger transportation.

INDUSTRY BACKGROUND

U.S. versus World Fleet Characteristics

tonnage measures

U.S. merchant fleet size

To position the U.S. merchant marine fleet—that is, to define its stature and characteristics relative to the world fleet—statisticians count the number of vessels in the fleet and their tonnages. Tonnage parameters, however, must be specified. For example, it makes a huge difference if statistics include only ships of 1000 or more tons, rather than 100 tons. Also, there are several tonnage measures such as gross register tons, a measure of the total capacity of a ship minus the motor compartment, fuel tanks, the crews' quarters, and so forth, with a *gross register ton* (GRT) being a unit volume equivalent to 100 cubic ft. There are also short tons (2000 lbs.), metric tons (2205 lbs.), and long tons (2240 lbs.). Another tonnage measure is *deadweight tons* (DWT), that is, metric tons of cargo, fuel, water, and supplies that can be loaded on a ship.

As indicated in Table 9.1, the U.S. fleet is the sixth largest in terms of vessels of 100 GRT or more. Surprisingly, it is smaller than either the fleet of Japan or the USSR, two major economic powers with smaller gross national products than the United States'. It is also smaller than Greece's fleet. Fur-

TABLE 9.1. Ten largest merchant fleets of the world in gross register tons (1983)[a]

Rank	Country	Tons	Percentage of Total
1	Liberia	67,564,000	16.0%
2	Japan	40,752,000	9.6
3	Greece	37,478,000	8.9
4	Panama	34,666,000	8.2
5	USSR	24,549,000	5.8
6	United States	19,358,000	4.6
7	Norway	19,230,000	4.6
8	United Kingdom	19,121,000	4.5
9	China, People's Republic of (includes Taiwan)	11,554,000	2.7
10	Italy	10,015,000	2.4
	Other Countries	138,303,000	32.7
	TOTAL	422,590,000	100.0%

[a]Vessels of 100 gross register tons (GRT) or more.

Source: Lloyd's Register of Shipping Statistical Tables: 1983 (London: Lloyd's, 1983), p. 3. (Reprinted with permission.)

thermore, Liberia, a small African nation, has a fleet more than three times the size of the U.S. merchant marine fleet, and Panama's fleet is also larger than the U.S. fleet.

registry decision

One important decision made by people interested in operating ships in international commerce is where to register vessels. Each ship must be registered in only one country. The choice can affect what traffic the ship hauls, which ports it can visit, the size and costs of the crew, the amount of corporate taxes paid, eligibility for promotion and subsidy payments, and the use of the ship for military purposes during wartime. The choice might also save a ship and crew from sinking, if, during a war, the merchant ship's country of registry is either a neutral, nonparticipating, nation in the war or an ally of the country whose planes or ships are deciding whether to fire on the merchant vessel.

types of registries

Shipowners who are U.S. citizens have a choice of registering vessels (1) domestically, (2) in many of the countries where their ships make port calls, or (3) in flag-of-convenience nations. Countries in the latter group, which include Liberia and Panama, among others, may seldom see ships bearing their colors arriving at their ports. As *flag of convenience* implies, these nations of registry often simply provide more flexibility and greater economic benefits for shipowners. Registries will be discussed later in the section on tankers. For now, the important point is that many millions of tons of shipping capacity owned by U.S. citizens are registered abroad.

world fleet size

In the aggregate, the world fleet in 1983 consisted of 76,106 vessels of 100 GRT or more, and their capacity totalled 422,590,000 GRT. All categories of ships from fishing vessels to oil tankers to dredges and cable layers are included in these statistics. More than 6400 vessels had U.S. registries.[3]

U.S. Fleet Categories

The U.S. merchant fleet is usually acknowledged to be much smaller than the 6400 vessels with U.S. registries, because ships less than 1000 GRT tend to be excluded. Using the 1000-GRT minimum, a more realistic portrayal of the international U.S. shipping fleet is possible. Table 9.2 segregates the fleet into active and inactive vessels and divides these categories into ship types by commodity classes: (1) tankers, which are liquid bulk ships whose cargo is loaded directly into holds; (2) intermodal, bulk cargo, and general cargo ships; and (3) combination passenger/cargo ships, which haul people, as well as freight.

active fleet

There were 827 vessels in the U.S. merchant marine fleet in 1983, but only 473 were active. Most of the remaining 354 were "mothballed," that is, idle and not available for service without extensive overhauling. Of the active fleet, 224 were in domestic ocean service in the coastwise, intercoastal, and noncontiguous trade (see Chapter 8). Of the remaining active fleet, 70 vessels

international fleet

operated under charters signed with the U.S. government. Consequently, only the last 179, which operated in the private sector in international commerce, hauled cargo from one country to another. Note that only 29 U.S. flag tankers operated in foreign commerce. Imported oil rarely sails on U.S.-owned, U.S.-

TABLE 9.2. Deployment of U.S. flag ocean-going merchant fleet[a] (March 1, 1983)

Types of Vessels and Deployment	Tankers	Intermodal, Bulk Cargo, and General Cargo Ships	Combination Passenger and Cargo Ships	Total
Active Vessels				
In foreign trade				
Overseas foreign	15	140	4	159
Foreign to foreign[b]	14	6	0	20
Subtotal	29	146	4	179
In domestic trade				
Coastwise	69	7	0	76
Intercoastal	81	3	0	84
Noncontiguous	36	27	1	64
Subtotal	186	37	1	224
U.S. Government Charters	32	33	5	70
Total Active Vessels	247	216	10	473
Inactive Vessels	56	253	45	354
TOTAL VESSELS	303	469	55	827

[a]Vessels of at least 1000 GRT. Excludes vessels operating exclusively on the Great Lakes and inland waterways, as well as vessels such as Army-owned dredges and tugs.

[b]Service by a U.S. flag vessel between two non-U.S. ports.

Source: U.S. Maritime Administration, Office of Trade Studies and Statistics, as cited in *Seatrade U.S. Yearbook 1983*, 5th ed. (London: Seatrade Publications, 1983), p. 21.

registered, U.S.-citizen-crewed, and U.S.-built ships. U.S. flag tankers operate almost exclusively in the domestic sector where goods are restricted to vessels registered in the United States. The term for this protective domestic restriction is *cabotage.*

freighter fleet

container fleet

Figures for the U.S. foreign trade intermodal, bulk cargo, and general cargo ship fleet are deceiving. Although the number of vessels appears small (146), in reality U.S. flag ships are a major force in world commerce. For example, the United States had the world's largest cellular (100% container) containership fleet comprised, as of November 1, 1983, of 85 vessels, 1,695,090 GRT, and 94,819 TEU.[4] Containerships carry large boxes, which are truck trailers without chassis. (The TEU equals a 20-ft.-long equivalent unit, i.e., a container typically 20 ft by 8 ft high by 8 ft wide.) The freighter statistics also fail to show that, although the United States has one of the oldest fleets in the world (27% of the vessels of 100 GRT or larger are at least 20 years old),[5] the nation's intermodal fleet is quite modern and includes containerships, *roll-on/ roll-off vessels* (i.e., ships that can lower ramps to permit wheeled and mobile cargo to be driven aboard), and barge-carrying ships (lighters). The intermodal fleet will be explained more fully later.

U.S./world fleet differences

Table 9.3 details some of the distinctions between the U.S. flag fleet and the world fleet. The U.S. fleet has a higher percentage of GRT in tankers (48.5% versus 40.2%), a significantly higher proportion of its tonnage in intermodal

TABLE 9.3. Comparison of U.S. fleet to world fleet (Vessels of 100 GRT[a] or more)

Vessel Type	Percentage of Fleet GRT	
	U.S. Fleet	World
Tankers	48.5%	40.2%
General Cargo Ships	17.5	18.5
Ore and Bulk Ships[b]	10.6	29.4
Intermodal Ships	14.1	4.3
Other[c]	9.3	7.3
TOTAL	100.0%	100.0%

[a]Gross register tons.

[b]Includes OBOs (i.e., vessels capable of carrying ore, bulk, and oil).

[c]Fish factories and carriers, fishing vessels, ferries and passenger vessels, supply ships and tenders, tugs, dredges, livestock carriers, icebreakers, research ships, and miscellaneous.

Source: Derived from *Lloyd's Register of Shipping Statistical Tables: 1983* (London: Lloyd's, 1983), pp. 8, 9, 13.

ships (14.1% versus 4.3%), and less ore and bulk ship tonnage (10.6% versus 29.4%). U.S. flag owners concentrate heavily on the domestic oil trade and intermodal general cargo foreign trade; therefore, for international bulk transportation, U.S. shippers may have to use ships of foreign registry.

liners

The maritime (merchant marine) industry is also divided into liner and tramp service. Liner service is characterized by regularly scheduled arrivals and departures at designated ports along a defined trade route. Liner service managers must decide which routes and ports to serve, the frequency of service—in essence, how often one of the company's ships will arrive at a particular port—and how fast service will be. Influencing ship speed is the circuity of the routing and the number of ports to be visited. Trade-offs often have to be weighed, such as between making numerous port calls to improve shipper accessibility to carrier services and making fewer stops to increase port-to-port vessel speeds. Liner service usually means the assignment of several ships to a particular route, with each subsequent vessel following the one ahead of it from port to port. For instance, a ship in the port of Seattle departs for Honolulu, a ship at San Francisco leaves for Seattle, and a vessel in Long Beach leaves for San Francisco. Regularly scheduled sailings are advertised, such as departures every Monday from New York to London. Liner service is called *common carriage* because ships serve the general public charging published rates and offering scheduled departures and arrivals. Liners primarily haul general cargo—manufactured and packaged goods, as opposed to unpackaged liquid bulk or dry bulk items.

tramps

The alternative to liner service is *tramp shipping*. Under this scheme, unscheduled ships ply the seas with supply and demand dictating origin and destination ports, routes, and rates. Tramps are like taxis roaming the seas and answering the customized demands of the marketplace. Their cargos are typically homogeneous bulk commodities such as sugar, grain, oil, or coal. For the most part, tramp-ship operators provide contract services. Contracts, called *charter parties,* specify the requirements of both the charterer (customer) and the shipowner. Normally, but not always, the charterer is a single party who accepts the entire ship's capacity.

charter parties

Shipping Alternatives

Shippers (cargo owners) also have strategic choices to make. They can own their own ships and engage in private carriage, pay a liner operator for common carrier service, or purchase charter services. Since the liner trade is general-cargo oriented, shippers of liquid and dry bulk traffic must often find answers in the private and charter options.

private carriage

Many high-volume bulk shippers choose to own a number of specialized vessels that can be deployed productively year-round and rely on independent shipowners to supply chartered vessels to accommodate peak period (high demand) needs. Charter parties are negotiated directly between a shipper and a vessel owner or through ship brokers, who are intermediaries between shippers and shipowners. Three types of charters are available: voyage (spot lease), time, and bareboat charters. Of the three types, the most common is the *voyage charter,* a one-trip, port-to-port ship contract. Its popularity stems from its convenience and short duration. The major drawback of the voyage charter is the risk that in high-demand periods, the charterer may have to pay a high price for the services received.

voyage charter

time charters

Time charters secure for the shipper the use of a vessel for longer terms, typically for one, three, or five years. Among the advantages is control of the ship's capacity for use wherever needed and greater rate stability. On the negative side, if cargo demand decreases, time charters lock shippers into unneeded capacity or into higher rates than those available in the spot market.

bareboat charters

Unlike the previous two options in which the shipowner retains responsibility for operation of the ship, the bareboat charter transfers full control to the charterer. Thus the shipper (ship operator) must hire and manage the ship's crew, purchase fuel, and maintain the ship. Payment to the shipowner is based on the carrying capacity of the ship. Bareboat charters usually last for periods of more than one year. Their primary advantages are total control of the ship and crew and possible savings from operating the vessel at lower cost than what it would cost the shipowner, such as savings derived by paying crew members less salary. Sometimes, bareboat charters cost more than time charters because unexpected costs materialize. For instance, shippers may experience unanticipated ship repair costs.

risks and opportunities

Maritime transport, then, is a high-risk business, and the timing of decisions is important. Shipowners and shippers who have entered the market at the right time have been known to make millions of dollars on a single voyage. The shipowner's goal is to have vessels available when cargo demand is escalating, for shipping rates are then high. Cargo shippers, by comparison, hope to purchase ship capacity at low prices, while simultaneously enjoying high prices for the commodities they are selling. If either party misses the market, great losses are possible. For example, new ships have been scrapped—dismantled and sold as scrap steel—before ever making a single revenue-generating voyage. A good illustration is the oil glut of the early 1980s, which created huge surplusses in tanker tonnage. With oil demand depressed, fewer ships were needed, and cargo shipping prices fell significantly. Rather than pay charges to store ships, management often reduced the number of ships owned.

GOVERNMENTAL PARTICIPATION

Policy

U.S. maritime policy, as defined by Title I of the Merchant Marine Act of 1936, establishes the necessity for a strong merchant marine capable of handling a substantial portion of the nation's commerce and serving as a naval and military auxiliary in time of war or national emergency. Furthermore, the policy states the desirability of having the fleet owned and operated by U.S. citizens, composed of vessels constructed in U.S. shipyards, and crewed by citizens of this country.[6] Thus carriers and shippers are not the only focus of maritime policy. Other beneficiaries are the national defense, U.S. merchant marine sailors and shipyard workers, who have greater job security because ships are to be manned by U.S. citizens and constructed domestically, and shipyard owners, who obtain shipbuilding contracts. The achievement of the desired objectives, however, often proves to be costly. Inflated ship purchase prices and high labor costs are two results that will be discussed later in this chapter.

Economic Regulation

The Federal Maritime Commission (FMC) regulates the economic aspects of the U.S. maritime trade, specifically, international water transportation to or from the United States. The FMC is not to be confused with the Federal Maritime Administration, called MARAD, a unit of the U.S. Department of Transportation whose principal function is promotion of the U.S. merchant marine (see Fig. 4.2).

Shipping Act of 1916   The origin of the FMC can be traced to the Shipping Act of 1916, which created the U.S. Shipping Board (as of August 12, 1961, renamed the Federal Maritime Commission) and gave it the authority to regulate and promote privately owned shipyards and vessels. An important power given to the Shipping Board was the authority to grant limited antitrust immunity to international shipping cartels known as *liner conferences.* The latter are associations whose memberships consist of operators of vessels engaged in the common carriage of international waterborne traffic.[7] To this day, the FMC's primary role is to regulate the conduct of conferences and their common carrier members.

FMC duties

The FMC certifies international water common carriers; licenses ocean freight forwarders; and more important, approves or rejects conference agreements. It also attempts to police the activities of common carriers who discuss, fix, and control rates, cargo space, and other conditions of service; pool or apportion traffic, revenues, earnings, or losses; allot ports or restrict or otherwise regulate the number and character of sailings between ports; limit or regulate the volume of cargo to be carried; and control, regulate, and prevent competition in international ocean transportation.[8] In most sectors of U.S. business, such activities are strictly forbidden but not in international water commerce.

conferences

Conferences emerged about 1895 as a result of common carriers trying to achieve economic efficiencies. Conference agreements were intended to control excess capacity problems by limiting shipping services among all carriers operating on a particular trade route. Unfortunately, some conferences began to abuse their powers by using fighting ships to exclude, prevent, or reduce competition. A *fighting ship* is a vessel that underprices nonconference–member–competitor rates on a particular route. In the past, conference members would share the losses on the fighting ship until the competitor left the trade or joined the conference. Another controversial practice was the deferred rebate—the returning of a portion of the freight charge to a shipper as a consideration for the shipper's giving all, or part, of its shipments to a common carrier.

provisions of the
Shipping Act of 1916

Although U.S. sentiment favored free enterprise, at the beginning of the twentieth century Congress was faced with the dual realities that it could not dictate world maritime policy and the world-accepted liner conferences. Thus the U.S. Shipping Act of 1916 was a compromise that accepted conferences but imposed restrictions aimed at ending monopolistic abuses on conferences serving the U.S. trade. Conference membership was to be open, indicating that any common carrier could join, every conference rate agreement had to be approved by the Shipping Board before it could go into effect, and fighting ships and deferred rebates were prohibited.[9] The United States thus became the only country in the world having a regulatory commission like the Shipping Board (later, the FMC); even today, in other nations, antitrust laws in general not only do not apply to international shipping, but also conferences that serve non–U.S. trades are free to limit membership, because they are closed, rather than open, conferences.[10] Since the U.S. economy generates the largest single portion of the world's ocean cargo, however, ships of foreign registries are drawn into serving U.S. trade routes. When they do, they are subject to FMC rules. Consequently, U.S. maritime policy has a powerful influence on international waterborne commerce.

threats

In the 1970s and 1980s, Congress became increasingly aware of threats to U.S. flag liner operations, such as in the form of increased competition from a highly subsidized Soviet commercial fleet and demands from third-world countries that their flag vessels haul a much larger portion of the tonnage between the United States and their respective home nations. Specifically, in 1983, Article 2 of the United Nation's Conference on Trade and Development

Convention, called the *UNCTAD Code,* was ratified, became effective, and called for closed conferences and a bilateral allocation of cargos among the trading countries.[11]

UNCTAD Code and Article 2

Article 2 specifies that liners of bilateral (two-nation) trading partners shall have equal rights to traffic between the two countries, and third-country shipping lines (cross-traders) shall have the right to acquire a significant part of the trade, such as 20%. The trade press calls this the 40–40–20 rule, but the terms are not that precise, for it does not limit outsiders to 20%. Nevertheless, Article 2 increased pressure on exporters and importers to use carriers flying the flags of the origin and destination countries. Consequently, less traffic is available for cross-traders. The United States did not ratify the UNCTAD Code on the basis that it would negatively affect U.S. carrier traffic in markets where a U.S. port was neither the origin nor destination, for example, a movement from South Korea to the United Kingdom.[12]

The Shipping Act of 1984. Thus Congress felt the need to make a decision about how best to improve the U.S. maritime industry, trading off the country's strong desire to deregulate transportation and the realities of the international market—in short, that the world would not prohibit liner conferences. The result was the Shipping Act of 1984, which not only continued to sanction conferences but also made it much easier for common carriers to sign and modify conference agreements.

Congressional goals

The Shipping Act of 1984 is similar to other deregulation acts affecting transportation because its intent is to give carriers more flexibility. On the other hand, it is also different because it increases, rather than decreases, antitrust immunity and does little to weaken collective ratemaking. The Staggers Rail Act of 1980 reduced the powers of railroad rate bureaus, but the Shipping Act of 1984 left most conference powers intact. In fact, the Shipping Act of 1984 was the strongest endorsement of shipping conferences ever made by the U.S. government. The goal was to make U.S. flag common carriers more competitive against foreign flag operators.

deregulation comparisons

A significant provision of the Shipping Act of 1984 was the specification that unless the Federal Maritime Commission rejects a proposed conference agreement, it becomes effective 45 days after filing or 30 days after being published in the *Federal Register,* whichever is later. In the past, the FMC could delay the effective date of agreements until it was satisfied the conference would fully comply with U.S. maritime regulations—a process that in some cases took years. Now, most go into effect in 45 days or less. The FMC can block the implementation of an agreement today only by obtaining a court injunction. The objective is increased flexibility, which permits U.S. and other flag carriers to adjust more quickly to the changing marketplace.

expedited FMC approval of agreements

Another important provision of the 1984 act was the authorization for common carriers or conferences to enter into service contracts with shippers or shippers' associations. This provision permits carriers to agree to provide a certain amount of space to customers who agree to ship a certain amount of cargo during a period of time. The Shipping Act of 1984 defined *shippers'*

service contracts

shippers' associations   *association* as a group of shippers that consolidate or distribute freight on a nonprofit basis for the members of the group to secure volume rates or contracts. Shippers' associations can now negotiate rates on behalf of their members, and shipowners are prohibited from refusing to negotiate with them.

other provisions   The Shipping Act of 1984 requires that each conference be open, giving nonmembers the right to join, conference members the right to withdraw, and past members the right to be readmitted to a conference. In addition, each conference member can exercise the right of independent action on any rate or service, which means that a carrier does not have to follow the exact terms of the conference agreements (Sec. 5, 98 *Statutes at Large,* p. 71). Each common carrier or conference serving the United States also must file tariffs with the FMC. Regarding *controlled carriers* (i.e., an ocean common carrier, as in the Soviet case, whose assets are either directly or indirectly owned or controlled by the government under whose registry the vessels of the carrier operate), the FMC has been given increased powers to disapprove rates found unjust and unreasonable—a measure aimed at stopping predatory pricing (Sec. 9, 98 *Statutes at Large,* p. 76). Finally, in keeping with past regulations, fighting ships, deferred rebates, and other forms of competitive abuses or unfair discrimination are prohibited in the U.S. trades (Sec. 10, 98 *Statutes at Large,* p. 78). Overall, the objectives of the Shipping Act of 1984 are to encourage the development of an economically sound and efficient U.S. flag liner fleet.

Promotion and Subsidy

Most governments offer some form of special financial aid to their maritime industries,[13] and the United States is no exception. U.S. concerns about maintaining not only a merchant fleet ready to meet wartime needs, but also a shipbuilding industry and skilled officers and crews, led to the creation of two major subsidy programs and several other incentives.

ODS   The first subsidy program is called *operating differential subsidy (ODS).* Created by Title VI of the Merchant Marine Act of 1936, ODS is a fund that pays much of the differences between the costs of operating a U.S. flag vessel and the estimated costs of the same items on vessels operated under foreign registry in international trade. Primarily, the subsidy covers higher U.S. crew costs, and payments can be large. Sometimes a U.S. flag ship's crew costs 4–5 times as much as a foreign flag crew does. Thus the goal of ODS has been to neutralize the cost advantage of foreign competitors by enabling U.S. flag ODS recipients to maintain competitive rates that do not reflect their higher operating costs. Rates of foreign competitors also tend to be subsidized. Without ODS, more U.S. citizens would probably register their vessels under foreign flags. Although not all U.S. flag ships collect ODS, both liners and tramps are eligible. Through the early 1980s, ODS grants contributed more than $6 billion to shipowners.[14]

CDS   In 1981, the Reagan Administration ended the *construction differential subsidy (CDS)* program, a second major aid program, which since 1936 had provided more than $3 billion to U.S. shipyards.[15] The CDS program was cre-

logic of CDS changes   ated to enable U.S. shipyards to compete against foreign ship builders, who for years had been underbidding domestic ship price quotations. The CDS program paid for up to 50% of the cost of a ship built in a domestic shipyard. The intent was to maintain a U.S. shipbuilding capability and, under the Merchant Marine Act of 1970, expand the U.S. flag merchant fleet. However, this objective never materialized as planned, so the administration changed strategies. Simultaneously with the ending of the CDS program, the administration encouraged the building, buying, and reconstruction of ships in foreign shipyards for subsequent U.S. flag registry and ODS eligibility. This decision resulted in plans for 36 new merchant ships and 12 reconstructions in foreign yards. It also prompted a strong rebuke from U.S. shipyard interests, unhappy that they did not receive these ship orders.[16]

other forms of maritime aid   Other forms of maritime aid include tax deferrals, in which tax payments are delayed until companies can take advantage of tax breaks; loan guarantees, leading to lower interest rates and available capital; low-interest financing; government purchases of retired vessels at good prices; cargo preference laws, which give U.S. flag carriers first right to haul all U.S. military cargo and 50% of all government-generated traffic; and cabotage, which requires that domestic traffic be carried in U.S. flag vessels. All these programs are tied closely to the goal of trying to fulfill U.S. maritime policy; they aid carriers, shippers, defense, labor, and shipyards. Despite the benefits, however, some U.S. flag lines, such as Sea-Land (to be discussed later), in the past refused to accept them and chose instead for the right to run their affairs as independently of federal red tape as possible. Others argue that U.S. aid programs are inadequate compared with what foreign nations do for their shipping interests. Regardless, federal promotion and subsidy have played a large role in the U.S. merchant marine business.

GENERAL CARGO TRADE

Ocean cargo is categorized as either dry or liquid matter. Dry cargo includes general cargo and bulk. Similarly, liquid traffic can also be divided that way if, for example, such items as bottled wine versus wine in bulk are distinguished. Typically, however, *general cargo* includes smaller shipments of packaged miscellaneous freight (e.g., stereo equipment, furniture, and carpets). *Bulk*, by comparison, usually includes shiploads of single commodities like coal or oil. For simplicity, however, let us direct our attention to three broad shipping markets: the general cargo, tanker, and dry bulk trades.

Breakbulk Freighters

During the 1960s, general cargo primarily moved in multipurpose ships called *breakbulk freighters* or freighters. These were deployed in liner and tramp operations; were relatively small (i.e., about 450 ft long, with a draft of about

28 ft, at a deadweight tonnage of approximately 10,500 tons), carried their own lift equipment (i.e., onboard handling equipment such as booms, rigging, and winches), and stowed breakbulk cargo in several holds accessible at deck level. Breakbulk refers to loose individual items of cargo. For example, a freighter shipment might be 63 boxes of manufactured goods or 10 pallet loads.

advantages and
disadvantages
of freighters

Freighters were, and still are, practical vessels. Because of their self-unloading/loading capabilities, they can work ports lacking shore-based cranes and handle cargo of almost any size in their holds or stowed on deck. However, their strengths are also their weaknesses. Loading and unloading can be agonizingly slow, taking typically several days at each port of call. In fact, most vessels of this type spend more time in port than at sea. With today's ship economics, this can be a costly and unproductive use of capital—a problem that prompted changes in the general cargo trade.

Sea-Land and Containerization

The catalyst behind a revolution in general cargo shipping was Malcolm McLean, who took an old concept called *containerization* and made it succeed. His answer was Sea-Land, a company started in 1956; although no longer under McLean's ownership, it is still the world's largest container shipping company.

container concept

Containerization is a simple concept: Cargo handling can be expedited and shipping efficiency, productivity, and service can be improved by consolidating shipments in large boxes of standard measurements. Sea-Land developed containers 35 ft by 8 ft by 8 ft (Fig. 9.1) and loaded them on reconstructed ships hauling up to 490 containers. These first ships carried an onboard crane that moved on rails linearly fore and aft on the ship. From that beginning, the container business emerged and evolved on larger, faster ships. A good illustration is American President Lines' M. V. *President Lincoln* (see Fig. 9.2), a ship 860 ft long, which is capable of carrying 1250 40-ft equivalent units (FEU's) (up to 1250 containers, each 40 ft by 8 ft by 8 ft) at a maximum speed

knot defined

of 23.9 knots.[17] A *knot* is one nautical mile or 6076 ft per hour, or the equivalent of approximately 1.15 mph. Measured another way, it would take a train more than 10 miles long to haul this load of containers. Today, even larger containerships are being introduced. United States Lines, Inc. in 1983 placed an order for 14 vessels capable of carrying nearly 4400 20-ft-equivalent units (TEUs)[18] or the equivalent of a 17-mile train.

changing shipping
characteristics

Containerization has drastically altered importing and exporting, shifted much of the cargo handling efforts from ports to inland origin and destination warehouses where container stuffing and unloading occur, and turned general cargo shipping into a production line business. The changes have enabled ship owners to keep vessels costing up to $50,000 or more per day at sea by condensing port calls to a matter of hours. Consequently, breakbulk general cargo vessels (i.e., freighters) have been pushed into lesser roles in the liner trades, particularly at leading world ports, where huge containerports and

FIGURE 9.1.
Since pioneering containerized ocean shipping in 1956, Sea-Land Service, Inc. has expanded its network to include 71 ports of call around the world. Sea-Land operates 60 vessels and more than 83,000 containers. (Photo courtesy of Sea-Land Industries Investments, Inc.)

FIGURE 9.2.
M. V. *President Lincoln.* (Photo courtesy of American President Lines)

FIGURE 9.3.
Shore-based gantry crane working a containership at the port of Savannah, Georgia. (Photo courtesy of Georgia Ports Authority)

shore-based gantry cranes have become common structures (see Fig. 9.3). Nonetheless, freighters—albeit more commonly in the 20,000 DWT, 30-ft draft, and 15-knot ranges—remain popular in tramp service.

container traffic

container benefits

container problems

By the 1980s, containers, hauling anything from appliances to automobiles to refrigerated and frozen foods, dominated the liner trade. For instance, more than 80% of the general cargo handled by the port of New York and New Jersey today is moved in containers. Containerization succeeded because shippers recognized, and were willing to pay for, the benefits of better security against loss and theft; expedited routings, due to shorter periods in ports and faster ships; reliable, frequent schedules; faster inland service via truck or rail; better protection against damage at sea; and in general, improved cargo control. However, containerization is not immune to problems. For example, direct service from local ports to desired ports is not always available, and it may be less so in the future. As giant containerships enter service, carriers are establishing load centers; thus decisions are being made to serve only one port in a region. An illustration is the selection of Savannah as United States Lines' only port in the southeastern United States. Another problem for some ports is that they do not have the demand or the required shore-based gantry cranes to handle these modern vessels.

Myriad Types of Ship Designs

One fascinating aspect of maritime transportation is the myriad types of ship designs that exist. Perhaps no sector of transportation is more responsive to changing market conditions and economic shifts than is ocean shipping, nor is equipment more customized than in this industry. For example, escalating oil prices virtually neutralized the profit potential of a group of Sea-Land–owned super-fast, steam-turbine containerships called SL-7's. Sea-Land's response was to order more fuel-efficient, diesel-powered ships. Fortunately for the owners, the U.S. government purchased the SL-7's for the reserve (inactive) fleet. Other illustrations of newer ship technology are roll-on/roll-off (Ro-Ro), LASH, and SEABEE vessels—ships built to haul container, trailer, and barge loads of traffic.

Ro-Ro ships

Roll-on/roll-off ships differ from containerships in that wheeled and mobile cargo can be driven aboard using a ramp configuration, such as the stern, bow, or side ramps that extend over the pier to permit access to or from the vessel. Inside the vessels, ramps somewhat similar to those in parking garages provide access to various deck levels. Ro-Ro ships come in many designs. Hybrids feature both a drive-on capability and space for crane-loaded containers (see Fig. 9.4).

LASH ships

LASH, meaning *lighter-aboard-ship,* vessels haul 80–90 nonself-propelled barges (lighters). The LASH ship functions in a long-haul, ocean transport capacity, and the barges, measuring approximately 60 ft by 30 ft by 13 ft, are the actual storage containers. Barges enable ocean vessels to serve remote or difficult-to-reach shallow harbors inaccessible to deeper-draft, large ships. By collecting and dispersing the barges at ocean ports, shipowners keep costly ocean-going vessels at sea. Like the containership, a LASH ship minimizes time in port by loading and unloading fewer individual units. The difference is that with the LASH vessel, the units are moved on water versus by highway or rail in the case of a containership.

FIGURE 9.4.
This roll-on/roll-off ship uses a stern ramp to allow vehicles to be driven on or off the vessel. Also, this vessel carries containers as shown in the far right of the photo. (Photo courtesy of Georgia Ports Authority)

SEABEE ships

SEABEE and
LASH differences

Another barge-hauling ship is the SEABEE, which stands for *sea barge*. Lykes Brothers Steamship Company, Inc., a U.S. company, pioneered the development of these vessels. Although they are similar to LASH vessels, several notable design differences exist. For example, a SEABEE ship handles fewer barges (38), but they are larger (97.5 ft by 35 ft) than are a LASH vessel's barges. If two of these SEABEE barge units were secured end-to-end, they would exactly equal the size of a standard 195 ft by 35 ft U.S. dry bulk barge. Thus SEABEES (the barges) are easily integrated in inland waterway tows. Another difference is in capacity. Whereas a LASH barge can be loaded with up to 375 tons of cargo, a SEABEE barge can handle 834 tons. A third distinction involves the loading and stowage systems. SEABEE ships have a 2000-ton submersible elevator that comes under the barges and is capable of lifting two barges simultaneously to one of three deck levels. Wheeled dollies then transport the barges forward to stowage locations. LASH ships use a 500-ton onboard gantry crane (see Fig. 9.5), which moves linearly on rails fore and aft along the ship. At the ship's stern, it will lift a single barge from the water. As the crane moves forward toward the bow of the ship, it hauls the barge to a fixed cellular stowage location.

Liner Conferences

Approximately 200 liner conferences serve U.S. ports.[19] Liners must choose between joining the conference that serves a particular trade route or trying to compete in the market as an independent, nonconference competitor. Most

FIGURE 9.5.
Waterman Line vessel *Sam Houston* with a White Stack Towing Company tug nudging a barge (lighter) up to the ship's specially adapted stern so that the onboard crane can lift the barge onto the vessel. (Photo provided by the Port of Charleston, South Carolina State Ports Authority)

carriers join conferences to minimize excess capacity and to avoid rate wars. Conferences and independent common carriers must file and publish rates; however, the business is characterized by much pricing freedom. Rarely in the past has the FMC used its power to disapprove rates on the basis of their being unreasonably high or low.

competition

In the general cargo trade, competition exists between conference lines, independents, and tramp ships. Sea-Land may be the largest container line in the world, but it has less than a 10% market share in the important trans-Pacific arena; numerous lines, many of which have strong nationalistic ties, compete for limited traffic. In fact, Sea-Land dropped out of the Trans-Pacific Freight Conference in the early 1980s, when its profits had been reduced to unacceptable levels by lower priced, independent competitors. Sea-Land's strategy was to cut prices below conference levels and meet the competition head-on. As a result, it regained market share, weakened the independents, and forced the conference to allow its members to have some independent rate flexibility.

General Cargo Economics: Profits

A worldwide recession in the early 1980s hurt the general cargo trade. Overall profits for the U.S. liner fleet were in general lean, with the exceptions of Sea-Land and American President Lines (APL), which both posted dramatic profit gains. In almost all cases, carriers, in the face of stagnated demand, focused on reductions in operating costs, improved asset utilization, and higher yielding cargo. In 1981, sales and profits for U.S. flag liner carriers totalled $4.7 billion and $100 million, respectively.[20]

TANKER TRADE

The second shipping market—the tanker trade—is a business of ships (tankers) hauling liquid bulk commodities. Included are oil, liquefied natural gas (LNG), chemicals, and other liquids. Oil, however, clearly dominates traffic in the tanker trade. Nations dependent on imported oil have little choice but to use ships. With few exceptions, seas must be crossed to link exporters and importers.

Although U.S. flag tankers play a minor role in international trade, U.S. citizens control one of the largest, if not the largest, oil tanker fleets in the world. Ships are registered for the most part, however, in foreign countries. As noted in Table 9.2, only 29 U.S. flag tankers operated in 1983 in foreign trade markets. Most U.S. flag tankers (186) serve the domestic trade, where traffic is protected from foreign competition by cabotage rules.

Tanker Evolution and Economics

At the end of World War II, the T-2 tanker—a ship of 16,600 DWT, with a length of 523 ft—was one of the largest and most popularly deployed ships in the oil trade. Today the T-2 is a dwarf compared to supertankers in the

100,000–500,000-DWT range. For example, the *Seawise Giant,* the largest ship afloat, can handle 564,764 DWT. It measures more than 1500 ft long and 226 ft wide, and it draws more than 97 ft when fully loaded.[21] Its cargo, if placed on a 100-yard-long football field, would reach a height of nearly 500 ft—just about the length of the T-2.

emergence
of supertankers

What caused the emergence of supertankers? Actually, there were several reasons, but economics was primarily responsible. Supertankers create economies of scale. A *VLCC*—a very large crude carrier, which is a ship measuring at least 160,000 DWT, but under 320,000 DWT—or a *ULCC*—an ultra large crude carrier of 320,000 DWT or more—can dramatically reduce the delivered cost per ton of oil. For example, the *Seawise Giant* has approximately the same number of personnel as a T-2, but the former can handle the same cargo as 34 T-2 tankers. Also stimulating supertanker development was the 1967 Middle East conflict, which closed the Suez Canal and forced petroleum interests to find an economical way to ship oil around the Cape of Good Hope and Africa from the Persian Gulf to Europe. Finally, the first supertankers proved that large-ship technology was feasible and that shipyards could create acceptably safe huge tankers. Thus, in a short time, the transportation of international oil traffic became dominated by VLCCs and ULCCs. With their advent, smaller vessels were relegated to serving domestic coastal trades and shallower draft ports.

economies of scale: crews

The early 1980s were not good years for tanker interests. The combination of high oil prices and conservation cut worldwide demand for crude petroleum, driving oil inventories to oil glut proportions. Nowhere was this more vividly illustrated than in the United States, which reduced its daily oil imports from 8 million barrels per day in 1978 to 4 million by 1982.[22] Complicating the situation were the worldwide recession and increasing use of alternate fuels, mainly coal. Collectively, these factors led to severe excess tanker capacity, depressed shipping rates, and the scrapping of tonnage—namely, salvaging ships for their raw steel value—as shipowners struggled with slumping oil transportation demand. In the early 1980s the trend toward building even larger tankers thus came to an abrupt halt.

recent tanker problems

Foreign Registries

In discussing tankers, it is important to understand the logic of foreign registries, in essence, why U.S. citizens register ships abroad and why the U.S. government permits such practices. As discussed previously, ships may be registered in a country in which the operator will make port calls to discharge or take on cargo, or they may be registered in a flag-of-convenience nation. Consider Exxon, a U.S.–based multinational corporation. In 1978, Exxon and its affiliates owned the world's largest fleet under private ownership, and its 140 tankers were registered in 14 countries. More than half carried the Liberian and Panamanian flags, and the remaining registries were divided among 12 other countries including the United States, the United Kingdom, France, and West Germany. In addition, Exxon's fleet of about 50 long-term chartered tankers was registered in 10 countries.[23]

Exxon fleet example

Why register abroad?

Many arguments are presented in favor of foreign registries by U.S. shipowners. The overriding objective would appear to be the improvement of profits through lower costs, greater efficiencies, and improved ship utilization, but there are other motivations. For instance, some countries, such as France and Spain, have cargo preference rules; ships registered in those countries are favored for hauling oil to them. In cases like this, an oil company would desire the registry there to participate actively in the trade.

flag-of-convenience advantages

Flag-of-convenience registries—that is, the registry of vessels in countries whose ports an owner may never or seldom send ships to—are another matter. Ships are usually registered in these countries (e.g., Liberia, Panama, Cyprus, the Bahamas, Bermuda, Singapore, Hong Kong, and Honduras) for economic reasons or for operating flexibility, or for both. The logic is as follows: U.S. registries can be costly and restrictive. Before 1981, to be eligible for ODS, U.S. flag vessels had to be built in U.S. shipyards. In general, capital acquisition costs were therefore higher than if ships were purchased abroad. Another restriction required, and still requires, that U.S. flag ships be crewed by U.S. citizens. Furthermore, ships must be repaired in U.S. yards or be subject to duties of up to 50% of the cost of repairs executed in foreign yards. Thus domestic requirements and economic disincentives encouraged businesspeople to find alternatives. One answer was the flag-of-convenience registry. By 1978, U.S. interests led the world with a 32% share of the aggregate flag-of-convenience tonnage.[24] Most of this U.S. capacity was in oil tankers.

U.S. flag-of-convenience participation

U.S. flag-of-convenience policy

Although it seems logical that the U.S. would be ardently opposed to flag-of-convenience registries, the record proves otherwise; in fact, the government was instrumental in their development. During the early years of World War II, the United States wanted to aid the United Kingdom in its conflict with the Germans; however, it also wanted to retain the state of neutrality. Its answer was to supply its allies using Panamanian registries of U.S.–owned ships staffed by non–U.S. crews. In 1949, Edward Stettinius, a former U.S. Secretary of State then acting as a private citizen, helped create laws establishing Liberia as a flag-of-convenience nation. Today, there is no strong political movement to end flag-of-convenience registries and bring U.S.–owned ships under the stars and stripes. Besides, there is no guarantee that laws requiring U.S. registries would strengthen the U.S. merchant marine. On the contrary, it is possible that higher U.S. flag costs would place the nation's ship operators in a difficult market position. Unless costs could be brought in line with those of foreign competitors, a federal mandate eliminating or restricting foreign flag registries might lead to U.S. citizen disinvestment in the shipping business.

advantages to registering country

Why would a country desire to become a flag-of-convenience nation? The primary answer is money. Each registered ship pays fees for the privilege. Prestige is another benefit. A small country like Liberia is the world leader in registered tonnage.

Liquefied Natural Gas (LNG)

Among the more controversial elements of the tanker trade are *liquefied natural gas* (LNG) vessels. Their origin can be traced to the 1970s and to rising oil prices, oil supply problems, and the urgent need to find non-oil energy alternatives. LNG ships are controversial because of safety concerns.

As a result of domestic natural gas supply shortages and favorable import prices, during the 1970s, U.S. interest in importing natural gas for home heating and industrial use intensified; however, problems had to be surmounted before long-haul gas transport by water could be made viable. Gas is difficult to ship in its natural state, for it has virtually no weight per cubic foot. Thus

U.S. ship designers proposed vessels that would carry gas in a liquefied state, since liquefaction reduces gas to one-six-hundredth of its original volume. Transforming natural gas to a liquid is accomplished by chilling it to 260 degrees below zero Fahrenheit. Once there, the problem is to keep it at that temperature during long sea voyages. This problem was solved by loading LNG in cryogenic tanks, which act like huge thermos bottles (i.e., these tanks are highly insulated to prevent heat exchange and vaporization). These tanks, in turn, are built into the superstructure of LNG ships (Fig. 9.6).

At first, it looked as though LNG shipping would develop rapidly; then the environment changed. First, the safety of LNG ships was questioned. Inquiries were made about the possible dangers of a liquid so cold it could crack steel plating, as well as the dangers of the gas, which is highly flammable and explosive.[25] Mainly, safety concerns centered on potential disaster risks. For example, suppose a cryogenic tank ruptured in port? No major accidents in fact occurred with LNG ships used in U.S. trade, but the adverse publicity about the possibilities created doubts about the desirability of LNG development. Also, during the late 1970s and early 1980s, political disparities in the Middle East interrupted supplies of LNG and raised delivery reliability ques-

FIGURE 9.6.
Liquefied Natural Gas (LNG) ship. (Photo supplied by Panhandle Eastern Corporation)

tions. Furthermore, the partial deregulation of domestic natural gas prices spurred exploration, leading to increased domestic gas supplies. Finally, oil prices started to fall. Collectively, the changing environment lessened the demand for LNG shipping.

Safety and Ecological Concerns

Although some types of maritime vessels are safer than others, no ship is entirely risk free or totally safe. Everytime a ship goes to sea, accidents and disasters are possible. Recognizing this possibility, as well as the inherent risks of transporting oil and other hazardous liquids, the government seeks a balance between the need to move commerce and the need to protect lives and the ecology. Spilled oil, for example, can have a devastating effect on fish and Coast Guard role fowl; yet, U.S. citizens need oil. The U.S. Coast Guard polices shipping in U.S. waters to ensure compliance with ship and crew safety requirements. The IMO role United Nations International Maritime Organization (IMO) similarly focuses on international shipping safety and pollution control. Still, it is impossible to control all the actions of irresponsible shipowners and operators or the laws of nature (e.g., violent storms and huge, unexpected waves). Deaths, injuries, and ecological destruction are inevitable, as long as ships go to sea. The goal, nevertheless, should be to minimize necessary risks and the consequences of maritime disasters.

DRY BULK TRADE

In addition to tankers and general cargo vessels, some ships specialize in the dry bulk trade—hauling iron ore, grain, coal, phosphates, and other solids. Worldwide, this third major shipping market is in general characterized by large vessels plying somewhat regular trade routes from raw material source countries to import markets. The trend has been toward larger vessels, many exceeding 60,000 DWT, and some of which are as large as 300,000 DWT. Like tankers, opportunities for reduced delivered costs per ton have been the motivating force behind the development of such vessels.

Design Features

Dry bulk ships typically have a series of deep holds designed to handle high volumes of unpackaged cargo. Loading is commonly accomplished by conveyor belt, gravity-fed chutes, pneumatic systems, and power shovels—in essence, by highly mechanized, non-labor intensive, capital-intensive equipment. Unloading is also highly capital intensive. A particular hold could stow practically any dry cargo, but that is not always optimal. For instance, a ship designed to haul iron ore, a dense cargo, efficiently may be inefficient at hauling grain, which is less dense and which needs more cubic capacity.

OBO ships

A major concern of shipowners is finding backhaul cargos. Since fuel is a high cost in ocean shipping, revenue-producing traffic on the return trip, even if not ideal, is desired. In fact, to resolve this problem, multipurpose ships called OBOs, which were introduced in the 1960s, permit the hauling of *ore*, other dry *bulk* cargo, and *oil* in their holds. Although this flexibility requires additional onboard equipment and capacity, because there are separate holds for dry bulk commodities and oil, and increases ship construction costs, the added versatility enables these vessels to haul, for example, iron ore from Brazil to Japan and oil from the Persian Gulf to Brazil. OBOs tend to be large, with some in the 170,000 DWT range.[26]

Bulk Trade Economics

The United States, which is significantly involved in the bulk trades, is a major importer of iron ore and bauxite, from which aluminum is created, and a leading exporter of coal and grain. U.S. citizens are also involved in ship ownership, even though few dry bulk ships fly the U.S. flag. Similar to tankers, most U.S.-owned bulk ships have foreign registries.

industry problems

The late 1970s and early 1980s were difficult years for bulk carriers. Iron ore, grain, and coal accounted for about 90% of global dry bulk traffic.[27] Unfortunately, when steel demand slumped as a consequence of the worldwide recession, so did iron ore shipping. Likewise, U.S. grain exports were hurt by U.S.–imposed embargoes against the Soviet Union. Only worldwide coal shipping increased. Even in the latter case, however, the growth forecasts for coal seem to have been overstated. Declining oil prices during the 1982–1986 period removed some of the optimism from the coal business. Again, it is worth restating that energy markets are volatile and interdependent. Changes in oil prices and supplies set off chain reactions affecting not only gas and coal demand, but also shipping tonnages of these cargos.

SHORE SUPPORT ROLE

Facilities and Organizations

Efficient, strategically placed shore facilities and support organizations are critical to the success of shipping operations for all commodities. First, ships come into port to collect and discharge traffic, take on supplies, be repaired, and change crews. Shore facilities and organizations answer these needs and provide a number of other services, including freight solicitation, documentation, billing, intermodal cargo transfers, and cargo customs clearances. In essence, the ships carry cargo at sea solely because shore personnel make it possible.

ship agents

Ship operators rely on land-based specialists familiar with each country's local environment. A key organization is the ship agency, whose function is to trouble-shoot for the ship's captain and answer the needs of the ship. Ship agents arrange for bunkering (fuel), supplies (e.g., food, water, etc.), and steve-dore gangs (dock workers), among other requests. They also solicit cargo for the ship's operator.

international freight forwarders

International freight forwarders, of which there were 1506 licensed by the U.S. Federal Maritime Commission in 1981, are an extended carrier sales arm. They solicit freight, consolidate shipments into higher volume loads, and arrange for landside and ocean-going transportation for shippers.

NVOCCs

Nonvessel operating common carriers (NVOCCs) can enter into joint through-rates with ICC carriers and freight forwarders, as well as FMC–regulated water carriers. Thus a NVOCC can quote a single price for the entire intermodal movement from inland points via a U.S. ocean port transported across the oceans to the foreign port. NVOCCs are common carriers that provide ocean shipping services without operating ships themselves. Primarily serving less-than-containerload shippers, they provide pick-up and delivery services, stuff (load) containers, prepare export documents, assume responsibility for the safe carriage of the cargo, and are financially liable to the cargo owner for cargo losses and damages.[28]

other specialists

Other specialists work for fees to facilitate foreign trade transactions. Included are customshouse brokers, who help shippers clear the regulations, paperwork, and taxing barriers of importing countries, as well as financial and insurance experts, export/import advisors, lawyers, and accountants.

PORT DEVELOPMENTS

Container Stuffing

Trends in international water transportation have initiated four important port developments: container stuffing, port competition, bridge services, and deep draft ports. Container stuffing is a labor dispute concerning the right to load containers. Before the advent of containerships, longshoremen earned their livings by handling breakbulk shipments at the pier. However, containers can be loaded anywhere. Thus containers have cost many longshoremen their jobs; fewer stevedore gangs are needed because containerships are loaded more quickly than breakbulk vessels formerly were, and inland loading and unloading of containers are also occurring. The International Longshoremen's Association (ILA), the union representing longshoremen on the Atlantic and Gulf coasts, fought hard for job protection against this threat, and in 1985 won an important victory when the U.S. Supreme Court upheld the 50-mile container rule. As a result, the ILA now has the right at the pier to strip and restuff all liner containers containing freight moving to and from points within 50 miles of the port. Rules do not apply to containers owned or leased by shippers—that is, those not owned or leased by liner companies.[29] Although container stuffing rules protect ILA jobs, they result in unnecessary work, added shipping costs, and increased risks of loss and damage. Container stuffing exemplifies ever-present conflicts in transportation, such as this trade-off between the needs for job protection and carrier efficiency.

Port Competition

Ports, as well as ship operators, compete with one another. Competition exists between domestic ports and between ports in different countries. Domestically, for example, Seattle, Washington, competes with Portland, Oregon; East Coast ports compete with Gulf of Mexico ports; and small ports compete with major ports like New York.

port
equalization charges

To a great extent, federal policy and carrier pricing dictate the desired level of competition. One controlling mechanism is *port equalization charges—* rail rates to different ports from a particular origin that approximately equal one another regardless of the costs to each port. Greater pricing freedoms in the rail and truck sectors, however, have considerably undermined the port equalization concept. U.S. ports also compete with Canadian ports. In fact, the diversion of U.S. traffic to Canadian ports is one example of a response by U.S. shippers dissatisfied with domestic rates and services.

Bridge Services

land-bridge

The need for improved intermodal activities has resulted in bridge services. *Land-bridge* refers to a rail movement across the contiguous United States with both a former and subsequent ocean shipment. For example, a container that originates in Japan is shipped to a U.S. Pacific port, loaded on a rail car for an Atlantic port, and then shipped by water to England. Neither the origin nor destination is in the United States. The goal is to use surface transpor-

mini-bridge

tation to reduce delivery times. In addition, a *mini-bridge* substitutes rail service for port-to-port ocean transport. A container from Japan destined for New Orleans would land at a West Coast port and be shipped by rail to New Orleans. Although New Orleans is a port, the container must pass through

micro-bridge

another port (in this case, a port on the West Coast). *Micro-bridge* services connect an inland U.S. point with a foreign port, for example, a container shipped by rail from Pittsburgh to New York and subsequently sent from there to Rotterdam by containership. Under any of these three bridge services, cargo moves under a single bill of lading—land and water services are combined under a single contract. In each case, the ocean carrier assumes responsibility for paying the costs of surface movements, but these fees are recouped from shippers.

double-stack trains

Double-stack trains are an outgrowth of containerization and bridge services. In the early 1980s, American President Lines, United States Lines, NYK Lines, and other intermodal steamship lines acquired articulated cars and contracted with railroads for linehaul overland services (see photo, Fig. 6.9). In 1986, double-stack trains were typically hauling between 200–250 containers, each 40–45-ft long, in dedicated unit trains. Each lightweight railroad car was approximately 270-ft long and was capable of carrying 10 containers. This feat was accomplished by stacking two containers on each of the five platforms that comprised a car. Double-stack trains were introduced because they increase railroad productivity and reduce surface transportation rates. Unfortunately, in 1984 serious backhaul problems emerged as traffic moving from West-to-East outnumbered East-to-West container loads by a wide margin. Steamship companies, needing to fill empty containers returning to West Coast ports, began selling container services to domestic shippers, such as people desiring to move freight from Chicago to Seattle, Oakland, and Los Angeles. This marketing initiative by ocean carriers triggered a rate war with railroads. Burlington Northern Railroad and Southern Pacific Transportation Company, for instance, responded in July 1984 by cutting piggyback rates in these westbound traffic lanes.[30]

Deep Draft Ports

The trend toward large, deep draft tanker and dry bulk vessels has also affected port development plans. Few U.S. harbors are deep enough to serve these ships without substantial dredging of channels to match ship draft capabilities. Thus, if the United States wants the economies of huge ships, ports must be modernized. Otherwise, small ships must be used, or *lightering* (e.g., the process by which a deep draft vessel has some of its cargo taken off in deep water to permit the vessel's entry into a port) is necessary.

LOOP   In response to this problem, several oil pipeline companies built the Louisiana Offshore Oil Port (LOOP) to handle VLCCs and ULCCs. *LOOP*, an offshore deepwater mooring system, allows supertankers to discharge oil directly into a submerged pipeline for delivery to land-based storage facilities and eventual movement through the U.S. pipeline system. After years of planning and development, LOOP opened in May 1981. Technologically, the system has worked well. Financially, however, it has had difficulties. Built to handle high volumes of oil and to respond to projections of rising imports, LOOP has borne the impact of shrinking U.S. oil imports. It was a sound idea victimized by a dynamic environment.

coal ports   The forecast of burgeoning U.S. coal exports encouraged the development and use of *super colliers*—large coal-hauling ships. Unfortunately, these ships also draw too much water for direct access to practically all U.S. coal ports. Thus, in the late 1970s, a push for deep draft coal ports developed. The goal is still being pursued today. Most proponents want U.S. taxpayers to fund extensive dredging activities. They argue that deep draft ports are needed if U.S. coal is to be competitive in the world marketplace; otherwise, high shipping costs linked to the necessity of using small ships will make U.S. coal exports nonprice competitive. This is a complex, unresolved issue involving multiple federal policy concerns.[31] However, Reagan's administration has opposed total federal financing of deep draft ports. Therefore deep draft ports in the immediate future are unlikely without user taxes and local taxpayer aid.

OCEAN PASSENGER TRANSPORTATION

One substantive change in transportation has been the resurrection of ocean passenger travel. Just when many thought liner passenger service was dead, entrepreneurs introduced the idea of floating resort hotels voyaging to scenic ports of call. Today, the cruise line business is one of the fastest growing transport sectors.

U.S. operators
ports

The United States serves two roles in this business. First, two companies operate ocean-going cruise vessels: American Hawaii Cruises and Delta Steamship Lines. Secondly, the U.S. ports of Miami, Fort Lauderdale, San Francisco, Los Angeles, and New York are important traffic originators. In fact, in the passenger trade, the U.S. port role is more significant than the U.S. flag ship role. Of the more than 150 cruise ships operating worldwide, only a few are U.S. flag ships.

industry facts

During the 1984 calendar year, 1,639,913 North American passengers boarded cruiseships, compared with 1,100,000 in 1979. Most passengers (83%) choose a cruise of one week or less—either a seven-day or a three- or four-day roundtrip offering. Ticket prices vary according to accommodations and duration. Air-sea packages whose fares include both air travel to and from the port and cruise services are popular. With few exceptions, passengers return to their port of embarkation or original point; hence, it is a roundtrip business.[32]

popularity

The increasing popularity of cruises can be traced in part to satisfied customers; positive word-of-mouth advertising; and strong marketing, particularly in sales through travel agencies. Another major catalyst in the trade's development has been *Loveboat,* a popular U.S. television program showing the excitement of the cruise liner business.

developments

Overall, the cruise liner business forecast seems promising. On the other hand, the traditional point-to-point international passenger ocean liner trade has been nearly obliterated by international jet airline services. In the North Atlantic—once the busiest market for ocean liners—only the *Queen Elizabeth II* operates today on a regularly scheduled pattern of crossings and only for about six months a year.

SUMMARY

Most of the world's international cargo is transported by oceangoing ships flying the flags of practically all nations. U.S. shipping interests involved in this business include shipowners; cargo merchants—both sellers and buyers; labor, including crewmembers, longshoremen, and shipyard workers; shipbuilders; and various shore support organizations, such as ship agents, ship brokers, international freight forwarders, port authorities, and customshouse brokers. Also significantly linked to this trade are inland transportation modes such as trucking and railroads, which create intermodal links with ocean carriers. Whereas the main function of merchant vessels is long-haul, efficient water transportation, inland carriers generate cargo and make ultimate deliveries possible.

International water transportation can be segmented into the general cargo, tanker, and dry bulk trades. Ship designs for these sectors are determined by the specialized needs of the various cargos transported and changing ship economics. Trends toward giant ships to haul containers, oil, and mine and farm products have their origin in economies of scale. As vessels increase in size, delivered costs per ton tend to decrease. Accompanying these larger ships, however, are business and ecological risks that remain troublesome. For instance, accidents involving large tankers, because of their capacities to carry vast quantities of oil, can be devastating. In response, the United States, acting unilaterally, as well as multinational agencies such as IMO, have been implementing policies and programs to reduce calamities.

Relative to the size of the U.S. economy, the U.S. flag fleet is small. However, due to foreign registries, U.S. citizens own and control one of the world's largest fleets, and the U.S. intermodal fleet is the largest in the world. Still, the federal government, worried about the threat of increasing foreign-flag competition, enacted the Shipping Act of 1984 to improve the economics and the efficiency of the U.S. flag liner fleet.

Overall, the merchant marine is an exciting transportation component offering equipment variety in a volatile business setting. Slight changes in energy prices and supplies, world politics, port developments, and ship technology present both risks and opportunities for those placing their fortunes on the line. Thus this business is only for clear-thinking strategists who have done their homework.

STUDY QUESTIONS

1. Explain your understanding of the conference (liner) system as it operates in the U.S. foreign trades.

2. Explain the options available to U.S. shipowners for registering a vessel. Why might they choose each option?

3. How has containerization affected the ocean movement of general cargo shipments?

4. What factors motivated shipowners to buy supertankers?

5. What types of managerial decisions must liner operators make?

6. Provide a definition and an example of a landbridge movement and how this service might benefit shippers.

7. What is the U.S. government's policy toward flag-of-convenience registries by U.S. citizens?

8. How might the Shipping Act of 1984 encourage the development of an economically sound and efficient U.S. flag liner fleet?

ENDNOTES

1. U.S., Bureau of the Census, *Statistical Abstract of the United States: 1986*, 106th ed. (Washington, D.C.: Government Printing Office, December 1985), p. 807.

2. U.S., Federal Maritime Commission, *20th Annual Report*, FY ended 30 September 1981 (Washington, D.C.: Government Printing Office, 1981), p. 2.

3. *Lloyd's Register of Shipping Statistical Tables: 1983* (London: Lloyd's, 1983), p. 13 (hereafter cited as *Lloyd's Register*).

4. *Shipping Statistics Yearbook: 1984* (Bremen, West Germany: Institute of Shipping Economics, 1984), p. 45.

5. *Lloyd's Register*, p. 29.

6. Public Law 835, 74th Congress, Sec. 101, 49 *Statutes at Large*, p. 1989.

7. U.S., Congress, House, *Shipping Act of 1984*, House Report No. 98-53, Part 1 to Accompany H.R. 1878, 98th Cong., 2d sess., 1983, pp. 5–6 (hereafter cited as Congress, *Shipping Act*, Part 1).

8. *Shipping Act of 1984*, 98 *Statutes at Large*, p. 70.

9. U.S., Congress, *Shipping Act of 1984*, House Report No. 98-53, Part 2 to Accompany H.R. 1878, 98th Cong., 2d sess., 1983, p. 2 (hereafter cited as Congress, *Shipping Act*, Part 2).

10. Congress, *Shipping Act*, Part 1, p. 9.

11. Congress, *Shipping Act*, Part 2, p. 4.

12. Information received by telephone from Robert A. Ellsworth, Office of International Affairs, U.S. Federal Maritime Commission, 5 April 1983.

13. U.S., Maritime Administration, Department of Commerce, *Maritime Subsidies* (Washington, D.C.: Government Printing Office, January 1981), p. v.

14. Based on H. David Bess and Martin T. Farris, "U.S. Maritime Policy: A Time for Reassessment," *Transportation Journal* 21, no. 4 (Spring 1982):9.

15. Ibid.

16. "Shipbuilders' Head Hits Administration Policies," *Traffic World*, 8 November 1982, p. 48.

17. Marc Felice, "First U.S.–Built Diesel Containership Joins American President Lines' Fleet," *The Maritime Review*, 15 November 1982, p. 4.

18. "First U.S. Lines Jumbo Containership—*American New York*," *Maritime Engineering/Log*, August 1984, p. 61.

19. Congress, *Shipping Act*, Part 2, p. 3.

20. *Seatrade U.S. Yearbook: 1982* (New York: Seatrade North America Inc., 1982), pp. 7, 13 (hereafter cited as *Seatrade*).

21. *Lloyd's Register of Ships 1981–82*, vol. P–Z (London: Lloyd's Register of Shipping, 1981), p. 687.

22. (a) "Tankers and the Flags They Fly," a background paper prepared by Exxon Corp., June 1979, p. 6 (hereafter cited as "Exxon Report"); and (b) *Seatrade*, p. 25.

23. "Exxon Report," p. 8. By 1981, Exxon listed 19 ships under its U.S. affiliate, *Fairplay 1982 World Shipping Year Book* (London: Fairplay Publications, 1982), pp. 110–114.

24. Citing a report of the United Nations Conference on Trade and Development (UNCTAD) in "Exxon Report," p. 11.

25. Peter Van der Linde, *Time Bomb* (Garden City, N.Y.: Doubleday & Company, 1978), pp. 16–17.

26. For a good discussion of OBOs, see Roy L. Nersesian, *Ships and Shipping, a Comprehensive Guide* (Tulsa, Okla.: PennWell Books, 1981), pp. 72–73.

27. Ibid., p. 49.

28. "NVOCCs Play Growing Role in World Trade," *Traffic Management*, October 1983, pp. 79–80.

29. "Supreme Court Affirms ILA Rule on Containers By Six-to-Three Margin," *Traffic World*, 1 July 1985, p. 7.

30. (a) David Field, "Shippers' Agents Debate Linertrain; Opportunity, Threat to Future Seen," *Traffic World*, 10 June 1985, pp. 19–23; and (b) Robert J. Kursar, "Double-Stack Influx Forces Rail Rate Cuts on TOFC Moves to West," *Traffic World*, 29 July 1985, p. 21.

31. See Frederick J. Stephenson and Arnold E. Balk, "Fast Tract Legislation—Public/Private Sector Roles in Harbor and Channel Deepening Projects," *ICC Practitioners' Journal* 50, no. 3 (March–April 1983):310–321.

32. Telephone call with James Neel, Cruise Lines International Association, New York, 21 April 1986.

ADDITIONAL READINGS

Abecassis, D. W. *Marine Oil Pollution*. Cambridge, England: University of Cambridge, 1976.

Abrahamsson, Bernard J. *International Ocean Shipping: Current Concepts and Principles*. Boulder, Colo.: Westview Press, 1980.

Bess, H. David, and Farris, Martin T. *U.S. Maritime*

Policy: History and Prospects. New York: Praeger Publishers, 1981.

Branch, Alan E. *The Elements of Shipping.* 4th ed. London: Chapman and Hall, 1977.

Cairis, Nicholas T. *Passenger Liners of the World Since 1893.* Rev. ed. New York: Bonanza Books, 1979.

Campbell, Thomas C., and Dalton, Amy. "Coal Exports: A Problem in Energy and Transportation." *Transportation Journal* 22, no. 3 (Spring 1983):34–46.

Carlisle, Rodney. *Sovereignty for Sale: The Origins and Evolution of the Panamanian and Liberian Flags of Convenience.* Annapolis, Md.: Naval Institute Press, 1981.

Cooke, James Aaron. "Port vs. Port: Steamship Lines Will Reduce Their Ports of Call in the Future to Gain Economies of Scale." *Traffic Management,* October 1983, pp. 65–66.

Corkhill, Michael. *The Tonnage Measurement of Ships.* 2d ed. London: Fairplay Publications, 1980.

du Jonchay, Yvon. *The Handbook of World Transport.* New York: Facts on File, Inc., 1978.

Frankel, Ernst G. *Regulation and Policies of American Shipping.* Boston: Auburn House Publishing Co., 1982.

Hazard, John. "A Competitive U.S. Maritime Policy." *Transportation Journal* 22, no. 2 (Winter 1982):32–62.

Heine, Irwin M. *The U.S. Maritime Industry: In the National Interest.* Washington, D.C.: National Maritime Council, 1980.

Kendall, Lane C. *The Business of Shipping.* 3d ed. Centreville, Md.: Cornell Maritime Press, 1979.

Kilmarx, Robert A. *America's Maritime Legacy: A History of the U.S. Merchant Marine and Shipbuilding Industry Since Colonial Times.* Boulder, Colo.: Westview Press, 1979.

Kyle, Reuben, and Phillips, Laurence T. "Cargo Reservation for Bulk Commodity Shipments: An Economic Analysis." *Columbia Journal of World Business* 18, no. 3 (Fall 1983):42–49.

Leeper, John H.; Tomassoni, Mark E.; and the Office of Technology Assessment. *Coal Exports and Port Development.* 2d ed. Centreville, Md.: Cornell Maritime Press, 1982.

Marks, Alex. *Elements of Oil-Tanker Transportation.* Tulsa, Okla.: PennWell Books, 1982.

Mostert, Noel. *Supership.* New York: Warner Books, 1975.

Peterson, Roger A. "Cargo Preference Legislation and the U.S. Tanker Fleet." *Transportation Journal* 19, no. 4 (Summer 1980):15–22.

Public Involvement in Maritime Facility Development. Washington, D.C.: National Academy of Sciences, 1979.

Rinman, Thorsten, and Linden, Rigmor. *Shipping—How It Works.* Gothenburg, Sweden: Rinman & Linden AB, 1978.

Rose, Warren. "Facilitating U.S. Oil Imports: Deepwater Ports in the Gulf of Mexico." *Transportation Journal* 20, no. 2 (Winter 1980):41–49.

Sletmo, Gunnar K., and Williams, Ernest W., Jr. *Liner Conferences in the Container Age.* New York: Macmillan Publishing Co., 1981.

Taylor, L. G., Captain. *Portrait of a Port.* Glasgow: Brown, Son & Ferguson, 1978.

von Schirach–Szmigiel, Christopher. *Liner Shipping and General Cargo Transport.* Stockholm: The Economic Research Institute, Stockholm School of Economics, 1979.

Waters, W. G., II; Heaver, T. D.; and Verrier, T. *Oil Pollution from Tanker Operations—Causes, Costs, Controls.* Vancouver, Canada: Centre for Transportation Studies, 1980.

PART 5 DIVIDES the U.S. pipeline industry into its three major components—oil pipelines, natural gas pipelines, and coal slurry pipelines. In this third modal mini-book, the text describes what each pipeline segment does, how it developed and why, and how it is regulated. The text reveals similarities and differences between the various types of pipelines, the nature of pipeline economics and competition, types of pipeline decisions, and the interface between the oil, gas, and coal industries and transportation pipelines that haul energy resources. Pipelines, because they are usually buried underground and are relatively inconspicuous, tend to be forgotten and taken for granted by the public. Their role, however, is vital to the citizens of the United States. Part 5 clarifies the pipeline industry's importance to the nation.

5 Pipeline Transportation

Pipeline Transportation

10

Pipelines are a rather unique mode of transportation. Unlike the four other modes (railroad, water, highway, and air transportation), which use moving vehicles to haul stationary cargo, *pipelines* are stationary vehicles whose cargo moves. Another distinction is that pipelines have no backhaul problems because traffic flows are one-directional. Pipelines are also known for minimal circuitous routings, no deadheading, a low degree of excess capacity, no commodity packaging requirements, an excellent safety record, and a superb level of service reliability.

Pipelines are far more important to U.S. citizens than perhaps most individuals realize. Because they tend to be buried underground and are invisible, they do not receive the exposure and attention that the country's other modes receive. Virtually everyone, however, depends on pipelines. Community water and sewerage systems are forms of pipelines. Pipelines are also primary movers of oil and natural gas—energy resources that fuel the economy and keep people warm in the winter and mobile year-round.

Interstate oil pipelines, natural gas pipelines, and coal slurry pipelines are the focus of Chapter 10. These three key components of the pipeline industry are described and analyzed to reveal how each segment developed and why this occurred, how each industry is regulated, what the economics of each segment look like, and what decisions carriers and users in the various pipeline industries make. As revealed in this chapter, both similarities and differences exist among the three forms of pipelines.

OIL PIPELINES

History of Development

Oil pipeline development can be traced to several events. The driving force behind the initial growth of the industry was the need to develop more efficient low-cost transportation to haul oil discovered in the rugged mountains of western Pennsylvania. At the time, the only option was unreliable, relatively expensive, horse-drawn wagons. Samuel Van Syckel is credited with starting the first successful oil pipeline—a 2-in.-diameter, 6-mile-long line. Van Syckel's pipeline, which began service in Pennsylvania in 1865, cut freight rates from $2.50 to $0.50 per barrel and simultaneously improved service reliability.[1] Both attributes—low prices and reliability—are still the two primary reasons shippers move oil by pipelines.

seamless pipe

Oil pipeline development was also helped significantly by events occurring at the turn of the twentieth century. Wildcatters discovered huge oil fields in Kansas, Texas, and California. Their remoteness from refineries and eastern markets created a need for improved long-haul pipeline technology, for existing pipe was too weak to withstand high-volume hydraulic pressures. Engineers responded with the invention of seamless pipe and electric welding between pipe sections. Both advancements reduced the loss of oil from pipeline leaks.

World War II

A third important factor was World War II. Crucial oil supplies needed along the U.S. East Coast were lost when German submarines sank 55 U.S. oil tankers. The threat of an oil shutoff spurred the federal government to support the construction of two large-diameter pipelines. The first, called the "Big Inch," was a 24-in. crude oil line from Longview, Texas, to Phoenixville, Pennsylvania. The second, nicknamed the "Little Big Inch," was a 20-in. product line—a pipeline moving refined oil—from Beaumont, Texas, to Linden, New Jersey, just west of New York City.[2] Together, these lines proved that large-diameter technology was feasible, verified that such systems could produce cost economies of scale, and established pipelines as the mode least vulnerable to enemy attack. The modern pipeline industry had been launched.

Operations

The heart of the oil pipeline business is operations. Unlike trucking, railroading, or air transportation, oil pipeline companies invest relatively little effort in marketing. What dictates success for the most part is high technology—choosing machines and computers and combining the two so that a pipeline works cost efficiently and reliably.

Virginia
Gasoline example

Few people realize that most of the gasoline transported to market moves by pipeline. For example, gasoline sold in Virginia may come from Alaskan crude, which is transported by the Trans Alaska Pipeline System (TAPS) (Fig. 10.1) to the port of Valdez, shipped by supertanker to Panama, carried by the

FIGURE 10.1.
The Trans Alaska Pipeline zig-zags across the barren, snow-covered North Slope. The
design converts pipe thermal expansion and movement from other forces into a controlled sideways movement. (Photo courtesy of the Alyeska Pipeline Service Company)

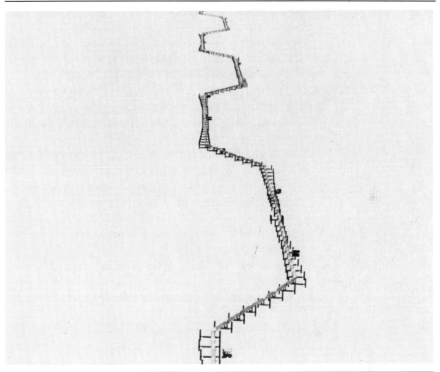

Trans Panama Pipeline System (TPPS) to the Caribbean side of the Isthmus,
reloaded on tankers destined for the Houston area, refined there, and shipped
by Colonial Pipeline to Virginia for local truck delivery to retail locations. Not
one, but three, distinct pipeline movements made the retail sale possible.

Pipeline System.　As the Virginia gasoline example implies, oil pipeline
traffic falls into the two categories of crude oil and refined oil products. Typically, a pipeline moves one or the other, but not both. In fact, a breakdown
of the 227,066-mile system in 1980 shows 145,770 miles of crude oil pipelines
and 81,296 miles of product pipelines. Crude oil pipelines can then be divided
into gathering lines (67,798 miles) and trunk lines (77,972 miles), with the gathering lines collecting oil from individual wells and feeding the larger volume
trunk lines. Trunk lines haul oil to refineries or interline points. Once petroleum is refined, gasolines, light oils, and heavy oils, among other items, move
numbers of firms　on product pipelines to end users or distributors. In 1982, 67 pipelines trans-

ported crude oil, 42 moved refined oil products, and 27 hauled both commodity categories for a total of 136 oil pipelines.[3]

pipeline similarities

Crude oil trunk lines and product pipelines are similar in several ways. First, both use large-diameter pipe (e.g., TAPS is a 48-in. line) and handle large daily volumes. Colonial Pipeline in 1983, for example, delivered 1.61 million barrels per day.[4] Both also require large investments in fixed assets such as pipe, stations, pumps, control and metering equipment, terminals (origin and destination points), tanks, and computers.

how a pipeline works

Terminals perform collection and distribution functions. Oil must be fed directly into a main line or accumulated in holding tanks to reach minimum tender (i.e., shipment size) requirements prior to entering the linehaul system. Once in the system, oil cannot be seen with the naked eye; therefore metering devices measure flow rates, and detectors check specific gravities (i.e., oil densities) to tell operators where particular batches are located. Exit tanks are also important, for oil must come off the line rapidly, since more oil under high pressure is following. What builds pressure is pumps, which push oil through the main lines at forces approximating 600 lbs. per square in. (psi). Pumps are housed, along with monitoring, measuring, and control devices, at origin terminals and at intermittent main-line stations typically spaced at 20- to 50-mile intervals.

deliveries

Modern oil pipelines can feed oil to spur lines—smaller lines branching off from main lines—and make heartcut deliveries from main lines directly to local distributors. A heartcut delivery is the diversion of, for example, 5000 barrels from the mid-section of a 50,000-barrel batch, without stopping the mail line flow. More specifically, after 10,000 barrels of the batch pass a particular point, a valve opens to draw the delivery from the next 20,000–30,000 barrels passing the valve. Once the correct amount is diverted to the spur line, the valve is closed.

computers and central control

Computers allow operators to move oil throughout the system from a central control room. Colonial Pipeline, the largest product pipeline in the United States with a route system running from Houston to Linden, New Jersey (just outside of New York City), can run its entire system from its control center in Atlanta. Its sophisticated computerized information system, in conjunction with advanced engineering, allows Colonial to adjust pumps and valves hundreds of miles away.

sizing

Crucial Decisions.   Because the oil pipeline industry is extremely capital intensive, adequate returns on investment are important if capital is to be raised. Two important management decisions are whether to build a pipeline and, if the choice is to build, where to locate the route. Pipelines must also be sized properly, since they must have the right capacity. Helping shape these decisions is the choice of commodities (crude oil or refined products) to be moved and the locations and volumes of supply and demand. For instance, a crude oil pipeline could be fed by domestic gathering lines, water carriers providing domestic or imported petroleum, interlining U.S. oil pipelines, or foreign lines such as those reaching the border from Canada or Mexico.

capacity One measure of pipeline capacity is pipe diameter; however, a more accurate device is the flow rate. Pipelines are constantly kept full; therefore larger diameter pipes hold more volume than smaller tubes. Nevertheless, output can be changed either by adding booster pumps or by changing pump impellers to accelerate flow rates to push oil through the pipeline faster. Impellers act like rotors or blades to draw the liquid forward.

risks of oversizing
or undersizing Since pipeline builders run the risks of oversizing or undersizing lines, they must forecast demand carefully. Given the 30- to 40-year projected lives of these projects, however, a degree of uncertainty always exists. LOOP is a good example of the risks involved (see Chapter 9). Built larger than initially needed to handle the expected growth in oil imports, LOOP quickly developed a severe excess capacity problem as the demand for imported oil steadily declined. If oversizing occurs, pipelines try to sell the additional pipeline capacity to independent oil producers, who do not own part of the pipeline. Failing to do this, pipeline owners must spread fixed costs throughout the remaining traffic or absorb the losses. If a pipeline is undersized, possible economies of scale are missed, demand exceeds supply, and competition is encouraged to enter the market to capture the excess traffic. The greatest risk is that a larger pipeline will be built seeking the present traffic as well.

looping The goal, then, is to build lines that will run at capacity 24 hours per day, 365 days a year for the life of the project. If a line is undersized, a loop line—a parallel pipeline constructed over the same right-of-way—can be added. The importance of careful sizing takes on further meaning when it is noted that a 36-in.-diameter line has the same capacity as 17 12-in.-diameter lines and 100 6-in.-diameter lines.[5] In addition to the greater throughput capacity of the large pipe, friction is also lower, since less liquid touches inner pipe wall surfaces than in the case of multiple smaller pipes. How fast oil moves through

flow rates a pipeline, however, depends on the number of working pumps, their horsepower, the pipe diameter, and fluid viscosity (i.e., properties in the liquid resisting movement). In general, though, speeds range from 3–8 mph.

Traffic

Pipelines moved 556.1 billion ton-miles of oil in 1983, representing 41.2% of the crude oil and 53.7% of the petroleum product traffic carried by all modes in the United States (see Tables 10.1 and 10.2). Furthermore, they did this work with less than 22,000 employees. In other words, oil pipelines moved the equivalent of 67.1% of the total railroad ton-miles in 1983, with only 6.4% of the railroad's work force of 341,507 people.[6] Pipelines have high labor productivity.

grades of oil Like wheat and other commodities, crude oil varies in quality and properties. In fact, crude oils are distinguished by color, specific gravity, temperature, vapor pressure, water, sediment, and organic makeup. Thus it is nec-

separation essary to separate crude oil shipments to protect the property rights of owners.

The segregation of refined products can be even more important. Product pipelines tend to move light oil products such as gasoline, jet fuel, kerosene,

TABLE 10.1. Ton-miles of crude oil transported by mode in domestic U.S. trade (1983)

Mode	Ton-Miles (billions)	Market Share (%)
Water Carriers	471.2	58.5%
Pipelines	332.4[a]	41.2
Motor Carriers	2.0	0.2
Railroads	0.5	0.1
TOTALS	806.1	100.0%

[a]Preliminary.

Source: Association of Oil Pipe Lines, "Pipelines and Water Carriers Continue to Lead All Other Modes of Transport in Ton-Mile Movement of Oil in 1983," Press Release (Washington, D.C.: AOPL, 18 April 1985), Table 2. (Adapted with permission.)

product pipeline commodities

and number 2 heating oil, rather than heavier oil products such as residual fuel oil and asphalt. Colonial Pipeline, for instance, in 1982 handled about 55 different grades of refined products.[7] Some lines also move liquefied gases

customers

such as ethylene, propane, and butane. Typically, a pipeline's list of customers is not extensive: For example, Colonial served 76 customers in 1983.[8]

Shippers expect to receive the same grade of oil that they give to a pipeline. Since shippers retain ownership of the oil transported by for-hire oil pipelines, carriers must carefully monitor and control batches of oil shipments

contamination

and take actions to minimize contamination, the situation in which adjoining batches mix together at the interface point and harm the marketability of the commingled liquid. For example, if adjacent batches of heating oil and gasoline are mixed, the contaminated barrels cannot be sold as gasoline.

Pipelines minimize contamination by advance scheduling, large minimum

scheduling

tenders, proper sequencing, and moving products in turbulent flow condition. Pipelines usually require shippers to specify the nature of their pipeline needs at least 30 days in advance of service. Likewise, carriers specify large mini-

minimum tenders

mum tenders. On Colonial, for instance, the minimum tender is 75,000 barrels or the equivalent of a stream 12-miles long in its 36-in.-diameter line. Large

TABLE 10.2. Ton-miles of petroleum products transported by mode in domestic U.S. trade (1983)

Mode	Ton-Miles (billions)	Market Share (%)
Water Carriers	159.3	38.3%
Pipelines	223.7[a]	53.7
Motor carriers	22.2	5.3
Railroads	11.3	2.7
TOTALS	416.5	100.0%

[a]Preliminary.

Source: Association of Oil Pipe Lines, "Pipelines and Water Carriers Continue to Lead All Other Modes of Transport in Ton-Mile Movement of Oil in 1983," Press Release (Washington, D.C.: AOPL, 18 April 1985), Table 3. (Adapted with permission.)

minimum tenders reduce the number of shipments and the opportunity for commingling. A third way to reduce the costs of contamination is planned shipment sequencing. The objective is to put compatible products next to one another in the pipeline. For example, if a batch of regular no-lead gasoline precedes a batch of premium no-lead gasoline, interface barrels can be sold as regular no-lead; the mix is merely a better product than regular no-lead.

batch sequencing

A common pipeline practice in the past was to insert spherical pigs between shipments. Pigs could weigh in excess of 1000 lbs., and by design had diameters slightly smaller than the inside diameter of the pipe. They served two purposes: (1) They lessened the degree of commingling by acting as a partial barrier between batches, and (2) they scraped the inside of the pipe cleaning it as they rolled along ahead of the moving oil. A picture of some spherical pigs is provided in Fig. 10.2.

spherical pigs

Although pipelines still use pigs for cleaning purposes, most major pipelines no longer use them for separation. Instead, they move product in turbulent flow condition. This movement agitates the liquids and lessens the tendency for heavier oil to settle to the bottom of a pipe and commodities of lower specific gravity to float to the top. In other words, by keeping molecules moving, turbulent flow condition lessens contamination. Despite all these precautions, however, it is possible that up to two miles of oil in a pipeline can be contaminated as a result of commingling. If incompatible products mix, refining is necessary.

turbulent
flow condition

FIGURE 10.2.

Employees at a pumping station along a large pipeline serving the Gulf Coast and Eastern Seaboard receive a spherical pig—a large rubber ball that traversed a section of the pipeline. Today, such pigs are used primarily to scrape wax residue and debris from the pipeline. The spheres are also used by some pipelines to mark the interface between two distinct products such as between gasoline and distillate fuel oil. (Photo courtesy of Colonial Pipeline Company)

Competition

intramodal
competition

A major difference between oil pipelines and natural gas pipelines is that the latter have a far greater tendency toward monopolistic market conditions than do the former. Crude oil pipelines face competition from other crude oil pipelines in moving petroleum from oil fields to refineries. For instance, 13 crude oil pipelines connect the West Texas fields and the Texas Gulf Coast refining area. Similarly, product pipelines like Colonial and Plantation compete for traffic moving from Houston to the Northeast. Sometimes crude oil pipelines compete against product pipelines because choices are made, such as between shipping crude oil from Texas to the midwestern refineries for local sales, or shipping Texas refined oil to midwestern markets. In addition, many crude oil pipelines and product pipelines compete with water carriers—for example, competition for refined oil moving from the Texas Gulf states to cities like New York, Philadelphia, and Boston. Oil could just as easily move by tanker as by pipeline, and it often does.

intermodal
competition

Tables 10.1 and 10.2 imply far more intermodal competition exists for oil movements than is actually true. As noted in Chapter 8, Alaskan oil traffic is moved by cooperative, not competitive, efforts of water carriers, oil pipelines, and trucking companies. Shippers cannot move crude oil from Alaska to California by pipeline because no pipeline exists to accommodate the traffic. Therefore, although oil pipelines experience far greater intermodal competition than do natural gas pipelines, it is best to examine individual market situations, rather than to rely on aggregate oil traffic statistics and modal market shares to determine the degree of oil pipeline competition. Many people are concerned with the degree of competition in the oil pipeline business because it can have a significant impact on rates. It will also influence pending decisions on whether to deregulate the oil pipeline industry.

Regulation

FERC responsibilities

At the federal level, the Federal Energy Regulatory Commission (FERC) regulates interstate oil pipelines. The FERC's jurisdiction is economic regulation, and its focus is on the rates and services of common carriers. All interstate pipelines that at any point in history hauled oil belonging to any party other than the pipeline's owners are automatically categorized and regulated as common carriers. The FERC's main objective has been to ensure that independent oil shippers, non-pipeline owners, are not unduly or unjustly discriminated against in gaining access to the pipeline system. For the most part, oil pipelines are owned by oil producing and refining companies. Therefore shippers and carriers tend to be one and the same. Thus the FERC's interest resides in protecting independent oil shippers from pipeline rate and service abuses.

origin of regulations

Federal economic regulation of oil pipelines started in 1906, when the Hepburn Act amended the Act to Regulate Commerce of 1887 (subsequently called the Interstate Commerce Act), placing interstate pipelines under the jurisdic-

other regulations

tion of the ICC. There they remained until the authority was transferred to the FERC by the Department of Energy Organization Act of October 1977. Nevertheless, the Interstate Commerce Act as amended is the legal basis of oil pipeline regulation. Intrastate economic regulation of oil pipelines, however, is the domain of state public service commissions or similar agencies. With the exception of Hawaii, every state contains oil pipelines. Pipeline safety is regulated by the U.S. Department of Transportation and comparable state agencies.

absence of regulations

Interstate oil pipeline managers have considerable freedom to make business decisions. Entry rules or prohibitions against route expansion are nonexistent. As noted earlier, carriers wishing to offer for-hire interstate services are automatically made common carriers by the FERC. There are no regulations governing exit, abandonment, mergers, or the issuance of securities.

rates

Common carrier oil pipeline rates must be filed with the FERC and published in tariffs. Since contract carriage is nonexistent, rates are nonnegotiable; shippers must adhere to tariffs or, if dissatisfied, try to have tariffs changed in the future. The FERC has the power to set maximum, minimum, and actual rates, but it rarely uses this authority. On the other hand, the FERC expects just and reasonable rates. It also has the authority to adjust joint rates between interlining pipelines. Actually, the FERC has focused much of its energies on the question of the reasonableness of rates of return and decides whether to approve or disapprove tariff changes after determining whether a carrier's rate of return is adequate. For instance, a rate increase may be granted if the FERC believes the change is necessary to increase a carrier's profitability to an acceptable level.

minimum tenders

One area the government watches closely is *minimum tenders* or shipment sizes. The FERC does not want pipelines setting unreasonably high minimum tenders that would deny access to small-batch shippers. If necessary, the FERC can prevent this problem by requiring smaller minimum tenders, for example, 10,000 barrels (bbl). Common carriers help small shippers meet these minimums by accepting *common stream* (joint batch) tenders, which allow two or more shippers to combine a similar grade of petroleum into a batch size that equals or exceeds the minimum tender.

prorationing

A potential problem exists when demand for pipeline capacity is high (i.e., when demand exceeds supply). Federal law requires that pipeline owners guarantee access to independent oil shippers. When independents request capacity on a pipeline that is already fully scheduled, a process called *prorationing* occurs: Those owning the line must reduce their shipments to apportion space for independents. If independents are dissatisfied with the space allocated, they can seek FERC relief.

Promotion and Subsidy

A feature of pipelines that is unparalleled in the transportation industry is that they have been built and operated virtually independently of public promotion and subsidy. Today's oil pipelines are totally owned by private inves-

Big Inch and
Little Big Inch

eminent domain

tors without federal or state aid. This includes the Trans Alaska Pipeline System (TAPS), built at an estimated cost of $9.2 billion. The "Big Inch" and "Little Big Inch" lines were exceptions; as previously mentioned, the U.S. government backed these projects as part of the war effort. However, these lines eventually passed to the private sector when both were purchased by the Texas Eastern Transmission Company and converted into natural gas pipelines.[9] Another exception to government nonintervention is the right of eminent domain, that is, the government-granted power to obtain rights-of-way either by buying property or by acquiring easements despite land owner resistance. Eminent domain has been given to oil pipelines by the federal government, as well as by individual states, where civil authorities decided the public interest would best be served by forcing property owners to sell their property. Although pipeline carriers almost always acquire rights-of-way without court action, eminent domain can be crucial in minimizing delays in completing projects.

Ownership Decisions

staying independent

single ownership

multiple ownership

One controversial aspect of oil pipelines is corporate ownership. Many oil pipelines are owned by their largest shippers, which creates the potential for discrimination against independent oil shippers. A common practice to lessen the risk of discrimination is to invite all shippers to participate in the ownership and financing of new pipelines. However, some shippers prefer to remain independent, partly because of prorationing, which forces common carrier owners to provide space if independents ask for pipeline capacity. Furthermore, shippers may not want to invest cash in pipelines when their capital is short or there are opportunities for better returns elsewhere.

Pipelines are owned by single or multiple firms. In *single ownership,* one company finances, builds, and operates a pipeline; moreover, the owner may or may not be a major oil company. There are two forms of multiple ownership. In *multiple ownership stock company corporations,* two or more parties build, own, and operate a pipeline as a single common carrier. Owners provide capital for the project usually in proportion to their expected throughput—namely, traffic. Colonial, with 10 stockholders, is an example. The second form of multiple ownership is the *undivided interest type.* This form of ownership makes each owner a separate common carrier, which must publish its own tariffs and try to use its share of the line's total capacity. Therefore owners could be viewed as competitors when demand is down and independents are being approached for business. One owner is usually chosen as the general contractor to build, operate, and maintain an undivided interest pipeline. The Trans Alaska Pipeline System is an example of this form of ownership, and in this case, Alyeska Pipeline Service Company is the operator. Advantages of multiple ownership are access to reasonably priced capital and the potential economies of scale from using large-diameter pipe. Pooling traffic facilitates much greater throughput.

Economics

investments

In 1981, oil pipeline capital investment was $21.2 billion.[10] The industry is highly capital intensive; pipelines must be completed before a single barrel of oil can be delivered. Once a pipeline is operating, the objective is to maximize the use of its capacity to spread fixed costs over as many ton-miles as possible.

revenues and yields

Pipeline revenues, by comparison, are relatively low. In 1981 they totalled only $6.7 billion, despite the industry's substantial traffic volumes. One major reason for low revenues is low yields. In 1984, the average rate per ton-mile was 1.268 cents.[11] As a specific illustration of oil pipeline prices, in 1983 Colonial moved gasoline 1534 miles from Houston to Linden, New Jersey, for less than 2.4¢ per gallon.[12] Low prices primarily resulted from cost efficiencies derived from large-diameter pipes, improved pumps, reduced maintenance and downtime, excellent use of pipeline capacity, and considerable insulation against inflationary variable cost elements such as labor.

cost efficiencies

rate factors

Oil pipeline rates are governed by operating costs and a carrier's need to finance debt, earn an acceptable return, and stay competitive. In this business, there are no rate bureaus. Consequently, individual carriers must prescribe rate levels, which they do by quoting charges on a per barrel basis, with an oil barrel being a standard measure of 42 gallons. Since costs are approximately the same regardless of the commodity moved, charges per barrel do not vary much between commodities. Tapering rates are customary in the business; thus transportation charges increase with distance but at a decreasing rate. For example, the charge for a shipment might be $400 to go 200 miles, $600 to go 400 miles, and $700 to go 600 miles.

income

Income is the most controversial aspect of oil pipeline transportation because the FERC, as already noted, makes rate increase decisions on the basis of whether a pipeline needs higher prices to earn adequate rates of return. At the center of the controversy is the knowledge that much of the pipeline system is owned by its oil company customers. The question therefore arises whether rates charged to independent oil shippers are excessive, since pipeline profits are channeled back to the competitors of these independents.

William's Pipe Line Company cases

On November 30, 1982, the FERC issued its decision in the *William's Pipe Line Company* case.[13] For more than a decade, the ICC (the FERC's predecessor) and then the FERC had been trying to decide what valuation should be used to determine the need for rate increases. Pipelines were entitled to earn a fair rate-of-return, but on what basis—Return on equity? Return on total capital? Return on some other measure? The FERC concluded in its 1982 decision that oil pipelines needed returns high enough to service debt and also provide "a real entrepreneurial rate-of-return on the equity component of the valuation rate basis."[14] On June 18, 1985, the FERC in the *William's Pipe Line Company* case adopted *net depreciated trended original cost* as the model for calculating rate bases and for determining rate requirements.[15]

high leverage
Consent Decree

In the oil pipeline industry, 9:1 debt-to-equity ratios are the norm, whereas in most economic sectors leverage of this magnitude is considered inordinately risky. What skewed the equity-debt balance was the 1941 Elkins Act Consent

Decree, which revolutionized pipeline finances. In the months prior to the December 23, 1941, Consent Decree date, the Antitrust Division of the Justice Department wanted a decree enjoining the major oil pipeline companies from paying unlimited dividends to their shipper-owners and argued such dividends were illegal rebates. However, the Justice Department was under pressure to halt its war on oil companies so that the oil companies could help the United States prepare for war. The result was a voluntary action by most shipper-owned pipelines to sign the Consent Decree.[16] This action resulted in two significant oil pipeline changes: (1) In no calendar year could dividends paid to a pipeline's equity owners exceed 7% of the valuation of such common carrier's property; and (2) most capital invested in pipelines thereafter took the form of debt, rather than equity. Since interest paid on debt did not count against the Consent Decree's 7% ceiling, borrowing became a viable alternative that could be used to attract investment capital.[17]

throughput
agreements

What made 9:1 debt financing acceptable to the investment community, however, was *throughput agreements*—that is, contracts obligating multiple ownership pipeline owners to use or pay for a portion of an oil pipeline's capacity. This guarantee, combined with a strong belief that U.S. oil consumption would increase in the future, reduced the perceived risks to lenders. Furthermore, favorable interest rates acted as an incentive to investors.

impact on
pipeline
rates-of-return

The switch to extremely high debt financing significantly changed oil pipeline returns on equity, as the following illustration verifies. If a pipeline earned $100 million on total capital of $1 billion, with the latter comprised of $100 million in equity and $900 million in long-term debt, the rate-of-return is 10% on total capital—equity plus long-term debt—or 100% on equity. Shippers wanting rate reductions argue that returns on equity are excessive. Pipeline investors counterargue that to lower rates-of-return would lead to pipeline disinvestment. What makes the debate even more interesting are the low numbers of shipper rate complaints over the years, the pipeline industry's low charges per ton-mile, the ability of pipelines to minimize inflationary trends, and the fact that taxpayers have not been burdened with financing pipeline investments or operations. Nevertheless, a relevant question is whether rates, even though low, could not be lower.

Lakehead Pipe Line Company Illustration.   To better understand oil pipeline economics, let us examine Lakehead Pipe Line Company, Inc., a crude oil trunk carrier operating a 2601-mile system in North Dakota, Minnesota, Wisconsin, Michigan, Illinois, Indiana, and New York. Table 10.3 is presented to facilitate the discussion.

revenues,
earnings,
and returns

In 1983, Lakehead had revenues of $194,151,000 and after-tax earnings of $52,810,000 for an after-tax income-to-gross revenues return of 27.2%. These figures compare with returns in 1983 of less than 5% for the trucking and airline industries. The operating ratio of total expenses before interest and income taxes ($90,665,000 minus $5,162,000 minus $86,000, or $85,417,000), divided by total transportation revenues of $188,710,000, was 45.3%. By comparison, the Class I railroad industry's operating ratio in 1983 was 93.2%. With total equity of $99,793,000 (not shown), the after-tax return

TABLE 10.3. Income statement Lakehead Pipe Line Company, Inc. (1983)	
Revenues	
Transportation revenues	$188,710,000
Interest income	5,441,000
total	$194,151,000
Expenses	
Power	$38,174,000
Operating and administrative	25,425,000
Property and other taxes	8,121,000
Provision for depreciation	13,697,000
Interest on long-term debt	5,162,000
Amortization of discount and expense on long-term debt	86,000
total	$90,665,000
Earnings before corporate income taxes	$103,486,000
Income taxes	50,676,000
Earnings (after tax)	$52,810,000

Source: SEC File No. 2-2681501–03 SIC 461, 10-K, Lakehead Pipe Line Company, Inc., 1983, p. II–6.

on equity was 52.9%. After-tax return on capital (equity plus long-term debt, or $168,933,000, a figure also not shown) was 31.3%. After-tax return on net depreciated assets at $232,864,000 (also not shown) was 22.7%. In 1983, Lakehead paid $48,000,000 in dividends to equity stockholders; it was not a party to the Consent Decree of 1941. As for costs, power—the cost of buying energy to run pumps and other equipment—was the company's leading expense item at $38,174,000 (42.1% of total expenses).[18] This situation is substantially different from the railroad case, where labor expenses are dominant.

leading cost item

Changing Environment

As the oil pipeline industry progresses into the future, more traffic growth is expected. New oil discoveries, such as the recent finds off Santa Barbara, California, will continue to interest investors in pipeline development. Tempering growth are the usual problems created by the depletion of oil fields and an unstable petroleum market. Also on the horizon is the possibility of oil pipeline deregulation. These variables necessitate the best planning possible in anticipation of what might lie ahead. In any case, the United States in the immediate future will remain an oil-based economy dependent on oil pipelines.

NATURAL GAS PIPELINES

The second major component of the pipeline mode is the U.S. natural gas pipeline industry. This huge system encompasses more than 1 million route miles and an investment in excess of $50 billion. Oil may be the leading source of energy consumed in the United States, but natural gas is the leading source

natural gas production and consumption

TABLE 10.4. Annual U.S. end-use energy consumption and production by energy source (1983)

Energy source	Consumption		Production	
	Quadrillion (10^{15}) Btu[a]	Percentage	Quadrillion Btu[a]	Percentage
Coal	15.860[b]	22.43%	17.225	28.20%
Petroleum	30.076	42.53	18.392	30.11
Natural gas	17.535	24.79	18.577[c]	30.42
Hydroelectric	3.880	5.49	3.510	5.75
Nuclear electric power	3.235	4.57	3.235	5.30
Other[d]	0.135	0.19	0.135	0.22
TOTAL	70.721	100.00%	61.074	100.00%

[a]Given the different properties of energy resources, the Btu (British thermal unit) is used to compare sources. A Btu is the heat energy required to raise the temperature of one pound of water one degree Fahrenheit. Btu's per unit of coal or other resource vary with product quality; thus these are approximations.

[b]Based on 15.877 quadrillion Btu's of coal less 0.017 quadrillion Btu's of imported coal coke.

[c]Includes 16.482 quadrillion Btu's of dry natural gas and 2.195 quadrillion Btu's of liquid natural gas.

[d]Includes only electricity produced by geothermal, wood, waste, wind, photovoltaic, and solar thermal energy sources connected to electric utility distribution systems.

Source: U.S. Department of Energy, Energy Information Administration, *Monthly Energy Review September, 1984* (Washington, D.C., 24 December 1984), pp. 3, 4.

of domestically produced energy (Table 10.4). Approximately 50 billion cubic ft of gas are consumed daily by more than 200,000 industrial users, more than 3 million commercial customers, and more than 47 million residential consumers.[19] This consumption is equivalent to nearly 9 million barrels of oil in Btu equivalents (see footnote "a" in Table 10.4). The United States has the largest, and one of the most sophisticated, natural gas pipeline systems in the world.[20]

comparisons with oil pipelines
In many ways natural gas pipelines are similar to oil pipelines, because they also require large capital investments and have high fixed costs; use pipe, stations, and computers; have one-directional flows; and tend to be affiliated with energy producers. However, there are also differences. First, most natural gas shipped by pipelines is owned by the pipelines and not by their customers. Also, natural gas pipelines use compressors to move lighter-than-air gas, whereas oil pipelines use pumps to move liquids. Furthermore, natural gas pipelines do relatively little interlining with other pipelines, rarely participate in intermodal movements, face far less intramodal competition, and are consequently much more tightly regulated.

importance
Gas pipelines have been virtually neglected in traditional transportation management education. Because the natural gas business is fascinating, and with changes in natural gas regulation and the importance of energy to the economy, transportation students need to be aware of the gas industry's characteristics and complexities. Therefore this section reviews the system, its development, the regulatory environment, gas pricing, the economics of the industry, and the Alaskan natural gas predicament.

Major Participants

Three major participants in the natural gas business are producers, transmission lines, and distributors. Gas originates both from gas wells and some oil wells, the latter of which bring both oil and gas to the surface. Nationally, the number of producing gas wells in 1981 was 189,609; however, about 70% of domestic production is currently divided equally between Louisiana and Texas. *Transmission lines,* which are large-diameter natural gas pipelines, collect natural gas at the wellhead and transport it to market. Transmission lines, in fact, are significantly involved in wholesaling, since most buy natural gas from producers and sell it to distributors. Distributors, after receiving the gas, odorize it to give it a smell for safety reasons and sell it to industrial users, commercial accounts like office buildings, and residences. Like the transmission lines, distributors are also in the pipeline business. Thus, from wellhead to home furnace, gas moves through a network of pipes. Rarely does gas require intermodalism.

numbers of firms

Approximately 3700 producers sell gas to more than 100 interstate and 1300 intrastate transmission lines, which in turn serve about 1600 distributors.[21] Transmission lines often buy from several producers and sell to several distributors. In some cases a particular distributor is totally dependent on a single transmission line.

Gas Pipeline System

gathering

Figure 10.3 diagrams a natural gas pipeline system. Pipeline functions include gathering, conditioning, processing, metering, compressing, linehauling, storing, and distributing natural gas. *Gathering* is the collection of gas from individual wells prior to conditioning, metering, and shipping it on main lines. For this purpose, the natural gas pipeline industry has placed in operation, as of 1981, a network of more than 86,000 miles of small-diameter lines. Usually the pressure emanating from wells is sufficient to push gas through these initial lines to the processing and conditioning plant; if needed, however, compressors can be added to boost line pressure.

conditioning, processing, and metering

Prior to compression, natural gas is conditioned to remove dirt and other impurities such as water vapor, carbon dioxide, and nitrogen. If water vapor, for example, is allowed to enter a compressor or pipeline, water could freeze and block the system. Processing separates gas from petroleum and natural gas liquids. In addition, gas passes through metering devices that measure flow rates and volumes.

compressing

Next, gas enters a compressor that accelerates the movement through the transmission line by increasing line pressure to levels as high as 1300 lbs. per square in. (psi). In fact, what moves gas is *pressure drop*—that is, the difference in pressure between the input and output ends; gas flows toward lower pressure settings. Like oil pipelines, which have booster stations spaced along the main line, natural gas transmission lines construct stations about every 75 miles. Stations house compressors as large as 15,000 horsepower. With the

FIGURE 10.3.
Natural Gas Pipeline System.

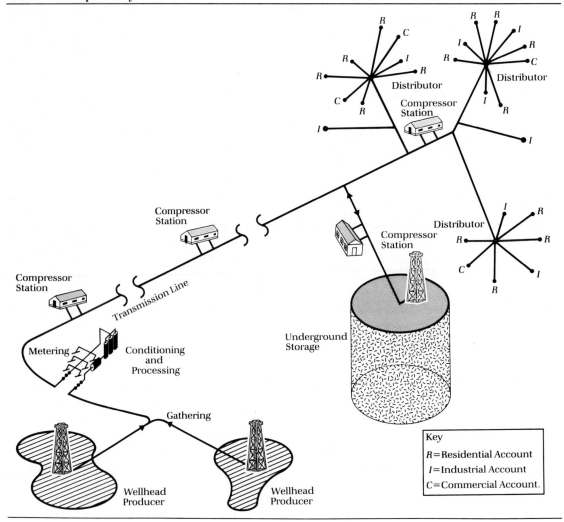

right equipment, gas can be moved at flow rates approaching 15 mph. Compressors also reduce the size of the volume shipped. At 1000 psi, the gas compresses to $\frac{1}{70}$ of its normal cubic volume at standard temperature. If this were not possible, it would be expensive to ship the much larger volume of weightless gas. Natural gas is not compressed further, however, because of higher compression costs, the need for much stronger pipe, and the concern for public safety. Natural gas is highly combustible, particularly under high pressure. Nevertheless, even at 1500 psi, it still has only one-tenth the energy density of gasoline.[22] Another alternative, LNG, liquefies gas by cooling the substance, but that too has risks and is hard to handle (see Chapter 9). Thus natural gas pipelines are uniquely efficient in enabling the product in its gaseous state to reach the ultimate consumer.

linehauling

In 1981 there were 270,000 miles of transmission lines that linehauled gas to market. Pipe used by these transmission lines is as large as 50 in. in diameter, and it is manufactured from seamless high-tensile-strength steel. Management must size a natural gas pipeline properly to maximize operating and cost efficiencies. If further capacity is needed, two solutions are adding or changing compressors and looping.

storing

Unlike oil pipelines, which benefit from reasonably balanced seasonal demand, the gas industry faces exceptional demand in the winter months because of the popularity of gas for heating buildings. To avoid severe excess capacity problems in other seasons, the industry has developed an extensive network of 385 underground storage reservoirs that have a combined capacity of 7.2 trillion cubic ft.[23] In the warmer months, gas is moved by the transmission lines to these holding points. Located in 26 states, these storage reservoirs are owned 50% by interstate pipelines and 50% by other parties such as distributors. Practically all these reservoirs occupy depleted salt domes, oil or gas fields, or aquifers—porous or permeable rock once filled with water. Gas enters storage reservoirs under pressure, and this same force propels it out from the ground when needed. Unfortunately, more than 50% of the stored gas, called *base gas,* must be kept below surface at one time to push

distributing

the retrievable gas out of the reservoir. After discharge, gas is moved by transmission line to the more than 708,000 miles of the main line distribution system. From there, it is disseminated through thousands of additional miles of small lines like those serving residences.

changing
pipeline technology

Like oil pipelines, natural gas pipelines use computers, central control, and automated monitoring and operation in running their systems. Technological advances now make natural gas pipelines highly reliable and virtually leakproof, which is quite different from the early days of the business in the late 1870s. At that time, pipes, which were made of wrought-iron and joined by bolts, would lose up to 50% of the gas shipped. Not until 1925, when acetylene welds were introduced for connecting pipe sections, were long-haul movements practical.

Regulation

federal
and state powers

The production, transmission, and distribution of natural gas is highly regulated but undergoing regulatory change. The regulation of interstate natural gas pipelines and intrastate shipments of gas moving through interstate pipelines is the domain of the Federal Energy Regulatory Commission (FERC). Distributors and transmission lines operating entirely within a state's borders, however, are heavily regulated by state agencies. In fact, most states give distributors and transmission lines exclusive, monopoly rights to operate pipeline systems in designated areas. In return, federal and state regulated carriers must maintain adequate service and follow FERC or state agency rate and abandonment rules. Safety is closely monitored and regulated by both federal and state officials. At the federal level, Part 192 Title 49 of the *Code of Federal*

Regulations sets minimum standards on pipeline materials, design, welding, operations, and maintenance.

origin of
federal regulations

Federal economic regulation originated with the Natural Gas Act of 1938, which established gas pipelines as natural monopolies and placed them under the jurisdiction of the Federal Power Commission (FPC). Then, in 1977, the FERC assumed the responsibility for regulating natural gas pipelines, in addition to regulating the natural gas, electric utility, hydroelectric power, and oil pipeline industries. At that point, the FPC was dissolved. An equally important event was the November 9, 1978, enactment of the Natural Gas Policy Act, which partially deregulated the gas business, exempting high-cost gas, newly discovered gas, and gas from new onshore wells from FERC jurisdiction. The NGPA's primary purpose was to encourage domestic gas production. A result, however, was the stratifying of natural gas into 28 categories, with each eligible for a different wellhead price. Because the law allows producer costs to be passed through to transmission lines and subsequently to distributors and end users, the NGPA's pricing provisions have been controversial. On the positive side, the NGPA did help to alleviate immediate shortages in interstate gas, for it encouraged gas exploration that resulted in increased gas supplies.

Natural Gas
Policy Act of 1978

regulatory focus

Services and rates are the focal points of federal regulation of interstate natural gas pipelines. The FERC's goals are to ensure that the nation's consumers have an adequate supply of gas at reasonable rates and that interstate natural gas pipelines earn rates of return sufficient to encourage capital investment. Specifically, the commission tightly controls entry and line expansion by requiring prior approval of most proposals to build and operate lines. The FERC can also order expansion or improvement of services, obligate a transmission line to assure future supply and to serve all customers, and require a transmission line to guarantee a specified annual throughput. Again, the tendency of distributors being dependent on single sources of gas is reflected in these unusual regulatory powers. Similarly, tight control on abandonment is a regulatory characteristic aimed at ensuring that consumers receive supplies of gas.

rates

Rates also receive much regulatory attention. The regulatory environment could encourage unnecessarily high costs and monopolistic pricing tendencies, so the FERC attempts to maintain just and reasonable rates. Thus the FERC administers a uniform system of accounts to judge the merits of rate increase proposals, requires filing of notice of proposed tariff changes, requires the filing of tariffs, monitors filed tariffs, investigates charges of rate or service discrimination, and approves or denies rate increases.[24] If the FERC desires, it can also apportion pipeline costs among various classes of pipeline customers, such as raising industrial user rates and lowering residential charges.

Gas Pricing Controversy

Despite FERC controls, rapidly escalating gas prices in the early 1980s spurred widespread criticism of interstate transmission lines. The latter were accused of recklessly negotiating contracts with producers, paying for high-priced gas they did not need, and using government pricing mechanisms to pass cost excesses onto the consumer.[25] Because gas pipelines are significantly involved in gas production, objections are raised that transmission lines have few incentives to negotiate for the lowest wellhead prices. The NGPA allows a transmission line to pay its own producing affiliate a price as high as the highest price it pays to independents, as long as that charge meets federal price controls. Distributors and industrial users, obligated by law to pay interstate transmission lines for a fixed percentage of their gas entitlements even if they refuse deliveries, demanded that pipelines reduce charges.

take-or-pay contracts

For years, transmission lines have signed long-term agreements with gas producers. Lasting 20 or more years and called *take-or-pay contracts,* the main goal of these contracts has been to guarantee gas supplies. As previously stated, adequacy of supply is a key federal objective. In addition, natural gas pipeline owners recognize how difficult and expensive it can be to relocate lines to other gas fields. Contracts minimize this risk, ensure the availability of future supplies of gas, and help guarantee the financial future of the pipelines. Take-or-pay contracts essentially mean that, during the life of the contract, pipelines will take delivery of the amount of natural gas specified in the agreement or pay for a percentage of the agreed-on volume if they choose not to take delivery of all the gas ordered. Usually, they must pay for a minimum of at least 75% of the gas volume specified in the contract. Producers find the take-or-pay contracts attractive because they guarantee sales and cash flow.

changing market conditions

Several factors brought take-or-pay contracts to national attention. First was the enactment of the NGPA, which deregulated certain categories of gas sold in interstate markets. Before the NGPA, gas prices were often deregulated for sales within a state. Consequently, gas was diverted to more attractive intrastate markets, leading to an interstate supply shortage in 1976–1977. The NGPA restored adequate supplies over the interstate transmission lines, but much of the new volume came from higher priced gas. Then the gas environment changed. Pipeline managers who signed costly take-or-pay contracts, when supply was short and demand appeared strong, failed to anticipate the worst recession in decades, declining oil prices, and conservation efforts by gas consumers. In 1982, the gas industry confronted a drop in gas demand and a simultaneous surplus in supply. When free-market conditions were driving down gas prices, transmission lines simultaneously remained obligated to

changing prices

buy unwanted gas at high prices. How much prices changed is documented by a government report indicating that from 1967 to 1981, consumer gas prices rose from $0.57 to $3.50 per thousand cubic ft (mcf). During the same period, average wellhead charges jumped from $0.17 to $2.15 per mcf. It also showed that transmission fees (i.e., actual transportation rates) from 1971 to 1980 increased from 22.6¢ to 77.2¢ per mcf.[26]

pipeline actions

Gas transmission lines gradually made efforts to improve the industry's dilemma. They tried, with some success, to renegotiate take-or-pay contracts cutting supplies and prices. They also used market-out provisions to reduce distributors' minimum bills.[27] These provisions included in some contracts allow pipelines to set lower prices for gas they cannot sell, and if producers refuse to accept lower prices, the gas covered by the market-out provision is released for sale elsewhere. Some transmission lines simply refused to honor their contracts, and in some cases, were sued.

RM85-1-000

One significant outcome of rising gas transmission prices is a new set of rules issued by the FERC on October 9, 1985.[28] Commonly referred to as Docket No. RM85-1-000, the rules will give millions of consumers and businesses access to cheaper natural gas by giving transmission lines the right to accept an optional blanket certificate. If a natural gas pipeline accepts the blanket certificate, it is required to provide carriage on a nondiscriminatory basis to customers who merely desire transportation services. In effect, customers of pipelines who accept blanket certificates are free to negotiate purchases of gas from producers, and they do not have to buy transported gas from transmission lines.

energy competition

The origin of the FERC's 1985 rulemaking can be traced to energy competition. As gas pipeline rates escalated, large industrial gas users threatened to buy substitute fuels if they were not allowed to buy gas directly from producers and use the pipelines as common carriers. Fearing the loss of traffic, gas pipelines gave in. Thus, instead of 100% of the gas being owned by pipelines, a rapid increase in common carrier traffic occurred. During 1984, 36% of the interstate gas moving in pipelines was owned by shippers.[29] Under the new rules, the shipper-owned percentage will rise. If a pipeline carries gas owned by someone other than the pipeline directly from a producer to a customer, it will be required to transport gas directly for all customers. Thus interstate gas pipelines have a decision to make. They can either accept the terms of the blanket certificate or deny everyone the right to move shipper-owned gas. The FERC's ruling, however, does allow carriers to pull out of common carriage after accepting the certificate, but they have to do so totally.

Gas Pipeline Economics

The transmission lines in 1981 had sales of $50.9 billion and net income after taxes of $3.1 billion.[30] High revenues substantially reflect the costs of buying and selling gas, which can represent more than 70% of total expenses. Balance sheet data for 1981 show depreciated assets of $45.9 billion, equity of $18.4 billion, long-term debt of $12.2 billion, and total capitalization of $30.6 billion. After-tax returns were 6.8% on assets, 16.8% on equity, and 10.1% on total capital. Thus gas pipelines are not nearly as leveraged as oil pipelines. In addition, with the utility (i.e., monopoly) type regulation now in force, rates are allowed to rise to maintain acceptable returns and adequate investment.

future concerns

Gas pipelines are concerned about their future sales and profitability. Revenues are threatened by a loss of gas sales if more shipper-owned gas moves on the pipelines. A loss of revenues will probably mean a loss of profits on those sales. Consequently, many pipelines disagree with the FERC's RM85-1-000 decision.

Alaskan Natural Gas.   One frustrating problem in any business is having a valuable resource that cannot be developed because of logistical barriers.

A classic case is Alaskan gas, for hidden beneath the surface of Prudhoe Bay are 26 trillion cubic ft of known natural gas reserves that have no way to get to market. The problem is far less technological than economic. Systems could be developed to transport the gas, but delivered price is the key issue. Will the gas be saleable?

ANGTS

The proposed solution approved by the U.S. government in 1977 was the construction of a 48-in., 4800-mile gas pipeline running parallel to the Trans Alaska Pipeline System—namely, the oil pipeline—to Fairbanks and then parallel to the Alcan Highway to a point near Calgary, Alberta, Canada. There it would fork with one leg going to the San Francisco Bay area and another to Dwight, Illinois (near Chicago). If the line is completed as planned, the Alaska Natural Gas Transportation System (ANGTS) would supply about 5% of the U.S. daily gas needs for about 25 years.

TAGS

Unfortunately, inflation, lower oil prices and an abundant oil supply, and declining domestic gas demand have forced backers to delay completing the project. Projected capital costs have ballooned to $43 billion from the original $10 billion estimate, and some oil executives believe crude oil would have to sell for $50 a barrel to allow Alaskan gas prices to inflate to profit-generating levels.[31] Meanwhile, Alaskan producers are daily pumping 1 billion cubic ft of natural gas back into the ground. An Alaska state committee has therefore proposed constructing an 820-mile Trans Alaska Gas System (TAGS), a natural gas pipeline that would move gas from Prudhoe Bay to the Kenai Peninsula, where it would be converted to LNG and shipped to Japan.[32] This plan only aggravates others who believe that Alaskan gas, like Alaskan oil, is too valuable a natural resource to be exported.

super LNG subs

One interesting suggestion is the deployment of a fleet of huge LNG submarine tankers—each 90-ft deep, 140-ft wide, and 1400-ft long—to transport gas under the Polar ice cap to eastern Canada or Europe. General Dynamics, the proponent of the idea, said these vessels would load LNG from submerged transfer terminals and then transverse the water under the ice cap at a depth of about 300 ft.[33] Although it is difficult to predict what the answer to the Alaska gas dilemma will be, it is equally difficult to believe that the gas will be left in the ground indefinitely.

COAL SLURRY PIPELINES

Coal slurry pipelines are the third and final major component of the pipeline industry to be discussed in this chapter. They work in a way similar to oil pipelines, for they carry a mixture of pulverized coal suspended in water, although other liquids might be used, like oil.

existing coal slurry pipelines

In 1985, only two U.S. coal slurry piplines existed (the Black Mesa pipeline in Arizona and Nevada, and the Consolidation Coal pipeline in Ohio); however, only the Black Mesa was operational. The Black Mesa, which has been in service since 1970, covers a 273-mile route from Kayenta, Arizona, to a power plant in southern Nevada. Annually, it moves about 4 million tons of coal through its 18-in.-diameter pipe, and it has been an economic and technical success for its owner, Southern Pacific Pipe Line, a subsidiary of Southern Pacific Company.[34]

reason for
chapter coverage

Coal slurry pipelines are a specialized component of U.S. transportation, and there has been strong interest, since the late 1970s and early 1980s, in developing nearly 9000 miles of new lines capable of annually hauling up to 200 million tons of coal.[35] Thus it is important to know how coal slurry pipeline technology works, and why, at least for the near term, the successful completion of ambitious coal slurry plans seems improbable.

Slurry Technology and Operations

From an operational perspective, coal slurry pipelines use pumps, like oil pipelines, to propel a water solution through large-diameter underground pipe. For slurries to function properly, coal is ground into particles no larger than $\frac{1}{8}$ inch in diameter and mixed approximately 50:50 with water. The water acts as a buffer to minimize the abrasive effects of coal rubbing on pipewalls, and it facilitates the flow rate through the line. Coal slurry pipeline operations must avoid solids settling and plugging the line. Therefore both the water in the mixture and careful system maintenance are extremely important.

preparation
transmission

At the mine, coal is stockpiled, cleaned, ground into particles, and combined with water. The mix, called coal slurry, is then stored in tanks equipped with mechanical agitators to prevent settling. Next, pumps inject the solution into the pipeline and propel the slurry at approximately 3–4 mph to the next booster station, some 50–150 miles distant. At destination, slurry normally enters agitated storage tanks until needed.

dewatering

What happens next depends on the desired end use for the coal. To be burned as a fuel for generating electricity, dewatering is usually necessary. Natural settling, vacuum filtration, and centrifuge methods can be used to remove the water from coal.[36]

need to keep
pipelines full

Similar to the case of oil pipelines, lines must be kept full to prevent damage caused by air in the pipes. Whereas oil pipeline operators resort to slowing the flow rate to accomplish this objective, coal slurry pipeline managers insert batches of 100% water in a line, called *water slugs*, between slurry batches when coal demand is depressed.

Coal Slurry Pipeline Development Problems

Interest in coal slurry pipeline development can be traced to optimistic forecasts of escalating coal demand linked to the viability of coal as a substitute for oil. Much has previously been said in the railroad and water transportation chapters about U.S. coal supplies and market opportunities both in the United States and abroad. Coal slurry advocates, such as electric utility companies, coal producers, and pipeline builders, were confident that coal slurry pipelines would provide an efficient, low-cost mode of transportation. Pipeline backers also saw coal slurry pipelines as a new source of income.

railroad,
rancher, and
farmer opposition

Pipeline proponents, however, met stiff resistance from railroads, ranchers, and farmers. Railroads opposed coal slurry pipeline development on economic grounds: For example, coal slurry pipelines might divert coal traffic from the railroads, force their coal transportation rates to unacceptable levels, and reduce railroad profitability. Consequently, railroads refused to allow coal slurry pipelines to cross their tracks. Ranchers and farmers in water-scarce parts of the country, such as in Wyoming where the coal-rich Powder River Basin is located, did not want coal slurry pipelines taking their limited water supplies. Nevertheless, the biggest problem was railroads, for they halted pipeline construction efforts.

eminent domain

Coal slurry pipeline proponents consequently appealed to Congress for the right of federal eminent domain. An intense lobbying effort failed, however, when the House of Representatives voted 285 to 182 in September 1983 to defeat H.R. 1010, the proposed Coal Pipeline Act of 1983. This bill would have given pipeline builders the right to take over property, or go over or under railroad tracks, to construct coal slurry lines.[37] Ironically, both oil pipelines and natural gas pipelines have federal eminent domain. This situation left coal slurry pipeline proponents with a much riskier strategy of trying to obtain eminent domain powers from each state along a proposed pipeline's path. If any one state fails to grant eminent domain, however, the pipeline probably cannot be built.

Status of Coal Slurry Pipelines

A major development of coal slurry pipelines will probably not be forthcoming in the immediate future. The coal boom, victimized by oil surpluses and declining oil prices, failed to materialize. Furthermore, during the two decades when coal slurry pipeline advocates fought for railroad cooperation and then eminent domain, pipeline economics changed for the worse. Delays in building pipelines, for example, resulted in dramatically increased construction costs. These costs would have to be recovered by increasing transportation rates, thus lessening the major pipeline advantage of low competitive prices. The loss of competitive advantage was magnified by railroad deregulation efforts. Using pricing freedoms, railroads successfully signed long-term contracts with coal shippers, thereby securing traffic coal slurry pipelines were planning to haul.[38] Consequently, coal slurry pipelines are rapidly losing their attractiveness to shippers who want low coal transportation rates and to pipeline investors who question their potential profitability. The barriers to coal slurry pipelines are numerous and difficult to overcome, and interest is waning.

SUMMARY

Pipeline transportation is specialized carriage. Unlike rail transportation, which carries vast numbers of different commodities, pipelines carry oil, natural gas, and coal. Oil pipelines and natural gas pipelines are extremely important to the United States because they haul nearly one-half of the U.S. crude oil, more than 50% of the petroleum products traffic, and practically all of the natural gas. Few U.S. citizens escape their positive impacts. Coal slurry pipelines, in contrast, are only a minor market factor. In the 1970s plans were made to construct more than 9000 miles of coal slurry lines capable of hauling up to 200 million tons of coal per year. Today, only one coal slurry pipeline is operating in the United States, and few plans exist to build new ones.

Pipelines are truly unique compared to other modes. They are the only mode where the vehicles do not move but the cargo does. They also have no backhauls. In general, the public and the carriers cannot see the commodities shipped because they are inside opaque pipes, and these pipes are buried in the ground. Among internal industry differences, natural gas pipelines tend to be regulated monopolies, but oil pipelines are common carriers; shippers own the oil in oil pipelines, yet natural gas pipelines (i.e., transmission lines) own most of the gas they transport; and oil and natural gas pipelines have federal eminent domain, but coal slurry pipelines do not.

Controversy surrounds the pipeline mode. Although oil pipeline rates are low, are independent oil shippers still paying unnecessarily high prices? Why are natural gas prices so high when there is a surplus of gas? Are transmission line charges excessive? Will coal slurry lines deplete scarce water resources? Such is the nature of this capital intensive transportation mode, which hauls the energy resources that fuel the U.S. economy.

STUDY QUESTIONS

1. Explain why there was considerable criticism of interstate natural gas transmission line prices in the early 1980s.

2. Why is it important to size oil pipelines properly?

3. What roles do oil pipelines, natural gas pipelines, and coal slurry pipelines play in the transportation of U.S. energy resources?

4. What caused oil pipeline capital financing to become so highly leveraged?

5. What measures has the federal government taken to minimize the risks of discrimination by interstate oil pipelines against independent oil shippers?

6. Why has the Alaska Natural Gas Transmission System never been completed?

7. How do oil pipelines, natural gas pipelines, and coal slurry pipelines handle excess capacity problems and manage to keep their lines filled?

8. What has stopped coal slurry pipeline development in the United States?

ENDNOTES

1. George S. Wolbert, Jr., *U.S. Oil Pipe Lines* (Washington, D.C.: American Petroleum Institute, 1979), p. 2.

2. Ibid., p. 21, citing A. Johnson, *Petroleum Pipelines and Public Policy* (1967), with no other information provided.

3. *Oil Pipelines of the United States: Progress and Outlook* (Washington, D.C.: Association of Oil Pipelines, March 1983), p. 1 (hereafter cited as *Oil Pipelines*).

4. Colonial Pipelines Company, *Performance & Trends 1983* (Atlanta: Colonial Pipeline Com-

pany, 1984), p. 1 (hereafter cited as *Performance & Trends 1983*).

5. *Petroleum Pipeline Primer* (Washington, D.C.: Association of Oil Pipelines, 26 June 1980), p. 10.

6. Association of American Railroads, *Railroad Facts 1985 Edition* (Washington, D.C.: AAR, August 1985), pp. 9, 56.

7. Colonial Pipeline Company, *Performance & Trends 1981* (Atlanta: Colonial Pipeline Company, 1982), p. 20.

8. *Performance & Trends 1983*, p. 1.

9. D. Philip Locklin, *Economics of Transportation*, 7th ed. (Homewood, Ill.: Richard D. Irwin, 1972), p. 608.

10. *Oil Pipelines*, p. 1.

11. Frank A. Smith, Senior Associate, *Transportation in America*, 3d ed., July 1985 Supplement (Washington, D.C.: Transportation Policy Associates, July 1985), p. 11.

12. *Performance & Trends 1983*, p. 8.

13. 21 FERC 61568, meaning *FERC Reports*, vol. 21, p. 61,568.

14. 21 FERC 61644.

15. (a) 31 FERC 61831, para. 61,377, FERC Opinion No. 154-B, Docket Nos. OR79-1-000 and 002 (Phase I); and (b) Stewart C. Meyers, A. Lawrence Kolbe, and William B. Tye, "Regulation and Capital Formation in the Oil Pipeline Industry," *Transportation Journal* 23, no. 4 (Summer 1984), 25–49.

16. United States v. Atlantic Refining Company, Civil Action No. 14060 (U.S.D.C.D.C.), issued 23 December 1941.

17. 21 FERC 61637, 61638, and 61639.

18. SEC File No. 2-2681501—03 SIC 461, 10-K, Lakehead Pipe Line Co., Inc., 1983, pp. I–2, II–4, II–5, and II–6.

19. *Gas Data Book* (Arlington, Va.: American Gas Association, 1982), pp. 3, 12 (hereafter cited as *Gas Data Book*).

20. U.S., Department of Energy, Federal Energy Regulatory Commission, *FERC 1980 Annual Report* (Washington, D.C.: Government Printing Office, March 1982), p. 25.

21. U.S., Congress, House, Committee on Energy and Commerce, Subcommittee on Fossil and Synthetic Fuels, *Natural Gas Regulation Study*, Committee Print 97-GG, 97th Cong., 2d sess., July 1982, pp. 19 and 196 (hereafter cited as *Natural Gas Regulation*).

22. Ibid., p. 106.

23. *Petroleum Storage & Transportation Capacities Vol. VI., Gas Pipelines* (National Petroleum Council, December 1979), p. 3.

24. U.S., Department of Energy, Federal Energy Regulatory Commission, *First Annual Report: Fiscal Year 1978* (Washington, D.C.: Government Printing Office, August 1979), p. 31.

25. (a) "Fed Up with Pancaked Rates, Customers Call on FERC to Investigate United," *Inside FERC*, 2 May 1983, p. 8; and (b) *Inside FERC*, 31 January 1983, p. 12.

26. *Inside FERC*, 4 April 1983, p. 4.

27. (a) Jerome J. McGrath, President, Interstate Natural Gas Association of America, Year-End Statement entitled "The Natural Gas Pipeline Industry Faces 1983," 19 January 1983, p. 3 (reprint provided by the Interstate Natural Gas Association of America); and (b) *Natural Gas Regulation*, p. 142.

28. (a) 33 FERC para. 61,007, *Regulation of Natural Gas Pipelines after Partial Wellhead Decontrol*, Docket No. RM85-1-000 (Parts A–D), issued 9 October 1985; and (b) "FERC's Final Rule on Transportation, Rates: What It Says, How It Works," *Inside FERC*, 14 October 1985, pp. 5–8.

29. (a) Robert E. Taylor and Bryan Burrough, "Energy Upheaval: Scheduled Rule Switch Would Aid Gas Users but Imperil Pipelines," *Wall Street Journal*, 8 October 1985, p. 1; and (b) Robert E. Taylor and Bryan Burrough, "FERC Approves Rule That Will Give More Customers Access to Cheaper Gas," *Wall Street Journal*, 10 October 1985, p. 3.

30. *Gas Data Book*, p. 19.

31. "Alaskan Energy: Shorter Is Better, Japanese Is Best," *The Economist*, 12 March 1983, p. 73.

32. Roger Lowenstein, "Alaska Proposing Japan Connection," *Wall Street Journal*, 17 January 1983, p. 26.

33. Robin Nelson, "The Ice Above, the Giant Below," *Popular Mechanics*, March 1982, 118–119.

34. Based on a paper prepared by J. G. Montfort, Vice-president and General Manager, Black Mesa Pipeline, entitled "Operation of the Black Mesa Pipeline System," and dated 9 November 1978. A copy of this paper was received by the author from Black Mesa Pipeline, Flagstaff, Arizona, in June 1983.

35. Based on a map and table prepared by the Slurry Transport Association of America, entitled "U.S. Coal Slurry Pipeline System," Washington, D.C., Slurry Transport Association, 11 August, 1982.

36. *Coal Slurry Pipelines—An Overview* (Washington, D.C.: Slurry Transport Association, 24 February 1983), pp. 3–4.

37. Albert R. Karr, "Coal-slurry Pipeline Measure Is Rejected by House as Railroad Lobbying Succeeds," *Wall Street Journal,* 28 September 1983, p. 6.

38. Bill Richards, "Lost Contract Raises Doubts on Coal Slurry," *Wall Street Journal,* 22 August 1983, p. 17.

ADDITIONAL READINGS

Barfield, R. S. "Trans-Panama Pipeline System Links Alaska Oil to Eastern U.S." *Pipeline & Gas Journal,* June 1983, p. 28.

Bright, Donald B. "Sohio Crude Oil Pipeline: A Case History of Conflict." *Transportation Law Journal* 2, no. 2 (1980):243–289.

Campbell, Thomas C. "Eminent Domain: Its Origin, Meaning, and Relevance to Coal Slurry Pipelines." *Transportation Journal* 17, no. 1 (Fall 1977):5–21.

Energy Journal 3, no. 4 (October 1982). A Special Issue on natural gas deregulation.

Farris, Martin T., and Shrock, David L. "The Economics of Coal Slurry Pipelining: Transportation and Nontransportation Factors." *Transportation Journal* 18, no. 1 (Fall 1978):45–57.

Hale, Dean. "Arctic Prospects Strong; New Pipelines Depend on Market." *Pipeline & Gas Journal,* September 1983, pp. 20–22.

———, and Watts, Jim. "Pipeline Construction Forecast: Modest Construction Year Seen for U.S., Canada Pipelines." *Pipeline & Gas Journal,* January 1984, pp. 28–30.

Johnson, James C., and Schneider, Kenneth C. "Coal Slurry Pipelines: An Economic and Political Dilemma." *ICC Practitioners' Journal* 48, no. 1 (1980):24–37.

Rose, Warren. "Facilitating U.S. Oil Imports: Deepwater Ports in the Gulf of Mexico." *Transportation Journal* 20, no. 2 (Winter 1980):41–49.

"Ships May Tap Giant Arctic Wells." *Resource Development,* Fall 1981, pp. 43–45.

U.S. Congress, House, Committee on Energy and Commerce. *Coal Slurry Pipeline Issues. Hearing before the Subcommittee on Commerce, Transportation, and Tourism.* Serial No. 98-37. 98th Cong., 1st sess., 14 July 1983.

———. *Coal Slurry Pipelines. Hearing before the Subcommittee on Commerce, Transportation, and Tourism.* Serial No. 97-196. 97th Cong., 2d sess., 6 August 1982.

———. *Natural Gas Contract Renegotiations and FERC Authorities. Hearings before the Subcommittee on Fossil and Synthetic Fuels.* Serial No. 98-7. 98th Cong., 1st sess., 10 and 22 February 1983.

———. *Oil Pipeline Deregulation. Hearings before the Subcommittee on Fossil and Synthetic Fuels on H.R. 4488 and H.R. 6815.* Serial No. 97-179. 97th Cong., 2d sess., 10 May and 23 September 1982.

———. *U.S. Energy Outlook: A Demand Perspective for the Eighties.* Committee Print 97-Q. 97th Cong., 1st sess., July 1981.

U.S. Congress, House, Committee on Public Works and Transportation. *The Coal Pipeline Act of 1983. Hearings before the Subcommittee on Surface Transportation on H.R. 1010.* 98th Cong., 1st sess., 13 and 19 April 1983.

U.S. Congress, Senate, Committee on Energy and Natural Resources. *Petroleum Pipeline Regulatory Reform Bill. Hearing before the Subcommittee on Energy Regulation on S. 1626.* Publication No. 97-95. 97th Cong., 2d sess., 21 May 1982.

U.S. Department of Energy, Federal Energy Regulatory Commission. *Proceedings of the Informal Public Conference on the Availability and Pricing of Natural Gas and Alternative Fuels,* vol. 2, April 1980.

Wildenradt, Wayne C. "Changing Economic Factors Affect Pipeline Design Variables." *Pipeline & Gas Journal,* July 1983, p. 20.

Wood, Donald F., and Johnson, James C. *Contemporary Transportation.* 2d ed. Tulsa, Okla.: PennWell Books, 1983. Chapter 6.

IN CONTRAST TO PIPELINE TRANSPORTATION, HIGHWAY TRANSPORTATION, the subject of the fourth modal mini-book, is very visible. It is difficult to imagine anyone in the United States unaffected by roads and the vehicles that use them.

Part 6 contains three chapters. Chapter 11 introduces readers to highway transportation by focusing on three important industry components—highways, the U.S. intercity bus industry, and the intercity trucking industry. Without roads, there would not be any need for buses and trucks; hence, readers are first exposed to the policies and mechanisms responsible for the nation's highways. Bus transportation is the means by which hundreds of millions of passengers move between cities, and yet it is a troubled industry that needs to be portrayed and analyzed. The remainder of Chapter 11 presents a detailed overview of a trucking industry in evolution. Regulatory reform measures that have greatly altered trucking industry traffic, economics, and competition are emphasized. This trucking introduction sets the stage for Chapters 12 and 13, which concentrate on general commodity trucking and specialized trucking.

Since most trucking revenues are generated by general commodity traffic, Chapter 12 addresses the needs, decisions, and strategies of regular route and irregular route common carriers, contract carriers, and intermediaries in this important trucking market segment. Chapter 13 reveals just how differentiated and segmented the trucking industry is by focusing on the roles, characteristics, and participants in specialized trucking. In particular, it looks at three specialized trucking industries—household goods carriage, heavy hauling, and the for-hire exempt agricultural trucking industry.

6 Highway Transportation

Introduction to Highway Transportation

The United States is the most highway-oriented country in the world. Every day its citizens rely on highway transportation to carry them to work, school, shopping, and play, as well as to supply most of their household needs.

What makes highway transportation function efficiently is a strong alliance between public and private investment and decision making. Unlike railroad or pipeline transportation, where rights-of-way are the responsibilities of carriers, taxpayers constructed and maintain most of the nearly 4 million miles of roads in the United States. Over this network, privately owned and operated motorized vehicles in the form of automobiles, buses, and trucks circulate subject to the rules of the road. Here again, government officials define speed limits, specify vehicle sizes, set taxes, such as the amount of tax paid per gallon of gasoline, and so forth.

Chapter 11 introduces students to three important industry components. The initial discussion covers the characteristics and problems of the highway system and some of the proposed and implemented answers. Next, the focus shifts to the U.S. intercity bus industry. Concluding the chapter is an introduction to the U.S. trucking industry, including a review of the sweeping economic regulatory changes instituted since 1976 and a synopsis of the economic state of this sector.

This chapter begins a three-chapter sequence on highway transportation. The next two chapters discuss the specialized characteristics and needs of *packaged* and *unpackaged* freight—general commodity trucking and the special commodity trucking businesses, respectively. Private automobiles and urban transit buses are not included in these chapters, because they will be discussed extensively in Chapters 17 and 18. The primary orientation of Chapters 11 through 13 is for-hire intercity transportation. Private trucking was covered in Chapter 3.

U.S. HIGHWAY SYSTEM

Public Highways

As noted in Table 11.1, the U.S. highway network is a 3,852,697-mile system of publicly owned roads plus thousands of other miles under private jurisdiction. Public highways are functionally segmented into local roads, arterials, and collectors. By far the largest component in route miles is local roads, with

local roads 2,653,138 miles and nearly 69% of the system mileage total. Local roads, such as the one in front of a residence, provide access to, and egress from, the higher speed collectors and arterials. Of equal importance, local roads are the means for accomplishing many home–to–work, home–to–school, or home–to–shopping trips.

As the name implies, a principal task of the more than 800,000 miles of

collectors collectors is to feed vehicular traffic from local roads to high-speed, high-
and arterials traffic-volume arterials. Arterials represent another 390,526 miles of the highway system. The most famous arterial system is the National System of Interstate and Defense Highways, or, as it is commonly called, the Interstate Highway System. When completed, this 42,500-mile network of uniform, limited-access, divided highways will link metropolitan areas and industrial centers of 50,000 or more population into a unified whole (see Fig. 11.1). The arterial system also includes 133,346 miles of other principal arterials (e.g., U.S. 1, which runs through the eastern states in a north–south direction) and 214,912 miles of minor arterials (see notes, Table 11.1).

Traffic Generation and Component Roles

Another way to analyze the U.S. highway system is by examining traffic generation. Table 11.1 shows the importance of the arterial system in terms of millions of vehicle-miles traveled (MVMT). Although arterials comprised only 10.2% of the U.S. route mileage in 1981, they accounted for 68.5% of the vehicular traffic. The most important traffic generator is the Interstate Highway System, which carried nearly 20% of the MVMT in 1981, with only 1% of the route mileage. In comparison, local roads, which had 68.9% of the route mileage, accounted for merely 13.6% of the traffic. These figures clearly establish the role of the arterials for intercity and interstate travel and the short-haul nature of local roads.

The U.S. highway network is not only the largest in the world in route mileage, but also the busiest, having generated an estimated 1.55 trillion

vehicle miles vehicle-miles in 1981. Nearly 84% of the route mileage is found in rural locations. Public officials in the geographically dispersed United States assign

TABLE 11.1. U.S. public highway system mileage and travel by functional category (1981)

	Rural	Urban	Total Miles[a]	Percent	Travel (MVMT)[b]	Percent
Arterial system						
Principal arterials[c]						
Interstate highway system[d]	32,959	9,309	42,268	1.1%	305,212	19.7%
Other	81,655	51,691[e]	133,346	3.5	451,823	29.1
Minor arterials[f]	148,826	66,086	214,912	5.6	305,495	19.7
Collector system[g]	739,924	69,109	809,033	21.0	277,290	17.9
Local[h]	2,217,320	435,818	2,653,138	68.9	210,451	13.6
TOTAL	3,220,684	632,013	3,852,697	100.1%[i]	1,550,271	100.0%

[a]Due to factoring procedures, individual components may not be compatible to other figures in the text. For example, as of 12/31/81, one source shows 40,756 miles of interstate mileage.

[b]Millions of vehicle-miles traveled.

[c]In rural areas, a network of routes that primarily serve travel of statewide or interstate significance; that serve virtually all urban areas over 50,000 population; that provide high overall travel speeds with minimum interference to through activity; that serve the highest traffic volume corridors and the longest trip lengths; and that carry a high proportion of urban area travel.

[d]Consists of routes of highest importance to the nation that connect, as directly as possible, the principal metropolitan areas, cities, and industrial centers, including important routes into, through, and around urban areas; serve the national defense and, to the greatest extent possible, connect at suitable border points with routes of continental importance in Canada and Mexico. The Interstate Highway System is a subset of the primary system.

[e]Includes urban freeways and expressways.

[f]In rural areas, a network of routes that provide access to principal arterial routes and, in conjunction with principal arterials, that link cities and larger towns to facilitate interstate and intercounty service. In urban areas, this system serves trips of moderate length at a somewhat lower level of travel mobility. Such routes interconnect with and augment the principal arterial system and may carry local bus routes and provide intracommunity connectivity.

[g]In rural areas, a network of routes that generally serve travel of a localized nature and on which predominant travel distances are shorter than on arterial routes. The rural collector system is stratified as follows: (1) major collectors—serving county seats and other traffic generators not directly served by arterials and (2) minor collectors—linking locally important traffic generators with small communities. In urban areas, such routes distribute trips to and from arterials. Such routes provide for local traffic movement within residential neighborhoods, commercial zones, and industrial areas.

[h]Roads used primarily for access to homes and land.

[i]Rounding error.

Source: U.S. Congress, House, *Report of the Secretary of Transportation: The Status of the Nation's Highways: Conditions and Performance* (Committee Print 98–14, 98th Cong., 1st sess., 1983), pp. 15–17, 63.

THE NATIONAL SYSTEM OF INTERSTATE AND DEFENSE HIGHWAYS

STATUS OF IMPROVEMENT AS OF June 30, 1983

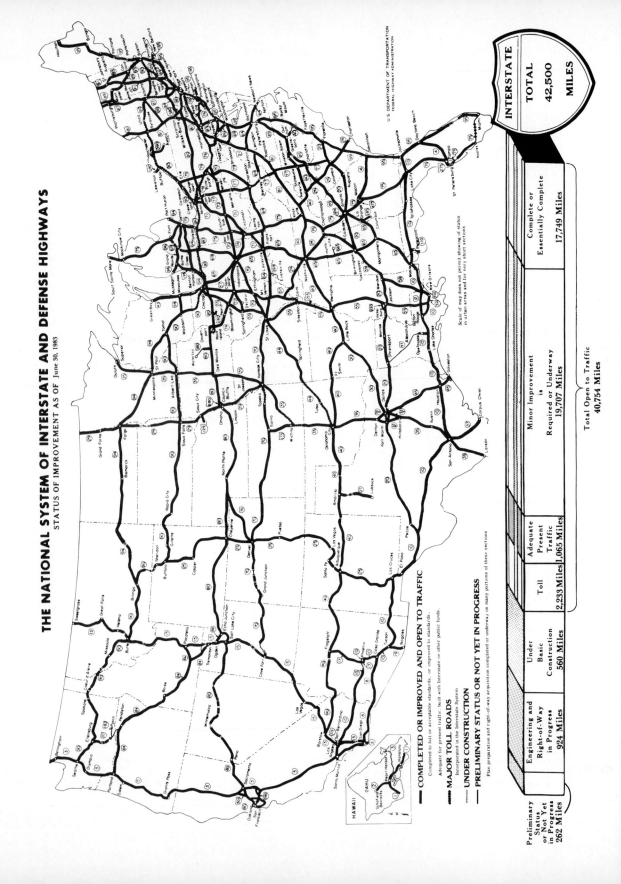

U S DEPARTMENT OF TRANSPORTATION
FEDERAL HIGHWAY ADMINISTRATION

Scale of map does not permit showing of status
in urban areas and for very short sections

HAWAII

OAHU

Schofield Barracks   Pearl Harbor   Honolulu

COMPLETED OR IMPROVED AND OPEN TO TRAFFIC
Completed to toll or acceptable standards, or improved to standards.

MAJOR TOLL ROADS
Incorporated in the Interstate System

UNDER CONSTRUCTION

PRELIMINARY STATUS OR NOT YET IN PROGRESS
Plan preparation and right-of-way acquisition completed or underway on many portions of these sections

Adequate for present traffic, built with Interstate or other public funds.

Preliminary Status or Not Yet in Progress 262 Miles	Engineering and Right-of-Way in Progress 924 Miles	Under Basic Construction 560 Miles	Toll 2,233 Miles	Adequate Present Traffic 1,065 Miles	Minor Improvement is Required or Underway 19,707 Miles	Complete or Essentially Complete 17,749 Miles

Total Open to Traffic
40,754 Miles

INTERSTATE

TOTAL

42,500

MILES

high priority to providing practically every citizen, regardless of location, with road access. U.S. public decision makers have developed an integrated system capable of feeding highway vehicles from homes over local roads and streets to collectors and arterials and then redistributing these vehicles back through the system to local destinations. As a result, the highway system has emerged as the most widely used transportation component in the United States.

Promotion and Subsidy

Sources and Uses of Funds.   What has made the highway system a reality is extensive promotion and subsidy. Of central importance is the Federal Aid Highway Program, which had its start in 1916, but soon it was joined by funding efforts at the state and local levels. From 1960 through 1981 alone, these joint promotional efforts contributed nearly $520 billion for roads (Table 11.2). In 1981, for example, disbursements totaled $41.1 billion, with funds expended for capital outlays (construction, reconstruction, major widening, bridge improvements, rehabilitation, restoration, and resurfacing), maintenance (pothole repair, snow removal, paint stripping, and grass cutting, among other uses), operation, administration, highway patrol and safety needs, and debt retirement and interest on debt (Table 11.3).

user taxes

Public highways are funded through user and non-user taxes. During 1982, users contributed 67% of total highway revenues; however, in comparison to the 83% contribution in 1960, there was a noticeable decline in participant funding.[1] Historically, federal and state governments have supplied more than three-fourths of all highway revenues (Table 11.2) and have relied on motor-fuel taxes, vehicle registration fees, tolls, and other charges to meet highway needs.

In contrast, local governments depend heavily on non-user fees such as

---

TABLE 11.2. Highway revenues by governmental jurisdiction (1960–1981)

	Receipts ($ Billions)	Percent
Federal	$140.972	27.1%
State	270.291	52.0
Local	108.430	20.9
TOTAL	$519.693	100.0%

Source: U.S. Congress, House, *Report of the Secretary of Transportation: The Status of the Nation's Highways: Conditions and Performance* (Committee Print 98-14, 98th Cong., 1st sess., 1983), p. 34.

◀**FIGURE 11.1.** (See Facing Page)
Map of the National System of Interstate and Defense Highways. (*Source:* U.S. Department of Transportation, Washington, D.C., 1984)

TABLE 11.3. National highway disbursements by expenditure category (1981) (billions)[a]

Capital outlays	$18.786
Maintenance and operation	11.713
Administration	3.246
Highway patrol and safety	3.979
Debt retirement and interest	3.402
TOTAL	$41.126

[a]Preliminary

Source: U.S. Congress, House, *Report of the Secretary of Transportation: The Status of the Nation's Highways: Conditions and Performance* (Committee Print 98-14, 98th Cong., 1st sess., 1983), p. 27.

non-user taxes   residential property taxes and general revenue funds to finance highway commitments. During 1982, only 18% of locally generated highway revenues were derived from user taxes.[2] Furthermore, $2.8 billion in state and local highway user revenues were expended for nonhighway purposes in 1980, yet simultaneously, non-user taxes in the form of federal revenue sharing, Department of Housing and Urban Development block grants, and economic development funds were spent on highway projects.

Federal Aid Highway Program.   The Federal Aid Highway Program (FAHP) provides funds to states for highway improvements. Responsible for administering the FAHP is the Federal Highway Administration, a unit of the U.S. Department of Transportation. Primarily, Washington has focused its attention on highways that are high generators of vehicle-miles—the arterials and collectors. Federal involvement is also oriented toward capital projects— buying land and building highways, bridges, and tunnels. In general, though, federal funding priorities have been expanded to provide some aid for preserving roads already in place. However, the federal government owns few miles of roads; almost all of the 828,526-mile Federal Aid Highway System is owned by the states and local municipal and county governments.

primary program   Today's Federal Aid Highway System benefits from four major funding packages: the primary, including the interstate and 4R interstate, secondary, urban, and bridge programs. The primary program provides funds for a system of interconnected main roads important to interstate, statewide, and regional travel. It consists of 227,000 miles of rural arterials and 28,600 miles of their urban extensions into and through cities. In fact, virtually all rural arterial, and 30% of urban arterial, mileages are included in the primary network, which connects all urbanized areas of 50,000 or more population and nearly all communities of at least 25,000 residents. Of course, a key part of the primary system is the interstate system. The origin of the primary program can be traced to the Federal Highway Act of 1921. (Table 11.4 provides a chronology of consequential federal highway promotion and subsidy programs for use throughout this section.) With the exception of the interstates,

---

TABLE 11.4. Chronology of highway promotion and subsidy programs

1916	Federal Aid Road Act formalized a federal concern for a basic primary system of roads envisioned as a 6200-mile rural road network.
1919	First road-user taxes were levied.
1920	All states were applying some type of use tax.
1921	Federal Highway Act of 1921 required that federal aid be spent on a designated system of interconnected roads as designated by the states. This act formally established the *primary* system.
1944	*Secondary* system was established.
1956	Federal Aid Highway Act of 1956 and the accompanying Revenue Act established the Highway Trust Fund with the purpose of constructing the *interstate* system.
1970	Federal Aid Highway Act of 1970 established the *urban* system. Its goal was to alleviate traffic congestion and minimize the differences in characteristics between urban functional and Federal Aid systems.
1976	*Interstate 3R program* was established for the resurfacing, restoration, and rehabilitation of interstate highways.
1978	Surface Transportation Assistance Act of 1978 established the *Highway Bridge Replacement and Rehabilitation Program* (HBRRP) to aid states in alleviating bridge deficiencies.
1981	Federal Aid Highway Act of 1981 added a fourth R (reconstruction) to the interstate 3R program and tripled preservation authorizations.
1982	Surface Transportation Assistance Act of 1982 significantly increased federal road-use taxes in an effort to increase substantially highway spending for completion of the interstate system, to maintain conditions on the primary system, to increase significantly funding for repair and replacement of deficient bridges, and to raise moderately the level of funding for urban and secondary systems.

Source: U.S. Congress, House, *Report of the Secretary of Transportation: The Status of the Nation's Highways: Conditions and Performance* (Committee Print 98-14, 98th Cong., 1st sess., 1983), pp. 8, 14, 23, 113, 115–118.

---

eligible primary roads receive 75% of their developmental funding from federal aid. States contribute the remainder.

interstate and 4R interstate programs

Two Federal Aid programs pertain to the interstates. The original program, created in 1956, was designed to build the 42,500-mile network. With the project still only 96% complete, funds continue to be appropriated to finalize the system. However, recognizing the deteriorating conditions of existing interstate highways, Congress in 1976 established the 3R interstate program to provide for the resurfacing, restoration, and rehabilitation of interstate highways. With the enactment of the Federal Aid Highway Act of 1981, which added a fourth R (reconstruction), this program is now called the 4R interstate program. Both the interstate and 4R interstate programs provide 90% federal funding; states contribute 10%.

secondary program

The Federal Aid secondary program provides 75% federal aid, matched with 25% state monies, to provide roads that serve as major rural collectors.

Unlike primary highways, secondary roads do not form an interconnected network of highways; instead, they funnel traffic onto and off the primary highways. Today, some 400,000 miles of highways comprise the secondary system of highways.

urban program

Urban arterials and collectors exclusive of urban extensions of the Federal Aid primary system comprise what is known as the urban system. This widely used part of the federal highway system carried 44% of all urban vehicular traffic in 1981. Funding is on a 75% federal, 25% state and local basis.

bridge program

The last and newest program is the Federal Aid bridge program. This program was created in 1978 as an incentive to state and local governments to prepare plans and to accelerate the rehabilitation and replacement of bridges.

other federal highway roles

federal, state, and local cooperation

These programs illustrate the partial transition of the federal role from highway construction to highway maintenance. The federal government also makes important contributions to highway safety and enforcement of the rules of the road. Furthermore, the success of the highway system is closely correlated to the degree of cooperative efforts of all levels of government. Much of the aggregate highway cost is borne by state and local governments, whose role it is to maintain and police the system in a far bigger way than that assumed by federal authorities. Also noted is the fact that more than 80% of the U.S. road system was built virtually independently of federal aid, for local roads in general fall outside the domain of the Federal Aid programs.

Surface Transportation Assistance Act of 1982.   On January 6, 1983, President Reagan signed the Surface Transportation Assistance Act of 1982 (STAA) (P.L. 97-424), which concluded a long debate on the need to increase highway taxes. In addition to raising federal gasoline and diesel fuel taxes from 4¢ to 9¢ per gallon, the STAA, if it had not been modified in 1983, would have levied an annual flat-rate tax of $1600 on an 80,000-lb. truck as of July 1984.[3] Although truckers were pleased with STAA provisions guaranteeing the right to operate heavier (80,000-lb.) trucks, longer single trailers (48 ft), and twin trailers (each 28 ft in length) in all states of the United States, they bitterly protested the annual flat-rate tax.

justification: deteriorating highways

Justification for STAA taxes can be traced to rapidly deteriorating roads and bridges, escalating capital and maintenance requirements, and declining user tax collections. In 1981, approximately 9400 miles of interstate highways, 215,000 miles of arterials, and 410,000 miles of collectors—in other words, a total of 634,400 miles of the Federal Aid Highway System—were deemed deficient from either a physical, operating, or safety perspective.[4] Furthermore, 244,241 of the 553,310 U.S. highway bridges were in need of repair or replacement.[5] How bad the situation had become was tragically evident in the collapse in 1983 of a section of the Connecticut Turnpike (I-95).

causes of road problems

The highway system suffers from excessive use, age, weather, and pounding from heavy vehicles. Why were the recognized problems not expeditiously corrected? Simply explained, there was a shortage of money. The federal share of total highway revenues, for example, was projected to reach a 20-year low in 1982; moreover, total dollars collected by all units of government in 1982, although 65% higher than the amount collected 10 years earlier, actually were worth 28% less in constant dollars because of inflation.[6] A net reduction in fuel consumption because of reduced vehicular travel and more fuel-efficient vehicles affected tax revenues. With federal fuel taxes fixed at 4¢ per gallon, the only direction collections could go was down. Government studies re-

immediate and long-term needs vealed that between $286 billion to $314 billion would be needed in 1980 dollars to maintain the highway system at its present levels, or $427 billion to $456 billion would be necessary to eliminate the system's physical and oper-ating deficiencies by the year 2000, taking into account highway travel growth of 2.0% to 2.8% annually. These estimates do not include an estimated $37.75 billion to complete the interstate system, any funding required from local au-thorities for roads outside the Federal Aid program, and inflation.[7]

STAA goals and amended taxes Thus the STAA was designed to increase highway tax collections, partic-ularly from heavy trucks that Congress believed were causing much of the highway and bridge damage. Truckers argued they were being told to pay more than their fair share of the taxes and that many financially troubled carriers could not afford the cost increases. In addition, truckers believed that if the federal government wanted to tax the carriers doing the most road damage, then it should tax vehicles on a more appropriate highway use basis rather than by applying an annual flat-rate tax: For example, a truck weighing 80,000 lbs. and driven 150,000 miles per year does more damage than another 80,000-lb. truck driven 60,000 miles annually. Congress responded to this line of reasoning with H.R. 4170, a bill signed by President Reagan in July 1984 that amended the STAA provisions. Starting August 1, 1984, the federal diesel fuel tax was raised to 15¢ from 9¢ per gallon, and larger trucks were directed to pay an annual tax of $100 plus $22 for each 1,000 lbs. over 55,000 lbs. Thus an 80,000-lb. truck pays an annual flat-rate tax of $550, instead of the $1,600 figure under the original STAA provisions.[8] Congress assumes the increased heavy truck highway taxes will be recovered from productivity gains derived from using larger vehicles.

impact The Surface Transportation Assistance Act of 1982 will inject an estimated $4.4 billion annually in new capital into the highway program. In addition, between 1977 and 1982, 31 states and the District of Columbia increased their fuel taxes to as high as 14¢ per gallon.[9] Recognizing the need for cash injec-tions, government decision makers fulfilled their responsibilities. Without question, tax increases were necessary, even if unpopular; however, the de-bate concerning the fairness of the tax levies continues.

U.S. INTERCITY BUS INDUSTRY

A major beneficiary of good highways is intercity bus transportation. This important mode in 1981 carried more passengers (approximately 375 million) and served more communities (about 15,000) than did any other for-hire mode.[10] For many people, bus transporation is the only alternative available.

types of carriage

In discussing bus transportation, we must distinguish between interstate and intrastate carriage. Between 800–850 bus companies operate across state lines making them subject to Interstate Commerce Commission (ICC) jurisdiction.[11] Approximately 600 other intercity firms operate exclusively on an intrastate basis. Most interstate carriers, however, also have intrastate authority. In addition to carrying passengers and their baggage, bus operators handle package express shipments, mail, and newspapers.

history

From a humble beginning, which some trace to the early days of horse-drawn coaches and which others link to the 1910 period when motor coaches first moved over the highways, the intercity bus industry has emerged as a $2 billion business employing about 49,000 workers. It is a vital transport sector essential for the continuing mobility of millions of individuals lacking access to an automobile or other modes. For many other people, it is a popular choice that takes them to virtually every scenic, historic, and cultural location across the United States. However, it is also a troubled industry whose environment has changed dramatically, leaving the industry's managers groping for answers.

Market Sectors

Passenger Service.   Today's intercity bus industry can be stratified into four major revenue-generating components: regular route, charter and special, and local passenger services, as well as package express services. Traditionally, regular route intercity passenger service has been the industry's main source of revenues. This sector is characterized by fixed routes connecting cities and serving urban terminals and roadside bus stops. Regular route carriers publish schedules and fares, and regardless of demand, buses are dispatched as advertised to the public.

regular route
intercity service

charter and
special bus services

Charter bus services and special bus services are more similar to contract, rather than common, carriage. Operators concentrate on hauling full bus loads of passengers on customized intercity routings. Schedules and fares are not usually published; in fact, trips that cannot be fully booked are often cancelled. Charter bus services are planned and booked by travel agents, brokers working with organizations wishing to obtain bus services, schools, teams, and groups or organizations other than a bus company itself. An example is a travel agent who arranges for a charter bus trip to a ski resort, agrees to pay the bus company for its services, and sells tickets to the general public. The special bus services market is similar to the charter bus market, except that the bus company plans the trip and sells the seats. No intermediary is involved, nor is the trip customer-initiated. Charter and special bus services represent the fastest growing market sectors in the bus industry.

local bus service

The third intercity passenger market sector, local bus service, involves people commuting from suburbs or nearby cities or towns to urban locations or retracing their routes on the return trip. These are intercity, not urban, transportation movements. Most are intrastate operations, such as a 20-mile ride into Minneapolis from a smaller city such as Anoka. Others, like bus routes hauling Connecticut residents into New York City, are interstate movements. Actually, it can be difficult at times to differentiate regular route intercity passenger services from local bus services as in the case of passengers commuting to work in Wilmington, Delaware, from Philadelphia. In general, though, local bus services imply short-haul intercity suburb to urban location trips versus movements from one urban location to a second large city.

charter, special, and local bus traffic

Table 11.5 shows that 250.2 million passengers of the total of 375 million intercity bus passengers in 1981 were customers of charter, special, and local bus service carriers. Charter and special bus service companies in 1981 hauled just under 55% of the 375 million passengers.[12] Table 11.5 also indicates that 223.0 million passengers (89.1% of the 250.2 million charter, special, and local passengers in 1981) were transported by non-Class 1 carriers, with annual sales below $3 million.

regular route traffic

Regular route service, by comparison, is dominated by Class 1 carriers, which generate $3 million or more in sales—especially by Greyhound and Trailways, the country's two nationwide operators (see Fig. 11.2). Table 11.5 reveals that Class 1 carriers transported 98.4 million (78%) of the industry's 124.8 million regular route passengers in 1981. However, Greyhound, with 57% of the market, and Trailways, with another 17%, controlled a combined 74% share of the Class 1 regular route passengers.[13] Until January 1985 when Greyhound announced it would begin franchising and licensing other carriers to operate as part of its intercity bus network,[14] Greyhound directly owned, controlled, and operated its own buses over a network that approximated 90,000 miles. Franchising is intended to help reduce Greyhound's overhead costs, increase its revenues, and lower its fares on many routes serving small towns. Trailways System is an intercity bus company that combines Trailways Inc.—a bus line Trailways Systems operates, 14 wholly owned bus subsidiaries, and 40–50 independently owned bus company affiliates in a national marketing and operating network.[15]

TABLE 11.5. Intercity bus passenger profile by service category and size of firm (1981 estimates)

	Class 1[a] Passengers (millions)	Non-Class 1[b] Passengers (millions)	Total Passengers (millions)
Regular route	98.4	26.4	124.8
Charter, special, and local	27.2	223.0	250.2
TOTAL	125.6	249.4	375.0

[a]An ICC-regulated bus company with annual revenues of $3 million or more.
[b]An ICC regulated bus company with less than $3 million in annual revenues.
Sources: American Bus Association, *Bus Facts: Intercity Bus Industry in 1981 and Decade of 70's*, 1982 ed. (Washington, D.C.: ABA, 1982), p. 3. (Adapted with permission.)

FIGURE 11.2.
Greyhound *Americruiser 2* bus. (Photo courtesy of Greyhound Lines, Inc.)

Package Express Service.   The bus industry actively began to promote package express services in the 1970s in response to a need for added (incremental) revenues and because it recognized the potential that buses had to help fill a void in the small shipment market. Package express services vary somewhat by carrier. For instance, Greyhound in April 1986 would handle shipments weighing up to 100 lbs. and no larger than either 33 in. by 33 in. by 48 in. or 24 in. by 53 in. by 74 in. In some locations, pick-up and delivery services are available from some bus companies for a fee, but shipments normally must be brought to the bus terminal and picked up by the consignee at destination.

In general, package express service is limited to regular route intercity *operating issues* bus carriers. Some buses have been specially altered by eliminating some seats for expanded freight capacity, but the bulk of the traffic is loaded in compartments under the passenger floor. (Fig. 11.2 shows access doors.) Contrary to popular opinion, bus seats were not elevated primarily for better passenger viewing but to facilitate and expand cargo handling capabilities.

Vehicles and Terminals

Intercity buses are built for passenger comfort and greater sustained speeds. The U.S. intercity fleet numbered 21,200 vehicles in 1981. In 1982, the average acquisition cost of both new and used buses was $127,000, up from $56,000 *fleet characteristics* in 1971.[16] Although the ages of bus fleets vary from carrier to carrier, many buses are quite new; Greyhound, for example, entered 1983 with 29% of its fleet less than one year old.[17] Virtually all intercity buses in service today are manufactured by Provost Company, Inc.: two Greyhound subsidiaries doing business as Transportation Manufacturing Corporation and Motor Coach Industries; and Trailways Manufacturing, Inc. and Eagle International, two units of Trailways' parent company, New Trails. Most buses are equipped with 43 coach service seats, but some buses feature better accommodations such as bigger, more comfortable seats.

terminals   One unique feature of regular route intercity bus carriage is that most terminals are privately owned and operated, and most are controlled by either Greyhound or Trailways. Terminals sell tickets and serve originating or departing passengers with such amenities as dining and baggage service. A high percentage of both passengers and packages require interlining between carriers or transfer between buses, so bus terminals also provide these relay services.

Ridership Characteristics

During 1981, the average trip distance among all intercity bus passengers was 72 miles, reflecting the short-haul nature of the business. A more significant statistic—because it better represents regular route services—shows an average trip length of 139 miles for passengers traveling on Class 1 carriers in 1982.[18] Both figures, however, are skewed by charter and special service trips that tend to be considerably longer than average. Many bus passengers are non-automobile drivers; many others simply prefer not to drive. The senior citizen market, for example, is an important market target group of the bus industry.

Economics

The U.S. intercity bus industry has many problems, as revealed in the data in Table 11.6. Class 1 intercity bus carriers sustained a 38.8% decline in passengers, an 11.8% reduction in revenue passenger-miles, and cutbacks of 24% in buses and 20% in employees between 1971 and 1981 or 1982. Despite an 80.7% gain in operating revenues and impressive sales increases in charter and special services, as well as package express, Class 1 carriers are having trouble with their ability to attract regular route business at yields high enough to cover rising costs. As a result, the Class 1 carrier operating ratio has risen, and profits have shrunk.

10 largest   Table 11.7 describes the financial situations at the 10 largest bus com-
bus companies   panies. Greyhound, with 62% of the Class 1 sales in 1982, had a 99.9% operating ratio in the 12 months ending on March 31, 1983. Furthermore, five of the eight largest Trailways units lost money in the same period. At the heart of the present regular route intercity carrier problems are intense competition, high operating costs, the impact of the recession, and a weak public image.

competition   Consider competition. Greyhound and Trailways are intense rivals who regularly battle each other in tough fare wars that depress yields (Table 11.8).

TABLE 11.6. Class 1 intercity bus carrier operating and financial statistics

Item	1971		1981	1982		Percentage Change
Revenue passengers, all services (millions)	166.8			102[a]		(38.8%)
Revenue passenger-miles, regular route service (billions)	17.94		15.83			(11.8)
Buses owned	9,900			7,526		(24.0)
Employees	34,731			27,775		(20.0)
Operating revenues ($ millions)		%			%	
Regular route	540.1	71.2		932.6	68.1	72.7
Charter and special	85.5	11.3		186.6	13.6	118.2
Local	12.6	1.7		5.2	0.4	(58.7)
Package express	104.1	13.7		216.2	15.8	107.7
Mail, stations,[b] other	16.1	2.1		29.7	2.2	84.4
TOTAL	758.4	100.0%		1,370.3	100.1%[c]	80.7
Operating expense ($ millions)	664.4			1,344.2		102.3
Operating ratio (%)	87.6			98.1		(12.0)
Net income after taxes ($ millions)[d]	64.5			29.5		(54.3)

[a]Preliminary figure.

[b]Revenues from terminal services, such as food and drink and sales of reading material.

[c]Rounding error.

[d]Net income includes not only operating income, but also fixed charges, non-operating income, income taxes, and extraordinary and prior period items.

Sources:
1. American Bus Association, *Bus Facts: Intercity Bus Industry in 1981 and Decade of 70's,* 1982 ed. (Washington, D.C.: ABA, 1982), pp. 5, 7.
2. Office of Transportation Analysis, Interstate Commerce Commission, *The Intercity Bus Industry, a Preliminary Study* (Washington, D.C.: ICC, 1983), pp. 3, 5, 10, 11, 17, App. 1–Table 3.

high costs

Deep discount airline fares and other intermodal competitive pressures from automobiles and AMTRAK have compounded the problem. Inroads by these modes into the bus market are revealed by a comparison of 1969 and 1979 data, which show passenger-mile gains of 32% in intercity auto travel, 63% for AMTRAK since it initiated service in 1971, and a 92% jump in airline travel. During the same period, Class 1 bus traffic declined 2.2%.[19] Class 1 bus carriers have also had little success in competing in the rapidly growing charter and special bus service sectors. With business customarily given to low-cost bidders, the more unionized, higher cost Class 1 carriers have lost out to smaller, lower cost operators. The smaller companies can still earn profits at greatly reduced yields. In addition, they tend to be quite successful in building brand loyalty and obtaining repeat business from faithful customers. The highest cost area for Class 1 carriers is payroll and fringe benefit costs, which in 1981 accounted for 58.3% of operating expenses.[20]

TABLE 11.7. Ten largest class 1 bus companies by revenues (Year ended March 31, 1983)

	Operating Revenues (millions)	Net Income[a] (millions)	Operating Ratio	Return on Equity (%)
Greyhound Lines, Inc.	$841.8	$17.8	99.9	5.25%
Trailways, Inc.[b]	49.2	2.9	102.1	3.42
American Bus Lines, Inc.[b]	41.9	(2.3)	109.3	(neg)[c]
Trailways Bus System, Inc.[b]	36.8	0.5	91.8	9.42
Safeway Trails, Inc.[b]	31.3	(1.3)	107.6	(neg)[c]
Trailways Southern Lines, Inc.[b]	29.3	1.5	86.5	43.03
Carolina Coach Co.	27.2	2.6	82.7	20.28
Trailways Southeastern Lines, Inc.[b]	17.9	(1.4)	93.8	(neg)[c]
Trailways Tamiami, Inc.[b]	17.1	(1.3)	100.6	(neg)[c]
Trailways Tennessee Lines, Inc.[b]	14.7	(0.4)	96.5	(neg)[c]

[a]Net income, after including fixed charges, non-operating income, taxes, unusual or infrequent items, earnings attributable to discontinued segments, and certain extraordinary items.

[b]A Trailways-owned company.

[c]Negative return on equity.

Source: Bureau of Accounts, Interstate Commerce Commission, *Large Class 1 Motor Carriers of Passengers, Selected Earnings Data* (Washington, D.C.: ICC, 1983), pp. 1, 2, 3.

recession and other problems

The bus industry, like most other transportation segments, was badly weakened by the recession of the early 1980s. Bus management experiments with discount fares proved that would-be patrons caught in a money squeeze were still bypassing trips rather than travel by bus. Because regular route carriers also confronted a relatively poor bus-industry consumer image, they were challenged to establish consumer trust and satisfaction. To attract primary demand and retain present riders, carriers must improve passenger per-

TABLE 11.8. Class 1 carrier average passenger fares: regular route intercity service (cents per mile)

Year	Current Dollars	Constant 1977 Dollars[a]
1977	5.12¢	5.12¢
1978	5.82	5.40
1979	6.73	5.62
1980	7.55	5.55
1981	8.43	5.62
1982	8.01	5.03

[a]Taking inflation into account.

Source: U.S. Department of Labor, Bureau of Statistics data as cited in Office of Transportation Analysis, Interstate Commerce Commission, *The Intercity Bus Industry, a Preliminary Study* (Washington, D.C.: ICC, 1983), p. 9.

ceptions of bus station security, driver courtesy, and so forth. Similarly, bus companies must redefine routings and schedules, trading off such alternatives as greater speed via more direct routings against traditional circuitous runs characterized by frequent stops aimed at building traffic volumes. What is needed is clearer market segmentation and targeting, deviation from the tendency of trying to be all things to all people, and major changes in costs and productivity.

Greyhound's Labor Strategy

One noteworthy action was Greyhound's demands in November 1983 that its employees accept a 9.5% salary cut and that employees begin making a 5% contribution to the pension plan. Greyhound also wanted to create a two-tier wage system whereby new employees would be paid lower starting salaries than currently employed workers. Management argued that Greyhound's current labor costs were 30% to 50% higher than its major competitors' labor costs; if these labor costs were not reduced, the company could not compete with regional airlines and bus companies.[21]

strike outcome

When 12,000 Greyhound workers struck the company, Greyhound notified them that they should either return to work or be replaced by people drawn from a pool of 45,000 job applicants.[22] The striking Amalgamated Transit Union members refused to acquiesce, and Greyhound's management carried out its threat by using substitute workers to keep the bus line operating. After several weeks, the union voted to accept Greyhound's modified offer and return to work. As a result, Greyhound obtained a 14% labor wage and benefit concession from current employees and a right to establish a two-tier pay program. Greyhound estimated that the contract terms would save the company $160 million in three years.[23]

Bus Regulatory Reform Act of 1982

Another measure, which is significantly changing the intercity bus industry, is the Bus Regulatory Reform Act of 1982 (Public Law 97-261, 96 *Statutes at Large* 1102 to 1129). The Bus Act significantly lessened federal and state powers over entry, exit, and rate matters. For example, it is now easier for carriers

entry and expansion

to start new or expanded regular route, charter, and special services. In general, regular route certification is granted today if the applicant has adequate liability, unless the ICC finds the service inconsistent with the public interest (49 U.S.C. 10521). Furthermore, applicants wishing operating authority in the charter or special service sectors need only establish adequate liability.

mixing and
other rights

Other provisions of the Bus Act permit the mixing of regular route, charter, and/or special service passengers on the same vehicle and automatically grant authority for bus operators with ICC passenger certificates to transport newspapers, express packages, and mail on the same vehicle with the passengers. Public Law 97-261 likewise eliminates most state-imposed prohibitions against picking up and discharging passengers within a state's borders—intrastate transportation—as part of an interstate routing. For example, a bus on an interstate route from Tulsa to Dallas could board passengers in Texas and drop them off in Dallas. In the past, carriers were often denied this "fill-up rights" privilege. Restrictions prohibiting roundtrip travel and intermediate stops on a route were also abolished by the Bus Act. Thus a carrier once limited to hauling passengers from point *A* to point *B,* but not from point *B* to point *A,* can now serve the *B* to *A* market. In addition, it may also pick up passengers at places between points *A* and *B,* whereas it previously may have been restricted to traffic only at points *A* and *B.*

abandonments and service reductions

What may turn out to be even more significant is the preempting of much of the states' powers to stop route abandonments and service reductions. In the past it was difficult for regular route interstate carriers to discontinue or alter services or even change schedules on unprofitable routes. Now states can do little to stop interstate carrier abandonment plans that affect intrastate traffic.

rate freedoms

Under the Bus Act, carriers also have substantially more freedom to change fares and freight rates without ICC interference. Key provisions establish a zone of reasonableness that gives carriers practically unlimited freedom to raise or lower rates. For instance, the only limit imposed on charter and special carriers is that they are prohibited from setting prices so low they are predatory (49 U.S.C. 10708).

rate bureau limits

Rate bureau powers are likewise limited by the Bus Act. Bureau members may not discuss and vote on any single-line rate—one that affects continuous carrier service from origin to destination—and they also may not discuss or vote on any rate applicable to special or charter transportation services. Although bureau members may still discuss and vote on general rate increases, they may not discuss and vote on joint rates—that is, rates for services provided by interlining carriers—proposed by one or more regular route carriers.[24]

purpose

It is apparent that the backers of the Bus Act, such as the American Bus Association, felt that tough measures were necessary to loosen the control of state authorities over rates and operating jurisdictions. Also clear is that this measure was principally aimed at helping regular route intercity carriers restore their financial prosperity. However, as is true for most regulatory reform

regulatory trade-offs

measures, efforts to help some interests adversely affect others. Greyhound has already announced plans to eliminate hundreds of service points, and in response the National Association of Regulatory Utility Commissioners asked for a change in the Bus Act. Once again, the difficulty in trying to balance common carrier obligations and private sector profitability needs is evident.

U.S. TRUCKING INDUSTRY: OVERVIEW

The Industry before 1977

The freight side of the for-hire highway transportation business is the trucking industry. As recently as 1976, it was one of the most stratified, fragmented parts of U.S. transportation. The industry was divided then into distinct, and often mutually exclusive, market segments because of economic regulations forcing carriers to limit their services according to geographic, route, and commodity restrictions explicitly stated in their operating authorities. For example, a company could be a common carrier or a contract carrier, but almost always not both, or the firm might have been an interstate regular route common carrier of general commodities or an interstate irregular route common carrier of general commodities. Some had special commodity common carrier authority to haul building materials; others using similar equipment were restricted to hauling slabs of granite. At the time, entry into the interstate trucking business was tightly controlled, and only certain types of truck operators such as private carriers and exempt-commodity firms escaped federal and state economic regulation. Figure 11.3 better explains why the trucking industry was called the trucking industries. In short, the legal classes of trucking firms were so specialized that companies often competed against only other truckers with the same authority.

brokers and surface freight forwarders
   Figure 11.3 is actually incomplete, for it leaves out brokers and surface freight forwarders—regulated intermediaries who work closely with trucking firms and shippers. Brokers try to match trucking companies desiring traffic with shippers needing trucking services. Surface freight forwarders, as mentioned in Chapter 6, collect and consolidate small shipments going to common destinations and tender consolidations to carriers. In 1976, brokers and forwarders found their operating authority limited by ICC regulations. It was virtually impossible to be both a forwarder and a common or contract carrier or to be both a broker and a carrier. A firm desiring to participate in interstate commerce was thus subject to many constraints. Then came 1977 and the regulatory reform movement.

Regulatory Reform Changes: Operating Authority

The initial sign that the legal structure of the interstate trucking industry would change occurred with the decision in *P. C. White Trucking Inc.* vs. *ICC*, 551 F 2nd 1326 (D.C. Cir. 1977). Prior to this ruling, ICC decisions about granting entry into the common carrier sector required consideration of three criteria: (1) whether entry would serve a useful purpose, (2) whether existing carriers could provide the proposed service, and (3) whether existing carriers would be harmed—*Pan American Bus Lines Operation*, 1 MCC 190, 203 (1936). The *P. C. White* case eliminated the second criterion.

deemphasis of protecting established carriers

Motor Carrier Act of 1980
   Subsequently, many changes occurred in the federal economic regulations governing the interstate trucking industry. Many modifications resulted from ICC decisions, but by far the most significant event in recent trucking history was the Motor Carrier Act of 1980 (94 *Statutes at Large* 793-826). Enacted July 1, 1980, this law significantly lessened entry regulations that dated to the Motor Carrier Act of 1935, a statute that originally regulated interstate motor carriage of property. Several significant entry changes include the following:

common carrier entry
- *Liberty Trucking Co. Extension—General Commodities*, 130 Motor Carrier Cases (MCC) 243, 246, and 133 MCC 573, 576, decided September 12, 1978, and Section 5 of the Motor Carrier Act of 1980, July 1, 1980 (MCA), shifted

FIGURE 11.3.

Legal structure of the U.S. trucking industry, 1976.

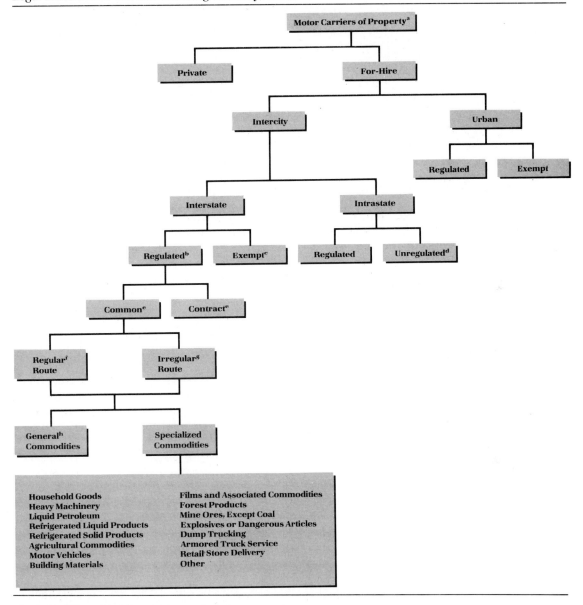

[a]Cargo (as differentiated from motor carriers of passengers).

[b]Regulated means subject to economic regulation.

[c]Exempt motor carriage refers to transportation of commodities, such as unprocessed agricultural goods, livestock, and newspapers, across a state line; it is transportation not subject to federal economic regulations.

[d]Unregulated means a state has not imposed economic regulations on motor carriers of property or has totally deregulated trucking.

[e]As in the case of railroads (see Chapter 5), a common carrier needs a certificate of public convenience and necessity. A contract carrier needs a permit.

[f]Regular route means regularly scheduled service over designated roads.

[g]Irregular route authority allows a carrier to provide services from any point within an area (e.g., Iowa) to any point in another area (e.g., Illinois) by any route cleared for safe operations.

[h]Although general commodities include cargo not under specialized commodity authority, they usually imply boxed, bagged, or containerized items (packaged freight).

the burden from the applicant to the protester to prove why a new carrier should not be allowed to enter the trucking business. If the protester fails to prove the proposed service is inconsistent with public convenience and necessity, the ICC can issue a certificate of public convenience and necessity allowing the applicant to engage in common carriage. The ICC must find the applicant fit, willing, and able, and the applicant must show the proposed service will serve a useful purpose responsive to a public demand or need.

private carrier rights ▪ Several changes also made it much easier for firms to engage in private carrier operations. First, in *Toto Purchasing and Supply Co., Inc.,* 128 MCC 873 (March 24, 1978), the ICC decided to allow private carriers to seek and obtain for-hire authority as common carriers to haul freight for the public over the carrier's backhaul routes. Section 9 of the MCA, which deals with intercorporate hauling, allows private carriers to haul on a compensated basis freight owned by any 100% owned corporate family member. Also, in 1982 the ICC ruled that private truck carriers could trip lease to authorize carriers. A *trip lease* is a contractual agreement under which a driver, tractor, and trailer can be used for a one-time journey. As noted in Chapter 3, a 1982 U.S. Supreme Court decision likewise enabled private carriers to engage in *single source leasing*—the right to lease equipment and drivers from unregulated sources. ICC decisions on June 25, 1986 subsequently (1) allowed private carriers and shippers to lease equipment and drivers from ICC regulated sources, such as a common carrier trucker (Ex Parte MC-43, Sub. 17) and (2) permitted single source leases with unregulated entities to run less than 30 days (Ex Parte MC-122, Sub. 2). The 1982 decision previously set a 30-day minimum lease limitation. Essentially, each of these changes was designed to minimize two major roadblocks to the establishment of private carrier fleets: empty backhauls (i.e., finding traffic at the destination to carry back to the origin) and operating cost economies (i.e., spreading costs over more traffic).

temporary authority ▪ Another change implemented by the MCA (Section 23) involved temporary authority and emergency temporary authority to carriers wishing to provide trucking service. The MCA defined rules for expeditiously granting such requests.

independent truckers ▪ Congress, sympathetic to the needs of independent truckers, included in Sections 5 and 10 of the MCA special provisions to permit owner-operators to obtain common carrier certificates and contract permits to carry regulated traffic under their own names and without meeting all the usual entry control tests. Authority was to be granted for owner-operators to haul regulated movements of food and other edible products, subject to certain limitations, contingent on proof that applicants were fit, willing, and able.

rail-truck: special circumstances doctrine eliminated ▪ As discussed in Chapter 5, the ICC in January 1983 eliminated the "special circumstances doctrine," making it easier for railroads and rail affiliates to obtain unrestricted motor carrier rights. When in force, the doctrine limited railroad truck services almost exclusively to movements involving prior or subsequent rail transportation. This regulation changed with Ex Parte MCC-156, *Applications for Motor Carrier Operating Authority by Railroads and Rail Affiliates,* 132 MCC 978.

TOFC/COFC truck deregulation	■ A 1981 ICC decision eliminated regulation of TOFC/COFC over-the-road movements on rail owned equipment (Ex Parte MC-230, Sub-No. 5, served February 19, 1981).
specialized markets	■ Section 5 of the MCA significantly lessened the entry requirements for trucking firms desiring (1) to provide services to communities not regularly served by certificated truck common carriers, (2) to replace abandoned rail services, (3) to haul U.S. government property other than used household goods, hazardous or secret materials, or sensitive weapons and munitions, or (4) to transport shipments weighing 100 lbs. or less if carried in a motor vehicle in which no package exceeds 100 lbs. Applicants need only prove they are fit, willing, and able.
removal of operating restrictions	■ Some of the most significant changes of the regulatory reform period eliminated operating restrictions. Section 6 of the MCA mandated the end of gateway and circuitous routing requirements, which had forced carriers to route vehicles through specified intermediate points or over specified routes. A gateway example would be authority to serve Pittsburgh and Albany, New York, via New York City. Now, the carrier could move cargo by a more direct route from Pittsburgh to Albany. These restrictions were originally imposed by the ICC to protect the traffic of more direct regular route common carriers. Other forms of restrictions removed by the MCA were prohibitions against serving intermediate points and limits governing the size of a carrier's geographic territory or the types of commodities a carrier could haul. In fact, the ICC encouraged carriers to seek broader authority such as 48-state rights.
contract carriage	■ Other changes eliminated the "rule of eight," which once restricted contract truckers to a maximum of eight customers. It had been believed by the ICC that a contract trucker who served more than eight customers was acting like a common carrier without accepting all of the common carrier duties—to serve, charge reasonable rates, avoid undue or unjust discrimination, and deliver the goods. Today, no limit exists on the number of clients a contract carrier serves. In addition, contract truckers can enter into contracts with surface freight forwarders, which they could not previously do; are no longer restricted to serving particular industries or geographic areas; and can seek and simultaneously hold contract and common carrier authority (Section 10 of the MCA). The latter is called
dual authority and mixing	dual authority, and it was authorized for common carriers as well. Today, it is also possible for a firm holding dual authority to transport property moving under its certificate and other shipments moving under its contract authority in the same vehicle. If the carrier wants to, it can also mix exempt traffic with regulated freight on the same vehicle (Section 21 of the MCA).
exemptions and regulatory freedoms	■ Other barriers either eliminated or lessened by the ICC or MCA include total deregulation of motor carrier transportation of property in conjunction with prior or subsequent movements by air (Section 7, MCA) and expanded privileges for agricultural cooperatives. The latter, who as shippers' associations cater to farming interests by consolidating small shipments for their members to gain volume rate savings, could haul up to 25% of their total traffic in the form of nonmember tonnage (Section 24 of the MCA). Changes also included an expansion of the list of exempt

agricultural and fisheries commodities (as per Section 7 of the MCA), an expansion of the geographic limits of the exempt urban areas known as commercial zones and terminal areas (because of *Commercial Zone Expansion,* Ex Parte No. MC-37, Sub-No. 26, decided December 17, 1976), and a lessening of the requirements for becoming an ICC-licensed broker, as a result of Section 17 of the MCA. Finally, surface freight forwarder restrictions were significantly eliminated by an ICC decision in *Freight Forwarder Restrictions (49 CFR Part 1137)*, Ex Parte MC-142, Sub. 2, 132 MCC 832, decided July 19, 1982.

Impact of Reform

Some of the implications of this significant liberalization of the federal entry rules can already be seen. The number of authorized ICC-regulated motor carriers of property increased by 102%; in 1976, there were 16,472 firms, and on December 12, 1985, there were 33,283.[25] As of February 1, 1986, approx-

numbers of regulated firms

imately 1100 companies with 12,000 subsidiaries had notified the ICC of intentions to engage in intercorporate hauling.[26] Signs reveal rapid expansion in the contract trucker and property broker sectors (i.e., an intermediary involved in the general commodity sector of trucking that tries to link shippers and carriers together). The number of broker authority applications granted rose from 603 during the first year under the MCA to 769 and 901, respectively, in the second and third years. For the fiscal year ending September 30, 1985, the ICC granted authority to 1872 brokers. Also, in February 1986 more than 4000 trucking companies held nationwide general commodity authority.[27]

indifference

In other ways, changes in operating authority have been surprisingly slight. For instance, the record shows relatively minimal interest by private carriers in seeking *Toto*-type for-hire authority. In addition, relatively few of the tens-of-thousands of owner-operators have shown interest in obtaining authority to serve the regulated sector under Section 5 provisions of the MCA. Only 533 general commodity operating authority requests were approved by the ICC between the signing of MCA in July 1980 and March 31, 1983.

hidden impact

Numbers, however, do not tell the entire story. Although it is important to know how many firms have authority, these figures do not show their activity levels. Furthermore, previous statistics do not reflect the impact of broadened commodity and geographic authority or the consequences of the removal of operating restrictions. The market is dynamic and should stay that way during the transitional years of regulatory reform. Many carriers are expanding their operations at the same time others are losing market share.

industry blurring

The trucking industry today is being condensed into fewer market segments. With the legal dividers falling, there is a blurring of for-hire and private carriage, urban and intercity operations, truckload common carriage and contract trucking, regular route and irregular route sectors, and general commodity and specialized cargo industries. Furthermore, the roles of intermediaries and carriers are not as distinct as they once were. In addition, there has never been more intermodal interest and cooperative activity among carriers of different modes.

emerging markets

The trucking industry is rapidly redefining its boundaries and opportunities. Deregulation and competition are now segmenting the business, rather than entry regulations. Emerging are truckload, less-than-truckload, and less than 100-lb. markets; price-oriented and service-oriented segments; specialized equipment (e.g., dump trucks) and multipurpose equipment (e.g., flat-bed trailers) sectors; and modal (e.g., trucking) and multi-modal, one-stop (e.g., a company offering truck, rail, and water services) segments. Some carriers are choosing to compete in only one trucking industry market; others follow a multi-market approach. All need to decide what strategy to follow, however, because the freer market environment demands better decision making.

Rate Reform

Easing federal entry regulations was the heart of the reform movement in the trucking industry, for entry is the means by which low-cost competitors can become market factors. However, rate flexibility is also necessary to enable these firms to effect change. Thus the Motor Carrier Act of 1980 contained two rate regulation changes of major consequence to the trucking industry.

zone of reasonableness

rate bureaus

First, Section 11 of the MCA established a zone of rate freedom that enabled carriers to raise or lower individual rates by 10% annually without fear of ICC interference. Subsequently, these limits were increased to ± 15%. Secondly, Section 14 promulgated new rules for trucking rate bureaus, forbidding carriers from voting on any rate unless they have the authority to provide the service in question and after July 1, 1984, prohibiting bureau discussion and voting on single-line rates. Clearly, the goal was to encourage more independent pricing. Another change was the requirement that bureau proceedings and individual votes by the members be made available to the public. Nevertheless, the MCA did not eliminate the right of a bureau's membership to discuss and vote on general rate increases (across-the-board percentage price changes on all items) or joint rates. Nonetheless, bureaus could eventually turn into rate publishing houses if Congress follows the wishes of the

Motor Carrier Ratemaking Study Commission

Motor Carrier Ratemaking Study Commission, a group created by the MCA to study the collective ratemaking process. On February 24, 1983, that group voted 6 to 4 in favor of ending antitrust immunity for joint rates, general rate increases, and freight classifications.[28]

impact on rates

In calendar year 1979, the 10 major motor carrier rate bureaus took action on 27,141 independent rate actions; for the three preceding years, the average was 20,639 per year. For the year ended June 30, 1982, however, the number was 180,829.[29] Clearly, carriers have exercised their new rate freedoms. The MCA, furthermore, was successful in effecting various rate discounts. Although general rate increases continued to be approved by the bureaus, many carriers flagged out—an industry term meaning they chose not to increase their rates, such as because of extreme competitive pricing pressures.

Other Provisions of the Motor Carrier Act of 1980

The MCA also contained provisions covering minimum levels of insurance and financial responsibility (Sections 29 and 30), issuance of securities (Section 18), and motor carrier mergers (Section 18).[30] Note, however, the omission of any reference in the MCA to exit/abandonment provisions. Unlike the bus industry, there never have been any substantive federal exit rules for the interstate trucking sector. The Motor Carrier Act of 1935 was designed to protect carriers from too much, not too little, competition. Moreover, when companies left the trucking business, others were usually waiting to replace them. This situation is still true today.

State Economic Regulation of Trucking

Public economic controls at the state level are as important as federal economic regulation. For the most part, intrastate regulation of trucking was modeled after provisions of the Motor Carrier Act of 1935. There were exceptions; for example, most of the for-hire trucking in New Jersey was unregulated long before the MCA. However, strict regulations on entry and rates prevailed in most states, and for the most part, they still do. Several states like Florida, Arizona, Wisconsin, and South Dakota deregulated trucking or lessened controls within their respective borders in the early 1980s, but most states are still highly regulated. This lack of uniformity among the states and between most states and Washington, as explained in Chapter 4, is a continuing problem for carriers.

Traffic and Economics

From a traffic and economic perspective, the early 1980s were difficult for the trucking industry. Between 1980–1982, the ICC-regulated trucking sector endured a 21.8% decrease in tonnage. Like railroads and other modes of transportation, truckers suffered from the national recession; nothing done by the industry, including heavy discounting from 10% to 30% below published rates, had much effect in stimulating traffic demand. In 1982, the financial performance for ICC carriers was the worst in recorded history.

Role of Trucking Industry.   To analyze the current economic situation in more depth, it is useful to know the overall role of the trucking industry relative to the aggregate transportation business. Clearly, one important contribution is its share of the nation's freight bill. In 1984, U.S. transportation freight users spent an estimated $274.2 billion. Of this amount, an estimated $208.3 billion, or 76.0%, was expended on truck services, equipment, and related costs.[31] Trucking dominates the market for the haulage of food, beverages, and most of the household items everyone uses. In fact, more than 75% of the tonnage in sporting equipment, televisions, clothing, carpets, bakery products, meat, and beverages moves on highway vehicles. Although intercity truckers carry only about 20% of the nation's traffic, the industry transports most of the high-valued traffic. As a result, yields are usually high, and these high revenues per ton-mile are the key to the trucking industry's revenue impact.

Troubled Trucking Industry. In the early 1980s, the trucking industry was troubled with declining income levels, low returns on equity, reduced tonnage, and rising operating costs. According to an ICC report covering the 12-month period ending on March 31, 1983, and summarized in Table 11.9, the largest U.S. carriers saw revenues drop 2.6%, net carrier operating income decline by 18.6%, net income fall by 30.3%, and return on equity lowered 29.0% from previous-year levels. Small trucking firms faced similar problems. The aggregate market was smaller, there were more carriers fighting for a share of the reduced tonnage, and costs were rising. Desperate to deploy excess capacity and meet the competition, carriers had little choice but to discount prices. Unfortunately, cost increases outpaced revenue gains, thus raising operating ratios to nearly 98% in 1983 and lowering returns on equity from more than 17% in 1978 to 11.1% in 1981, 7.70% in 1982, and 5.5% in 1983.[32]

TABLE 11.9. Selected traffic and financial U.S. data of 100 of the largest trucking common carriers[a] (Twelve months ended March 31, 1982 and 1983)

	1982	1983	Percent Change
Operating revenues	$15,673,782,000	$15,268,303,000	(2.6%)
Net carrier operating income[b]	$398,214,000	$323,962,000	(18.6)
Net income[c]	$228,129,000	$158,948,000	(30.3)
Operating ratio	97.5%	97.9%	(0.4)
Return on equity[d]	7.70%	5.45%	(29.0)
Revenue tons hauled[e]	168,875,000	153,830,000	(8.9)

[a]Excludes United Parcel Service, Inc. and United Parcel Service, Inc. (New York), which in terms of sales are the nation's two largest trucking companies; contract truckers, because the data filed were substantially reduced in scope; and several of the largest 100 carriers whose data had not been received in time.

[b]The difference between operating revenues and operating expenses.

[c]Net income (after fixed charges, non-operating income, income taxes, and other extraordinary items were included).

[d]Ratio of net income before net extraordinary charges for write-down (devaluation) of operating rights to shareholder's equity less intangible property.

[e]Includes tons hauled under common and contract carrier service.

Source: Bureau of Accounts, Interstate Commerce Commission, *Class 1 Motor Carriers of Property Selected Earnings Data* (Washington, D.C.: ICC, 1983), p. 1.

selected prosperity

Although this is not a promising picture, it is also somewhat misleading. For fiscal years ending September 30, 1984, and September 30, 1985, returns on equity were 14.58% and 11.01%, respectively.[33] Also, some firms have tripled and quadrupled revenues and seized new marketing opportunities made possible by regulatory reform. The growth in contract trucker and brokerage sectors is further proof of market share restructuring and selected prosperity. However, the record also shows that since mid-1980, 1993 intercity trucking companies failed,[34] including McLean Trucking Company, one of the industry's largest firms. After combining these statistics with projected significant increases in federal and state user taxes and continued growth in the number of firms in the trucking business, it is easy to understand carrier fears. Even as the economy improved in 1984 and 1985, additional companies closed their doors. Survivors groped for answers to secure their corporate futures.

SUMMARY

Highway carriers of passengers and property have been struggling during recent years. The intercity bus industry has had to contend with rising costs and intense downward pricing pressure from airlines, AMTRAK, and intramodal competition. Regular route intercity bus companies like Greyhound and Trailways need to increase yields and profits, but they have been reluctant to raise prices for fear of losing traffic to low-price competitors. The recession also hurt the bus industry. Even discount prices could not adequately stimulate passenger traffic.

Trucking companies faced many similar problems—rising costs, the recession, a decline in aggregate cargo demand, and competition. In 1977, the ICC began lessening entry restrictions. Then the Motor Carrier Act of 1980 became law, and a flood of new low-cost carriers entered the interstate trucking business. These carriers, as well as established trucking companies, began aggressively discounting rates, which motivated other trucking companies to respond in kind. In the ensuing intramodal battle, nearly 2000 intercity trucking companies went out of business.

If these problems were not enough, bus and truck carriers faced deteriorating highways and rising highway user taxes instituted by federal and state governments seeking to raise revenues to improve U.S. roads and bridges. Heavy-truck operators, in particular, objected to what they perceived were excessive, unfair tax levies. The federal government allowed the use of larger trucks expecting that productivity gains would neutralize cost (tax) increases. In addition, it altered the tax structure in 1984, increasing diesel fuel taxes but lowering annual flat-rate taxes.

Like the trucking industry, the interstate bus sector was deregulated. The Bus Regulatory Reform Act of 1982 and the Motor Carrier Act of 1980 were intended to improve bus, as well as truck, companies' efficiencies. Both acts have given carrier managers considerably more freedom to make decisions.

History, however, will show the wisdom of the acts and corporate management choices.

STUDY QUESTIONS

1. Discuss the profitability of the 10 largest bus companies in 1983, and explain why this financial condition existed.

2. How does the Federal Aid Highway Program act as an incentive for states to build new highways?

3. Why were the taxing provisions of the Surface Transportation Assistance Act of 1982 amended?

4. What is responsible for the increased number of ICC-regulated trucking companies from 1976 to 1985?

5. What actions has Greyhound's management taken to try to improve the profitability of the company's intercity bus operations?

6. Explain how the purposes of the interstate and 4R interstate highway programs differ.

7. What caused the deterioration in the returns on equity of the 100 largest U.S. trucking firms from 17% in 1978 to 11.1% in 1981, 7.70% in 1982, and 5.5% in 1983?

8. How might the Bus Regulatory Reform Act of 1982 help or hinder bus passengers in small towns?

ENDNOTES

1. U.S., Congress, House, *Report of the Secretary of Transportation: The Status of the Nation's Highways; Conditions and Performance*, Committee Print 98-14, 98th Cong., 1st sess., 1983, pp. 3, 19 (hereafter cited as *Status of the Nation's Highways*).

2. Ibid., p. 23.

3. "House-Senate Conferees Order DOT to Study Weight-Distance Taxes," *Traffic World*, 2 July 1984, p. 120 (hereafter cited as "House-Senate Conferees").

4. *Status of the Nation's Highways*, p. 97.

5. Ibid., p. 77.

6. Ibid., p. 22.

7. Ibid., pp. 97, 98, 100, and 104.

8. (a) "House-Senate Conferees," p. 120; and (b) "President Reagan Signs Tax, Drinking Measures," *Traffic World*, 23 July 1984, pp. 20–21.

9. Patrick Fitzgerald, "States Fuel Drive for Gas Tax Hikes," *USA Today*, 12 November 1982, p. 1B.

10. American Bus Association, *Bus Facts: Intercity Bus Industry in 1981 and Decade of 70s*, 1982 ed. (Washington, D.C.: ABA, 1982), p. 2 (hereafter cited as *Bus Facts*).

11. *Bus Regulatory Reform Act of 1982*, U.S. Code, 97th Cong., 2d sess., Vol. 3, p. 2311.

12. American Bus Association, *The Intercity Bus Industry: A New Era Dawns, the 1982 Annual Report of the American Bus Association* (Washington, D.C.: ABA, 1982), p. 18.

13. Office of Transportation Analysis, Interstate Commerce Commission, *The Intercity Bus Industry, a Preliminary Study* (Washington, D.C.: ICC, 1983), pp. 19, 21 (hereafter cited as *Intercity Bus Industry*).

14. "Greyhound Will Offer Franchises on Routes to Boost Bus Network," *Wall Street Journal*, 9 January 1985, p. 33.

15. *Intercity Bus Industry*, p. 2.

16. Ibid., p. 17.

17. Ibid., p. II.

18. Ibid., p. 7.

19. Derived from *Bus Facts*, p. 5.

20. (a) Ibid., p. 7; and (b) Rush Loving, "The Bus Lines Are on the Road to Nowhere," *Fortune*, 31 December 1978, p. 60.

21. Damon Stetson, "Greyhound Girds for Strike Today," *New York Times*, 3 November 1983, p. A25.

22. "Greyhound to Replace Strikers if Return Date Is Not Set by Monday," *Wall Street Journal*, 8 November 1983, p. 20.

23. (a) Leonard M. Apcar, "Greyhound's Tentative Pact with Strikers Includes Important Concessions by Union," *Wall Street Journal*, 5 Decem-

ber 1983, p. 3; and (b) "Greyhound to Resume Full Services," *Athens Banner-Herald,* 20 December 1983, p. 8.

24. Section 10, Bus Regulatory Reform Act of 1982, Public Law 97-261 (H.R. 3663), 20 September 1982, 96 *Statutes at Large* 1109.

25. (a) Office of Policy and Analysis, Interstate Commerce Commission, *The Effect of Regulatory Reform on the Trucking Industry: Structure, Conduct and Performance, Preliminary Report* (Washington, D.C.: ICC, 1981), p. 33 (hereafter cited as *Effect of Regulatory Reform*); (b) Office of Transportation Analysis, Interstate Commerce Commission, *Staff Report No. 9, Highlights of Activity in the Property Motor Carrier Industry* (Washington, D.C.: ICC, 1983), p. 6 and (c) information supplied by Joseph Edwards, Bureau of Accounts, Interstate Commerce Commission, by phone, on 21 April 1986 (hereafter cited as Edwards).

26. Information supplied by Brinkley Garner, Office of Transportation Analysis, Interstate Commerce Commission, by phone on 21 April 1986 (hereafter cited as Garner).

27. (a) Office of Transportation Analysis, Interstate Commerce Commission, *Staff Report ` No. 9, Highlights of Activity in the Property Motor Carrier Industry* (Washington, D.C.: ICC, 1983),

p. 6 (hereafter cited as *Staff Report No. 9*); and (b) Garner.

28. Robert M. Butler and Robert J. Kursar, "Truck Industry 'Resentment' Grows over Actions by Rate Study Group," *Traffic World,* 7 March 1983, p. 49.

29. (a) *Staff Report No. 9,* p. 16; and (b) Office of Policy and Analysis, Interstate Commerce Commission, *The Effect on Regulatory Reform on the Trucking Industry: Structure, Conduct and Performance, Preliminary Report* (Washington, D.C.: ICC, 1981), p. 77.

30. For an excellent review of these and other provisions, see Donald V. Harper, "The Federal Motor Carrier Act of 1980: Review and Analysis," *Transportation Journal* 19, no. 2 (Winter 1980):5–33.

31. Frank A. Smith, Senior Associate, *Transportation in America,* 3d ed., *July 1985 Supplement* (Washington, D.C.: Transportation Policy Associates, July 1985), p. 4.

32. (a) *Effect of Regulatory Reform,* p. 89; (b) *Staff Report No. 9,* p. 33; and (c) Bureau of Accounts, Interstate Commerce Commission, *Class I Motor Carriers of Property Selected Earnings Data* (Washington, D.C.: ICC, 1983), p. 1.

33. Edwards.

34. Garner.

ADDITIONAL READINGS

Beilock, Richard, and Freeman, James. "Carrier and Shipper Perceptions of Motor Carrier Deregulation in Florida." Transportation Research Forum. *Proceedings of the Twenty-third Annual Meeting.* Oxford, Ind.: Richard B. Cross Company, 1982, pp. 250–257.

Boisjoly, Russell P., and Corsi, Thomas M. "The Aftermath of the Motor Carrier Act of 1980: Entry, Exit, and Merger." Transportation Research Forum. *Proceedings of the Twenty-third Annual Meeting.* Oxford, Ind.: Richard B. Cross Company, 1982, pp. 258–264.

Brown, Terance A. "Shippers' Associations: Operations, Trends, and Comparative Prices." *Transportation Journal* 21, no. 1 (Fall 1981):54–66.

Chow, Garland. "Studies of Intrastate Trucking Regulation—A Critique." *Transportation Journal* 19, no. 4 (Summer 1980):23–32.

Coyle, John J.; Bardi, Edward J.; and Cavinato, Joseph L. *Transportation.* St. Paul, Minn.: West Pub-

lishing, 1982, pp. 345–353. (Provides a concise summary of the provisions of the Motor Carrier Act of 1980.)

Cunningham, Lawrence F.; Howard, Jeffrey; and Florin, Nanci A. "The Motor Coach Industry and Tourism: State-of-the-Art and Future Research Opportunities." Transportation Research Forum. *Proceedings of the Twenty-third Annual Meeting.* Oxford, Ind.: Richard B. Cross Company, 1982, pp. 616–619.

Dean, Donald L. "A Service Strategy Model for Estimating Trunkline Intercity Bus Service to Rural Communities." Transportation Research Forum. *Proceedings of the Twenty-third Annual Meeting.* Oxford, Ind.: Richard B. Cross Company, 1982, pp. 608–615.

Enis, Charles, and Morash, Edward A. "The Economic Losses from the Devaluation of Motor Carrier Operating Rights." *ICC Practitioners' Journal* 50, no. 5 (July–Aug. 1983):542–555.

Forkenbrock, David J., and Hoefer, Constance A. "Variable Motor Fuel Taxes: Problems and Prospects." *Transportation Quarterly* 37, no. 1 (January 1983):23–40.

Freeman, James W. "A Survey of Motor Carrier Deregulation in Florida: One Year's Experience." *ICC Practitioners' Journal* 50, no. 1 (Nov.–Dec. 1982):51–75.

Harmatuck, Donald J. "The Effects of Economic Conditions and Regulatory Changes upon Motor Carrier Tonnage and Revenues." *Transportation Journal* 24, no. 2 (Winter 1984):31–39.

Harper, Donald V. "Consequences of Reform of Federal Economic Regulation of the Motor Trucking Industry." *Transportation Journal* 21, no. 4 (Summer 1982):35–58.

Horn, Kevin H. "Entry into Regulated Interstate Trucking: Shipper Perspectives and Carrier Prospects." *Transportation Journal* 24, no. 2 (Winter 1984):55–72.

Kahn, Fritz R. "Motor Carrier Regulatory Reform—Fait Accompli." *Transportation Journal* 19, no. 2 (Winter 1979):5–11.

Krall, Farrel L., and Rossow, Gary W. "Heavy Truck Safety . . . The Need to Know." *Transportation Quarterly* 35, no. 3 (July 1981):337–358.

Larson, Thomas D., and Rao, Kant. "Capital Investment, Performance and Pricing in Highways." *Transportation Journal* 21, no. 3 (Spring 1982):22–33.

McGee, Michael P., and Carlock, Margaret. "Motor Carrier Market Segmentation: A Function of Shipper Cost Sensitivity." Transportation Research Forum. *Proceedings of the Twenty-third Annual Meeting.* Oxford, Ind.: Richard B. Cross Company, 1982, pp. 202–207.

McGillivray, Robert G. "Should the Intercity Bus Industry Be Subsidized?" *Traffic Quarterly* 33, no. 1 (January 1979):99–115.

Mentzer, John T., and Krapfel, Robert E. "Reactions of Private Motor Carriers to *Toto* and Compensated Intercorporate Hauling Rights." *Transportation Journal* 20, no. 3 (Spring 1981):66–72.

Morash, Edward A., and Enis, Charles R. "Investor Perceptions of the Impact of Deregulation on Motor Carrier Earnings." *The Logistics and Transportation Review* 19, no. 4 (1983):309–323.

Morrison, Steven A., and Winston, Clifford. "The Demand for Intercity Passenger Transportation: The Impact on the Bus Industry in a Changing Environment." Transportation Research Forum. *Proceedings of the Twenty-fourth Annual Meeting.* Oxford, Ind.: Richard B. Cross Company, 1983, pp. 526–534.

Mulvey, Francis P. "The Nature of Rail/Bus Competition in Inter-urban Passenger Transport Markets." Transportation Research Forum. *Proceedings of the Twenty-second Annual Meeting.* Oxford, Ind.: Richard B. Cross Company, 1981, pp. 302–310.

Nupp, Byron. "Trends and Choices for Intercity Passenger Transportation in an Era of Resource Stringency—A Problem Posed." *Transportation Journal* 19, no. 4 (Summer 1980):48–52.

Office of Transportation Analysis, Interstate Commerce Commission. *Small Community Services Study.* Washington, D.C.: ICC, 1982.

Pautsch, Gregory R.; Hamlett, Cathy A.; and Baumel, C. Phillip. "Impact of Alternative Changes in the Surface Transportation Assistance Act of 1982." Transportation Research Forum. *Proceedings of the Twenty-fourth Annual Meeting.* Oxford, Ind.: Richard B. Cross Company, 1983, pp. 331–340.

Pustay, Michael W. "Regulations of the Intrastate Motor Freight Industry in Ohio." *ICC Practitioners' Journal* 50, no. 4 (May–June 1983):415–432.

Rakowski, James P. "The Trucking Industry in the United States: A Study of Transportation Policy in Transition." *Transportation Quarterly* 35, no. 4 (October 1981):623–638.

Semmens, John, and Roth, Gabriel. "The Road to Privatization of Highway Facilities." Transportation Research Forum. *Proceedings of the Twenty-fourth Annual Meeting.* Oxford, Ind.: Richard B. Cross Company, 1983, pp. 154–165.

Stevens, Charles L., and Norris, Paul R. "The Role of the Intercity Bus Industry in Isolated Rural Regions of Oregon." Transportation Research Forum. *Proceedings of the Twenty-fourth Annual Meeting.* Oxford, Ind.: Richard B. Cross Company, 1983, pp. 535–541.

Wagner, William B. "Exit of Entry Controls for Motor Common Carriers: Rationale Reassessment." *ICC Practitioners' Journal* 50, no. 2 (Jan.–Feb. 1983):163–175.

12

General
Commodity Trucking

Chapter 12 focuses on the most important part of the for-hire trucking business in terms of revenues generated—general commodity trucking. As Fig. 12.1 shows, general freight—that is, general commodity—carriers produced 59.6% of the industry's sales dollars in 1981, compared to 40.4% of the industry's revenues derived by specialized motor carriers.

The ICC defined general commodity carriers rather vaguely as common and contract carriers transporting commodities in general, except such commodities as require special equipment or service (Ex Parte No. MC-10, decided August 9, 1937, 2 MCC 709). In simpler terms, general commodity carriers haul boxed, bagged, or containerized items in van (closed trailer) service. Unpackaged cargo that can be carried in a van-type trailer, such as tires and manufactured steel parts, also fit the general commodity category. Trucking companies that use specialized equipment such as flat-bed trailers, milk trucks, and so forth, are specialized motor carriers, which will be discussed in Chapter 13.

This chapter examines regular and irregular route general commodity common carriage; contract carriage; general commodity specialists like United Parcel Service (UPS), property brokers, and pool consolidators and distributors; traffic and economics; and management concerns and strategies.

GENERAL COMMODITY COMMON CARRIAGE

The general commodity trucking industry's most important component is general commodity common carriage. By definition, motor common carriers of

FIGURE 12.1.
Distribution of revenues by type of carrier in 1981. (*Source:* Patricia Lisciandro, *Financial Analysis of the Motor Carrier Industry 1982*, Washington, D.C.: American Trucking Associations, 1983, p. 5.)

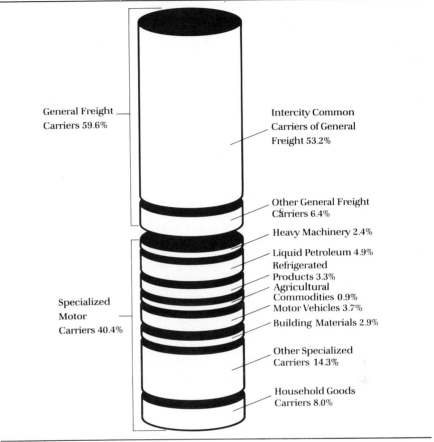

General Freight Carriers 59.6%

Intercity Common Carriers of General Freight 53.2%

Other General Freight Carriers 6.4%

Heavy Machinery 2.4%

Liquid Petroleum 4.9%

Refrigerated Products 3.3%

Agricultural Commodities 0.9%

Motor Vehicles 3.7%

Building Materials 2.9%

Specialized Motor Carriers 40.4%

Other Specialized Carriers 14.3%

Household Goods Carriers 8.0%

property are people holding themselves out to the general public to provide motor vehicle transportation for compensation over regular routes, or irregular routes, or both—49 U.S.C. 10102 (12). An applicant intending to serve interstate markets as a common carrier must obtain a certificate of public convenience and necessity from the Interstate Commerce Commission. Similar to common carrier freight railroads, a certificate both constitutes a trucking company's operating authority and obligates the possessor to adhere to the four common carrier duties of (1) serving the public, (2) delivering the goods, (3) avoiding undue or unjust discrimination, and (4) charging reasonable rates. These requirements were previously explained in Chapter 3.

Entry and Growth Problems

Of all the sectors of regulated interstate trucking, general commodity common carriage has been the most difficult to enter. If a carrier already held a certificate, it was also difficult to expand the scope of the existing business. The ICC interpreted its duty prior to deregulation as protecting existing common carriers from excessive intramodal competition. Therefore applications for certificates of public convenience and necessity were usually rejected. Carriers, recognizing the probabilities of being denied common carrier entry and knowledgeable of the legal costs and delays of applying for certificates, found the acquisition of, or the merger with, an established common carrier to be preferable, because certificates for operating authority could be transferred to the new owners. Consequently, certificates became valuable, and carriers even listed operating rights on balance sheets as intangible assets. Then came

devaluation of certificates regulatory reform, which made the process of obtaining a certificate much easier. This reform in turn lessened the value of these intangible assets to practically nothing. Thus there was no need to buy operating authority.

New Entry Rules

To obtain an ICC certificate, as explained in Chapter 11, applicants must file a request for operating authority; prove they are fit, willing, and able; and establish that the proposed service will serve a useful public purpose responsive to a public demand or need. Protesters have the burden of proving that the entry would be inconsistent with the public convenience and necessity (Section 5, the Motor Carrier Act of 1980). Thus applicants today can gain entry primarily by proving financial responsibility and by having prospective shippers say they need and would use the service. Consequently, either entering into the general commodity common carrier sector of trucking or expanding the scope of a firm's present common carrier authority is relatively easy.

As Chapter 11 noted, barriers have been removed to allow private carriers, owner-operators, contract truckers, and other industry participants to hold common carrier authority. As a result, the industry has experienced a

rapid expansion rapid expansion in the number of ICC common carriers, as well as broadened operating territories for many of the previously established common carriers. Today, the single largest obstruction to entry is not certification but financial impediments—the cost of buying trucking equipment and terminals.

Regular versus Irregular Route Common Carriage

Regular Route Service.   General commodity common carriers are divided into regular route and irregular route companies. The regular route common carrier sales leaders in 1984 were as follows: Roadway Express, Inc.; Yellow Freight System, Inc.; Consolidated Freightways Corporation; Ryder/P-I-E Nationwide; McLean Trucking Company; Overnite Transportation; and Arkansas Best Corporation. These and hundreds of other firms in the business are characterized by national, regional, and local networks of terminals linked by linehaul operations—the part of the operations transporting loads on long-haul intercity trips.

LTL and TL mix

With some exceptions, regular route common carriers traditionally built businesses around LTL traffic—shipments weighing less than 10,000 lbs.—supplemented by TL (truckload) traffic—shipments weighing 10,000 lbs. or more. TL traffic helped solve backhaul problems in unbalanced traffic lanes, where LTL traffic flows were heavily one-way oriented, and it typically generated 20% to 40% of corporate operating revenues. Regular route common carriage is a business characterized by many competitors but dominated by only a small number of large regional and national carriers. National carriers today commonly operate hundreds of terminals, own their tractors and trailers, do little interlining with each other or with smaller carriers, and are highly unionized. (Overnite, a noted exception, is a large non-unionized firm.) Scheduled departures, preplanned trip itineraries, and published rates distinguish the regular route side of the business.

Irregular Route Service. The other half of general commodity common carriage is irregular route service. Firms in this sector have broad operating authority and the freedom to use any routes available to deliver cargo to market. An illustration of an irregular route carrier is a company with authority to serve any point in Ohio connecting with any point in Iowa.

TL emphasis

The most noticeable difference between irregular route and regular route operations is the irregular route carriers' nearly total concentration on truckload traffic. Mostly they carry goods from the shipper's dock to the consignee's door and avoid much of the high variable costs associated with handling LTL· shipments that regular route carriers experience. Irregular route carriage is also characterized by a large number of relatively small firms, the absence of large dominating carriers, heavy reliance on independent owner-operators, who own and drive their trucking equipment, to supply vehicles and drivers, demand-activated or unscheduled departures, and few unionized firms. Irregular route carriage today is far more similar to contract trucking than to regular route common carriage. Consequently, the irregular route common carrier and contract units of the American Trucking Associations recently merged into the Interstate Carriers Conference.

Regular Route Common Carrier Terminals

Successful regular route common carriage relies on origin terminals as sources of traffic and destination terminals to enable shipments to be delivered. In between, most carriers establish breakbulk and relay terminals. The terminal network idea is based on the belief that customers desire single carrier service. Therefore a carrier should serve not only the consignor, but also the consignee. However, to succeed, carriers must build sufficient loads to common destinations to cover costs and make profits.

Local Terminals.   Local terminals dominate the regular route business in the number of units and the diversity of functions performed. Usually, these small facilities employ a minimal work force, including a terminal manager responsible for operations and terminal administration, a salesperson, a clerk, dispatchers, dock workers, and drivers. In larger cities, of course, facilities can be considerably larger. Often the terminal manager at small facilities assumes the salesperson role, as well as supervises operations.

terminal functions

Every day, personnel solicit, collect, and distribute shipments among their localized customers. A typical day might include the routing of several peddle-run trucks—vehicles that follow planned routings stopping at shipper docks to drop off inbound freight and pick up outbound shipments. In addition, some drivers have in-cab radios enabling them to receive directions to make pick-ups at unscheduled shipper facilities. Moreover, an increasing tendency is to reduce peddle-run activities and send vehicles only to places where shipments are ready for transportation. This economy move is aimed at reducing fuel, labor, and other operating costs wasted when peddle-run trucks stop at shipper docks where there is no business.

dock and linehaul operations

Peddle-run drivers return to the terminals by about 4 P.M., at which point cargo is put on the dock, sorted, and loaded on over-the-road (linehaul) vehicles. When linehaul trailers are filled to capacity or the clock reaches a pre-designated cutoff time, vehicles are dispatched either to breakbulk terminals or directly toward destination terminals. Local terminals also receive inbound trailers and sort shipments for local delivery.

importance of local terminals

Local terminals are important to ensure that regular route common carriers succeed. Since local terminal personnel are the customers' key contact points with the company, shippers rely heavily on these employees for rate and service information, tracing to locate shipments and obtain shipment status information, billing, claims, and many other forms of assistance. If a carrier plans to make a profit, terminal personnel must perform their operating, maintenance, and marketing jobs well. Productivity, cost controls, and good customer rapport are essential. Therefore terminal managers strive to reduce unnecessary vehicle miles, save fuel, avoid in-service equipment failures, minimize loss and damage problems, and establish positive and helpful employee attitudes. Success is often determined by doing little things right.

profitability keys

Breakbulk Terminals.   Breakbulk terminals receive loads from local, other breakbulk, and relay terminals and sort the cargo for shipment to further points. For example, a local terminal routes an assortment of shipments in a single trailer to a breakbulk facility. Cargo is then unloaded and sorted, according to destination and further shipment points (see Fig. 12.2). For instance, all cargo going to St. Louis and beyond would be consolidated and loaded into a trailer soon to be dispatched to that city. Again, these terminals attempt to use equipment efficiently by using the full cubic capacity and weight-hauling capacity of each trailer. At the other end of the journey, another breakbulk facility receives this vehicle and those from other terminals, sorts cargo, and ships freight to local terminals for delivery to customers. Sometimes breakbulk facilities also act as local terminals serving nearby cus-

FIGURE 12.2.
A drag line is used to haul shipments from inbound trailer locations in Overnight Transportation Company's breakbulk terminal in Gaffney, South Carolina, to locations throughout the facility. In this case, a continuously moving cable is located beneath the floor. When carts are ready for moving to other terminal areas, a dock worker attaches them to the drag line that subsequently pulls the carts to the right places. There, other dock workers disengage the carts and load materials on outbound trailers. (Photo courtesy of Overnight Transportation Company)

tomers. Breakbulk facilities further tend to accommodate regional management personnel and perform extensive maintenance work.

Relay Terminals. In the regular route common carrier sector, most carriers use relay terminals primarily to expedite cargo movements and comply with driver needs. These facilities are located within a 10-hour driving range of several breakbulk terminals, or at intervals of approximately 400–450 miles, depending on average driving speeds and highway congestion. At a relay terminal, the inbound driver leaves the tractor, and another sits behind the wheel to drive to the next breakbulk or relay terminal. Another strategy is to send a driver from his or her domicile or home terminal in, for example, an easterly direction and another driver from his or her home terminal in a westerly direction. At a midpoint, approximately 200–225 miles from each domicile, drivers switch vehicles and head for their respective domiciles. Most regular route carriers do not use two-person crews or sleeper cabs as is more common in the private carrier side of the business. Thus regular route carriage is similar to the old Pony Express, except today the driver is able to rest, while the truck keeps going.

Equipment

As previously noted, general commodity carriage relies almost entirely on conventional van trailers. Equipment selection varies according to several criteria such as the cargo density (weight per cubic foot), the amount of emphasis

selection criteria

given to fuel efficiency, driver considerations, planned vehicle use (i.e., for linehaul or peddle-run purposes), maneuverability, and compliance with federal and state laws.

new vehicle
size limits

In the Surface Transportation Assistance Act of 1982, the federal government mandated that states allow the operation of motor vehicles with minimum limits of 20,000 lbs. carried on any one axle and 34,000 lbs. on a tandem (double) axle, as well as 80,000 lbs. overall maximum gross weight, including cargo and net vehicle weight. The same act allows minimum single trailer lengths of 48 ft and twin-trailer (double-bottom) minimums of 28 ft for each trailer. On designated highways, vehicles within these limits operate free of state interference. Furthermore, because of the Department of Transportation Appropriations Act of December 18, 1982, vehicle widths of 102 in. (versus the former 96 in.) are now allowed.

equipment
considerations

Given the right to acquire larger vehicles, carriers must decide whether to purchase larger tractors and trailers, and if acquisitions seem like the appropriate action, then what equipment to buy. Twin 28-ft trailers, for example, can increase the productivity of a truck driver by more than 30% over a conventional single 45-ft van if a carrier can fully use the available increased cubic capacity. However, if the carrier cannot use all the increased space because traffic demand is too low or because the traffic density is too great, indicating that shipments are so heavy that the vehicle weights-out (i.e., it reaches its gross maximum weight limit), then there is less justification for purchasing double-bottoms.

equipment strategies

Major regular route common carriers buy equipment to replace existing vehicles or to expand the fleet; furthermore, they tend to place large orders for tractors and specify engines, transmissions, clutches, and other equipment carefully. They also emphasize standardization, operating efficiency, and easy maintenance, rather than glamorous equipment. Trailers, too, are often produced to customer specifications. Regular route carriers tend to buy approximately two 45-ft or 48-ft trailers per tractor and three double-bottom trailers, called pups, per tractor. This arrangement permits one trailer to be dropped for loading or unloading, while the others are in road service. Decisions to use double-bottom equipment necessitate purchases of dollies like the one shown in Fig. 12.3. A dolly is positioned behind the first pup; it serves as the front axle of the second pup and links both pups together.

CONTRACT CARRIAGE

Contract carriage, another key component of the general commodity business, is experiencing rapid growth. *Contract carriers* of property are defined as people who provide motor vehicle transportation for compensation under continuing agreements with one or more people "(i) by assigning motor vehicles for a continuing period of time for the exclusive use of each such person; or (ii) designed to meet the distinct needs of each such person" [49 U.S.C. 10102(13)].

FIGURE 12.3.
A double-bottom dolly like the one in the photograph is positioned between the first and second trailers; it serves as the front axle of the second trailer and links both trailers (pups) together. (Fred Stephenson photo)

definition

As previously noted, contract trucking is a truckload-oriented, door-to-door business. The growth of this sector is attributable to the ease of entry and to minimal initial cash outflow requirements. A carrier can start without a terminal network or hundreds of customers. Basically, only a single rig and one customer with two-way traffic are required.

Impact of Deregulation

Deregulation has accelerated the development of contract carriage. To enter the business, applicants must now receive an ICC-approved permit by proving they are fit, willing, and able and that the service would be consistent with the public interest and the National Transportation Policy (Section 10 of the MCA). The MCA makes it much harder for protesters to raise objections and stop the applicant from receiving a permit today than in the past. As a rule, the ICC is generous in granting permits. Ending the rule-of-eight has also helped carriers. When the rule was enforced, contract truckers often turned down business from a prospective eighth customer for fear that this last customer might force the carrier to miss a better opportunity coming available in the future. Ending the rule-of-eight encouraged contract carriers to be more aggressive marketers. With their labor costs lower than the costs experienced by many of their unionized common carrier competitors, contract carriers have used low prices to capture a large portion of the truckload traffic that used to move by common carriage.

GENERAL COMMODITY SPECIALISTS

United Parcel Service

The general commodity business is also served by specialists. One of the most successful U.S. transportation companies is United Parcel Service of America, Inc. (UPS). With 1984 sales of $6.8 billion and net income after interest and taxes of $477 million,[1] UPS is an excellent example of the fruits of good management and a productive work force.

General Characteristics.   What is UPS? Its certificate reads that it is a general commodity carrier;[2] however, unlike most trucking companies that *role* provide a wide assortment of services, UPS limits its activities to the small package market, handling shipments in 1984 no heavier than 70 lbs. each and measuring no more than 108 in. in length and girth. This strategy has not only paid off handsomely for the owners, but it also proves that the transportation industry is a huge business offering great opportunity for those finding a niche and accomplishing the job to the satisfaction of their shipper customers.

history and size UPS began in 1907 as a small messenger service in Seattle, Washington. Gradually, the company expanded its route system, and during 1984 the company delivered 1.9 billion packages, served 669,000 steady customers, employed 141,000 workers, and operated a fleet of 72,413 vehicles.[3]

services UPS provides three types of services: standard parcel service or surface transportation, UPS Next Day Air Service, and UPS Second Day Air Service. With deregulation, the company has been able to integrate its surface and air operations; the same delivery and pick-up vehicles generate and dispense both surface and air packages. UPS has interstate motor carrier authority in the 48 contiguous states, Washington, D.C., and all the Hawaiian Islands. It also possesses intrastate authority in all 48 contiguous states except Texas. Finally, UPS Second Day Air Service, once known as Blue Label Air Service, connects the 48 contiguous states, Washington, D.C., and all parts of Hawaii. This service depends on the company's fleet of 148 aircraft, as does UPS Next Day Air Service, which serves 44 states and the District of Columbia.

Keys to Success.   UPS remained financially successful and growing, even during the recession of the early 1980s. With approximately 90,000 Teamster employees, UPS employs more union workers than does any other transportation company, and it pays its employees well. In fact, 61.5¢ of each *labor costs* $1 of revenues in 1984 were used to cover the pay and benefits of all its *and advantages* employees. However, several differences exist between the UPS Teamster contract and the National Master Freight Agreement (NMFA) governing most other Teamsters in the trucking industry. UPS negotiates separately and nationally, and its contract has its own terms. For example, UPS drivers are all paid on an hourly rate. None receives mileage fees as is the practice with road (line-haul) drivers under the NMFA. In addition, UPS has the right to use part-time workers during peak periods. Both UPS provisions contribute significantly to high productivity levels and cost efficiencies.

profit sharing and employee ownership

A second key to the success of UPS is profit sharing. More than 79,000 UPS employees participate in a voluntary profit-sharing plan; furthermore, UPS stock is almost totally owned by 10,685 UPS managers and supervisors. With a vested interest in the company, managers and employees have common grounds for working together and harder. Thirdly, UPS has an informal management style. As a people-oriented, open-door, first-name-basis company, it stresses teamwork and promotion from within.

selective marketing

productivity

Finally, although UPS accepts its responsibilities as a common carrier, its certificate does not require that UPS solicit business from everyone. Consequently, it does not.[4] UPS caters to steady, volume customers. If individuals want to use UPS, they can, but they often discover that customer counters are hard to find. UPS is a premier consolidator that wants multiple shipments picked up at, and delivered to, single points. This volume generates the economies and productivity permitting low prices, which, when joined with a superior corporate record of dependability and convenience, have made UPS the most relied on privately run small-package company in the United States.

Operations. The UPS operating system is divided into regions that are subsequently separated into districts, then into divisions, and then into operating centers. Nationally, UPS has more than 100 highly mechanized sorting hubs and hundreds of operating centers. Hubs perform many functions similar to general commodity common carrier breakbulk terminals, whereas operating centers perform most of the same activities as common carrier local terminals. In addition, operating centers perform retail functions; customers can drop off packages and pay in advance for UPS service.

hubs and operating centers

package cars and feeders

Every day, parcels received at an operating center from hubs are sorted and loaded on what UPS calls *package cars* (see Fig. 12.4). Package-car drivers start their routes early in the morning delivering each parcel. Later the same day drivers again start at the beginning of their routes and repeat the cycle making pick-ups before returning to the operating center. That evening, inbound parcels from package cars are sorted for local delivery or loaded on feeders (tractor-trailer rigs) for hubs (see Fig. 12.5). Feeders linehaul packages between operating centers and hubs, hubs and hubs, or hubs and centers. Feeders are designed to provide maximum cubic capacity. Unlike typical general commodity van-type trailers, UPS trailers are molded around the wheels, because UPS hauls light-density traffic. Since feeders cube-out faster than they weight-out, this trailer design aids productivity.

Property Brokers

Another general commodity specialist is the property broker. Of all the changes resulting from trucking deregulation, the rapid development and growth of property brokers is possibly the most significant.

FIGURE 12.4.
United Parcel Service (UPS) package car. (Photo courtesy of United Parcel Services of America, Inc.)

FIGURE 12.5.
United Parcel Service (UPS) feeder. (Photo courtesy of United Parcel Service of America, Inc.)

definitions

The federal government defines *broker* to mean "a person, other than a motor carrier or an employee or agent of a motor carrier, that as a principal or agent sells, offers for sale, negotiates for, or holds itself out by solicitation, advertisement, or otherwise as selling, providing, or arranging for, transportation by motor carrier for compensation" [49 U.S.C. 10102(1)]. Another definition is the following one:

> It is a company that takes a shipper's freight and finds a carrier to haul the freight. It is a freight forwarder without cargo liability and without tariffs, and a shipper's agent that handles more than just piggyback freight. In today's transportation supermarket of many price service options, a broker is a transportation consultant that secures the best transportation package available for shipper clients and lines up freight for carrier clients.[5]

broker compensation

Brokers either charge an owner-operator or carrier a commission, usually ranging from 5% to 10% of the freight bill, or add a charge to the established freight bill. In some cases, brokers establish the rate on contract carriage. In other words, the broker acts as a contract carrier. Today it is common to see a broker with more than 100 carriers working for it.

historical function

new niche

Prior to regulatory reform, brokers primarily served the exempt interstate agricultural sector as go-betweens for shippers and independent owner-operators hauling such commodities. Today, much of the activity and most of the growth is in the general commodity sector, the realm of property brokers. The law now permits property brokers to serve private carriers, who possess common carrier or contract carrier interstate authority, contract carriers, common carriers, and even other brokers. In fact, some companies have formed nationwide brokerage franchise systems, with each franchise holding its own brokerage license and all franchised brokers tied together by computers.[6]

Entry and Growth.   Entry into the property brokerage business, exclusive of those wishing to be brokers in the household goods industry, is controlled by provisions of 49 U.S.C. 10924(b). A license is granted by the ICC to applicants who establish that they are fit, willing, and able and who will comply with the law and the regulations of the Interstate Commerce Commission. With few exceptions, entry is available for the asking. Furthermore, since brokers require no trucking equipment and minimal office facilities, financial start-up costs are not a burden. Thus firms have entered the brokerage business by the thousands.

reasons for growth

Once licensed, brokers automatically have 50-state authority to serve almost anyone holding an ICC trucking certificate or permit. In addition, the Commission's lax lattitude toward enforcement of federal rules and regulations[7] has also prompted the dramatic rise in interest and activity in property brokerage.

The growth in property brokerage can also be explained by several other factors. Liberalized licensing removed legal entry obstacles and restrictions that formerly had limited the broker's business functions—what they could do and who could use them. The broker today is recognized as someone who can help small carriers find traffic, since few of these carriers have extensive sales forces. Shippers, confused by the greater assortment of trucking rate/service options, likewise see the property broker as someone who can sort through the piles of marketing information and find quality trucking services at low rates. Brokers can do this service in part by relying on lower cost, non-unionized trucking companies. Finally, brokers can facilitate backhaul problems by finding traffic to fill vehicles that otherwise might travel empty.

Opportunities and Risks.   Even though the property brokerage industry is still in its infancy, it is a sector with great opportunities. Most brokers are relatively small, but they are aggressively marketing their services. Furthermore, expansion is possible if brokers seek opportunities to become shippers' agents, surface freight forwarders, air freight forwarders, and/or non-vessel operating common carriers for ocean freight. Moreover, property brokers may be totally deregulated in the near future, as the U.S. Department of Transportation desired in 1983.

shipper concerns   Will shippers accept the idea of giving traffic to people who do not own equipment or do not have drivers on their payrolls? This situation is a risk in property brokerage. Shippers who want to negotiate with firms that directly control equipment and labor are reluctant to use brokers. Also, shippers may have concerns about cargo liability and should ask brokers to define the limits of their insurance.

Pool Consolidators and Distributors

background   A third group of general commodity trucking industry specialists that has gained popularity in recent years is pool consolidators and distributors. *Pooling,* an old concept, originated when LCL freight was loaded on rail boxcars and shipped to distant warehouses. From this period of "pool cars," there gradually developed numerous local cartage (short-haul trucking) companies that resided in major transportation centers across the country. These firms performed similar functions for the long-haul common carrier truckers, collecting and distributing LTL shipments within urban commercial zones—ICC-defined geographic areas that contain most of a city's industrial/commercial economic activity.

new role   With truck deregulation came the development of a broader niche. As a result of the expansion of the larger LTL common carriers into the smaller markets, local cartage companies found their interline traffic and role diminishing. Some went out of business; others found an opportunity in pooling. Actually, they discovered a void in the market between the LTL shipment sector and the truckload business, and they stepped forward to fill it.

Operations.   How does general freight pooling work? First, shippers need to transport numerous small shipments from a single origin point to multiple dispersed consignees but at reasonably low rates. They can do so with pooled shipments tendered under a master bill of lading and transported by an intercity irregular route common carrier to a breakbulk warehouse for subsequent short-haul delivery of separate smaller shipments to consignees. At origin and destination, pool agents—consolidators and distributors, the same local cartage companies that were described previously, for the most part— are responsible for the pick-up and delivery of shipments.

illustration

For example, the ACE Manufacturing Company of Omaha, Nebraska, is contemplating shipping air conditioners to 20 different customers located within a 100-mile radius of Memphis, Tennessee. Each air conditioner weighs 250 lbs. One option is to ship each unit separately by LTL common carrier. Another is to pool them into a 5000-lb. load, but this pooling will require holding the freight until ACE has the 5000 lbs. It could ship smaller consolidations, for example, four units, but to realize fully the advantages of volume rate savings, ACE needs about 5000 lbs. Therefore, to reduce its transportation costs, ACE choses the pooling option.

Next, the ACE traffic manager contacts an Omaha consolidator, who agrees to pick up the 5000 lbs. and haul the shipment to the consolidator's Omaha warehouse (Fig. 12.6). This shipment and other similar traffic for the Memphis region are soon consolidated and tendered to an irregular route common carrier, which agrees to perform over-the-road TL service to Memphis. Then the same agent, if that agent has warehouse and distribution capabilities, or a second agent, if necessary, sorts the inbound load and arranges delivery. If destinations reside outside the commercial zone or beyond the agent's operating authority, LTL service is arranged by the agent, usually with a regular route common carrier.

Success. Pooling sales are increasing primarily because shippers can cut their door-to-door transportation bills, but improved services also commonly result. Savings are realized primarily from lower cost long-haul, bulk volume irregular route common carrier service. As previously noted, these are mostly non-unionized firms using their own equipment and drivers or purchased transportation (employment of owner-operators). Consolidating necessitates few pick-ups, which lowers costs. In addition, pool agents can often perform all origin and destination duties (e.g., pick-up, consolidating, sorting, and delivery) at relatively low price levels because of their own low-cost structures. Collectively, total door-to-door charges are often 10% or more below discounted direct LTL regular route service rates.

reasons for growth

shipper concerns

For many shippers, pooling makes sense, yet others cannot use it or refuse to shift from LTL carriage. One concern is control. Using pool agents usually means that more people and companies will handle the freight than with the LTL option, which in turn increases the risks of loss and damage. Shippers also worry that the pool consolidators and distributors or the carriers they use might go bankrupt or that they will have problems collecting on loss and damage or overcharge claims.

DACA

Consequently, Distributors and Consolidators of America (DACA), a network of about 50 pooling agents in the U.S. and Canada, was created. DACA

FIGURE 12.6.
Pooling illustration.

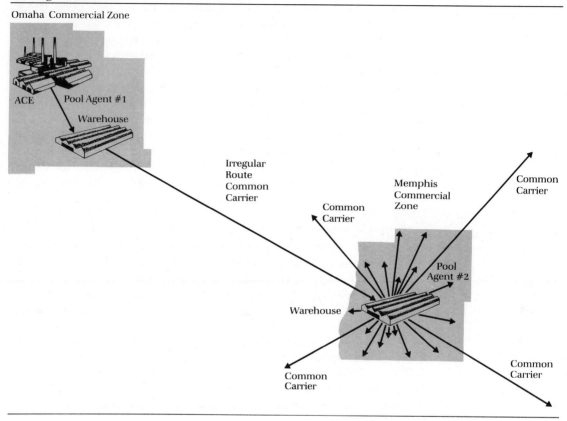

is an example of a sales and marketing organization whose members depend on each other to do the job properly. The DACA member originating freight must have confidence another DACA member will take just as much care and responsibility delivering shipments. DACA members failing to meet these and other standards are removed from the organization.

TRAFFIC AND ECONOMICS

Commonalities and Distinctions

General commodity motor carriers exhibit both differences and similarities in their traffic and economics. One commonality is an industry cost structure that is predominantly variable. First, the rights-of-way are publicly owned, operated, and maintained. Compared with railroads, for example, fixed assets are minor and limited to terminals and trucking equipment; moreover, for firms in the truckload business, even these assets are not particularly necessary. Shipments go from consignor (shipper) warehouse to consignee (receiver) dock, and there is heavy use of tractors and trailers supplied by owner-operators. Secondly, it is a labor-intensive industry.

Another commonality is private ownership, for there is little government ownership of motor carriage, except for U.S. postal operations. Few firms, however, offer public stock offerings. Most are owned by small groups of investors or managers and employees.

distinctions

To generalize is difficult in other areas, since there are small, as well as large, firms, short-haul carriers and carriers whose average length of haul exceeds 1000 miles, union and non-union firms, carriers concentrating on LTL freight and others with TL orientations, firms owning all their equipment and others owning little, and so forth. Therefore industry averages must be interpreted carefully, because there are many exceptions.

Roadway Express, Inc.

One chapter cannot cover all aspects of the general commodity trucking business, so one sector will be analyzed here in depth. The largest general commodity common carrier in the United States, Roadway Express, Inc., will be used to illustrate large LTL carriers. Financial analysts recognize Roadway as one of the best managed, most financially secure firms in trucking. It is also an LTL specialist recognized for its productivity. The information provided is based on Roadway's operations from January 1 through December 31, 1984.

Company Description. In 1984, Roadway operated a network of 541 terminals serving all states except Hawaii.[8] It employed 19,942 people, and its fleet numbered 29,532 tractors, straight trucks (i.e., single-unit vehicles, rather than tractor-trailer rigs), and trailers.[9] Legally defined, its business is regular route common carriage and, to a minor extent, contract carriage. In fact, during 1984 the former accounted for 94.3% of Roadway's intercity freight revenues. Like most major regular route common carriers (RRCCs), Roadway owns its vehicles and has its drivers on the company payroll. The company minimally uses purchased transportation (the use of owner-operator or leased trucking equipment and drivers).

size

regular route
common
carrier orientation

Financial Situation. Table 12.1, a 1984 income statement, reveals a company doing well despite deregulation, increased competition, recession, and high costs. On revenues of $1.4 billion, Roadway achieved after-tax income from continuing operations of $82 million and an operating ratio of 90.4. Its after-tax return on stockholders' equity of $607 million was 13.5%.

revenues
and earnings

Table 12.1 shows that Roadway was profitable in 1984, despite high employee costs accounting for 68.25% of all operating expenditures. Contrary to popular opinion, high-cost unionized firms like Roadway can make money in the trucking industry today. Note also that only a small percentage of dollars was spent for fixed assets. The items "depreciation and amortization" and

labor and fuel costs

TABLE 12.1. Roadway Express, Inc. income statement (January 1—December 31, 1984)

	($ Thousands)	Percent	($ Thousands)
Operating revenues			$1,400,907
Expenses			
Salaries and expenses	$864,725	68.25%	
Supplies and expenses	204,518	16.14	
Operating taxes and licenses	42,218	3.33	
Insurance	27,449	2.17	
Communications and utilities	22,915	1.81	
Depreciation and amortization	48,239	3.81	
Revenue equipment rents and purchased transportation	42,206	3.33	
Building and office equipment	3,705	0.29	
Loss (gain) on disposition of assets	(317)	(0.03)	
Miscellaneous expenses	11,403	0.90	
Total operating expenses		100.00%	$1,267,061
Net carrier operating income			133,846
Other income/deductions[a]			16,011
Ordinary income			149,857
Income taxes			67,373
Income from continuing operations after taxes			$82,484

[a]Mostly interest income. Roadway had no long-term debt fee and paid no interest.

Source: Roadway Express, *Motor Carrier Annual Report "M" to the Interstate Commerce Commission, MC Docket 2202, for the Period Ended December 31, 1984.*

"building and office equipment" show that Roadway can subsist without major obligations for equipment and facilities. Fuel and fuel taxes, which were part of "supplies and expenses", represented 7.14% of Roadway's 1984 costs. This figure is low compared with airline cost structures, where fuel expenses typically exceed 20% of costs. However, Roadway paid $90 million for fuel and taxes in 1984 (not shown). With the potential of saving nearly $1 million annually for each 1% reduction in the fuel bill, efficiency is nevertheless important.

    Table 12.2 depicts Roadway's expenses by business activity. The percentages shown are most important, for they indicate cost-cutting priorities. Linehaul operations (with 39.03% of the cost dollars), platform activities (with

activity costs

TABLE 12.2. Roadway Express, Inc. expenses by activity area (Period January 1—December 31, 1984)		
Activity	Cost ($ Thousands)	Percent
Linehaul	$494,577	39.03%
Platform	275,945	21.78
Pick-up and delivery	249,969	19.73
Terminal	90,923	7.18
General and administrative	48,187	3.80
Traffic and sales	43,089	3.40
Maintenance	27,204	2.15
Billing and collecting	22,819	1.80
Insurance and safety	14,348	1.13
Total operating expenses	$1,267,061	100.00%

Source: Roadway Express, *Motor Carrier Annual Report "M" to the Interstate Commerce Commission, MC Docket 2202, for the Period Ended December 31, 1984*, pp. 38, 39.

21.78%), and pick-up and delivery operations (with 19.73%) collectively accounted for 80.54% of all expended dollars. Thus a regular route common carrier must try to control these cost areas, because positive changes there can produce the most company impact. It also illustrates why irregular route and contract carriers can usually offer lower TL rates: they are not burdened by high platform (terminal) and pick-up and delivery costs. Another important discovery (not shown in the table) is that salaries, wages, and benefits accounted for 56.9% of Roadway's linehaul costs, 75.4% of its pick-up and delivery fees, and 91.8% of its platform charges (terminal receiving, sorting, consolidating and loading work).

profitability keys

How can Roadway make money with such a cost structure? In simple terms, the company is profitable because of productivity and high yields. Like UPS, Roadway is known for high labor productivity. It pays well, but it expects workers to earn that income. Secondly, the company collects more per ton-mile than the costs of the service. Roadway averaged 21.6¢ per ton-mile, while operating expense tallied 19.6¢ in 1984.[10] In part, this high yield can be traced to a dedicated effort to sell LTL services. Moreover, Roadway had no long-term debt and earned millions of dollars from invested capital (Table 12.1, "Other Income").

Traffic Trends. In 1978, Roadway transported 6,990,000 tons of freight of which 43.8% was truckload business. However, by 1982, truckload traffic had been reduced from 3,065,000 tons to 1,549,000 tons—a drop of 49.5%.[11] The erosion of TL freight reflects the difficulties of competing against lower cost TL carriers, the impact of the recession, and a shift in Roadway's marketing orientation toward the LTL sector. Nevertheless, during the same period, LTL tonnage also declined by 16.6% from 3,925,000 tons to 3,273,000.[12] The recession was primarily responsible. However, Roadway, aided by high

LTL yields and the long-haul nature of its operations (the average ton in 1982 traveled 1077 miles), continued to be highly profitable. Long hauls produce higher aggregate revenues than short hauls tend to do. In 1984, LTL traffic represented 67.8% of Roadway's tonnage, 98.5% of Roadway's shipments, and 85.4% of the company's revenues.[13]

Final Assessment.   In 1984, Roadway averaged $3.02 in revenues per intercity mile. This figure is relatively high in the trucking industry and indicates that Roadway has found market niches where shippers are willing to pay higher prices for trucking services that satisfy their needs. Roadway also averaged 13.93 tons per intercity vehicle-mile and had an average haul of 1109 miles per ton.[14]

Collectively, Roadway has done a better job than most trucking companies at target marketing, obtaining the yields and longer hauls, and filling its vehicles to above-average weights. The company has proven that a trucking company can maintain earnings despite major changes in the economy and high labor costs if it is well managed and implements sound business strategies.

MANAGEMENT CONCERNS AND STRATEGIES

Problems

Not all general commodity truckers have adjusted to change as well as Roadway has. In fact, the 1980s have been a period of despair for many carriers. Rapidly rising fuel costs, labor expenses, and user taxes were not just a burden but also an omen of future impediments to corporate prosperity. When truckers believed they had run the gauntlet, the insurance crisis of 1985 hit, extracting an additional costly toll. In one year, the trucking industry saw insurance rates increase 300% to 500%.

insurance crisis   Such hefty insurance price jumps were due to falling interest rates, poor insurance company investments of premiums, and high jury awards. Insurance companies, as a result of insurance industry competition, had bid down insurance premiums for about six years prior to 1985 to increase market shares, which was not a problem as long as premiums could be reinvested at higher interest rates. However, when the prime rate fell, the insurance industry suffered billions of dollars in losses. An aggravating factor was the increasing tendency of courts to award high settlements to accident and other victims both inside and outside the trucking industry. In summary, however, trucking companies were told they would substantially share the financial burden of the insurance industry's shortcomings.[15]

rising costs   Rising costs are a corporate problem almost anytime, but in a deregulated environment where discounting is rampant and carriers are trying to compete with lower cost trucking companies for business from price-sensitive shippers, they can be devastating. Particularly hard pressed were unionized regular route common carriers, for many were driven out of the TL sector, and others were put entirely out of business. Regular route common carriers were **discounting** also thrust into a new battle featuring LTL discounting. Leading the way was Overnite Transportation Company, a large general commodities common carrier that decided to capitalize on its lower cost and non-unionized status to lower its prices. Great disparity exists between what unionized and non-unionized trucking firms pay their employees. Thus major improvements in a high-cost regular route common carrier's profits require tighter cost controls and increased productivity. Otherwise, a carrier must increase yields by performing services for which shippers will pay higher rates. None of these strategies will be easy to implement, but they could be important to corporate survival.

Labor

As recently as 1979, the most powerful U.S. transportation union was the International Brotherhood of Teamsters. At that time the Teamsters had 300,000 over-the-road and local truck drivers and dock workers and a contract signed by more than 700 trucking companies. This was a unique situation, for unlike the rail or airline sectors, where virtually each large carrier had to handle multiple unions, the Teamsters stood practically alone in negotiations with trucking management. Approximately every three years, the Teamsters sat across the bargaining table from Trucking Management, Inc. (TMI), the carriers' negotiating team, and hammered out the new National Master Freight Agreement (NMFA)—a single national labor contract. Deregulation, however, has significantly weakened the union's power. By 1982 an estimated 100,000 union members were out of work, and the Teamsters and the carriers employing them returned to the negotiating table to try to save both the companies and workers from self-destruction.

1982
Teamsters contract
As a result of the 1982 negotiations, the Teamsters agreed to a wage freeze and work-rule concessions aimed at helping their employer firms withstand the joint pressures of recession and deregulation, as well as return laid off workers to their jobs. The new 37-month contract effective March 1, 1982, however, placed a cap on cost of living allowance (COLA) increases. On April 1, 1982, the rate of pay for an hourly worker was set at $13.26 per hour plus about $4 more per hour in benefits—about $35,000 in annual wages and benefits per worker, excluding overtime.

Reasons for Cost Levels. How did labor costs reach this level? The answer lies in the previous regulated environment, which effectively shut the door on people who could have qualified for trucking industry jobs and who would have worked for less but who had little opportunity because of rigid entry regulations that kept new carriers out of the industry. Moreover, existing carriers were allowed to pass labor cost increases through to the shipping public by applying for and receiving general rate increases. During this highly regulated period before 1980, there was practically no price competition in the LTL sector. Virtually all carriers raised prices simultaneously. Shippers either paid the for-hire rate or looked beyond regular route common carriage for answers, and there was no guarantee of the latter solutions. Thus rates of pay rose rapidly, particularly after COLA provisions were included in the contract. The only difference today is that, while general rate increases are still granted, carriers are not sure they can raise rates for fear that lower cost firms will underprice them.

Carrier and Union Responses to Competition. In response to this mounting competitive threat, unionized carriers have taken several measures. First, hundreds of carriers refused to sign the 1982 NMFA. In fact, only about 285 out of 700 signed, and many others tried (some, successfully) to amend the contract wage and work-rule provisions at the local level to compete against non-unionized firms in their local areas.[16] Trying to prevent bankruptcies and job losses, some union workers have been unofficially working for less than NMFA wage levels. To save jobs and return laid-off workers to the job, Teamster officials tried to convince the membership to agree to lower pay scales, but the union membership would not support them. Still, there is both a lessening of demands and a willingness to compromise on organized labor's part, as well as resistance from the membership to lessen pay for more work. The labor cost disparity problem is real and will not disappear. It must either be solved, or high pay scales will mean nothing to unemployed workers whose firms are in bankruptcy.

ERISA and MEPPAA

Some firms can neither afford bankruptcy nor afford to stay in business. In 1974, Congress passed the Employee Retirement Income Security Act (ERISA) (93 *Statutes at Large*, p. 935), and in 1980, it amended ERISA with the Multi-Employer Pension Plan Amendments Act (MEPPAA) (94 Stat. 1208). These laws altered employer pension plans and obligated participating carriers to pay at the time of withdrawal or partial withdrawal from a plan not only the amounts of employer contributions but also liabilities far in excess of these contributions, and often far beyond the net worth of the company.

The problem at present is twofold, and the industry is seeking amendments. First, companies cannot control the factors used to determine pension liability. These factors are set by pension fund trustees, who are primarily union appointees. Secondly, some unprofitable firms that need to file for bankruptcy cannot exit the business because it costs more to cease operations than to continue hauling freight.[17]

Needs. Because of these problems, the managers of troubled firms and their unions must work together to survive and prosper. Whether pay scales were earned and legitimate, or whether other industries pay their workers more is irrelevant in a deregulated environment. What is crucial to survival on both sides today is what supply and demand are dictating in the deregulated trucking market. Companies anticipate that increased vehicle weight and length limits will increase labor productivity, but non-union firms have the same opportunities to spread costs over more units of output. It will require far more effort and results by labor and management to return firms to more cost-competitive positions.

Operating Strategies: Costs and Productivity

To regain strength, firms should analyze all cost areas. No major improvements may be possible in any one area, but if a company could save a little in each activity or bolster productivity by a few percentage points, the sum of these improvements could be significant. For instance, can a carrier reroute vehicles to save fuel or better use labor and equipment? Is it necessary to stop daily at every shipper's dock? Can smaller vehicles be used on peddle runs? Can more fuel-efficient vehicles be bought? Can costly breakdowns and big repair bills be avoided by implementing planned maintenance programs? Can unnecessary paperwork be eliminated? Can the computer be used more wisely? Are people doing tasks that are totally useless, or if they have value, can either their output be improved or their input effort reduced? To succeed, firms must continuously ask: "Why are we doing it this way?" This is management's challenge, and both owners and labor are counting on managers to produce the right answers.

Marketing Strategies

Before deregulation, marketing in the trucking industry was rudimentary compared to the sophistication of marketing endeavors in such industries as toiletries and grocery products. Trucking organizations did little, if any, market research to find out what customers wanted. Instead, they operated sales organizations and traffic departments, often independently of one another. Traffic departments had two basic tasks: determining rate levels and providing rate information. Salespeople tried to convince shippers to use their companies' services at the established rate levels. There were exceptions, of course. However, as previously stated, there was practically no LTL price competition and only limited competition between common and contract TL sectors. Basically, service competition prevailed, primarily because of the regulatory environment; there was no compelling need for marketing sophistication.

Ratemaking in the Regulated Environment. In this previously regulated environment, Traffic Department personnel determined desired rate levels by following a blend of cost of service and value of service pricing the-

theories ories (the same theories explained in Chapter 5). Because the trucking industry has high variable costs, however, it would have been foolish to set rates too low. Furthermore, truckers were restricted from doing so by federal and state minimum rate regulations. Accordingly, rates reflected such measures as weight, distance, density, and the need for special equipment or handling. Traffic personnel, who also appraised the market's willingness to pay rates above fixed and variable costs, examined such items as intramodal and intermodal competition, the economic health of the particular shipping industry, and the value of the goods to be transported.

TABLE 12.3. Motor carrier rate bureaus
Central and Southern Motor Freight Traffic Association
Central States Motor Freight Bureau
Eastern Central Motor Carriers Association
Middle Atlantic Conference
New England Motor Rate Bureau
Middlewest Motor Freight Bureau
Niagara Frontier Tariff Bureau
Pacific Inland Tariff Bureau
Rocky Mountain Motor Tariff Bureau
Southern Motor Carriers Rate Conference

rate bureaus and the
rate change process

Once rate proposals satisfied traffic personnel, they sent proposed changes to the appropriate trucking rate bureaus. There were, and still are, 10 of these bureaus, as listed in Table 12.3. Most rate proposals filed with the rate bureaus were for rate reductions. A common practice, however, was for other carriers to match proposed rates if the bureau approved them. Rarely, however, would a carrier propose a rate increase. Similar to railroads, price increases typically were handled by general rate increases, which were also bureau approved or rejected. Proposals clearing the bureau then went to the ICC for formal approval or rejection. Most often, the ICC approved bureau requests without holding a hearing.

Ratemaking in the Deregulated Environment.   Deregulation did not eliminate federal rate regulations or eliminate the legal rate-setting function of rate bureaus, but it certainly weakened both. The ICC retained the power to set minimum, maximum, or actual rates. Common carriers must still file rate change proposals and publish rates. Rates still must be just and reasonable. Furthermore, the Motor Carrier Act of 1980 even added new powers, enabling the ICC to require joint rates and through services; thus carriers could be required by the ICC to interline.

ICC rate powers

rate impact

Deregulation, however, gave carriers far greater latitude and encouragement to set rates independently, outside the bureau collective ratemaking process, and free from ICC interference. Furthermore, the ICC has shown little interest in taking action against rates set outside the zone of reasonableness. Price competition, consequently, has become an explicit element in the general commodity trucking business.

Marketing Changes.   The slumping U.S. economy in the early 1980s, plus intense competition, forced many general commodity trucking companies to search for marketing improvements. Marketing is more than sales and pricing. It is a corporate game plan integrating carrier service, pricing, promotion, and network (route and terminal) strategies; and its focus is corporate profitability and not market share, sales growth, maintaining customers at any

corporate game plan

cost, tonnage, shipments, or what is best for individual profit centers like the local terminal. Marketing, as well as corporate, success will probably be closely correlated to the accuracy with which pricing specialists know corporate, as well as individual shipment, costs. In a discount-oriented market, a price set too high could mean the loss of a customer to a lower-priced carrier; a price set too low could mean the carrier would fail to cover variable costs.

market research

market segmentation

More sophisticated market research could be another key. Failure to find out what shippers want in terms of rates and services might result in lost business opportunities or wasted resources providing services shippers do not want. Market segmentation is also advisable as a preliminary measure to target marketing. The market can be segmented in many ways such as by commodities shipped (e.g., chemicals, automobile parts, or textiles), by customer type (e.g., corporate traffic managers versus plant traffic managers, purchasing agents versus traffic managers, or office personnel versus traffic specialists), and by the sizes of shipments (e.g., less than 150 lbs., 150 to 1000 lbs., 1000 to less than 10,000 lbs., or truckload weights of 10,000 or more lbs.). Other ways to segment are by speed of delivery or length of haul.

target marketing

Target marketing is also crucial. Some market opportunities are far more potentially lucrative than others, and it encourages firms to stop trying to serve everyone and concentrate limited corporate human and capital resources where they are likely to produce the best results. Similar to the UPS case mentioned earlier, common carriers are obligated to serve the public, but they do not actively have to pursue traffic that is only marginally profitable. Targeting encourages carriers to specialize in market segments where they have a market price or service advantage and a good probability of maintaining that edge against intramodal or intermodal competition. Success depends on a carrier's knowing not only its strengths and weaknesses, but also understanding its competitors' capabilities.

marketing goals

Specific marketing goals might be selling high-yielding freight services; soliciting backhaul traffic for an imbalanced market lane (a route between two points); giving discounts in competitive market lanes where they are needed to compete for traffic but avoiding discounting in less competitive markets—in other words, practicing selective, not universal, discounting; shrinking the size of the business and concentrating on a more profitable, yet smaller, market share; and totally revamping the sales incentive program to deemphasize myopic goals like increased sales or tonnage and encouraging efforts to boost corporate earnings.

differentiating services

In the deregulated trucking environment, marketers must hesitate from overreacting and doing what everyone else does, such as matching the prices of anyone else in the market. High-cost carriers must differentiate their services so that they can command higher yields to cover higher costs. This goal can be accomplished in many ways, such as through more reliable services, better pick-up and delivery schedules, better credit terms, an above-average loss and damage record, better tracing and control, faster delivery times, or simplified paperwork.

Finally, marketers must be given more freedom and budgets to institute

budgets
and innovation

innovative ideas. How important is national television advertising to Federal Express? To borrow an example from the air cargo business, Federal Express gambled and spent millions of dollars on television advertising to build a corporate identity. How many general commodity trucking companies, however, advertise on television? Is now the time to alter promotional strategies?

motivation for
better marketing

In the deregulated environment, carrier managers and not bureaucrats will decide corporate futures. Shippers are becoming more sophisticated. The competition is also rapidly learning how to manage better. Thus each general commodity trucking company's managers should become improved strategists and decision makers. Marketing should be a high priority to ensure corporate survival and prosperity.

SUMMARY

Carrier managers in the general commodity trucking industry have begun to ask more of the right questions and search harder for the answers. In less than a decade, traditionally protected common carriers have seen their market share, revenues, and profits erode. To a great extent, the large regular route common carriers have lost much of their truckload traffic to new and expanding non-unionized low-cost carriers. Simultaneously, rate freedoms and heavy discounting by large and small lower cost firms have forced industry leaders to reposition themselves in the market.

General commodity trucking management is tackling myriad problems. Carrier managers are examining ways to trim costs, improve labor and capital productivity, and increase yields and revenues. Some firms like Roadway Express and United Parcel Service continue to prosper, but the industry in general has been struggling with ways to cut excesses to survive in an environment now dictated by market supply and demand.

The general freight market is being segmented rapidly by consumers rather than by bureaucrats, as it was in the past. Service-oriented markets and price-oriented segments are emerging. Shippers of less than 500 lbs., 500 to 5000 lbs., and 5000 to 10,000 lbs., as well as truckload shippers, all have different requirements. Never has there been a greater need for carriers to decide what the market wants, where they can best find niches and hold the competitive edge, and how to earn profits.

STUDY QUESTIONS

1. How is regular route general commodity common carriage different from irregular route general commodity common carriage?

2. What caused Roadway Express to lose much of its truckload (TL) business?

3. Why has property brokerage been one of the fastest growing sectors of transportation?

4. Now that the Surface Transportation Assistance Act of 1982 has cleared the way for larger trucks, what might delay the purchase of double-bottoms by regular route common carriers?

5. Why do shippers use pool consolidators and distributors?

6. Why is it more important today than before de-

regulation for trucking companies to have accurate cost information?

7. Explain how Roadway Express continued prospering, despite declining traffic, increased competition, and high labor costs.

8. What prevents trucking companies today from using general rate increases to raise freight rates?

ENDNOTES

1. United Parcel Service of America Inc., 10-K Disclosure, SEC File No. 0-4714, for year ended December 31, 1984, Washington, D.C., p. 18 (hereafter cited as UPS Disclosure).

2. Information supplied by the Boston Regional Office of the Interstate Commerce Commission.

3. Unless otherwise stated, statistics were obtained from UPS Disclosure.

4. John D. Williams, "The Brown Giant: UPS Delivers Profits by Expanding Its Area, Battling Postal Rates," *The Wall Street Journal*, 25 August 1980, p. 1.

5. Robert C. Dart, "Freight Brokers Seek New Identities as Transportation Options Multiply," *Traffic World*, 4 April 1983, p. 15.

6. Office of Policy and Analysis, Interstate Commerce Commission, *Staff Report No. VII, Highlights of Recent Activity in the Motor Carrier Industry* (Washington, D.C.: ICC, November 1981), p. 15.

7. Kenneth E. Siegel, Esq., "The Re-Emergence of Property Brokers," *Terminal Operator*, August/September 1981, p. 8, as reprinted from *ATA Sales & Marketing Council Bulletin*, August 1981.

8. Roadway Services, Inc., *1984 Annual Report* (Akron, Ohio: Roadway Services, Inc., 18 February 1985), insert page (hereafter cited as Roadway Services).

9. Roadway Express, Inc., *Motor Carrier Annual Report "M" to the Interstate Commerce Commission, MC Docket 2202, for the Period Ended December 31, 1984*, pp. 52, 54 (hereafter cited as Roadway Express).

10. Derived from ibid., pp. 11, 49.

11. Roadway Services, pp. 18, 19.

12. Ibid.

13. Roadway Express, p. 50.

14. Ibid., p. 49.

15. (a) Allen Wastler, "Insurance Industry Woes Source of Rising Costs for Trucking, Says CRS," *Traffic World*, 2 December 1985, pp. 47–48; and (b) "ATA Asks for ICC Probe of 'Insurance Crisis,'" *Traffic World*, 26 August 1985, p. 8.

16. Robert S. Greenberger, "Teamsters Reject Truckers' Plea for More Relief," *The Wall Street Journal*, 4 February 1983, p. 6.

17. Patricia Lisciandro, *Financial Analysis of the Motor Carrier Industry 1982* (Washington, D.C.: American Trucking Associations, 1983), p. 46.

ADDITIONAL READINGS

"All Aboard to Be a Broker." *Distribution,* May 1983, pp. 69–72.

Anderson, David L. "Strategy: Turning 'Haulage' into 'Logistics.'" *Fleet Owner,* January 1983, pp. 70–74.

Baker, Gwendolyn H. "The Carrier Elimination Decision: Implications for Motor Carrier Marketing." *Transportation Journal* 24, no. 1 (Fall 1984):20–29.

Barrett, Colin. "Contract Carriage: No Golden Age." *Distribution,* September 1983, pp. 58–59.

Beilock, Richard, and Freeman, James. "Deregulated Motor Carrier Service to Small Communities." *Transportation Journal* 23, no. 4 (Summer 1984):71–82.

Brown, Terrence A. "Freight Brokers and General Commodity Trucking." *Transportation Journal* 24, no. 2 (Winter 1984):4–14.

Bruning, Edward R., and Morash, Edward A. "Deregulation and the Cost of Equity Capital: The Case of Publicly Held Motor Carriers." *Transportation Journal* 23, no. 2 (Winter 1983):72–81.

Cooke, James Aaron. "ERISA: No Exit." *Traffic Management,* May 1983, pp. 53–55.

Deierlein, Bob. "Strategy: Equipment Selection Must Fit the Plan." *Fleet Owner*, January 1983, pp. 80–82.

Duncan, Thomas W. "Deregulation Creates a Boom for Freight Brokers." *Fleet Owner*, April 1984, p. 58.

Ferguson, Wade, and Glorfeld, Louis W. "Modeling the Present Motor Carrier Rate Structure as a Benchmark for Pricing in the New Competitive Environment." *Transportation Journal* 21, no. 2 (Winter 1981):59–66.

Gallagher, Patrick. "Pooling—the LTL Alternative." *Handling & Shipping*, August 1981, pp. 38–40.

———. "Ten Ways to Boost Trailer-Fleet Productivity." *Handling & Shipping Management*, August 1982, pp. 35–37.

———."Struck with Overcapacity, Truckers Await the Recovery." *Handling & Shipping Management*, January 1983, pp. 26–30.

Goldner, Leslie M. "LTL-Carrier Pricing Practices for Individual Shippers: The Aftermath of Deregulation." *Traffic World*, 11 February 1985, pp. 83–88.

"Great Trucking Wars." *Distribution*, November 1982, pp. 30–31.

Henjum, Scott E. "Transus: More Than a New Name." *Fleet Owner*, September 1983, pp. 90–94.

Mabley, Robert E., and Strack, Walter D. "Deregulation—A Green Light for Trucking Efficiency." *Regulation: AEI Journal on Government and Society,* July/August 1982, pp. 36–42.

Marien, Edward J. "Formula Rates: Their Time Has Come Again." *Distribution*, January 1982, pp. 54–58.

"Motor Carriage: A Bright Future, But Only for Big Truckers." *Distribution,* January 1983, pp. 48–52.

Poist, Richard F., and O'Conner, Lawrence M. "Use of Fuel Conservation Devices and Techniques by Motor Freight Carriers: A Survey Report." *Transportation Journal* 18, no. 4 (Summer 1979):5–19.

Quinn, Francis J. "Contract Carriers Start to Flex Their Muscles." *Traffic Management*, September 1983, pp. 84–85.

"Strategy: How to Build Your Fleet's Future." *Fleet Owner*, January 1983, pp. 58–61.

Sugrue, Paul K.; Ledford, Manfred H.; and Glaskowsky, Nicholas A., Jr. "Operating Economies of Scale in the U.S. Long-Haul Common Carrier, Motor Freight Industry." *Transportation Journal* 22, no. 1 (Fall 1982):27–41.

"Trailers: Spec'ing for Low Maintenance and Longer Life." *Fleet Owner*, January 1981, pp. 61–63.

"Trucking Industry." *The Wall Street Transcript*, 16 May 1983, pp. 69, 800–69, 805.

Specialized Trucking

13

By definition, specialized trucking involves motor carriers of property that usually require specially designed equipment not ordinarily used in the movement of general commodities. The Interstate Commerce Commission first defined specialized classes of for-hire carriage in 1937 (2 MCC 703) to facilitate its task of making entry decisions. At the time, existing ICC carriers were interested in protecting their traffic from new competition, as well as in clarifying what commodities they could haul legally. Thus were born specialized classes of trucking, such as household goods, heavy machinery haulers, agricultural commodities, and so on, and the distinction between specialized and general commodity trucking emerged. Today, specialized trucking has been broadened to include exempt traffic, as well as regulated freight haulage.

Specialized trucking industries tend to be unique. Although several of these sectors compete intermodally with rail or other transportation modes, intramodal competition prevails; competition tends to be limited to firms within a specialized trucking class. For example, dump truck operators do not compete with armored truck carriers, nor do bulk milk carriers worry about bulk petroleum haulers. Each specialized trucking class tends to have customized equipment, operations, and needs.

Chapter 13 examines specialized trucking, particularly three industry components, namely, household goods carriage, heavy hauling, and for-hire exempt agricultural trucking. Independent owner-operators, on whom the specialized trucking industries rely heavily, will also be discussed.

BACKGROUND

Specialized trucking is for-hire, door-to-door transportation by thousands of irregular route common carriers, contract carriers, and exempt truckers. Most firms are small, few are unionized, and there is significant reliance on independent owner-operators. Within the various specialized trucking industries, however, vast differences exist in infrastructure, economics, and operating practices.

Classes of Specialized Trucking Companies

As previously noted, the origin of specialized trucking industries can be traced to the ICC and in particular to 2 MCC 703, decided on August 9, 1937, which defined 15 classes of regulated ICC specialized trucking companies as follows.

household goods
Household goods carriers include firms, both common and contract, engaged in the transportation of property commonly used in a home, such as furniture, fixtures, and equipment; property of an office, museum, institution, hospital, or similar establishment when it is a part of the stock, equipment, or supply of such establishment; furniture, fixtures, and equipment of a store; and works of art, furniture, musical instruments, display exhibits, and articles requiring the specialized handling and special equipment usually employed in moving household goods.

heavy machinery
Heavy machinery haulers include carriers, both common and contract, engaged in the hauling of heavy machinery and equipment, including such items as road machinery, structural steel, oil-field rigs, and oil-field equipment.

liquid petroleum products
Carriers of *liquid petroleum products* include firms that transport petroleum products like gasoline, other liquid motor fuel, road oil, crude oil, fuel oil, kerosene, and similar products in tank vehicles or drums (Fig. 13.1). Carriers of butane, propane, and other derivatives of petroleum are included in this group when such products are transported in tank vehicles. Also included in this group are carriers of coal-tar products and chemicals, if transported in tank vehicles. Carriers may be either common or contract operators.

refrigerated liquid products
Refrigerated liquid product carriers are either common or contract firms specializing in the transportation of temperature-controlled perishable liquid products such as fruit juices.

refrigerated solid products
Carriers of *refrigerated solid products* include both common and contract companies transporting perishable commodities requiring the use of special refrigeration or temperature-controlled equipment. Commodities transported include fresh fish, meats and meat products, fruits and vegetables, dairy products, and so forth.

agricultural commodities
ICC-regulated carriers of *agricultural commodities* are firms engaged exclusively in the transportation of unmanufactured or unprocessed agricultural commodities. This category includes carriers of milk, regardless of the type of vehicle used, but it does not include carriers engaged in the transportation of fruit juices or other processed agricultural commodities.

FIGURE 13.1.
Tank truck. (Fred Stephenson photo)

motor vehicles

Carriers of *motor vehicles* are firms transporting new and used motor vehicles, including automobiles, trucks, trailers, chassis, bodies, and automotive display vehicles, whole or partially assembled, in interstate or foreign commerce.

building materials

Carriers of *building materials* include both common and contract carriers engaged in the transportation of building materials for compensation, except for sand, gravel, crushed stone, or other building materials ordinarily transported in dump trucks. They include haulers of lumber, cut stone, slate, tile brick, cement, plaster in sacks, or other similar materials usually transported on flatbed vehicles. Most other building materials can be, and usually are, hauled in small lots as general commodities. Commodities in this category usually move in connection with a construction project, in truckloads, and for comparatively short distances. The transportation of lumber between manufacturing plants and from mill to retail yard is an important service rendered by carriers in this group.

films and associated commodities

Carriers of *films and associated commodities* are both common and contract carriers engaged in the transportation of motion picture and sound-reproducing films; recording, reproducing, and amplifying devices; supplies and accessories for the operation of motion picture theaters or places of exhibition, including the transportation of tickets, advertising matter, displays, and exhibits such as are found in lobbies of motion picture theaters; and furnishings and supplies necessary in the maintenance and operation of such theaters. This type of operation requires unusual delivery schedules.

Carriers of *forest products* are both common and contract carriers en-forest products

gaged primarily in the transportation of logs, poles, fence posts, shingle bolts, pulpwood, and fuel from the forest to processing points or to market. This group does not include carriers engaged in the transportation of rough or finished lumber or processed products derived from raw forest products or other operations grouped under "carriers of building materials."

mine ores

Carriers of *mine ores,* not including coal, are both common and contract firms engaged primarily in the transportation of mining products in the rough (e.g., iron, copper, or other ores) from the mine to the smelter or from the mine to connecting carriers. It also includes the transportation of products of smelters to refineries or foundries. Not included are coal or coal products or refined or manufactured products of ores, which are classified under other groupings.

explosives or dangerous articles

Carriers of *explosives or dangerous articles* transport dangerous, less dangerous, or relatively safe explosives, including nonexplosive material such as fuses, cartridge cases, dummy cartridges, and so forth; inflammable oxidizing materials; corrosive liquids; compressed gases; poisonous articles; and other dangerous articles, except inflammable liquids, in tank vehicles.

dump trucking

Carriers engaged in *dump trucking* are both common and contract carriers who operate dump trucks and similar vehicles used in the transportation of sand, gravel, dirt, debris, coal, and other similar commodities.

armored-truck service

Trucking firms in *armored-truck service* are common or contract carriers, which because of the commodity transported (i.e., gold, silver, currency, valuable securities, jewels, and other property of high value) use specially constructed armored trucks and provide police protection to safeguard the commodity while it is being transported and delivered. This category includes carriers operating ordinary equipment in the transportation of high-value commodities when guards are necessary to accompany the shipment.

retail store delivery service

Carriers engaged in *retail store delivery service* render specialized delivery services for establishments wishing to serve their customers. Usually, operations are confined to municipal areas, and these carriers may be regarded as city cartage operations.

Gradually, Congress and the ICC have both lessened the importance placed on defining specialized trucking classes and exempted some commodities, such as fresh fruits, vegetables, and other agricultural, horticultural, and fisheries items, from federal economic regulation. Since the Motor Carrier Act of 1980, the ICC has furthermore encouraged applicants for specialized common or contract trucking authority to ask for broad commodity authority, and it has generously granted such entry. Thus applicants now seek *bulk* authority rather than being more specific as was required before deregulation when they asked for refrigerated solid products or heavy machinery-hauling authority. Bulk authority allows specialized carriers to haul anything, except household goods or explosives. Nevertheless, because companies still buy specialized equipment suited for specific customer needs, continue to refer to their services by the traditional ICC-specialized trucking industry names, and compete in segregated unique markets, the earlier trucking classes continue to be important.

However, our emphasis is on specialized trucking markets and the carriers serving them, rather than on ICC-defined regulated classes of specialized trucking.

Special Commodity and General Freight Operating Differences

role of truck stops

One major difference between specialized trucking and regular route general commodity common carriage is the former's tendency to dispatch vehicles over routes that take many of them far from carrier terminals or other facilities. Consequently, drivers are more on their own to find fuel sources, repair facilities, and places to rest. Independent truck stops meet many of these needs; they provide lodging, food and drinks, mechanical services, fuel, and ample parking areas.

sleepers and driver teams

Another distinction is that many special commodity tractors are sleepers; in essence, they have a bunk behind the cab seats. In general, a driver works alone, putting in the legal number of hours and then resting or sleeping. Driving teams are still used by some carriers, however, particularly when expeditious trip-times are needed. Teams allow one driver to sleep or rest while the other drives the rig.

HOUSEHOLD GOODS TRUCKING

Characteristics

As discussed in Chapter 1, people in the United States are extremely mobile. Every year, 17% of the U.S. population changes residences, 50% of the 22–24 year olds move, and 84% of the newly married Americans relocate.[1] By one estimate, typical U.S. citizens move 13 times during their lifetimes,[2] and each time personal effects (e.g., furniture, clothes, equipment, and appliances) must be moved. People can hire a household goods (HHG) carrier; move the property themselves using privately owned vehicles; or rent moving equipment from U-Haul, Ryder, or other leasing specialists. Considering the high costs of moving in money, time, and possible emotions, as well as its high incidence, the HHG segment is a frequently used, important transportation segment.

Few sectors of the transportation industry are more unique or confusing than the HHG business. For example, HHG carriage is the leading source of registered ICC complaints,[3] yet major HHG carriers regularly achieve exceptionally high service performance records. For instance, in 1982 major carriers achieved a 97.2% on-time delivery record.[4] In addition, although the HHG industry has above-average operating ratios, it also has above-average industry returns on equity. Such contrasts make the HHG business ideal for analysis and review.

Industry Structure

HHG carriage is a three-tiered system of carriers, agents, and owner-operators who, with few exceptions, mutually depend on each other to earn profits. In 1982 there were approximately 3,000 ICC-authorized interstate moving companies, 8,000 local moving companies (agents or local moving companies without interstate authority), and 25,000 independent owner-operators in the industry.[5] However, not all were active in the market as some previously obtained authority was not being used. Firms who lease equipment to "do-it-yourself" movers are not included in these figures since this chapter focuses on the for-hire moving industry.

Carriers.   For the most part, HHG movers are common carriers offering transportation services to the general public at published rates. Figure 13.2

FIGURE 13.2.
Types of household goods carriers. (*Source:* Adapted from definitions included in Edward A. Morash, "Household Goods Agency Systems," *The Transportation Journal* vol. 19, no. 4 [Summer 1980]: 38–47.)

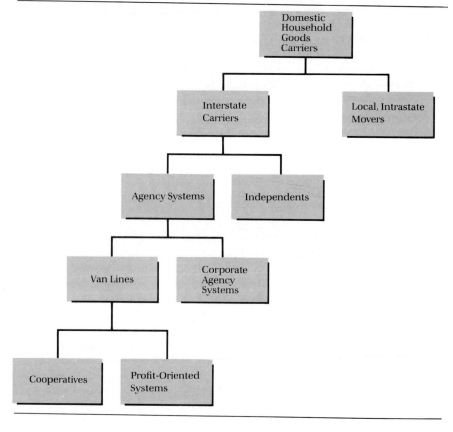

local movers

divides the carriers first into local movers and interstate operators. The former group handles numerous short-haul moves within an urban setting or between cities in a particular state. Thus this is an important group, since most for-hire moves are intrastate relocations.

interstate carriers

Interstate carriers, by comparison, move traffic across state lines. Of the more than 1000 active interstate HHG firms, approximately 90% are called independents, and the remaining firms are labeled agency systems.[6] The key distinction resides in the assignment of business responsibilities. Agency systems make extensive use of HHG agents, whereas independents do not.

agency systems

Although vastly fewer in number than independents, agency systems are the dominant force in traffic and sales generation. Agents are depended on to perform various support services. If agents book shipments (finalize service contracts), those using them to do so are called van lines. Van lines also extensively use owner-operators. Examples are North American Van Lines and Aero-Mayflower. Another important distinction for van lines is the difference between *cooperative* and *profit-oriented* agency systems. Several large van lines are in fact owned by their agents, and, hence, are called cooperatives. Under such an ownership pattern, profitability of the parent company is a secondary concern to profitability of the agents. Examples of such cooperative van lines are Allied Van Lines and United Van Lines. However, the more typical van line is a separately owned, profit-oriented parent company. Examples are North American Van Lines, Aero-Mayflower Transit Company, and Wheaten Van Lines. Agency systems that do their own booking but use agents for limited roles, such as providing pick-up or delivery services, are labeled corporate agency systems. Neptune World Wide Moving is an example.[7]

van lines

The origin of van lines can be traced to the desire of groups of agents to band together to achieve economic and operating efficiencies. By joining the operating authorities of independent local carriers into long-haul networks, geographically dispersed local agents found a way to combine several shipments on a particular vehicle and also to circumvent serious backhaul problems. The van line home office controls the operating authority and provides central dispatching, such as routing and scheduling advice, to drivers. The home office also acts as a clearing house for the division of revenues and for the settlement of shipper claims, provides national advertising and promotion, is held responsible for ICC reporting, offers technical assistance to agents, and is responsible for the acts of agents. When a shipper books with a van line agent, traffic moves on equipment bearing the logo of the van line, even though the trailers are primarily owned by local agents and the tractors almost always belong to owner-operators working under a lease agreement with the agent or van line. The largest of the van lines have agreements with hundreds of agents and thousands of owner-operators. North American Van Lines, for instance, works with more than 600 agents.[8]

cargo authority

If classified as a household goods carrier, then the leading source of the firm's traffic is household goods, which by ICC definition includes the following three categories or provisos of freight.[9]

- ■ *Proviso 1:* Personal effects and property used in residential homes.
- ■ *Proviso 2:* Furniture, fixtures, equipment, and property of businesses, museums, institutions, or other establishments.
- ■ *Proviso 3:* Articles, including objects of art, displays, and exhibits that, because of their unusual nature or value, require specialized handling.

The bulk of the industry's traffic is *proviso 1* traffic, but carriers today are paying increasing attention to the potential of *provisos 2* and *3* traffic, as well as to nontraditional forms of freight.

Agents.   The second tier of the HHG business includes agents, who are important to the carriers, as well as the owner-operators who work with them. The top 20 carriers in 1980 all used agents.[10] On the same move, agents may

functions   provide the customer with a price estimate, sell packing containers to the shipper, perform packing services prior to loading, arrange for or make a local pick-up, arrange for laborers to assist the owner-operator with the loading of the cargo on the van, provide storage in transit, arrange local delivery of loads, unpack the goods of an inbound shipment, connect appliances like clothes washing machines, and/or assist with the processing and settlement of claims for lost or damaged goods. Van lines look to the agents for the provision of most equipment and facilities, for local marketing assistance, and for help when owner-operators request aid. However, many agents wear two hats, acting on behalf of van lines selling nationwide services and running their own moving and storage businesses as independent local or interstate operators.

multiple agents per shipment   A single shipment usually involves multiple agents, such as one at the origin, one possibly for storage in transit, and one at the destination. With so many people involved, activities must be closely coordinated and steps taken to ensure quality services on a door-to-door basis. Agents and van lines are so mutually dependent that they try to choose partners carefully. Once agreements between carriers and agents have been established, however, relationships often tend to be long-term.

Owner-Operators.   Owner-operators are also important contributors to the HHG industry. HHG owner-operators are independent businesspeople who lease themselves and their equipment to carriers or agents. In HHG trucking, though, it is more common for the owner-operator to sign a lease with the agent, who in turn signs a lease with a carrier. In 1977 the ICC issued a report estimating that more than 90% of the HHG vehicle-miles were accomplished by owner-operators.[11] No other category of ICC regulated carriage relies more on owner-operators than does the HHG sector.

involvement and responsibilities   As an illustration of the extent of owner-operator involvement in the trade, Allied Van Lines, one of the nation's two largest HHG carriers, owns virtually no equipment and directly employs no drivers.[12] Another unusual characteristic of the business is the way owner-operators are used to perform certain functions that are not normally their responsibilities in other trucking industries. For example, HHG owner-operators are expected to load and unload the van and often pack or unpack individual items.

operating characteristics
Like nomads, HHG owner-operators roam the states picking up and delivering freight as demand dictates until they eventually return to their domiciles (homes). For example, a driver domiciled in Los Angeles but currently in Rhode Island with loads on board for Arlington, Virginia, and Birmingham, Alabama, may be directed to Syracuse, New York, to pick up a third shipment to Houston. In the process of picking up and discharging individual HHG shipments, the owner-operator may be on the road for weeks before returning to California. Another problem is seasonal peaking. Because approximately 40% of all household goods shipments move from June 1 to September 30, during the peak season driver demands are compounded.

Equipment. Another distinct element of the HHG industry is the specialized design of the linehaul equipment. Figure 13.3 pictures a typical tractor-trailor with its sleeper tractor and trailer. Trailers are built to maximize cubic capacity, provide ease of access to the various shipments on board (vans usually have side doors), and minimize the possibility of damage. On average, household goods weigh about 7 lbs. per cubic ft, compared to 12–14 lbs. per cubic ft for general commodity cargo. Because of this light density, weighting out is not usually a problem; therefore the van drops into the well between the tractor and trailer axles to gain cubic capacity. The lowered floor also facilitates loading and unloading.

Special shock absorbers and other features cushion the vehicle's contents against pounding and jolts. Household goods not only tend to be breakable, but also their value exceeds the limits of dollars and cents. The fact that house-

FIGURE 13.3.
Household goods tractor–trailer rig, showing the sleeper compartment just behind the window on the driver's side of the cab (tractor), the side door on the trailer for easier loading and unloading, and the shape of the trailer to maximize cubic capacity. (Photo courtesy of Allied Van Lines, Inc.)

hold goods carriers handle irreplaceable items and memories is in part the reason why the HHG business leads the transportation industry in registered ICC complaints. Customers are demanding, and rightly so.

Industry Economic and Traffic Analysis

In the early 1980s, the HHG trade was strongly affected by a deep housing recession, high mortgage interest rates, and the reluctance on the part of many people—whether job transferees or those desiring to relocate for other reasons—to move. In addition, the cost of employee relocations was, and still is, discouragingly high. In 1982, according to Merrill Lynch Relocation Management, Inc., corporations paid an average of $46,800 per executive transfer.[13] Although the cost of moving household goods typically represents only a few thousand dollars of the total relocation expense, if the aggregate cost acts as a disincentive to transfers, household goods firms also suffer.

largest carriers: trends   Household goods shipments were down 4.1%, tonnage was off 5%, and operating revenues declined 3.2% in 1982 versus 1981 for the nation's 15 largest HHG carriers.[14] These figures may be somewhat misrepresentative of the industry as a whole, however, since larger carriers typically do better than smaller firms in this business. Nevertheless, since the HHG industry is highly concentrated, it makes sense to study the 15 largest firms, for they account for approximately 75% of total industry revenues.[15]

Financial Statistics of Largest Carriers. Table 13.1 highlights selected economic statistics for the largest HHG carriers. These data show high individual and aggregate operating ratios, yet surprisingly high returns on equity in comparison to figures quoted in Chapter 11 in the discussion of ICC common carriers for 1983. The table, specifically Allied and United Van Lines, shows operating ratios at or above 100%, but returns above 13%. Net income, however, includes not only transportation charges but also income derived from the sale of such items as packing containers and tape, packing and unpacking fees, and warehouse charges. These other revenue sources are extremely important; in 1981, 112 HHG carriers reported $42 million in carrier operating income but $67 million in noncarrier operating earnings before taxes.[16] Thus the HHG business is not restricted to selling transportation services alone.

diversification and general commodity revenues   Deregulation, resulting from the combination of the Motor Carrier Act of 1980, the Household Goods Transportation Act of 1980 (94 Stat. 2011), and ICC rule changes, has encouraged household goods carriers to enter the general commodity sector in addition to expanding *provisos 2* and *3* opportunities. Consequently, United, Aero-Mayflower, Bekins, Global, North American, and American Red Ball have diversified. North American, by far the most active in this respect, produced $196 million (nearly 40% of its corporate revenues) during the year ending March 31, 1983, from general freight sales.[17] In 1983, North American ranked as the largest irregular route general commodity carrier of truckload freight in the United States.

TABLE 13.1. Selected statistics, largest class I household goods carriers
(Twelve months ended 3/31/83)

	Operating Revenues ($ thousands)	Net Income ($ thousands)[a]	Operating Ratio (%)[b]	Return on Equity (%)[c]
North American Van Lines[d]	299,168	19,548	94.1%	14.91%
Allied Van Lines, Inc.[d]	276,009	2,166	100.0	13.06
United Van Lines, Inc.[d]	237,309	2,549	100.3	13.92
Aero-Mayflower Transit Co.[d]	193,442	3,885	97.0	17.87
Bekins Van Lines Co.[d]	164,952	3,745	97.3	15.76
Atlas Van Lines, Inc.[d]	126,667	4,776	96.4	16.80
Global Van Lines, Inc.[d]	67,775	671	98.4	7.07
Burnham Van Services, Inc.	48,963	2,453	90.4	55.67
Wheaton Van Lines, Inc.	31,585	987	97.1	9.03
American Red Ball Transit[d]	24,297	(42)	98.6	0
Neptune World Wide Moving	17,997	389	97.5	8.89
National Van Lines, Inc.	16,629	(460)	101.9	0
Pan American Van Lines, Inc.	13,963	423	95.1	60.17
Cartwright Van Lines, Inc.	12,823	35	98.3	3.68
Interstate Van Lines, Inc.	11,029	125	97.9	8.83
TOTAL, 15 carriers	1,542,608	41,250	97.4%	15.03%

[a]Includes carrier and noncarrier income after taxes.

[b]Operating expenses divided by operating revenues.

[c]Return on equity less intangible property (i.e., less the value of operating rights). It is the ratio of net income to shareholders' equity. The symbol "0" indicates a deficit.

[d]Net income and return on equity reflect general freight earnings.

Source: Interstate Commerce Commission, Bureau of Accounts, *Large Class I Household Goods Carriers Selected Earnings Data* (Washington, D.C.: ICC, 1983), pp. 1–4.

purchased transportation

Another key variable affecting operating ratios and returns on equity is the abundant use of owner-operators. In 1981, purchased transportation (fees for leased equipment and drivers) consumed 53.3% of reported HHG industry revenue dollars.[18] When a carrier uses owner-operator and/or HHG agency equipment, it can expense the charges. This situation not only increases the numerator of the operating ratio (for a review of the ratio, see Chapter 2), causing that figure to be high, but also minimizes the size of the company's assets, thereby lowering the potential need for a large equity base. (It produces a smaller denominator in the return on equity ratio.) Consequently, returns on equity are higher than what might be expected.

market segments

To understand HHG revenue data, knowledge of market segments, yields, and the division of revenues among carriers, agents, and owner-operators is also useful. The market can be segmented into individual accounts (called C.O.D. accounts, because individuals typically are expected to pay at the time personal effects are delivered), national accounts (employer-paid moves), and military shipments (government-paid shipments of personal effects). In 1982, the industry revenue split was C.O.D. (31%), national (55%), and military (14%).

yields

Yields tend to be relatively high compared to other sectors of the trucking industry. Whereas Roadway's yield in 1984 was 21.6¢ per ton-mile (Chapter 12), in 1981 C.O.D., national, and military traffic for the largest 15 HHG carriers averaged 62.5¢, 73.7¢, and 55.6¢ per ton-mile, respectively. Of course, these figures reflect more than just transportation yields, which were 42.3¢, 42.8¢, and 33.0¢ per ton-mile, respectively.[19] What motivates these high yields is the need to recover high labor costs, due to the labor-intensive nature of the business, and the high-value nature of the freight.

division of
linehaul charges

Finally, in terms of the division of aggregate linehaul charges, owner-operators receive 55%–65%, agents receive about 20%, and carriers receive the remaining 15%–25%.[20]

Future Strategies.   The future of the for-hire HHG industry offers a combination of promise and risk. When the economy began to improve in the early 1980s, housing starts rose dramatically in response to declining mortgage interest rates. These changes helped to produce mild increases during the first half of 1983 in HHG shipments (up 1.0%), tonnage (up 2.2%), and revenues (up 1.5%) among the nation's top 20 carriers and in comparison to the first six months of 1982.[21] In another encouraging sign, population in the highly mobile 25–44-year-old age group was forecast to grow by 30% in the 1980s.[22] However, other evidence, such as the continuing high costs of relocation and the resistance of employees to move from present locations, dampens the outlook.

reasons for optimism

reasons
for pessimism

carrier choices

Because of the relaxed regulatory situation, carriers are reevaluating corporate strategies. Some have decided to remain in the traditional HHG domain. Others have diversified. Still others are striving for growth in both sectors— HHG and general commodities. Those staying in the HHG market are likely to experience even greater competition, for not only have entry freedoms encouraged more competitors in the marketplace, but deregulation has also prompted extensive price competition. The business today is characterized by a high level of independent price initiatives. Although the Household Goods Carriers' Bureau remains the industry's national rate clearinghouse, there is increasing use of discounts, contract services, binding estimates locking carriers to pre-move bids, an assortment of liability coverages at different costs to the shippers who select them, and service guarantees with penalties for carrier deficiencies.

pricing activities

diversification
initiatives

Diversification presents other opportunities. Because HHG operators have suitable equipment, they are successfully attracting high-value, time-sensitive, LTL traffic under a combination of existing HHG and new operating authority. They can also offer attractive rates compared to what unionized general commodity carriers charge because of low operating costs linked closely to the use of owner-operators. Overall, HHG carriers, like other forms of trucking, are reacting to changes in their economic, demographic, and regulatory world. They are broadening their operations to serve a more diverse assortment of customers and aggressively marketing their services.

HEAVY HAULING

Characteristics

Equipment.   A second specialized trucking industry is heavy hauling—transportation of items such as highway construction equipment, structural steel, prestressed concrete beams, and boilers. Unlike HHG vans, which are designed for maximum cubic capacity, flatbeds and lowboys (i.e., trailers built low to the ground to facilitate the loading of heavy construction equipment, such as the one shown in Fig. 13.4) mark this industry. Vehicles are designed to transport dense, as well as overdimensional, objects that exceed legal weight, length, or height limitations. Figures 13.5 and 13.6 show the capabilities of some of these vehicles, which are designed for strength, ease of loading, and flexibility; for example, trailers with frames that will stretch for long objects.

Use of Owner-Operators.   Like HHG carriers, heavy haulers make extensive use of owner-operators. Although average yields of 10.87¢ per ton-mile in 1981 are far below the yields of HHG carriers, heavy haulers can also keep assets and equity requirements low by using purchased transportation. In fact, this sector had a 10.52% after-tax return on equity in 1981.[23] Heavy haulers contract with either an individual (that is, an owner-operator who has one truck and drives it) or fleet operators (individuals who own more than one truck and hire drivers). Both forms of contract operators represent lessors, and as independent contractors they are not classified as employees of the heavy hauler. Consequently, carriers are not responsible for payroll taxes and benefits, nor must they be concerned with the unionization of contracted equipment operators. This situation tends to lessen labor costs.

contract operators

FIGURE 13.4.
A front-end loader secured on a five-axle unit. The trailer is approximately 24 in. from the ground. Overall dimensions are 12 ft wide and 14 ft 3 in. high, with a total weight of 90,000 lbs. (Photo courtesy of Moss Trucking Company, Inc.)

FIGURE 13.5.
Transporting an evaporator vessel, 16 ft 8 in. in diameter, 42 ft long, and weighing 68,000 lbs. Note that the vessel is self-supporting—that is, supported on a saddle front and rear and a two-wheel dolly system. The evaporator was transported 300 miles. (Photo courtesy of Moss Trucking Company, Inc.)

responsibilities   Standard industry practices call for the contract operator to pay for the capital costs of the tractor, fuel, fuel taxes, collision and comprehensive insurance, license plates, maintenance and repairs, and the driver's wages. In general, heavy haulers (lessees) provide the trailer and furnish terminal service, freight solicitation, cargo insurance, public liability insurance, billing, collection, accounting service, and general management expertise. Heavy haulers that supply trailers are usually responsible for trailer maintenance, repairs, and licenses. For their efforts, contract operators either receive a percentage

FIGURE 13.6.
With a steerable dolly to help maneuver the turn, a 174-ft-long distillation column, weighing 140,000 lbs., is moved at an average speed of 15 mph. The equipment consists of a three-axle tractor, four-axle lowbed trailer, and a five-axle steerable dolly. (Photo courtesy of Moss Trucking Company, Inc.)

of the gross revenue or a fixed fee per mile, which may vary between loaded and empty trips.

Operating Authority. In today's deregulated environment, there are heavy haulers with nationwide irregular route authority, authority to haul other special commodity traffic, general commodity rights, or any combination of these operating authorities. Diversification, however, typically necessitates the acquisition of non-flatbed trailers to meet divergent traffic needs.

Routing

Routing can be complex in the heavy hauling sector. Suppose a shipper requests service requiring a carrier to transport an overdimensional shipment across the country. The shipment is 10 ft wide, thereby exceeding the 102-in. legal limit. How does the carrier route this traffic? In fact, many variables must be considered. The season of the year (e.g., Is snow a problem?), terrain to be crossed, driver routing preferences, and the location of the carrier's terminals frequently influence the choice. In addition, states require permits for overdimensional shipments, and the fees assessed for these road-use privileges impact routing decisions. After all factors have been considered, the shortest trip path in actual miles is seldom selected.

cross-hatching

To help the customer predetermine shipping costs, the industry has developed what it calls *cross-hatching*, which is a published list of permit fees between any two states regardless of the final route selected. For instance, this list quotes a single binding charge from Oregon to West Virginia, even though the heavy hauler may pay more or less depending on the route taken.

Competition

The heavy hauling sector of trucking has become competitive in recent years. Traditionally, irregular route common carriers joined the National Association of Specialized Carriers, Inc. (NASC), and raised or lowered rates through this organization, as well as through memberships in more specialized rate bureaus such as the Steel Carriers' Tariff Association, Inc. However, independents, who have chosen to remain outside the NASC bureau structure (e.g., Blue Hen Lines, Inc.; Roadrunner Trucking, Inc.; and Anderson Trucking Service, Inc.), and general commodity truckers with special commodity divisions have become important market factors. This competition, coupled with the shortage of traffic during the recession of the early 1980s, weakened NASC's rate-setting abilities. The problem today is that although NASC carriers, for the most part, need to increase rates to keep up with rising costs, it is difficult to obtain the bureau members' approval of general rate increases. Where rate increases are sanctioned by the bureau, individual carriers are under great pressure from shippers to flag out (i.e., not implement the rate boost across all customers).

rate bureaus

competitors

Ironically, one victim of this rate compression is the independent con-

impact of
rate compression

tractor—one key reason for profitability in this industry. Low revenues have not only driven a number of these entrepreneurs from the market, but they also have discouraged others from making their services available. The economy has improved, but heavy haulers still find it difficult at times to attract enough vehicles and drivers to haul their freight. (More will be said on the problems of independent owner-operators at the end of this chapter.)

EXEMPT AGRICULTURAL TRUCKING

Agricultural commodities are hauled by refrigerated liquid products carriers, refrigerated solid products carriers, private carriers, and even general commodity carriers; however, in this section our focus is exempt agricultural trucking—the primary mode of produce transportation in the United States. In Florida alone in 1979, more than 22,000 trucking firms hauled exempt agricultural commodities.[24]

Interstate Exemption from Regulation

The basis for interstate exempt agricultural trucking is 49 *United States Code Annotated* 10526 (a)(6). By definition, the interstate agricultural exemption applies to commodities hauled by truck, rather than to trucking firms themselves. Although a trucking company does not hold exempt authority, cargo carried on any truck—regardless of whether it is operated by a common, contract, or private carrier—is exempt if that traffic is any of several hundred commodities specifically listed by the federal government as being exempt. The list covers not only agricultural items, but also horticultural items, fish, meat, and various other specialized commodities. Shipments must cross state lines to be exempt. In many cases, identical items shipped on an intrastate basis are regulated by state authorities. Because interstate traffic is exempt, carriers do not need a certificate or permit and are free to change rates and services whenever it is desirable. Management has total decision-making power without government interference except in such matters as safety and taxes.

Specialization

grain haulage

Exempt agricultural trucking is fragmented, with carriers grouped into grain haulers, produce specialists, and other components. Segments are distinguished by the specialized nature of the traffic. Trailers are designed to handle high density commodities, such as wheat, corn, and soybeans, weighing as much as 60 lbs. per bushel, as well as to facilitate loading and unloading. Because of the density, higher walled trailers are impractical, since vehicles quickly weight out.

refrigerated
transportation

In contrast, if the shipment includes apples, strawberries, lettuce, and so forth, the carrier needs more cubic capacity and temperature-controlled equipment. Shelf life and perishability are key shipper concerns. Therefore refrigerated vans are the trademark of this type of traffic.

Operating Problems and Decisions

Unlike manufacturing, which provides the managerial prerogative to produce and ship materials on a steady monthly or weekly basis, latitude and weather dictate agricultural harvest times. In any one particular location, the entire crop may need to be harvested within a month or two. Thus exempt agricultural trucking is highly seasonal. An illustration is Georgia and South Carolina peaches, which are ready for picking in July and August. Another case is Florida, where 52% of the state's produce traffic by weight occurs in the March–June period, whereas the next four months yield only 6% of the aggregate annual volume.[25] Seasonality forces truckers to relocate operations, and many travel around the country to points where crops have different harvest periods.

backhauls

Another important factor in this sector is the backhaul problem. Produce flows from growing centers like the Brownsville area of Texas, the Salinas Valley of California, and the Yakima Valley of Washington to the great urban markets like Los Angeles, Chicago, New York, and Boston. Once trailers are unloaded, agricultural carriers or owner-operators must decide just how much time or deadheading miles they will endure to find backhaul traffic, which will generate cash to take them back to the produce-growing regions. In New England it is not unusual for carriers to deadhead to Maine, pick up a load of potatoes, haul this produce to Atlanta, and then deadhead to the Orlando area for traffic heading north. Others try to obtain loads of exempt seafood for transportation south. Illegal loads of traffic are not uncommon occurrences either. The latter refers to the carriers transporting regulated traffic without having ICC-operating authority.

backhauls: regulated and private carriers

In other cases, regulated common and contract truckers and private haulers may view the agricultural exempt haul itself as the backhaul. In other words, a firm might haul granite to Texas from the northern states as the primary haul and carry rice as a revenue-generator for the backhaul. This procedure insulates the firm from what often is a bad backhaul problem.

grain hauler differences

Exempt grain haulers of the Great Plains states often bypass backhaul freight in favor of returning as rapidly as possible to origin elevator locations. Many of these truckers are farmers who operate only during the periods when weather makes farming impossible. Do not confuse the need to transport grain from field to initial storage facility with haulage from rural or regional elevators to major grain markets. For the latter haulers, growing seasons are far less important than market demands in triggering long-haul transportation needs. Grain is stored in elevators for months or years. Therefore moving grain during the winter is quite commonly done.

Brokers

Help in finding traffic is needed by independent owner-operators and even established carriers like regulated general freight carriers who desire exempt loads. Hundreds of brokers thus locate traffic and link shippers and carriers trying to find one another.

functions
Long before property brokerage became both legal and popular, these agricultural sector intermediaries handled communications from in-bound truckers, arranged loads and pick-up schedules, provided monetary advances to help drivers with short-term cash needs, processed shipping claims, and took responsibility for documentation. Brokers do not physically handle cargo themselves (although some do control their own trucking operations), but they provide useful functional services for truck operators, who respond by paying the broker typically between 8%–14% of the gross shipping revenues.[26] Fee levels are influenced by the extent of services provided. Brokers' abilities to minimize delays, deadheading, and excess capacity problems are what has made them valuable partners to truck operators, and it is expected that these intermediaries will continue to fill vital market needs in the future.

Lumpers

Owner-operators also depend on lumpers, individuals who are compensated for loading or unloading trailers at warehouses, terminals, ports, and other facilities. However, because some lumpers abused these responsibilities, illegal activities by lumpers have been the subject of debate and Congressional action. Some lumpers were found to be requiring truckers to hire people to load or unload trucks even when not needed or coercing truckers into paying illegal or exorbitant fees for assistance whether it was performed or not. Section 11109(a) of Title 49 U.S.C. thus states that shippers or receivers who require loading or unloading assistance will either provide such help or compensate the trucker for all costs pertinent thereto. The law also forbids unlawful lumping practices and sanctions fines and prison terms for convicted violators. The federal government has no quarrel with honest lumpers, but industry abuses will not be tolerated.[27]

OWNER-OPERATORS

In the discussion of the trucking industry, many references have been made to owner-operators. The media portrays these individuals as autocratic sorts, nomads, cowboys, and even folk heros. However, their continued existence will really depend primarily on their astuteness as small businesspeople adjusting to a significantly altered working environment. Owner-operators represent some of the most hardworking, productive people in the U.S. transportation business, but they are surprisingly one of the more endangered species of the trade.

Problems

Fuel Costs and Supplies. Being an owner-operator is risky. Their positioning between carriers or agents and shippers makes them vulnerable to cost surges and rate reductions. Consider the fuel situation. Starting with the

1973 Arab oil embargo, truckers experienced two periods of fuel shortages and rapid price increases (1973 and 1979). In response to owner-operator protests, the federal government instituted a series of fuel "surcharge" programs to channel revenues back to owner-operators, who were paying the increased fuel bills. Unfortunately, several plans used during the years they were operational were not without flaws, and many owner-operators were not treated fairly. At times carriers did not pass fuel cost increments (i.e., price increases to cover higher fuel costs) onto their owner-operators, other carriers refused to increase transportation charges when not mandated by law, and rate wars also took their toll. Another major weakness was that surcharges applied only to owner-operators under permanent lease to regulated carriers; thus exempt-sector owner-operators never benefitted.[28] Finally, effective July 23, 1983, truck-companies were freed from further ICC responsibility to reimburse owner-operators for fuel expenses.[29]

financial vulnerability

Today, with fuel costs representing approximately 20%–25% of their vehicle-mile costs, owner-operators are vulnerable to even slight changes in yields or delays in receipt of carrier payments for services rendered. They must meet fuel, as well as other operating expenses, to stay in business. To protect owner-operators from regulated carrier leasing abuses and to expedite payments to these same individuals, the ICC on November 10, 1982, instituted a series of rule changes.[30]

Competition. Competition has also taken its toll on owner-operators. Thousands of new firms have entered the trucking industry, resulting in heavy downward pricing pressure in the truckload sector. Similarly, railroad competition, particularly in the piggyback area, has intensified. Also, the economic recession, with its consequent aggregate reduction in freight transportation demand, compounded the problem. Thus many independents were driven out of business, and others were forced to survive on barely adequate revenues. Although it is difficult to pin down the precise number of failures, estimates speak in terms of tens of thousands who have departed from the industry since the 1979–1980 period.[31] Although approximately 100,000 to 150,000 owner-operators remain in service, the future is threatening for many at the margin.

Yields. Yields are clearly a problem. It was estimated that owner-operators as of 1983 had to realize at least $1.10 per vehicle-mile to meet operating costs and, more important, to set aside money for a replacement rig when the present vehicle became worn out.[32] Furthermore, as self-employed businesspeople, owner-operators, from their net of revenues less operating expenses, must fully cover all their own social security premiums, which for company employees are either in part or fully the firm's burden, as well as bear the full cost of family health or life insurance and retirement income. When carriers cut rates or competitive pressures force prices to low levels, there are no parallel reductions in costs.

It appears, then, that carriers use owner-operators as economic shock absorbers in hard times, yet if bumped too hard or too often, even shock absorbers fail. For these reasons, frustrated owner-operators have struck three times nationally since 1973. History has shown that others emerge to take the place of owner-operators who have left the business, but there is no guarantee of adequate resupply. As previously noted, heavy haulers have been experiencing difficulty attracting contract operators. The key seems to be yields. If they are adequate, the supply of owner-operators will grow.

Strategy

Owner-operators must take a close look at their businesses and do what every manager or company owner should be doing: reexamine their purpose for being in business, strategy, goals, competition, and so forth. It is no longer true that being a good, hardworking driver is adequate to ensure success in this side of the transportation business.

Some owner-operators must choose between continuing in their present operating status or becoming a driver employee of a regulated or private carrier. Others may find it advisable to seek another, more profitable occupation. With deregulation, more options are available to choose from, but relaxed entry has encouraged more companies to compete for freight in each market sector. Owner-operators will not disappear, but they must adjust to their changing environment.

SUMMARY

Trucking companies whose principal revenue source is other than general commodity traffic are engaged in specialized trucking. At one time, the ICC strictly segregated these specialists into distinct legal categories, but today many of these parochial barriers have been eliminated. Nevertheless, because of specialized equipment needs and other factors, unique subset industries are still found within the trucking business. Examples are the household goods, heavy hauling, and exempt agricultural trucking sectors. Competition tends to be not only highly intramodal, but also limited to truckers within that particular trucking segment. For example, for-hire household goods carriers compete with other household goods truckers.

Household goods carriers serve a highly mobile U.S. population. When citizens relocate, they must move personal effects from old to new residences. That task falls in considerable measure on the shoulders of van lines, their agents, and thousands of owner-operators. Hurt by the economy, rising relocation costs, and changes in people's attitudes about moving, industry traffic and finances took a turn for the worse in 1982 before starting a slight rebound. Pessimism about household goods growth, combined with regulatory freedoms, have encouraged these carriers to diversify.

A second specialized trucking industry is heavy hauling. Different from household goods transportation, this trade uses flat-bed and lowboy trailers to move high density or overdimensional cargo. When special problems arise because loads exceed legal maximum widths, lengths, or weights, heavy haulers attempt to solve these problems and meet shippers' needs.

Exempt agricultural trucking is a third important specialized trucking industry. Within this category are found both grain transporters and produce haulers, which differ in equipment and operations. Exempt agricultural truckers depend on brokers and lumpers—intermediaries who respectively link carriers with shippers and load or unload trailers.

In the last decade, many independent owner-operators have been driven from the trucking industry by a combination of fuel cost and supply problems, increased competition, and compressed yields. In frustration, many owner-operators participated in strikes that affected many parts of the United States. The economic survival of owner-operators, however, is likely to be closely correlated to their ability to become better businesspeople and to adjust to the changing trucking environment.

STUDY QUESTIONS

1. What factors have driven many owner-operators out of the trucking business?

2. Now that the ICC has relaxed its entry regulations and is granting broad operating authority to applicants seeking specialized trucking authority, what prevents carriers from serving a wide variety of specialized trucking industry markets (i.e., sectors like household goods, heavy hauling, and exempt agricultural trucking)?

3. When is a household goods carrier called a van line?

4. Explain why it is important to an interstate household goods van line that its agents be reliable.

5. What is purchased transportation and how does it help to explain high household goods operating ratios and yet relatively high returns on equity?

6. Discuss the role of contract operators in the heavy hauling trucking industry.

7. Discuss backhaul strategies for interstate agricultural exempt truckers.

8. What functions do brokers perform in the agricultural exempt trucking industry?

ENDNOTES

1. Council of Better Business Bureaus, *Tips on Interstate Moving* (Arlington, Va.: Better Business Bureaus, 1983), p. 2.

2. Household Goods Carriers' Bureau, "Household Goods Moving Industry Statistics" (Arlington, Va.: Household Goods Carriers' Bureau, 1982), single page unpublished statistical summary (hereafter cited as Household Goods Carriers' Bureau).

3. U.S. General Accunting Office, *Report to the Congress: The Household Goods Moving Industry: Changes Since Passage of Regulatory Reform Legislation* (Washington, D.C.: G.A.O., June 10, 1983), p. 45 (hereafter cited as U.S. General Accounting Office).

4. Based on 1982 carrier annual performance reports (ICC–OCP 101 Form).

5. Household Goods Carriers' Bureau.

6. Derived from Edward A. Morash, "Household

Goods Agency Systems," *Transportation Journal* 19, no. 4 (Summer 1980):38.

7. Ibid., p. 39.

8. U.S. General Accounting Office, p. 96.

9. Ibid., p. 1.

10. Morash, "Household Goods Agency," p. 38.

11. Edward A. Morash, "Owner-Operators in the Household Goods Moving Industry," *Transportation Journal* 19, no. 2 (Winter 1979):18.

12. Morash, "Household Goods Agency Systems," p. 38.

13. Allied Van Lines, Inc., *Mobility Trends* 12, no. 2, a newsletter published by Allied Van Lines, Inc., July 1983, p. 1.

14. Household Goods Carriers' Bureau, *1982 Moving Industry Financial Statistics* (Arlington, Va.: Household Goods Carriers' Bureau, 1983), pp. 12, 14.

15. U.S. General Accounting Office, p. 3.

16. Patricia Lisciandro, *1982 Financial Analysis of the Motor Carrier Industry* (Washington, D.C.: American Trucking Associations, Inc., 1983), p. 31.

17. Interstate Commerce Commission, Bureau of Accounts, *Large Class I Household Goods Carriers Selected Earnings Data* (Washington, D.C.: ICC, 1983), p. 4.

18. Lisciandro, *1982 Financial Analysis*, p. 31.

19. Household Goods Carriers' Bureau, *Transportation Report of the Moving Industry: 1981 Continuing Traffic Study Statistics* (Arlington, Va.: Household Goods Carriers' Bureau, 1983), pp. 4–5.

20. U.S. General Accounting Office, p. 20.

21. Household Goods Carriers' Bureau, *Quarterly Statistics, First 6 Months, 1983* (Arlington, Va.: Household Goods Carriers' Bureau, n.d.), pp. 2, 6, 10.

22. U.S. General Accounting Office, p. 52.

23. Lisciandro, *1982 Financial Analysis*, p. 32.

24. Richard Beilock and George Fletcher, "Exempt Agricultural Commodity Hauler in Florida," Transportation Research Forum. *Proceedings of the Twenty-fourth Annual Meeting* (Oxford, Ind.: Richard B. Cross Company, 1983), pp. 444–445.

25. Richard Beilock, "Toward a Balanced Delivery System for Fresh Fruits and Vegetables," *Transportation Journal* 21, no. 2 (Winter 1981):28, citing United States Department of Agriculture, *Fresh Fruits and Vegetable Shipments: by Commodities, States, and Months* (Washington, D.C.: USDA, various issues 1950–1980).

26. Charles A. Taff, "A Study of Truck Brokers of Agricultural Commodities Exempt from Economic Regulation," *Transportation Journal* 18, no. 3 (Spring 1979):9.

27. Interstate Commerce Commission, *Illegal Lumping* (Washington, D.C.: U.S. Government Printing Office, 1980), various pages.

28. Thomas M. Corsi and J. Michael Tuck, *The ICC and Owner-Operators: The Fuel Surcharge Program* (Washington, D.C.: ICC, April 1982), p. 15.

29. "ICC Diesel Fuel Program for Independents Ended; Base Rates Left Intact," *Traffic World*, 18 July 1983, p. 41.

30. "ICC Boosts Protection for Owner-Operators in New Leasing Rules," *Traffic World*, 15 November 1982, pp. 4–10.

31. "Independent Truck Owners Want No More Shutdowns, Press Table Group Told," *Traffic World*, 30 May 1983, p. 33.

32. (a) Bill Richards, "Rough Road: Independent Truckers Who Hailed Deregulation Reconsider as a Rate War Rages and Taxes Rise," *Wall Street Journal*, 31 March 1983, p. 56; and (b) "Independent Truck Owners," p. 34.

ADDITIONAL READINGS

Adam, Everett, E., Jr. "Independent Owner/Operator and Agent Attitudes, Special Commodity Company Management Attitudes, and Attitude Congruence." *Transportation Journal* 19, No. 2 (Winter 1979):34–43.

Barber, G. K., and Kratochvil, J. D. "A Cost of Service Model for Irregular Route Truckload Perishables Carriers—From a Shipper's Perspective." *Transportation Journal* 19, no. 4 (Summer 1980):78–81.

Becker, H. G. "The New Movers and Shakers." *Handling and Shipping Management*, March 1982, pp. 74–76.

Corsi, Thomas M. "The Impact of Multiple-Unit Fleet Owners in the Owner-Operator Segment on Regulatory Reform." *Transportation Journal* 19, no. 2 (Winter 1979):44–59.

——, and Tuck, J. Michael. *The ICC And Owner-Operators: Leasing Rule Modifications.* Washington, D.C.: ICC, April 1982.

——; Tuck, J. Michael; and Gardner, Leland L. "Owner-Operators and the Motor Carrier Act of 1980." *The Logistics and Transportation Review* 18, no. 3 (1982):255–277.

Kogon, Gary B. "Contracting Household Goods Transportation." *Distribution,* September 1983, pp. 68–69.

——. "Regular Route Motor Common Carrier Special Commodity Divisions: An Introduction." *Transportation Journal* 19, no. 3 (Spring 1980):61–68.

Maze, T. H. "The Value of Information in Unregulated Truck Service Markets." *Transportation Journal* 20, no. 2 (Winter 1980):57–62.

McGee, Michael P., and Carlock, Margaret. "Motor Carrier Market Segmentation: A Function of Shipper Cost Sensitivity." Transportation Research Forum. *Proceedings of the Twenty-third Annual Meeting.* Oxford, Ind.: Richard B. Cross Company, 1982, pp. 202–207.

Morash, Edward A. "Household Goods Agency Systems." *Transportation Journal* 19, no. 4 (Summer 1980):38–47.

——. "Operating Practices of Interstate Household Goods Carriers." Transportation Research Forum. *Proceedings of the Twenty-first Annual Meeting.* Oxford, Ind.: Richard B. Cross Company, 1980, pp. 180–188.

National Association of Truck Stop Operators. *A Study of Truck Stop Operations in the United States, 1980 Edition.* Alexandria, Va.: National Association of Truck Stop Operators, 1980.

Paxson, David S. "Changes in Intercity Truckload Costs & Service, 1950–1980." Transportation Research Forum. *Proceedings of the Twenty-second Annual Meeting.* Oxford, Ind.: Richard B. Cross Company, 1981, pp. 508–515.

Pederson, Larry E.; Mittelhammer, R. C.; and Casavant, Kenneth. "Factors Affecting Interstate Backhauling of Exempt Agricultural Commodities by Regulated Motor Carriers: A First Look." *Transportation Journal* 18, no. 4 (Summer 1979):46–52.

"Reefer Fleet's Advice: 'Don't Blame Dereg; Use It!'" *Fleet Owner,* December 1982, pp. 68–72.

Shafer, Laurie A. "Moving Toward Brighter Horizons, and in New Directions." *Handling and Shipping Management,* April 1983, pp. 68–70.

U.S. Interstate Commerce Commission, Office of Policy and Analysis. *The Independent Trucker: Follow-up Survey of Owner-Operators.* Washington, D.C.: ICC, November 1979.

Whipple, Glen D.; Casavant, Ken L.; and Mittelhammer, Ron. "Evaluation of State Regulation of Primary Agricultural Motor Carriers in Washington." Transportation Research Forum. *Proceedings of the Twenty-second Annual Meeting.* Oxford, Ind.: Richard B. Cross Company, 1981, pp. 25–32.

Wyckoff, D. Daryl. *Truck Drivers in America.* Lexington, Mass.: Lexington Books, 1979.

——, and Maister, David H. *The Owner-Operator: Independent Trucker.* Lexington, Mass.: Lexington Books, 1975.

UNLIKE THE PREVIOUS FOUR MINI-BOOKS, PART 7 examines air transportation, a mode that is primarily passenger-oriented. In an overview of the structure and environment of today's U.S. aviation industry, Chapter 14 defines air transportation terminology; analyzes the most important part of aviation—certificated commercial air transportation; and discusses commuter airlines, private air transportation, safety issues, and the roles of travel agents and others in aviation.

Chapter 15 is a unique chapter that systematically examines and analyzes the strategies enacted by, and decisions made by, the 10 largest domestic airlines as they have tried to compete profitably in the deregulated airline industry. It is an analytical review of corporate changes—a case study provided with the intent of teaching readers how to improve skills in locating, computing, and interpreting business data. It illustrates the application of business theories, concepts, and strategies such as cost controls, productivity measures, yields, and controlling interest payments—carrier management tactics proposed in Chapter 2.

Chapter 16 examines two important specialized aviation sectors. International air transportation is the initial topic. Specifically, international aviation policy, air transportation statistics, and concerns of U.S. flag carriers are covered. The remainder of Chapter 16 analyze the deregulated domestic air cargo industry.

7

Air
Transportation

U.S. Air Transportation

14

The four transportation modes discussed thus far have the common characteristic of being either predominantly or totally freight oriented. Air transportation, in comparison, is a passenger-oriented mode, as well as the nation's most recognized, publicized, and praised transportation system. It is also in evolution. During the last 10 years, the airline industry has changed significantly as a result of dynamic environmental and industry forces. The recession of the early 1980s, inflation, the second OPEC oil embargo, deregulation, and a national air traffic controller strike have all impacted on, and helped transform, the U.S. airline industry. In the process, the airline business has fluctuated between record profits in 1978 and 1984 and severe operating losses in 1980, 1981, and 1982. The industry is a business of contrasts. Braniff International collapsed into bankruptcy in May 1982, Continental filed for reorganization in 1983, and Eastern came precariously close to failing. Simultaneously, USAir (formerly Allegheny) and Piedmont, two former regional airlines, experienced rapid growth and unheard of prosperity. At a time when many carriers were struggling to survive, a new carrier like People Express was able to enter the airline business in 1981 and grow in just a few years to become a carrier with sales above $500 million. The last decade has proven to be a period of great risk for some and an unequaled opportunity for others. But in all cases, it was a period of radical change.

Chapter 14, the first of three air transportation chapters, begins with an initial description of the changing structure and environment of air transportation. It next analyzes certified commercial air transportation, the backbone of the air transportation mode, and then reviews the commuter airline industry and general aviation. In conclusion, aviation safety is discussed.

AIR TRANSPORTATION TODAY

integrated business

Air transportation is an integrated business. Although airlines receive most of the recognition for the industry's accomplishments, they could not function without the contributions of aircraft equipment suppliers like Boeing, McDonnell Douglas, or Lockheed (which produce airframes) or Pratt & Whitney or General Electric (which produce jet engines). Likewise, there could be no flights without airports and airways (the airspace used by air carriers to connect origin and destination airports). Travel agents and air freight forwarders also play instrumental roles. Travel agents annually sell billions of dollars worth of passenger tickets, while air freight forwarders are intermediaries who solicit shipments and tender consolidated loads to airlines. Working hand in hand, all these components make the air transportation system both possible and more efficient.

Definitions

U.S. air carrier, foreign airline, and foreign air commerce

By definition, a *U.S. air carrier* is any citizen of the United States who engages in air transportation. A *foreign airline* refers to air carriage by non-U.S. citizens whose aircraft are registered in another country—Air France, for example. Foreign airlines become the concern of the U.S. government when they link foreign and U.S. markets or fly over U.S. airspace. Within this context, *foreign air commerce* refers to flights connecting the United States or its territories or possessions and places outside the United States, its territories, or its possessions. It also includes flights connecting two non-U.S. points. When Northwest Airlines flies from Minneapolis to Tokyo, it illustrates a U.S. air carrier engaging in foreign air commerce.

interstate, overseas, and intrastate air commerce

Legal classes of air carriage in addition to foreign air commerce are interstate, overseas, and intrastate air commerce. If an aircraft operates over a route connecting two states or a state and the District of Columbia, or involves a flight connecting two points in a state through airspace over any place outside thereof (e.g., Baltimore, Maryland, via West Virginia, to Cumberland, Maryland) or between points in a U.S. territory, a possession, or Washington, D.C., it has engaged in *interstate air commerce. Overseas air commerce* refers to any flight connecting a point in a state or the District of Columbia and a U.S. territory or possession, or a flight between a U.S. territory or possession and another U.S. territory or possession. An example is a Puerto Rico to Virgin Islands flight. *Intrastate air commerce* is air transportation within a state's borders. Interstate, overseas, and intrastate air commerce all represent forms of domestic air commerce.

Airlines can also be differentiated according to functions. *Combination carriers* haul people, baggage, cargo, and mail or people and any combination

combination
carriers, all-cargo
carriers, and
all-cargo aircraft

of the other three commodities, whereas *all-cargo carriers* haul either property (cargo) only, or both property and mail (Fig. 14.1). However, some combination airlines also operate *all-cargo aircraft* (freighters). These planes contain no passenger seats, and they are configured for maximum cargo payloads (weight or cubic capacity).

Segmentation is also possible by operating characteristics. Most airlines are *scheduled carriers*, which implies they publish timetables and try to adhere to them. In contrast, *charter airlines* key departures more to full plane loads of passengers or cargo; precise departure and arrival times become secondary. Other names for charter carriers are *nonscheduled airlines* and *supplementals.* Although scheduled airlines may fly charter flights, they are primarily scheduled operators of aircraft.

scheduled and
charter airlines

Certificated airlines are firms holding certificates of public convenience and necessity authorizing operations of large aircraft. They are either Section 401 airlines that operate as scheduled or charter carriers or Section 418 companies that are certificated all-cargo airlines. The numbers 401 and 418 refer to sections of the Federal Aviation Act of 1958 as amended (49 U.S.C. 1301 et seq.).

certificated
Section 401 and
Section 418 carriers

Also frequently mentioned are *Part 298 carriers.* The source is 14 *Code of Federal Regulations* (C.F.R.) Part 298, which is concerned with *exempt air taxi operators and commuter airlines*—firms not subject to federal economic regulation. Part 298 carriers include any air carrier of people, property, or mail (or any combination of these forms of traffic) that registers with the Department of Transportation and that operates no aircraft holding more than 60 passengers or carrying more than 18,000 lbs. of payload [14 C.F.R. 298.2(i)]. The air taxi operator term includes Part 298 carriers providing only charter services, as well as commuter airlines—air taxi operators carrying passengers on at least five roundtrips per week on at least one route between two points according to its published flight schedules [14 C.F.R. 298.2(f)].

Part 298 exempt air
taxi operators and
commuter airlines

General aviation aircraft (personal and business aircraft) and *public air-*

FIGURE 14.1.
Federal Express aircraft. (Photo courtesy of Federal Express Corporation)

general
aviation aircraft

craft (not-for-hire government aircraft) are also exempt; however, they are not Part 298 carriage. (More will be said about Part 298 carriers and general aviation later in the chapter.)

trunk and
local service airlines

Before October 2, 1980, the Civil Aeronautics Board classified long-haul scheduled carriers as *trunk airlines,* and short-haul, regional carriers that fed passengers to the trunk airlines as *local service airlines.* Examples of trunk airlines were United and American; illustrations of local service airlines were Ozark, Piedmont, and Republic. On October 2, 1980, the Civil Aeronautics Board dropped these classes and established four new airline categories: majors, nationals, large regionals, and medium regionals. As of January 1, 1984,

majors, nationals,
large regionals, and
medium regionals

majors have annual revenues of more than $1 billion, *nationals* produce sales between $100 million and $1 billion, *large regionals* are in the revenue range of $10 million to $99,999,999, and *medium regionals* either (1) have operating revenues of less than $10 million or (2) exclusively operate aircraft either with 60 seats or less or carrying no more than 18,000 lbs. of payload. All are *certificated* airlines; therefore Part 298 carriers are excluded from these classes.

Economic Regulation

before deregulation

For nearly 50 years before the Air Cargo Deregulation Act of 1977, entitled the Federal Aviation Act of 1958—Insurance Risks (91 Stat. 1284), and the Airline Deregulation Act of 1978 (92 Stat. 1705), the U.S. commercial air transportation business was one of the most regulated sectors in the U.S. enterprise system. With the passage of the Civil Aeronautics Act of 1938, Congress imposed strict laws designed to develop a fledgling airline industry, protect its established certificated scheduled interstate carriers, and ensure a high level of passenger safety. Rigid entry and rate rules were the methods used. For instance, of the 79 applications filed by companies wanting to enter the domestic scheduled certificated airline industry between 1950 and 1974, not one was approved by the Civil Aeronautics Board.[1] In this highly protective environment, route expansion efforts, rate changes, and merger plans had to pass before the scrutinizing eyes of the Civil Aeronautics Board. This process took time and resulted in large expenditures for legal fees by applicants seeking CAB approvals. Nevertheless, many requests were granted, and the air system expanded substantially.

after deregulation

Today's legal environment is much different. The domestic air cargo business is considerably deregulated, and the economic regulations of the domestic passenger side of the industry have also been significantly lessened. Deregulation, however, was directed at the domestic passenger and freight businesses, leaving foreign air commerce regulations virtually unchanged. In addition, the Airline Deregulation Act of 1978 did not totally end domestic airline controls. Many provisions of the Federal Aviation Act of 1958 remain, albeit transferred from the defunct CAB primarily to the U.S. Department of Transportation as a result of the Civil Aeronautics Board Sunset Act of 1984, signed into law by President Reagan on October 4, 1984 (98 Stat. 1703, et seq.). The only exception was the U.S. Postal Service, which is responsible for determining rates for the carriage of mail in interstate and overseas air transportation (92 Stat. 1745).

existing regulations

As summarized in Table 14.1, a U.S. citizen today who wishes to operate as a Section 401 for-hire domestic scheduled passenger airline flying aircraft containing more than 60 seats still requires a certificate of public convenience and necessity; is obligated to provide safe and adequate service; has certain prohibitions against terminating, reducing, or suspending services; is subject to some rate rules; could see any merger plans scrutinized by the Department of Transportation;[2] and will meet the government's reporting and accounting requirements.

ease of entry

rate freedoms

Two substantive differences exist between today's regulatory environment and that which preceded deregulation. First, entry is now not only possible, but also relatively easy, and route changes are much faster. Secondly, although the government retained certain powers to alter rates, such as determining whether predatory pricing exists, federal officials did not aggressively try to stop such abuses. With few exceptions, carriers today raise or lower prices as they please. The combination of route and pricing freedoms has given carriers broad powers to decide their corporate fates subject only to market conditions and their internal skills and financial resources. Federal regulators have been told to remove themselves as much as possible from the for-hire airline business, and in terms of economic regulations, they have in general complied. (See Chapter 4 for a review of deregulation goals.)

Noneconomic Regulations

Noneconomic regulations also affect airline operations and management decisions. Noise restrictions, airport security precautions against hijacking threats, and safety regulations are only a few of the types of rules carriers must abide by. Table 14.2 lists air regulatory provisions and their sources.

Promotion and Subsidy

Without question, U.S. air transportation would never have reached its present stage of development without federal, state, and local aid. For the most part, airports have been financed and constructed by local governmental units. Management of the airways has been, and still is, a federal responsibility. Federal tax dollars are derived mainly from user taxes authorized primarily by the Airport and Airway Development Act of 1970 (84 Stat. 219). That law created the Airport and Airway Trust Fund to finance airway and airport capital improvements and airway system research and development. In addition to user taxes, hundreds of millions of dollars annually are also channeled from federal general revenue funds into the air transportation industry.

airports and airways

Section 406
subsidy program

Two forms of direct operating assistance are Section 406 and Section 419 subsidies. Section 406 of the Federal Aviation Act of 1958 (72 *Statutes at Large,* p. 763) pertains to subsidies created by Congress in 1958 to compensate air carriers for hauling U.S. mail. As time passed, the Section 406 program be-

TABLE 14.1. Key implications of airline deregulation on domestic scheduled passenger carriers[a]

ENTRY

(1) U.S. citizens wanting to fly aircraft containing more than 60 seats[b] must prove they are fit, willing, and able to perform air transportation properly and conform to the provisions of the Federal Aviation Act of 1958 as amended (the Act), but no longer do they need to show the air transportation is consistent with the public convenience and necessity. This altered Sec. 401(d)(1) and (2) of the Act as per Sec. 1601(a)(1)(A) of the Act effective, 12/31/81.

(a) Carriers can hold a domestic charter certificate at the same time they have scheduled certificated authority. This changed Sec. 401(d)(3) of the Act as per Sec. 1601(a)(1)(A) of the Act.

(b) Carriers can commingle, on the same flight, scheduled and charter passengers. This changed Sec. 401(n)(1) of the Act as per Sec. 1601(a)(1)(E) of the Act, effective 12/31/81.

(c) The government cannot specify terminal and intermediate points (i.e., route points). This changed Sec. 401(e)(1) of the Act as per Sec. 1601(a)(1)(C) of the Act, effective 12/31/81.

(2) If citizens only want to fly aircraft with 60 or less seats, certificates are not required, and exemptions to operate under Sec. 416(b)(4) of the Act apply. Exemptions do not apply in certain Alaskan markets.

SERVICE

(1a) The fact that carriers were authorized to provide certificated air service does not necessarily mean they are required to do so. Sec. 404(a) of the Act was changed by Sec. 1601(a)(1)(F) of the Act, effective 12/31/81.

(b) Carriers are required to continue to provide safe and adequate service, but certificated carriers no longer are subject to other provisions of Sec. 404 of the Act such as the requirement for through (i.e., connecting carrier) service, as per Sec. 1601(a)(2)(B) of the Act, effective 1/1/83.

EXIT

(1a) The CAB lost its power over terminations, reductions, and suspensions of service except with respect to essential air services in which case strict procedures apply. Sec. 1601(a)(1)(D) of the Act changed Sec. 401(j)(1) of the Act, effective 12/31/81.

(b) Essential air service matters were transferred to the Department of Transportation on 1/1/85 as per Sec. 1601(b) of the Act.

RATES

(1a) Carriers are no longer required to file and publish tariffs. Sec. 403 of the Act was terminated by Sec. 1601(a)(2)(A) of the Act, effective 1/1/83.

(b) The CAB lost the power to prescribe maximum or minimum rates. Sec. 1601(a)(2)(D) of the Act changed Sec. 1002(d)(1) of the Act, effective 1/1/83.

(c) The CAB lost the power to suspend rates. This changed Sec. 1002(g) of the Act as per Sec. 1601(a)(2)(D) of the Act, effective 1/1/83.

(d) The CAB lost the power to establish joint rates. This changed Sec. 1002(i) of the Act as per Sec. 1601(a)(2)(D) of the Act, effective 1/1/83.

(e) The zone of reasonableness was retained. See Sec. 1002(d)(4)–(8) of the Act.

(f) The government retained power to alter individual or joint rates if found to be unjustly discriminatory, or unusually preferential, or unduly prejudicial, or predatory. Sec. 1002(d)(3) of the Act applies.

MERGERS

(1) Authority was transferred to the Department of Transportation 1/1/85 and continues until January 1, 1989, when it shall cease. See Section 408 of the

Act as per Sec. 1601 (b)(1)(c) of the Act and Sections 3(a) and 3(c) of the Civil Aeronautics Board Sunset Act of 1984, 98 Stat. 1703.

REPORTS, ACCOUNTS

(1) The government (the CAB and now the DOT) retained the power to require reports from air carriers, as per Sec. 407(a) of the Act.

(2) The government (the CAB and now the DOT) retained the power to prescribe the forms of any and all accounts, as per Sec. 407(d) of the Act.

(3) The government (the CAB and now the DOT) has the power of access to inspect accounts and property, as per Sec. 407(e) of the Act.

CAB SUNSET

(1) The CAB was abolished 1/1/85. See Sec. 1601(c) of the Act and 98 Stat. 1703 et seq.

ᵃThis limited review focuses only on domestic scheduled passenger carriers and excludes all-cargo, charter passenger carriage, and foreign air carriage.

ᵇRevised from 55 to 60 seats by the CAB in ER-1123, effective May 17, 1979.

TABLE 14.2. Selected federal aviation regulatory provisions and their sources

Provision	Source
Federal Aviation Act of 1958 as Amended	49 U.S.C. 1301 et seq.
Airline Deregulation Act of 1978	92 Stat. 1705 et seq.
Federal Aviation Act of 1958—Insurance Risks (i.e., the Air Cargo Deregulation Act)	91 Stat. 1284 et seq.
International Air Transportation Competition Act of 1979	94 Stat. 35 et seq.
Civil Aeronautics Board Sunset Act of 1984	98 Stat. 1703 et seq.
Applications for Certificates of Public Convenience and Necessity, Entry	49 U.S.C. 1371(d) 14 C.F.R. 201
Certification and Operating Rules for Operators of Large Aircraft	14 C.F.R. 121
Exemptions for Air Taxi Operators	14 C.F.R. 298
Essential Air Service	14 C.F.R. 270 14 C.F.R. 398
Terminations, Suspensions, and Reductions of Service	14 C.F.R. 323
Domestic Cargo Transportation	14 C.F.R. 291
Indirect Air Transportation of Property (Air Freight Forwarders)	14 C.F.R. 296
Tariffs	14 C.F.R. 221
Mergers	14 C.F.R. 315
Air Taxi Operators and Commercial Operators	14 C.F.R. 135
Accident Investigations	49 C.F.R. 831
Hazardous Materials	49 C.F.R. 175
Noise Standards	14 C.F.R. 36
Federal Aid to Airports	14 C.F.R. 151

came the basis for compensating eligible local service airlines for providing air passenger and mail services to small communities (49 U.S.C. Section 1376).

Section 419 subsidy program

Another subsidy program, Section 419 of the Federal Aviation Act of 1958 (92 Stat. 1732), provides compensation for airlines who provide essential air transportation services to small communities (49 U.S.C. 1389). Much of the Section 419 financial assistance today is paid to eligible commuter airlines that have been replacing the former local service airlines in these small airport markets. Essential air transportation is scheduled air transportation of people to a point under such criteria as the CAB (now the Department of Transportation) determines satisfies the needs of the community for air transportation to one or more communities of interest. It ensures access to the country's air transportation system at rates, fares, and charges that are not unjust, unreasonable, unjustly discriminatory, unduly preferential, or unduly prejudicial. Regarding air transportation to any point (except Alaska), in no case shall essential air transportation be specified as fewer than two daily roundtrips, five days per week, unless the level of service to such point was less frequent in 1977, in which case that level of service applies (92 Stat. 1739). (More will be said about essential air transportation later in the chapter.)

CERTIFICATED COMMERCIAL AIR TRANSPORTATION

Since certificated commercial (for-hire) air transportation is the most important segment of the U.S. air transportation system in terms of revenues and traffic, this section will examine its characteristics, operations, problems, and economics.

Characteristics

Blurring of Airline Sectors.   One salient characteristic of this segment is all the new names in the market. New York Air, People Express, and Midway did not exist prior to deregulation. The interstate market is also expanding from the addition of companies like Pacific Southwest and Southwest, which were formerly intrastate California and Texas carriers, respectively. Formerly local service carriers, such as Allegheny (now USAir) and Piedmont, are now major carriers, and both have used the advantage of route freedoms to end their local service images. Several former certificated charter airlines also moved into the scheduled carrier sector. They were motivated by the loss of their low-price marketing advantage over scheduled airlines and by relaxed entry rules that made it much easier to become scheduled carriers. With deregulation, scheduled carriers matched low charter prices with deep-discount fares. As the competition intensifies in commercial air transportation, airline categories are blurring.

Route Competition.   In the airline business, market competition is route competition. It is a battle of carriers fighting for passengers in each origin-destination market pair. Hence, management must attract and retain the passenger or freight shipper not across the system, but in specific markets like the New York to Los Angeles route. Consequently, emphasis is placed on entry and exit—the right to serve a particular city pair or leave the market if service is not profitable.

number of firms

As a result of deregulation, not only can airline *X* expand rapidly, but so can others—and they can expand into the more lucrative routes of airline *X*. Thus there has been a surge in market entry. For instance, in June 1978 there were only 29 certificated U.S. airlines. By 1983 there were 94 Section 401 certificated airlines and approximately the same number of Section 418 all-cargo carriers, and on January 3, 1986, a total of 180 Section 401 and Section 418 carriers were operating.[3] The former trunk airlines have thus faced an influx of new firms. Simultaneously, trunk airlines have expanded rapidly into each other's markets.

entry control powers

As shown in Table 14.1, as of January 1, 1982, the CAB essentially lost its power over route matters. However, flight frequencies, departure times, non-stop or multistop flight itineraries, and aircraft choices are still left predominantly to management discretion. The exception today would be rules governing terminations, reductions, and suspensions of guaranteed essential air services, mainly small-town air services. Even in the latter case, carriers can exit markets, but the law requires that the federal government (i.e., the Department of Transportation) find a substitute carrier. This subject is discussed further in the section on commuter airlines.

Peaking. Airline flights and traffic tend to cluster during daylight hours, the 6–9 A.M. and 4–7 P.M. workday times, and the busy Thanksgiving and Christmas–New Year periods. This peaking (high demand/high supply periods) reflects not carrier choice, but carrier responses to passenger expectations. Passengers resist night flights; businesspeople, who comprise approximately half of the certificated airlines' travelers, want to leave early and return late to maximize their productive working hours; and vacation travelers like to go home for the holidays. However, maintaining a fleet and staff capable of serving traffic peaks can be expensive. Underutilization of capacity in off-peak periods is the problem. Just the same, the public demands that seats be available whenever requested.

Airports and Airways. In 1983 the United States had 372,953 miles of airways linking 16,029 airports.[4] Included in the latter figure are military airports that permit civil aircraft operations. Actually, though, for the year ending December 31, 1983, U.S. commercial air transportation served 500 certificated points in the 50 states, the District of Columbia, and other U.S. areas, but even this figure is misleading. During 1983, 97.1% of the industry's enplaned revenue passengers (i.e., paying passengers boarding certificated major, national, and regional air carriers' aircraft, including originating, stopover, and transfer passengers) boarded aircraft at 121 air traffic hubs. Rather than airports, hubs are cities and Standard Metropolitan Statistical Areas gener-

commercial airports

hub airports

ating high levels of airline passenger traffic. An SMSA is a county that contains at least one city of 50,000 population, or twin cities with a combined population of at least 50,000, plus any contiguous counties that are metropolitan in character and have similar economic and social relationships. Hubs are further classified as follows: (1) a large hub accounts for 1.0% or more of total U.S. commercial air transportation enplaned revenue passengers, (2) a medium hub accounts for 0.25% to 0.99% of enplaned revenue passengers, and (3) a small hub has between 0.05% and 0.24% of revenue passengers enplaned. The remaining airline service points are called nonhubs.[5] The 26 large hubs in 1983 accounted for 72.6% of the total enplaned revenue passengers.[6] The largest U.S. hub, New York, enplaned 8.84% of the industry's passengers at its three major airports—Kennedy, La Guardia, and Newark.

top 20 airports

The top 20 airports are listed in Table 14.3. Note, however, that many of the passengers enplaned at these facilities did not originate there but were merely changing aircraft. As a result, traffic figures shown in the table and

TABLE 14.3. Top 20 U.S. airports (12 Months ended 12/31/83)			
Rank	Airport	Enplaned Revenue Passengers	Percentage of Total Industry Enplaned Passengers
1	Atlanta	18,648,189	6.13%
2	Chicago (O'Hare)	18,197,199	5.99
3	Los Angeles International	14,265,641	4.69
4	Dallas–Ft. Worth Regional	12,738,376	4.19
5	Denver	11,401,005	3.75
6	San Francisco International	10,269,536	3.38
7	New York (Kennedy)	9,794,648	3.22
8	New York (La Guardia)	8,786,003	2.89
9	Newark	8,300,298	2.73
10	Boston	8,044,651	2.64
11	St. Louis	7,815,390	2.57
12	Miami International	7,337,567	2.41
13	Washington National	6,559,868	2.15
14	Minneapolis/St. Paul	5,781,536	1.90
15	Houston Intercontinental	5,676,551	1.86
16	Pittsburgh/Wheeling	5,544,359	1.82
17	Honolulu	5,375,172	1.76
18	Seattle–Tacoma International	4,954,028	1.63
19	Detroit Metropolitan Wayne City	4,888,149	1.60
20	Phoenix	4,800,711	1.58
	Top 20 as Percentage of Industry Total		58.89%

Source: U.S. Department of Transportation, Federal Aviation Administration, and U.S. Civil Aeronautics Board, *Airport Activity Statistics of Certificated Route Air Carriers 12 Months Ending December 31, 1983* (Washington, D.C.: U.S. Government Printing Office, 1984), pp. 14–15.

later in the chapter tend to overstate the true number of air travelers. In a multiple-stop routing, a single passenger would be counted every time the plane he or she was on takes off.

large airport market entry

The large airports, because of their passenger-generating potential, have attracted the most market entrants. Much of the entry has been by established certificated scheduled airlines attempting to fill in holes in their national route networks. However, new airlines, such as New York Air, have also chosen to compete for large-airport business. One result of this intensified competition is price discounting, particularly in the medium- and long-haul routes such as between New York and Miami, and between Los Angeles and Newark. This discounting has produced great benefits to price-sensitive travelers in these markets.

Operating Decisions

schedules

hub-and-spoke versus point-to-point networks

Routes and schedules are important variables in determining carrier success or failure. A few minutes' difference in departure times between two carriers can mean a gain or loss of passengers. Other decisions and trade-offs can be as simple as whether to give free peanuts on a flight or as complex as trying to decide whether to operate a hub-and-spoke system or a point-to-point network.

hub-and-spoke example

A *hub-and-spoke system* uses a large- or medium-sized airport as a central collector of traffic emanating from several radial feeder routes that reach out to passengers. The strategy is to schedule complexes—periods lasting approximately 30 minutes to one hour—during the day when, for instance, 30 of an airline's aircraft converge at the airport from various other airports, and passengers and baggage are transferred between aircraft before they again take off. For example, Atlanta's Hartsfield Airport is the main hub of both Delta and Eastern, and between them, they account for nearly 700 departures each weekday. Ten times daily, waves of Delta and Eastern planes converge on Hartsfield. During early September 1984, to be precise, the two carriers scheduled a combined total of 85 arrivals between 7:55 A.M. and 8:30 A.M., and 89 departures between 9 A.M. and 9:34 A.M.[7] Hub-and-spoke operations are designed to boost productivity by increasing passenger traffic on outbound flights, but they can also result in passengers transferring to competitive carriers that fly more direct nonstop or point-to-point *routes.* Still, the choice belongs to the airline on whether to establish hub-and-spoke operations or fly point-to-point routes such as back and forth between two airports.

Recent Problems

Air Traffic Controller Strike.   In recent years, certificated carriers have had to handle some unusual and difficult problems. One of the most damaging problems, from an operating perspective and because of its possible repercussions on public sector unions, was the strike of the Professional Air Traffic Controllers Organization (PATCO) in August 1981. When President Reagan or-

firings and
flight cutbacks

dered the illegally striking government employees to return to work or be fired, PATCO members called his bluff, and 11,400 controllers eventually lost their jobs. Subsequently, the Federal Aviation Administration ordered significant flight reductions until staffing could be restored. Hardest hit were certificated carriers serving the country's busiest airports. Ironically, although deregulation had finally allowed carriers to expand their route systems expeditiously, the carriers were not only restrained, but actually forced to reduce flights. Although most flight restrictions had been lifted by the FAA by the summer of 1984, the FAA was still 1,000 controllers shy of its goal of 14,300 workers.[8] Pan American World Airways Chairman, C. Edward Acker, complained in June 1984 that delays caused by air traffic controllers had become so serious that they were threatening the economic well-being of Pan Am.[9]

hub-and-
spoke problems

Delays at Large Airports. Deregulation and the proliferation of hub-and-spoke activities must also share the blame for flight delays. During January–June 1984, 189,473 flight arrivals and departures were delayed across the United States. This figure represented a 73% increase compared with the same period in 1983. Six airports—Newark, Atlanta, Denver, Chicago's O'Hare, and New York's La Guardia and Kennedy—accounted for 76% of these delays.[10] To compete with each other for traffic, carriers try to offer the most attractive flight schedules. Unfortunately, these decisions create severe flight peaking problems, as previously illustrated by the busy morning flight activities at Atlanta's Hartsfield Airport.

airline
scheduling
committees

As the crisis worsened, Secretary of Transportation Dole in 1984 asked the airlines to adjust their schedules voluntarily to spread flights across more time.[11] When unilateral actions failed, and with carriers under the threat by the FAA that it would regulate schedules if the carriers would not, the CAB in September 1984 granted Eastern Airlines' request that airlines be given antitrust immunity to form committees to set schedules at the six airports previously listed.[12] That same month, carrier committees changed flight schedules, and some small carriers were upset by the flight arrangements. Zenith International, as a case in point, said it had lost its right to make eight roundtrip flights through O'Hare airport.[13] Others, like People Express and Southwest Airlines, were concerned that larger, older airlines would force them to accept schedules that would be noncompetitive.[14]

continuing airport
capacity problems

Thus the battle over airline scheduling at large airports continues, and the delay problem will probably become worse. The CAB granted antitrust immunity to airline scheduling committees for only 45 days. Secondly, the FAA forecast that the number of enplaned revenue passengers would increase by 43% by 1990, from the 1983 level of 318 million to 454 million.[15] Finally, the demand for landing slots (a *slot* is the right to schedule one take-off or landing at an airport at a particular time) at large airports is intensifying. Unless measures are taken to expand the number of slots available, airline flight operations will be stymied by airport capacity constraints.

Airline Ticketing. A different, but equally troublesome, problem is airline ticketing. For more than 30 years, airline tickets were sold exclusively either by airlines or by travel agents licensed by the Air Traffic Conference of America, an airline sanctioning board. Throughout the years, agency sales increased in volume until, by 1983, the nation's approximately 22,000 licensed

travel agents travel agents sold nearly 70% of the airline industry's tickets. For their services, which cost the ticket purchaser nothing additional, agents in the early 1980s received from the airlines commission rates, determined by individual airlines, but ranging from 8% to 12% (10% was the norm). In comparison, the pre-1980 rate was 7%. Payments from the airlines in 1982 for these services

deregulation totalled $2.1 billion.[16] On December 16, 1982, the CAB deregulated airline ticket
of ticket sales sales, which opened the business to literally anyone interested. Not surprisingly, the decision was denounced by the American Association of Travel Agents, a group representing most of the country's established travel agencies.

Although it is too early to be definitive about the impact of deregulation,
impact of some observations are possible. First and quite surprisingly, there was no rapid
deregulation influx of new firms trying to sell tickets. Perhaps airlines avoided aggressively endorsing new ticket sellers, because they feared a backlash from established agents. Based on recent history, agents have market channel power to influence commission rates, and they are not afraid to use it. In the early 1980s, proposals by some airlines to lower commission rates from 10% to 9% were met with warnings that agents would promote the sales of competitors' tickets. The carriers subsequently retracted the proposals.

Perhaps the largest change occurred in commissions paid to in-plant agen-
in-plant agencies cies—namely, ticket sellers located on the premises of large companies and who issue tickets to company personnel. Before deregulation, airlines paid in-plant agencies a 3% commission rate. Corporations demanded higher commission rates believing they deserved the same commission rates paid to independent (non–in-plant) travel agencies. Airlines who disagreed with their corporate customers argued that in-plant agencies do less for the money, since they do not promote air travel. Furthermore, the airlines argued they could not financially afford to lose any additional revenues. However, not wanting to lose corporate business that in many cases can exceed $1 million in revenues annually from a single corporate account, airlines increased in-plant commission rates, either through announced commission rate changes or unofficially through rebates (i.e., returned portions of ticket prices). Thus airline agency costs rose because airlines feared the loss of revenues and traffic to other carriers paying higher agency commissions.

Economics

Which Is the Largest U.S. Airline? If the question is asked, "Which is the largest airline in the United States?" what is the correct response? Actually, the answer depends on the criterion and the year. On an operating revenue basis, the largest airline in 1984 was United, with $6.10 billion in sales (see

TABLE 14.4. Top 10 U.S. airlines: operating revenues[a] (Twelve months ended 12/31/84)

Rank	Name	Revenues (in $ thousands)
1	United	$6,096,845
2	American	5,087,382
3	Delta	4,496,735
4	Eastern	4,363,898
5	Trans World	3,646,839
6	Pan American	3,381,580
7	Northwest	2,463,357
8	USAir	1,629,696
9	Republic	1,547,232
10	Continental	1,196,827

[a]Revenues from the performance of air transportation and related incidental services including international and domestic, scheduled and charter, all classes of traffic, and nontransport revenues consisting of federal subsidy (where applicable).

Source: U.S. Department of Transportation, Research and Special Programs Administration, *Air Carrier Financial Statistics December 1984* (Washington, D.C.: U.S. D.O.T., 1985).

Table 14.4). United also carried the most passengers (Table 14.5) passing Eastern, which ranked first in 1983. United again appears at the top of Table 14.6 as the leader in passenger-miles, whereas Eastern slips to the third position behind American (see Fig. 14.2), because of American's longer average enplaned passenger trip length of 1076 miles versus Eastern's 772 miles. From a different perspective, United has the largest fleet (see Table 14.7). Who, then, was the most profitable? In terms of dollars of operating profits, again United ranked first with $550 million (Table 14.8). Yet if the standard is pre-tax op-

TABLE 14.5. Top 10 U.S. airlines: scheduled revenue passenger enplanements[a] (Twelve months ended 12/31/84)

Rank	Name	Passengers
1	United	41,010,000
2	Eastern	38,081,000
3	Delta	37,341,000
4	American	34,123,000
5	Trans World	18,487,000
6	USAir	17,047,000
7	Republic	15,177,000
8	Piedmont	14,274,000
9	Pan American	13,913,000
10	Northwest	13,216,000

[a]The total number of passengers boarding aircraft. Excludes charter passengers.

Source: U.S. Department of Transportation, Research and Special Programs Administration, *Air Carrier Traffic Statistics December 1984* (Washington, D.C.: U.S. D.O.T., 1985).

TABLE 14.6. Top 10 U.S. airlines: revenue passenger-miles[a]
(Twelve months ended 12/31/84)

Rank	Name	Passenger–Miles (in thousands)
1	United	46,687,187
2	American	36,705,451
3	Eastern	29,408,649
4	Pan American	28,405,784
5	Trans World	28,303,717
6	Delta	27,055,068
7	Northwest	20,131,363
8	Continental	10,924,669
9	Western	9,416,970
10	Republic	8,594,042

[a]All services. Includes charter, as well as scheduled, passengers.

Source: U.S. Department of Transportation, Research and Special Programs Administration, *Air Carrier Traffic Statistics December 1984* (Washington, D.C.: U.S. D.O.T., 1985).

erating income as a percentage of gross operating revenues, Evergreen occupied the first spot, followed by Air Wisconsin, Southwest, and USAir (Table 14.9), while United ranked eighth.

Traffic and Financial Trends and Causes. Table 14.10 shows industry figures and trends for four key airline industry measures. It is useful

statistics and trends

FIGURE 14.2.
American Airlines' Boeing 747 Luxury Liner. (Photo courtesy of American Airlines)

TABLE 14.7. Top 10 U.S. airlines: fleet size (1984)

Rank	Name	Aircraft
1	United	319
2	Eastern	285
3	American	260
4	Delta	229
5	Republic	160
6	Trans World	159
7	United Parcel Service	148[a]
8	USAir	133
9	Northwest	120
10	Pan American	116

[a]Nearly 100 airplanes are small aircraft.

Source: Air Transport Association of America, *Air Transport 1985* (Washington, D.C.: ATA of A, June 1985), p. 9, and *10-K's* and *Annual Reports* filed with the SEC. (Adapted with permission).

in pinpointing industry problems and positive changes and verifying the cyclical nature of airline profitability. Note first the marked growth progression from 1975 through 1978 in revenue passengers, revenue passenger-miles (RPMs), operating revenues, and operating income. Record operating income of $1.365 billion was recorded in 1978, followed by 1979 records in revenue passengers (317 million), RPMs (262 billion), and operating revenues ($27.2 billion). Then, for the first time in modern U.S. airline history, passenger and RPM traffic declined for two consecutive years, bottoming out in 1981. The year 1980 also showed a drop of $1.166 billion in operating profits, from the 1979 level of $1.365 billion to $199 million. It was an omen of worse times to

TABLE 14.8. Top 10 U.S. airlines: operating profits[a] (Twelve months ended 12/31/84)

Rank	Name	Profits
1	United	$550,006,000
2	American	339,065,000
3	Delta	287,344,000
4	USAir	192,724,000
5	Eastern	189,631,000
6	Piedmont	125,750,000
7	Continental	107,546,000
8	Flying Tiger/Metro International	102,191,000
9	Republic	100,002,000
10	Northwest	96,842,000

[a]System operating revenues less operating expenses, excluding non-operating income and expenses, nonrecurring items, interest, and income taxes.

Source: U.S. Department of Transportation, Research and Special Programs Administration, *Air Carrier Financial Statistics December 1984* (Washington, D.C.: U.S. D.O.T., 1985).

TABLE 14.9. Top 10 U.S. airlines[a]: ratio of pre-tax operating income to gross operating revenues[b] (Twelve months ended 12/31/84)

Rank	Name	Percent
1	Evergreen[c]	22.55%
2	Air Wisconsin	13.23
3	Southwest	12.78
4	USAir	11.83
5	Piedmont	11.08
6	Transamerica[d]	10.43
7	Zantop[c]	9.15
8	United	9.02
9	Continental	8.99
10	Flying Tiger/Metro International	8.85

[a]Only includes airlines required to file CAB Form 41 with annual sales more than $25 million.
[b]Operating income divided by operating revenues.
[c]Cargo carrier.
[d]Principally a charter carrier.

Source: Derived from U.S. Department of Transportation, Research and Special Programs Administration, *Air Carrier Financial Statistics December 1984* (Washington, D.C.: U.S. D.O.T., 1985).

TABLE 14.10. Selected air transportation statistics (1974–1984)[a]

	Revenue Passengers[b] (in thousands)	Revenue Passenger–Miles[b] (in thousands)	Operating Revenues[c] (in $ thousands)	Operating Income[c] (in $ thousands)
1974	207,458	162,918,594	$14,699,125	$725,740
1975	205,062	162,810,057	15,355,921	127,879
1976	223,318	178,988,026	17,501,215	721,933
1977	240,326	193,218,819	19,924,800	908,040
1978	274,719	226,781,368	22,883,955	1,364,863
1979	316,863	262,023,375	27,226,665	199,055
1980	296,903	255,192,114	33,727,806	(221,615)
1981	285,976	248,887,801	36,662,555	(454,770)
1982	294,102	259,643,870	36,407,635	(733,435)
1983	318,638	281,829,148	38,953,672	310,410
1984	343,264	304,458,727	43,825,047	2,151,511

[a]Calendar years.
[b]Scheduled services only, i.e., excludes charter passengers.
[c]All services for majors, nationals, and large regionals.

Source: Air Transport Association of America, *Air Transport 1985* (Washington, D.C.: ATA of A, June 1985).

come. For three straight years, the airline industry experienced increasingly larger operating losses of $222 million, $455 million, and $733 million. During 1982, airline revenues declined for the only time during the 1974 to 1984 period; however, on a positive note, passenger and RPM traffic finally started expanding again. In 1983, the U.S. airline industry established new records for passengers, RPMs, and operating revenues and a return to operating profitability. Each of these figures was topped in 1984 as passenger traffic hit 343 million, RPMs reached 304 billion, and operating revenues neared $44 billion. In addition, the $2.2 billion in operating income was an all-time record. What was responsible?

super-saver fares

It is not possible to isolate precise causes of these trends, but a key factor in the 1975–1978 growth trend certainly was American Airlines' introduction of super-saver fares on April 24, 1977. These discount roundtrip fares were restricted to individuals who agreed to fly on certain days of the week and stay a minimum period at destination. Originally implemented as a marketing device to counteract the diversion of scheduled passengers to charter airlines, these fares had two significant consequences. First, their success at generating traffic surprised everyone, including American itself. Secondly, by April 1978, practically all the trunk and local service airlines offered system-wide super-saver fares. These fares were designed to stimulate primary demand by attracting potential passengers who refused to fly at previous fare levels. With industry load factors (i.e., the ratio of revenue passenger-miles to available seat-miles) approximately 55% in 1976, the industry had a problem, and found a mechanism to fill empty seats at marginal added costs. At the same time, the restrictions were designed to keep the one-day roundtrip business traveler paying the full coach fare.

deregulation

Also contributing to the traffic growth trend were the Airline Deregulation Act of 1978 and CAB de facto deregulation. The latter deregulation included CAB rule changes that eased airline entry rules and encouraged domestic discount passenger pricing initiatives, prior to the enactment of the Airline Deregulation Act of 1978. Thus the airline business soared to new heights before it began its nosedive to record losses from 1980 through 1982.

recession

Recession, inflation, and management errors likewise had a hand in the slump. When the economy soured, cash-short travelers suddenly viewed air transportation, even at discount prices, as too much of a luxury. As Table 14.10 reveals, 20 million fewer passengers flew in 1980 than in 1979. By the time the slump bottomed out in 1981, passenger traffic had dropped 9.7%, and passenger-miles had declined 5.0% from 1979 levels. This decline was not a precipitous drop, but for an airline industry already committed to orders for new aircraft in anticipation of rapid traffic growth (see passenger and passenger-mile trends from 1975–1979 in Table 14.10), it was devastating. The combination of less traffic, more airlines fighting for pieces of a smaller pie, and the exercise of increased pricing freedoms forced many carriers to discount fares or lose ridership.

inflation

The timing of the recession could hardly have been worse, for the airline industry was struggling through one of the highest periods of inflation in history. Rising labor, aircraft, fuel, and capital costs demanded that airlines increase yields. The urgency of that need is clearly depicted in Table 14.11, which shows that average fuel prices rose from a 1978 level of 39.210¢ per gallon to 104.152¢ per gallon in 1981. In three years, the fuel bill of the trunk and local service carriers had jumped an incredible $5 billion. At one point, every time the fuel price increased a penny per gallon, it was costing the U.S. airline industry $110 million annually in operating expenses. Where market conditions permitted fare increases, they normally happened. Thus operating revenues continued to rise through 1981. However, competition did not always allow full cost recoveries.

management
errors: labor

A final cause of industry problems from 1979 through 1982 can be traced to questionable airline management decisions. Much of the industry's financial troubles derived from the relatively high-cost structures of the established airlines versus new competitors in the market. Particularly burdensome are high labor costs. The origin of the cost disadvantage of the established carriers can be traced to the protective prederegulation environment. At that time, the lack of competition from smaller, low-cost firms unable to enter the airline business; the absence of true price competition (then, certificated carriers

TABLE 14.11. Airline fuel costs: trunks and local service carriers (Calendar years)

Year	Average Price per Gallon (cents)	Total Fuel Expenses (in $ thousands)
1972	11.963¢	$1,093,337
1973	13.071	1,254,083
1974	24.329	2,060,900
1975	29.072	2,444,286
1976	31.649	2,746,637
1977	36.147	3,273,972
1978	39.210	3,622,922
1979	57.850	5,587,869
1980	89.310	8,173,706
1981	104.152	8,592,235
1982	98.488	7,807,561
1983[a]	89.200	8,639,000
1984	84.000[b]	(not available)

[a]Majors and nationals, excluding Continental Airlines and Air Florida.

[b]Average price of jet fuel for U.S. scheduled airlines, January 1985.

Sources:
1. For years 1972 through 1982, the source is Financial and Cost Analysis Division, Office of Economic Analysis, Civil Aeronautics Board, *Long-Term Fuel Expense: Consumption, Unit Prices and Total Expense, System Trunks and Locals* (Washington, D.C.: CAB, 31 March 1983).
2. For 1983, the source is Air Transport Association of America, *Air Transport 1984* (Washington, D.C.: ATA of A, June 1984), p. 10.
3. For 1984, *The Airline Quarterly*, September 1985, p. 153.

competing against one another in the same market invariably charged the same fare); and pressure to avoid strikes, which would drive customers to the competition—all contributed to management's allowing salaries, wages, and benefits to escalate far too rapidly. Suddenly the rules changed, the entry gates were opened, and the United States discovered that pilots, mechanics, flight attendants, and even white-collar airline professionals were willing to work for less compensation. Present managers are now carrying the burden for the false sense of security created in prior years by a combination of protective laws and managers too generous in times of airline prosperity.

management errors: overexpansion

Other questionable management decisions involved overexpansion. Braniff can be isolated as a case where management expanded its route system too rapidly and unwisely into some questionable markets. Braniff's bankruptcy in 1982 might have been avoided if expansion had occurred at a different point in history, but Braniff spread itself too thin just before traffic slumped. The business world demands that managers make choices and take risks. Unfortunately, sometimes the decisions are not the best, and when they are not, employees and owners share the consequences.

more recent results and causes

The positive trends of the 1983–1984 period can be traced to a combination of environmental and industry changes. As the country emerged from the recession, more people started to travel. Also helpful was a reduction in the inflation rate. In particular, the reduction in the average price per gallon of fuel from 98.488¢ in 1982 to 89.200¢ in 1983 saved the airline industry nearly $1 billion in 1983. Increased competition was another contributing factor, for without question, discount air fares stimulated revenue passenger and RPM traffic growth. However, the airlines must be given credit for managing their capital and labor better. Considerable improvements were made in productivity and cost controls. These and other airline strategies and actions are discussed in detail in Chapter 15.

COMMUTER AIRLINES

Federal Policy and Subsidy Programs

Commuter airlines and other air taxi operators represent one of the fastest developing components in the airline passenger business. Commuter airlines now account for approximately one-third of all scheduled U.S. aircraft operations.[18] The United States is committed to both a national air system and to providing air service to small communities. The emphasis is on linkage, the ability to get from here to there by air transportation without isolating less developed areas from the potential benefits that scheduled air services can produce. The U.S. government consequently makes services available to non-hub airports and small hubs that do not voluntarily attract and retain scheduled airline operations.

federal goals

Small-town air service is not a new problem nor are the efforts to solve it a new response. Since 1946, airlines have been subsidized to provide scheduled services to small communities. In the early years, trunk carriers and eventually local service airlines received federal aid for this purpose, such as under the 406 subsidy program. A secondary goal was to use subsidized carriers to feed traffic to trunk carriers.

impact of subsidy programs

Without federal direct operating subsidies, many small communities would certainly have lost certificated airline service. Just the same, the subsidy program did not guarantee continued service. In fact, in the 10 years prior to the Airline Deregulation Act of 1978, 137 communities lost all certificated air service. Ironically, one primary consequence of the Section 406 subsidy effort was to encourage local service airlines to purchase jet aircraft too large and costly to serve the numbers of passengers boarding at smaller airports.[19] Then, local service carriers wanted to abandon small towns to fly the jet aircraft between larger airports and over longer distances. Faced with the choice of increasing subsidies or reducing the number of service points, the government turned to commuter air carriage.

Part 298 Exempt Carriers

For more than three decades, U.S. citizens have been able to enter the air taxi business and operate in nearly total freedom from federal economic regulation. In 1952, when the CAB issued a general exemption later embodied as Part 298 of its regulations, no one really cared much about air taxi operators. After all, their traffic was minuscule, and they posed no real competitive threat to certificated trunk air carriers, which the CAB wished to protect. Later, on July 1, 1969, the Board broadened the exemption to include a new category of airlines, commuter carriers.

entry rules

A Part 298 carrier must file a registration statement showing proof of a valid Federal Aviation Administration operating certificate and minimum liability insurance. Since February 26, 1981, new commuter applicants must also prove fitness. Once authorized to fly, commuter airlines have few economic regulatory restrictions, with the noted exception being the rules added by Section 33 of the Airline Deregulation Act of 1978, which amended the Federal Aviation Act of 1958 (49 U.S.C. 1389). The effect of these provisions was to guarantee essential air services for 10 years to 555 communities that received certificated service on October 24, 1978. The number of points was thereafter increased to include eligible communities that had lost certificated service before deregulation.[20]

guarantee of essential air services

deregulation impact

Thus deregulation actually increased regulation over commuter airlines, for if a commuter operator was providing essential air services, it could no longer terminate, reduce, or suspend operations without CAB clearance. Now, with the CAB's sunset, clearance must be obtained from the Department of Transportation, which has to find a substitute airline or subsidize the present commuter carrier to stay in the market to maintain essential air services. Before the Deregulation Act of 1978, subsidies to commuter carriers were prohibited. However, deregulation had a positive impact on commuter airlines.

By accelerating the exit of trunk and local service airlines from small airports, it opened those market opportunities to eager commuter carriers.

In 1980, Section 401 certificated air carriers served approximately 300 airports, whereas commuter airlines reached 816 points in the United States, including Alaska and Hawaii. Of 286 commuter airline operators, 240 carried passengers.[21] Moreover, of the 555 eligible essential service communities, 145 previously served by certificated carriers were receiving replacement service by commuter-type airlines. Of the 137 other communities that had lost certificated service prior to October 24, 1978, commuters flew into 17 of these airports. Meanwhile, of 203 subsidy ineligible service points that had been receiving noncertificated service on October 24, 1978, 102 lost all air service since that date.[22] In 1981 approximately 90% of the industry's commuter carriers received no operating subsidies. Only 16 firms received aid to serve a total of 40 communities.[23]

statistics (margin note)

Role of Commuter Airlines

Deregulation changed a three-tier scheduled airline system of trunk, local service, and commuter carriers into a two-tier structure of large aircraft operators (i.e., majors, nationals, and regionals) and small aircraft airlines (i.e., taxis and commuter airlines). What exactly is the commuter airline's role beyond flying small aircraft into communities that generate small traffic volumes? First, commuter airlines are important feeders of traffic to the jet carriers flying longer haul flights. Commuter airline operations have a high tendency toward using hub-and-spoke routings, shuttling approximately 60% to 70% of their passengers to and from connecting flights with majors, nationals, and regionals. Although some local (one-carrier) service exists, high short-haul air fares relative to surface transportation rates tend to discourage this kind of commuter airline use. Connecting service usually means joint fares, which proportionately lower commuter prices enough to attract travelers. Nevertheless, on average, the typical commuter airline passenger, connecting or otherwise, is on board the Part 298 carrier for only about 115 miles.[24]

feeder to first tier carriers (margin note)

short-haul carriers (margin note)

Growth Trends

Commuter airline carriage has been growing rapidly despite a number of stubborn obstacles that, as previously noted, severely affected certificated airlines during the late 1970s and early 1980s. As depicted in Table 14.12, between 1972 and 1980 the number of operating commuter carriers grew by 55.4%, fleet size jumped 133.8%, there were 26.9% more airports and 60% more passenger markets served, enplaned passengers increased 270%, passenger-miles rose 146.2%, and the passenger-mile market share jumped 400%. Furthermore, these figures would have been even higher, except that 25 former commuter airlines opted to obtain Section 401 certificates to haul passengers and another 22 applied for and received Section 418 all-cargo certificates. Growth is attributed to a Part 298 carrier's ability to fill a hole in the air system

statistics (margin note)

causes (margin note)

TABLE 14.12. Growth in commuter air carriage	1970–1973	1980–1982[a]	Percentage Growth
Carriers Reporting to CAB	184	286	55.4%
Aircraft in Commuter Fleet	687	1,606	133.8
Airports Served	643	816	26.9
City Pair Passenger Markets Served[b]	1,304	2,087	60.0
Enplaned Passengers (in thousands)	4,270	15,800	270.0
Passenger-Miles (in thousands)	528,144	1,300,404	146.2
Aggregate Share of Airline System Revenue Passenger–Miles	0.3%	1.5%	400.0%

[a]Excludes 25 former Part 298 companies that became certificated passenger carriers after deregulation and 22 firms that are now Sec. 418 certificated all-cargo carriers.

[b]Each pair of origin-destination points, such as Eugene, Oregon, to Portland, Oregon.

[c]Would be 1.3 million higher with traffic of former commuters (see note "a").

Sources:

1. U.S. Department of Transportation, Federal Aviation Administration, *FAA Statistical Handbook of Aviation Calendar Year 1981* (Washington, D.C.: Government Printing Office, 31 December 1981), pp. 72, 74.
2. U.S. Congress, Senate, Committee on Commerce, Science, and Transportation, *U.S. Commuter Airline Industry, Hearings,* 97th Congress, 1st Session, 1981, Statement of Duane H. Ekedahl, President of the Commuter Airline Association of America, p. 42.
3. U.S. General Accounting Office, *The Changing Airline Industry: A Status Report Through 1982* (Washington, D.C.: GAO, 6 July 1983), p. 28.

vacated by certificated airlines and to meet passenger desires and cargo shippers' needs for more frequently scheduled service at reasonable prices.

Future

The future of commuter aviation appears encouraging, but success is in no way guaranteed. On the positive side, the law now exempts 60-seat aircraft,[25] which is a definite improvement over the early years when the effective limit was 10 seats.[26] Without question, rising capacity limits have encouraged de-

larger planes

velopment of improved aircraft such as the DeHavilland Dash-7, a four-engine, quiet, 50-passenger airplane. Furthermore, a federal loan guarantee program has aided Part 298 carriers in the purchase of aircraft by lowering interest rates and keeping capital costs more reasonable. Since 1978 the commuter airline industry has committed $1 billion toward the purchase of new aircraft.

It just may take larger, more comfortable aircraft to sustain industry

rider complaints

growth, however. Many people do not fly on commuter airlines because they fear flying in small aircraft. Even among users, there are complaints. One study, for instance, revealed passenger displeasure over loud and crowded airplanes.[27] Other criticisms include objections to the lack of an onboard restroom, low interior ceilings, and the inability to stretch one's legs. These are common characteristics of a fleet that in 1980 averaged 13 seats per aircraft. Nevertheless, traffic increases imply growing consumer satisfaction with commuter airline services, and studies back this up.[28]

airports and airways

Another possible future problem is airport treatment. Will airport operators provide landing slots at busy airports and first-class terminal treatment, or will they relegate commuter airlines, as has been the case far too frequently in the past, to second-class status? In addition, commuter carrier service and reliability are limited as long as small airports lack proper runway lengths for the larger planes and precision all-weather landing aids. In this respect, the Airport and Airway Improvement Act of 1982 should help by injecting millions of dollars into small airports and improved airway navigation equipment.

financial barriers

A final set of concerns centers on the financial aspects of entering and succeeding in the industry. Although entry regulations are minimal, entry costs are high. It might be argued that it does not cost much to obtain a few small aircraft. In reality, though, it is costly enough to require investment capital and adequate cash flow to survive the difficult start-up period. Therein lies a big industry problem. Between 1969 and 1980, 533 commuter airlines existed, and between 1977 and 1980, 346 entered the business.[29] Since only 286 remained in 1980, obviously, many failed; as a result, investors assign high risks to this market. Therefore obtaining financial support is difficult, and where it is available, capital costs remain high.

optimism

Despite these numerous challenges, there is still room for optimism. The historical record is quite clear that commuter airlines—if not as an entire industry, then as successful separate companies—are succeeding. Moreover, the positive aspects of the Act of 1978 and an improving economy are heartening. Finally, no other industry is more available, willing, and capable of providing small-town air services and feeding passengers to traffic-hungry certificated airlines. Commuters fill an important role, and statistics indicate that both the government and consumers are increasingly accepting and supporting their efforts.

GENERAL AVIATION

General aviation is the private, not-for-hire, sector of air transportation. Included within this category are personal and corporate aircraft used primarily, but not necessarily exclusively, for passengers. Some corporate aircraft are used to haul cargo.

pilots

General aviation statistics reveal large numbers of pilots, aircraft, and airports used relative to what is found in the commercial airline sector. As of December 31, 1981, 595,602 of the 764,182 U.S. certificated pilots participated in general aviation, and the remaining 168,580 were commercial pilots. Of the 764,182 certificated pilots, 47,721 were female, 43,620 of whom flew general

aircraft

aviation aircraft. As of January 1, 1982, the general aviation fleet totaled 213,200 aircraft comprised of 167,900 single-engine and 25,500 multi-engine piston aircraft; 4,700 turboprop airplanes; 3,200 turbojets; 7,000 helicopters; and 5,000 balloons, dirigibles, and gliders.[30] Private sector aircraft pilots use most of the nation's 16,029 airports unless access is prohibited by law. Sup-

support personnel porting the needs of general aviation aircraft owners and pilots were 398,000 people, including 263,000 mechanics.

Equipment Suppliers

Any discussion of general aviation would be incomplete without mentioning equipment suppliers. Names like Beech, Cessna, and Piper are quite familiar to many people in the United States, for these names appear on small aircraft all over the country. Probably not so recognizable are aircraft manufacturers, such as Gulfstream, Fairchild, or Mooney, or engine manufacturers like Teledyne Continental Motors, but all play key roles in enabling the private pilot to fly.

changing
sales patterns

Some dramatic changes have occurred in general aviation aircraft sales in recent years. For instance, only 4,266 fixed-wing general aviation aircraft, as differentiated from helicopters, were delivered in 1982, compared with a record-setting 17,811 in 1978. Causes of this precipitous decline include the recession, rising fuel costs, and rising interest rates. In October 1981 the average price of aviation gas had risen to between $2.16 and $2.28 per gallon. In addition, according to industry officials, once interest rates passed the 12% level, aircraft dealers became reluctant to carry aircraft in inventory. Subsequently, sales of the lower priced piston aircraft plummeted. Many individuals wanting to buy airplanes for personal use could not afford them.

The early 1980s, at any rate, did produce one positive sales trend. While industry revenues fell from nearly $3 billion in 1981 to $2 billion in 1982, the higher priced business jet and turboprop market remained strong. For example, Gulfstream Aerospace Corp., which produces the Gulfstream III, an 8–12 passenger executive jet, which retailed in 1982 at about $13 million per unit, reported increased sales. High resale values, quality, and the ability of the high-speed aircraft to save an executive's time and help close business deals were credited for the company's success.[31]

General Aviation Analysis

The corporate aircraft market remained stronger overall in the early 1980s than the personal airplane business, because corporations are more capable of handling inflation. In 1983, the estimated average cost of a new single-engine piston aircraft—the type most desired for personal ownership—was $82,000. This price was much lower than the average estimated prices of $345,000 for a multi-engine piston plane, $1,556,000 for a turboprop, or $4,571,000 for a jet,[32] the type that corporations prefer, but more relevant is the question of who has an easier time justifying the outlay and producing the money. Nevertheless, general aviation manufacturers as a whole have rebounded from previous sales declines and are optimistic that an improved economy and newer, more technologically advanced aircraft in terms of flight range, fuel efficiency, and reliability will again boost revenues and profits.

AVIATION SAFETY

The U.S. government has never wavered from its commitment that air travel be safe. Section 102(a)(1) of the Federal Aviation Act of 1958 explicitly charged the CAB to consider "the assignment and maintenance of safety as the highest priority in air commerce." At first, what motivated this concern was the recognition that air commerce would probably not develop unless passengers could feel confident of safe passage; fear of flying had to be minimized to encourage people to leave the ground. Today the motivation is far less developmental and far more a simple desire to protect life and limb.

Government Agencies

Federal Aviation Administration

Air safety matters fall primarily under the Federal Aviation Administration's jurisdiction, specifically under 14 C.F.R. 121 (Certification and Operating Rules for Operators of Large Aircraft) and 14 C.F.R. 135 (Air Taxi Operators and Commercial Operators). It is the FAA's job (1) to run the airway system through the administration and operation of air traffic control facilities, equipment, and personnel and (2) to set standards for aircraft equipment, maintenance, and operation and the training and certification of pilots, crew members, and mechanics.

National Transportation Safety Board

Another key agency is the National Transportation Safety Board (NTSB). Once an independent agency housed within the U.S. Department of Transportation, since 1974 the NTSB has been an entirely independent governmental agency. The NTSB has priority over all other organizations investigating aviation accidents, as well as surface transportation disasters. Unlike the FAA, whose charge is to prevent accidents from happening, the NTSB analyzes aviation mishaps and recommends corrective action to prevent or minimize similar future happenings.

How Safe Is U.S. Air Transportation?

How safe is U.S. air transportation? Based on statistical data, commercial aviation has in general been quite safe compared to other modes. In the 26 months prior to January 1982, U.S. commercial aircraft subject to 14 C.F.R. 121 flew more than $\frac{1}{2}$ billion passengers more than $\frac{1}{2}$ trillion passenger-miles on more than 10 million flights without a catastrophic crash of a jet airplane.[33] During 1980, domestic scheduled air transportation, on the basis of passenger fatalities per 100 million passenger-miles, was 4 times as safe as passenger trains, 15 times as safe as buses, and 132 times as safe as passenger automobiles and taxis.[34]

pressing safety concerns in 1986

Regardless, air safety was a major concern for U.S. citizens as they started 1986 and for good reasons. The public has been vividly reminded of terrorist attacks on aircraft, airports, and airline passengers, so security is a concern. There has been conveyed an increasing anxiety about several reported near mid-air collisions that happened since the firing of air traffic controllers in 1981. There is also a growing dependence on commuter airlines, and fears of flying in small planes have passengers more carefully examining commuter airline safety records. But by far what made safety so prominent an issue were the air disasters of 1985 that killed 523 people in five accidents by U.S. certificated airlines and more than 2000 worldwide in aviation accidents. During 1985, the media constantly reminded U.S. citizens of the risks of flying. What the public should want to know, therefore, is whether 1985 was an anomaly or a clue to future disasters. Perhaps it is best to study the historical trends and facts first and then address some of the more current, specific questions about aviation safety. It is important to look at statistics, and, while not attempting to diminish the tragedies of lost loved ones, to try to remove some of the sensationalism associated with airline accidents. Two underlying objectives of the analysis are (1) to assess the true risks of flying versus traveling by other modes and (2) to try to determine if the federal government needs to take actions to reduce aviation risks.

14 C.F.R. 121 aircraft

Analysis of Safety Statistics.   The approach followed in examining the aviation industry's safety record is to study in sequence the safety records of 14 C.F.R. 121 scheduled service airlines (i.e., operators of large aircraft), 14 C.F.R. 135 commuter air carriers, and general aviation aircraft. This examination should help to clarify effectively the more, from the less, safe sectors of air transportation. Table 14.13 highlights statistics and trends for large aircraft scheduled service operators. It shows an airline industry that was safer in 1982 than in 1973, 1974, or 1978, in terms of accident rates per 100,000 aircraft hours and per 100,000 departures. It also verifies the risks of flying. With approximately 5,000,000 departures annually (an average of 13,700 take-

TABLE 14.13. Safety record of 14 C.F.R. 121 scheduled service airlines

				Fatal Accident Rates	
Year	Total Accidents	Fatal Accidents	Fatalities	Per 100,000 Aircraft Hours	Per 100,000 Departures
1973	36	8	221	0.136	0.156
1974	43	7	460	0.110	0.127
1975	31	2	122	0.037	0.043
1976	22	2	38	0.036	0.041
1977	21[a]	3	78	0.052	0.061
1978	21[a]	5	160	0.083	0.100
1979	24[a,b]	4	351	0.060	0.074
1980	15	0	0	0.000	0.000
1981	25[c]	4	4	0.061	0.077
1982[d]	16[a]	5	235	0.062	0.080

[a]Contains one accident involving a scheduled commuter carrier.
[b]Contains one accident involving a deregulated all-cargo air carrier.
[c]Contains two accidents involving deregulated all-cargo air carriers.
[d]Preliminary.

Source: National Transportation Safety Board, *Annual Report to Congress 1982* (Washington, D.C.: NTSB, 23 March 1983), p. 38.

offs every day of the year), some accidents and fatalities are likely. However, in 1982, the probability of a fatal accident on board a 14 C.F.R. 121 aircraft was only 1 in 993,800 departures.

commuter carriers

Table 14.14 indicates a higher number of accidents (21 versus 16 in 1982), yet fewer absolute fatalities (13 versus 235), for commuter air carriers than for scheduled 14 C.F.R. 121 operators. Still, the fatal accident rates per 100,000 aircraft hours (0.330 versus 0.062) and per 100,000 departures (0.210 versus 0.080) were higher than for the large aircraft operators. A review of the fatal accident rates for each year from 1975 through 1981 also confirms a consistent pattern of greater risks flying on commuter aircraft. Commuter aircraft activities, regarding aircraft hours and departures, are significantly less (approximately 19% and 38%, respectively, in 1982, of the 14 C.F.R. 121 totals). Consequently, fatal accident rates were larger. This fact continues to be troublesome, yet commuter air carrier fatal accident rates in 1982 were encouragingly better than in previous years.

general aviation

Unquestionably, the most dangerous sector of aviation is general aviation (Table 14.15). Although it is encouraging to note favorable trends in fatal accident rates per 100,000 aircraft hours, the 1982 figures reveal 3276 accidents, 1164 deaths, and a fatal accident rate 25 times higher for the general aviation sector than for the scheduled 14 C.F.R. 121 carriers (1.59 versus 0.062) and 4 times greater than for commuters (1.59 versus 0.33). Safety problems are partially due to less experienced pilots in general aviation than in commercial air transportation. Another cause is flying into smaller airports that lack the level of air traffic control sophistication found in larger airports.

Scheduled Airline Safety Record in 1985.   Thus the facts through 1982 show that the commercial airline industry is safer than the private aviation sector and within the scheduled airline industry, large aircraft operators—the companies flying the aircraft that most travelers will use in the future—have the best safety records. Table 14.13 also showed that fatal airline accidents and fatalities have occurred with rather random frequency. The preregu-

				Fatal Accident Rates	
Year	Total Accidents	Fatal Accidents	Fatalities	Per 100,000 Aircraft Hours	Per 100,000 Departures
1975	48	12	28	1.280	0.820
1976	35	9	27	0.930	0.590
1977	44	9	32	0.780	0.520
1978	61	14	48	1.080	0.700
1979	52	15	66	1.280	0.800
1980	38	8	37	0.680	0.450
1981	33	10	36	0.810	0.540
1982[a]	21	4	13	0.330	0.210

TABLE 14.14. Safety record of 14 C.F.R. 135 commuter air carriers

[a]Preliminary data.

Source: National Transportation Safety Board, *Annual Report to Congress 1982* (Washington, D.C.: NSTB, 23 March 1983), p. 39.

TABLE 14.15. Safety record of U.S. general aviation (All operations other than those reported under 14 C.F.R. 121 or 14 C.F.R. 135)

Year	Total Accidents	Fatal Accidents	Fatalities[a]	Fatal Accident Rates Per 100,000 Aircraft Hours
1973	4090	679	1299	2.52
1974	4234	689	1327	2.47
1975	4034	638	1247	2.24
1976	4005	648	1187	2.15
1977	4069	658	1281	2.08
1978	4223	723	1563	2.07
1979	3800	629	1219	1.62
1980	3594	621	1247	1.65
1981	3504	657	1288	1.79
1982[b]	3276	574	1164	1.59

[a]Includes commercial air carrier deaths from collisions with general aviation aircraft.

[b]Preliminary data.

Source: National Transportation Safety Board, *Annual Report to Congress 1982* (Washington, D.C.: NTSB, 28 March 1983), p. 41.

lation years of 1973–1975 showed a high number of fatalities as did the deregulation years of 1978 and 1979. Similarly, there were safe years in 1976 and 1977, as well as in the deregulated years of 1980 and 1981. Still, the focus must return to 1985 and its 523 deaths. Actually, though, 14 C.F.R. 121 scheduled carriers accounted for 197 fatalities in 1985. The remaining deaths occurred in charter airline accidents. Accordingly, the U.S. scheduled airlines had a safer year in 1985 than in 1973, 1974, 1979, and 1982. Therefore the record does not substantiate that there is a safety crisis among carriers in the scheduled airline sector.

Safety During/After the Controller Strike.   Concerns about an increase in near accidents and an apparent breakdown in the air traffic control system following the firing and during the retraining period of replacement personnel were addressed by the National Transportation Safety Board in a report released on May 12, 1983, entitled the "Special Investigation Report, Followup Study of the United States Air Traffic Control System." It found, among other items, that there was no increase in air traffic control involved accidents since the strike, but that a number of near accidents were not reported. The report commended the outstanding cooperation and dedication of individual controllers but warned that improvements were still necessary in the training and supervision of air traffic controllers.[35]

Corrective Actions

The recent growth in airline traffic, relaxed entry procedures that have enabled many new, and often less experienced companies to operate commercial aircraft, and the rise in fatal airline accidents and deaths during 1985 raise valid concerns about the continuing need to evaluate and improve airline safety. Two recent developments verify the federal government's renewed commitment to air safety. First, the Airport and Airway Improvement Act of 1982 pledged billions of dollars for improved air navigation equipment and airport modernization. Secondly, the U.S. Department of Transportation began taking a harder look at potential safety problems. In 1983 Transportation Secretary Dole ordered an in-depth review of all transportation safety procedures and stated that airlines that show evidence of problems may lose their operating licenses. Furthermore, heavy fines were levied in 1986 on several airlines found guilty of aircraft maintenance violations. These actions will not eliminate aviation disasters nor will they eliminate safety risks, but they do reflect the government's support in making the airways as safe as possible. Still, if aviation safety problems persist, there may be a need to increase the number of qualified Federal Aviation Administration inspectors and air traffic controllers and increase safety regulations, safety checks, and safety violation fines or other penalties. The public expects the government to keep the airlines, airways, and airports safe.

SUMMARY

Air transportation in the United States is an integrated business of airlines, travel agents, equipment suppliers, and airport and airway operators each trying to earn a living while simultaneously making air transportation more efficient. Air transportation can be segmented into legal categories (certificated and exempt), by operating authority (interstate, overseas, foreign, and intrastate), by market target (passengers and cargo), by revenues (majors, nationals, and regionals), by operations (scheduled and charter), by aircraft size (more or less than 60 seats), and in several other ways.

Analyses of certificated commercial air transportation, commuter airlines, and general aviation reveal roles, peculiarities, strengths, and weaknesses by sector. Dominating the passenger traffic and sales statistics are the certificated carriers, the first tier of scheduled airlines in the United States. While 1984 produced record industry traffic and profits, certificated airlines have been struggling with substantial financial problems in a significantly altered environment. In contrast, the nation's second tier, the commuter airline industry, has made great headway to become the fastest growing segment in the airline passenger business.

General aviation is private air transportation. Although this sector shows the most pilots, aircraft, and airports used of any air transportation component, recently the personal use, individually owned, aircraft side of the business has been experiencing a number of problems. Escalating aircraft prices and fuel costs, for instance, have prevented many people from buying their own planes. Others have been forced to restrict personal aircraft use. The other part of general aviation—corporate flying, because it was less affected by inflation—continued to grow in the early 1980s.

General aviation is the least safe component of air transportation. Overall, the U.S. commercial airline industry has an excellent safety record, but a series of fatal commercial airline accidents in 1985 served warning of the need to continue to assign high priority to aviation safety.

STUDY QUESTIONS

1. What was the largest U.S. airline in 1984?

2. During the 1979 through 1982 period, what prevented U.S. domestic scheduled passenger airlines from raising prices as high as they might have desired to keep pace with rapidly rising costs?

3. What factors contributed to the achievement of record operating income by the U.S. scheduled airline industry in 1984?

4. How safe are the operations of scheduled 14 C.F.R. 121 airlines?

5. What is a Part 298 air carrier, and how does a U.S. citizen obtain Part 298 operating authority?

6. What must a U.S. citizen do to gain Section 401 air carrier authority?

7. Explain the role of general aviation in U.S. air transportation.

8. How much power do travel agents have in setting the commission rates paid to them by airlines? Why?

ENDNOTES

1. U.S. Congress, Senate, *Report of the Subcommittee on Administrative Practice and Procedures, Committee on the Judiciary on Civil Aeronautics Board Practices and Procedures* (Committee Print), 94th Cong., 1st sess., 1975, p. 78. This report is commonly called the *Kennedy Report.*

2. "D.O.T. Proposes Rulemaking for Former CAB Functions," *Traffic World,* 11 February 1985, p. 42.

3. (a) Air Transport Association of America, *Air Transport 1979* (Washington, D.C.: ATA of A, June 1979), p. 29; (b) U.S. Civil Aeronautics Board, *CAB Air Carrier Financial Statistics, June 1983* (Washington, D.C.: U.S. Government Printing Office, 1983), p. ii; and (c) information provided by phone by the Office of Aviation Information Management, U.S. Department of Transportation, 3 January 1986.

4. U.S. Department of Transportation, Federal Aviation Administration, *FAA Statistical Handbook of Aviation Calendar Year 1983* (Washington, D.C.: Government Printing Office, December 1984), pp. 8, 35.

5. U.S. Department of Transportation, Federal Aviation Administration, and U.S. Civil Aeronautics Board, *Airport Activity Statistics of Certifi-*

cated Route Air Carriers 12 Months Ended December 31, 1983 (Washington, D.C.: Government Printing Office, 1984), p. v (hereafter cited as *Airport Activity Statistics).*

6. Ibid.

7. (a) Christopher Conte, "Airline and Government Officials Clash as Meetings Begin on Snarled Schedules," *Wall Street Journal,* 6 September 1984, p. 5; and (b) Scott Kilman, "Delays at Atlanta's Hartsfield Airport Should Lessen under Revised Schedules," *Wall Street Journal,* 14 September 1984, p. 18.

8. Christopher Conte, "Improved Air Traffic Control Is Called Solution to Airlines' Schedule Quandary," *Wall Street Journal,* 11 September 1984, p. 6.

9. Christopher Conte, "Pan Am, Consumer Group Charge FAA Isn't Controlling Air Traffic Adequately," *Wall Street Journal,* 21 June 1984, p. 6.

10. Christopher Conte, "Transport Agency's Dole Vows to Restrict Traffic at Six Busy Airports if Carriers Don't," *Wall Street Journal,* 16 August 1984, p. 6.

11. Ibid.

12. "CAB Grants Antitrust Immunity Bid for Airline

Scheduling Committees," *Traffic World*, 20 September 1984, p. 34 (hereafter cited as "CAB Grants Antitrust Immunity").

13. Christopher Conte, "Four New Airlines Say Rescheduling Is Unfair to Them," *Wall Street Journal*, 13 September 1984, p. 10.

14. "CAB Grants Antitrust Immunity," p. 35.

15. Bill Coker, "Coping with the Airport Crunch," *Airline Executive*, March 1984, p. 30.

16. Harlan S. Byrne, "Travel Agents Watch Profits Shrink in Face of Airline Wars and Tougher Competition," *Wall Street Journal*, 14 June 1983, p. 37.

17. Eric N. Berg, "Agents, Airlines Feuding," *Athens (Georgia) Banner Herald*, 21 August 1983, p. 7c, presenting Mr. Berg's *N.Y. Times News Service* article.

18. U.S. Department of Transportation, Federal Aviation Administration, *FAA Statistical Handbook of Aviation Calendar Year 1981* (Washington, D.C.: Government Printing Office, 31 December 1981), p. 13 (hereafter cited as *FAA Statistical Handbook*).

19. Kenneth C. Williamson, Lawrence F. Cunningham, and Marc G. Singer, "Scheduled Passenger Air Service to Small Communities: A Role for State and Local Governments," *Transportation Journal* 21, no. 4 (Summer 1982):27–28 (hereafter cited as "Scheduled Passenger Air Service").

20. U.S. General Accounting Office, *The Changing Airline Industry: A Status Report Through 1982* (Washington, D.C.: GAO, 6 July 1983), p. 24 (hereafter cited as U.S. General Accounting Office).

21. (a) "Scheduled Passenger Air Service," p. 29, citing Commuter Airline Association of America, *1980 Annual Report*, pp. 55–62; and (b) *FAA Statistical Handbook*, p. 74.

22. U.S. General Accounting Office, p. 24.

23. Statement of Elizabeth E. Bailey, Member, CAB, U.S., Congress, Senate, Committee on Commerce, Science, and Transportation, *U.S. Commuter Airline Industry, Hearings*. 97th Cong., 1st sess., 1981, p. 74 (hereafter cited as Statement of Bailey).

24. "Scheduled Passenger Air Service," p. 30.

25. CAB, ER-1123, effective 17 May 1979.

26. Statement of Bailey, p. 79.

27. J. Richard Jones and Sheila I. Cocke, "A Performance Evaluation of Commuter Airlines: The Passenger's View," Transportation Research Forum. *Proceedings of the Twenty-second Annual Meeting* (Oxford, Ind.: Richard B. Cross Company, 1981), p. 251.

28. Ibid., p. 254.

29. Edward R. Bruning and Larry E. Oberdick, "Market Structure and Economic Performance in the Commuter Airline Industry," *Transportation Journal* 21, no. 3 (Spring 1982):77, citing Clinton V. Oster, Jr., "Competitive Strategies in the Commuter Airline Industry," paper presented at the 22nd Annual Meeting of the Transportation Research Forum, 4–7 November 1981.

30. General Aviation Manufacturers Association, *General Aviation Statistical Databook 1983 Edition* (Washington, D.C.: GAMA, 1983), pp. 10, 14, 18.

31. Beau Cutts, "Gulfstream Jets Are the Ultimate in Private Flying," *Atlanta Journal/Constitution*, 12 December 1982, p. 1E.

32. Derived from unpublished General Aviation Manufacturers Association data, Washington, D.C., 1983.

33. National Transportation Safety Board, *Annual Report to Congress 1982* (Washington, D.C.: NTSB, 23 March 1983), p. 4.

34. U.S. Department of Transportation, Federal Aviation Administration, *FAA Statistical Handbook of Aviation Calendar Year 1983* (Washington, D.C.: Government Printing Office, December 1984), p. 162, citing the National Safety Council's "Accident Facts."

35. National Transportation Safety Board, *Special Investigation Report, Followup Study of the United States Air Traffic Control System* (Washington, D.C.: NTSB, 12 May 1983), pp. 64–65.

ADDITIONAL READINGS

Bright, Elise M. "Secondary Impacts of Airports: An Assessment of Planning Procedures." *Transportation Quarterly* 36, no. 1 (January 1982):75–97.

Bruning, Edward R., and Oberdick, Larry E. "Market Structure and Economic Performance in the Commuter Airline Industry." *Transportation Journal* 21, no. 3 (Spring 1982):76–87.

Chapman, R. Stanley. "Once Divided Airlines Now United in Supporting Deregulation Law." *Traffic World*, 30 May 1983, pp. 12–14.

Cunningham, Lawrence F.; Williamson, Kenneth C.; and Wood, Wallace R. "Planning Decisions in Commuter Airlines." *Transportation Journal* 23, no. 3 (Spring 1984):53–62.

Davis, Grant M., and Dillard, Jr., John E. "The Professional Traveler and the Airline Deregulation Act of 1978: An Appraisal." Transportation Research Forum. *Proceedings of the Twenty-third Annual Meeting.* (Oxford, Ind.: Richard B. Cross Company, 1982), pp. 419–426.

Graham, David R., and Kaplan, Daniel P. "Airline Regulation Is Working." *Regulation* (May/June 1982):26–32.

Havens, Arnold I., and Heymsfeld, David A. "Small Community Air Service under the Airline Deregulation Act of 1978." *Journal of Air Law and Commerce* 46 (1981):641–686.

Hu, Michael, and Bruning, Edward. "Prior Experience and Misperceptions of Airline Service." *The Logistics and Transportation Review* 20, no. 3 (September 1984):213–222.

James, George W., ed. *Airline Economics.* Lexington, Mass.: Lexington Books, 1982.

Kahn, Alfred E. "Applying Economics to an Imperfect World." *Regulation* (November/December 1978):17–27.

Kennedy, Edward M.; Casey, Albert V.; Muse, M. Lamar; Colodny, Edwin I.; and Robson, John E. "Competition in the Airlines." *Regulation* (November/December 1977):24–35.

Kennelly, John J. "Aviation—The Need for Uniform Legislation." *Journal of Air Law and Commerce* 48, no. 3 (1983):613–646. (An article discussing litigation problems arising from airplane crashes.)

Levin, Robert E. "Aircraft Delays at Major American Airports Can Be Reduced." *Traffic Quarterly* 34, no. 10 (October 1980):493–509.

Magathan, Wallace C., III, and Franks, Victoria A. "Domestic Airline Passenger Remedies." *Journal of Air Law and Commerce* 48, no. 3 (1983): 647–664.

Meyer, John R.; Oster, Clinton V., Jr.; Morgan, Ivor P.; Berman, Benjamin A.; and Strassmann, Diana L. *Airline Deregulation: The Early Experience.* Boston, Mass.: Auburn House Publishing Company, 1981.

Monastirsky, Steve S., and Rosenberg, Larry J. "The Airlines Face the Challenge of Overbooking." *Transportation Journal* 18, no. 4 (Summer 1979):85–91.

Moore, Thomas Gale. "Deregulating Transportation." *Regulation* (March/April 1978):37–44.

Notis, Mitchell J. "In Defense of PATCO." *Journal of Air Law and Commerce* 47 (1982):317–336.

O'Connor, William E. *An Introduction to Airline Economics.* 2d ed. New York: Praeger Publishers, 1982.

Park, Choon Y.; Porter, Alan L.; and Connolly, Terry. "An Analysis of Federal Airport Funding Policies." *Traffic Quarterly* 34, no. 3 (July 1980):333–354.

Pavlicek, Michael J. "O'Hare International Airport: Impervious to Proposed State Efforts to Limit Airport Noise." *Journal of Air Law and Commerce* 47 (1982):413–448.

Rassenti, S. J.; Smith, V. L.; and Bulfin, R. L. "A Combinatorial Auction Mechanism for Airport Time Slot Allocation." *Bell Journal of Economics* 13, no. 2 (Autumn 1982):402–417.

Rider, Miriam. "A Chronological Listing of Legislation Affecting Civil Aviation 1938–1980." *Journal of Air Law and Commerce* 47 (1981):257–271.

Ruppenthal, Karl M., and Toh, Rex. "Airline Deregulation and the No Show/Overbooking Problem." *The Logistics and Transportation Review* 19, no. 2 (1983):111–121.

Sauter, John. "Airline Data Reporting Requirements: Costs and Benefits for Large Carriers and Aircraft Manufacturers." *Transportation Journal* 22, no. 2 (Winter 1982):74–83.

Stephenson, Frederick J., and Beier, Frederick J. "The Effects of Airline Deregulation on Air Services to Small Communities." *Transportation Journal* 20, no. 4 (Summer 1981):54–61.

Thayer, Frederick C. "Airline Regulation: The Case for a 'Public Utility' Approach." *The Logistics and Transportation Review* 18, no. 3 (1982):211–234.

Thornton, Robert L. "Channel Structure Changes and Passenger Air Deregulation." Transportation Research Forum. *Proceedings of The Twenty-second Annual Meeting.* (Oxford, Ind.: Richard B. Cross Company, 1981), pp. 285–293.

Toh, Rex S. "Airline Overbooking Model for Terminator Flights," *International Journal of Transport Economics* 2, no. 3 (December 1975):241–251.

U.S. Congress, House and Senate, House Committee on Science and Technology, Subcommittee on Transportation, Aviation, and Materials, and Senate Committee on Commerce, Science, and Transportation, Subcommittee on Aviation. *Future of General and Commuter Aviation Technology and Trade, Hearings,* 97th Cong., 1st sess., 27 August 1981.

Warren, William D. "Changing Air Transportation Services for Smaller Metropolitan Regions: 1980–1982." *Transportation Quarterly* 38, no. 2 (April 1984):245–266.

Whempner, Robert J. *Corporate Aviation.* New York: McGraw-Hill Book Company, 1982.

Wiliamson, Kenneth C., and Cunningham, Lawrence F. "Commuter Air Carriers and Federal Equipment Loan Guarantees: History Repeating Itself?" Transportation Research Forum. *Proceedings of the Twenty-second Annual Meeting.* (Oxford, Ind.: Richard B. Cross Company, 1981), pp. 230–238.

Coping
with Change:
Strategies
of Major Domestic
Combination Airlines

15

In the course of airline history, there has never been a period of rapid corporate change to match what has transpired since 1978. Stung by inflated fuel prices and suddenly thrust into a totally unfamiliar deregulated domestic airline environment, most established carriers felt considerable pressure not just to act, but to do so expeditiously. Among the decisions that had to be made were whether to acquire more fuel-efficient aircraft, which markets and routes to add or delete, how to compete on a price basis when costs were so much higher than those of the new airlines, and how to handle a severe recession. In reality, the period since 1978 has been a challenging time marked with great opportunities but also significant risks.

Chapter 15 is a study of corporate strategy and decision making. Much can be learned from examining carrier initiatives, as well as defensive reactions, to competitors' moves. Thus this chapter examines labor costs and trends, fleet and fuel strategies and issues, marketing and operating tactics, and changing airline finances. In essence, it is an in-depth case study of the 10 largest U.S. passenger airlines (see Table 14.4): United Airlines, American Airlines, Delta Air Lines, Eastern Airlines, Trans World Airlines, Pan American World Airways, Northwest Airlines, USAir, Republic Airlines, and Continental Airlines.

Chapter 15 provides a unique opportunity to apply concepts learned from previous courses such as economics, finance, and marketing or touched on throughout this book. It demonstrates applied business theory; examines management strategy, logic, and actions; ties together measures aimed at controlling costs, increasing productivity, and generating revenues; portrays the risks associated with making decisions without perfect information; and expresses labor and management needs, as well as capital versus labor trade-offs.

LABOR STRATEGIES AND ISSUES

Labor Costs

The highest cost area in the airline passenger business is employee compensation—salaries, wages, and benefits (S/W/B). S/W/B includes dollars expended for every airline worker from the chairperson of the board to filing clerks and airplane cleaners. Retirement costs are also included. Table 15.1 verifies that S/W/B represented nearly 40% of the domestic trunks' total operating expenses in 1982. If carriers expect to make significant headway with cost-

TABLE 15.1. Domestic trunk operations[a] percentage distribution of operating expenses by objective groupings (Twelve months ended 12/31/82)

Expenses	Percentages
Salaries/Wages and Related Fringe Benefits	
Salaries/Wages	30.7%
Benefits	8.9
Subtotal	39.6
Materials Purchased	
Aircraft Fuel and Oil	28.4
Maintenance Material	2.2
Passenger Food	3.3
Other Materials	1.4
Subtotal	35.3
Services Purchased	
Advertising and Promotion	2.4
Communications	1.3
Insurance	0.3
Outside Flight Equipment Maintenance	0.8
Traffic Commissions	6.1
Other Services	3.3
Subtotal	14.1
Landing Fees	1.5
Rentals	2.0
Depreciation	5.5
Amortization	1.1
Other	0.8
TOTAL	100.0%

[a]The CAB chose to make an exception from the use of the new carrier groupings (i.e., majors, nationals, and regionals) and use "trunks" for this source.

Source: Financial and Cost Analysis Division, Office of Economic Analysis, U.S. Civil Aeronautics Board, *Recent Trends in Airline Cost Elements, U.S. Certificated Route Carriers by Group* (Washington, D.C.: U.S. CAB, 9 August 1983), Table 16.

fuel costs

control tactics, they must address areas that offer the most potential for improvements—the largest of the cost items. Aircraft fuel and oil is another key cost item, with a 28.4% share of total costs. Interest expenses do not appear in Table 15.1. Although debt payments have become high-cost items at many carriers, interest is not an "operating" expense.

S/W/B Costs as Percentage of Operating Costs. Table 15.2 provides S/W/B data for the separate airlines for 1978 and 1984. It shows the relative rankings and trends and the relative magnitudes of the S/W/B cost elements as percentages of total operating expenses. As noted in the table's footnotes and sources, data for this table, as well as for most subsequent ones, were derived from, or found directly in, the 10-K and annual reports filed by the airlines with the Securities and Exchange Commission. All carriers file these reports for years ended 12/31 except Delta, which ends its year on 6/30. Moreover, mergers and acquisitions influence the tables' figures. Continental combined with Texas International in 1982; Pan American acquired National in 1979; and Republic resulted from the merger of North Central Airlines and Southern Airways in 1979 and the acquisition of Hughes Airwest in 1980. USAir was formerly known as Allegheny, but there was no merger—only a name change.

explanations

Table 15.2 acknowledges that each carrier's S/W/B costs as a percentage of total operating costs declined from 1978 to 1984. At first glance, this decline appears to be the result of effective cost controls. Looks are deceiving, however, as verified by data in Table 15.3. S/W/B costs increased by at least 28.1% at every airline except Continental, and at some carriers, increases were substantially higher. For example, the percentage changes at Delta (102.9%), USAir (154.1%), and Northwest (187.9%) are significant. Some of these trends are explained in footnotes in Table 15.3 as being strike, or merger or acquisition,

declining percentages

rising S/W/B dollar costs

TABLE 15.2. Salaries/wages/benefits as percentages of total operating costs (Annual)

Airline	1978 (%)	1984 (%)
American	41.40%	36.85%
Continental	42.75	21.18
Delta[a]	45.07	41.65
Eastern	43.82	36.89
Northwest	30.74	27.23
Pan American World	38.00	32.11
Republic	43.65	35.03
Trans World (TWA)	40.76	36.10
United	44.39	36.90
USAir	43.20	40.66

[a]Six years: 7/1/78 through 6/30/84. Delta files data on a fiscal year basis.

Sources: 10-K's and *Annual Reports* filed with the Securities and Exchange Commission.

TABLE 15.3. Dollars paid for salaries/wages/benefits (By year)

Airline	1978	1984	Percentage Change
American	$1,083,387,000	$1,749,803,000	61.5%
Continental	308,527,000	228,218,000	−26.0
Delta[a]	831,818,000	1,687,899,000	102.9
Eastern	1,000,300,000	1,539,760,000	53.9
Northwest[b]	222,200,000	639,606,000	187.9
Pan American World[c]	780,976,000	1,129,175,000	44.6
Republic[d]	115,227,000	506,905,000	340.0
TWA	1,008,800,000	1,292,362,000	28.1
United	1,444,175,000	2,086,582,000	44.5
USAir	230,090,000	584,579,000	154.1

[a]Six years: 7/1/78 through 6/30/84.

[b]Long strike reduced labor costs in 1978.

[c]Includes National's S/W/B in 1984.

[d]North Central figure in 1978.

Sources: 10-K's and *Annual Reports* filed with the SEC.

related. Other increases are correlated to such items as pay raises and increased staffing. Continental's 26.0% reduction in S/W/B costs is primarily attributed to the fact that it filed Chapter 11 bankruptcy papers in September 1983, voided its labor contracts, and slashed wages and benefits.

fuel cost impact   Since S/W/B costs continued to rise at most airlines, how can the percentage declines in Table 15.2 be explained? The primary answer is rising fuel costs (Table 15.4). In a percentage table such as Table 15.1 with a 100% ceiling, if one area of expenses increases faster than another, the relative importance

TABLE 15.4. Fuel costs as percentages of total operating costs (Annual)

Airline	1978 (%)	1984 (%)
American	19.67%	22.99%
Continental	20.40	30.31
Delta[a]	20.70	23.15
Eastern	16.62	24.04
Northwest	22.08	29.47
Pan American World	19.41	24.82
Republic	16.30	24.83
TWA	19.25	22.26
United	19.90	24.19
USAir	17.78	21.62

[a]Six years: 7/1/78 through 6/30/84.

Sources: 10-K's and *Annual Reports* filed with the SEC.

of the latter declines. Significant rises in fuel costs in the 1978 through 1981 period (see Table 14.11) reduced the labor cost percentage figures in Table 15.2. Thus labor costs were not quite as important in 1984 as they were in 1978; in dollars, however, they remained the industry's largest cost burden and still are today.

impact of
unionization

As shown in Table 15.2, Delta had the highest S/W/B burden in 1984 (41.65%). That percentage seems odd, since Delta has been the least unionized carrier of the majors; only about 10% of its employees are unionized, versus about 60% for the typical airline in the table. Thus it is necessary to probe further into factors affecting airline labor costs.

Employment Trends.   Table 15.5 displays changes in employment levels among the carriers. For most airlines, staffing increased. However, real growth must be distinguished from the consequences of mergers and acquisitions. On the basis of real growth, USAir seems to have expanded the most rapidly, with its 43.2% increase due to enlarged operations. Northwest's 42.2% growth is similarly explained. Higher levels of employment were also primarily responsible for Northwest's 187.9% and USAir's 154.1% jumps in S/W/B costs (Table 15.3). It cannot explain all of Delta's S/W/B costs, however. A 12.1% increase in employees alone is not enough to cause a 102.9% boost in S/W/B expenses. Neither can Republic's 340.0% change in S/W/B costs (Table 15.3) be totally explained by a 200.2% jump in workers. Observe also the employment reductions at TWA (−23.3%), Continental (−13.1%), United (−7.9%), and Pan Am (−2.6%). Continental's smaller work force was a result of the bankruptcy actions, which at one time cut staffing to 4000 workers. Table 15.5 does not reveal the full magnitude of airline furlough and other staff reduction actions during the recession. For instance, United employed 55,000 workers in 1979,

TABLE 15.5. Airline employment trends (Number of employees)

Airline	1978	1984	Percentage Change
American	38,115	39,600	3.9%
Continental	11,502	10,000	−13.1
Delta[a]	33,340	37,389	12.1
Eastern	37,100	38,400	3.5
Northwest	10,680	15,185	42.2
Pan American World	26,968	26,262	−2.6
Republic	4,460	13,390[b]	200.2[b]
TWA	35,700	27,384	−23.3
United	52,000	47,900	−7.9
USAir	8,745	12,524	43.2

[a]Six years: 7/1/78 through 6/30/84.
[b]Mainly due to the merger and acquisition.
Sources: 10-K's and *Annual Reports* filed with the SEC.

dropped down to 41,000 employees in 1982, and only recently brought the level up to 47,900 people. Still, since S/W/B costs at United increased by 44.5% (Table 15.3), with employment down from 52,000 in 1978 to 47,900 in 1984, retained workers received better compensation.

S/W/B costs per employee

With the exception of Continental, which cut average S/W/B costs per worker by 14.9%, average employee costs increased a minimum of 46.5% during the 1978 to 1984 period (Table 15.6). Significant increases of 102.5%, 80.9%, and 78.8% were recorded respectively at Northwest, Delta, and USAir. Table 15.6 also shows TWA, USAir, and Delta as the highest paying airlines in 1984, with average S/W/B costs per worker at $47,194, $46,677, and $45,144, respectively. Clearly, Delta's high compensation per worker and generous pay and fringe benefit boosts contributed substantially to explain why the airline ranked first in S/W/B costs as a percentage of total operating expenses in 1984 (Table 15.2). It is not quite so easy to explain the Northwest figures. Part of the 102.5% growth in S/W/B costs per worker resulted from a 109-day strike in 1978 that significantly lessened total S/W/B costs (Table 15.3) and 1978 compensation per worker (Table 15.6). The number of employees was not reduced for statistical purposes, but strikers lost pay. More relevant is the finding that in 1982 Northwest had the lowest S/W/B costs per worker of $34,826. Unfortunately, this knowledge plus the 1984 figure of $42,121 that appears in Table 15.6 (a 20.9% increase) leads to the suspicion that Northwest has been giving above-average compensation boosts lately. Adding relevance to this observation is the fact that American and Delta increased average S/W/B compensation in the 1982–1984 period by 6.2% while United actually reduced average

TABLE 15.6. Yearly salaries/wages/benefits per employee and trends

Airline	1978	1984	Percentage Change
American	$28,424	$44,187	55.5%
Continental[a]	26,824	22,822	−14.9
Delta[b]	24,950	45,144	80.9
Eastern	26,962	40,098	48.7
Northwest[c]	20,805	42,121	102.5
Pan American World[a]	28,959	42,997	48.5
Republic[a]	25,836	37,857	46.5
TWA	28,258	47,194	67.0
United	27,773	43,561	56.8
USAir	26,110	46,677	78.8

[a]With airlines that merged or acquired other carriers, 1978 figures reflect the leading predecessor airline, e.g., North Central in 1978 versus Republic in 1984.

[b]Six years: 7/1/78 through 6/30/84.

[c]1978 figures reflect a long 1978 strike that reduced S/W/B.

Sources: 10-K's and *Annual Reports* filed with the SEC.

payments by 3.4%. In fact, most airlines from 1982 to 1984 implemented measures to try to hold the line on employee cost increases.

S/W/B Findings.   The discussion so far can be summarized as follows:
(1) S/W/B costs usually represent the largest airline operating expense; this
was true in 1978 as well as in 1984. (2) S/W/B costs as a percentage of total
operating expenses have declined primarily due to faster rising fuel costs. (3)
Aggregate dollar S/W/B payments escalated at most airlines, and in some cases,
by large amounts. (4) Employment trends have been mixed, reflecting some
growth and some shrinkage. (5) Airline employees are usually well compensated. (6) Average S/W/B costs per worker for the most part increased quite
substantially in the post-deregulation period; however, many airlines found
ways to slow employee cost rises from 1982 to 1984.

Causes of S/W/B Trends

prosperity and
inflation arguments

Prosperity and inflation are two key reasons for labor cost increases in the
1978–1984 period. When airlines are profitable, labor expects improvements
in pay and benefits. Even when airlines are struggling financially, employees
demand pay raises to keep pace with inflation and to maintain and improve
their standards of living. Management is sympathetic to this line of reasoning;
managers have the same personal goals.

fear of strike
consequences

As a general rule, airlines have attempted to avoid strikes. They feared a
loss of traffic and revenues and understood the known difficulties of returning to normal in a post-strike period.

regulation

Regulation is another factor explaining escalating labor costs. In the days
of service competition, when all airlines in a particular market charged the
same coach fares and there was no price competition, there was not much
pressure to control S/W/B costs. If labor received more money, an airline asked
the CAB for fare increases. When this increase was approved, as was normally
the case, other carriers raised their prices to the new fare levels as well. The
process made it easier for management to grant labor concessions than remain firm and endure strikes. Thus management often acquiesced too quickly.

entry delays

Entry was closed to new low-cost airlines before 1978. Right after deregulation, not much changed either. Therefore, in 1978, record profits were
earned and shared with workers through new multi-year contracts. Not until
the established carriers felt the full force of the recession and price competition during the 1979 through 1981 period did they sense the urgency to
control labor costs.

Drastic Labor Measures

staffing cuts,
two-tier pay
systems,
and pay cuts

As a result, with the start of the 1980s, management began implementing a
number of drastic labor measures. Significant staffing cuts were made. For
example, nearly 14,000 jobs at United and 10,000 positions at both TWA and
Pan American were eliminated. Secondly, in unprecedented moves, every airline except United and USAir succeeded in reducing salaries and benefits of

at least some workers by early 1984. Furthermore, many asked for and received union agreement to the establishment of two-tier pay structures. American, for instance, started paying certain categories of new union workers between 30% and 50% less than what senior wage earners received for similar work. In a more extreme move, Continental told its workers to accept 50% pay cuts and work rule changes, or they would be replaced. In another case, Eastern's management warned its employees to accept one-year pay cuts of from 15% to 22% in 1984 in exchange for company stock or run the risk of the firm's collapse. Eastern's unions accepted the plan and in turn received company stock, making employees the owners of 25% of the airline.

motivation for labor changes By 1983 the message became clear to most airline management teams that labor costs had to be trimmed and labor productivity improved. Low fares were taking their toll on income and retained earnings, and the time had come to start taking unpopular but necessary corrective measures. Labor also began to understand the urgency of the situation, thus making concessions to help airline profits and protect jobs. Still, in many cases labor blamed poor management decisions for the predicaments that necessitated such drastic labor penalties.

Case Study: Delta

Much can be learned from a brief review of corporate labor philosophies at Delta and Northwest, the two most profitable U.S. airlines. Delta has been cited in this chapter for its high and rising labor costs. As previously noted, Delta employees are well paid; furthermore, their jobs have been secure, for management has never deviated from its policy of not laying off permanent employees. Without question, maintaining that policy in the recession of the early 1980s was centrally responsible for Delta's first losses in its history. The question now is whether Delta's employees will return the favor. If the past record is a realistic predictor, they will, for Delta's employees have great respect for their airline's owners and managers. For example, as a pilot nearing retirement, Captain Joseph H. Moss had the full-page announcement in Fig. 15.1 published at personal expense in the September 13, 1982, edition of the *Atlanta Constitution.* In the early 1980s, for another example, Delta employees paid for and gave the corporation a new Boeing 767 airplane in gratitude for what Delta had done for them. The aircraft was appropriately named "The Spirit of Delta" (see Fig. 15.2).

Case Study: Northwest

efficiency first Northwest followed a much different strategy than Delta, but it also proved to be a wise choice. Northwest management has had a reputation for taking strikes and fighting hard for reasonable labor contracts. Its thesis has been that the best security employees can have is to work for a lean, efficient, profitable company; a firm in prosperous, as well as lean, times must consistently strive for cost efficiency. In previous years, management endured the harsh words of its employees and the ridicule of its competitors but persisted

FIGURE 15.1.
"A Personal Message of Thanks," from Captain Joseph H. Moss.

A Personal Message of Thanks for Some Very Fine People

In February 1946 I made my first flight as a new co-pilot with Delta Air Lines. Our company operated only one type of airplane at that time. It could carry a maximum of 21 passengers at a speed of 160 miles per hour.

Tomorrow, I will make my last flight as a Delta pilot. This time it will be as Captain of a large jetliner that transports more than 300 passengers at speeds of 600 miles per hour. This airplane can take off at weights of five hundred thousand pounds and fly non-stop to cities in Europe and the Caribbean. All of this would have been incomprehensible in 1946.

During the years between these two flights it has been my privilege to work with the finest group of human beings that God ever created. Delta doesn't have just a large number or even a high percentage of good employees. The fact is, they are all exceptional people. This unusual circumstance is due to a rare spirit shared by all personnel and can be traced directly to the founder of the company.

It has been my good fortune to work in an industry that has grown from the first day of my career to the last. Examined over a period of years, this growth has been truly phenomenal. Recently, there has been a slowing of this historic pattern as the industry adjusts to the continuing uncertainties of deregulation. If there is any one overriding observation I take into retirement, it is that our industry has been through 37 consecutive years of some type of uncertainty. But the discipline of deregulation will surely produce a more efficient, more responsive, and eventually more profitable group of companies. The real beneficiaries will be the traveling public.

It has also been my good fortune to work for an organization that has been exceedingly well managed. This, too, can be traced to the founder of our company, a man of rare vision, who never, for a single instant, lost sight of the need to be financially strong. Were he alive today, Mr. Woolman would be proud of Delta's present management. While others in our industry have overreacted and underreacted to recent conditions, our company has expanded steadily into new areas and new services.

I thank the workers, management, and share-owners of McDonnell-Douglas, General Dynamics, and Lockheed Corporation. Each of the aircraft manufactured by these companies represented an advancement over those that preceded it. These airplanes permitted large gains in productivity while offering improvements in safety and comfort.

Today, it is easy to forget the high incidence of air sickness a few years ago or how uncomfortably cold or hot those airplanes sometimes were. The high percentage of schedule completions today would have been inconceivable at the outset of my career. At that time every flight required a ceiling of at least 400 feet and a visibility of one mile in order to land. The airplane I fly tomorrow will make automatic landings with zero ceiling and visibility of only 600 feet. Tomorrow's airplane will be even better.

I also thank the design engineers, production workers, managers, and shareholders of United Technologies, General Electric, and Rolls Royce Corporation. Aside from the automobile, no single invention of man has done as much to change the traveling habits of people throughout the world as that of the jet aircraft engine. Each of the engines on the Lockheed Tri Star that I will fly tomorrow is 40 times more powerful and 100 times more reliable than those on that first DC-3. Still greater technological advancement is a certainty.

I thank the maintenance, engineering, and mechanical personnel of Delta. Their precise work made my job a lot easier. Besides the obvious consideration of safety, these employees helped keep mechanical delays, cancellations, and reroutes to a minimum.

I thank the many air traffic controllers who have assisted my flights over the years. Like airline employees, these professionals work day and night in good weather and bad. It is not always easy to control traffic on the ground and in the air at terminals like La Guardia, Hartsfield, and O'Hare, but the quality of traffic control has constantly improved.

I thank the many flight attendants with whom I have worked. Their conscientious efforts to coordinate the requirements of cabin and cockpit have worked to the betterment of everybody. The flight attendant's job is not an easy one as they serve large numbers of passengers in the high speed airplanes of today. Only at this late date in my career will I admit that their job is as important as that of the pilots.

My thanks also to the many others in Delta including dispatchers, crew schedulers, meteorologists, and cabin service employees, along with those in operations, the ticket counters, and reservations.

I thank Captain Dolson, Chief Pilot, later President and Board Chairman of Delta for hiring me at a time when many other ex-military pilots were looking for the same job. I came to work with little in the way of immediately useful equipment but with a strong desire to earn a living as a commercial airline pilot. I still can't think of a better profession.

Above all, a special gratitude to the many passengers who made it all possible.

Joseph H. Moss

Source: Atlanta Constitution, 13 September 1982, pg. 12–A. Reprinted with permission of the author.

FIGURE 15.2.
The Spirit of Delta, a Boeing 767 purchased by Delta Air Lines' employees and given to their employer. (Photo provided by Delta Air Lines; reprinted with permission)

with its strategy, and it paid off. While other carriers have been struggling and taking drastic labor measures in the 1980s, Northwest has grown, maintained employment for practically all its employees, and continued to grant compensation increases. Northwest dared to make unpopular decisions but appears now to have had great foresight. However, rising S/W/B costs since 1982 would indicate a change in Northwest's management philosophy and a weakening of its comparative cost advantage.

FLEET AND FUEL STRATEGIES AND ISSUES

Airlines recently have been under pressure to modernize their aircraft fleets. Motivating factors include age (inevitably, maintenance costs will become excessive and reliability less certain), technological advancements presenting opportunities for improved cost efficiencies and productivity gains, and marketing and operating needs, for example, corporate strategies might require smaller planes than a carrier presently has to serve smaller airports. In the past, an airline also felt compelled to fly the latest models so passengers would not opt for carriers that had them. Still, in the present era, the overriding justification for aircraft purchases has been the urgency attached to increasing fuel efficiency.

Fleet Characteristics

fleet sizes and changes

Table 15.7 shows fleet sizes and changes, fleet mixes, and brief comments on carrier fleet actions. As noted, most fleets have increased in size, growing either as the result of mergers or acquisitions (combinations) or to accommodate expansion efforts. Spectacular growth in fleet size, such as the 135.3% gain for Republic and the 63.2% increase for Continental is linked to combinations. Growth at Delta, Eastern, USAir, and Northwest has been due to expansion—specifically, the enlarging of the route system and increased flight schedules. In contrast, some fleets were reduced. TWA, for example, flew 94 fewer aircraft in 1984 than in 1978.

fleet mixes

According to Table 15.7, United has one of the more balanced fleets of large, medium, and small aircraft (21.3%, 47.7%, and 31.0%, respectively), although most carriers tend to have a broad variety of aircraft in terms of seating capacity. Pan American and Northwest in 1984 were the most large-aircraft oriented, which is not surprising considering their heavy involvement in long-haul international operations. At the other extreme are Republic and USAir, whose fleets were primarily comprised of small aircraft.

Fleet Strategies

reconfiguration

As indicated in the "Comments" section of Table 15.7, most airlines have attacked fleet needs with the implementation of two strategies: reconfiguring aircraft and acquiring new ones. Reconfiguration refers to an action whereby airlines remove seats from existing aircraft and replace them with an increased number of seats to boost available seat-miles. By using lighter weight, more compact seat designs, carriers have expanded systemwide capacity by as much as 20% without adding aircraft to their fleets. To gain a perspective on how much capital this strategy has saved airlines, see the prices of aircraft in Table 15.8. Another term for reconfiguration is high-density seating.

fuel-efficient aircraft

Initially, two aggressive airlines ordering large numbers of new aircraft were Delta and Eastern. Delta purchased B-767s (Fig. 15.2) and B-757s. Eastern initially ordered B-757s. Both types of aircraft are primarily designed to produce significantly higher fuel efficiency than the aircraft they replace. Both the B-767 and B-757 are also two-engine, two-person cockpit crew aircraft. The advantage of the latter is labor savings over the three-person cockpit crews on replaced vehicles. More specifics on the capabilities of these aircraft are provided in Table 15.8. As noted in Table 15.7, most airlines have followed Delta and Eastern's lead and are acquiring more fuel-efficient aircraft. Specifications on other aircraft models are also found in Table 15.8.

standardization

Fleet strategies actually encompass far more variables than mentioned so far. One consideration is the trade-off between a broad mix of various aircraft models and standardization. In other words, there are advantages to having just the right aircraft for just the right traffic demand in terms of matching the number of seats with the number of passengers, but there are also costs. With greater fleet diversity, a carrier faces increased spare-parts inventory

TABLE 15.7. Fleet characteristics of the 10 largest combination airlines

Airline	Number of Aircraft			Estimate of 1984 Distribution of Aircraft by Seating Capacity (Plane Size) (%)[a]			Comments
	1978	1984	Percentage Change	Large[b]	Medium[b]	Small[b]	
American	248[c]	260	4.8%	20.4%	64.6%	15.0%	Reconfigured aircraft; has been adding many new medium-sized airplanes; ordered 67 MD-80s.
Continental	68	111	63.2	11.7	46.0	42.3	Reconfigured aircraft; fleet grew because of the acquisition; has made limited fleet changes; ordered B-737-300s.
Delta	200	229	14.5	16.6	59.0	24.4	Reconfigured aircraft and has been making aggressive move to acquire fuel-efficient medium and small aircraft; has youngest fleet.
Eastern	250[c]	285	14.0	20.7	40.4	38.9	Reconfigured aircraft; has been obtaining many new medium capacity planes; is buying fuel-efficient planes.
Northwest	106	120	13.2	45.0	47.5	7.5	Reconfigured aircraft; has ordered large- and medium-sized planes.
Pan American	87	116	33.3	53.4	32.8	13.8	Reconfigured aircraft; has been acquiring some medium and large aircraft; fleet grew primarily because of the National acquisition.

continued

TABLE 15.7. *Continued*

Airline	Number of Aircraft			Estimate of 1984 Distribution of Aircraft by Seating Capacity (Plane Size) (%)[a]			Comments
	1978	1984	Percentage Change	Large[b]	Medium[b]	Small[b]	
Republic	68	160	135.3	0	16.3	83.7	Added replacement aircraft; added medium-sized aircraft; added a few DC-9-80 fuel-efficient aircraft; grew primarily from the merger and acquisition.
TWA	253[c]	159	−37.2	32.7	41.5	25.8	Reconfigured aircraft; has been reducing fleet size; has been replacing some large- and medium-sized aircraft; has oldest fleet; has been making some fuel-efficient plane purchases.
United	352	319	−9.4	21.3	47.7	31.0	Reconfigured aircraft; ordered 6 B-747s and 110 B-737s; mainly obtaining small aircraft.
USAir	93	133	43.0	0	10.5	89.5	Reconfigured aircraft; added medium-sized planes and some small planes; has been buying B-737-300s.

[a]Includes all-cargo aircraft of comparable size.

[b]"Large" includes aircraft of 240 or more seats; "medium" includes 140 to 239 seat aircraft, "small" means less than 140 seats.

[c]Reflects fleet at 12/31/77.

Sources: Derived from *10-K's* and *Annual Reports* filed with the SEC.

TABLE 15.8. Various statistics on new jet aircraft

Model	Manufacturer	Seats	Range (Miles)	Average Price[a]
B-747	Boeing	300–500	up to 7000	$100,000,000[b]
DC-10-10	McDonnell Douglas	250–380	6300	45,465,000[c]
L-1011-100	Lockheed	250–400	4000	41,607,000[d]
A-300B	Airbus	251–345	N/A	34,137,000[d]
B-767-300	Boeing	255	6000	60,000,000[e]
B-767-200	Boeing	210	5700	38,477,000[f]
B-757-200	Boeing	186–220	2800	30,834,000[f]
B-727-200	Boeing	145	2240	12,251,000[f,g]
B-737-300	Boeing	150	N/A	30,000,000[h]
B-737-200	Boeing	115	2100	14,840,000[f]
DC-9-80	McDonnell Douglas	167	3000	23,293,000[d]

[a]Prices reflect contract terms.

[b]July 1984.

[c]Third quarter 1982.

[d]Fourth quarter 1982.

[e]February 1985.

[f]First quarter 1983.

[g]Reflects low price at end of production run. Price was $20.4 million in 2nd quarter 1982.

[h]September 1984.

Sources:

1. Office of Economic Analysis, U.S. Civil Aeronautics Board, *Number and Average Price of New Jet Aircraft Purchased and Delivered During the Four Quarters Ended March 1983* (Washington, D.C.: CAB, 9 August 1983).
2. "Specifications," *Aviation Week and Space Technology*, 8 March 1982, pp. 118–119.
3. William M. Carley and Peter Truell, "Boeing to Sell $1 Billion of 747s to Saudi Airline," *Wall Street Journal*, 18 July 1984, p. 3.
4. "Boeing Co. Unit Gets Order From Delta Air for 4 More 767-300s," *Wall Street Journal*, 28 February 1985, p. 6.
5. "USAir Orders 10 Boeing Jets for $300 Million," *Wall Street Journal*, 4 September 1984, p. 8.

costs, higher maintenance expenses, and pilot utilization problems. Normally, since pilots are certified for only one aircraft, management can find itself short of crews for some flights and overstaffed for others.

increasing block hours

Another way to increase fleet productivity is to fly each aircraft more hours per day. Rarely, though, are carriers able to average 10 hours of block time per day. *Block time* is the period from the moment a plane's *blocks*—that is, wedges placed around the wheels to prevent rolling—are pulled and the plane is ready to leave the terminal gate until the blocks are placed around the wheels at destination. The problem for scheduled combination airlines is that passengers resist flying at night. Although carriers try to increase block time, most fleets average close to 7.5 hours of block time per day.

disposal of old aircraft

A third issue is the disposal of old aircraft. In recent years, many have been sold either directly or through aircraft brokers—namely, intermediaries who work between sellers and buyers—to foreign airlines, emerging all-cargo carriers like Emery or Federal Express, and new passenger airlines. Ironically, it is the latter who have then used these planes in competition against the majors from whom they had acquired the aircraft.

ownership
versus leasing

It also is important to understand how new aircraft are acquired. Northwest in 1984 owned its entire fleet. By comparison, 118 of American's 260 aircraft were leased. In most cases, the costs of new aircraft (as shown in Table 15.8) and the numbers needed force carriers to sign long-term capital leases—basically, a long-term debt arrangement—to obtain portions of their fleets.

Fuel Strategies

ASMs/gallon

Airline Fuel Productivity Statistics.   Despite great differences in fleet strategies (see Table 15.7), every airline improved its fuel productivity since 1978, as shown in Table 15.9. The biggest surprise is in who made the greatest gains in available seat-miles (ASMs) per gallon. Available seat-miles are the products of seats multiplied by the miles they are flown. The leader, with a 39.11% productivity improvement was Trans World, a carrier that has made few new airplane purchases. Other airlines making significant gains were USAir (35.17%) and Delta (34.93%). In 1984, the leaders in ASMs per gallon were Trans World (49.69 ASMs/gal.), United (49.32 ASMs/gal.), and Delta (46.05 ASMs/gal.). Of the three carriers, only Delta had substantially added new fuel-efficient aircraft to its fleet by 1984. Only USAir failed to achieve 40 ASMs/gal. for its fleet in 1984.

RPMs/gallon

The problem with ASMs/gallon is that seats are not necessarily occupied. Therefore a more appropriate measure is revenue passenger-miles per gallon, for it reflects used available seat-miles. *Revenue passenger-miles* are the products of the number of paying passengers multiplied by the miles they fly, whereas available seat-miles reflect the product of seats and miles. Table 15.10

TABLE 15.9. Fuel productivity as measured by available seat miles/gallon

Airline	ASMs/Gal.		Percentage Change
	1978	1984	
American	35.36	45.91	29.84%
Continental	38.26	45.49	18.90
Delta[a]	34.13	46.05	34.93
Eastern	35.79	42.70	19.31
Northwest	35.64	41.41	16.19
Pan American	37.61	45.65	21.38
Republic	31.90[b]	40.19	25.99
Trans World	35.72	49.69	39.11
United	39.24	49.32	25.69
USAir	29.06	39.28	35.17

[a]Six years: 7/1/78 through 6/30/84.
[b]North Central.

Sources: Derived from *10-K's* and *Annual Reports* filed with the SEC.

TABLE 15.10. Fuel productivity as measured by revenue passenger-miles/gallon

Airline	RPMs/Gal.		Percentage Change
	1978	1984	
American	22.53	28.72	27.5%
Continental	22.71	28.53	25.6
Delta[a]	20.23	23.60	16.7
Eastern	23.08	24.31	5.3
Northwest	17.49	25.07	43.3[b]
Pan American	23.01	29.32	27.4
Republic	18.15[c]	20.18	11.2
TWA	22.58	30.90	36.8
United	25.16	29.83	18.6
USAir	17.76	23.00	29.5

[a]Six years: 7/1/78 through 6/30/84.
[b]In part strike related, as 1978 RPMs were abnormally low.
[c]North Central.

Sources: Derived from *10-Ks* and *Annual Reports* filed with the SEC.

indicates that Northwest experienced the most improvement, with a 43.3% jump in RPMs/gallon between 1978 and 1984. The second and third best gains were made by TWA (36.8%) and USAir (29.5%). The most fuel-efficient airlines in 1984, nevertheless, were TWA (30.90 RPMs/gal.), United (29.83 RPMs/gal.), and Pan American (29.32 RMPs/gal). Two of the more confusing figures are the low 1984 RPMs/gallon for Delta (23.60) and USAir (23.00). Obviously, other variables besides more fuel-efficient aircraft impact on RPMs/gallon.

Fuel Savings Strategies. Airlines have saved fuel by implementing conservation and productivity measures. Conservation tactics include using flight simulators to train pilots as opposed to the actual flying of airplanes; reducing cruising speeds; following more direct routings; taking better advantage of jet stream tail winds; using auxiliary power units rather than running jet engines to operate air conditioning and lights when aircraft are on the ground; smoothing the airframe to reduce aerodynamic drag; and reducing gross vehicle weight by such measures as carrying less fuel on board, replacing heavy seats with those made from lighter weight materials, and even stripping paint off the fuselage of the aircraft. These and other measures reduce fuel requirements.

conservation tactics

The goal of productivity tactics is to increase ASMs and RPMs per gallon of fuel consumed. High-density seating probably produced the greatest gains in ASMs per gallon. Measures that also helped improve ASM and RPM fuel productivity were as follows: (1) grounding the most fuel-inefficient planes; (2) substituting more fuel-efficient aircraft in their place; (3) reducing frequent flights of small aircraft and replacing them with fewer flights by wide-bodied

productivity tactics

aircraft, which are airplanes capable of accommodating seven or more seats side-by-side; (4) better matching of the right size aircraft, in terms of seats and flight range, to the markets; and (5) increasing aircraft utilization. Likewise, better marketing and operations were instrumental in increasing RPMs and load factors, that is, the percentage of ASMs filled with RPMs. The right operating decisions position aircraft in markets where the correct prices or services create high levels of demand.

Capacity and Traffic Trends.   Table 15.11 shows ASM and RPM

ASM changes

changes for the airlines from 1978 to 1984. Although several airlines that did not participate in mergers or acquisitions added capacity (ASMs) in significant ways (e.g., Northwest, USAir, and Delta), the leading carrier in ASMs/gallon in 1984—TWA (see Table 15.9)—added very little capacity (only a 6.7% growth in ASMs). This happened, however, despite a fleet reduction of 94 aircraft (Table 15.7).

The RPM data of Table 15.11 indicate that, with the exception of North-

RPM changes

west, Continental, and Pan American, each other airline increased RPMs by less than it increased ASMs. In general, this situation reflects one problem with ordering and receiving new aircraft. The timeframes are such that traffic often lags increased ASMs. Trends also reflect dramatic route expansion activities. Upon entering new markets, an airline usually endures a period of time when RPMs trail ASMs by wide margins, which is why Northwest's record is so unusual. During the 1978–1984 period, Northwest raised ASMs 128.4% and RPMs by 181.7%. These results are not simply strike-related. Strike bias can be minimized by examining trends from 1977, a normal year, through 1984. During that period, Northwest's ASMs grew by 42.2% from 22.968 billion to 32.664 billion, but RPMs jumped 78.1% from 11.100 billion to 19.772 billion. Consequently, from 1977 to 1984, RMP growth increased at a pace that was

TABLE 15.11. Changes in ASMs and RPMs (1978–1984)

Airline	Percentage Change in ASMs	Percentage Change in RPMs
American	29.0%	26.6%
Continental	19.8	26.6
Delta[a]	45.0	25.3
Eastern	31.8	16.4
Northwest	128.4	181.7
Pan American	26.9	33.3
Republic	405.7	346.4
TWA	6.7	4.9
United	19.4	12.7
USAir	107.5	98.8

[a]Six years: 7/1/78 through 6/30/84.

Sources: Derived from *10-K's* and *Annual Reports* filed with the SEC.

85% faster than the growth in ASMs.[1] This growth is unmistakable proof that Northwest effectively carried out operating and marketing strategies. Table 15.12 verifies this finding by showing that from 1978–1984, Northwest's load factor increased 23.22%, the best increase for any airline. As the Table notes, 7 of 10 carriers endured reduced load factors in this period.

load factors

Because of above-average lead factors (Table 15.12), TWA, United, and Pan American had the most fuel-efficient fleets in 1984, while low load factors are primarily responsible for low RPMs/gallon at Eastern, Delta, and Republic (Table 15.10). TWA, United, and Pan American limited ASM growth and aggressively attempted to fill available seats. As previously noted, Delta was assertively expanding its system, adding 45.0% to its ASMs from 1978–1984. It only increased RPMs by 25.3% in the period, however, causing a 13.65% reduction in its load factor.

fuel costs per ASM

Another airline objective is to pay the lowest possible price for fuel supplies. Airline success in accomplishing this goal can be measured by examining fuel costs per ASM or per RPM, as shown in Table 15.13. In 1984, TWA was the most efficient carrier, having paid an average of 1.75¢ (in fuel costs) per ASM. Behind it in rank order were United (1.77¢/ASM) and Delta (1.84¢/ASM). Data not shown in the table provide evidence that United's success was primarily derived from high ASMs/gallon (Table 15.9), but not from particularly advantageous fuel prices per gallon.

High percentage increases in cents/ASM among all airlines reflect the surge in fuel prices per gallon during the period; however, TWA, USAir, and American appear to have gained ground over the other carriers, since their costs increased the least (56.3%, 58.8%, and 64.6%, respectively). Not so fortunate were Continental (86.1%), Northwest (89.3%), and Eastern (101.0%). In 1984,

TABLE 15.12. Load factors and trends (Scheduled service)

Airline	1978	1984	Percentage Change
American	63.7%	62.6%	−1.72%
Continental	59.4[a]	62.7	5.56
Delta[b]	59.3	51.2	−13.65
Eastern	64.5	56.9	−11.78
Northwest	49.1	60.5	23.22
Pan American	61.2	64.2	4.90
Republic	56.9[c]	50.2	−11.78
TWA	63.2	62.2	−1.58
United	64.1	60.4	−5.77
USAir	61.1	58.6	−4.09

[a]Continental before acquisition by Texas International.
[b]Six years: 7/1/78 through 6/30/84.
[c]North Central.
Sources: Derived from *10-K's* and *Annual Reports* filed with the SEC.

TABLE 15.13. Fuel costs per ASM and RPM and trends					
	Cents per ASM		Percentage Change	Cents per RPM		Percentage Change
Airline	1978	1984		1978	1984	
American	1.13¢	1.86¢	64.6%	1.78¢	2.97¢	66.9%
Continental	1.01	1.88	86.1	1.71	2.99	74.9
Delta[a]	1.09	1.84	68.8	1.84	3.59	95.1
Eastern	0.97	1.95	101.0	1.50	3.42	128.0
Northwest	1.12	2.12	89.3	2.27	3.50	54.2
Pan Am	1.16	2.00	72.4	1.89	3.11	64.6
Republic	1.27[b]	2.10	65.4	2.23[b]	4.18	87.4
TWA	1.12	1.75	56.3	1.77	2.82	59.3
United	1.00	1.77	77.0	1.56	2.93	87.8
USAir	1.36	2.16	58.8	2.23	3.69	65.5

[a]Six years: 7/1/78 through 6/30/84.
[b]North Central.

Sources: Derived from *10-K's* and *Annual Reports* as filed with the SEC.

USAir had the highest cost at 2.16¢ per ASM, which correlates to its being the least fuel-efficient carrier in ASMs/gallon (Table 15.9).

fuel costs per RPM   In terms of 1984 fuel costs/RPM, TWA was again the low-cost leader, with a 2.82¢/RPM expense. Next were United at 2.93¢/RPM and American (2.97¢/RPM). TWA's lead is a product of fuel efficiency as measured in RPMs/gallon (see Table 15.10). TWA gained ground on United by combining improved fuel prices and a more favorable increase in RPMs/gallon (Table 15.10). Rapidly rising RPMs relative to increasing ASMs account for Northwest's achieving the lowest escalation in fuel costs per RPM (54.2%). Not so fortunate were Delta and Eastern, which experienced the highest increases in fuel costs per RPM at 95.1% and 128.0%, respectively. Load factor declines were primarily responsible. The two airlines with the highest fuel costs per RPM in 1984, however, were Republic (4.18¢/RPM) and USAir (3.69¢/RPM).

analysis limitations   ASMs and RPMs should not be used as the sole productivity and cost measures. They presume that all the carrier's costs and all the fuel consumed are linked only to scheduled revenue passengers, which is not true for any of the airlines studied. Each carrier has other revenue sources such as cargo, mail, and charter sales. Actually, scheduled passengers acounted for between 81% and 93% of the revenues of these 10 airlines. This percentage range implies that the data overstate by a small amount fuel costs/ASM and costs/RPM. However, data would be far more distorted and less informative if available ton-miles and revenue ton-miles had been used, because it is confusing to describe passengers in ton-miles. In reality, little relative bias is introduced by the use of ASMs and RPMs since the overwhelming business of the studied airlines is passenger service.

TABLE 15.14. Employee and fuel costs as percentages of total operating costs (Calendar years)

Airline	1978 Employee and Fuel Costs (%)	1984 Employee Costs (%)	1984 Fuel Costs (%)	1984 Employee and Fuel Costs (%)
Continental	63.15%	21.18%	30.31%	51.49%
Northwest	52.82	27.23	29.47	56.70
Pan American	57.41	32.11	24.82	56.93
TWA	60.01	36.10	22.26	58.36
American	61.07	36.85	22.99	59.84
Republic	59.95	35.03	24.83	59.86
Eastern	60.44	36.89	24.04	60.93
United	64.29	36.90	24.19	61.09
USAir	60.98	40.66	21.62	62.28
Delta[a]	65.77	41.65	23.15	64.80

[a]Years ended 6/30/78 and 6/30/84.

Sources: Derived from *10-K's* and *Annual Reports* filed with the SEC.

relevance of fuel cost percentages

Table 15.4 can be enhanced by the data in Table 15.14 which ranks the 10 airlines in terms of combined employee and fuel costs as a percentage of total operating costs. First, it shows the relative importance of employee and fuel costs to the respective carriers in 1984. This figure is used in pinpointing Delta and USAir as the carriers most needing to address these two leading cost areas. Secondly, it compares 1984 versus 1978 totals to establish how total percentages for employee and fuel costs have changed for each carrier. Nevertheless, totals are relative statistics. For example, Delta had the highest total employee and fuel percentage in 1984 (64.80%), but it also had the lowest percentage expense level for all other operating costs (see Table 15.1). Each airline's total operating costs equal 100%. Thus Table 15.14 merely notes which airlines need to address S/W/B and fuel costs the most.

MARKETING AND OPERATING STRATEGIES AND ISSUES

Successful airlines depend not only on labor, fleet, and fuel strategies but also on closely coordinated operating and marketing strategies. Since the airline business sells services produced by the operations department, which engages in flying and maintaining aircraft, and promoted by marketing people, who determine services and prices and solicit traffic, if either group pursues parochial objectives, carrier profits can be negatively affected.

Therefore this section focuses on the marketing-operating interface. It will examine such topics as the geographic derivation of revenues, the revenue splits between scheduled passengers and other sources of sales dollars, changing airport and route strategies, operating tactics, and other marketing developments. Its objective is to position the airlines as they struggle for market identities, market shares, and financial prosperity.

Domestic and International Orientations

Pan Am

As shown in Table 15.15, most of the described carriers are fundamentally domestic operators. Pan Am is the exception, with 79.5% of its 1984 revenues ($2.688 billion of a total of $3.382 billion) derived from international operations. For the year ended 12/31/84, Pan Am was the second leading U.S. airline in sales in the Atlantic and Pacific markets, and the leader in the Latin–American market. Trans World was ranked first in Atlantic revenues. Northwest was the leader in Pacific revenues.

United

United was the leading domestic carrier, with 1984 sales of $5.946 billion. It was also the largest U.S. airline in total domestic and international revenues ($6.097 billion). Although United did little business outside North America in the past, this situation will change rather dramatically in 1986 because United received permission to acquire all of Pan Am's transpacific routes except U.S.-mainland to Hawaii service.[2] As indicated in Table 15.15, Republic and USAir were the only two airlines not engaged in international operations in 1984.

Revenue Split

scheduled passenger orientation

Another way to see an airline's marketing focus is by studying revenue split, that is, the division of sales dollars by commodity hauled. As mentioned in the prior section of this chapter, the primary business of each of these carriers is scheduled passenger operations. As Table 15.16 shows, about the only dif-

---

TABLE 15.15. Geographic distribution of air carrier operating revenues (Billions)

Airline	Total Operating Revenues	Total Domestic Revenues[a]	Atlantic Revenues	Latin American Revenues	Pacific Revenues	Total International Revenues
American	$5.087	$4.737	$0.086	$0.264	$0	$0.350
Continental	1.197	0.949	0	0.044	0.204	0.248
Delta	4.497	4.305	0.128	0.064	0	0.192
Eastern	4.364	3.969	0	0.395	0	0.395
Northwest	2.463	1.345	0.168	0	0.950	1.118
Pan American	3.382	0.694	1.479	0.420	0.789	2.688
Republic	1.547	1.547	0	0	0	0
Trans World	3.647	2.044	1.603	0	0	1.603
United	6.097	5.946	0	0	0.151	0.151
USAir	1.630	1.630	0	0	0	0

[a]Revenues earned from Canadian flights are included in domestic totals.

Source: U.S. Department of Transportation, Research and Special Programs Administration, *Air Carrier Financial Statistics December 1984* (Washington, D.C.: U.S. D.O.T., 1985).

TABLE 15.16. Revenue split by percentages of total operating revenues (Year ended 12/31/84)

Airline	Scheduled Passenger (%)	Cargo and Mail (%)	Charter and Other (%)
American	85.3%	6.1%	8.6%
Continental	89.3	——10.7ᵃ——	
Deltaᵇ	93.0	6.0	1.0
Eastern	91.4	4.8	3.8
Northwest	81.2	16.9	1.9
Pan American	87.4	8.2	4.4
Republic	91.5	5.0	3.5
Trans World	85.0	5.8	9.2
United	87.0	5.8	7.2
USAir	93.3	3.1	3.6

ᵃCombines cargo, mail, charter, and other.
ᵇYear ended 6/30/84.
Sources: Derived from *10-K's* and *Annual Reports* filed with the SEC.

ference between airlines is the degree of passenger emphasis. At the high end, USAir and Delta derived 93.3% and 93.0% of their sales dollars from scheduled passenger traffic. At the other end, Northwest and Pan American generated sizeable cargo and mail revenues. In addition, TWA can be singled out for the highest percentage of "charter and other" sales.

pros and cons of sales diversification

Sales diversification has advantages and disadvantages. Cargo and mail frequently contribute high marginal profits. When passenger fares are set to recover flight costs, cargo and mail can be carried at relatively low incremental costs. The logic is that the flight is going anyway, so freight produces bonus revenues. Furthermore, charter traffic can help offset scheduled passenger traffic downturns. In the winter, for example, when scheduled travel to Europe diminishes, charter flights to the tropics can be flown.

From a negative perspective, diversification can interfere with scheduled passenger services, such as by delaying departures to load cargo. Overall, few airlines assign high priorities to the freight or charter sides of the business. In recent years due to shifts in marketing emphasis, most airlines have increased their scheduled passenger orientations. A leading example is Republic's increase in scheduled passenger sales from 83.1% of total sales in 1978 (when it was called *North Central*) to 91.5% in 1984.

Route Strategies

hub-and-spoke developments

The recent development of point and route strategies likewise presents learning opportunities. As might be expected, when deregulation provided airlines with the opportunity to add airports—points—to existing networks, every carrier did just that. They all sought to add to their systems large airports that they had not been serving and to fly longer haul routes for efficiency and traffic-generating purposes. Since 1978 there was also an accelerated rush to expand and develop hub-and-spoke operations. By 1983, each carrier had at least two operating hubs, and most had more. For instance, Delta added four hubs to complement its extensive Atlanta base of operations. By 1983 Pan Am claimed no less than 5 hubs and 4 gateways—U.S. airports serving international departures and arrivals. Thus the 1980s have become the decade of the hub-and-spoke operators.

point strategies

Beyond these commonalities, each of the study-group airlines followed different point strategies. American added the most points. In 1978, it served 49 cities, but by the end of 1984, it flew to 114 airports. Delta increased the number of cities served from 85 domestic points in 1978 to 94 domestic and 7 international cities in 1984. However, in the interval, Delta went through a massive restructuring process, culling out weak traffic-generating points and adding better opportunities. Other airlines, too, eliminated points after initial airport additions had been made. In 1978, North Central served 90 cities, but following the merger with Southern, the acquisition of Hughes Airwest, and other point additions, in 1980 Republic served nearly 200 points. By 1984, it had reduced the number of cities served to 100. Another illustration of dynamic point activity is the Continental case. Continental served 34 cities in 1978, 71 cities in 1982, 25 cities after the filing of Chapter 11 papers in 1983, and 44 cities in 1984.

hub-and-spoke specialists

Route strategies also differed between carriers. Continental, after its Chapter 11 filing, concentrated on a radial operation emanating from, and mostly returning to, its Denver and Houston hubs with relatively few routes between other points. Northwest placed importance on its Minneapolis/St. Paul hub to feed both its domestic and Pacific routes. Quite different was Republic, which initially offered a number of "bridge" routes. In other words, Republic added a number of point-to-point routes linking cities in the upper midwest to points in the south and bypassing the major hubs. Also, Republic added longer haul flights from its hubs to other large airports.

bridge routes

national networks

Overall, though, the carriers described in this chapter tried to build national networks by filling in the holes in their route systems and by establishing service to new regions. Illustrations are USAir's development of routes to the southwest from Pittsburgh, United's efforts to expand midwest–Florida service, and Delta's expansion to the Texas markets and the southwest. Each carrier had to make choices about which points to add or delete; which points to link together or to link to hubs; whether to concentrate on linking original network points, old-to-new points, or new-to-new airports; whether to substitute small planes for larger ones and vice versa; how to alter the schedules and frequency of flights in a market; and so forth. Often carriers experimented to test the market potential. In essence, because of deregulation, far more decisions on how to operate airlines and market services were left solely to management. As governmental controls diminished, the private sector responded, and the airline business changed.

Price Theory and Practice

product
differentiation

Before deregulation, scheduled passenger airlines competed almost exclusively on a service basis, trying to outdo one another by enticing consumers with plane decor, better meals, free drinks, baggage services, and so forth. This situation still exists; however, price competition has become a major market factor. Since deregulation, standard coach seats are being offered at different price levels in a particular market. The consumer can choose from low prices with limited services, often called "no-frills service," to exquisite services at relatively high prices, as well as everything in-between. Marketers would call this phenomenon product differentiation—in other words, different quality services at different price levels and aimed at selective market targets.

aggressive
unrestricted
discounters

Pricing Practices. The 10 airlines described in this chapter positioned themselves by 1984 between the extremes of no-frills and unheard-of-frills. All would be considered full-service airlines because they offered first class and coach service and in-flight passenger amenities, but some evident differences are also apparent. Only Continental became an aggressive discounter offering unrestricted coach discounts; tickets were sold on a one-way basis to anyone who wanted to buy one and with no purchase constraints. Thus businesspeople and other short-term travelers could advantageously use Continental's low prices. Motivating Continental was its desire to reposition itself as the nation's largest discount airline and to take advantage of its lower labor costs.

American

For the most part, the other carriers followed the strategy of matching the discount prices introduced by Continental and other new low-price competitors, but they did not initiate them. Of course, there are exceptions. American, for instance, started the Super-Saver program even before deregulation (see Chapter 14) and in 1985 launched its Ultimate Super Saver program, which offered discounts at up to 70% below standard coach prices.[3] However, the primary difference between pricing tactics by these airlines and Continental

restricted discounts

is the restrictiveness of the discounts. Restricted discounts usually mean purchasers must buy roundtrip tickets, the number of discount seats on a given flight is limited, tickets must be purchased in advance of departure dates, travel can occur only on certain days of the week, the traveler must stay at destination a minimum number of days, such as through the weekend, and/or penalties must be paid, such as forfeiting 25% of a ticket's price, for cancellation of travel. Restricted discounts are intended to attract primary demand, while ensuring that present full-fare-paying customers do not buy discount seats, lowering airline yields.

yield erosion

The theory did not work particularly well in practice, since about 85% of the domestic riders in 1983 traveled on some type of discount fare. Delta, for example, watched the percentage of discount passengers surge from 27% in 1978 to more than 90% in the April–June 1983 quarter. This increase resulted in overall yield deterioration. For a company like Delta with 1984 sales of $4.5 billion, every time the average price per RPM drops 0.1¢, if there is no gain in traffic, there is approximately a $28 million loss in revenues. Subsequently, increasing yields became a central goal at most major airlines.

standard coach fares

Fare Changes.   Table 15.17 shows price changes in three particular airline markets. First, observe that the one-way standard coach fares rose in each of the three markets. In the long-haul Atlanta to San Francisco market, the standard coach fare increased 133.8% in only 7 years from $195 to $456. In the intermediate-haul market (Boston to Minneapolis), a 177.3% increase is discovered, as the fare changed from $119 to $330. Finally, the short-haul Charleston to Raleigh fare jumped by 256.6% from $53 to $189. Note particularly the 1985 yields and how they vary as distances increase. Short-haul fares can be high, as the 85.9¢ per RPM Charleston–Raleigh charge reveals. Lower long-haul fares reflect the application of the tapering rate principle. Rates are also affected by the degree of competition in a particular market. If a carrier is the only airline connecting point *A* and point *B,* there is no real pressure on the carrier to reduce prices. Where another carrier provides low-price competition, other airlines tend to match fare levels.

lowest discount fares

Discounts primarily reflect reductions from standard coach fares or introductory offers, such as a low price for the first 30 days of service in a market. The discount prices of $99 between Atlanta and San Francisco, $59 between Boston and Minneapolis, and $45 between Charleston and Raleigh offered substantial savings compared to standard coach prices. Low fares have

TABLE 15.17. Changing one-way airline fares[a]						
	11/1/78	12/20/85				
Market (Route Miles)	Standard Coach Fares	Lowest Standard Coach Fare	Percentage Price Change	Yield per Revenue Passenger– Mile	Lowest Discount Fare[b]	Yield per RPM
Atlanta to San Francisco (2139)	$195	$456	133.8%	21.3¢	$99.00	4.6¢
Boston to Minneapolis (1124)	$119	$330	177.3%	29.4¢	$59.00	5.2¢
Charleston, S.C., to Raleigh, N.C. (220)	$53	$189	256.6%	85.9¢	$45.00	20.5¢

[a]Selected to show one long-haul, one medium-haul, and one short-haul route.
[b]Part of special roundtrip fares available for travel during the December 25–27, 1984 period.
Source: Official Airline Guide: North American Edition (Oak Brook, Ill.: Reubin H. Donnelley Co., 1 November 1978) and travel agency information.

made air travel attractive to consumers. It is no wonder that air traffic grew to record levels in 1983 and 1984 (see Table 14.10).

price strategy Scheduled certificated airlines, because of rapidly rising costs, have tried to raise standard coach fares to improve revenues and profits. However, increased competition and discounting have made this goal rather elusive. In the second quarter of 1985, the average yield for U.S. scheduled airlines (all services) was 11.1¢.[4] This average was the lowest yield for the industry in two years, and the figure was 1.0¢/RPM lower than the 1984 average of 12.1¢.[5]

Changing Market Shares

Market shares are also changing, and not always in the direction that carriers desire. For instance, Table 15.11 showed that some airlines increased RPMs far more than did others between 1978 and 1984. Table 15.18 provides more comprehensive evidence of market adjustments in the deregulated environment. Although the 10 airlines in question came close to maintaining the 78.46% share of industry revenues, with a 1984 figure of 77.43%, only Delta, Northwest, Republic, and USAir increased their revenue-share percentages. Republic's figure, though, was biased by the merger and acquisition. Study-group carriers, on the contrary, lost a sizeable part of the RPM market, dropping collectively from a 1978 share of 94.11% of the RPMs to a 1984 total of 76.90%. Only Northwest, Republic, and USAir increased their market shares, but Republic's trend again must be discounted because of the merger and acquisition. Obviously, nongroup carriers have grabbed a portion of the market once collectively held by the 10 study-group airlines. In fact, the RPMs of smaller airlines have been increasing faster than the RPMs of the largest scheduled airlines.

future strategies Major airlines would like to regain market share, as well as experience growth, which to some extent explains the increase in route points—a process that should continue into the future. Recently, the airlines have been returning to small airport cities using newly acquired small aircraft or by acquiring small airlines or by signing interline argreements with commuter airlines. The objective is to capture a greater share of the passengers originating in small towns who are taking medium- to long-haul trips. Major airlines have discovered that small-town passengers are important elements in the total market. If a passenger from a small town starts on an air transportation trip on another carrier, the large certificated carrier has no guarantee it will ever see that passenger board one of its planes for the long-haul flight. Consequently, majors are changing operations to board the passenger at the origin point. Secondly, with most majors serving most large hubs, there will not be much interlining between the largest airlines or with the nationals who are also expanding their route networks. If an airline is not capable of delivering a passenger to the destination point, the likelihood is that a competitor can. The risk is that the first airline will lose the passenger. Again, this is a good reason for continued expansion of route networks. However, expansion requires money.

TABLE 15.18. Airline revenue passenger–miles and revenue market-share distributions (1978 and 1984)

| | Revenue Passenger–Miles | | | | Revenues | | | |
| | 1978 | | 1984 | | 1978 | | 1984 | |
Airline	(in millions)	Percentage share	(in millions)	Percentage share	(in millions)	Percentage share	(in millions)	Percentage share
United	41,436	20.11%	46,687	14.68%	$3,523	15.39%	$6,097	13.92%
American	29,407	14.27	36,705	11.54	2,736	11.95	5,087	11.62
Eastern	25,228	12.24	29,409	9.24	2,380	10.40	4,364	9.97
Delta	23,853	11.57	27,055	8.50	2,242	9.79	4,497	10.27
Pan American	23,661	11.48	28,406	8.93	2,173	9.49	3,382	7.72
Trans World	28,206	13.69	28,304	8.90	2,475	10.81	3,647	8.33
Northwest	7,220	3.50	20,131	6.33	794	3.47	2,463	5.62
Republic	1,925[a]	0.93	8,594	2.70	299[a]	1.31	1,547	3.53
USAir	4,243[b]	2.06	8,433	2.65	567[b]	2.48	1,630	3.72
Continental	8,772	4.26	10,925	3.43	771	3.37	1,197	2.73
TOTAL		94.11%[c]		76.90%[d]		78.46%[c]		77.43%[d]

[a]North Central, only.

[b]Allegheny.

[c]As percentage of total for certificated route carriers; all services.

[d]As percentage of total for majors, nationals, and large regionals.

Sources:

1. Office of the Controller, U.S. Civil Aeronautics Board, *CAB Air Carrier Traffic Statistics December 1978* (Washington, D.C.: CAB 1979).
2. Office of the Controller, U.S. Civil Aeronautics Board, *CAB Air Carrier Financial Statistics December 1979* (Washington, D.C.: CAB, 1980).
3. U.S. Department of Transportation, Research and Special Programs Administration, *Air Carrier Traffic Statistics December 1984* (Washington, D.C.: U.S. DOT, 1985).
4. U.S. Department of Transportation, Research and Special Programs Administration, *Air Carrier Financial Statistics December 1984* (Washington, D.C.: U.S. DOT, 1985).

FINANCIAL STRATEGIES AND ISSUES

Before deregulation there was considerable debate about how increased competition would change the airline business. Surely, it was postulated, American, Delta, and other large carriers were endowed with sufficient cash reserves to withstand market intrusions by new airlines or growth-oriented local service carriers. When the rate wars were over, according to this theory, the more established carriers would have increased their market shares and prosperity. Not all agreed, however. A second opinion was that the established airlines, because of their high-cost structures, were vulnerable to competition. Low-cost non-unionized entrants would not only survive but would also prosper at the expense of the more established major airlines.

Preliminary Findings

Today, it looks as though the truth lies between these extreme views. Preliminary findings, as already mentioned, show that collectively the majors have lost some aggregate market share to other competitors. Individually, some carriers like Northwest and USAir have significantly increased their RPMs (Table 15.11), yet others like Continental experienced a Chapter 11 filing, and Braniff International went bankrupt. Although 1984 was a prosperous year for the majors, 1982 was the year of the worst financial losses in airline history. Consequently, to obtain a better comprehension of how secure or vulnerable the study-group carriers really are, it makes sense to examine financial information. Profitability, debt, interest payments, equity positions, and competitive cost data are quite revealing.

Profitability

Table 15.19 establishes that eight of the airlines enjoyed operating profits in 1984, with only Trans World and Pan American showing losses of $86.3 million and $135.2 million, respectively. Figures compare quite favorably to the 12 months ending June 30, 1983, when United had an operating loss of $58 million, Eastern lost $50 million, Delta lost $208 million, Pan Am lost $222 million, TWA lost $120 million, Republic lost $78 million, and Continental lost $109 million. TWA, Pan Am, Eastern, Texas Air Corporation (parent of Continental Airlines and New York Air), and Republic had negative five-year average returns on equity in the 1979 through 1983 period, which further reveals the seriousness of the situation.[6] Table 15.19 also shows net income or losses after income taxes—a measure more relevant than operating income. By this standard, most carriers' earnings were reduced below operating income levels, and many by substantial amounts. Eastern is the most visible, showing a net loss of $37.9 million, rather than the more impressive $189.6 million in operating income.

TABLE 15.19. Airline operating income (loss), interest expense, and net income (loss) after income taxes[a] (Annual, year ended 12/31/84)

Airline	Operating Income (Loss)[b] (in $ Thousands)	Interest Expense (in $ Thousands)	Net Income or (Loss) after Income Taxes (in $ Thousands)
American	$339,065	$153,337	$208,606
Continental	107,546	78,910	28,657
Delta	287,344	114,461	258,641
Eastern	189,631	287,121	(37,927)
Northwest	96,842	9,714	87,004
Pan American	(135,216)	170,750	(206,836)
Republic	100,002	97,000	13,709
Trans World	(86,348)	118,495	29,885
United	550,006	126,693	235,856
USAir	192,724	27,552	118,331

[a]Airline only; disregards subsidiaries or other parts of the holding company, if appropriate.
[b]Airline operating revenues less operating expenses.
Source: U.S. Department of Transportation, Research and Special Programs Administration, *Air Carrier Financial Statistics December 1984* (Washington, D.C.: U.S. DOT, 1985).

Leverage Problems

A closer review of Table 15.19 indicates that one of the biggest financial problems in the airline industry is high interest payments. Eastern by far had the most severe problem with interest costs of $287 million in 1984. However, the 10 airlines shown in Table 15.19 collectively paid $1.184 billion in interest in 1984. Only Northwest and USAir seem to have kept their interest obligations suppressed.

debt-to-equity ratios

Table 15.20 establishes the magnitude of borrowing levels and the dangerously high debt-to-equity ratios that several carriers experienced in 1984. Four carriers owed more than $1 billion, and Pan American's debt-to-equity ratio was 4.57:1, Eastern's was 6.89:1, and Republic's was 20.20:1. Extremely leveraged, too, was Continental, but because it had negative stockholders equity of $41 million, its debt-to-equity ratio could not be calculated. Only Northwest was virtually debt free. Its debt-to-equity ratio was a minuscule 0.13:1.

reasons for high leverage

Airlines borrow deliberately or by necessity. If a company borrows at a lower interest rate (e.g., 10%) and earns a higher rate of return from its investment of the borrowed funds (e.g., 15%), it makes money with other people's cash. This is good business. Unfortunately, more often airline leverage comes from necessity. An example is a carrier with low liquid assets that needs to acquire aircraft. Long-term debt may be the only alternative available. The hard-pressed carrier then faces two additional problems. First is the timing

TABLE 15.20. Airline debt and equity data[a] (12/31/84)

Airline	Total Noncurrent Liabilities (in $ Thousands)	Stockholders Equity (in $ Thousands)	Debt-to-Equity Ratio	Retained Earnings (in $ Thousands)
American	$1,839,581	$1,455,296	1.26:1	$767,231
Continental	518,989	−41,130	——	−227,549
Delta	634,567	1,177,424	0.54:1	971,693
Eastern	2,242,934	325,433	6.89:1	−323,968
Northwest	113,302	892,985	0.13:1	738,738
Pan American	1,032,612	225,899	4.57:1	−371,384
Republic	740,229	36,640	20.20:1	−118,176
Trans World	1,231,447	729,402	1.69:1	122,108
United	768,611	1,463,167	0.53:1	405,913
USAir	264,798	663,749	0.40:1	419,307

[a]Airline only; disregards subsidiaries or other parts of the holding company, if appropriate.

Source: U.S. Department of Transportation, Research and Special Programs Administration, *Air Carrier Financial Statistics December 1985* (Washington, D.C.: U.S. DOT, 1985).

of the borrowing. If the firm must have cash when interest rates are high, the debt will cost more than usual. Secondly, a financially weak carrier is a greater risk to lenders—this situation boosts interest rates. Both problems forced some majors to pay interest rates above the prime rate in recent years.

leverage risks   Airlines with debt-to-equity ratios exceeding 2:1 are considered bordering on financial risk. Leverage assumes that carriers will earn adequate operating income. Failure to do so means an airline must tap its cash reserves or other current assets, sell some of its fixed assets like aircraft, or refinance borrowed capital. In each case, the solution can jeopardize a carrier's future.

Cash Reserves and Equity

It is often argued that the biggest airlines have such large cash reserves that they have the dual capabilities of enduring losses suffered in rate wars or expanding operations at will. Frequently cited, too, are the sizes of stockholders equity, such as Delta's $1177 million and American's $1455 million (Table 15.20). Actually, there is a risk in assigning too much corporate power or security to these amounts.

negative   Table 15.20 shows that Eastern, Pan Am, and Republic have much weaker
retained earnings   equity positions than several other carriers of comparable sales levels (for sales, see Table 15.15). Next, look at retained earnings levels (Table 15.20). By definition, retained earnings equal accumulated income less accumulated dividends paid to stockholders over time. Note that Pan Am, Eastern, Continental, and Republic showed negative retained earnings in 1984. There are two ways to reach a negative retained earnings position: either by paying out too much in dividends or by generating excessive operating losses. The latter cause is

primarily responsible for the airlines' negative retained earnings. Furthermore, the only ways to remove negative retained earnings are by generating future operating profits or by undergoing a corporate balance sheet restructuring to reduce stockholders' equity. Thus some equity positions are misleadingly high. Suppose, nevertheless, that a large carrier has a book value of $1 billion in equity. Of course, management cannot spend this $1 billion as it pleases. Since equity equals assets less liabilities, true net worth can only be known at the time all assets are sold.

equity analysis

Nevertheless, assume that same airline has $1 billion in current assets, including cash, short-term investments, and receivables. This situation does not mean, however, that the carrier can spend it all, for the airline just might have a similar amount of current liabilities. Even if current assets far exceed current liabilities, it is financial folly to have a company in a cash-short position. Contingency risks, such as a possible surge in fuel prices, or a recession, are too great.

current assets analysis

Another argument is that the largest of the major airlines have the ability to sustain long-term operating losses. Although true, this suggestion would seem to be a rather imprudent corporate strategy to follow. During the five-year period through 1983, TWA, Eastern, Pan American, and Republic had deficit five-year average returns-on-equity, and American and United had five-year returns-on-equity of only 2.9% and 0.3%, respectively.[7] It is not logical that investors will allow such trends to continue indefinitely.

ability to sustain losses

Consider also the true costs of expansion and modernization. In 1984, American announced an order for 67 MD-80 aircraft and options to buy 100 more.[8] At a conservative estimate of $20 million each, if all the planes are eventually delivered, this request will require a capital commitment of $3.34 billion. Of course, some capital will be raised by the sale of used aircraft, but this is a huge capital need. Compared with aircraft expenditure requirements, $1 billion today in equity or current assets is not much money, even if a carrier could spend it all. Thus the majors are not as cash rich as might be expected. They also are not as financially secure as they might initially seem. Sustained profits are essential for big firms, as well as for small companies.

capital needs capital deficiencies

Competitive Costs

Are the majors truly hindered by a large cost disadvantage in competing on a price basis with aggressive smaller airlines? Table 15.21 combines operating costs and interest payments and expresses the totals in terms of costs per ASM and costs per RPM by carrier. Piedmont, Southwest, and People Express were added to the study group because they have been profitable, rapidly growing and/or low price competitors.

The most cost-efficient major airline in 1984 was Continental, with an average cost per ASM of 6.64¢ and 10.58¢ per RPM. The highest cost carriers for the same year were USAir at 10.17¢/ASM and Republic at 17.97¢/RPM. To be a fair comparison, though, longer haul operators, as measured by average flight lengths, should have cost advantages over short-haul operators. Thus

cost leaders

TABLE 15.21. Comparable costs per scheduled available seat–mile and revenue passenger–mile and average flight lengths (Year ended 12/31/84)

Airline	Cents/ASM[a]	Cents/RPM[a]	Average Flight Length[b] (Miles)
American	8.36¢	13.36¢	849
Continental	6.64	10.58	813
Delta	8.18	15.97	569
Eastern	8.65	15.20	605
Northwest	7.22	11.93	852
Pan American	8.44	13.14	1150
Republic	9.02	17.97	396
TWA	8.13	13.07	968
United	7.35	12.15	786
USAir	10.17	17.38	374
Piedmont	8.96	17.04	347
Southwest	6.05	10.35	321
People Express	5.56	7.96	531

[a]Combines total operating expenses, plus interest on long-term debt and capital leases.
[b]This is the aircraft flight-stage length, not the average passenger-trip length. The latter is larger.
Sources:
1. U.S. Department of Transportation, Research and Special Programs Administration, *Air Carrier Financial Statistics December 1984* (Washington, D.C.: U.S. DOT, 1985).
2. U.S. Department of Transportation, Research and Special Programs Administration, *Air Carrier Traffic Statistics December 1984* (Washington, D.C.: U.S. DOT, 1985).

part of the difference in costs between Continental and USAir and Republic is distance-related, but not all. Southwest shows a shorter average flight length (321 miles) than USAir (374 miles) or Republic (396 miles), but a considerable cost advantage. Continental has become a strong low-cost competitor on the basis of cost-cutting actions taken since 1983. Another low-cost competitor among the study-group carriers is Northwest. Its efficiency can be traced to lower labor costs established over a period of decades. United is also benefiting from a cost advantage relative to other carriers in the group. Continental reduced its costs per RPM from 14.06¢ for the year ended 6/30/83 to 10.58¢ (24.8%). On another positive note, Northwest, Pan American, TWA, United, and USAir also lowered costs/RPM during the same period.

Piedmont, Southwest, and People Express

Piedmont's growth and prosperity are not obviously closely correlated to a cost advantage. As Table 15.21 indicates, Piedmont's costs per ASM and per RPM in 1984 were 8.96¢ and 17.04¢, respectively. The cost per RPM approximates the figure for USAir. However, as previously noted, another short-haul carrier, Southwest, had considerably lower costs than either USAir or Piedmont. Only People Express managed to attain a lower cost/ASM than Southwest (5.56¢ versus 6.05¢). Southwest also had lower costs per RPM than all the study-group airlines. Its 10.35¢ was second only to People Express's 7.96¢

in cost efficiency. Southwest, however, provided more services for the ticket price than People Express, which until 1986 was a no-frills airline.

conclusions

Table 15.21 confirms several beliefs. First, some carriers have clear cost advantages. For example, Southwest in 1984 was flying passengers at an average cost of 10.35¢ per mile, compared to USAir's cost of 17.38¢, or in other words, for 40.4% less. People's cost difference relative to USAir was 54.2%. It should be noted that USAir is a full-service airline, which People Express at the time was not. Secondly, the majors in general have succeeded in reducing costs per RPM, and some, like Continental, Northwest, and United, have more favorable cost structures than do others like Delta or Eastern. Thirdly, if lower cost carriers remain in the market, and there is no real evidence as of 1986 that they will not, and if they continue to use their cost advantages to compete on a low-price basis, they will pose serious threats in head-to-head competition with airlines with higher cost structures, because low-cost carriers can make profits at lower average yields than high-cost companies can. Moreover, some high-cost carriers have been profitable in the deregulated period because there wasn't effective competition in enough of their markets to depress yields. High costs are not a problem if yields exceed costs/RPM. A definite threat to high-cost carriers is increasing market entry into carriers' more monopolistic routes. Southwest and Continental should be viewed as definite threats to expand their operations into the more protected markets of high-cost carriers. In fact, the process has already begun. Furthermore, although small airlines tend to start operations flying small planes and show short average flight lengths, they have aircraft capable of intermediate or long-haul flights. Most airplanes they fly can easily travel 1000 miles nonstop.

Survival Strategies

All the majors are potentially vulnerable to selective market competition from discount airlines.[9] Although some new airlines, such as Air Florida, have failed, others continue to step forward to replace them, providing a constant source of price competition. Recognizing this threat, most majors have tried to cut costs and/or increase productivity. They have also been able to match the prices of low-cost carriers by selling the seats that would have been empty otherwise. This practice works, however, only as long as carriers are successful in booking enough full-fare passengers. Unfortunately, more and more passengers, including business travelers, are finding ways to buy discount tickets, so yields have deteriorated. Thus many airlines seem to be relying quite heavily on the size of their liquid assets to give them more staying power than the smaller airlines have to survive rate wars. This strategy assumes that discounting is a temporary phenomenon, which seems rather doubtful. As previously noted, moreover, several of the majors have serious financial problems and questionable staying power.

mergers
and acquisitions

Another theory, reportedly expressed by members of the investment community, is that airlines will seek merger partners or will attempt to acquire other airlines. This view assumes that there will be only two types of airlines in the post-deregulation period—super-size airlines and relatively small-niche carriers.[10] The author is not so convinced that mergers and acquisitions would improve corporate profitability; however, several carriers must believe it because in 1986 Delta offered to acquire Western, and Northwest bought Republic, Ozark Air Lines' owners accepted TWA's offer to buy Ozark, and Texas Air Corporation reached an agreement to acquire Eastern Airlines. Mergers and acquisitions should increase staying power if that is the corporate objective; however, nothing is guaranteed. For example, People Express bought Frontier Airlines in 1985, but they agreed under financial duress to be acquired by Texas Air Corporation in 1986.

cost-efficiency and productivity

All things considered, it would seem that the best hedge in the deregulated environment is for the majors to become more cost-efficient and productive. In general, they need to become more competitive on a price basis, since low yields are likely to continue for some time to come. If airlines cannot bring their costs/RPM in line with the market, they must be able to sell differentiated services, because they will struggle otherwise as discounters. Imperative, too, is the need for companies to reduce, or at least control, interest payments. If airlines fail to improve profitability by these measures, then shrinkage of the firm to a more manageable and profitable size might also be considered. In addition, employee participation in company ownership should also be carefully examined as a way to improve worker motivation.

final analysis

Without question, there will be further changes in the airline industry. Some firms are insecure and could be forced to leave the industry. Others will increase market shares. In the final analysis, the future of the study-group airlines will reside more in the decisions of management and in the cooperation of labor rather than in forces external to the firm. If there is one crucial action that is recommended, nonetheless, it is that majors improve their competitive positions by changing their cost structures to be more in line with the deregulated environment.

SUMMARY

The deregulated domestic airline business has presented established carriers with exceptional opportunities, as well as substantial new risks. The challenge has been particularly significant for the 10 largest U.S. scheduled passenger airlines, yet managers have accepted it with enthusiasm. Carriers have taken labor, fleet and fuel, marketing and operating, and financial initiatives.

There is no blueprint for success in the airline business. In fact, numerous examples of divergent strategies and actions were cited. Salaries, wages, and benefits continue to receive considerable attention from management. Rising fuel prices, too, have forced airlines to become more conservative and more productive, and fuel efficiency has been improved by means other than by just buying fuel-efficient aircraft. Increasing load-factors is one example. The airline business is now characterized by national network systems and selective route specialists. Thus the majors know they cannot depend too heavily on interlined traffic. Price competition is also a factor in the airline industry, and it has forced high-cost carriers to reexamine their operating and marketing orientations. Debt financing, too, is a particularly severe problem for many major airlines.

Most of the largest airlines have serious cost disadvantages, and these have placed some carriers in vulnerable positions in competing against lower cost operators. Analyzing how managers of the largest U.S. carriers have made decisions in these areas during one of the most turbulent periods in aviation history sets the stage for better understanding the future of the U.S. airline industry.

STUDY QUESTIONS

1. Explain the primary reasons why Delta's S/W/B dollar costs (Table 15.3) increased 102.9% from 7/1/78 through 6/30/84.

2. What actions have airlines taken in recent years to control labor costs?

3. Compare and contrast Delta's and Northwest's corporate labor philosophies. How has each airline's strategy helped carrier profitability?

4. What can major airlines do to prevent yield erosion?

5. Explain why Eastern's fuel costs in cents/RPM increased 128.0% from 1978 to 1984.

6. Why have most majors offered only restricted discounts?

7. Discuss the advantages and disadvantages of a scheduled passenger airline engaging in cargo and charter operations.

8. Why should majors try to reduce their total costs per RPM?

ENDNOTES

1. Derived from *10-K's* and *Annual Reports* filed by Northwest Airlines during the 1977 through 1984 period, various pages.

2. (a) "United Orders up to 116 Jets Worth $3 Billion from Boeing," *The Atlanta Constitution,* 8 November 1985, p. B-2; (b) "United to Get Pan Am Pacific Unit under Tentative Decision by Dole," *Traffic World,* 21 October 1985, p. 40; and (c) John Koten, "UAL to Get Pan Am Landing Rights in Japan but Friction Seen Continuing," *Wall Street Journal,* 27 January 1986, p. 4.

3. John Koten and Laurie P. Cohen, "New Discount Fares Could Make Flying More Expensive for Many," *Wall Street Journal,* 24 January 1985, p. 33.

4. *The Airline Quarterly,* September 1985, p. 115.

5. Air Transport Association of America, *Air Transport 1985* (Washington, D.C.: ATA of A, June 1985), p. 2.

6. "Air Transport," *Forbes,* 14 January 1985, p. 55.

7. Ibid.

8. "American Airlines Places Big Order with McDonnell," *Wall Street Journal,* 1 March 1984, p. 7.

9. See also William M. Carley, "Rough Flying: Some Major Airlines Are Being Threatened by Low-Cost Carriers," *Wall Street Journal,* 12 October 1983, p. 1.

10. Dean Rotbart, "Some Investors Believe Texas Air Might Bid for Pan Am as Airline Industry Consolidates," *Wall Street Journal,* 7 January 1986, p. 63.

ADDITIONAL READINGS

"Airline Woes Catch up with Delta." *Business Week,* 8 November 1982, p. 131.

Barnes, Lawrence. "A New Braniff is Ready To Test Its Wings." *Business Week,* 29 December 1983, p. 35.

———. "Special Report: A Painful Transition for the Transport Industry." *Business Week,* 28 November 1983, p. 83.

Berger, Robert G., and Mitchell, Stephanie J. "Predatory Pricing in the Airline Industry: A Case Study—The Policies and Practices of the CAB." *Transportation Law Journal* 13, No. 2 (1983): 287–305.

"Bitter, Deadly Dogfights." *Time,* 10 October 1983, pp. 44–45.

Carlton, Dennis W.; Landes, William M.; and Posner, Richard A. "Benefits and Costs of Airline Mergers: A Case Study." *Bell Journal of Economics* 11, no. 1 (Spring 1980):65–83.

Caves, Douglas W.; Christensen, Laurits R.; and Tretheway, Michael W. "Airline Productivity Under Deregulation." *Regulation: AEI Journal on Government and Society* (November/December 1982): 25–28.

Chapman, R. Stanley. "Labor and Management Maneuver as Airlines Strive to Cut Costs." *Traffic World,* 29 August 1983, pp. 40–41.

Cunningham, Lawrence F., and Wood, Wallace R. "Diversification in Major U.S. Airlines." *Transportation Journal* 22, no. 3 (Spring 1983):47–63.

Ellison, Anthony P. "The Structural Change of the Airline Industry Following Deregulation." *Transportation Journal* 21, no. 3 (Spring 1982):58–69.

Ghoshal, Animesh. "Price Elasticity of Demand for Air Passenger Service: Some Additional Evidence." *Transportation Journal* 20, no. 4 (Summer 1981):93–96.

Gritta, Richard F. "Air Carrier Financial Strategies: A Contrast—Pan Am and Delta." Transportation Research Forum. *Proceedings of the Twenty-fourth Annual Meeting.* Oxford, Ind.: Richard B. Cross Company, 1983, pp. 684–691.

———. "Bankruptcy Risks Facing the Major U.S. Airlines." *Journal of Air Law and Commerce* 48 (1982):89–108.

———. "The Effect of Financial Leverage on Air Carrier Earnings: A Break-Even Analysis." *Financial Management* (Summer 1979):53–60.

Hunsaker, James Kirk. "The Changing Shape of America's Airline Industry: An Analysis of the Deregulation Strategies of Five Airlines." Transportation Research Forum. *Proceedings of the Twenty-second Annual Meeting.* Oxford, Ind.: Richard B. Cross Company, 1981, pp. 449–456.

Keyes, Lucile Sheppard. "A Preliminary Appraisal of Merger Control under the Airline Deregulation Act of 1978." *Journal of Air Law and Commerce* 46 (1980):71–100.

Mandell, Robert W. *Financing the Capital Requirements of the U.S. Airline Industry in the 1980s.* Lexington, Mass.: Lexington Books, 1979.

Meyer, John R., and Oster, Clinton, V., eds. *Airline Deregulation: The Early Experience.* Boston, Mass.: Auburn House Publishing Company, 1981.

Pustay, Michael W. "Airline Competition and Network Effects." *Transportation Journal* 19, no. 4 (Summer 1980):63–72.

Putnam, Howard D. "Never Stop Trying." *Journal of Air Law and Commerce* 48, no. 3 (1983):471–481. (An article about Braniff Airlines.)

Rhodes, Lucien. "That Daring Young Man and His Flying Machine." *INC,* January 1984, p. 42. (An article on People Express.)

Richardson, J. D. *Essentials of Aviation Management.* 2d ed. Dubuque, Iowa: Kendall/Hunt Publishing Company, 1981.

Rose, Warren. "Three Years after Airline Passenger Deregulation in the United States: A Report Card on Trunkline Carriers." *Transportation Journal* 21, no. 2 (Winter 1981):51–58.

"Shootout in the Skies: As the Air-Control System Rebuilds, Pan Am Sets Off an Air-Fare Battle." *Time,* 28 September 1981, pp. 70–72.

Smith, Jon L. "Market Performance in Domestic Airline Markets." *Transportation Journal* 24, no. 1 (Fall 1984):51–57.

Soliman, Afi, and Brown, John L. "Air Transportation and Energy—A Systems Management Approach." *Transportation Quarterly* 37, no. 1 (January 1983):57–72.

Solomon, Mark B. "Labor-Management Confrontations Continue to Plague Air Industry." *Traffic World,* 6 February 1984, pp. 38–40.

Talley, Wayne K., and Eckroade, William R. "Airline Passenger Demand in Monopoly Flight Segments of a Single Airline under Deregulation." *Transportation Journal* 24, no. 2 (Winter 1984):73–79.

Taneja, Nawal K. *Airline Planning: Corporate, Financial, and Marketing.* Lexington, Mass.: Lexington Books, 1982.

———. *Airlines in Transition.* Lexington, Mass.: Lexington Books, 1981.

Toh, Rex S., and Higgins, Richard G. "The Impact of Hub and Spoke Network Centralization and Route Monopoly on Domestic Airline Profitability." *Transportation Journal* 24, no. 4 (Summer 1985):16–27.

Voorhees, Roy D., and Coppett, John. "New Competition for the Airlines." *Transportation Journal* 20, no. 4 (Summer 1981):78–85.

White, Lawrence J. "Economies of Scale and the Questions of 'Natural Monopoly' in the Airline Industry." *The Journal of Air Law and Commerce* 44, no. 3 (April 1979):545–573.

Specialized Aviation Sectors: International Air Transportation and the U.S. Air-Cargo Industry

16

International air transportation and the air-cargo industry are two important specialized aviation sectors. International sales for U.S. major, national, and large regional carriers for the year ending December 31, 1984, totaled $7.9 billion (18.0% of total U.S. airline sales).[1] Air-cargo and mail revenues also represented as much as 16.9% of the sales of one of the nation's largest airlines (see Table 15.16) and obviously constituted practically all the sales dollars for all-cargo carriers like Flying Tiger and Federal Express. Economics aside, there is no substitute for the speed that air transportation can deliver in moving passengers and cargo over long distances. Both international air transportation and air cargo fill unique roles in U.S. transportation. Chapter 16 will clarify the functions, characteristics, and concerns of each of these key transportation industry components.

INTERNATIONAL AIR TRANSPORTATION

The study of international air transportation includes discussion of international and U.S. aviation policy, route considerations, rate matters, U.S. international aviation statistics, and concerns of U.S. international carriers. Initially, however, it is necessary to clarify some terminology.

Definitions

Foreign, that is, international, air commerce refers to flights carrying passengers and/or cargo between different nations. Serving routes linking the United

435

States and other nations are *U.S. flag airlines* and *foreign flag airlines*. The former register their aircraft in the United States and display the U.S. flag (see Fig. 16.1). All other aircraft, from the U.S. perspective, are operated by foreign flag carriers. For the most part, U.S. flag airlines fly traffic to and from the United States. To a much lesser degree, they operate commercial, for-hire, services between foreign airports as part of a flight itinerary beginning or ending in the United States: for example, a flight by a U.S. flag carrier from Manila in the Philippines to Hong Kong and then continuing on to Seattle.

U.S. role   The United States plays several important roles in international aviation. The United States represents the largest single aviation market in the world. Secondly, the country has played a major role in the development of international aviation policy and in the establishment of the system of bilateral, two-nation, air transport agreements, which to this day are the bases for most international air service. Thirdly, U.S. flag airlines lead the world in aggregate market share. Fourthly, the United States remains the principal supplier of the world's commercial aircraft. Finally, the United States is the only major country in the world committed to a privately owned system of airlines.[2]

Aviation Policy

A major difference between the domestic and international aviation sectors is the higher degree of political involvement in the latter. Diplomacy plays a crucial part in the success or failure of international air service, and the need to establish a structure for reconciling political, economic, and social differ-

FIGURE 16.1.
U.S. flag on a Pan American World Airways' Boeing 747 aircraft. (Photo courtesy of Pan American World Airways)

ences between nations was recognized early in aviation history. No one country is in the position to dictate world aviation policy. This was true in the 1920s when international air transportation began to develop and remains so today. Consequently, a basic knowledge of aviation policy is necessary to understand the international airline business. The focus here will be on policies and actions important to U.S. international air transportation.

Havana Convention of 1928.   The Havana Convention of 1928 resulted in one of the first aviation documents ratified by the United States. At issue was control of the air space—deciding who could fly aircraft over another country's borders. The Havana Convention led to an agreement among nations of the Western Hemisphere that each country has complete and exclusive control of the air space above its borders and over its territorial waters; therefore, foreign flag airlines cannot unilaterally decide to fly their aircraft across another country's borders; they need permission from that country. However, the Havana Convention allowed a foreign carrier to request permission to enter another country's air space. Thus was established the mechanism for permitting aircraft of foreign nations to serve other political states.[3]

Chicago Convention of 1944.   A second major agreement resulted from the Chicago Convention of 1944. At the invitation of the United States, allied and neutral powers met to try to create a multilateral forum for solving international aviation problems. At this meeting, U.S. negotiators advocated the need for, and advantages of, free competition as opposed to strict economic regulation. They also requested that civil, nongovernment-owned aircraft be granted the following five freedoms[4]:

five freedoms

- *First freedom:* The right to fly over the territory of another country without landing, providing the overflown country is notified in advance and approval is given. This freedom is called the "right of innocent passage."
- *Second freedom:* The right to land in another country for technical reasons, such as for refueling or maintenance, without offering any commercial service to or from that point.
- *Third freedom:* The right of an airline to carry traffic from its country of registry to another country.
- *Fourth freedom:* The right of an airline to carry traffic from another country to its own country of registry.
- *Fifth freedom:* The right of an airline to carry traffic between two countries outside its own country of registry as long as the flight originates or terminates in its own country of registry (called *beyond rights*).

convention results

The Chicago Convention of 1944 rejected the U.S. proposal for free competition and accepted only the first two of the proposed five freedoms. This meant that the third through fifth freedoms, the bases for commercial international air services, would have to be resolved not by multilateral, many-nation, forum, but through bilateral agreements.[5]

Bermuda I. It was apparent from the Chicago meeting that most nations, unlike the United States, favored tight economic regulation of international airlines. At the same time, they, like the United States, wanted to expedite air transportation development. Thus, for this development to occur, policy rifts between the pro-competition United States and pro-regulation other nations had to be resolved. A case in point was ideological differences between the United Kingdom (a pro-regulator) and the United States. In an effort to find an agreeable solution, these two countries met in Bermuda and signed the Bermuda Agreement of 1946. Now called *Bermuda I*, this historic accord was the first bilateral air agreement. Under the terms of Bermuda I, each nation granted the other country the five freedoms advocated in Chicago. Of equal importance, Bermuda I accelerated the growth of U.S.–United Kingdom air traffic. For approximately 30 years, Bermuda I guided international airline policy developments.

Discontent. In the 1970s, signs of political discontent began to emerge. One of the first indications was the U.S. passage of the International Air Transportation Fair Competitive Practices Act of 1974 (88 Stat. 2102 et seq.). This measure notified the world that U.S. flag airlines were not to be discriminated against nor subjected to unfair competitive practices by foreign governments or their carriers.

U.S. discontent

The British were also dissatisfied with international aviation developments and announced intentions to terminate Bermuda I effective June 1977. Understanding the potential consequences on international airline services of the absence of an agreement, the United States and the United Kingdom returned to the negotiating table. The outcome was Bermuda II, signed July 23, 1977. Its provisions gave the United Kingdom some of its desired rate and capacity restrictions, and the United States achieved new route authority between 15 U.S. cities and London.[6] Bermuda II also authorized the entry of new competitors like Laker Airways, Delta, and Braniff International in the U.S.–London market. Overall, though, Bermuda II might well be most remembered for opening the door to far more liberal U.S.–foreign nation airline agreements. An example is the U.S.–Israel bilateral agreement, which permitted U.S. flag airlines to serve any point in Israel from any point in the United States. In exchange, Israeli flag airlines received rights to New York and three other U.S. cities.[7]

British discontent

Bermuda II

Changing U.S. Policy. In the late 1970s, the United States became an aggressive campaigner for deregulation of international aviation. Some argue that domestic airline deregulation was responsible for the change in mood. For one thing, the CAB interpreted the Airline Deregulation Act of 1978 as a directive to extend deregulation principles to the international sector. Thus it began trying to convince foreign countries to liberalize routes, prices, and charter rules.[8] Encouraged by domestic deregulation results, Carter's administration also joined in the crusade by issuing a statement entitled, "The Policy

"Open Skies" policy

of Conduct of International Air Transportation Negotiations." Signed on August 21, 1978, this policy was so liberal that it was soon called the *"Open Skies" policy.* It specified seven points as U.S. negotiating objectives in bilateral talks:

1. Creation of new and greater opportunities that will encourage and permit use of new price and service options to meet the needs of different travelers and shippers.
2. Liberalization of charter rules and elimination of restrictions on charter operations.
3. Expansion of scheduled service through elimination of restrictions on capacity, frequency, and route and operating rights.
4. Elimination of discriminatory and unfair competitive practices faced by U.S. airlines in international transportation.
5. Flexibility to designate multiple airlines in international air markets. (As opposed to the past practice of limiting entry in a new route to one U.S. flag airline and one foreign flag carrier, several carriers could start services between two points.)
6. Encouragement of maximum traveler and shipper access to international markets by authorizing more cities for nonstop or direct service and by improving the integration of domestic and international airline services.
7. Flexibility to permit the development of competitive air-cargo services.[9]

International Air Transportation Competition Act of 1979. Next in the sequence of emerging U.S. air policy came the enactment of the International Transportation Competition Act of 1979 (IATCA) on February 15, 1980 (94 Stat. 35 et seq.). The IATCA amended the Federal Aviation Act of 1958 to promote competition in international air transportation, provide greater opportunities for U.S. air carriers, and establish goals for developing U.S. international aviation policy. For the most part, the IATCA incorporated and expanded the ideas of the Carter "Open Skies" policy (for specifics, see Table 16.1).

Post-1980 Period. Since 1980, the U.S. government has continued to push for deregulation of international aviation. Still advocated were multiple airport designations, rather than the usual designation of only one airport at each end of a new route, multiple carriers in a market, and maximum pricing flexibility. About the only U.S. policy change from previous years seemed to be a more conscientious effort to ensure that the results of negotiations were fair to U.S. flag carriers.[10] This responsibility fell heavily on the U.S. Department of Transportation, the agency playing the main role in bilateral negotiations and, following the CAB's demise, administering U.S. international air transport economic regulation.[11] Also involved today in the agreement process are the Department of State, which is concerned with the impact of airline agreements on foreign affairs, and the president, who can disapprove international air carrier certificates or permits on the basis of negative foreign relations ramifications or national defense considerations (92 Stat. 1970).

U.S. government
responsibilities

> **TABLE 16.1. Goals for international aviation policy**
>
> **(b)** In formulating United States international air transportation policy, the Congress intends that the Secretary of State, the Secretary of Transportation, and the Civil Aeronautics Board shall develop a negotiating policy which emphasizes the greatest degree of competition that is compatible with a well-functioning international air transportation system. This includes, among other things:
>
> **(1)** the strengthening of the competitive position of United States air carriers to at least assure equality with foreign air carriers, including the attainment of opportunities for United States air carriers to maintain and increase their profitabililty, in foreign air transportation;
>
> **(2)** freedom of air carriers and foreign air carriers to offer fares and rates which correspond with consumer demand;
>
> **(3)** the fewest possible restrictions on charter air transportation;
>
> **(4)** the maximum degree of multiple and permissive international authority for United States air carriers so that they will be able to respond quickly to shifts in market demand;
>
> **(5)** the elimination of operational and marketing restrictions to the greatest extent possible;
>
> **(6)** the integration of domestic and international air transportation;
>
> **(7)** an increase in the number of nonstop United States gateway cities;
>
> **(8)** opportunities for carriers of foreign countries to increase their access to United States points if exchanged for benefits of similar magnitude for United States carriers or the traveling public with permanent linkage between rights granted and rights given away;
>
> **(9)** the elimination of discrimination and unfair competitive practices faced by United States airlines in foreign air transportation, including excessive landing and user fees, unreasonable ground handling requirements, undue restrictions on operations, prohibitions against change of gauge, and similar restrictive practices; and
>
> **(10)** the promotion, encouragement, and development of civil aeronautics and a viable, privately owned United States air transport industry.

Source: Section 17, International Air Transportation Competition Act of 1979, 94 Stat. 42.

ICAO   Most international airlines today, in addition to participating in bilateral negotiations, are members of two multilateral organizations—the International Civil Aviation Organization (ICAO) and the International Air Transport Association (IATA). Founded in 1947, the ICAO is now an official agency of the United Nations. Its objectives are to promote international civil aviation through the development of airports, airways, and air navigation facilities; to promote safety; to develop techniques for international air navigation; and to ensure that the rights of member countries are fully respected so that every member country has a fair opportunity to operate international air carriage.[12]

IATA   IATA is a tariff setting and trade association representing 112 airlines from 90 countries.[13] (IATA's role will be explained in depth in the rate discussion later in this chapter.)

Routes

entry: U.S.
flag airlines

Route awards are of paramount importance in international civil aviation. Since U.S. flag airlines cannot compete unless they are authorized entry into a market, U.S. flag applicants today must receive certificates of public convenience and necessity from the U.S. Department of Transportation, and these are necessary for each new route sought (94 Stat. 37). The issuance, transfer, amendment, suspension, or revocation of international certificates is also subject to review and possible disapproval by the president of the United States.

foreign flag permits

To fly international routes, a U.S. flag carrier needs permission or authorization from the governments of the foreign countries it intends to serve. Upon receiving such permission, the airline must comply with the laws and regulations of host countries. Permits, authorizations, and rights vary considerably among the sovereign states. Similarly, foreign flag carriers desiring to serve the United States must receive a permit from the U.S. Department of Transportation (94 Stat. 38) and follow U.S. laws and procedures when in U.S. territory.

consequences
before late 1970s

Prior to the late 1970s, bilateral air transport agreements between the United States and foreign countries typically specified exact routes that could be operated and cities that could be served. This policy usually meant that the United States designated one of its flag airlines, and the foreign country did likewise, to serve the specific route. The effect was to limit schedule frequencies and capacities; moreover, restrictions, such as required intermediate stops, were commonplace occurrences.

results since
the late 1970s

Since the late 1970s, U.S.–foreign bilateral agreements have been characterized by expanded route freedoms. As a result, many new U.S. and foreign flag carriers have entered scheduled service; numerous new U.S. gateways have been opened providing direct air service from interior U.S. airports (like Dallas and Minneapolis) to international markets; and more services have been offered between existing U.S. and foreign airports. Expanded routes and fewer capacity limits distinguish the period.

Rate Matters

Former IATA Role and Power.   Rates have also been the focus of much international deliberation. Until the 1960s, IATA was powerful in its role as a multilateral international rate negotiation forum. Even then, however, some limits on IATA's influence were visible. As an exclusive association of scheduled airlines, IATA has never had any rate-setting powers over charter airlines. Also, since IATA membership is voluntary, some scheduled non-IATA carriers set rates independently of the IATA structure.

IATA
rate-setting process

IATA's mechanism for setting rates is the traffic conference, an organization of IATA carriers that compete in a market area. An example is the United States–Europe Traffic Conference. Periodically, a conference is called to debate and vote on tariff matters. Proposals are approved only if the vote of the traffic conference membership is unanimous. Achieving that, IATA must then wait for each respective government to sanction the IATA agreed-on rates. Until the 1960s, government approval of IATA rates usually meant that all IATA scheduled carriers in a city-pair market (e.g., New York–London) charged the same IATA price. Hence, rate competition among IATA carriers was virtually nonexistent.

In the 1960s, however, IATA's rate-setting influence began to ebb. The catalyst was more liberal international air policies, which both relaxed charter airline rules and lessened scheduled carrier entry and pricing restrictions.[14] When non-IATA charter airlines capitalized on their low costs and full airplanes to underprice substantially IATA airlines, IATA carriers demanded pricing freedoms. This demand led to the introduction of group inclusive tour fares (GITS) in 1967, excursion fares (1970), and advanced purchase excursions (APEX) in 1974—forms of discount air fares.[15] Nevertheless, the charter carrier market share remained intact. Another source of market pressure was Laker Airways, a privately owned non-IATA member British airline that offered no-reservation, low-priced scheduled service.

During the 1970s it became evident that IATA carriers could not reach a pricing strategy consensus. Frustrated by the IATA rule that rate changes needed unanimous approval of a traffic conference and by their inability to have discount rates quickly approved by IATA, IATA carriers in the North Atlantic commenced independent pricing. The introduction of low-priced standby, budget, and super-APEX fares followed.[16] The rate war had begun in earnest.

IATA Reorganization.   IATA had further problems. Arguing that IATA traffic conference procedures were not in the public interest, the U.S. Civil Aeronautics Board in June 1978 issued a show cause order questioning why U.S. flag carriers should continue to receive antitrust immunity allowing them to participate in IATA.[17] Delta and Pan American subsequently resigned from IATA, with Delta's reason stated as the need for greater flexibility to handle the changing competitive environment.[18]

Cognizant of its weakening posture, IATA reorganized to segment itself into a trade association and a tariff-setting component. Airlines today are free to join either IATA unit, both, or neither. Legal, technical, baggage, and ticketing matters are the trade association's responsibilities, and rate matters fall under the IATA traffic conference organization.[19] Although the reorganization calmed U.S. government objections to IATA, it did not fully restore IATA's power. Several U.S. airlines today are not IATA members, and some IATA members do not belong to the tariff-setting bodies. Most of the larger, older carriers—both U.S. and foreign—since the early 1980s have openly disregarded IATA agreed tariffs.[20] Illegal discounting by IATA carriers is also commonly observed.[21] Thus what was once a structured, non-price competitive international airline passenger industry became quite price competitive, particularly in the 1980s.

Margin notes: diminishing IATA power; charter competition; Laker Airways; independent pricing and rate wars; CAB show cause order of 1978; IATA still weakened

U.S. International Aviation Statistics

Passenger Traffic and Market Shares. U.S. flag carriers can be positioned within the aggregate international aviation market by an analysis of selected statistics. The earlier claim that U.S. flag carriers are a significant factor in this business is easily substantiated by the data in Table 16.2. In 1984, U.S. airlines carried 22,154,615 (49.4%) of the 44,819,172 passengers departing from or arriving in the United States. On a regional market basis, the highest U.S. flag market share was in the Caribbean (69.9%).

Table 16.2 is also useful in revealing the relative significance of the U.S.–world regional markets, the most important of which by far is the U.S.–Europe arena. With nearly 18 million passengers in 1984, the U.S.–European market far exceeded traffic levels in each of the next three most important markets: the U.S.–Caribbean (8.4 million), U.S.–Central America/Mexico (7.0 million), and U.S.–Far East (6.5 million) markets.

international versus total traffic

According to another data source, in calendar year 1984, U.S. registered airlines made 23,614,000 scheduled international revenue passenger enplanements, representing 6.9% of the total of 343,264,000 scheduled passenger enplanements. The balance (319,650,000) was domestic traffic. However, international traffic represented 21.0% of the industry's scheduled revenue passenger-miles. The difference (21.0% vs. 6.9%) is traced to much longer average international flight lengths. International operations also produced 30.9% (2,064,000) of the U.S. airline industry's charter passenger enplanements; 40.8% (5.6 billion) of its charter revenue passenger-miles; and 32.7%

TABLE 16.2. U.S. flag carrier international passenger traffic and market share: arrivals plus departures[a] (Calendar year 1984)

U.S. to or from This Market	U.S. and Foreign Flag Total Passengers	U.S. Flag Carrier Passengers	U.S. Flag Carrier Market Share (%)
Europe	17,719,186	8,366,856	47.2%
Caribbean	8,405,168	5,828,437	69.9
Central America and Mexico	7,049,866	3,071,036	43.6
Far East	6,535,229	2,782,317	42.6
South America	2,458,099	939,084	38.2
Oceania	1,409,462	631,006	44.8
Middle East	819,989	316,748	38.6
Africa	422,173	219,131	51.9
TOTAL	44,819,172	22,154,615	49.4%

[a]Reflects scheduled and charter commercial traffic only in markets where U.S. flag carriers provide services.

Source: U.S. Department of Transportation, Research and Special Programs Administration, *U.S. International Air Travel Statistics Calendar Year 1984* (Cambridge, Mass.: Transportation Systems Center, 1985), derived from Tables Ia and Id, but based on data collected from the U.S. Immigration and Naturalization Service.

of its charter freight, express, and mail revenue ton-miles.[22] The cargo figure is somewhat inflated, however, since some domestic traffic is not reported by exempt firms.

key U.S.
international
markets

More specific market information is shown in Table 16.3, which ranks U.S.–foreign country markets by passenger traffic totals. Only passengers boarding U.S. flag airlines are reported. The United Kingdom ranks first with 3.8 million passengers. Ranked second in 1984 was Mexico, followed in order by Japan, West Germany, and France.

Busiest U.S. Points of Embarkation.   Table 16.4 lists the 10 busiest U.S. points of embarkation. Figures include all commercial passengers leaving the United States regardless of the registry of the airline. By far the most important international airport city is New York, as indicated by the more than 7.3 million passengers it served in 1984. New York dominates the U.S.–European market and ranked first to the Middle East and Africa as well. Miami

TABLE 16.3. Top 20 U.S. flag carrier international air passenger markets[a] (Calendar year 1984)

Market	Passengers	Rank
United Kingdom	3,848,345	1
Mexico	2,595,386	2
Japan	2,112,634	3
West Germany	1,341,290	4
France	838,388	5
Bermuda	823,684	6
Italy	798,265	7
Netherlands Antilles	643,771	8
Jamaica	616,030	9
Dominican Republic	595,303	10
Hong Kong	331,276	11
Barbados	311,166	12
Greece	304,385	13
Spain	292,056	14
Haiti	288,616	15
Venezuela	267,933	16
Brazil	250,427	17
Panama Republic	244,626	18
Israel	224,294	19
Switzerland	220,920	20

[a]Commercial traffic only; arrivals and departures on U.S. flag airlines only; selected statistics; Canadian traffic figures are included in U.S. domestic traffic statistics.

Source: U.S. Department of Transportation, Research and Special Programs Administration, *U.S. International Air Travel Statistics Calendar Year 1984* (Cambridge, Mass.: Transportation Systems Center, 1985), derived from pp. IV–18 through IV–21, but based on U.S. Immigration and Naturalization Service data.

TABLE 16.4. Top 10 U.S. points of embarkation[a] (Calendar year 1984)

U.S. Departure Point	Total Passengers	Destinations (passengers)							
		Europe	Caribbean	Central America and Mexico	Far East	South America	Oceania	Middle East	Africa
New York[b]	7,347,874	4,791,755	1,218,990	206,808	282,633	291,102		366,416	190,170
Miami	3,342,882	382,220	1,466,005	695,851	186	796,724		1,884	12
Los Angeles	2,190,423	608,575	13,997	844,750	496,804	71,265	154,803		229
Honolulu	1,566,413				1,148,328		418,085		
Chicago	843,373	497,761	23,834	214,957	104,833			1,988	
San Francisco	691,973	197,203		155,287	339,430		53		
Houston	655,975	111,317	43,139	489,833		4,023			
Boston	647,094	502,561	107,837	959		617		34,860	7,663
Atlanta	587,878	332,919	209,429	45,530					
Seattle	496,533	128,736		32,023	335,774				260

[a]Passengers leaving the United States on either a U.S. flag or foreign flag airline, commercial traffic only.
[b]Excludes Newark.

Source: U.S. Department of Transportation, Research and Special Programs Administration, *U.S. International Air Travel Statistics Calendar Year 1984* (Cambridge, Mass.: Transportation Systems Center, 1985), Table IIId, but based on U.S. Immigration and Naturalization Service data.

ranked second overall, with 3.3 million departing international travelers; however, it was first in service to the Caribbean and South America. Leading as a departure point for Central America and Mexico and ranked third overall was Los Angeles. Honolulu was fourth overall on the strength of its number-one ranking to the Far East and Oceania (Pacific islands, Australia, etc.). Table 16.4 also shows the importance of inland gateways like Chicago and Atlanta and some surprising findings such as the importance of Los Angeles in serving Europe. Most Los Angeles passengers fly the polar route over the Arctic to Europe.

Pan Am, TWA, and Northwest

Financial Statistics.   Since the late 1970s, U.S. flag carriers have been struggling with profitability problems. Of the three largest U.S. international airlines—Pan American, TWA, and Northwest (see Table 15.15), only Northwest is financially sound. As noted by Table 16.5, TWA reported 1984 international operating profits of $161 million. In the black, too, was Pan Am with $133 million. However, the carriers cannot disregard domestic operating prob-

---

TABLE 16.5. Operating revenues and operating profits (losses)[a] for U.S. flag airline international services (Year ended December 31, 1984)

Airline	Operating Revenues	Profits (Losses)
American	$ 349,792,000	$ 25,686,000
Continental	248,055,000	24,083,000
Delta	191,841,000	24,787,000
Eastern	394,907,000	(21,490,000)
Northwest	1,118,582,000	61,856,000
Pan American	2,687,677,000	132,876,000
Trans World	1,602,639,000	161,498,000
United	151,201,000	(7,387,000)
Western	65,000,000	(2,142,000)
Capitol	26,001,000	(1,700,000)
Flying Tiger	679,291,000	82,322,000
People Express	62,021,000	6,441,000
World	92,195,000	14,202,000
American Trans Air	75,218,000	4,395,000
Buffalo	3,886,000	(24,000)
Global	5,003,000	(1,131,000)
Overseas National	58,131,000	(11,115,000)
Ryan	6,582,000	336,000
South Pacific	33,202,000	2,944,000
Tower Air	58,775,000	(973,000)

[a]Includes majors, nationals, and large regionals.

Source: U.S. Department of Transportation, Research and Special Programs Administration, *Air Carrier Financial Statistics December 1984* (Washington, D.C.: U.S. D.O.T., 1985).

lems that continue to hurt their finances. TWA lost $86 million, and Pan Am lost $268 million, in 1984, on domestic operations.[23] Both carriers have been struggling to survive, and unless matters improve systemwide, losses could affect their international operations and traffic. In fact, one result already was Pan Am's decision to sell most of its Pacific operations to United.

tough
competitive
environment

U.S. flag carriers compete in a difficult international environment. This competition particularly exists for Pan American and Trans World Airlines, which were important international carriers long before route freedoms let in many new U.S. and foreign competitors. Every U.S. flag airline is privately owned and expected to succeed on its business acumen, even if that means competing against nationalized, subsidized airlines.

industry losses

One particularly revealing piece of evidence indicating the seriousness of international airline problems is the $7.1 billion loss experienced by IATA carriers between 1979–1983.[24] Deficits have been blamed on discounting, the worldwide recession, high interest rates, and inflated fuel costs. Furthermore, IATA expected losses to continue until 1986 when a modest upturn was predicted.[25] Non-IATA airlines have also paid a price, as exemplified by the financial collapse of Laker Airways in 1982.

declining
U.S. market share

Market share losses are of particular concern to U.S. carriers. In 1971, U.S. flag airlines commanded a 56.5% share of the passenger traffic in international markets they served.[26] By 1984, the figure was 49.4% (see Table 16.2). More specifically, the U.S. share in the European market dropped from 48.0% to 44.9% in 1982, before rising to 47.2% in 1984; in the Far East, the U.S. share dropped from 55.9% to 39.3% in 1982, before climbing to 42.6% in 1984; and in the Oceania market the reduction was from 61.6% to 44.8%.[27]

Concerns of U.S. Flag Carriers

open skies

U.S. Aviation Policies.   Blamed for U.S. carrier problems are U.S. aviation policies, the policies of foreign countries, and foreign discrimination against U.S. flag airlines. Pan Am has criticized the U.S. government's "Open Skies" policy, which favors competition between carriers and between different routes.[28] Before the United States opened new routes to Europe from new gateway cities, Pan American was fed traffic that originated at inland points and was carried by domestic airlines to Pan Am's gateways such as New York. When the United States opened new routes to Europe from new interior gateway cities, it most often gave these new routes not to Pan Am but to other U.S. airlines. Consequently, these carriers now haul passengers to Europe, and Pan Am has lost business. Foreign governments, given the same power as the United States received to designate carriers for new routes, tended to favor a single carrier—the state-owned airline. As a result, Pan Am also faces strengthened foreign competitors.

conflicting
national airline goals

U.S. policy goals stress consumer benefits and economic efficiency—that is, low prices, expanded services, and carrier self-sufficiency through the earning of profits. None of these goals is universally accepted abroad. Foreign airlines may exist to earn hard currency from foreigners, to provide a market for domestic aircraft manufacturing industries, to promote tourism, and to provide airline jobs. Other reasons are to "fly the flag" as an instrument of national prestige, to provide diplomatic services connecting nations, to promote foreign policy, to provide an expanded military airlift capability, and even to serve as an instrument for espionage.[29]

Of course, U.S. international airlines do fulfill many of these same objectives, but emphases among nations definitely differ. U.S. airlines must still earn profits, whereas most foreign airlines face no such constraint. On the contrary, subsidies are provided. For example, the French government assumed Air France's amortization and financing costs for the carrier's supersonic transport Concorde aircraft.[30] U.S. carriers feel disadvantaged against such subsidized, nationalized competition, and some like Pan Am have questioned the wisdom of their own government trying to intensify competition against foreign airlines.

Foreign Political Actions.   International air services carry far greater risks than domestic operations. Political unrest and wars can cause U.S. carriers to suspend services as Pan Am was forced to do in recent years in El Salvador and Iran.[31] Terrorism against U.S. aircraft and passengers has also hurt commerce. Few people are likely to forget either the catastrophe of September 1, 1983, when a Soviet aircraft shot down a Korean Airlines Boeing 747, killing all 269 persons on the flight.[32] As these examples show, carrier managers worry about suddenly losing markets they spent years developing, or worse, losing the lives of passengers and crew.

Foreign Discrimination.   During the 1970s, the number of complaints increased against foreign governments or their airlines for discriminating and engaging in unfair competitive practices against U.S. flag airlines (see Table 16.6). The United States responded with a much tougher negotiating position in new or renewed bilateral talks. The IATCA of 1979 also gave the United States increased powers to retaliate against these foreign abuses of U.S. carriers (see 94 Stat. 36–38 and 94 Stat. 44–45), such as suspending a foreign flag airline's permit to serve the United States. These problems are not directed at U.S. carriers alone, but reflect what any foreign airline could face in serving a particular nation. The U.S. position basically says that foreign countries should treat U.S. airlines the same way the United States treats foreign airlines. Often, they do not.

short-term prospects

Assessment.   There are signs that the U.S. international air sector is improving. U.S. carriers need a stronger world economy, and aggregate traffic needs to be stimulated. Thus the 7.1% growth in world passenger traffic in 1983 was encouraging, particularly since it ended two years of declines.[33] Another good sign was a 12.8% increase in U.S. flag carrier international passenger trips during the 1982–1984 period.[34] A contributing cause was a

TABLE 16.6. Complaints of discrimination and unfair competitive practices against U.S. flag airlines (Samples)

1. Problems obtaining access to foreign airline computer reservation systems (West Germany).

2. Excessive airport user charges at Heathrow Airport in England and in Australia.

3. Unjustified "noise" charges on Boeing-747 equipment, which are quieter than aircraft operated domestically by Japanese carriers (Japan).

4. Higher prices on fuel sold to U.S. airlines than to local carriers (Spain, Peru, Bolivia, Israel, Columbia, and Venezuela).

5. Excessive route navigation charges (Brazil).

6. Delays in approving plans for cargo handling facilities (Korea).

7. Inability to expand landing slots at Narita Airport (Tokyo, Japan).

8. Ground handling monopolies that do not allow U.S. carriers to control their freight, but rather force them to use the services of the native airline (SAS, Sweden).

Sources:

1. U.S. Civil Aeronautics Board, *CAB Reports to Congress, FY 1979 Annual Report,* (Washington, D.C.: U.S. Government Printing Office, November 1982), pp. 100–102.

2. U.S. Congress, House, Committee on Public Works and Transportation, *International Air Transportation Competition Act of 1979, Hearings,* before the Subcommittee on Aviation, House of Representatives, 96th Cong., 1st sess., 1979, statement and testimony of Dan Colussy, President, Pan American World Airways, Inc., pp. 235–236, 276.

stronger U.S. dollar, which encouraged U.S. citizens to fly abroad in search of travel bargains, in essence, more for the dollar.

U.S. flag airlines remain the dominant force in international commercial
longer
term concerns   aviation, yet they do not command the preeminence they once possessed. Although recent signs are generally favorable, the market is quite dynamic, and competition remains fierce. Complicating matters is international politics. Terrorism, for instance, caused many U.S. citizens to cancel European travel plans in 1986, producing traffic and revenue declines for U.S. carriers. Further U.S. market improvements, therefore, are far from certain.

U.S. AIR-CARGO INDUSTRY

Air cargo is defined as the transportation of property and mail by aircraft. In volume, it represented a minuscule 0.28% of the total ton-miles handled in the United States in 1984,[35] but this figure is misleading. Air cargo is a multibillion-dollar business, and for most large combination airlines, cargo sales can make the difference between operating profits and losses. Furthermore, air transportation alone has the ability to move goods hundreds or thousands of miles in a few hours. Used wisely, it can reduce distribution costs, improve sales, and produce highly desired levels of service. It is an indispensable shipper tool.

Evolving Air-Cargo Sector

The air-cargo industry today is in evolution. Before 1977, restrictive entry rules left the market with only three certificated all-cargo airlines: Flying Tiger, Seaboard, and Airlift International. Shippers desiring service could use one of these carriers or pay one of the combination carriers to haul the goods either in one of their passenger aircraft or in a freighter, which is an all-cargo aircraft. Most freight moved on approximately 25 scheduled airlines. Today there are far more carriers in the market.

Air-Cargo Deregulation Act of 1977

What changed the air-cargo business was the Federal Aviation Act of 1958—Insurance Risks (91 Stat. 1284 et seq.), or as it is more commonly called, the Air Cargo Deregulation Act. Signed on November 9, 1977, this act not only deregulated the domestic air cargo business but also precipitated legislation deregulating the air passenger, motor carrier, railroad, and intercity bus industries. In fact, the Air Cargo Deregulation Act was enacted to test the waters before proceeding with the other deregulation bills. International air cargo was not deregulated by this domestic bill, however.

Entry Deregulation.   The main themes of air cargo deregulation were entry and rate decontrols. Provisions contained in the Air Cargo Deregulation Act and the Airline Deregulation Act of 1978 and CAB actions significantly increased entry into the market. Today, if a U.S. citizen wants to become a direct air carrier, that is, one who owns and operates aircraft, several options are available. If plans call for exclusively flying aircraft with a maximum payload or cargo contents of 18,000 lbs. or containing no more than 60 seats, that person only has to register with the government as a Part 298 exempt air taxi or commuter carrier. If the choice is to fly larger planes, the applicant needs to request a certificate of public convenience and necessity from the DOT. Two forms of authority are available. As in the past, the applicant can seek a Section 401 certificate. Essentially, this is the type of authority a Flying Tiger or American Airlines has held. Alternatively, the person can seek Section 418 all-cargo air service authority. Sections 401 and 418 refer to parts of the Federal Aviation Act of 1958 as amended.

The Air Cargo Deregulation Act of 1977 made entry much easier than it had been. Grandfather provisions enabled any certificated 401 airline to obtain 418 authority if it had flown at least one scheduled all-cargo flight during the January 1, 1977, through November 9, 1977, period [49 U.S.C.A. 1388(a)(1)]. Likewise, experienced all-cargo Part 298 carriers and certificated charter cargo airlines were given 418 authority for the asking [49 U.S.C.A. 1388(a)(2) and (a)(3)]. Also, as of November 9, 1978, any U.S. citizen could receive 418 authority within 180 days of filing unless the CAB (now DOT) found the applicant not fit, willing, and able to provide the service or comply with rules or regulations promulgated by the Board [49 U.S.C.A. 1388(b)(1)(B)]. By June 30, 1983,

Part 298 carrier

certificated carrier

Section 418 entry requirements

there were 115 Section 418 carriers. Of these, 58 simultaneously held Section 401 authority.[36]

indirect air carriers

Indirect air carriers—that is, air freight forwarders and shippers' associations—were also affected by deregulation. Before the 1977 Act, indirect air carriers could not own and operate aircraft, and as a result, they had to rely on purchased transportation from scheduled or charter direct air carriers, that is, companies that could own and operate aircraft. Shippers' associations, who worked for the betterment of their members, collected small shipments, consolidated them to common destinations, and achieved volume shipment rate savings from the airlines. Similarly, air freight forwarders were intermediaries soliciting shipments from shippers and tendering consolidated loads to direct air carriers. They earned profits by living off the spread between the higher rates per 100 lbs. collected from shippers and the lower rates per 100-weight paid to airlines. Expedited service and control were what the forwarders sold. These functions are still provided by forwarders; however, with deregulation, indirect air carriers could apply for direct air carrier authority.

entry rules

Deregulation made entry into indirect air carriage simple. Before deregulation, a firm filed an application that was screened by the CAB. Since October 1981, however, entry has been totally deregulated, and neither shippers' associations nor forwarders need register any longer. Given this freedom, the number of air freight forwarders jumped from a July 1974 level of 257 to approximately 1500–2000 firms by 1984. Precise figures are unknown because deregulation ended forwarder reporting requirements.

Other Air-Cargo Deregulation Changes.

rates

Entry rights carry with them broad operating privileges today. Except for restrictions imposed on intrastate Alaskan or Hawaiian routes, Section 418 airlines have 50-state route freedom [49 U.S.C.A. 1388(b)(2) and (3)]. Usually, forwarders can operate wherever they please. Furthermore, airlines and forwarders are exempt from tariff filing requirements and can now alter rates almost totally free from government interference (see 14 C.F.R. 291.31). Only if cargo rates cause unjust discrimination, undue preference, or predatory problems can the U.S. DOT (formerly the CAB) suspend or forbid a carrier from charging such rates (91 Stat. 1286 and 1287). Furthermore, it makes no difference whether cargo is flown in freighters or in combination aircraft; rate freedoms apply in either case.

liability

Air cargo liability has also been deregulated. Carriers and forwarders must inform their customers of cargo liability limits, but each carrier can set its own limits.[37] Also, indirect air carriers have been almost totally deregulated from all federal economic regulation, but they are subject to antitrust rules [14 C.F.R. 296.10 (a) and 296.11].

surface
truck movements

One final, yet consequential, change resulted from the Motor Carrier Act of 1980 (94 Stat. 797). Since air-cargo shipments originate and terminate by truck, for years the degree of regulation necessary for surface portions of air cargo movements has been disputed.[38] Because of Section 7(b)(8) of the Motor Carrier Act of 1980, motor vehicle transportation incidental to air transportation, or in other words linked to a subsequent or prior airline movement, has become totally deregulated.

Structural Changes.   Deregulation significantly altered the structure of the air-cargo business. Already discussed was the increase in the number of competitors. Perhaps more significant was the move by several leading forwarders into direct air carriage. Emery, Airborne, Air Express International, and United Parcel Service (UPS)—all took advantage of new rules and quickly acquired all-cargo aircraft fleets (see Fig. 16.2). Principally, they accomplished this move through expanded charter operations or Section 418 certificates. Section 418 authority also enabled Federal Express to shift from its Part 298 air taxi authority and fly larger jets. It furthermore allowed Federal Express to continue to enjoy considerable decision-making freedom and, through the use of larger airplanes, gain operating economies.

What prompted forwarders to invest heavily in their own aircraft was the unreliability of overnight air service. As most combination carriers in the early 1970s began taking delivery of jumbo jets such as the B-747, DC-10, and L-1011, they began phasing out their freighter aircraft fleets. From an airline perspective, it made sense to fill belly space on these large combination aircraft. However, as the freighters were withdrawn, forwarders began to experience night flight capacity problems. Unlike freighters, few jumbo jets flew at night because passengers preferred flying during daylight hours. Consequently, forwarders found it increasingly difficult to provide reliable overnight air service.[39] Since this was their perceived market niche, forwarders started chartering airplanes and then acquiring them.

(margin notes:) new all-cargo airlines and why

night flight capacity problems

FIGURE 16.2.
View of a portion of the Emery Worldwide fleet that surrounds the Dayton hub each night as cargo is loaded and unloaded. (Photo courtesy of Emery Worldwide)

end of United
and American
freighter operations

Not all forwarders immediately assumed direct air-carrier responsibilities. Two of the largest companies—Burlington Northern Air Freight, Inc. (BNAFI) and CF Air Freight—continued to rely on combination airlines for direct air carriage. Both were jolted, therefore, by decisions in 1984 by United and American to cease all freighter operations that same year. In both cases, the reason was the disappointing economics of their all-cargo operations.[40] American and United had been two of the last majors to fly freighters.

forwarder responses

BNAFI's response to the actions by United and American was to lease aircraft and create a sorting hub at Fort Wayne, Indiana.[41] CF Air Freight's solution was to sign an innovative three-year agreement with Eastern Airlines that gave the forwarder exclusive use of the cargo space on seven Eastern Airbus A-300 airplanes. Nightly, these aircraft in early 1985 were linking nine major U.S. cities through the Houston hub. In addition, they were hauling passengers at low one-way prices (from origin to Houston for $49 and from Houston to destination for $49).[42]

forwarder
importance

Most small forwarders, however, lacking the traffic volume of a CF Air Freight, are in no position to sign a similar type agreement with a combination airline and will therefore continue to gamble on finding belly space on individual flights by combination aircraft. Still, the importance of forwarder business to the airlines should not be underestimated. Despite the move by forwarders to establish their own airlines, in 1982 the Air Transport Association of America reported its members derived almost 50% of their shipments from forwarders, and the percentage was increasing. In 1978, the forwarder share was 43.6%.[43]

air-truck
developments
and why

Another structural development was the aggressive move by small-package trucking companies into the air-cargo business. Although UPS had held air freight forwarder authority since 1953, with deregulation, it foresaw new market opportunities and moved assertively into overnight air services. Another market factor was Purolator Courier, which became an air-cargo carrier in 1977.

Airlines like American and Flying Tiger went in the opposite direction by developing supporting intercity trucking operations.[44] These expansionary efforts gave carriers the freedom of choice between routing shipments hundreds of miles by highways to connecting air services or in many cases simply leaving the short-haul shipments on the ground. The carriers believed that shippers wanted expedited service and what mode carried the cargo was of lesser importance.

Marketing Issues

Segmentation by Shipment Characteristics.   The air-cargo market can be segmented by shipment characteristics and time-sensitivity. Three characteristic shipment segments are courier service, small package express (SPE), and air freight. Courier service is the expeditious, overnight or faster, movement of documents and specially designed envelopes and tubes. Usually, these are limited to 5-lb. shipments. SPE traditionally has been defined as time-sensitive, overnight or sooner, shipments weighing up to 70 lbs. Following Federal Express's lead in 1984, some SPE competitors have now raised the limit to 150 lbs. Anything else is called air freight. Quite often, this freight involves larger shipments or traffic that may not be quite as time-sensitive as SPE services provide.

commodities

Most air-cargo commodities are high-valued manufactured goods, but aircraft also handle a wide variety of goods ranging from perishables like strawberries and flowers to live animals. For example, in 1983, Northwest flew 1598 cattle in 14 charter flights from Minneapolis to Seoul, Korea, for breeding purposes.[45]

SPE and Federal Express

Without question small package express has been the air-cargo success story in the last decade. Much of the credit is due to the Federal Express Corporation and its Chairman, Frederick W. Smith. Smith conceived the idea that shippers would pay a premium for reliable overnight air services and then made the theory work with a coordinated system of air transportation, sorting, ground handling, and door-to-door delivery under one ownership. Federal Express began operations in 1973 and grew to an annual sales level of $2.03 billion in the year ending May 31, 1985.[46] The leader in SPE, Federal had FY 1984 SPE sales of $626 million and another $639 million in courier—document and letter—revenues. Total FY 1984 sales were $1.436 billion.[47] Net income after taxes for FY 1984 was $115 million. Before-tax income on operating revenues was 11.5%.[48] Federal's success over the years spurred the entry of Airborne, Emery, UPS, and Purolator into the air SPE market.

yields

Federal's yields are truly surprising. While Section 401/418 operators averaged 44.3¢ per revenue ton-mile during 1983, Federal collected an average of 413.4¢ per revenue ton-mile.[49] In the first quarter of fiscal year 1986, Federal averaged $3.43 per lb.,[50] or about twice what passenger traffic was producing for the major combination airlines. Even more impressive is Federal's revenues per pound for overnight letter service—about $90 for two-ounce letters.[51]

Segmentation by Time-Sensitivity. Federal's success reaffirmed what the forwarders had been saying for years about the time-sensitive nature of most air cargo shipments. What used to be a business separated into overnight and second- or third-day service has been even more segmented in recent years. Choices now include same day, next morning (delivery by 10:30 A.M., for example), next afternoon (12 noon to 5 P.M.), next day (after working hours), second-day, and third-day service.

Passenger-hauling airlines are heavily promoting same day service. With thousands of daily daylight flight departures, this service is a natural product for them to sell. Overnight offerings, in contrast, are heavily marketed by forwarders and all-cargo airlines, since freighter flights are usually scheduled for nighttime departures. Finally, second- and third-day services are sold primarily by premier consolidators like UPS and by the combination airlines. The latter, according to the Air Transport Association of America, have a serious belly freight excess capacity problem, having achieved only a 28% load factor in 1982.[52] To fill more space, airlines need consolidated container loads, but this need requires more ground time resulting in second- or third-day services.

How Shippers Choose Carriers. With so many air-cargo options available, how do shippers choose a particular air carrier? In 1980, 560 traffic managers across the United States responded to a national survey to see what variables most influenced their selection of an air-cargo carrier. As summarized in Table 16.7, the rankings show little difference among the courier, SPE, and air freight market segments. Speed—that is, "total time in transit"—was found to be important to air freight purchasers, as well as to buyers of the courier or SPE services. However, consistent on-time delivery ranked first on each market segment list.

shopping for air-cargo services

Table 16.7 shows that "low rates" was far less important in carrier selection than services in all three market segments. For small package express customers, in fact, "low rates" was ranked last in importance. Thus rates appear to be a factor only after service considerations have been deemed ac-

---

TABLE 16.7. Air cargo carrier selection variables by market segments: rating means and rankings

Variable	Importance Rating (Means and Rank[a])		
	Courier	Small Package Express	Air Freight
Convenience of contacting previously used carrier	3.71(13)	3.26(11)	3.40(13)
Carrier reputation among shippers	3.33(11)	3.08(9)	3.23(12)
Prompt settlement of claims	3.06(8)	2.54(8)	2.66(8)
Total time in transit	1.24(2)	1.27(3)	1.30(2)
Consistent on-time delivery	1.16(1)	1.14(1)	1.20(1)
Carrier's ability not to lose shipments	1.35(3)	1.16(2)	1.31(3)
Carrier's ability to minimize damage to shipments	1.84(5)	1.58(4)	1.55(4)
My ability to obtain flight space when needed	2.38(7)	2.15(7)	2.12(6)
Low rates	3.08(9)	3.35(13)	3.05(10)
Tracing capability	1.89(6)	2.01(6)	1.75(5)
Accurate rate information	2.42(12)	3.18(10)	2.94(9)
Overall liability coverage	3.22(10)	3.27(12)	3.10(11)
Pick-up and delivery service	1.71(4)	1.83(5)	2.33(7)

[a]Importance rating response categories ranged from 1 ("Extremely important") to 7 ("Not at all important"). Ranks shown in parentheses.

Source: John W. Vann and Frederick J. Stephenson, "Air-Cargo—One Market or Three?" *Transportation Journal* 21, no. 1 (Fall 1981):17. (Reproduced by permission of the American Society of Transportation and Logistics, publisher of the *Transportation Journal.*)

ceptable. Nevertheless, because carriers and forwarders price independently, the range between high and low charges can be quite broad. Users are cautioned to make sure they understand air-cargo charges, including the amount charged, for it can be quite high, and what is offered for the money. Rates that appear to be a bargain may not include pick-up and delivery services or adequate liability coverage. Similar services must be examined in rate comparisons.

Market Targets. Not all air-cargo firms participate in all three of the courier, SPE, and air freight segments and in each time-sensitive market. UPS, for example, is the biggest package specialist in the transportation business. In 1984 UPS handled about 6.5 million packages per day.[53] Except for 180,000 air shipments, all packages moved by surface modes. Although UPS originally concentrated on the second-day air-cargo market using its "Blue Label" air freight forwarding service, it entered the overnight SPE air segment on September 20, 1982, and the courier overnight letter sector in June 1985. Nevertheless, it remains the biggest second-day air package carrier in the industry.

UPS

Purolator Courier Services, a specialist in overnight package and document or courier service, is a strong market force in the less than 350-mile range.[54] About 85% of its shipments move exclusively by truck, but Purolator has also been an important competitor in the air sector. Another firm, Flying Tiger Line, Inc., is one of the world's largest scheduled air-cargo carriers[55] and the leader in the high-weight shipment-size end of the air freight business. In January 1982, however, it, too, entered the small package door-to-door business.

Purolator

Flying Tiger

Airborne Freight Corporation traditionally was an air freight specialist. Since 1980 it has been emphasizing SPE and courier service, and with great success. In 1983 its SPE and courier shipments increased 66% and 52%, respectively.[56] A significant competitor, too, is Emery Worldwide, the largest U.S. air freight forwarder. Unlike most firms, Emery takes a broad approach, marketing with equal fervor SPE, courier, and air freight services and shipments of any size and any weight and for any destination.[57] Emery Worldwide is recognized as the industry leader in the 70–500 lb. segment. Approximately 98% of its aggregate shipments are delivered the next day.[58]

Airborne

Emery

Trends and Characteristics

Deregulation certainly contributed to recent air-cargo trends. From the quarter ended September 1977 through the quarter ended June 1983, average domestic cargo yields per revenue ton-mile for majors and all-cargo nationals increased from 32.76¢ to 43.38¢, or 32.4%. However, the 1983 figure was 3.86¢ below the December 1980 peak of 47.24¢.[59] Deregulation did not prevent rates from rising, but it seems to have moderated inflationary trends.

average yields

Nevertheless, between 1977 and 1982 domestic revenue ton-miles rose 25%, according to the CAB.[60] The gains were not balanced, however. Air freight tonnage declined three years in a row (1980–1982), whereas SPE traffic grew

traffic

at an annual rate of about 25%. The former is more sensitive to the level of general economic activity than the latter, which advanced despite the recession. The latter is a reflection of shippers' reducing inventories and using air transportation for faster, last-minute deliveries.

discounting

The deregulated air-cargo business is also characterized by heavy discounting. A general trend has been for larger forwarders and carriers to offer rate savings to customers who provide a large number of shipments or revenues during a prescribed timeframe. For example, Flying Tiger reported that these volume contracts accounted for about 30% of its domestic volume in early 1983.[61] Clearly, the larger carriers have intensified national (corporate) accounts sales efforts. Much of the discounting has happened in the air freight market segment. The combination carriers have also been trying to use price incentives to increase belly-freight traffic. For the most part, though, price wars have not been a characteristic of the more time-sensitive courier and SPE markets. Even in these segments, however, discounts are available for big shippers.

types of rates

Commodity characteristics seem far less important in air-cargo pricing than do weight or distance variables. *Flat rates*—charges that do not vary because of distance—often prevail between any two points on a carrier's national system. For example, overnight letter service might cost $11.00 anywhere in the United States that the airline or forwarder can reach. Carrier-provided envelopes or tubes often carry one price as long as maximum weights are not exceeded. However, as a customer requests faster delivery services, prices tend to rise. For example, next morning service normally costs more than next day service.

Some carriers deviate from flat rates by using a multiple zone pricing scheme to better factor varying shipping distances into their prices. In other words, the price from zone 1 to zone 2 (close-by zone) is less than the charge from zone 1 to zone 3 (a farther away zone). Freight-all-kinds (FAK) container rates, which allow a shipper to mix commodities in a single container while essentially purchasing container space on the aircraft, are also commonly used by carriers. Likewise, density discount rates frequently are offered to encourage shippers to use better aircraft cubic capacity. Such prices lower the rates per pound if cargo weighs more than a predetermined number of pounds per cubic foot. The carrier's objective is to increase the number of pounds flown because aircraft usually cube-out first. Only in the air freight segment are prices more closely linked to commodity descriptions.

Air-Cargo Forecasts and Developments

In 1984 Kidder, Peabody analyst Alfred Norling predicted annual increases in the air-cargo industry of 10% for the next several years for packages (SPE) and 25% a year for documents (courier service).[62] The Boeing Company was less optimistic, predicting an annual growth rate for scheduled domestic air-cargo movements throughout the world of 4.0% through 1985.[63] Others, critical of the Boeing estimate, argue that it fails to place enough emphasis on high-technology trends. These trends, they say, should produce small, high-valued commodities more suitable for air-cargo service.[64]

opportunities
and problems

It would appear that the better opportunities continue to be in the time-sensitive courier and SPE markets. The underdeveloped international air cargo market also looks promising. However, no one is predicting rapid expansion of the air freight market. Improved trucking services at highly competitive rates act as a deterrent to anything more than moderate domestic air freight growth. However, the ability of the U.S. economy to emerge from recession should help traffic. Another positive sign was the Air Transport Association's report of a 46.6% gain in small package express air shipments in the first quarter of calendar year 1984 versus the same quarter of 1983.[65]

electronic document
transmission service

An uncertain trend in the air-cargo business may be same-day electronic document transmission services, the blending of transportation and communications services. Federal Express began offering its Zap-Mail electronic mail service in 1984, combining surface truck pick-up of a document, electronic image transmission by satellite, printing at a distant Federal Express facility, and delivery by Federal Express truck, all within two hours.[66] Purolator responded with a competitive service offered in conjunction with MCI, the second largest U.S. telecommunications company.[67] But at the end of 1986, Federal Express dismantled Zap-Mail, because this service resulted in an after-tax writeoff of $190 million.

FIGURE 16.3.
Photo of STS-5 satellite deployment, using the Satellite Business System (SBS-3) spacecraft. (Photo reprinted courtesy of U.S. National Aeronautics and Space Administration)

space shuttle
The space age has made an impact on air-cargo transportation in another way. When the space shuttle Columbia blasted off on November 11, 1982, it thrust the United States into the for-hire satellite launching business (see Fig. 6.3). The National Aeronautics and Space Administration (NASA) charged each of two companies $8 million to haul their satellites aloft and launch them from the shuttle. As of November 1982, 33 companies, governments, and agencies were waiting in line with more than 100 satellites to be shuttle-launched.[68] Furthermore, the base price for the shuttle's entire cargo bay, which holds two or three satellites, was scheduled to rise to $71 million for fiscal years 1986 through 1988.[69] However, the world was stunned and saddened by the disaster of January 28, 1986.[70] The explosion and loss of the space shuttle Challenger on that date verified the risks of space transportation.

SUMMARY

International air transportation and air cargo represent two unique and important submarkets of U.S. aviation. From an economic perspective, each sector's revenues are relatively small compared with the revenues generated from domestic airline passenger traffic. However, if distances are great or time is critical, these sectors offer unmatched service capabilities.

The United States is the world leader in international aviation. Not only is this country the world's largest single aviation market, but U.S. flag airlines also rank first in aggregate market share. However, all is not well, as the overall U.S. flag carrier market share has declined. U.S. aviation policies, the aviation policies of foreign countries, and discrimination against U.S. flag airlines are blamed by some. International aviation is a risky business; U.S. carriers are still expected to survive by earning profits in a tough market where competition is comprised of many nationalized airline competitors.

Air cargo is an indispensable shipper tool. As a result of deregulation and bold carrier initiatives, the air-cargo business has rapidly changed. The courier and small package express segments of the market have been growing appreciably in recent years. Not so fortunate was the air freight segment, which was hurt by the recession and increased competition from an improved trucking industry. Marked by a flood of new entrants, the air-cargo industry is an extremely competitive business that provides a considerable array of price-service options.

STUDY QUESTIONS

1. What is the U.S. role in international aviation?
2. How are international passenger rates determined today?
3. Why did air freight forwarders start flying their own airplanes?

4. Based on the data of Table 16.7, what five variables most influence shipper choices of air carriers to haul their small package express shipments? Are rates not important?
5. How did the "Open Skies" policy and the avia-

tion policy of the International Air Transportation Competition Act of 1979 threaten Pan American World Airways?

6. Explain why air-cargo transportation is a good example of intermodal carriage.

7. What did CF Air Freight do to guarantee night-

flight cargo capacity in the wake of decisions by United and American to sell their freighter fleets?

8. Why has the United States not been able to deregulate international air transportation?

ENDNOTES

1. U.S. Department of Transportation, Research and Special Programs Administration, *Air Carrier Financial Statistics December 1984* (Washington, D.C.: U.S. D.O.T., 1985), pp. 1, 2 (hereafter cited as *Air Carrier Financial Statistics*).

2. U.S., Congress, House, Committee on Public Works and Transportation, *A Review of U.S. International Aviation Policy, Hearings,* before the Subcommittee on Investigations and Oversight, House of Representatives, 97th Cong., 1st and 2d sess., 1981 and 1982, testimony of Knut Hammarskjold, p. 869 (hereafter cited as *U.S. International Aviation Policy*).

3. Robert M. Kane and Allan D. Vose, *Air Transportation*, 8th ed. (Dubuque, Iowa: Kendall/Hunt Publishing Company, 1982), pp. 13–1, 13–2.

4. Betsy Gidwitz, *The Politics of International Air Transport* (Lexington, Mass.: Lexington Books, 1980), pp. 49–50.

5. Nawal K. Taneja, *Airlines in Transition* (Lexington, Mass.: Lexington Books, 1981), p. 42.

6. U.S. Civil Aeronautics Board, *CAB Reports to Congress, FY 1979 Annual Report* (Washington, D.C.: U.S. Government Printing Office, issued November 1982), p. 18 (hereafter cited as *CAB Reports*).

7. Gidwitz, *Politics of International Air Transport*, p. 62.

8. *CAB Reports*, p. 75.

9. Ibid., p. 97.

10. (a) "U.S. Reviewing European Fare Pricing Agreements," *Aviation Week & Space Technology*, 3 October 1983, p. 41; and (b) James Ott, "U.S. Stiffens Negotiating Stance," *Aviation Week & Space Technology*, 9 April 1984, pp. 28–29.

11. Ott, "U.S. Stiffens Negotiating Stance," p. 28.

12. Nawal K. Taneja, *The Commercial Airline Industry* (Lexington, Mass.: D. C. Heath and Company, 1976), pp. 280–281.

13. *U.S. International Aviation Policy*, p. 867.

14. Douglas L. Adkins, Martha J. Langelan, and Joseph M. Trojanowski, *Is Competition Workable in North Atlantic Airline Markets?* (Washington, D.C.: Bureau of International Aviation, U.S. Civil Aeronautics Board, March 1982), p. 6 (hereafter cited as *Is Competition Workable?*).

15. Ibid.

16. Ibid., pp. 10–11.

17. Gidwitz, *Politics of International Air Transport*, p. 98.

18. Sheila Tefft, "Delta Withdraws from Air Transport Group," *The Atlanta Constitution*, 13 November 1978, p. 10–D.

19. Joan M. Feldman, "IATA Faces Unresolved Fare Issues, Possible Hammarskjold Departure," *Air Transport World*, October 1983, pp. 66, 68.

20. Joan M. Feldman, "IATA's Rate Fixing Role Could Be Ending Soon," *Air Transport World*, December 1983, p. 20.

21. "Airlines Cite Need to Cut Fares to End Illegal Discounting," *Wall Street Journal*, 11 November 1982, p. 36.

22. U.S. Department of Transportation, Research and Special Programs Administration, *Air Carrier Traffic Statistics December 1984* (Washington, D.C.: U.S. D.O.T., 1985), pp. 1, 3.

23. *Air Carrier Financial Statistics*, pp. 16, 20.

24. "The Troubled World Airlines," *Dun's Business Month*, December 1983, p. 28.

25. Ibid.

26. *Is Competition Workable?*, p. 36.

27. Percentages for 1982 were derived from U.S. Department of Transportation, Research and Special Programs Administration, *U.S. International Air Travel Statistics Calendar Year 1982* (Cambridge, Mass.: Transportation Systems Center, 1983), Tables Ia and Id (hereafter cited as *U.S. International Air Travel Statistics*).

28. Pan American World Airways, Inc., *10-K Report,* filed with the Securities and Exchange Commission (S.E.C.), 31 December 1982, p. 25.

29. (a) Gidwitz, *Politics of International Air Transport,* pp. 20–22, 26–28; and (b) *Is Competition Workable?,* p. 29.

30. Jeffrey M. Lenorovitz, "Air France to Consolidate Gains in 1984," *Aviation Week & Space Technology,* 30 January 1984, p. 30.

31. (a) Pan American World Airways, Inc., *10-K Report,* filed with the S.E.C., 31 December 1980, p. 8; and (b) Pan American World Airways, Inc., *10-K Report,* filed with the S.E.C., 31 December 1978, p. 9.

32. "Soviet Su-15 Shoots Down Korean 747," *Aviation Week & Space Technology,* 5 September 1983, p. 25.

33. James Ott, "Forecasters Expect More Growth in Airline Traffic," *Aviation Week & Space Technology,* 12 March 1984, p. 185.

34. Based on (a) *U.S. International Air Travel Statistics;* and (b) Table 16.2 of the text.

35. Frank A. Smith, Senior Associate, *Transportation in America,* 3d ed., *July 1985 Supplement* (Washington, D.C.: Transportation Policy Associates, July 1985), p. 6.

36. U.S. Civil Aeronautics Board, Office of Economic Analysis, *Summary of Section 418 Domestic All-Cargo Financial and Traffic Results for the Six Months Ended June 30, 1983* (Washington, D.C.: C.A.B., 25 October 1983), p. 1 of the appendix (hereafter cited as *Section 418 Domestic All-Cargo*).

37. Frederick J. Stephenson and John W. Vann, "Air Cargo Liability Deregulation: Shippers' Perspective," *Transportation Journal* 20, no. 3 (Spring 1981):48–58.

38. Frederick J. Stephenson, "Air Freight Regulation: The Twenty-Five Mile Rule," *The Journal of Air Law and Commerce* 43, no. 1 (1978):55–69.

39. Frederick J. Stephenson, "The Night-Freighter Controversy," *Transportation Journal* 15, no. 4 (Summer 1976), 15–21.

40. Mark B. Solomon, "Airlines Drop Freighters, Force Change on Forwarders, Shippers," *Traffic World,* 5 November 1984, p. 87.

41. Mark B. Solomon, "New Hub System, Freighter Lift Puts BNAFI at Critical Juncture," *Traffic World,* 6 January 1986, p. 11.

42. Mark B. Solomon, "CF Air Freight, Eastern Sign Cargo-Space Pact on Coast-to-Coast Shipments," *Traffic World,* 18 February 1985, p. 8.

43. Joan M. Feldman, "Cargo Forecast 1984: Business Good and Getting Better," *Air Transport World,* January 1984, p. 36.

44. Ibid., p. 37.

45. Northwest Orient Airlines *Annual Report 1983,* (Minneapolis, Minn.: 1984), p. 9.

46. Joan M. Feldman, "Federal Express: Big, Bigger and Biggest," *Air Transport World,* November 1985, p. 48.

47. Federal Express Corporation, *10-K Report,* filed with the S.E.C., 31 May 1984, p. 4.

48. Feldman, "Federal Express," p. 48.

49. Derived from *Section 418 Domestic All-Cargo,* Table 1 (p. 1), Table 1 (p. 2), and Table 4 (p. 2).

50. Feldman, "Federal Express," p. 48.

51. Based on ibid., p. 47.

52. Feldman, "Cargo Forecast 1984," p. 36.

53. Michael Ward, "Creating a Niche in Semipriority Shipping," *Air Cargo World,* February 1984, p. 33.

54. Ibid., p. 34.

55. Patrick Fitzgerald, "Competition Big for Small Deliveries," *USA Today,* 15 December 1982, p. 2B.

56. "Airborne Freight," *The Value Line Investment Survey* (New York: Value Line, 1984), p. 254.

57. Beau Cutts, "Expanding the Fast-Courier Dogfight," *Atlanta Constitution,* 7 September 1982, p. 1-C.

58. Joan M. Feldman, "Small Package/Express Business Knows Few Bounds," *Air Transport World,* February 1984, p. 40.

59. U.S. Civil Aeronautics Board, Office of Economic Analysis, *Domestic Freight Yields and Traffic: Major and All-Cargo Groups* (Washington, D.C.: C.A.B., 3 October 1983), Table 1.

60. "CAB Tells Congress That Six-Year Deregulation Experiment Has Worked," *Traffic World,* 20 February 1984, p. 34.

61. Thomas A. Foster, "Buying Air Freight: Too Often an Afterthought," *Distribution,* May 1983, p. 46.

62. Feldman, "Small Package/Express," p. 40.

63. "Boeing Company Seers Predict Period of Air Freight Growth," *Traffic World,* 20 June 1983, p. 44.

64. Ibid.

65. "Small Package, Express Air Shipments Up 47%," *Traffic World,* 28 May 1984, p. 32.

66. James D. Parker, *Federal Express Corporation* (Atlanta, Ga.: Robinson Humphrey/American Express Inc., 24 April 1984), p. 6.

67. Feldman, "Small Package/Express," p. 41.

68. Dan Neuharth and Juan Palomo, "Columbia's Sales Pitch: 'We Deliver,' " *USA Today*, 12 November 1982, p. 2A.

69. Arlen J. Large, "Washington's Pricing Policy for Shuttle Cargoes Will Determine Future of Commercial Launches," *Wall Street Journal*, 21 March 1985, p. 64.

70. "Daring to Break the Bonds of Earth," *U.S. News & World Report*, 10 February 1986, p. 14.

ADDITIONAL READINGS

"Air Cargo, Inc., Loses Struggle To Retain Antitrust Immunity." *Traffic World*, 31 May 1982, pp. 10–11.

Alterman, Stephen A. "Air Freight Deregulation—Why Not?" *Air Cargo World*, March 1984, pp. 43–44.

Barks, Joseph V. "Forwarder Thinking." *Chilton's Distribution*, May 1982, pp. 34–35.

Barnum, John W. "Carter Administration Stumbles at Bermuda." *Regulation* (January/February 1978):18–30.

Bogosian, Richard W. "Aviation Negotiations and the U.S. Model Agreement." *Journal of Air Law and Commerce* 46 (1981):1007–1037.

"CAB to Suspend International Rates Only When 'Extraordinary Circumstances' Prevail." *Traffic World*, 7 February 1983, pp. 46–47.

"CAB Warns Peru, Brazil of Service Suspensions, But Grants Extensions." *Traffic World*, 14 May 1984, p. 42.

Cook, John C. *International Air Cargo Strategy*. 2d ed. Philadelphia: Air Cargo Research Institute, 1983.

Cummings, Sally. "Emery Goes 'World Wide.' " *Air Cargo Magazine*, February 1982, p. 26.

Dempsey, Paul Stephen. "Deregulation: The Great American Aviation Catastrophe." *Air Cargo World*, March 1984, pp. 44–46.

Eddy, Art. "Forwarder Hubs Make a Home in Mid-America." *Air Cargo Magazine*, November 1981, p. 20.

———. "Trucker Forum Assesses Impact of Deregulation." *Air Cargo Magazine*, May 1982, p. 12.

Feazel, Michael. "Europe Moves to Ease Regulation." *Aviation Week & Space Technology*, 30 January 1984, pp. 28–29.

Feldman, Joan M. "International Air Freight Outlook '84: Competition Heats Up." *Handling and Shipping Management*, February 1984, pp. 36–38.

Footer, Sheila. "Legal Issues and Answers for Commercial Users of the Space Shuttle." *Transportation Law Journal* 13, no. 1 (1983):87–101.

Gourdin, Kent N. "International Aviation Policy and Strategic Airlift: A Critical Appraisal." *Transportation Journal* 23, no. 2 (Winter 1983):20–27.

Hagen, Paul. "Flynn on Tigers." *Air Cargo World*, November 1983, pp. 36–38.

"IATA Aircraft Needs Surpass Revenue Level," *Aviation Week & Space Technology*, 24 October 1983, pp. 31–32.

"Is the U.S. Sabotaging Its International Airlines?" *Business Week*, 26 January 1981, pp. 74–78.

Johnson, Bruce. "Federal Express: High on Its Mighty 200's." *Airline Executive*, April 1984, pp. 40–41.

Lyon, Mark. "Federal Express: How the Rich Get Richer." *Air Cargo World*, February 1983, pp. 30–31.

"Pan Am Lives." *Air Transport World*, December 1983, pp. 38–43.

Phillips, Laurence T., and O'Connell, K. Michael. "The International Commercial Aircraft Market: Challenges and Opportunities for the 1980s." Transportation Research Forum. *Proceedings of Twenty-fourth Annual Meeting*. Oxford, Ind.: Richard B. Cross Company, 1983, pp. 183–192.

"Shipping by Air Comes of Age in the '80s." *Dun's Business Month*, February 1983, pp. 90–91.

Stephenson, Frederick J., and Vann, John W. "Deregulation: The Elimination of Air Cargo Tariff Filing Requirements." *Journal of Business Logistics* 3, no. 1 (1982), 59–72.

"U.S. Airlines Hurt Competitively by Overseas Bias, Reports GAO." *Traffic World*, 3 August 1981, pp. 34–37.

Veres, Robert. "Thinking Big in Small Packages." *Air Cargo World*, February 1983, pp. 16–21.

Part 8 examines three diverse, but equally relevant, topics. Chapter 17 addresses personal transportation management, strategy, and decision making. It is a special effort to examine transportation choices that can be beneficial to individuals, rather than to corporate employers or organizations. Primarily, the focus is on passenger transportation, and in particular, on automobile-related decisions. However, other transportation decisions that affect household budgets, personal safety, and lifestyles are also covered.

Chapter 18 is concerned with governmental decision makers. As in the preceding chapter, the orientation is directed away from corporations and toward public sector employees and officials who make transportation decisions. In particular, Chapter 18 examines public sector transit management, strategy, and decision making—choices made by government employees working in urban transportation settings. The goal is to identify public sector transit decision makers, examine the nature of their responsibilities and the impact of their decisions, show differences between public and private transportation decision making, and evaluate public sector transit management.

Chapter 19, which focuses on competition in the transportation industry, reviews theory, practice, and strategy. It initially examines economic and marketing theory, practice, and strategy. Price and service competition are reviewed. Then it combines information provided

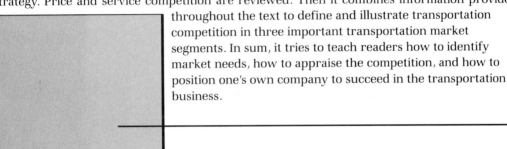 throughout the text to define and illustrate transportation competition in three important transportation market segments. In sum, it tries to teach readers how to identify market needs, how to appraise the competition, and how to position one's own company to succeed in the transportation business.

8 Selective Transportation Issues

17

Personal Transportation Management, Strategy, and Decision Making

Throughout their lives, U.S. citizens make transportation decisions such as what kind of car to buy, how to travel on vacation, and how to ship household goods when they move to another residence. Personal transportation decisions affect their household budgets, their happiness, their ability to use time more efficiently, and even their safety. Just as corporate managers need to plan transportation strategies and make wise transportation decisions, so do individuals. This chapter focuses on personal transportation management and strategy. Specifically, it addresses automobile decisions, transportation and location decisions, and other types of personal transportation choices.

AUTOMOBILE DECISIONS

The automobile is the single most important element in U.S. transportation. That fact is often forgotten. Consider the following items:

automobile facts

- Of the estimated $713.2 billion spent in 1984 for U.S. passenger and freight transportation, private automobile expenditures represented $375.7 billion (52.7%).[1]
- In 1981, there were 123,461,507 privately and publicly (government) owned cars registered in the United States.[2] That figure accounted for 37.3% of all the registered cars in the world (331,161,771).[3] In relation to the 1980 U.S. population figure of 226,545,805,[4] there were approximately 0.54 cars per man, woman, and child in the United States.

■ Government researchers in 1977 found that 86% of the nation's 75.4 million households had cars, and 36.5% of those households had two or more automobiles. Also, 22.8% of U.S. households owned trucks. There was an average of 1.5 motor vehicles (cars and trucks) per U.S. household.[5]

■ In 1982, U.S. drivers licenses totalled 144,610,000.[6]

Without question, the United States is one of the most automobile-oriented societies in the world. Cars are ingrained in the nation's social fabric, its economic base, and its people's lifestyles. At one time or another, most citizens own and/or operate automobiles.

New Car Strategy

case study

New Car Cost Summary.   Since many people buy new cars or plan to, an analysis of the economic consequences of the decision to buy a new automobile is pertinent. Consider the case of John Doe, a 22-year-old single man and a recent graduate of a four-year business school, who in June 1984, after he had found a full-time job, purchased a new 1984 Cutlass Supreme Coupe. John's car was comfortable but not as luxurious as he would have liked. For economic reasons, John rejected the options of a V-8 engine, power seats, reclining seats, and power windows. What he bought was a two-door, 6-cylinder car with a Landau vinyl roof, AM-FM stereo radio with a tapedeck, power steering, power brakes, automatic transmission, cruise control, tinted glass, side molding, and a rear window defroster. His intentions were to drive the car—his only vehicle—15 miles each way to work for 250 days per year (7,500 miles per year) and put another 12,500 miles on the car annually for pleasure and personal business reasons. John would reside in an apartment in Fulton County (Metropolitan Atlanta) and work in Atlanta.

What would be the estimated future costs of John's decision? Table 17.1 shows that the answer is $21,077 for three years, or an average of $7,026 per year, $585 per month, $19.25 per day, and 35.1¢ per mile for each of the 60,000 miles. As noted in the table, the highest cost items listed are depreciation ($6,515, or 30.91%), gasoline ($4,500, or 21.35%), insurance ($3,354 or 15.91%), and finance charges (interest of $2,073, or 9.84%).

Each cost item will be explained in detail in the following sections. Figures are based on primary (interviews, phone calls, etc.) and secondary (written) government and industry data. This illustration uses a precisely defined car model, and costs take into account John Doe's personal profile, including age, sex, marital status, job location, residential location, and driving plans. Although automobile costs vary from one location to another and between different types of drivers (for example, a 45-year-old man with a family versus John Doe), this illustration provides an accurate estimate of the costs in one location—Metropolitan Atlanta—and for one type of car owner. This illustration provides a benchmark by which other automobile owners can appraise their own situations.

TABLE 17.1. The cost of owning and operating a new automobile[a]

Cost Item	Three-Year Costs	Percentage
Sales tax	$563	2.67%
Depreciation	6,515	30.91
Finance charges (interest)	2,073	9.84
Insurance	3,354	15.91
Gasoline	4,500	21.35
Property taxes and registration fees	518	2.46
Repairs and maintenance	1,637	7.77
Tires	567	2.69
Garaging, parking, and tolls	1,350	6.40
Total three-year costs	$21,077	100.00%
Average cost per year	$7,026	
Average cost per month	$585	
Average cost per day (365 days per year)	$19.25	
Average cost per mile for each of 60,000 miles	35.1¢	

[a]Assumes a Cutlass Supreme Coupe was purchased new in 1984 and operated by a 22-year-old single man who lived in an apartment in Fulton County (Metropolitan Atlanta). Purchased on June 22, 1984, at a price of $11,250 plus sales tax, it was the only car owned by John Doe. John planned to drive it 20,000 miles per year for three years.

Sources:

1. Federal Highway Administration, *Cost of Owning and Operating Automobiles and Vans: 1982* (Washington, D.C.: U.S. Department of Transportation, 1982).
2. *N.A.D.A. Official Used Car Guide, Southeastern Edition, June 1984* (McLean, Va.: National Automobile Dealers Used Car Guide Co., 1984), p. v.
3. Communications with Georgia businesspeople and tax authorities. The methodology used is a composite approach based on the first source document (*Cost of Owning and Operating Automobiles*) and the author's original work.

Sales Tax.   The first cost item in Table 17.1 is a $563 sales tax. The automobile sticker price was $12,531, but John negotiated a purchase price including delivery charges and dealer preparation fees of $11,250. In Fulton County, the sales tax was 5% of the purchase price ($11,250).

Depreciation.   The second and most expensive cost John would face is depreciation. Rather than deal with down payment costs and the retirement of borrowed money, which would require monthly payments of principal and interest, an alternative methodology is to measure the loss in the vehicle's value over time. In other words, *depreciation* measures the difference between the value at the time of purchase and the resale value at any point in time thereafter. According to statistics from the U.S. Department of Transportation[7] and the National Automobile Dealers Association (NADA),[8] John's car would lose an estimated 57.9% of its value ($6515) during the first three years of use. This percentage figure is higher than normal due to high mileage (60,000 miles versus the normal 35,000 to 40,000 miles).

Finance Charges.   A third expense is finance charges. If John paid the sales tax in cash, paid a 20% cash down payment of $2250, and financed the remaining $9000 of the purchase price, aggregate interest costs would be $2073. This figure is based on a 36-month bank loan at an annual percentage rate (APR) of 14%. For informational purposes only, the monthly loan payment for principal and interest would have been $307.59. If John had opted to finance the $9000 debt over 48 months, he could have lowered the monthly payment to $248 per month. However, in return, the APR would have increased to 14.5%, and the total four-year interest cost would have been $2914 (an increase of 40%, or $841). APR rates and loan duration terms vary from region to region and between lenders, such as between manufacturer financing sources and banks.

Insurance.   Next on the list is automobile insurance. The estimate in Table 17.1 is from one of the largest U.S. automobile insurers. It assumes that John has had no previous accidents and no traffic violations. The policy will give John the recommended coverage of $100,000 (each person)/$300,000 (each accident) bodily injury, $50,000 property damage, $25,000 personal injury, and $100,000 (each person)/$300,000 (each accident) uninsured motorist protection. Deductibles, should John have an accident, would be $250 for collision and $250 for comprehensive, except for collision loss. In projecting the six-month charge to cover the three-year period, a 3.0% annual premium increase was factored in. Also taken into account was the trade-off between the declining car value and increasing insurance rates due to inflation. John maintained the same insurance protection but on a less valuable automobile as it became older.

female
insurance cost

John's high insurance costs are determined by his age (22), his sex (male), his marital status (single), his residential location (a major metropolitan area), and his car's value. If John's name had been Mary and if all other assumptions had remained the same, her estimated three-year insurance bill would have been $2914. Rural residents could expect to pay lower premiums. In contrast, many people will pay more. For example, a *Wall Street Journal* article stated that New Jersey drivers paid the highest average auto insurance premiums in the nation in 1983.[9]

Gasoline.   Gasoline, too, is a big cost item. Although John's automobile was advertised at 27 miles per gallon on the highway and 20 miles per gallon in town, a more realistic overall estimate is 18 miles per gallon. Because much of John's driving would be in traffic, gasoline efficiency would suffer. At 18 miles per gallon, John's car would burn 1111 gallons going 20,000 miles annually. Assuming that John would buy unleaded gasoline at the self-service pump and the average price per gallon would be $1.25 the first year, $1.35 the second year, and $1.45 the third year, the total three-year fuel bill would be $4500.

Property Taxes and Registration Fees.   In Fulton County, John would pay an estimated $518 over three years in ad valorem (i.e., property) taxes and vehicle registration fees. In the first year, John would pay no ad valorem tax, as the new car dealer is responsible for this expense. Thereafter, however, he would be looking at property taxes of approximately $253 in year two and $223 in year three. Registration, including license plates and tags, would be about $14 per year.

Repairs and Maintenance. One difficult expense to estimate is repair and maintenance costs. If John is fortunate, he will escape serious problems such as engine or transmission work. It is hoped that he will avoid accidents and not be billed for insurance deductibles. However, not knowing what good fortune or misfortune John might face, Table 17.1 relies on government average estimates.[10]

scheduled maintenance

Assumed in the car purchase price was the decision not to participate in optional warranty programs. Although this decision kept the purchase price down, there was a cost trade-off in case major work was needed later. Included in the $1637 three-year estimate is scheduled maintenance per the instructions in the owner's manual, including maintenance of emissions control and cooling systems, oil changes, safety checks, tune-ups, lubrication, repair parts, and labor. Nonscheduled repairs such as brake repairs, replacement of shock absorbers, and accessorial work (e.g., replacement of fan belts, light bulbs, wiper blades, etc.) were also factored in.[11] It was assumed that John was a mechanical novice who would pay others to work on his car.

Tires. John will need to replace four tires at some point before 60,000 miles of car use. Consequently, the $567 cost based on local advertising data is for top-quality steel belted radials—tubeless whitewalls. This price includes federal excise taxes, state sales taxes, tire balancing, and valve stems. Alignment (a likely action on John's part) would be included under the repairs and maintenance cost item.

Garaging, Parking, and Tolls. The last expense item listed—garaging, parking, and tolls—is also difficult to appraise. Georgia is a toll-free state, so no cost figure for tolls was included. If John lived in Florida or many northeastern states, he could face toll roads, bridges, or tunnels every day. Next, it was assumed that John's employer would provide him with a free parking space at work. However, John did not buy the new car to stay home in his nonworking hours. Therefore, $150 per year in meter and parking lot charges was assumed. Finally, John's monthly apartment rental rate includes a monthly fee of $25 for the provision of a parking space and access roads to his building. Collectively, residential and nonresidential parking costs would total $1350 for the three-year period.

classes of cars by weight

Hertz Study. As high as John Doe's cost figures may seem to be, they could be much higher. Table 17.2 shows car ownership and operating cost estimates in 20 of the largest U.S. cities. In 1983 Atlanta ranked 20th in car costs, with average per-mile expenses (41.59¢) 26.9% below those in Los An-

TABLE 17.2. Costs of owning and operating a 1983 compact car in 20 U.S. cities[a]

City	Cost in Cents per Mile	Rank
Los Angeles	56.86¢	1
San Francisco	54.61	2
New York City	54.50	3
Miami	50.03	4
Chicago	49.46	5
Denver	47.74	6
St. Louis	47.53	7
Seattle	47.06	8
20 City Average	46.53	—
San Diego	45.34	9
Boston	45.34	9
Minneapolis	44.99	11
Milwaukee	44.23	12
Houston	44.09	13
Pittsburgh	43.56	14
Detroit	43.44	15
National Average	43.28	—
Cleveland	43.21	16
Cincinnati	42.68	17
Dallas	42.27	18
District of Columbia	42.11	19
Atlanta	41.59	20

[a]Assumed a new 1983 Ford Fairmont was purchased by a family of four with one youthful male driver. Car options included automatic transmission, power steering, power brakes, air conditioning, and tinted glass. Two-thirds of the purchase price was financed with a 60-month loan. The car would be driven 10,000 miles annually for five years. Costs per mile reflect total vehicle costs for five years divided by 50,000 miles of travel.

Source: The Hertz Corporation, "1983 New Car Ownership & Operating Costs Fall $\frac{2}{3}$ Cents a Mile in 20 Top Cities, Latest Hertz Annual Study Shows" (unpublished press release, the Hertz Corporation, 26 March 1984). (Published with permission of the Hertz Corporation.)

geles, the most costly city in which to own and operate a car (56.86¢). Atlanta's cost figure was also lower than the national average (43.28¢). These findings imply that John Doe's costs most likely would have been greater in many locations across the country where taxes, insurance, fuel, and other costs exceed Atlanta's expense levels. The table also shows that average costs at each of the 20 cities, as well as the national average, exceed the 35.1¢ per mile estimate in John Doe's case. Since the two studies (the Hertz survey and the John Doe example) differ in several assumptions (e.g., Hertz assumes the car would be driven 10,000 miles per year for five years versus John Doe's 20,000 miles per year for three years), there is risk in trying to compare too closely the two studies' results. Nevertheless, the Hertz study validates how expensive new automobiles can be. Furthermore, the figures in Table 17.2 are for a compact car—one smaller and less costly to own and operate than John's intermediate-sized Cutlass. Compact cars weigh between 2800 lbs. and 3600 lbs., whereas intermediates weigh between 3600 lbs. and 4400 lbs. While classifying cars by weight (and because they will be referenced later), subcompacts weigh from 2000 lbs. to 2800 lbs., and large cars weigh more than 4400 lbs.

Cost Impact of Driving Less.   Why did John's newer, larger car cost less per mile? In part, the answer is found in the assumption of less miles of use per year. If John had been in the position of limiting his driving to 10,000 miles annually, the average cost per mile for the first three years and 30,000 miles would have been 55.8¢ (versus 35.1¢), because an estimated 66% of John's new car costs are fixed expenses. When he signed the automobile purchase agreement, he was obligated to pay the sales tax, finance charges, and other fixed costs regardless of the number of miles driven. By driving 20,000 miles per year, John spreads his fixed automobile costs over more miles, thereby lowering average total fixed and variable costs per mile. However, by driving 20,000 versus the hypothetical 10,000 miles per year, John would spend $4323 more during the three years in increased variable costs. In addition, increased automobile use wears vehicles out faster than conservative use.

Earnings Impact.   How would John's decision to buy a new car affect his earnings? As shown in Table 17.3, assume that John's first year salary would be $18,000. In subsequent years, if he received annual 10% pay raises, gross earnings would increase to $19,800 and $21,780, respectively. From this amount he would pay a three-year total of $16,980 in federal income taxes (16.4% rate), state income taxes (3.9%), social security taxes (6.7%), and state and local sales taxes (1.5%)—or in other words, 28.5% of his gross pay. These deductions would leave John with $42,600 in take-home pay, of which the new car would consume 49.5%. If he seems short on cash for rent, food, clothing, and dating, this shortage is due to his initial transportation decision.

TABLE 17.3. The impact of John Doe's new car purchase on his personal finances

Item	Amount
Earnings	
First year	$18,000
Second year	19,800
Third year	21,780
Total	$59,580
Less federal, state, and local taxes of 28.5%	−16,980
Take-home pay	$42,600
Auto cost (3 years)	21,077 (49.5%)
Net remaining take-home pay after auto expenditures	$21,523

Sources: Federal and state tax documents.

Controlling New Car Costs.   Buying a new automobile has become
more expensive than it was a decade ago. According to the Motor Vehicle
Manufacturers Association, the average purchase price of a new automobile,
including all classes of cars from small subcompacts to large luxury vehicles,
was $10,398 in March 1983. By comparison, the average price was $4,439 in
1974. During this period, then, average new car prices jumped 134%. In 1974,
28.7 weeks of earnings were required to equal the average new car purchase
price, whereas it required 37.9 weeks in 1983. However, that figure was less
than the 1950 level of 41.6 weeks. Nevertheless, the trend is not favorable for
potential automobile purchasers.[12]

rising new car costs

How could John have reduced his new car costs? One strategy is down-
sizing—buying a compact or subcompact rather than an intermediate-sized
car. Another tactic is to buy a more stripped-down car (one with fewer options). By lowering the car's purchase price, John should be able to cut the
amounts expended for the sales tax, finance charges, and property taxes. With
less value to lose, depreciation costs most likely would be less.

*reducing
new car costs*

Regardless of the model or options purchased, a new car buyer should
shop diligently. Sticker (list) prices on intermediate-sized cars tend to be 15%–
17% above dealer costs. With this fact in mind, buyers should bargain for a
lower purchase price. Other possible strategies for savings are to buy cars
that depreciate slowly and/or have excellent fuel efficiency. Small cars often
accomplish both. However, regardless of the model purchased, most new cars
will cost their owners at least 25¢ per mile. Decisions should be made accordingly.

The Used Car Option

Three of four car purchasers buy used, rather than new, cars. These vehicles
typically represent one-owner cars loaded with options, driven less than 30,000
miles by the previous owner, and intended to be used as the primary vehicle
in the household of the used car buyer.[13] In other words, this car is a substitute for a new car.

What are the drawbacks of buying a used car? First, cars are consumables
in the sense that most wear out eventually. The choice to buy a used car is
usually a decision to buy a car with a shorter remaining life; the buyer may
need to replace the used car sooner than a new car. The drawback is the
uncertainty involved. Why is the owner selling the car? Was it in an accident?
Does it have mechanical problems? Image is another risk. Can the buyer's ego
endure a used car? Finally, used car buyers may not be able to purchase the
exact model, color, and options they would prefer.

drawbacks

Economic and other advantages, however, can make the used car option
attractive. For example, if John Doe had elected in June 1984 to buy a 1983
Cutlass Supreme Brougham with a V-8, less than 10,000 miles of use, and just
about every option conceivable, he could have bought the car for $10,775 and
saved more than $1000 (his new car price including sales tax was $11,813).[14]
One great advantage of the used car purchase option is upgrading—buying a

advantages

more luxurious automobile. Upgrading is the only way that many consumers will ever be able to afford better quality in a car. Since the biggest cost for most new cars is depreciation, by buying a used, intermediate-sized car, the purchaser allows the previous owner to absorb about 30% of the depreciation expense the first year and approximately 50% or more during the first three years of ownership. Used cars tend to result in lower purchase prices, which subsequently reduce financing costs and property taxes. However, a buyer should be prepared to pay higher APR interest rates on used car loans. Still, money can be saved by borrowing less principal.

buyer advice

Prospective used car buyers should do their homework and shop wisely. Study the used car literature to check for price, quality, and safety information. Look for relatively new cars. In general, a good time to buy a used car is right after the new models reach the showrooms. For example, when the 1987 model arrived on the scene in the fall of 1986, buyers could shop for a 1985 model of the same car. In this way a 13–14-month-old low-mileage car might be found and two years of depreciation expenses saved (greater than 40%). Remember, too, that used cars are traded in at wholesale prices and offered to the market at retail price levels. Whether a used car is purchased from a new car dealer, a used car specialist, or directly from the owner, bargain for a price closer to the wholesale price. Publications found at newsstands, such as *Buyer's Guide Report/Auto Price: Used Car Prices,* list average wholesale prices, so there is little excuse for pricing ignorance. A buyer who has any doubt about a car's quality or condition should have the vehicle inspected by a qualified mechanic. This inspection may cost the buyer $50, but it could save hundreds of dollars later.

attitude changes

Used car buyers need to be flexible. Purchasers may not receive exactly the cars they want, but they can usually find satisfactory solutions. To salvage the ego problem, many used car buyers buy luxury cars. Also, attitudes about new cars as status symbols seem to be changing. People are keeping cars longer, as attested by the increasing average ages of automobiles. In 1972 the average age of a car on the road was 5.7 years. By 1982 it was 7.5 years.[15]

Present Car Option

If John had owned a used car, he could have kept it, bypassing both the new and used car purchase decisions. Often, this option can result in the lowest car costs per mile. If a car is paid for and is five or more years old, the owner faces no sales tax, low depreciation, no finance costs, lower insurance expenses, and reduced property taxes. However, depending on the car's model and condition, the owner could face higher fuel costs (it could be a gas guzzler) and repair and maintenance costs. Nevertheless, a driver can buy a considerable amount of gasoline and spend hundreds of dollars on repairs and often be ahead in relation to other car ownership options. In fact, owners who drive an older model in some cases can lower their costs to less than 15¢ per mile—the only way known to achieve such cost levels. One consulting firm,

Townsend-Greenspan & Company, estimated the expected life of 1980 model automobiles in the United States at 14 years and 5 months.[16]

Leasing

Leasing is another option. Nearly 10% of all cars today are leased, but few are leased by individuals. Corporations, government units, and independent businesspeople lease most cars for nonpersonal reasons. However, by 1987, research shows that 40% of the new cars in the United States may be leased.[17]

advantages and disadvantages   Why lease a car? Leasing usually requires no significant down payment. Leases may also produce lower monthly payments; however, low monthly payments may require a larger down payment. Another advantage might be that the user can drive a newer car. As new car ownership loans stretch to 60-month terms, more owners may trade owned cars after five years when the car is fully paid for. Leasing, in contrast, may give consumers a new car every three years. The most common disadvantage is that the user is not building equity, since the individual does not own the automobile after several years of payments. Those who lease should understand down-payment, monthly fee, mileage, maintenance, and future car purchase provisions. For example, the lessee may have to buy the car at the end of the lease. Since leases include a variety of financial arrangements, those who choose to lease should know what they are paying for.

Company-Provided Car

Many U.S. workers benefit from company-provided cars or monthly or mileage allowances offered in repayment for the use of privately owned vehicles. How much would a company-owned car have been worth to John Doe? For illustrative purposes, assume that his employer provided a car identical to the one John bought. (In reality, John probably would be eligible only for a downsized, stripped-down new automobile at his management position.)

Assume that John would annually drive as follows: (1) 7,500 miles between home and work (the same assumption as in the ownership case, 250 days at 30 miles per day); (2) 12,500 miles for personal reasons (the same as before); and (3) 20,000 miles making sales calls. Furthermore, John would pay his employer 5¢ per mile for nonbusiness use (a common practice). Otherwise, almost all auto expenses, including John's insurance, gasoline, repairs, and so on, are covered by the company. The noted exception is garaging and parking expenses. Assume that John would pay the $1350 for residential and nonresidential parking.

gross pay benefit   Computation of John's gross pay benefits from the company car appears in Table 17.4. As noted, John would draw benefits from the 7,500 miles driven to and from work and the 12,500 miles of pleasure travel. If he owned the car, he would have paid $2,632.50 going to and from work. Since this would be a fully compensated expense, it would be worth $2,632.50 to John. Also, the 30.1¢ savings per mile of personal travel ($0.351 per mile minus John's

TABLE 17.4. John Doe case: annual gross pay impact of receiving a company-owned 1984-model new car	
Item	**Value to John Doe**
(A) 20,000 miles of business travel making sales calls	No value; without the sales job, he would not have driven these miles. $0
(B) 7500 miles of commuting to and from the office	(7500 miles) ($0.351 per mile) = $2632.50
(C) 12,500 miles of personal use	(12,500 mi.) ($0.351 − 0.05 per mi.) = $3762.50
Gross take-home pay savings	$6395.00
Less personal garaging and parking costs	− 1350.00
Net take-home pay savings	$5045.00
Gross pay benefit taking into account John's 28.5% tax rate ($0.715x = 5045)	$7056.00

Source: Based on Table 17.1 of the text.

$0.05 per mile contribution) equates to another $3762.50. After the $1,350 garaging and parking costs, the new take-home pay benefit would be $5,045. After taxes are factored on that amount, the company car would equate to another $7,056 in annual gross pay benefits. In essence, John's gross pay in his first year of work would have to exceed $25,000 to be as good a deal as $18,000 gross pay and the new car. An added benefit of a company car is that John should receive a new car every third year, because the car would have 80,000 miles on its odometer after only two years. Few company cars are kept beyond 100,000 miles.

who receives company cars?

Which 22-year-old college graduates are likely to receive company cars? The answer is salespeople. Too often, people forget this fact when looking for jobs. Although job seekers obviously need to consider other reasons for accepting work, car benefits should not be ignored. Furthermore, as salaried employees advance to positions of greater corporate responsibilities, many not only receive cars, but also receive more luxurious models. As income levels rise and employees find themselves in higher income tax brackets, company car benefits only increase in value.

Car Selection

Whether an individual owns or leases a car, he or she often prefers a certain model. How people select cars is a function of needs, wants, and price. Invariably, people place considerable weight on styling, purchase price, fuel efficiency, dependability, and comfort.[18]

Needs.   One of the first decision variables is needs. Does the automobile operator have a family and need room for more than four people in the vehicle? Does the person have a baby and need plenty of storage space for hauling a playpen, diapers, and other luggage? Will the car be used for short-distance trips or longer trips? A vital question to ask is what the vehicle must do. For example, if the owner plans to haul a trailer into the mountains, a V-8 engine might be necessary. Often this situation prompts the one-car household to buy an all-purpose "family" car—large in size, high on power, and capable of meeting every driving need. The trouble is that such cars are far less efficient than smaller cars for the vast majority of trips U.S. citizens take.

Trip Use.   Although data are not available to analyze car trips exclusively, if we include other forms of privately controlled motor vehicles (e.g., vans, pickup trucks, motorcycles, self-contained recreational vehicles, and taxis), we will better understand transportation decision making.

applications   Table 17.5 shows that 83.7% of all person-trips in 1977 were taken in these kinds of vehicles (we will call them personal motor vehicles). Furthermore, personal motor vehicles accounted for 89.3% of the work-related (earning-a-living) trips, 88.4% of the family and personal business trips, and 84.3% of the vacation trips. As noted in the table, 32.9% of all motor vehicle trips were for work-related purposes in 1977, and another 32.3% accommodated family and personal business needs. Only one-tenth of 1% (one trip in a thousand) was for vacation purposes. This is an important finding, because many people buy such vehicles as cars and vans for vacation purposes, although 99.9% of their trips are not vacation oriented and cover only short distances. As data in Table 17.5 indicate, work-related trips averaged 9.6 miles; family and personal business trips averaged 5.9 miles; and all trips, including the 95.4-mile average vacation trip, averaged only 8.3 miles. Knowing these statistics, consumers might be wiser to rent or lease vacation vehicles or use other modes to get to and from the vacation spot. They could then acquire vehicles more efficient for 999 of the 1000 trips taken. Nevertheless, most U.S. citizens must have a privately controlled motor vehicle simply to earn a living and function in our car-based society.

There is, however, far less need for most households to own multiple vehicles. Again, individuals make those decisions, so there is room for considering alternatives such as public or private for-hire transportation (e.g., taxis, buses, rapid rail lines, subways, etc.); car pooling, which means more people in each car; van pooling, usually a company-backed program for picking up plant workers in a company-purchased vehicle; bicycling; or even walking. However, individual environments and needs will influence the feasibility of these alternatives.

Safety Considerations.   Too infrequently mentioned as a car model selection variable is automotive safety. How many buyers ask which cars have the lowest fatality rates or demand that additional safety equipment be installed as car purchase options?

TABLE 17.5. Personal motor vehicle trip statistics (1977)

Trip Purpose	Percentage of Person Trips[a] By Private Vehicles[b]	Percentage of Motor Vehicle Trips by Trip Purpose	Average Trip Length by Trip Purpose (miles)
Earning a living (work-related)	89.3%	32.9%	9.6
Family and personal business	88.4	32.3	5.9
Civic, educational, and religious	54.2	6.4	6.1
Social and recreational			
Visiting friends	85.8	8.4	11.2
Pleasure trips	96.2	0.4	15.7
Vacations	84.3	0.1	95.4
Other	85.5	10.4	9.1
Subtotal—social and recreational	N/A[c]	19.3	10.2
Other and unknown	N/A	9.1	9.8
All purposes	83.7%	100.0%	8.3

[a]The sum of all trips taken by all individuals, for example, four people going in the same car from one location to a concert is four person trips.

[b]Cars, station wagons, vans, pickups, trucks, motorcycles, self-contained recreational vehicles, and taxis (for personal use).

[c]Not available.

Source: MVMA Motor Vehicle Facts & Figures 1983 (Detroit, Mich.: Motor Vehicle Manufacturers Association, 1983), p. 40, citing U.S. Federal Highway Administration, *1977 National Personal Transportation Study.*

small versus large cars

In 1982 more than 60% of the new cars purchased in the United States were subcompacts or compacts.[19] Compared to 1972, when intermediates and large cars represented 61.8% of the new car market,[20] there has been an evident shift in consumer preferences. The obvious motivation for buying smaller cars is the need for greater fuel efficiency. As OPEC crude oil prices soared from $2.48 per barrel in 1972 to a peak of $34.00 in October 1981,[21] U.S. citizens traded in their gas guzzlers for cars capable of producing more miles per gallon. In the process of opting for economic efficiencies, however, small car buyers increased their safety risks.

Small cars have higher fatality rates than do larger cars. The U.S. Department of Transportation stated that the fatality rate for subcompacts was 3.5 deaths per 10,000 cars on the road. For compacts the rate was 2.4 deaths per 10,000 vehicles. By comparison, intermediate-sized and large cars had fatality rates of 1.9 and 1.5 deaths, respectively.[22] By these measures, the average subcompact is twice as risky as the typical large car. However, if a subcompact is involved in a nose-to-nose crash with a large car, with each traveling

40 mph, the occupants of the smaller car are 8.2 times more likely to die.[23] The problem is the mismatch in car weights and the subcompact's more limited crush space—the distance from the bumper to the leading wall of the passenger compartment. Another grim statistic shows that small-car occupants represented 55% of the nation's traffic fatalities from two-car collisions in 1979, yet in that year only 38% of the automobiles on the road were small cars.[24] Thus larger cars tend to be safer. How much is this worth to the individual?

Safety Issues and Decisions

mandatory safety equipment

Automobile Safety Equipment and Use.   All cars sold in the United States have mandatory car safety features. According to the U.S. Bureau of Labor Statistics, federally required seat belts, collapsible steering columns, penetration-resistant windshields, padded instrument panels, dual brakes, and other mandatory safety equipment added $515.01 (adjusted to 1981 dollars) to the retail price of a 1981 model automobile.[25] The negative aspect of these regulations is that they raise car prices, which can discourage car buying. On the positive side, an estimated 10,000 lives a year are saved because of these measures.[26] In this case, the government removed the individual's right to elect to pay for these safety items. Would the public buy them if not required to do so?

passive restraint systems

One controversial automobile issue in 1984 was the debate concerning the necessity of requiring that new automobiles be equipped with passive restraint systems. One such item is an *air bag,* a device positioned in the steering column or dash that would automatically inflate a balloon-type device in a front-end or near-front-end collision. This device would cushion the blow in a crash. Automatic coupling lap and shoulder *seat belts* are an alternative to air bags. These automatic seat belts are called passive restraint systems because they require no human effort to engage them; when a person sits down on the front car seat, the belts automatically move into position and lock themselves into place.

safety potential

According to the National Highway Traffic Safety Administration, up to 10,000 deaths and thousands of crippling or other serious injuries would be prevented annually in the United States by air bags in all cars.[27] On average, 21,000 people are killed each year in the front seats of cars, and the proportion of the deaths resulting from head-on or near-head-on crashes is 55%.[28] Thus, why do opponents resist air bags? The key factor is their price. Some car manufacturers offered this option in 1984, but the price was high ($880 on a Mercedes-Benz, for example).[29] Also, if an air bag activates, it would need to be replaced at further expense to the car owner. However, if air bags were mass produced, the estimated cost for a full seat unit would be in the $185–$230 range[30]—about equivalent to the price of an AM-FM stereo tapedeck. A far cheaper alternative would be for people to buckle-up using their present car's lap and shoulder belts, but this practice is not likely on a voluntary basis. The seat belt usage rate in the United States in 1983 was only about 14%.[31]

On July 11, 1984, Transportation Secretary Elizabeth Dole ordered that air bags or automatic seat belts be installed in new cars beginning in 1986. For example, 10% of the 1987 model cars produced in 1986 must have passive restraint systems. Unless enough states pass laws requiring use of manual seat belts (states accounting for two-thirds of the population), 100% of the 1990 car models must be equipped with passive restraint systems.[32]

seat belts and child safety seats

Although many people feel that seat belts are inconvenient, they save lives by reducing the number of people thrown against the windshield (or through it), dash, or steering column. Use of the shoulder belt, as well as the lap belt, lessens the probability of head injuries. People riding in the back seats should also use seat belts, and children should always be secured with safety belts or safety seats. According to the U.S. Department of Transportation, nearly 60% of the children who died in cars could have been saved by the use of child safety seats or safety belts.[33]

drinking and driving

Driving Decisions. Since 1941, a total of 1,788,400 people in the United States have died on the country's highways. This figure is more than three times the combined number of U.S. citizens killed in World War II, Korea, and Vietnam (519,264).[34] Another troublesome statistic is that life expectancy has increased for every age group in the United States except 15–24 year olds. In the latter case, the death rate is higher than it was 20 years ago, and the leading cause of death is alcohol-related motor vehicle crashes.[35] To a great extent, these tragedies are the results of poor human judgment—transportation decisions to drink and drive, to speed, or both.

Alcohol and driving do not mix. About 26,000 people each year die in alcohol-related traffic accidents. Of this total, 10,000 are young people.[36] How many of them are innocent victims of ill or irresponsible citizens? Statistics show that of every 2000 drunk drivers, only one is arrested, and that person's chance of receiving a serious penalty is statistically insignificant.[37] This means that the problem will not be lessened until all drinkers start monitoring themselves. A person who wants to drink should find a way home other than driving. This is one decision that really requires no more than common sense and a concern for other human beings.

speeding

Speed is another killer. All that is required to slow down is to lift a foot off the accelerator. This, too, is a decision each driver can make. A passenger in a speeding car should not be embarrassed to ask the driver to slow down. If the driver refuses, the passenger would be wise to find another way home, if possible. By increasing the car's speed from 45 mph to 60 mph, the chances of dying in a crash double. If the speed is raised to 70 mph, the death risk doubles again.[38] When the United States dropped its maximum speed limit in 1974 to 55 mph, traffic fatalities decreased from a 1972 total of 54,600 to a 1975 level of 44,500.[39] Although all the credit cannot be attributed to slower speeds, certainly it was more than coincidental that at least 10,000 fewer deaths occurred. Nevertheless, many drivers are increasing their speeds. Although speeding is against the law, most speeders will not be caught. Speeders, therefore, should consider the potential consequences of their poor decisions—to themselves and to the innocent bystanders they might injure or kill.

TRANSPORTATION AND LOCATION DECISIONS

Location decisions can have considerable impact on transportation costs and time commitments. When people accept jobs and make residential location decisions, they have defined their home-to-work transportation parameters. If they reverse the decision-making process and choose residences to decrease transportation costs, they may significantly increase apartment rent or home mortgage costs. For example, a home in the suburbs 10 miles from the central business district (CBD) is likely to cost more than a similar home 25 miles away, but its purchase could reduce travel costs to and from the CBD.

Cost of Commuting

Consider an example of the costs of commuting between home and work. John Doe's decision to live 15 miles from his Atlanta office cost him $2632.50 per year, assuming he drove to work 250 days a year at 35.1¢ per mile and 30 miles per daily round trip. Suppose, however, he had decided instead to accept a job in downtown Boston and live in Franklin, Massachusetts, a suburb southwest of the Boston CBD. How would these choices have altered John's commuting costs?

car mode and minimum mileage decision   Initially, assume John had decided to drive to work by the route that minimizes trip mileage. As explained in Table 17.6, the route would follow 30 miles of "back roads" and require 75 minutes in total door-to-door (home-to-work) time. Daily round trip commuting costs would be $29.06 (auto costs and parking). Annually, then, the expenditure would total $7265 for 250 round trips.

car mode and minimum trip-time decision   An alternative, if John wanted to minimize trip time, would be to drive by local roads to I-495, travel north on I-495 to the Massachusetts Turnpike (I-90), then drive east on I-90 into Boston. For the privilege of saving 20 minutes daily (this option is a 65-minute, one-way, door-to-door trip versus the other 75-minute trip), John, because of circuity, would drive another 40 miles per day (a total of 50 miles each way versus 30 miles each way using the backroads route). Compared with the prior routing, this alternative would add $16.44 to the daily commuting bill (82¢ per minute saved). Total costs, including tolls and parking, would be $45.50 per day and $11,375 per year.

parking implications   The $8 daily parking charge was the average rate near the Boston CBD in June 1984.[40] In contrast to the company-provided free parking in the Atlanta example, if John had been in Boston, he would have paid $2000 per year, $6000 for three years, and an additional 10¢ per mile if he drove 60,000 miles for three years ($6000 divided by 60,000 miles). This illustrates how automobile costs can vary substantially by region or by the change of an assumption such as from free parking to employee-paid parking. Another point is

TABLE 17.6. John Doe's auto and rail commuting costs, Franklin, Massachusetts, to the Boston central business district

Option	Commuting Costs	
(A) Drive the fewest miles via backroads (30 miles one-way)	Daily auto costs (60 miles per day) at ($0.351 per mile) =	$21.06
*75-minute one-way trip time	Parking	8.00
	Total per day	$29.06
	Annual commuting costs (250 days)	$7,265.00
(B) Drive the shortest route in time (local road to I-495 to Massachusetts Turnpike) (50 miles one-way)	Daily auto costs: (100 miles per day) at ($0.351 per mile) =	$35.10
	Parking	8.00
	Tolls	2.40
*65-minute one-way trip time	Total per day	$45.50
	Annual commuting costs (250 days)	$11,375.00
(C) Commuter rail	Daily round-trip rail fare	$3.79
*80 minutes door-to-door one-way trip time home to work	Auto costs to/from Franklin station (2 miles per day) at ($0.351 per mile) =	0.70
	Total per day	$4.49
	Annual commuting costs (250 days)	$1,122.50

Sources: Friends in the Boston area and a phone call to the Boston and Maine Railroad (Franklin Office), 2 July 1984.

that John would put 75,000 miles on his car in three years if he drove to and from work at the rate of 100 miles per day. This mileage would force John to replace his automobile prematurely.

commuter rail option

By deciding to live in Franklin, John would also have had a commuter rail or public transportation option. For example, the monthly cost for an unlimited-use train ticket between Franklin and Boston in June 1984 was $79.[41] Assuming John bought 12 monthly tickets at $79 each and made 250 annual roundtrips, the average cost per daily round trip would have been $3.79. Assuming that each day John drove one mile from home to the Franklin station, parked free at the station, and drove one mile home in the evening, the transit option would cost $4.49 per day and $1122.50 per year. Comparing the costs of the three alternatives, commuter rail could have saved John a minimum of $24.57 per day and $6142.50 annually. This saving would be equivalent to an $8591 annual pay raise in gross pay.

advice

What can be learned from this illustration? First, someone deciding to live a long way from work should be prepared to pay for the privilege, regardless of whether the commuting choice is to drive or use public transportation. Secondly, if the person's goal is to minimize trip-time, the individual should calculate the economics of circuitous routings. In our illustration, Franklin is poorly located for interstate highway travel to Boston. If John wanted to use the Massachusetts Turnpike, he should have chosen to live in a town closer to I-90. Thirdly, if there is a public transit alternative, one should examine its costs and consider using that alternative. Fourthly, when locating a residence, a person should look for one with a public transportation alternative. Even if he or she does not plan to use transit regularly, it could be used if necessary. Fifthly, car pooling can be a good alternative. Automobile costs drop rapidly if two or more people share the expenses. Finally, living closer to work may be best. If John had made a decision to live only 15 miles from the Boston CBD, he could have reduced his annual driving and parking costs by $2632.50 (30 versus 60 roundtrip miles per day @ 35.1¢ per mile times 250 days per year). With these savings, he could have spent another $219.38 per month on rent or on a mortgage ($2632.50 divided by 12 months). As a bonus, he would have been able to reduce his commuting time to work. Time is a precious commodity. Can we afford to use this limited resource unproductively commuting to and from a job?

saving a work-year   Think about this situation. If one individual commuted 80 minutes to work each way and another person, because of a decision to live close to work, accomplished the trip in 10 minutes, the second person would save 583.3 hours per year (80 minutes less 10 minutes, times 2 trips per day, times 250 days per year, divided by 60 minutes per hour) and 1750 hours every three years. This time-saving is nearly a full work-year (50 weeks @ 40 hours per week, or 2000 hours). Thus a critical variable is where to locate a household in respect to where one works.

Need To Minimize Commuting Time

Consider another illustration portraying how an individual might minimize commuting time by making intelligent transportation decisions during a 43-year career (age 22 to age 65). Assume that Jane Smith is married, has children, is religious, and is civic minded (participates in community affairs). In studying Jane's time commitments, try drawing a profile of your own plans and how your time use might differ. Table 17.7 summarizes the results.

time commitments   Begin with the assumptions that on a daily basis, Jane averages 8 hours of sleep, 2 hours of eating, and 1 hour of preparation (showering, drying her hair, dressing, changing clothes, etc). Presume, too, she shops an average of $\frac{1}{2}$ hour per day (this activity includes travel time), participates in religious activities 7 hours per week (an average of 1 hour per day), and contributes another 30 minutes per day to civic responsibilities. Personal business (e.g., reading the mail, balancing checkbooks, writing correspondence, answering telephone calls, reading papers or magazine articles, etc.) uses another hour per day. Chores consume another hour, and children's activities (parental driving, waiting, watching, and coaching) use 30 minutes daily. Finally, earning a living occupies 45 hours per week (about 6.5 hours per day spread over 7 days).

time remaining and needs   If this schedule was followed, 22 hours of every 24-hour day (for 365 days per year), 153.5 hours of each 168-hour week, and 39.44 total years of a 43-year career would be obligated. The balance available for anything else would be 2 hours per day, 14.5 hours per week, and 3.56 years during the career. (In short, as one manager remarked, with his time commitments, he cannot afford to be mad at anyone for more than 10 minutes.) Not included in Table

TABLE 17.7. Time obligations: daily, weekly, and during
a career[a]

Activity	Average Hours per Day	Average Hours per Week	Average Years per 43-Year Career
Sleeping	8.0	56	14.32
Eating	2.0	14	3.57
Preparation	1.0	7	1.81
Shopping	0.5	3.5	0.90
Religious activities	1.0	7	1.81
Civic responsibilities	0.5	3.5	0.90
Personal business	1.0	7	1.81
Chores	1.0	7	1.81
Children's activities	0.5	3.5	0.90
Work	6.5	45	11.61
Subtotal	22.0	153.5	39.44
Balance	2.0	14.5	3.56

[a]Assumes Jane Smith is married, has children, is religious, and is civic minded.

17.7 is time for recreation and *commuting to and from work*. If Jane was locked into two hours of commuting each day, she would have no choice but to sacrifice some other priority. Note again that the most critical determinant of commuting time is the location decision.

Potential Monetary Benefits

Consider another reason for locating wisely. Suppose Jane Smith had the choice of buying two homes identical in every way except that one was two miles closer to work. If her intentions were to drive to work and live in that home for the duration of a 43-year career, how much could be saved by choosing the home nearer to work? At 35¢ per mile and 250 roundtrips per year for 43 years, if Jane invested the $350 of annual transportation savings (4 miles @ 35¢ per mile × 250 trips) and earned 10% per year, at the end of the forty-third year, her accumulated savings would be $188,523.

Other Location Suggestions

The following location suggestions might prove to be helpful:

▪ Try to find a job in the suburbs. Traffic is heavier near the CBD. A person who works 10 miles from the CBD and lives farther out in the suburbs misses most of the traffic. Also, consider living in the city center and commuting to work in the suburbs. The advantage here is driving to and from work in the opposite direction from the movement of most traffic.

▪ Live to the east of one's job. The sun will be over a person's shoulder and not in his or her eyes while the person is commuting to and from work.

■ Table 17.5 shows that pleasure and vacation trips represent only five trips per thousand. Thus choosing a residential location that keeps work-related, family, and personal business trips short in distance and time is more practical than choosing one that is closer to the shore, the lake, or the mountains.

FURTHER PERSONAL TRANSPORTATION DECISIONS

Most U.S. citizens make a number of other transportation decisions. How to move household goods is one example. Another is how to ship small packages. Other decisions involve the best mode to use for a vacation or the selection of transportation modes to use on company-paid business trips. Finally, people make leisure transportation vehicle decisions.

Household Goods Movement Choices

moving company versus do-it-yourself

Most people move several times during their lives. Which is better: Hiring a household goods carrier, or renting a "do-it-yourself" truck or trailer such as U-Haul or Ryder equipment? Although the subject of for-hire household goods moving companies was discussed from a carrier perspective in Chapter 13, here we view moving decisions from a consumer perspective. The key decision variable is perhaps who is paying the freight bill. If the employer assumes this responsibility, a household goods carrier is the best choice. Moving requires a considerable amount of effort and is disruptive. Why assume this burden if it is not necessary? However, an individual who is paying for all or part of the move should obtain price estimates from several moving companies and compare their services. Moving company services and rental costs for do-it-yourself equipment should also be compared.

should you do your own packing?

People can save money when using a moving company by packing many things themselves. Buying boxes (used boxes can often be purchased cheaply from household goods moving companies), tape, and labels (e.g., name and address, "this side up," "fragile," etc.), and packing dishes and other items are relatively simple for those who do not mind investing time and energy. Since packing costs frequently represent as much as 50% of the total bill paid to a moving company, savings can be substantial. People who do pack their own property, however, should remember to do it well. Moving companies rarely assume responsibility for damaged goods packed by the owners.

released rates

Household goods moving carriers ask their clients to agree to, or reject, released value rates. Those who accept released value rates agree to pay lower transportation charges in exchange for reduced liability protection from the carrier. Those who want higher liability protection should not accept released value rates, but they will pay higher shipping charges. Although a homeowner's insurance policy might cover monetary losses above and beyond the released value rate of approximately 60¢ per lb. paid by the moving company, it is not a good idea to assume that this insurance protection will be given. Check personal insurance policies before moving.

Small Package Decisions

People are periodically faced with decisions on how to ship small packages to friends or relatives. Frequently, the shipments involve presents or "care packages" sent to children at school or camp. What is the best way to send packages? Actually, the individual's problems are similar to an employee's dilemma in shipping small packages for the firm. The best advice is to plan the shipment far in advance of the required delivery date and look for satisfactory service at reasonable prices. Items should be packed well but not excessively to avoid paying for unnecessary weight. Chapter 19 will present a detailed discussion of small package shipping alternatives.

Vacation Transportation Choices

driving or flying

Many people err in making vacation transportation decisions. For example, a person traveling alone might drive 1000 miles round-trip to a vacation point at 30¢ to 35¢ per mile ($300 to $350) when air fare might be as low as $79 each way. Often it is much faster and cheaper to take an airplane and rent a car at destination than to drive alone or with two people in the car. Cars are most cost-efficient when they contain four to six people.

using a travel agent

Another vacation decision people often face is whether to use a travel agent or book reservations directly with an airline. Travel agents are excellent sources of information, and airline tickets cost the same whether booked directly from the airline or from the travel agency. Fees paid to travel agents are deducted from the airline ticket prices at no added charge to the consumer. Whereas a carrier wants to sell seats on its airplanes, travel agents can try to find the best services at the right prices among all carriers.

ways to save money

When planning a vacation, consider carefully the time available and the savings that might be achieved by traveling in off-peak periods. Most airlines, for instance, offer substantial discounts if fliers travel during the carriers' least busy periods (at night, mid-day, mid-week, or Saturdays). Flexibility in choosing vacation destinations can also lead to savings. Look for markets where rate wars have reduced airline ticket prices. Consider varying surface transportation plans. For example, hundreds of dollars in family flying expenses might be saved by driving another 50 miles to an airport different from the one normally used but one offering discounts to the desired destination.

Employer-Paid Travel Decisions

Those whose travel is paid for by their employers should understand the consequences of their corporate transportation decisions. Is the employer adequately compensating employees for the use of their cars? An employee who is not reimbursed at the rate of 30¢ or more per mile is probably underwriting the employer's travel expenditures. Also, many individuals do not take advantage of programs that provide personal travel benefits. An example is an airline's frequent-flier program, which provides individuals with free travel when they have flown a certain number of miles or have taken a fixed number of trips on that particular airline. Although employers pay the airline charges for business-related trips, employees are often given the right to select the airline on which they wish to fly. Thus they should choose one that can benefit them personally if there is no added cost to their employer.

Leisure Transportation Decisions

Finally, U.S. citizens spend billions of dollars annually for leisure transportation. In the pursuit of rest and relaxation, people buy boats, aircraft, motorcycles, recreational vehicles, snowmobiles, bicycles, and pick-up trucks and then spend countless more dollars using them, maintaining them, or hauling them to places where they can be used. The following statistics show the popularity of these vehicles.

boating
- U.S. citizens spent $3.63 billion in 1981 for pleasure boats, motors, and accessories. Sales included 281,000 outboard boats, 51,000 inboard/outdrive boats, and 73,000 nonpowered sailboats. In 1981 there were 12.5 million pleasure boats used by more than 60.7 million people in this country.[42]

motorized and nonmotorized aircraft
- During 1981, 9,457 general aviation aircraft were sold for a total of $2.9 billion in factory net billings. The general aviation fleet, as of January 1, 1982, totalled 213,200 aircraft. Most were owned by individuals, and not corporations, and were used for personal reasons.[43]

motorcycles
- In the U.S. in 1981 there were approximately 7.3 million motorcycles and three-wheel all-terrain vehicles. More than $2.1 billion was spent on the purchase of an estimated 1.0 million new motorcycles in 1981, and considering other expenditures such as taxes, repairs, parts, and used equipment sales, the total economic impact in this sector was $8.1 billion.[44]

recreational vehicles
- Recreational vehicles (RVs) include travel trailers, truck campers, vans, motor homes, and camping trailers. Statistics show 1981 sales of RVs at $1.8 billion and 239,100 units. By one survey, an estimated 10% of all U.S. families own RVs.[45]

bicycles
- U.S. citizens purchased 8.9 million bicycles in 1981, resulting in retail sales of approximately $1 billion. Since 1972 more than 106 million bicycles have been sold in this country, and in 1983 it was estimated that there were 64.5 million bicycles in use by 105 million riders.[46]

snowmobiles
- In the United States in 1983 there were an estimated 1.9 million snowmobiles used by about 12 million people.[47]

pick-up trucks
- Pick-up truck sales in the U.S. from domestic and foreign production totalled 933,809 in 1981. Many owners use these vehicles in part for recreational purposes. The total privately and publicly owned truck registrations in 1981 were 34.9 million, the majority of which were pick-up trucks.[48]

Before buying expensive leisure transportation vehicles, people should forecast how much they expect to use them. Many people use them sparingly and at great cost per utilization period. Often these are expensive luxuries, but it is hard to deny that they can be great fun to play with.

SUMMARY

Personal transportation decisions can have considerable impact on individuals, households, and families. Owning a new car, for example, was found to cost a 22-year-old man $21,077 for three years—an average of $7026 per year, $585 per month, $19.25 per day, and 35.1¢ per mile for each of 60,000 miles. Most U.S. citizens need an automobile, but not necessarily a new one. By buying the right used car, a person could save not only money, but also buy a more luxurious model. The cheapest option is probably to retain the present automobile. Still better can be the receipt of a company-provided car. Under the right circumstances, a company car that can be used for personal reasons could be worth more than $7000 annually to an employee. Any automobile driver, however, can make safer transportation choices such as not drinking and driving, not speeding, or wearing seat belts.

People selecting an automobile should try to find a vehicle that does what it is needed to do the most—a car that efficiently takes care of home-to-work and other short-haul trip needs. On average, only one trip in 1000 is a vacation trip, and the remaining trips tend to be less than 10 miles in length. Thus many car buyers could save money by buying less expensive cars and finding alternative ways to travel to vacation points.

After people have chosen a job site and located a new residence, they have locked themselves into transportation costs and time commitments. If the location decision is made without adequate study and thought, the result could be expensive. There are ways to save both time and money by choosing residential locations more wisely.

Individuals should make intelligent transportation decisions at home as well as at the office. Chapter 17 explained some of the types of personal transportation decisions individuals make, their consequences, and how more intelligent choices might be made in the future.

STUDY QUESTIONS

1. If a person's only objective is to buy the most cost-efficient new car available, what general advice would you give?

2. What are the advantages of buying a used automobile instead of a new car? What are the disadvantages of used cars?

3. What are passive restraint systems, and why are more automobiles not equipped with them?

4. When is it usually less expensive to use air transportation than automobile transportation for taking trips? Why?

5. What types of leisure transport decisions do people make?

6. Why does it usually cost more to operate automobiles in cities like Los Angeles and San Francisco than in smaller cities or rural areas?

7. If an employer compensates an employee at the rate of 20¢ per mile for driving the employee's automobile on company business, who is receiving a good deal? Why?

8. Why would it usually cost more per mile for an individual to operate the same automobile 10,000 miles per year than 20,000 miles per year? Why then would it cost more in dollars per year to operate the car 20,000 miles rather than 10,000 miles?

ENDNOTES

1. Frank A. Smith, Senior Associate, *Transportation in America,* 3d ed., *July 1985 Supplement* (Washington, D.C.: Transportation Policy Associates, July 1985), pp. 2, 5.

2. Motor Vehicle Manufacturers Association of the United States, *MVMA Motor Vehicle Facts & Figures 1983* (Detroit, Mi.: Motor Vehicle Manufacturers Association of the United States, Inc., 1983), pp. 36–37 (hereafter cited as *MVMA Motor Vehicle Facts*).

3. Ibid.

4. U.S. Department of Commerce, Bureau of the Census, *U.S. Census of Population: 1920 to 1980, I,* as cited in U.S. Bureau of the Census, *Statistical Abstract of the United States: 1984,* 104th ed. (Washington, D.C., 1983), p. 6.

5. *MVMA Motor Vehicle Facts,* citing Oak Ridge National Laboratory, *Transportation Energy Conservation Data Book: Edition 4.*

6. U.S. Bureau of the Census, *Statistical Abstract of the United States: 1984,* 104th ed. (Washington, D.C., 1983), p. 616, citing U.S. Federal Highway Administration, *Drivers Licenses,* annual.

7. U.S. Department of Transportation, Federal Highway Administration, *Cost of Owning and Operating Automobiles and Vans: 1982* (Washington, D.C.: D.O.T., 1982), p. 4.

8. *N.A.D.A. Official Used Car Guide: Southeastern Edition, June, 1984* (McLean, Va.: National Automobile Dealers Used Car Guide Co., 1984), pp. iv and v.

9. Joanne Lipman, "New Jersey's High Insurance Rates on Autos Hurt Drivers and Insurers," *Wall Street Journal,* 11 October 1983, p. 23.

10. U.S. Department of Transportation, *Cost of Owning and Operating Automobiles,* p. 11.

11. Ibid., pp. 4–5.

12. (a) Heidi Ehrlich, "What It Costs to Buy a Car," *USA Today,* 16 May 1983, p. 1B, citing the Motor Vehicle Manufacturers Association; and (b) *MVMA Motor Vehicle Facts,* p. 42, citing (1) "Expenditure Per Car," unpublished data, U.S. Bureau of Economic Analysis;" (2) "Nonsupervisory Gross Weekly Earnings," U.S. Bureau of Labor Statistics; and (3) "Median Family Income," U.S. Bureau of the Census.

13. William G. Flanagan, "Computing Real Costs of Owning a New Car: No Wonder People Coddle So Many Clunkers," *Wall Street Journal,* 11 February 1980, p. 38.

14. *Buyer's Guide Reports/Autoprice: Used Car Prices* (Milwaukee, Wi.: Pace Publications, 1984), p. 24.

15. John Koten, "Auto Officials See Sales Rebound but Face Ticklish Pricing Decisions," *Wall Street Journal,* 16 June 1982, p. 29.

16. Cited in "Retiring Autos at 14," *New York Times,* 3 April 1983, p. 1F.

17. Bill Waters, Director of Marketing Services, Merrill Lynch Pierce Fenner & Smith, "High Prices, Interest Rates Lead Many to Lease New Autos," *The Bureau of Wholesale Sales Representatives News,* 10 October 1983, p. 12.

18. (a) John Koten and Amanda Bennett, "Sticker Stickler: Auto Makers Rethink Pricing Policies to Woo Still-Reluctant Buyers," *Wall Street Journal,* 23 October 1981, p. 1; (b) Leonard M. Apcar, "Idling Autos: Car Sales Slip As Prices, Loan Costs Rise; Slow Recovery Expected to Begin This Fall," *Wall Street Journal,* 28 April 1981, p. 56; and (c) Ruth Hamel, "We Still Think Japanese Cars Are a Better Deal," *USA Today,* 7 March 1983, p. 1B.

19. "U.S. Auto Makers Reshape for World Competition," *Business Week,* 21 June 1983, p. 85.

20. *MVMA Motor Vehicle Facts,* p. 18, citing *Automotive News, Market Data Book.*

21. "OPEC Price Cut Should Reduce Inflation 1%," *Atlanta Constitution,* 16 March 1983, p. 1–A.

22. U.S Department of Transportation, National Highway Traffic Safety Administration, *The Car Book: A Consumer's Guide to Car Buying* (Washington, D.C.: D.O.T., 1981), pp. 18–23.

23. (a) Dale D. Buss, "Death on the Road: Small Cars

May Save Fuel but Cost Lives, Safety Experts Think," *Wall Street Journal*, 27 April 1982, p. 1; (b) Sylvia Porter, "Small Car Owners Warned," *Athens Banner Herald*, 24 March 1981, p. 3; and (c) "Fatal Automobile Accidents on Rise Again," *Atlanta Constitution*, 26 May 1981, p. 9–A (reprinted from the *New York Times*.)

24. Sylvia Porter, "Small Car Owners Warned," *Athens Banner Herald*, 24 March 1981, p. 3.

25. (a) Buss, "Death on the Road," p. 20; and (b) *MVMA Motor Vehicle Facts*, p. 42, citing the U.S. Bureau of Labor Statistics.

26. Buss, "Death on The Road," p. 20.

27. Albert R. Karr, "Auto Air Bags: U.S. Resumes Debate on Use," *Wall Street Journal*, 29 November 1983, p. 35.

28. Kevin McManus, "The $100 Solution: Maybe, Just Maybe, the Airbag's Time Has Come," *Forbes*, 5 December 1983, p. 206.

29. "Auto Air-Bag Maker Says His New System Would Cost Far Less," *Wall Street Journal*, 16 March 1984, p. 17.

30. Karr, "Auto Air Bags," p. 51.

31. McManus, "The $100 Solution," p. 206.

32. "Dole Orders Air Bags for Cars," *Atlanta Constitution*, 12 July 1984, p. 1 (Associated Press release).

33. U.S. Department of Transportation, *The Car Book*, p. 24.

34. "Get the Drunks Off the Road," a message paid for by United Technologies Corporation, *Wall Street Journal*, 7 June 1984, p. 30.

35. Information compiled by the National Highway Traffic Safety Administration and distributed by Mothers Against Drunk Driving.

36. Editorial, "Why Deprive Many to Punish a Few?" *USA Today*, 2 December 1982, p. 10A.

37. Information distributed by Mothers Against Drunk Driving and provided by the National Highway Traffic Safety Administration and the National Safety Council.

38. Albert R. Karr, "Death on the Road: Driver Error, the Cause of Most Auto Mishaps, Defies Easy Solution," *Wall Street Journal*, 4 May 1982, p. 1.

39. Ibid.

40. Phone call from James Tilley, a transportation analyst in Boston, 30 June 1984.

41. Phone conversation with the Franklin, Massachusetts, Station Master of the Boston and Maine Railroad, 2 July 1984.

42. Standard and Poor's *Industry Surveys*, Vol. 1, October 1982, p. L29.

43. *General Aviation Statistical Databook 1982 Edition* (Washington, D.C.: General Aviation Manufacturers Association, 1982).

44. *1982 Motorcycle Statistical Annual* (Irvine, Calif.: Motorcycle Industry Council, Inc., 1982), pp. 6, 11.

45. Standard and Poor's *Industry Surveys*, Vol. 1, October 1982, p. L28, based on information provided by the Recreation Vehicle Industry Association and *R.V. Dealer*, May 1982, p. 29.

46. Information supplied by the Bicycle Manufacturers Association of America, Inc., Washington, D.C., December 1982.

47. Information provided by the International Snowmobile Industry Association, Annandale, Va., 22 December 1982.

48. Motor Vehicle Manufacturers Association of the United States, Inc., *MVMA Motor Vehicle Facts & Figures '82* (Detroit, 1982), pp. 14, 21.

ADDITIONAL READINGS

"The All-American Small Car Is Fading." *Business Week*, 12 March 1984, pp. 88–91.

Arnould, R. J., and Grabowski, H., "Auto Safety Regulation: An Analysis of Market Failure." *The Bell Journal of Economics*, 12, no. 1 (Spring 1981):27–48.

"Autos: Detroit's Struggle to Survive." *Business Week*, 11 January 1982, pp. 62–63.

Bettner, Jill. "Behold That Lowly Creature, the Gas-Guzzler: The Cost of a New Car May Make It a Bargain." *Wall Street Journal*, 22 September 1980, p. 46.

Bogdanich, Walt. "Purchases of Flight, Rental-Car Insurance Are Often Unnecessary, Many Experts Say." *Wall Street Journal*, 30 July 1984, p. 19.

Darlin, Damon. "Leasing a Car for Personal Use Could Be Good Alternative to Buying with a Loan." *Wall Street Journal*, 19 December 1984, p. 31.

"A Deal That Could Put a Brake on Car Costs." *Business Week*, 25 January 1982, p. 26.

Eck, Ronald W., and Stafford, Donald B. "National Freight and Passenger Mobility Indexes." *Traffic Quarterly* 34, no. 4 (October 1980):539–554.

Edwards, Jerry L., and Plum, Roger A. "Attitudes Toward Ride-Sharing: 3M Center Case Study." *Traffic Quarterly* 34, no. 2 (April 1980):287–304.

Flint, Jerry. "A Million Jobs to Go." *Forbes,* 23 November 1981, pp. 39–41. (An article about U.S. auto workers.)

———. "Wipe That Sneer." *Forbes,* 7 June 1982, pp. 38–41. (An article on Chrysler's comeback.)

Herd, Donald R.; Pigman, Jerry G.; and Rizenbergs, Roland L. "Analysis of Weekday, Weekend, and Holiday Accident Frequencies." *Traffic Quarterly* 34, no. 3 (July 1980):413–428.

Karr, Albert R. "The Rule-Slashers: Auto-Safety Agency Stalls in Deregulation after Setting Fast Pace." *Wall Street Journal,* 9 December 1983, p. 1.

Landro, Laura. "Market Share Sets off Fight at Avis, Hertz." *Wall Street Journal,* 21 July 1982, p. 31.

Oppenheim, Norbert. "Carpooling: Problems and Potentials." *Traffic Quarterly* 33, no. 2 (April 1979):253–262.

Owen, Wilfred. *The Metropolitan Transportation Problem.* Washington, D.C.: The Brookings Institution, 1966.

Shoup, Donald C. "Cashing Out Free Parking." *Transportation Quarterly* 36, no. 3 (July 1982):351–364.

Solomon, Barry D. "Gasohol, Economics, and Passenger Transportation Policy." *Transportation Journal* 20, no. 1 (Fall 1980):57–64.

Stevens, Charles W. "Car Buyers Start Returning to V-8 Engine: As Gas Prices Drop, Big Autos Sell Better." *Wall Street Journal,* 25 May 1983, p. 33.

———. "Lots Of Action: A Used-Auto Bonanza Helps New-Car Dealers Survive Their Slump." *Wall Street Journal,* 9 October 1981, p. 1.

———. "People Are Keeping Cars Longer as Costs Rise and Attitudes Change." *Wall Street Journal,* 7 January 1982, p. 23.

Taylor, James I. "Moral Dilemmas in Highway Safety Decisions." *Transportation Quarterly* 35, no. 1 (January 1981):85–95.

Tracy, Eleanor Johnson. "An Air Bag That Could Crash the Cost Barrier." *Fortune,* 29 October 1984, p. 88.

Viton, P. A. "On Competition and Product Differentiation in Urban Transportation: The San Francisco Bay Area." *The Bell Journal of Economics* 12, no. 2 (Autumn 1981):362–379.

Public Sector Transit Management, Strategy, and Decision Making

18

Previous chapters of *Transportation USA* have concentrated almost exclusively on the decisions and strategies of two of the transportation industry's primary participant groups—carriers and users (i.e., shippers and passengers). Less attention has been paid to the third key group involved in U.S. transportation—elected and appointed government officials who are responsible for making numerous important transportation choices. Fortunately, there is a yet unexposed but vital market segment that provides an excellent forum for improving one's understanding of public sector transportation management, strategy, and decision making. That area is urban mass transit.

Urban transportation means the movement of people or shipments between two points in a metropolitan area or in a particular city. Mass transit more specifically refers to the for-hire transportation of urban passengers by either private companies or publicly operated systems. In either case, carriers offer regularly scheduled services between homes, schools, jobs, retail shopping facilities, and other points within a town, city, or metropolitan area. As previously noted in Chapter 17, the dominant role played by privately owned motor vehicles is in supplying most U.S. passenger trips. Mainly the automobile fills this need. Nevertheless, this fact in no way diminishes the importance of mass transit. In 1980, mass transit vehicles carried more than 8.5 billion passengers, representing more than 12 times the number of people transported by the combination of intercity buses, airlines, and AMTRAK.[1] In addition, mass transit supplied an estimated 80% of the work trips into the central business districts—downtown areas—of New York City and Chicago.[2]

Like other sectors of transportation previously discussed in the text, mass transit serves a unique, important niche in the marketplace and in society. It differs from previously studied systems in its short-haul nature, because it is an intracity rather than an intercity business, with a 1980 average passenger trip length of 6.1 miles.[3] Furthermore, ownership and operation of mass transit systems are primarily in the public sector. The mass transit industry is controlled by municipal, county, regional, and state agencies; it is no longer an industry dominated by private sector capitalists.

Chapter 18 concentrates on public sector transit management, strategy, and decision making. After providing an initial review of the transfer from private to public ownership and control, this chapter identifies public sector decision makers and reviews their responsibilities. It next examines system, service, and economic decisions and strategies. Chapter 18 concludes with an update on the mass transit industry.

PUBLIC SECTOR TAKEOVER

private transit problems

Public mass transit management is a recent phenomenon. Prior to the 1960s, the private sector ran most of the buses, trolleys, and other transit vehicles in the United States as a way to make profits. After World War II, however, profits declined. Also, between 1945 and 1964 annual industry ridership dropped from 23.3 billion to 8.3 billion.[4] As a result, hundreds of firms failed. Backed by a powerful highway lobby, the United States had shifted its priorities to roads, streets, and automobiles. As the nation's love affair with cars blossomed, the country's mass transit systems declined. Only then was there

call for public ownership and control

a call for public ownership and operation. A driving force was the sudden realization that automobiles alone could not meet society's urban transportation needs; there just was not enough room on the roads and in the parking lots for everyone wanting to drive. Equally compelling was an assortment of automobile-related problems such as *urban sprawl,* which is the exodus of city dwellers and businesses to the suburbs, central city decay, and air pollution. Another stimulus was the availability for the first time of federal mass transit aid.

Urban Mass Transportation Act of 1964

Although federal aid for mass transit was introduced in 1961, a more significant development was the signing of the Urban Mass Transportation Act of 1964 three years later because it linked mass transit aid to public ownership. If an urban area wanted capital grant money for system development and equipment, its mass transit system had to be owned by the taxpayers—or in some cases, be leased by private owners to public agencies.[5] This situation prompted taxpayer (public) acquisition of private transit carriers.

public sector statistics

By 1980, 576 of the nation's 1044 mass transit systems (55.2%) were publicly owned. More significantly, in that same year, publicly owned mass transit systems supplied 94% of the mass transit industry's passenger trips, owned or leased 90% of the industry's vehicles, and operated 93% of the vehicle-miles.[6] The remaining private mass transit systems tended to be small, catering to particular market niches in large urban areas or providing a variety of services in small urban areas.

PUBLIC SECTOR DECISION MAKERS

transit authorities

There are four broad groups of public mass transit decision makers: local mass transit authorities, local elected officials, state governments, and federal administrators. Publicly held mass transit properties are administered by transit authorities. Typically, a board of directors supervises a general manager of the mass transit system. Responsibilities of transit authorities include assessing transportation needs, evaluating alternatives, recommending system changes such as routes and equipment, and operating the system by managing human and capital resources. An example is the New York Metropolitan Transportation Authority (NYMTA).

local officials

Transit authorities almost always are subject to official and/or unofficial review of their operations and finances by local officials such as mayors or metropolitan planning commissions, which are boards whose memberships come from political jurisdictions that receive transit services or pay taxes to support public mass transit—for example, towns, counties, or suburban cities or communities. Furthermore, transit authorities often recommend that a new system be funded, but the project cannot move forward until voters approve the measure by public referendum. Sometimes these efforts fail. For example, Houston voters in 1983 rejected a $2.35 billion bond issue for a new rapid transit line.[7]

state governments

With increasing frequency, state governments are participating in public mass transit decision making. The reason is funding problems; state approval of transit plans may be necessary if local tax dollars are inadequate for capital or operating needs and state promotion and subsidy dollars are to be provided.

federal administrators

With the advent of federal mass transit aid, Washington assumed a new role. The Urban Mass Transportation Administration (UMTA) was given the responsibility of selecting aid recipients. This selection process is not an easy task, considering the number of systems requesting and expecting to receive federal grants. Since funds are limited, every applicant will not receive funding approval.

SYSTEM DECISIONS AND STRATEGY

Modal Options

Some of the most crucial decisions made by mass transit managers are system choices: what types of equipment to operate, how large the route system should be, which neighborhoods should receive new services first, and whether to renovate the present system or replace it. Choosing among the mass transit modal options is one key decision managers face, and this choice cannot be separated from each of the other decisions.

motor bus More than 65% of all mass transit riders in 1980 were carried on motor buses operated by 1022 transit systems.[8] Motor buses are rubber-tired, self-propelled, manually steered vehicles that carry onboard fuel supplies. For the most part, they operate on the same streets and highways as automobiles and trucks. The exception would be found in cities with specialized traffic lanes that are restricted to bus use or shared with multiple-rider, privately owned motor vehicles, such as cars with at least three people in them.

heavy rail Mass transit vehicle railways constructed on exclusive rights-of-way—subways or elevated guideways limited to transit vehicles—and utilizing high-level platform stations—at the same level as the car's floor—are called *heavy rail mass transit systems*. They are powered by electricity usually supplied by a wheel-level third rail. Often, heavy rail is referred to as one form of rapid transit, because of its higher speed capabilities than vehicles operating on congested city streets. An example of a heavy rail mass transit system is the Washington Metro (see Fig. 18.1). The other form of rapid transit is *light rail transit* (LRT), which is a streetcar-type mass transit vehicle railway system constructed on city streets (the rail is placed in the pavement), semiprivate rights-of-way (no other vehicles operate on the tracks but streets cross the track), and exclusive rights-of-way. Some of the differences between LRT and heavy rail transit are the capability of LRT to operate in street traffic, its step-up boarding, like getting on a bus, and its normal use of an above-the-car electrical power supply. A photo of an LRT car in San Diego is shown in Fig. 18.2.

FIGURE 18.1.
Washington Metro's heavy rail mass transit vehicles in a subway station. (WMATA photo by Paul Myatt; reproduced courtesy of Washington Metro Area Transportation Authority—WMATA.)

FIGURE 18.2.
San Diego's light rail mass transit vehicle. (Photo courtesy of San Diego Metropolitan Transit Development Board.)

trolley coach

Trolley coaches—trolley buses—are rubber-tired mass transit vehicles that are manually steered and propelled by electric motors drawing current normally through overhead wires. Because these vehicles do not operate on rails, the operators have the ability, although limited, to maneuver more freely around street traffic.

commuter railroad

Commuter railroad systems provide urban passenger train service over railroad rights-of-way that are identical to the intercity railroad rights-of-way as described in Chapter 6 and use either locomotive-hauled or self-propelled railroad passenger cars. Usually, trains operate from nearby cities or suburbs and on radial routes feeding a central business district of a major city like Boston, New York, or Chicago. Radial routes resemble spokes on a bicycle wheel. Commuter railroad equipment more closely resembles AMTRAK's short-haul vehicles than rapid transit cars, because riders tend to ride longer distances on commuter railroads (estimates vary from 17.3 to 36 miles) than, for instance, on heavy rail equipment (an average of 6.3 to 10.2 miles).[9]

cable car

Transit vehicles such as San Francisco's cable cars (see Fig. 1.4) are operated in mixed street traffic as unpowered, individually controlled vehicles propelled by moving cables located below the street surface. The cable moves continuously and is powered by motors at a central location. When an individual car needs to move forward, the vehicle operator sets a clamp, which grabs the moving cable.

ferry boat

Passenger-carrying marine vessels providing frequent "bridge" service over a fixed route between two or more points and on a published time schedule are ferry boats. Perhaps the most famous is the Staten Island Ferry in New York (Fig. 18.3).

FIGURE 18.3.
Staten Island Ferry. (Fred Stephenson photo)

personal
rapid transit (PRT)

Computer-controlled automated (driverless) vehicles carrying small numbers of individuals on exclusive guideways are called *personal rapid transit* (PRT), or "people movers." An example is the Morgantown, West Virginia, system. Initial plans for PRT were to design urban systems featuring elevated guideways and numerous stops. Riders would go to a PRT stop, feed origin and destination data to a centralized computer, board a PRT vehicle capable of holding 4–6 people, and be routed by computer over the shortest time-path to the destination. In this design form, PRT offers the privacy of the automobile (service is nonstop), and there's no street congestion.

paratransit

Paratransit is a transportation system that can operate over the highway and street system in such forms as shared-ride taxis, carpools, and subscription bus services.[10] As differentiated from the scheduled services provided by previously defined systems, paratransit is more demand-activated. An example is dial-a-ride in which customers call a number requesting that a vehicle pick them up. Similarly, subscription buses provide customized services between specialized points. Customers agree to ride the bus regularly or pay fees (usually monthly) to have services available, such as from a suburban location to an urban CBD.

Political Problems and Their Consequences

infighting

Politics is one big obstacle in mass transit system decision making. So many public officials and levels of government are involved that it is difficult for transit managers to act, and decisions are time consuming. One problem is political infighting. Urban municipalities fight among themselves, suburban officials protest efforts by innercity politicians, and rural state representatives often oppose urban transit proposals. At stake are tax dollars, constituents' interests, and votes.

indecision and delays

Several examples demonstrate the planning and decision-making difficulties. In 1984, 42 state and local agencies had some degree of control over the New York Metropolitan Transportation Authority.[11] In Detroit, Mayor Coleman A. Young quipped that the metropolitan area had argued for 60 years about transit and, after studying 40 system alternatives, still had not reached a decision.[12] Also, it took 15 years from conception to the introduction of service on San Francisco's Bay Area Rapid Transit System (BART).[13] These examples reveal the slowness and inefficiency of public sector decision making.

cost overruns

Cost overruns are another problem. Regional voters authorized $792 million for BART. It cost $1.4 billion.[14] The 98-mile Washington Metro heavy rail system was estimated initially to cost $2.5 billion. However, costs may soar to $8.3 billion.[15]

voter influence

Mass transit decisions are affected by many other factors, not the least of which is voter appeal. Because of their high visibility, new transit systems and equipment are favored by public officials over renovation and maintenance efforts; voters see instant results when rapid transit lines or new buses enter service. An assortment of transit officials, federal administrators, and writers have noted that elections and votes sway public transit system decisions.[16] As one critic complained, "Transit has become a vehicle to carry people into public office rather than to jobs, homes, and stores."[17] Furthermore, political ambitions can lead to suboptimal transit system decisions. Although for one particular city, buses might be the best solution, public officials sometimes override management's recommendations and choose rapid transit.

rapid transit

Without question, the 1970s and early 1980s will be remembered by transit historians for the reemergence of rapid transit. Following the introduction of BART in 1972, new heavy rail service opened in Washington, D.C., Atlanta, Baltimore, and Miami. Los Angeles, Houston, and Honolulu have also shown serious interest in similar systems. Many other cities have chosen light rail systems. Big-city mayors favor rapid transit to reduce street congestion, control urban sprawl, and boost innercity economics through such benefits as high-rise office construction near stations, jobs, and added tax sources.

Federal Capital Grants

The real catalyst behind the development of rapid rail systems, however, was, and still is, the availability of federal capital grants. Realistically, few new rapid rail transit systems would have been built without the potential of obtaining $4 of federal taxpayer support for every $1 of local money.

Reasons for Federal Aid.   The Urban Mass Transportation Act of 1964 was legislated to assist in the development of improved mass transit facilities, equipment, techniques, and methods. Because of this act and subsequent federal funding authorizations, capital improvements were accomplished, as listed in Table 18.1. Federal capital grants signified a recognition by Congress that

TABLE 18.1. Equipment and facilities funded in part by U.S. government capital assistance, 1964–1980

42,692	Motor buses
678	Trolley coaches
3,218	Heavy rail cars
497	Light rail cars
1,720	Commuter railroad cars
96	Commuter railroad locomotives
16	Ferry boats
2	Inclined plane cars[a]
2	Automated guideway transit systems[b]
12	Miles of commuter railroad lines[c]
23	Miles of busways[c]
240	Miles of heavy and light rail lines,[c] plus bus garages, office buildings, passenger shelters, communications systems and many other items

[a]Cars that go up steep slopes.

[b]Includes one airport system.

[c]Includes only mileage actually under construction, in engineering, or completed. Mileage being planned is not included.

Source: American Public Transit Association, *Transit Fact Book 1981* (Washington, D.C.: American Public Transit Association, 1981), p. 30.

U.S. mass transit systems not only needed help, but that significant system improvements and increased ridership were not likely to be accomplished through private transit operators or local public officials.

Programs.   Between 1965 and 1980, the U.S. Government distributed $15.2 billion in capital grant funds under several programs to local transit authorities.[18] Of this total, $11.3 billion was awarded as Section 3 grants— "Section 3" refers to the section describing the program in the Urban Mass Transportation Act of 1964 (78 *Statutes at Large,* p. 303). Known also as the *discretionary capital assistance program,* Section 3 grants now cover 80% of the costs of new buses, fixed-guideway vehicles, and other transit equipment (49 *United States Code* 1602). Also, they can be used for the acquisition, construction, reconstruction, and improvement of mass transit facilities and equipment. Local transit authorities receiving Section 3 funds must raise the remaining 20% of the project's capital costs.

A second source of federal capital grant aid is Section 5 funds of the amended Urban Mass Transportation Act of 1964 (49 U.S.C. 1604). This program, known as *formula grant assistance,* referring to the way funds are distributed according to a population and population density equation, contributed $818 million between 1965 and 1980. It, too, provided an 80% federal contribution for acquisition, construction, and improvement of transit facilities and equipment.

Section 3 grants

Section 5 grants

The remaining federal funding amounts and sources during the period were $193 million under the urban systems program (Federal-Aid Highway Act of 1973, 23 U.S.C. 142) and $2.9 billion under the interstate transfer program (Federal-Aid Highway Act of 1973, 23 U.S.C. 103).[19] The former program supported highway public transit projects such as exclusive bus lanes, where no autos or trucks are allowed. The latter program allowed states to substitute transit projects for controversial or unwanted interstate highway sections in urbanized areas with populations of more than 50,000 people.[20]

Problems with Capital Grants.   Federal capital grants have been instrumental in modernizing transit systems and attracting new riders; however, they have simultaneously generated numerous criticisms, such as the following:

1. A Reagan budget document stated that the availability of steadily increasing federal transit funding has significantly inflated the prices for new rail transit.[21]

2. Testimony before a federal House of Representatives Subcommittee on Investigations and Oversight suggested that elements of the federal transit assistance program may be inhibiting development of the most rational responses to current urban transportation problems.[22]

3. Testimony in federal oversight hearings also raised troubling questions about incentives to "waste" capital created by 80% federal capital grants.[23]

4. In 1981, Jonathan H. Klein, chief mechanical officer of the Southeastern Pennsylvania Transportation Authority (SEPTA), criticized the process and consequences of federal aid for new rail transit vehicles. According to Klein, "There is no check on investment cost, they [the cars] are more costly to buy, more costly to operate, . . . more complex, more costly to maintain and have reduced availability, hence [these cars] have less ability to generate revenue."[24]

5. Robert Duncan, former chairman of the federal House Transportation Appropriations subcommittee, warned, "If the federal government assumes all or too much of the costs [of transit], there is an erosion of local responsibility resulting in overinvestment, unwise investment and no or reduced incentives for efficient operations."[25]

Few would question the need for federal capital grants to help restore and develop transit. However, does the federal aid program cause transit costs to rise, thereby unnecessarily wasting taxpayer dollars?

One major criticism of federal aid is that it comes with numerous strings attached. For example, the 1978 "Buy American" law placed a condition on transit grants: To be eligible for federal aid, 51% of the components of a rail car must be made in the United States, unless a special waiver is granted, and the car must be assembled domestically. This law can inflate car costs. In 1983, the New York MTA was threatened with a $91.2 million fine for buying subway cars produced by Bombardier Inc., a Canadian company.[26] Subsequently, the fine was lifted when the MTA agreed not to buy any foreign-made cars for three years, even though it could have purchased the cars it desired at a lower price abroad.[27] This illustration reveals how transit costs are increased by federal policies that protect U.S. jobs and manufacturers. The MTA could have refused federal aid, but that would have been foolish. There is no contest between a decision involving higher equipment costs and the potential loss of hundreds of millions in federal aid.

full accessibility

Another troublesome federal policy for mass transit decision makers until the early 1980s was the requirement of full accessibility for the elderly and handicapped. Section 16 of the amended Urban Mass Transportation Act of 1964 directed that special efforts be made in planning and designing new transit facilities and services to ensure that elderly and handicapped persons could effectively use them.[28] Again, federal capital grant aid was tied to meeting the full accessibility constraint. In April 1976, UMTA issued regulations requiring vehicle features such as interior handrails, stanchions, and nonskid flooring. The rules also mandated that bus manufacturers offer TRANSBUS— a full size, kneeling bus in which hydraulics would lower the bus and the first step for easier boarding; the bus is equipped with a low floor, wide front door, and either a ramp or a wheelchair lift at the front door.

Although the federal intent was commendable, average bus prices rose from $33,000 to $120,000 in the 10 years ending 1979.[29] According to a U.S. Congressional Budget Office report, full accessibility would have cost transit systems $6.8 billion in 30 years if the policy had not been changed.[30] As a result of heavy protests from the transit industry, legislation was approved by a House subcommittee rolling back federal regulations that required transit systems to equip all buses and many subway stations to handle handicapped persons. It did not, however, remove the responsibility of states to accommodate the disabled with special transit services, such as provided by vans equipped to handle wheelchair users.

federal priorities

A third problem with federal aid is that it encourages local officials to build systems that do not necessarily best match the area's needs, but that have the greatest probabilities of being funded. Federal funds are limited, and not all projects will be approved for aid. With 80% possible funding available, the selection process encourages transit managers to seek items high on the federal priority list.

federal leadership changes

Changes in the leadership at the Department of Transportation and UMTA that occur when presidents leave office are another problem. Local officials have no guarantee that they will receive federal aid to initiate a massive system start-up or expansion project such as heavy rail. Furthermore, if they are successful initially, they cannot be sure of future federal capital grants to finish the projects. Administrative priorities change. For example, President Carter wanted $50 billion for mass transit and favored heavy rail projects,[31] but President Reagan stated opposition to heavy rail systems because they are too costly.[32]

labor protective clauses

Two other complaints about federal aid are that it inflates construction costs and causes delay problems. Federal labor protective clauses require that transit system contractors and subcontractors pay wages to construction workers at rates not less than those prevailing at construction work in the local area (49 *United States Code* 1609). While helping labor, this policy can also significantly raise construction costs if transit construction wages are compared with the highest wage standards in a particular area. The second problem, and an equally troublesome one, is the time-consuming, costly paperwork process that must be completed prior to UMTA approval of a capital grant. An UMTA application contains 28 separate requirements such as civil rights assurances, labor protective clearances, an environmental impact statement, and aged and handicapped considerations.[33] If an applicant fails to satisfy fully each of these 28 requirements, the project is tabled by UMTA, the funding decision maker. As previously noted, delays lead to inflated system capital costs.

interference and higher costs

inadequate controls

In summary, federal aid is often the difference between transit system capital improvements and the continuance of declining ridership. Funds, however, come with many strings attached, and they cause local decision makers to lose considerable control over the choices they might wish to make. In addition, typically more money is paid for capital improvements than would have been spent if the federal government had not been involved. Moreover, higher levels of sophisticated equipment have produced added maintenance problems due to accelerated breakdowns and escalated repair costs.[34] Federal administrative goals are admirable, but not always practical. Too much federal priority is placed on choosing grant recipients and using transit to accomplish nontransit objectives, such as the "Buy American" program. Too little priority is attached to managing system costs. Capital grants have allowed transit managers to make stunning system improvements—but at inflated costs to the taxpayers.

SERVICE DECISIONS AND STRATEGY

Background

During the 1960s, 1970s, and early 1980s, a primary objective of federal mass transit investment efforts was an improvement in services that would lead to a growth in ridership. This goal was fueled by the belief that something had to be done to curtail auto-related problems. Cars drew harsh criticism for polluting the air, clogging city streets, and encouraging urban residents to move to the suburbs. Furthermore, the 1973 OPEC-caused oil crisis lessened supplies and raised fuel prices. A stunned federal government demanded national energy efficiency. Singled out for wasting fuel was the automobile. Cars per se were not fuel inefficient; how people were using them was. Excess capacity was the problem; on average, cars designed to hold 5 people were occupied by less than 1.5 people per vehicle.[35] Nearly 65% of U.S. workers drive alone to their jobs.[36] Suddenly, the government viewed mass transit as a way to improve fuel conservation by removing people from their cars.

tough competition
from automobiles

Accomplishing this objective was far more difficult. Automobiles are customized vehicles that often not only match the lifestyles of their owners, but also offer flexibility. They are available when their owners want them, can go to any destination, can stop along the way, and can be routed around traffic jams. To encourage people to abandon their cars, mass transit had to overcome a poor service image and be perceived as offering more for the money—maybe not superior service, but at least a bargain in relation to automobile costs. Mass transit managers were asked by government officials to overcome years of transit system neglect and restore consumer confidence.

reason for optimism

Nevertheless, public sector transit managers had reason for optimism. Unlike their private sector predecessors, public transit authorities benefited from the promise of capital grants, no pressure to make profits, and a changing citizen attitude. The public seemed ready to try mass transit and more understanding of its importance. Tired of traffic congestion, escalating fuel costs, and gas station lines, auto users were looking for alternatives.[37]

Service Decision Variables

Presented with this situation, decision makers faced service decisions that concentrated on ways to improve availability, door-to-door speed, and reliability—attributes necessary to induce mass transit use.

Availability. Availability of mass transit is critical. Before automobile owners will use bus service, for example, they need to be relatively close to a bus stop, want to know if the route can get them to their destination, need to verify the bus schedule to make sure they have service when they need it, and so forth. In other words, they expect the service to deliver reasonable time and place utility.

routes and schedules

peak
period demands

Consequently, mass transit managers must decide routes and schedules. In the process, they are constrained by financial limitations that do not allow them to meet the needs of all potential users, as well as pressured by politicians to serve their constituents better. Demands are placed on management to meet peak period (6:30 A.M. to 9 A.M. and 4 P.M. to 7 P.M. rush hour) needs, for it is during these periods that auto problems are maximized. If managers try to accommodate every passenger desiring service in the peak periods (the morning period is worse, because it is shorter), they create a huge excess capacity problem (idle equipment and employees) in the off-peak hours (9 A.M. to 4 P.M. and 7 P.M. to 6:30 A.M.). The public asks management to do something no rational businessperson would typically voluntarily do—buy enough capacity for a brief period. Such are the demands on transit operators, and they result in excessive operating costs.

Door-to-Door Speed. Another critical consumer decision variable is door-to-door speed. How long does it take to travel from home to the office, counting not only the time on the transit vehicle, but also the time to and from the stations or stops as well as waiting time? A simple example is commuter railroad service. If a train leaves at 6:15 A.M., can a person afford to arrive at the station at 6:14 A.M.? People arrive early and wait.

relevancy of speed

Speed is so relevant because mass transit users or potential riders constantly compare times to automobile door-to-door capabilities. What increases transit times are long walks, waits, and indirect routings. For example, riding a bus to the CBD, transferring to another vehicle, and actually riding back out

strategies

of the CBD to the destination is time consuming. To reduce transit times, transit managers strive for increased vehicle speeds, more direct routings, and fewer stops. Rapid transit is attractive because of its improved speed. There is a trade-off, however, for route miles are limited, and station availability is restricted. Fixed rail systems force consumers to choose between riding cars to stations that may be inconveniently located or just continuing by car the entire way to the destination. If transit service is too inconvenient, regardless of the fare levels, many people will simply not use it.

Reliability. The third important service variable is reliability. How can mass transit operators ensure that schedules are met? How can they keep rolling stock (vehicles) in service and out of maintenance shops? What does it take to ensure that vehicles have air conditioning or heat when needed? These are just a few of the criteria that can determine system success or failure. Passengers expect managers to deliver promised, as well as basic, services.

examples of unreliable service

Unreliability is one obvious deficiency in the nation's mass transit systems, as the following four examples illustrate. Breakdowns in the New York subway system increased from 43,683 in 1979 to 71,773 in 1980.[38] On a typical day in 1979, nearly one-fourth of the New York MTA's bus fleet of about 4000 buses was unavailable for service.[39] On a fall day in 1979, only 26 of the 220 Broad Street subway cars in Philadelphia were available for service.[40] Finally, the San Francisco Municipal Railway (Muni) transit system was averaging 10 accidents a day in 1984, and after an accident-plagued, disastrous year, rider confidence was shaken.[41]

causes of unreliable service

What makes these problems difficult to comprehend is that they showed up *after* billions of dollars had been spent on capital improvements. Obviously, capital efforts should be carefully differentiated from maintenance endeavors. The latter are the primary problem, but the two are inseparably linked. Even though much money has been spent on new equipment, more is needed to replace aged and worn out vehicles. Old buses were cited as a major factor behind some of the more serious San Francisco Muni accidents. A lack of spare parts is another critical shortcoming. The chief mechanical officer of SEPTA (Philadelphia) complained that obtaining parts for old equipment, as well as for the system's new light rail vehicles, was difficult.[42] Prices can be high, with replenishment lead times quite long. Other problems include new vehicles so sophisticated that maintenance employees do not know how to fix them, long delays caused by understaffing in the maintenance area, and chaotic maintenance practices.[43] A central problem is inadequate finances. As one union president noted, federal grant programs encourage systems to buy new, rather than repair old, equipment.[44] Unfortunately, new equipment is more complex and costly to repair, and thus it magnifies unreliability problems.

ECONOMIC DECISIONS AND STRATEGY

rising deficits

Economic decisions occupy a considerable portion of a senior public transit manager's time. Finding sources of capital for facilities and equipment is one concern. Another often is the urgent need to raise funds to offset mounting operating deficits. The last year the U.S. mass transit industry generated operating income was 1967. Since that time, operating deficits steadily increased from $62.6 million in 1968 to $3.946 billion in 1980 (see Table 18.2). Not included in the 1980 figure was a $537 million commuter railroad deficit.

shutdowns
and bankruptcies

How severe financial problems have become is illustrated by system shutdowns and near bankruptcies. In 1981, Birmingham stopped bus service for three months for lack of funds.[45] The Boston transit system (the MBTA), after running out of money for the second year in succession, was shut down for a day in 1980 and was taken over by the Commonwealth of Massachusetts.[46]

TABLE 18.2. Operating revenues, operating expenses, and operating income (deficits)[a]

Year	Operating Revenue (in $ thousands)	Operating Expense (in $ thousands)	Operating Income (Deficit) (in $ thousands)
1967	$1,556,000	$1,530,864	$25,136
1968	1,562,739	1,625,314	(62,575)
1969	1,625,633	1,744,989	(119,356)
1970	1,707,418	1,891,743	(184,325)
1971	1,740,700	2,040,453	(299,753)
1972	1,728,500	2,128,193	(399,693)
1973	1,797,640	2,419,837	(622,197)
1974	1,939,700	3,239,300	(1,299,600)
1975	2,002,400	3,752,500	(1,750,100)
1976	2,161,100	4,082,600	(1,921,500)
1977	2,280,000	4,366,600	(2,086,600)
1978	2,381,100	4,788,900	(2,407,800)
1979	2,524,200	5,611,400	(3,087,200)
1980 (preliminary)	2,568,200	6,514,200	(3,946,000)

[a]Excludes commuter railroad, urban ferry boat, and automated guideway systems (operated without crew members on board).

Sources:
1.   American Public Transit Association, *'74–'75 Transit Fact Book* (Washington, D.C.: American Public Transit Association, 1975), p. 12.
2.   American Public Transit Association, *Transit Fact Book 1981* (Washington, D.C.: American Public Transit Association, 1981), pp. 46–47.

Another case is the Chicago Transit Authority, the operator of one of the largest systems in the mass transit industry, which came close to bankruptcy in 1981.[47]

defining the problem

What is ailing public transit? First and foremost is the simple fact that fares are not keeping pace with surging operating costs. Between 1965 and 1980, industry passenger revenues (fare-box sales) increased 83.7% from $1.3401 billion to $2.4623 billion. However, operating costs rose 347.9% from $1.4544 billion to $6.5142 billion.[48] Several options are available to mass transit managers to lessen acute system financial deficits: raising fares, reducing services, deferring maintenance, cutting costs and improving productivity, and asking for greater taxpayer support. None is easy to implement.

possible solutions

Fare Strategies

unrealistically low fares

In 1980, the national average fare paid by a transit passenger was 38.4¢.[49] This figure is based on composite data for light rail, heavy rail, trolley coach, and motor bus users, and it includes transfer charges for customers changing vehicles en route. According to the U.S. General Accounting Office and other sources, transit fares are unrealistically low.[50] Chapter 17 noted that at times, transit fares can be exceptional bargains compared with costs for commuting to work alone by automobile. Whether fare increases are needed is the subject of heated debate in many cities.

Need for Fare Increases. Passenger fares provide only a limited amount of system revenues. Nationally, passenger revenues derived from regularly scheduled service accounted for only 39.0% of industry revenues in 1980 (Table 18.3). In some places, fares represent an even smaller revenue share, such as in Atlanta (34%)[51] and Boston (33%).[52] In Canada, by contrast, fares represent 53% of operating revenues; moreover, in the case of the highly praised Toronto system, riders provide 68% of the operating dollars.[53] Therefore there is good reason for asking riders to pay more.

Arguments against Raising Fares. Likewise, there are valid arguments inhibiting management actions to raise fares. Some people, such as the poor and the unemployed, cannot afford price increases. When the government chose to transfer mass transit ownership from the private to the public sector, one goal was to provide service to those in need. However, fare increases are a disadvantage to the poor and can impede employment opportunities if people cannot afford to commute to work. Another obstacle is political opposition to fare increases. Well aware of the power of urban transit riders' votes, city politicians tend to fight fare increases and prefer to transfer rising deficit burdens to suburban and rural taxpayers.[54]

some cannot afford higher fares

inner-city political opposition

rider objections

Even if transit riders can afford fare hikes, transit managers are reluctant to increase prices out of fear of ridership reductions. Users object to price hikes that seem to produce no better services and merely increase transit worker pay packages.[55] A good example is the reaction in Chicago: In 1981,

TABLE 18.3. Sources of mass transit industry revenues (1980)—preliminary data

Source	Percentage
Passenger revenues[a]	39.00%
Other operating revenues[b]	1.68
Non-operating revenues[c]	2.01
Federal operating assistance	17.33
State operating assistance	12.99
Local operating assistance	26.99
TOTAL	100.00%

[a]Farebox revenue.

[b]Revenues derived from charter and special (nonregular) routes and sales of advertising space aboard mass transit vehicles.

[c]Net revenue from affiliated facilities or operations rendering services other than the provision of transit services (e.g., some transit authorities generate and sell electricity) and net income from transit system facilities or operations not associated with providing transportation or transit services.

Source: American Public Transit Association, *Transit Fact Book 1981* (Washington, D.C.: American Public Transit Association, 1981), pp. 45, 75.

area commuters who had been hit by 8 fare increases in 13 years were riled by reports of excessive labor costs and wastes in the transit system.[56] Fare increases cannot be merely a conduit for increasing labor wages and benefits if mass transit managers expect to retain riders and public support. Most riders own cars and, if aggravated too much, would not hesitate to use them.

ridership losses   Fare increases are counterproductive to achieving the goal of increased ridership. The American Public Transit Association (APTA) has stated that each 1.0% increase in transit fares (above inflation) tends to produce a 0.3% decline in transit passenger trips.[57] SEPTA reported a 20% decline in ridership following a 60% commuter railroad fare increase and sharp service cuts in 1980.[58] Another example is what happened in New York City. Transit fares there increased from 20¢ to 35¢ in the early 1970s, and yearly ridership dropped from 1.7 billion to 1.4 billion.[59] Transit officials also blame rising fares for the slowdown in the growth rate of national transit ridership in the early 1980s.[60] Only if markedly improved services accompany fare increases is there much chance that ridership losses can be avoided.[61] Managers know this fact, and they are also well aware of the probability of facing a powerful coalition bent on freezing fare levels or, at the worst, holding increases to minimum levels.

Service Strategies

service reductions   A second strategy to combat rising deficits is service changes. One option is service reductions. Like the fare increase option, plans to reduce schedules, eliminate routes, or redesign routes tend to run into stiff opposition. System cuts, such as the elimination of bus service used by only a few people, may make excellent economic sense. However, public transit decisions are not necessarily motivated by economics; often, politics is the deciding factor. At the opposite end of the spectrum are service improvements. This strategy can work if the changes are targeted to the market and priced above marginal breakeven costs. Otherwise, increased services only compound the deficit problem.

service improvements

Deferred Maintenance Strategy

Earlier in this chapter in the discussion of system decisions, it was stated that an alternative to system development and new equipment acquisitions is the maintenance strategy. Without question, a balance needs to be struck between buying new versus repairing old equipment and facilities. However, when funds are short and opposition to fare hikes or service reductions is intense, many transit managers will reduce maintenance budgets. In the short-term, deferred maintenance can be used as an effective cost-cutting measure. Its biggest advantage is that it is a relatively discreet tactic not likely to spark the wrath of users or politicians. However, as previously explained, deferred maintenance can devastate a system's image, service availability, reliability, and ridership. It is one of the riskiest and potentially most costly actions mass transit management can take.

Cost Control and Productivity Strategies

Labor as a Factor.   Cost control and productivity tactics represent a fourth alternative in reducing financial deficits. To be successful in producing substantive gains, management must concentrate on high-cost areas. In the transit sector, this area is labor. As shown in Table 18.4, salaries, wages, and benefits accounted for 73.35% of industry operating expenses in 1980. Employee and

TABLE 18.4. Mass transit industry operating expenses[a] (1980)

Expense Category	Percentage
Salaries, wages, benefits	73.35%
Services	4.56
Fuel and lubricants	6.62
Tires and tubes	0.65
Other materials and supplies	5.28
Utilities	3.19
Casualty and liability costs	3.93
Other	2.42
TOTAL	100.00%

[a]Excludes commuter railroad and ferry boat services.

Source: American Public Transit Association, *Transit Fact Book 1981* (Washington, D.C.: American Public Transit Association, 1981), p. 49.

retiree expenses of $4.44 billion in 1980 were equal to 173% of operating revenues ($2.568 billion).[62] The huge deficit caused by the difference between farebox revenues and labor costs is a shared, major concern of mass transit managers, mass transit riders, and taxpayers. In particular, taxpayers were upset when facts like the following became known:

1. UMTA Administrator Arthur Teele stated that transit wages increased 160% from 1967 to 1980. In the same period, the Consumer Price Index (CPI), the nation's standard for measuring inflation, rose only 146%.[63]
2. Pension costs in the New York transit system increased 285% in the 1970s (10 years).[64]
3. An Atlanta bus driver earned wages totaling $150,188 in the three-year period ending in 1982, or an average of $50,063 per year. In 1981, the same year that this driver earned $56,135, the average pay for Atlanta police officers and firefighters was less than $13,600 annually.[65]
4. Testimony before a Congressional subcommittee documented that absentee levels among bus and railcar operators were running 50% to 200% higher than in the industrial work force in general or in the private transportation sector.[66]

labor's rebuttal

There is, of course, another side to the mass transit labor debate: Workers' wages and benefits had been suppressed during the last years of private system ownership. Wage and benefit increases were long overdue and necessary to catch up to earnings outside the mass transit industry. It is the same argument airline workers used to justify that they had a right to expect salary and benefit increases equal to or better than changes in the CPI. After all, according to this argument, employees deserve the right to improve their standards of living.

labor considerations

Labor's argument is valid, but it disregards several matters of consequence to urban areas. One issue is whether transit pay is fair in relation to the pay levels of other public sector employees, such as teachers, police officers, and firefighters. Related to this issue is whether pay inequities will lead less fortunate public sector employees, such as sanitation workers, to demand equal wage levels and benefits, thereby raising additional taxpayer burdens. A third consideration, also correlated to the first two, is the ability of riders or taxpayers to fund escalating labor costs. Another is whether mass transit pay levels are unnecessarily high. Would other qualified people do the same jobs as well as, and for less pay than, current workers? Should labor supply and demand be a factor? While asking what is fair to transit employees, should questions not also be asked about what is fair to transit riders, other public sector workers, the local area's taxpayers, and interested and qualified workers who cannot obtain transit jobs? In any event, why should the public tolerate high absentee rates? Why does management allow this problem to happen?

lack of management control

In reality, transit management has little control over labor costs and productivity. The labor force is comprised of an unusually high percentage of union and/or civil service workers, both of which have a high degree of job security. New York City is typical: Of 49,000 transit employees in 1984, only 600 were neither union nor civil service workers. Even transit management tends to be unionized, since there were 5000 middle managers in New York City under labor contracts.[67] How can management succeed in cutting labor costs and improving productivity when most of the front line managers have a conflict of interest between labor allegiances and their transit authority responsibilities? For the most part, the people running major public transit systems did not create these structural labor problems but merely inherited them from previous administrations. Nevertheless, present managers are expected to improve labor efficiency, although it can be nearly impossible to fire incompetent employees or motivate inefficient workers and middle managers.[68] Even the right to promote on the basis of performance is often absent; employee seniority tends to carry more weight. There is a big difference in knowing what needs to be done in the labor area and being able to accomplish it. Too many transit managers have too little control over subordinates. They are told to manage with no real power to do so.

Examples of Labor Successes.   Since the mid-1960s, mass transit unions have been successful in winning contract concessions. Among their accomplishments have been generous pay raises, cost-of-living allowances (COLAs), excellent pension programs, prohibitions against the hiring of part-time workers (job security measures), and favorable work rules. Since rapidly rising pay levels have already been discussed, let us look at the other four achievement areas.

COLAs

Despite the strong objections of mass transit management, labor succeeded in winning automatic cost-of-living allowances. Like all workers, transit laborers felt victimized by inflation. To offset losses in their members' buying power, unions fought for and won contract clauses providing periodic (3-month, 6-month, or annual) pay adjustments keyed to changes in the national Consumer Price Index. COLAs are a primary reason for higher labor costs. For example, from 1975 to 1981, hourly pay for an Atlanta bus driver increased from $5.84 to $10.34. In 1981, Alan Kiepper, then General Manager of MARTA, said, "In effect, because of the automatic cost-of-living escalator, we do not control our labor costs, which represent 73% of our budget. Our labor costs are set by the consumer price index."[69]

pensions

This chapter has mentioned rapidly rising retirement costs and a bus driver who earned more than $150,000 in a three-year period. These are related problems. In 1968, the New York Transport Workers Union (TWU) won contract pension terms providing half pay for retirement at age 50 for workers with 20 years' service.[70] Compared with the private sector, these are generous terms. Equally significant is the basis for computing pension payment amounts. The New York contract specified that payments were to be based on an employee's final year's earnings. Since the amount of overtime a driver could work was unrestricted by management, a senior employee was encouraged to work as many extra hours as possible. In this way, some employees earned pension payments in excess of normal annual wages. An example is a New York driver who earned $20,459 in overtime and raised his annual pension from what would have been $12,899 to $21,660.[71] The Atlanta bus driver who earned more than $150,000 in three years was doing the same thing. The pension cost problem is magnified because transit workers retired as soon as they became eligible, such as at the age of 50 in the New York City case.

part-time workers

For years, mass transit management has wanted the right to employ part-time workers to meet peak-period needs. However, transit workers, interested in job security and overtime earnings, have opposed the use of part-time workers. Thus management was often obligated to pay overtime to idle full-time workers when equipment was not in service during off-peak hours. Sometimes managers escaped paying time-and-a-half wage rates, but they were still required to pay for unproductive hours. A good example is the commuter railroad sector, where 80-hour work weeks were not unusual, yet train crews often did nothing from 9 A.M. to 4 P.M. and still drew pay for idle hours.

work rules

Transit literature yields numerous citings of work-rule problems that restrict productivity and inflate costs. New York Transport Workers Union members in 1980, for example, were only required to work $6\frac{1}{2}$ hours daily for 8 hours of pay. The other $1\frac{1}{2}$ hours were allowed for wash-up time and lunch and coffee breaks.[72] Other illustrations are the 100-mile rule (Chapter 6) and craft rules inherited by public transit managers when commuter railroad services were transferred from the former private sector railroad companies. The 100-mile rule, which still applies today, gives train crew members one day's pay for each 100 miles their trains operate. Craft rules dictate which unions can do which jobs. An example from SEPTA's commuter railroad files is union rules that in 1982 required separate efforts by members of four unions to fix an air conditioner, when one person actually could have done the job.[73] Craft rules protect union jobs but drive up costs in the process.

strikes

Reasons for Labor's Power.   The rise in labor power in the public transit industry was due to strikes, Section 13(C) of the Urban Mass Transportation Act of 1964, and binding arbitration. Unlike private sector employees, public transit employees tend to be prohibited by law from striking. This law has not, however, prevented work stoppages. Philadelphia experienced six strikes in the 1979–1981 period, and New York had major strikes in 1966, 1980, and 1983. Transit strikes are labor's way of trying to win contract concessions from management. Labor knows that local areas do not want to face transit strikes, and if strikes occur, there is considerable pressure to end them quickly. Transit strikes can cripple a city and extract high economic tolls. An example is the $12\frac{1}{2}$ day transit strike that hit New York City in 1966; by one estimate, it cost the city more than $1 billion.[74] Whenever transit systems cease operations in a place like New York City, where 80% of the CBD work trips are transit-provided, there is a tremendous outcry from users and politicians to restore transit services. Time works to the union's advantage. Unions also know that fines levied by the courts against illegally striking workers have tended to be dismissed as part of the agreement to reopen transit services.

For instance, the New York State legislature passed a bill, which was signed by Governor Nelson A. Rockefeller, removing all strike penalties administered as a result of the 1966 New York City transit strike.[75] Such precedents encourage transit workers to strike for wage, pension, job security, or work-rule concessions.

Section 13(C)

One controversial provision of the amended Urban Mass Transportation Act of 1964 is Section 13(C) (49 *United States Code* 1609). Section 13(C) requires that prior to approval of federal aid to a local transit system, the Secretary of Labor must determine that transit employees will not be adversely affected by such assistance. Transit managers insist that Section 13(C) gives transit unions the power to veto federal grant applications, and unions have used this leverage to force transit authorities to grant requested wage and benefit concessions. If labor's demands are not granted, labor either delays or refuses to sign capital grant applications, thereby denying funding to the transit authority.[76] A 1982 report by the Congressional Subcommittee on Investigations and Oversight said that Section 13(C) has become a formidable factor in local collective bargaining. It gives both labor and management an excuse for not confronting difficult issues and reinforces labor with a weapon of "national" scope.[77]

binding arbitration

Federal regulations under the Urban Mass Transportation Act of 1964 require that transit authorities and unions enter into binding arbitration as a way to resolve labor contract disputes.[78] Thus both parties must accept the arbitrator's contract terms. Transit managers contend that binding arbitration inflates labor costs, because arbitrators have the tendency to compare the local union's wage levels to what is being paid by the highest paying transit systems across the United States. For example, Boston mass transit operators might receive a wage increase because transit workers in Chicago have higher earnings. Local transit managers, such as in Atlanta, have argued that arbitrators should live in the local region—to understand better and to share in the consequences of their decisions—as well as to make their judgments based on regional, rather than national, wage levels and according to the ability of the area to pay for increased costs.[79]

Operating Subsidy Strategies

Section 5

The advent of public transit ownership opened a fifth avenue for remedying funding deficits—taxpayer operating subsidies. Assistance today derives from all three levels of government—federal, state, and local. Before federal aid was made available, local areas provided aid to transit authorities usually as soon as the transfer occurred from private to public ownership and operation. State aid then followed. In 1968, Pennsylvania enacted legislation to pay operating assistance; soon California and New York did likewise in 1971 and 1974, respectively.[80] The last governmental sector to provide operating funds was the federal government. As a result of the National Mass Transportation Act of 1974, Washington amended the Urban Mass Transportation Act of 1964 to award subsidies covering up to 50% of a local transit system's operating deficit. Funding was made as part of the Section 5 formula grant process, an effort that linked payments to a population and population density formula. Section 5 aid was considered a victory for transit lobbyists who had worked hard for federal help. From 1975 through 1980, government operating assistance totaled $13.720 billion, of which $6.497 billion (47.3%) came from local taxpayers, $3.275 billion (23.9%) was state awarded, and $3.948 billion (28.8%) was federally provided.[81]

distribution of taxpayer dollars

There is a rushing wave of resistance at all levels of government to operating subsidies. The Reagan Administration in 1981 called for a five-year phaseout of federal mass transit operating subsidies. Although this situation will probably not happen completely, federal transit operating subsidies were reduced from $1.37 billion in fiscal year (FY) 1982 to $1.2 billion in FY 1983.[82] Supposedly operating subsidies have not worked as predicted, and local systems have become too dependent on federal aid. Operating subsidies also removed some of the incentive for transit managers to increase efficiency and hold down labor costs.

federal resistance to aid

State governments, at the insistence of rural taxpayers, are also demanding reduced subsidies for urban transit systems. Non-urban residents have never been particularly pleased about aiding cities like Chicago, Atlanta, Boston, or New York, but two trends have intensified their drive to limit transit operating aid. First is the growing deficit. What was once considered a troublesome, yet small, financial commitment has grown to multimillion-dollar proportions. Secondly, in cases like Illinois, the balance of political power has shifted away from the city to the suburbs and rural districts. Chicago is no longer assured of sufficient votes in the state legislature to pass transit funding measures.[83]

state resistance to aid

In recent years, local taxpayers, who shoulder the largest share of operating subsidies, have also shown a greater resistance to transit funding demands. Caught between pressing needs for limited tax dollars, they seem more inclined to fight system wastes than to increase transit subsidy payments. Consequently, they are now demanding that transit authorities increase fares, cut transit services, and endure strikes to gain more equitable union contracts.

local resistance to aid

All levels of government seem to be placing more weight on the goal of economic efficiency and less on increased ridership. Fiscal responsibility is being demanded by the voting public, and the message is reaching political leaders and transit managers alike that excessive financial losses will not be tolerated. System operators are no longer assured of a taxpayer solution to transit deficit problems.

demands for fiscal responsibility

MASS TRANSIT INDUSTRY UPDATE

The switch from private to public mass transit ownership and operation caused an increase in ridership. Bolstered by billions of dollars in federal, state, and local capital assistance, the nation's transit systems were given a face lift and a more attractive image. However, other evidence is less encouraging. Despite growing transit ridership, the percentage of workers in the United States who rode mass transit to work in 1980 had declined to 6.4% from the 9.0% modal share in 1970.[84] Only in the West was there a reported gain in mass transit use (an increase from 4.6% to 5.0%). According to the U.S. Census Bureau, the Northeast mass transit use rate dropped from 19.1% to 14.2%; the North Central region showed a reduction from 6.7% to 4.9%; and in the South, only 3.3% of the area's workers used transit in 1980 versus 5.0% in 1970.[85]

causes of riderships trends

There are several explanations for these trends. Increased mass transit ridership since the 1960s can be traced to improved services on newer equipment and to increasing population (since the U.S. population grew, there should have been a parallel rise in transit use). Another factor was rising automobile operating costs. OPEC fuel price increases encouraged automobile users to reexamine transit alternatives.

reasons for modal share changes

There are three possible explanations for the loss in modal share. First, automobile users became more conditioned to higher fuel prices and gradually lost their economic incentive to use mass transit. Secondly, there was a growing dispersal of workers and jobs away from urban centers to places where transit services were minimal or nonexistent. Finally, rising transit fares and inferior transit services, compared to the automobile, encouraged people to use automobiles in increasing numbers.

Transit Management Problems

Public transit management is often the scapegoat for transit's failures. Management is not blameless, but much of the criticism is unfair and unwarranted. Managing a public mass transit system successfully is one of the most challenging tasks in the entire transportation industry. Mass transit managers have too many bosses, are subject to too much political interference, and must handle a highly protected labor force. To run a system effectively, these managers need support from bosses, labor, and the public; however, they often fail to receive this support, which delays or obstructs needed actions. In addition, system goals are vague and conflicting. Managers are expected to increase services without increasing costs or taxes—an impossible task.

deep-rooted obstacles

Mass transit managers also face more deep-rooted problems: aging, unreliable facilities and equipment; operating deficits; costly and protective labor contracts; and, above all, one of the toughest competitors in the transportation industry—the car. Mass transit managers are expected to be miracle workers, although in reality they have little power to make significant changes. In addition to knowing what needs to be done, they must figure out how to accomplish it and then carry out the plan.

Changing Transit Priorities

One significant change to affect mass transit management in recent years is the public demand for greater fiscal responsibility. Mass transit priorities are changing, and as a result, system goals are now more clearly defined. Tax-payers are demanding better cost controls, increased productivity, and higher fares. For the first time in two decades, elected and appointed officials have backed programs and legislation initiated by mass transit managers. Boston and Atlanta are two examples.

Boston

In response to mounting deficits, in the early 1980s the Massachusetts Bay Transportation Authority increased subway, trolley, bus, and commuter rail fares; reduced service 15%; and eliminated 775 jobs. The state legislature passed a law allowing the MBTA to reduce subway train crews from three to two workers and eliminated some restrictive work rules.[86]

Atlanta

The Georgia General Assembly in 1982 passed legislation that went a long way toward shifting the balance of power from labor to management. These tough new provisions freeze wages of Metropolitan Atlanta Rapid Transit Authority (MARTA) employees until a new contract is agreed on, limit overtime to 10 hours per week, and allow the hiring of part-time workers. Also, under the law, wages no longer go to binding arbitration unless management elects to do so. If arbitration is necessary, arbitrators must be local residents and must consider the following: (1) the ability of MARTA to pay wage and benefit cost increases; (2) the need for fare increases; (3) comparative wages, benefits, and working conditions of other Atlanta ground transportation workers; and (4) Atlanta's (not the U.S.) cost of living changes.[87] On July 9, 1985, however, a federal appeals court ruled that the 1982 Georgia law limits the bargaining rights of MARTA's union workers and that MARTA would be ineligible for federal funds unless it bargained in good faith.[88]

cost controls

These two examples reflect local efforts across the country to control mass transit costs in general, and labor costs in particular. As noted previously, labor is the industry's highest cost area. Management goals include increasing productivity by eliminating restrictive work rules and finding solutions to curb costs, such as part-time labor, controls on COLAs, restrictions on overtime hours, and subcontracting transit services to private firms that can provide these services at lower costs.

fare increases

Fares are also being raised. Riders are expected to pay a more realistic share of operating costs, because taxpayers are resisting higher subsidies. It is quite possible that what may develop is a change in subsidy programs, chan-neling cash to transit users who are poor but expecting other riders to pay more.

Increased Local Decision Making

The Reagan Administration said it wanted to return as much transit decision making to the local level as possible. In theory, this policy makes sense because it would reduce some of the delays and costs associated with federal grant applications. In practice, however, it is doubtful that this policy will be im-plemented. Most local areas not only want to continue federal capital and operating grant programs, but also many senators and representatives sup-port their efforts.[89]

Pressing Needs

The only thing that seems clear is that public mass transit—if it intends to succeed—needs considerable improvements. From the perspective of the potential benefits it can produce in curbing street congestion, saving fuel, helping the environment, and providing needed services for transit dependents (the elderly, the young, and the handicapped), it seems logical that now is not the time to become excessively frustrated by transit shortcomings. The challenge for transit managers is to maintain what they presently have, enhance system reliability, and recognize that the transit role is limited. It is not practical to assume that mass transit can serve every urban dweller's needs or desires. An acceptable balance satisfying users and taxpayers must be found. Success is more likely to arise out of the application of private sector business principles such as better marketing. Politics decides too many public mass transit issues, and mass transit will not be successful if the emphasis remains too focused on satisfying parochial interest groups. However, politics accompanies public ownership. Regardless, somehow transit managers must be given more power and the tools to do their jobs more effectively.

SUMMARY

The job of moving people in the urban setting has been assumed by the public sector from private owners with mixed results. The transfer was probably necessary. After decades of neglect, the loss of millions of transit riders to the automobile, and the failure of hundreds of private transit operators, the transit industry was on the brink of disaster. The federal government decided this disaster could not be allowed to happen and came forward with billions of dollars in aid.

In many ways, public sector mass transit management is more difficult than private sector management of railroads, airlines, or other modes. Decisions are similar—system, service, and other choices must be made. Public mass transit executives, however, have less clear—even conflicting—performance goals, too many bosses, and too little control over junior managers and labor. Politics interferes with decisions, delays actions, and forces suboptimal solutions.

Nevertheless, mass transit systems and equipment are improving, and ridership has increased during the last 20 years. Market share, however, has declined. Problems such as service breakdowns and escalating operating deficits remain, leaving room for improvements. However, the mass transit industry is changing. Demands for increased economic efficiencies are giving managers clearer mandates and improved controls. The balance of power is shifting from labor to management. This shift is of major significance, since labor is the industry's highest cost area.

Mass transit makes sense in this automobile-dominated country, for it can reduce street congestion, strengthen inner cities, save energy, reduce air pollution, and save most riders money in comparison to automobile use. Now is not the time to abandon mass transit, but public sector mass transit produces waste, and inefficiencies cannot be excused, either. The challenge, then, is to give management more power to improve U.S. mass transit efficiency and then hold these decision makers more accountable for their actions.

STUDY QUESTIONS

1. Why is it difficult to stimulate mass transit ridership?

2. How does the goal of trying to satisfy all peak-period mass transit demand impact on system costs and productivity?

3. Why do big-city mayors tend to favor rapid rail transit systems rather than other forms of mass transit investments?

4. Distinguish between federal capital grants and operating grants. What is each form of subsidy intended to accomplish?

5. Explain what this statement might mean: "If the federal government assumes all or too much of the costs of transit, there is an erosion of local responsibility resulting in over-investment, unwise investment, and no, or reduced, incentives for efficient operations."

6. Why have mass transit equipment breakdowns been increasing, despite record levels of capital improvements?

7. Why don't mass transit authorities raise fares to offset rising operating deficits?

8. Explain how Section 13(C) of the Urban Mass Transportation Act of 1964 increased union contract bargaining power.

ENDNOTES

1. American Public Transit Association, *Transit Fact Book 1981* (Washington, D.C.: American Public Transit Association, 1981), p. 12 (hereafter cited as *Transit Fact Book 1981*).

2. Ibid., p. 24.

3. Ibid., p. 40.

4. American Public Transit Association, *'74–'75 Transit Fact Book* (Washington, D.C.: American Public Transit Association, 1975), p. 16.

5. U.S. Department of Transportation, Urban Mass Transportation Administration, *Federal Assistance for Urban Mass Transportation* (Washington, D.C.: U.S. D.O.T., 1979), p. 9 (hereafter cited as *Federal Assistance*).

6. *Transit Fact Book 1981*, pp. 42–43.

7. Susan Tift, "Mass Transit Makes a Comeback," *Time*, 16 January 1984, p. 20.

8. *Transit Fact Book 1981*, p. 40.

9. Ibid., p. 57.

10. JKH & Associates, *Policy Guidance for Public Transportation Decision Makers*, a Training Course prepared for the Federal Highway Administration, Urban Mass Transportation Administration; and U.S. Department of Transportation, unpublished manual, (JHK & Associates, January 1979), p. VI–18.

11. Daniel Machalaba, "Train Master: Underneath New York, David Gunn Tackles a Monumental Task," *Wall Street Journal*, 25 April 1984, p. 22.

12. William Dunn, "Mass Transit for Motown? SEMTA 'Prefers' Light Rail," *Railway Age*, 8 August 1977, p. 40.

13. "Attacking the Mass Transit Mess," *Business Week*, 3 June 1972, p. 60.

14. "Making Mass Transit Work," *Business Week*, 16 February 1974, p. 79.

15. Michael Doan, "The Great American Transportation Mess," *U.S. News & World Report*, 31 August 1981, p. 21.

16. (a) Machalaba, "Train Master," p. 22; and (b) Douglas Martin, "Public Transit's Rocky Road," *Wall Street Journal*, 1 November 1979, p. 28.

17. Robert Roberts, "Transit Hardware: Shift To

Renovation," *Modern Railroads,* October 1981, p. 44.

18. *Transit Fact Book 1981,* p. 67.

19. Ibid.

20. JKH & Associates, *Policy Guidance,* p. IV–13.

21. Albert R. Karr, "Cities Say President's Budget Cuts Imperil Many Mass-Transit Projects," *Wall Street Journal,* 29 July 1981, p. 25.

22. U.S., Congress, House, Report by the Subcommittee on Investigations and Oversight, Committee on Public Works and Transportation, *Oversight of the Federal Public Transportation Assistance Program, the State of Public Transportation in the Nation, and a Recommended New Block Grant Concept,* Committee Print 97–42, 97th Cong. 2d sess., May 1982, p. 1 (hereafter cited as *Oversight of the Federal Public Transportation*).

23. Ibid., p. 6.

24. Roberts, "Transit Hardware," p. 44.

25. *Oversight of the Federal Public Transportation,* p. 6.

26. Jane Perlez, "U.S. Rules Against M.T.A. on Subsidy for Subway Cars," *New York Times,* 5 February 1983, p. 25.

27. Ari L. Goldman, "MTA Escapes Federal Penalty in Rail Car Deal," *New York Times,* 11 February 1983, p. B1.

28. *Federal Assistance,* pp. 21–22.

29. Martin, "Public Transit's Rocky Road," p. 28.

30. "House Panel Votes to Halt Requirement of Full Transit Access for Handicapped," *Wall Street Journal,* 2 March 1980, p. 22.

31. John D. Williams, "Commuter Rail Service, Still Deteriorating after Fuel Squeeze, Is Seen at Perilous Point," *Wall Street Journal,* 19 October 1979, p. 48.

32. "Transit: Shoot First, Ask Questions Later," *Railway Age,* 9 March 1981, p. 24.

33. JKH & Associates, *Policy Guidance,* pp. III-1, 2.

34. Kevin Tottis, "Malfunctions Plague Fancy New GM Buses, Forcing Cities to Make Expensive Repairs," *Wall Street Journal,* 2 June 1982, p. 27.

35. "Attacking the Mass Transit Mess," p. 62.

36. Public Transport Use for Work Fell 10.6% in 70s, Census Showed," *Wall Street Journal,* 20 April 1982, p. 20.

37. "The Mess in Mass Transit," *Time,* 16 July 1979, p. 52.

38. Doan, "Great American Transportation Mess," p. 21.

39. David A. Andelman, "Bus System in City Termed the Worst of All MTA Units," *New York Times,* 24 December 1979, p. D5.

40. Roberts, "Transit Hardware," p. 44.

41. Ken Wells, "San Franciscans Face Uphill Climb Despite Return of Cable Cars," *Wall Street Journal,* 26 June 1984, pp. 1, 31.

42. Roberts, "Transit Hardware," p. 44.

43. Wells, "San Franciscans Face Uphill Climb," p. 31.

44. *Oversight of the Federal Public Transportation,* p. 6.

45. Doan, "Great American Transportation Mess," p. 21.

46. (a) Harlan S. Byrne, "End of the Line? Mass Transit Is Facing a Financial Crisis; Service Cutbacks and Higher Fares Loom," *Wall Street Journal,* 2 April 1981, p. 56; and (b) "Boston Transit System Runs Out of Money; State Assumes Control," *Wall Street Journal,* 19 November 1980, p. 22.

47. "Chicago Transit Gets $70 Million Financing from Banking Group," *Wall Street Journal,* 9 September 1981, p. 41.

48. *Transit Fact Book 1981,* pp. 46–47.

49. Ibid., p. 60.

50. Albert R. Karr, "Mass-Transit Riders Are Facing Prospect of Higher Fares to Keep Systems Running," *Wall Street Journal,* 17 March 1981, p. 35.

51. Emily Ellison, "Kiepper: Four Good Reasons for MARTA Fare Hike," *Atlanta Journal and Constitution,* 7 June 1981, p. 6C.

52. Alan Freeman, "While Public Transit in U.S. Deteriorates, Canada's Subway and Bus Systems Flourish," *Wall Street Journal,* 31 December 1981, p. 9.

53. Ibid.

54. Henry Eason, "Politicians' Feuding Could Put Brakes on Chicago Transit," *Atlanta Journal and Constitution,* 7 June 1981, p. 6C.

55. Richard Reeves, "New York Subways 'Dying'," *Atlanta Constitution,* 30 January 1981, p. 5A.

56. Byrne, "End of the Line?" p. 56.

57. *Transit Fact Book 1981,* p. 31.

58. Byrne, "End of the Line?" p. 56.

59. "Making Mass Transit Work," p. 77.

60. Karr, "Mass-Transit Riders," p. 35.

61. "MBTA: Greater Stability Comes to Boston Transit," *Railway Age,* 11 October 1982, pp. 29–31.

62. *Transit Fact Book 1981,* pp. 46, 48.

63. *Oversight of the Federal Public Transportation,* p. 11.

64. John D. Williams, "New York Strike Threat Only a Symptom of Transit System's Long-Term Illness," *Wall Street Journal,* 31 March 1980, p. 14.

65. (a) Bill Shipp, "Union Pay: The Giant That Is Swallowing MARTA," *Atlanta Journal and Constitution,* 28 February 1981, p. 1B; (b) Carole Ashkinaze and Sharon Bailey, "MARTA Driver's Pay Hit $56,135 in '81," *Atlanta Constitution,* 5 February 1982, p. 1; and (c) "Twentieth Semi-Annual Report to the MARTA Overview Committee," *Atlanta Journal,* 12 February 1983, p. 11A.

66. *Oversight of the Federal Public Transportation,* p. 14.

67. Machalaba, "Train Master," p. 22.

68. Ibid., p. 1.

69. Ellison, "Kiepper," p. 6C.

70. Williams, "New York Strike Threat," p. 14.

71. Ibid.

72. "New York City Transit Union Told That State Can't Afford Demands," *Wall Street Journal,* 26 February 1980, p. 36.

73. Richard Koenig, "Philadelphia's Commuter Rail Deadlock Reflects the Problems That Conrail Faces," *Wall Street Journal,* 3 November 1982, p. 31.

74. "Transit Union Calls on New York City System to Give 30% Pay Rise," *Wall Street Journal,* 5 February 1980, p. 16.

75. "$1 Million in Fines Levied on 2 Unions in Transit Strike," *New York Times,* 9 April 1980, p. B3.

76. See (a) Alan Reed, "The Urban Mass Transportation Act and Local Labor Negotiation: The 13–C Experience," *Transportation Journal* 18, no. 3 (Spring 1979):56–64; and (b) Thomas Crosby, "Section 13(C): To Grant or Not to Grant," *Mass Transit,* May 1977, pp. 10–13.

77. *Oversight of the Federal Public Transportation,* p. 17.

78. Raleigh Bryans, "MARTA Asks Union to 'Think Atlanta' on Pay," *Atlanta Journal and Constitution,* 14 February 1982, p. 2B.

79. The Atlanta situation will be explained at a later point in the chapter.

80. James H. Miller, "An Evaluation of Allocation Methodologies for Public Transportation Operating Assistance," *Transportation Journal* 18, no. 1 (Fall 1979):40.

81. *Transit Fact Book 1981,* p. 46.

82. "Transportation Bill for $10.6 Billion Is Sent to Reagan," *Wall Street Journal,* 20 December 1982, p. 6.

83. John Curley, "Looming Shutdown of Chicago's Transit Heats up Rivalry Between City, Downstate," *Wall Street Journal,* 16 June 1981, p. 33.

84. John Herbers, "New Data Raise Issues of Mass Transit's Value," *New York Times,* 31 March 1983, p. B14.

85. Ibid.

86. "MBTA: Greater Stability," pp. 29–31.

87. Jerry Schwartz and Fran Hesser, "Assembly OK's MARTA Bill, Ends 1982 Session," *Atlanta Journal and Constitution,* 27 March 1982, pp. 1A, 5A.

88. Cathy S. Dolman, "Ruling Could Cost MARTA Patrons 15¢ More a Ride," *Atlanta Constitution,* 11 July 1985, p. 1D.

89. "Parkway to Deficits," Editorial, *Wall Street Journal,* 7 September 1984, p. 26.

ADDITIONAL READINGS

Altshuler, Alan. *The Urban Transportation System: Politics and Policy Innovation.* Cambridge, Mass.: MIT Press, 1979.

Appleyard, Donald. *Livable Streets.* Berkeley, Calif.: University of California Press, 1981.

Ashford, Norman; Bell, William G.; and Rich, Tom A., eds. *Mobility and Transport for Elderly and Handicapped Persons.* New York: Gordon and Breach Science Publishers, 1982.

Becker, A. Jeff, and Talley, Wayne K. "A Single Measure for Evaluating Public Transit Systems." *Transportation Quarterly* 36, no. 3 (July 1982):423–431.

Berg, W. D., and Koushki, Parviz A. "Improving Rural Mobility—A Practical Approach." *Transportation Quarterly* 36, no. 4 (October 1982):631–642.

Black, John. *Urban Transport Planning: Theory and Practice.* Baltimore: Johns Hopkins University Press, 1981.

Cervero, Robert. "Transit Cross-Subsidies." *Transportation Quarterly* 36, no. 3 (July 1982):377–389.

Dawson, John A. "Segmentation of the Transit Market." *Transportation Quarterly* 37, no. 1 (January 1983):73–84.

Fischer, Stanley I. *Moving Millions: An Inside Look at Mass Transit.* New York: Harper & Row, 1979.

Frankena, Mark W. *Urban Transportation Financing: Theory and Policy in Ontario.* Toronto: University of Toronto Press, 1982.

Glacel, Barbara Pate. *Regional Transit Authorities: Policy Analysis of Massachusetts.* New York: Praeger Publishers, 1983.

Gray, George E., and Hoel, Lester A., eds. *Public Transportation: Planning, Operations and Management.* Englewood-Cliffs, N.J.: Prentice-Hall, Inc., 1979.

Hendrickson, Chris; McNeil, Sue; and Pucher, John. "Socioeconomic Characteristics of Transit Riders: Some Recent Evidence." *Transportation Quarterly* 35, no. 3 (July 1981):461–483.

Hilton, George W. *Federal Transit Subsidies: The Urban Mass Transportation Assistance Program.* Washington, D.C.: American Enterprise Institute for Public Policy Research, 1974.

Lam, William, and Morrall, John. "Bus Passenger Walking Distances and Waiting Times: A Summer–Winter Comparison." *Transportation Quarterly* 36, no. 3 (July 1982):407–421.

Lave, Charles A. "Is Part-Time Labor a Cure for Transit Deficits?" *Traffic Quarterly* 34, no. 1 (January 1980):61–74.

Lieb, Robert C. "Urban Transportation Labor Issues in the 1980s." *Transportation Journal* 20, no. 2 (Winter 1980):50–56.

Nash, C. A. *Economics of Public Transport.* New York: Longman Inc., 1982.

Owen, Wilfred. *The Accessible City.* Washington, D.C.: The Brookings Institution, 1972.

Pucher, John. "Effects of Subsidies on Transit Costs."

Transportation Quarterly 36, no. 4 (October 1982):549–562.

Pushkarev, Boris S.; Zupan, Jeffrey M.; and Cumella, Robert S. *Urban Rail in America: An Exploration of Criteria for Fixed-Guideway Transit.* Bloomington, Ind.: Indiana University Press, 1982.

Robinson, Richard K., and Lovelock, Christopher H. *Marketing Public Transportation.* Chicago: American Marketing Association, 1981.

Roth, Gabriel, and Wynne, George G. *Free Enterprise Urban Transportation.* New Brunswick: Transaction Books, 1982.

Schaeffer, K. H., and Sclar, Elliott. *Access for All: Transportation and Urban Growth.* New York: Columbia University Press, 1980.

Schwartz, Martin L. "Motivations and Barriers to Riders' Acceptance of Bus Transit." *Transportation Journal* 19, no. 4 (Summer 1980):53–62.

Smerk, George M. "Federal Mass Transit Policy— 1981–1982: A Fall from Grace?" *Transportation Journal* 23, no. 1 (Fall 1983):38–86.

——. "The Transit Act That Never Was: Public Transportation Legislation 1979–1980." *Transportation Journal* 20, no. 4 (Summer 1981): 29–53.

——. "The Urban Mass Transportation Act at Twenty: A Turning Point?" *Transportation Journal* 24, no. 4 (Summer 1985):52–74.

——. *Urban Mass Transportation: A Dozen Years of Federal Policy.* Bloomington, Ind.: Indiana University Press, 1974.

Steiner, Henry Malcolm. *Conflict in Urban Transportation: The People Against the Planners.* Lexington, Mass.: Lexington Books, 1978.

Whitt, J. Allen. *Urban Elites and Mass Transportation: The Dialectics of Power.* Princeton, N.J.: Princeton University Press, 1982.

Competition in the Transportation Industry: Theory, Practice, and Strategy

19

In today's deregulated transportation environment, carriers must become more competitive to survive and prosper. Regulations that once protected less-efficient firms have been replaced by a new policy that primarily allows the marketplace to decide who succeeds or fails. Therefore, whether a firm prospers and grows or shrinks or becomes bankrupt then is likely to depend on each company's ability to compete. This competitive ability in turn will be closely correlated to the capabilities of corporate officers to grasp and apply economic, as well as marketing, theories and principles. Owners and managers need to know the limits of their own firms; the capabilities and deficiencies of their competitors; and the needs, strengths, and weaknesses of customers. They must also possess the flexibility and courage to face changes in a dynamic business climate.

Nothing is more symbolic of the new transportation environment than price competition. In the past, railroad, common carrier general commodity trucking, and scheduled passenger airline executives competed for business on a service basis. Between two points, intramodal competitors tended to charge identical prices; cargo and passenger business was therefore won or lost on the basis of which company had the best services. Now this narrow competitive focus has changed. Starting in the late 1970s, pricing regulations were lessened or eliminated. The results were price competition, heavy discounting, and an imperative need for carriers to reduce or control costs and bolster productivity.

Chapter 19 defines economic and marketing theories and concepts and applies them in real world transportation settings. The primary intent is to enable carrier managers to become more competitive. Secondly, it explains many of the modal and carrier strategic options available to transportation users. Specific topics to be discussed are price competition, service competition, and factors influencing modal and carrier competitiveness. Other issues include an analysis of the changing transportation competitive environment and an examination of competitors and competition in three major transportation markets.

PRICE COMPETITION

Price competition is defined as the struggle to obtain business through advantageous freight rates or passenger fares. Briefly, Chapter 2 introduced the basic determinants of pricing strategies—costs, demand, and the degree of competition. Chapters 5 through 18 subsequently provided much description of modes and specific illustrations of carrier pricing activities. All this information will now be used as a foundation on which to summarize pricing theories and concepts and build a greater understanding of pricing strategies. Carrier costs are considered first.

Costs

General Cost Terminology.   Costs, or the expenses of doing business, are important because they define the lower parameters of prices. Furthermore, in relation to prices and demand, costs help to determine profits. Besides fixed and variable costs (see Chapter 2, "Finance" section, for definitions), other forms of costs that affect transportation prices include joint costs and common costs. *Joint costs* are expenses unavoidably created by the decision to offer a particular type of service. Backhaul costs are an example: By accepting a load from point *A* to point *B,* a carrier will experience costs in returning equipment to point *A.*

joint costs

Common costs are variable or fixed expenses that result when various forms of traffic benefit from the same company expenditures. For example, when an airline decides to send an aircraft from one airport to another, fuel, a variable cost, is burned. However, passengers, baggage, mail, and cargo share the benefits of the service. Thus the fuel expenditure is a common or shared cost. The decision to construct an oil pipeline also creates a large fixed cost expense, but all commodities subsequently flowing through the pipeline benefit from the fixed costs. Consequently, it is difficult to trace common pipeline costs to a particular cargo item like gasoline or jet fuel.

common costs

Commodity Cost Factors.   Although fixed, variable, joint, and common costs form the basis for setting rates, these terms are quite general. Thus carrier marketing personnel seek more specific cost measures. Two major considerations are commodity cost factors and route cost factors. First, let us look at three types of commodity cost factors.

1. *Types of equipment needed.* Some cargo requires specialized equipment; examples are liquefied natural gas (LNG) needing expensive cryogenic (thermal) tanks; cash, checks, and other valuables requiring armored vehicle service; and frozen foods, which need refrigerated vehicles. Similarly, the passenger side of the business presents special needs. For instance, AMTRAK must supply dining and sleeping cars on long-haul trains. Because specialized equipment, such as an LNG ship, is uniquely designed to carry only certain commodities, its use is restricted. LNG ships, therefore, are often deadheaded home since no commodity is suitable for transportation on the backhaul. Specialized equipment often incurs higher operating costs; it can also be expensive to purchase.

types of equipment needed

2. *Loading characteristics.* Some items are easily loaded onto vehicles, whereas others are not. Examples of the latter are objects that are too long (telephone poles), too wide (industrial boilers), and too high (roof trusses). Others can be too heavy (granite blocks), too light (potato chips), or too awkward (canoes, which are unsuitable for stacking and wasteful of vehicle cubic capacity). The more time it takes to load and unload vehicles and the more cubic or weight-hauling vehicle capacity a commodity wastes, the higher the costs per 100 lbs. to the carrier.

loading characteristics

3. *Potential loss and damage problems.* The more susceptible an item is to loss and damage, the higher the cost to the carrier. Potential risks force carriers to use greater care (that is, take more time, which adversely affects productivity), make larger claims settlements when loss and damage occur, or provide greater insurance. All these factors raise carrier costs.

loss and damage risks

Route Cost Factors.   Other carrier costs are caused by route-related factors. Three specific considerations are as follows:

1. *Distance.* Variable costs increase as cargo and passengers are hauled longer distances. Carriers that haul traffic over circuitous routes to avoid interlining (e.g., a hub-and-spoke airline network) are voluntarily increasing distance-related costs. Equipment wears out the more it is used; thus fixed costs, such as those incurred when a railroad locomotive is purchased to replace a worn out existing locomotive, are also affected when vehicles move additional miles.

distance

2. *Traffic density.* Traffic density also affects costs. In cases of higher traffic densities, greater volumes of cargo or passengers are moved between any two points, thereby producing economies of density. This economy of density in turn can lead to lower fully distributed costs—variable costs plus a fair share of the fixed costs—and price reductions. In contrast, increased traffic densities might cause costs to rise. The decision to add one more rail car to a train, for example, might necessitate the addition of another locomotive. In this case, the efficient balance between power units, or locomotives, and cars with just enough power to climb the steepest hill is distorted by the increase in traffic density (the addition of one more car). Also, carriers must be careful not to create directional traffic im-

traffic density

balances. Severe backhaul excess capacity problems and increased joint costs can result from too much traffic in one direction.

3. *Operating conditions.* It costs more money to operate vehicles going up hills, around curves, through populated areas requiring more stops or continuous braking and accelerating, and through snowy country than over flat lands over straight routes between far-removed origins and destinations in good weather. Rates should reflect cost differences.

operating conditions

Demand

Demand, or the needed quantity of services, is just as important as costs to transportation pricing strategists. First consider the types of demand important to carrier managers.

Types of Demand. Chapter 5 already defined *derived demand.* Five other forms of transportation demand are aggregate, modal, company, market-lane, and primary demand.

1. *Aggregate demand* is the total demand for transportation services via all modes of transportation. Intercity passenger traffic is an example: Although automobiles, intercity bus lines, AMTRAK, and airlines are interested in this aggregate demand, an oil pipeline, a trucking company, or a freight railroad does not try to satisfy this market potential.

aggregate demand

2. *Modal demand* segments aggregate demand by modes; it refers to the total demand supplied by all carriers of a particular mode. For instance, if the aggregate demand for all for-hire and private intercity passenger-mile traffic is 100%, the airline modal demand (modal split market share) may be only 13% of the aggregate demand.

modal demand

3. *Company demand* segments modal demand into each carrier's share. An airline is interested in its share of the modal demand total. If it has 17% of the airline industry's total passenger-miles, a modal demand measure, its company demand would represent approximately 2.0% of the aggregate national intercity passenger-mile demand—17% × 13% × 100%.

company demand

4. *Market-lane demand* divides aggregate and modal demands into origin-destination pairs (lanes). Continuing the example, an airline would like to increase its share of the passenger-mile traffic moving between Chicago and New York City. It is at the market-lane level where competition really occurs. Carriers compete for specific traffic in specific market lanes. It is difficult for a particular carrier to address aggregate and modal demand, but by successfully winning the market-lane battle, a firm creates company demand.

market-lane demand

5. *Primary demand* represents present aggregate and modal demand that a carrier does not currently control, along with new, untapped potential not presently included in aggregate and modal demand. In other words, primary demand represents growth traffic that a carrier might obtain to increase its share of market-lane demand and to bolster company demand. An illustration, from an airline perspective, is trying to convince people to take their first airplane trips.

primary demand

Primary Demand Strategies.   Although carriers should constantly be concerned with satisfying present customers to retain their business, management's ability to satisfy primary demand will determine corporate growth. Several primary demand strategies are available.

intramodal diversion

1. *Intramodal diversion* is a plan that seeks to shift modal traffic from competitor carriers to a carrier's own particular firm. For example, airline *X* will try to convince passengers now flying on airline *Y* between Chicago and Denver to use its service.

intermodal diversion

2. *Intermodal diversion* is a strategy similar to intramodal diversion. The objective of managers using this tactic is to convince users to shift business from the present mode to the manager's own company (call this company *T*). Target customer groups could be company *T*'s present clients, who are also using carriers in other modes, or nonclients of company *T*. As a case in point, discount pricing programs have been successful in drawing travelers from automobiles and buses to air transportation.

other strategies

3. *Increasing aggregate or modal demand* is far more difficult. In theory, management's objective is to stimulate the total demand for cargo or passenger services and increase his or her mode's traffic levels. An example might be an advertising campaign to stimulate intercity bus travel (modal demand strategy) or travel in general (aggregate demand strategy). As modal demand (all bus travel) increases or aggregate demand (all intercity passenger travel) grows, a bus company hopes to haul more traffic than it did in the past.

Demand Variables.   Demand is influenced by prices and the economic conditions of the users. Consider price elasticity of demand, which indicates how price changes alter the quanitity of services demanded and revenues, assuming all other variables are held constant. In the transportation case, *quantity* usually refers to ton-miles or passenger-miles moved. If price reductions produce revenue gains, demand for the service is elastic. If revenues fall with price reductions, demand is price inelastic. Knowledge of price elasticity can guide pending decisions about price decreases or increases. For example, carriers whose market is demand elastic will know that price reductions should stimulate demand and revenues; therefore lower prices might be a good tactic.

price elasticity of demand

customer's ability to pay

Another key demand factor is the ability of the customer to pay. To increase prices at a time when a freight customer is struggling to survive financially could lead to a loss of all the user's business. The customer may either divert traffic to other carriers or entirely cease shipments. With the passenger trade the situation is similar. Passengers short of cash may switch to lower priced carrier services, postpone travel plans temporarily, or cancel trips entirely. Price increases make far more sense when customers are able to pay increased charges. However, a carrier should never assume that financially strong customers will automatically pay higher rates or fares. Much depends on the competition.

Forms of Competition

Carrier managers trying to set prices should be concerned primarily with five forms of competition: intramodal competition, intermodal competition, market competition, producer competition, and product competition.

Intramodal Competition.   One primary source of competition is between two carriers in the same mode: for example, one trucking company trying to compete against another trucking company. Sometimes the struggle is between two common carriers; at other times a common carrier duels a contract carrier. For-hire competition with private carriage is also a routine occurrence. In all cases in intramodal competition, competitors are members of the same mode.

Intermodal Competition.   When a carrier in one mode battles a carrier from another mode, intermodal competition is occurring. Illustrating this form of competition is water carrier and railroad competition for grain shipments.

Market Competition.   Market competition—competition for traffic between two carriers serving the same origin but different destination points—can also position one carrier against another. As an illustration, assume a coal mine owner in West Virginia could ship coal to Mobile, Alabama, or Norfolk, Virginia, for subsequent export to Europe (Fig. 19.1). Coal moving to Mobile

---

FIGURE 19.1.
Market competition.

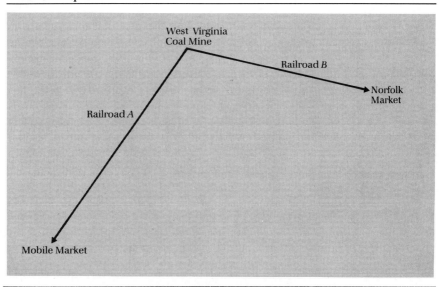

is transported by Railroad *A,* and coal to Norfolk is carried by Railroad *B.* Railroad *A* does not serve Norfolk, and Railroad *B* does not serve Mobile. To carry as much traffic as possible, Railroad *B* requires that most of the coal demand be in Norfolk. Otherwise, Railroad *A* receives the majority of the freight traffic. Thus the West Virginia–Mobile market competes with the West Virginia–Norfolk market. In such situations, each carrier is motivated to offer attractive rates.

Producer Competition.   Another form of competition is producer competition. Again referring to a coal example (see Fig. 19.2), an electric utility in Dallas could buy coal from West Virginia or Wyoming (the Powder River Basin). Thus the coal-producing areas compete for the Dallas business. If the Dallas utility selects Wyoming coal, Western Railroad will be the traffic beneficiary; if the West Virginia mine wins the contract, Eastern Railroad will receive the freight. Again, carriers should work with shippers, such as coal producers, to reach a competitive delivered price for the shipper's product. Failure to do so could mean lost sales to both producer and carrier.

Product Competition.   A final form of competition is product competition. When oil prices rose in the 1970s, a number of electric utilities switched from oil to coal as the natural resource for generating electricity. Reductions in oil demand hurt water and oil pipeline carriers, whereas increases in coal demand favored railroads. *Product competition* refers to the

FIGURE 19.2.
Producer competition.

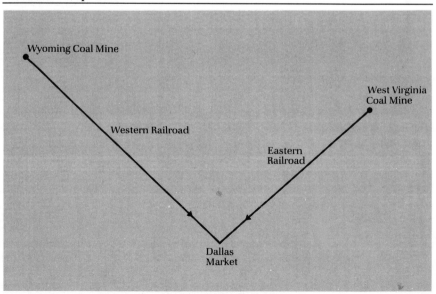

substitutability of one product for another. Because transportation is a derived-demand business, product competition can significantly alter modal and company demand. If customers do not demand the commodities a carrier transports, they do not need the carrier's services.

Economic Market Structures

Market structure, which includes the number of competitors in a market, the size and power of these competitors, as well as the ability of firms to enter and expand operations, also affects price competition. In developing pricing strategies, managers should recognize whether the firm is positioned in a pure monopoly, an oligopoly, a monopolistic competition, or a pure competition economic market structure, or something resembling one of these four structures.

Pure Monopoly.   Pure monopoly is a market structure in which a firm has no real competition. There is no substitute for the services it provides and no real threat from new-carrier competition; the firm has total control. A slight variation of this situation in the railroad industry is market dominance, interpreted to mean a lack of effective intramodal, intermodal, producer, or market competition. The closest example of a pure monopoly structure is the pipeline transportation of natural gas.

A carrier in a pure monopoly market, however, may still not have unlimited capacity to increase prices. Pricing specialists must never forget the economic conditions of their customers, as well as product competition—each of which affects demand. Carriers in pure monopoly markets are also frequently tightly regulated. Another constraint is the risk that abused or irritated customers will retaliate against a pure monopoly carrier by ceasing to give that carrier traffic in other non-monopoly markets. Big customers often have leverage and use it as necessary. Pure monopolies give carriers wider capabilities for raising prices, but an intelligent strategy is to seek price and demand levels that optimize profits without jeopardizing longer term market potential.

Oligopoly.   A second market structure is *oligopoly*—a market setting in which the competition is limited to a few sellers (carriers, in this case) and a small number of customers. Price or service changes by any one carrier force other carriers to respond, such as by duplicating the prices or services of the price or service initiator. Nevertheless, without *collusion*—that is, a secret, usually illegal, agreement among carriers—a competitor who initiates a price change cannot be sure of the reactions of other carriers in the market. For example, if one firm raises prices, what will prevent another carrier from maintaining present price levels?[1] The ability of one carrier to raise prices and maintain market share depends to a great extent on the degree of differentiation the carrier has established between its services and competitors' service offerings. If a carrier's services are relatively unique and superior (e.g., a higher degree of reliability or speed, less loss and damage, etc.), customers might pay higher prices than what the competition charges. If customers perceive little or no service differentiation, however, why would they pay a higher rate to one carrier if others will perform equally well for less? It is not easy to identify examples of transportation oligopolies because of the influence of intermodal competition. In some cases crude oil pipelines come close to meeting the oligopoly characteristics, since a few carriers serve a restricted number of shippers who want oil moved from oil fields to refineries or to ocean shipping terminals.

Monopolistic Competition. In contrast to the previous forms of market structures, monopolistic competition exists where there are many sellers (i.e., carriers) and buyers (i.e., shippers or passengers) and where services are differentiated. In this structure, price changes by one carrier are not likely to have a major effect on prices of other competitors. A mode that generally has the characteristics of monopolistic competition is trucking, with approximately 200,000 carriers and millions of customers in the market. Although firms often operate similar equipment, trucking companies strive for differentiated services, such as faster delivery times, better reliability, and less loss and damage.

Pure Competition. A fourth market structure is pure competition. Its characteristics include large numbers of sellers (i.e., carriers) and buyers (i.e., shippers and passengers), virtually no industry concentration (i.e., no market dominance by either one or a few carriers, virtually no service differentiation, total freedom for carriers to enter and exit markets, and perfect information, because buyers and sellers each know what the other is doing. The market therefore dictates prices, and sellers have no real control. If carriers raise prices above the market price, they reduce their demand to zero. However, if a carrier sets its prices at the market price, it can obtain all the traffic it can carry. One carrier's prices will not change the market price. In transportation, there are no real world examples of pure competition market structures.

Pricing Strategies

market penetration

Managers need to define corporate objectives clearly before implementing pricing changes. If the goal is market penetration by trying to increase market-lane and company demand, the most common strategy would be to use a relatively low price. Market penetration tactics are also appealing when firms have excess capacity, want to increase productivity through traffic growth, or both. Furthermore, penetration can be used to enter a market and convince new clients to try a carrier's services for the first time.

early cash recovery

A low price is also conducive to accomplishing the goal of early cash recovery. Users of this strategy will price services in ways that generate high volumes of traffic in the short term. The cash so generated is then used to meet current liabilities or investment opportunities.

With a third strategy, market skimming, carriers initially offer services at market skimming high prices and hope to attract enough demand to realize high short-term profits. Gradually, carriers using the market skimming strategy lower prices to create increasing volumes of demand from more price-conscious buyers.

risks Each pricing strategy contains inherent risks. There is a danger in the long run with low-price strategies, such as market penetration and early cash recovery. Because of rising costs or low profits, most carriers eventually need to increase prices. How will users respond to price increases and, in particular, to dramatic escalations during periods when they know a carrier's costs have not risen as appreciably as the price increases would indicate? In these situations, carriers are in trouble with both their customers and government regulators because of alleged monopoly abuses.

Carriers using value of service pricing (for an explanation, see Chapter 5) also err at times by setting prices at unnecessarily low levels. Managers should determine whether the low rate is necessary to obtain the traffic and whether prices actually cover variable costs. Low prices may protect market share, but they also may precipitate rate wars, especially in an oligopoly market structure. There are dangers, too, in market skimming. If a carrier sets prices too high, it may not generate enough sales to establish its presence in the market or to meet profit targets.

price leaders and followers Does the carrier want to be a price leader (i.e., one who initiates price changes) or a price follower (i.e., one who lets other carriers first adjust rates and then decides whether to respond and in what way with its own price changes)? Some carriers, such as American Airlines, are aggressive price leaders. Others are followers, such as Delta Air Lines.

broad and selective pricing strategies Another choice is between broad or selective pricing strategies. To illustrate the difference, one carrier might decide to reduce every rate offered systemwide by 10%—broad pricing strategy. A second firm may reduce rates in selective markets where competition or a market penetration strategy necessitates such action—selective pricing strategy. The selective strategy is advantageous because it does not lower yields in markets where demand will support higher prices.

restricted air fares Restricted and unrestricted air fares are refinements of these strategies. Carriers with restricted air fares offer discount airline tickets, but these fares are limited to a small number of seats per aircraft. Other sales conditions frequently imposed are advanced ticket purchasing requirements, departures restricted to certain days of the week, and a minimum number of days at destination before flying back to the origin point. Unrestricted air fares, in contrast, are available to all passengers and impose no such limitations. The primary objective of restricted fares is to maintain high yields generated by business (i.e., short-term) travelers—people who will fly regardless of price. unrestricted air fares Unrestricted fares are designed to stimulate primary demand—to attract new passengers to the airline—or to protect company demand and market-lane demand from intramodal competitors.

pricing considerations Carriers should try to avoid three common problems linked to pricing strategies. First, in the urgency of trying to attract primary demand, they should not neglect present customers and should never take the business of loyal customers for granted. Secondly, they should be careful not to price services in ways that encourage yield deterioration. Discounts should not cause present customers to shift traffic from one company service offering, such as railroad boxcar service, to another, such as railroad TOFC service. Without an increase in primary demand, this practice only lowers yields. Finally, if carriers have high costs that cannot be lowered to become more price competitive, the carriers should strive diligently for superior differentiated services, for example, more frequent service, greater reliability, and more convenient delivery times. Customers perceive high prices to be less unappealing if they perceive more value for their money.

SERVICE COMPETITION

The second broad basis for carrier competition is service competition. Services represent the non-price factors necessary to satisfy each customer's transportation needs and to obtain the customer's business. Carriers compete by trying to provide superior services to what other firms are offering. This section will address service competition by first reviewing cargo service factors (a subject introduced in the "Traffic Management" section of Chapter 3) and then by examining passenger service factors.

Cargo Service Factors

Figure 19.3 summarizes the various types of service factors influencing shipper modal and carrier choices. Few shippers expect a carrier to provide all the services in Fig. 19.3; expectations vary by shipper and by commodity shipped. The carrier's task is to discover the levels of importance that particular shippers place on variables like reliability, speed, accessibility, and control and liability.

service factor example

Since terms like *reliability* and *accessibility* were extensively defined in Chapter 3, they will not be redefined here. Instead, the meaning of these terms will be illustrated by an examination of the service needs of a shipper who in 1985 needed to transport a box weighing 80 lbs. The package was 72 in. long, 20 in. wide, and 16 in. high. Valued at $5000, the contents were fragile and were needed in five days at a destination approximately 2000 miles away. What service factors were likely to assume high shipper priorities in this case?

accessibility

Beginning with the factor of accessibility, the shipper would have wanted to know if a carrier served both origin and destination points. If the carrier served only one point, interlining would have been necessary, and shippers of fragile, high-value items usually desire one-carrier service to minimize cargo handling and maximize control (i.e., the carrier's ability to avoid losing or damaging shipments). Another accessibility priority is weight and measurement restrictions. The package weighed less than 150 lbs, so weight would have posed no problems if the shipper had wanted to give the shipment to Federal

FIGURE 19.3.
Service factors influencing shipper modal and carrier choices.

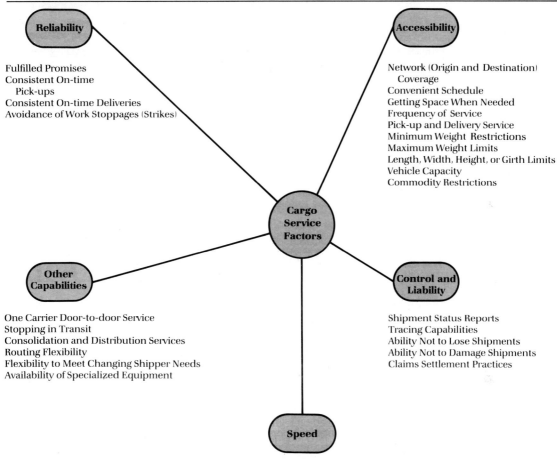

Express. However, Federal Express would have rejected the package because its length and girth (144 in.) exceeded the company's 120-in. maximum. Since United Parcel Service and U.S. Postal Service limited packages to 70 lbs., there was no accessibility to these carriers either. Accessibility is a critical factor; other carrier services are meaningless if companies refuse to handle the shipment.

reliability

speed

Since the shipper's package had five days to reach the destination, speed was not critical. However, if a mode slower than air transportation had been chosen, such as LTL trucking, reliability would have been more important: on-time pick-up and delivery would have been needed. If the reliability risk was too great, speed would have been more important.

control and liability

Finally, the value of the item ($5000) and its urgency (It *must* be at destination in five days) probably would have meant that high priorities were assigned to control and liability factors. Carrier-initiated status reports advising of the en-route location of the shipment would have been valuable, as would have been the shipper's ability to trace the shipment (i.e., shipper-initiated action). Because of the value of the item, the level of carrier overall liability protection would also have been a relevant consideration, although perhaps not as important as avoiding loss or damage entirely.

Passenger Service Factors

speed, reliability, and accessibility

Figure 19.4 diagrams and lists service factors that influence passenger choices of modes and carriers. Speed can be important. Likewise, on-time departures and arrivals—reliability—are often high-priority decision variables. Accessibility factors, too, can be critical determinants. Network coverage—that is, origin-destination capabilities—is important. Correlated with it are convenient schedules, the frequency of service (How long will the wait be before the next departure?), seating availability (There may be a departure, but can a passenger have a seat?), and interlining capability (Can the trip-taker improve services by transferring to another carrier for connecting service?). Two other passenger concerns are terminal access and egress: Is it convenient to get to and from carrier terminals, stations, or depots? Another factor is special passenger needs: Will the carrier accommodate children traveling alone or people in wheelchairs? Finally, can the transportation firm handle group travel?

terminal service

Whether the journey is an urban, intercity, or international trip, terminal services—services either prior to or subsequent to the passenger's boarding of a transportation vehicle—also affect modal and carrier choices. Since many users drive automobiles to terminals, one concern is parking: Is there a convenient, secure parking space available? Other terminal considerations are passenger processing (e.g., convenience of checking in, ticketing, and boarding vehicles), baggage (e.g., handling, convenience, security, and claims if loss or damage occur), and waiting room accommodations (e.g., seat availability and comfort). Walking distances are another decision factor. Further interests are restroom availability, cleanliness, the availability and clarity of information and directions, and employee courtesy and helpfulness. Terminal safety; food, drink, and shopping services; and lighting, heating, air conditioning, and uncrowded space are other passenger expectations.

vehicle services

Passengers can be even more demanding of vehicle services. Since the list of possible expectations in Fig. 19.4 is long and generally self-explanatory, the text will review only the more nebulous items, starting with classes of service. Can a passenger book better services, such as first class seating, or is service limited to single-class accommodations? Can a passenger buy a guaranteed reserved seat to avoid the hassles of having to compete with the crowd for available limited space? Will a passenger, because of the route, have a chance to sightsee during the trip? Does a traveler have sufficient privacy to escape

FIGURE 19.4.
Service factors influencing passenger modal and carrier choices.

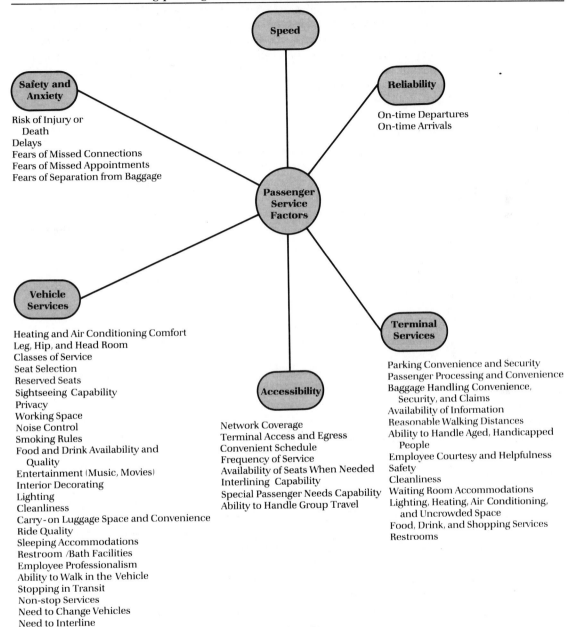

boisterous or obnoxious fellow travelers? Is there sufficient space to work on a project or use a portable computer? Is the ride quality smooth or bumpy? Are lounge chairs or sleeping accommodations available for night-time passengers? Other passengers may be more interested in employee professionalism (do workers really know their jobs?). A final question is whether passengers will be able to stop in transit for a short vacation and then later board another vehicle without incurring an additional charge.

safety and anxiety

Safety and anxiety may be major decision factors. An example is a passenger's perception of the risks of injury or death by taking one mode or carrier versus another. Some people fear flying and, regardless of an airline's safety record, it is difficult to coax them onto an aircraft. Transportation-caused anxieties are another problem. Tensions build as a result of delays, fears of missed connections in which a passenger arrives too late to board a departing vehicle, fears of missed appointments, and concerns about going somewhere while the baggage goes elsewhere. If any of these anxieties creates too much passenger discomfort, customers will divert to other carriers or modes or not travel at all.

Carrier Service Strategies

Because of this assortment of cargo and passenger needs and expectations, carriers that want to be competitive need to answer the following eight questions:

questions

1. What services do customers demand in return for their business?
2. How must a carrier change its service offerings to match customers' needs?
3. Are these operational changes within the carrier's capabilities?
4. How will these changes alter carrier costs, prices, demand, revenues, and profitability in both the short-term and the long-term?
5. How important is a particular group of customers' business?
6. Is it really worth making the necessary changes to match these customers' needs?
7. How will the carrier's competitors respond to its initiatives if the carrier decides to seek the traffic?
8. Does the carrier have the wherewithal to gain and hold a competitive edge in the market?

results and actions

These questions essentially force carriers to use market research and other management tools to make intelligent business decisions. The potential business may turn out to be poor and unworthy of price or service changes, or the potential may look excellent, but the carrier lacks resources to sustain a competitive edge. Ideally, the potential is attractive, and it looks as though the carrier could be an important market factor. This situation should trigger a response in the form of a carefully considered price/service initiative.

FACTORS INFLUENCING MODAL
AND CARRIER COMPETITIVENESS

Gaining the competitive edge and holding it, unfortunately, are not entirely within the control of individual carriers. As previously discussed, no matter how good a firm is, much depends on the competition. The quality of the competition's services, the strength of the rivals' finances, and the motivational level of the competitors' employees are three leading indicators of how difficult the challenge will be. Moreover, the strength of the competition in relation to a firm's market power is subject to external forces, which will be discussed in this section.

Governmental Regulations

As discussed throughout the text, the government does not regulate modes equally. This situation is true in economic, as well as noneconomic, forms of regulation. Traditionally, railroading was the most regulated mode of transportation. Railroads were supposed to compete against totally deregulated interstate agricultural exempt truckers for wheat, corn, soybeans, and approximately 600 other commodities, yet train operators were severely handicapped by restrictive pricing regulations. In comparison, exempt truckers were free to change their rates at will. Deregulation measures starting in 1977 improved, but did not entirely remove, economic regulatory imbalances between the modes.

advantages of being a less-regulated carrier

From the perspective of intermodal competition, less-regulated modes have the competitive edge in their ability to change prices and services. They can react quickly to competitor marketing and operating initiatives, cost increases, and a changing economy. More regulated firms, however, are handicapped by procedural delays and restrictive rules, such as route restrictions. Although deregulation has enabled the more regulated modes of the past to compete on a more equal footing today, handicaps still remain. The interstate transportation of wheat, corn, and soybeans, for example, is still regulated for railroads, so they do not have the advantages given to exempt truckers hauling the same commodities.

Governmental Policies

Sudden changes in federal policies also affect traffic and modal and company market share distributions. For example, President Reagan's 1981 decision to fire striking air traffic controllers (see Chapter 14) resulted in severe flight reductions at many large hub airports in the United States. This reduction, in turn, reduced modal demand as inconvenienced passengers, as well as those worried about airline safety, either diverted to other modes or postponed or eliminated planned trips. The carriers more closely tied to the busiest airports were more severely affected by the president's decision than those serving medium- and small-hub airports. Embargos, such as the 1979 grain embargo on Soviet trade (see Chapter 8), also severely hamper transportation demand, because they stop the flow of commerce.

Governmental Promotion and Subsidy

The government's allocation of transportation promotion and subsidy benefits, a blessing to recipients, can be a curse to nonrecipients. Unable to obtain federal eminent domain rights, even though oil and gas pipelines have this right, coal slurry pipeline development projects have been stymied. With the advantages of many billions of dollars in aid, automobiles, trucking companies, domestic water carriers, and airlines have successfully diverted a significant amount of freight traffic and virtually all intercity passenger traffic from the railroads. Of course, superior services played an equal part in many of these modal shifts. However, governmental promotion and subsidy lower the beneficiaries' costs, which lead to lower prices for the recipients. Modes receiving less aid and stuck with proportionately higher cost burdens do not have the same low-price capabilities. Furthermore, if their lower prices meet the competition's, while retaining only market share, they result in reduced profits. For example, regular route intercity bus operators ask if it is fair that they have to compete against AMTRAK, a government-owned, government-operated, and government-subsidized carrier whose passengers, on the average, pay only about 50% of their transportation costs. Such direct subsidies force nonsubsidized carriers to make difficult pricing decisions, such as lowering prices to maintain market share but risking yield erosion, maintaining prices but risking a loss of traffic, or reducing their operations.

Technological Advances

Technology is improving. Oil pipelines, for example, were superior to railroads in hauling crude oil. Containerships made many breakbulk ships obsolete. Aircraft and automobiles proved their worth against railroad passenger trains. Supertankers relegated smaller oil-bearing ships to lesser roles. Also, computers have assumed many jobs once occupied by transportation employees and simultaneously created the need for other workers.

Inventions should always be expected; no carrier can afford to become complacent or assume that its future is secure. When new ideas and inventions are introduced, they can strengthen the competitive position of the fortunate mode in relation to other market modes. More often than not, however, carriers control neither the design nor timing of the introduction of inventions. They can only try to be prepared when technological advances, helpful to their mode or beneficial to competitors, present themselves. One strategy is to acquire the latest technology. To do so, however, carriers must have financial resources.

Fuel Prices

Fuel prices have considerable impact on carrier competitiveness. Changing oil prices in the 1970s took a greater toll on some modes than on others. Hardest hit were airlines, truckers, automobile operators, and bus companies, which saw their costs rise more dramatically than did the more fuel-efficient modes like water carriers and railroads. Pipelines, which need electricity to run pumps or compressors, were even more fortunate, because they were not oil dependent—in essence, electricity can be generated from coal, natural gas, and other non-petroleum resources. For oil-dependent firms, increased fuel costs translated into higher transportation prices and a weakened price-competitive position compared with less oil-sensitive modes. As explained in Chapter 15, inflated fuel prices sent airlines scrambling for ways to reduce oil use—a necessary measure to stay price competitive.

The Economy

recession

Recession and inflation—products of U.S. governmental decisions, world policies, industrial production, consumption, and many other factors—affect transportation carriers in divergent and significant ways. Most transportation demand is harmed by an economic downturn, but some market participants do better in a weakened economy. For example, the recession of the early 1980s reduced railroad and trucking traffic but not small package air express movements. Recessions lead to reduced industrial production, inventory cutbacks, lower demand for raw-material shipments to production points, and less haulage of large numbers of finished products to distributor locations. Consequently, railroad and trucking traffic suffered. In a recession, manufacturers reduce production and inventories to lower costs and increase cash reserves. However, they try to maintain customer service levels to protect against lost sales and declining revenues. Small package air express companies provide a way to deliver goods in short timeframes. Therefore, their business increases during a recession because shippers require faster transportation services.

inflation

Inflation extracts another toll in carrier costs and price competitiveness. Because of inflation, highly unionized firms in particular face a greater cost burden than do non-unionized companies. Assume that a highly unionized firm paid its workers an average of $30,000 per year, and a non-unionized firm paid only $20,000 per person. If both organizations felt compelled to offer wage increases to match a 10% annual rise in the Consumer Price Index, the former's cost would increase by another $1000 per worker over the latter's (a $3000 versus a $2000 pay raise). In a period of inflation, a low-cost carrier tends to increase its cost advantage.

THE CHANGING COMPETITIVE ENVIRONMENT

The competitive environment of the transportation industry has changed significantly since the late 1970s because of deregulation. Intramodal trucking and air transportation competition has intensified because of the increased numbers of competitors and the development of price competition. Independent rate-setting has become common not only in these two modes, but in railroading as well. Furthermore, the powers of collective ratemaking bodies like railroad and trucking rate bureaus and the International Air Transport Association have been lessened by a combination of regulatory changes and market adjustments. Carriers, allowed by law to participate in general rate increases, have shown a reluctance to do so. In this environment, low-cost carriers have seized opportunities to underprice higher cost competitors.

increased intermodalism, intermodal companies, and unifications

The deregulated period has also witnessed increased intermodalism, increasing numbers of intermodal companies, and stepped-up unification activities. *Intermodalism* (i.e., intermodal carriage) refers to shipments moved by equipment combining the best features of several modes. For example, TOFC combines the short-haul advantages of trucking and the long-haul economies of railroading to move truck trailers over long distances. Another example is containerized shipping. An *intermodal company,* by comparison, is a firm that offers services by two or more modes. CSX Corporation is a good example; in 1985 it operated railroads (Chessie System and Seaboard System), a trucking company (Chessie Motor Express), aviation services (CSX Beckett Aviation Inc.), and a domestic water carrier (American Commercial Barge Line). As differentiated from intermodalism, an intermodal company, if it chose to do so, could keep a shipment on a single mode like trucking. An intermodal company merely gives the shipper a modal choice from a single carrier. Nevertheless, CSX also offered intermodal movements, such as TOFC/COFC service. Finally, *unifications* are mergers and acquisitions within a particular mode. Leading examples are the formations of several large railroads (see Chapter 5 for details). Intermodalism represents sources of competition for trucking companies, freighters (i.e., breakbulk cargo ships), and other single-mode carriers. The increase in intermodal companies and unifications implies that transportation companies are becoming larger and exploring ways to become stronger competitors.

blurring of sectors

Chapters 11 and 16 discussed the blurring of transportation sectors, another important competitive change. As regulatory barriers have been eliminated, the transportation industry has experienced movements of industry components (e.g., carriers, intermediaries, etc.) into once-forbidden territories. Examples used in earlier chapters are (1) private truck operators being able to obtain for-hire Toto authority, (2) dual authority allowing a common carrier trucking company to hold contract trucking authority, and (3) air freight forwarders now owning and operating aircraft. Chapter 16 also talked about the blurring of the air courier and telecommunications industries with the introduction of Zap-Mail by Federal Express. Blurring of sectors creates problems for carriers located in segments experiencing an influx of new competitors.

MARKET COMPETITORS

Who competes against whom in the transportation industry and on what basis? Three markets particularly important in traffic and revenue production are the small package, general commodity, and domestic intercity passenger markets. This section will emphasize each market's major competitors.

Small Package Competitors

Small package competitors are carriers handling individual shipments of 150 lbs. or less. As shown in Fig. 19.5, the market can be arbitrarily segmented into four submarkets—same day, next day, second- or third-day, and later than third-day services—according to the time sensitivity or urgency of delivery.

more or less than 400 miles

Same Day Service.   A deciding factor in identifying effective competitors in the small package same day service segment is distance. To deliver a shipment to a consignee on the same day as it is accepted from the consignor means that speed is imperative. From a practical standpoint, few surface modes routinely attempt to provide reliable same day service at distances greater than 400 miles. At 50 mph, same day service in a 400-mile market is possible, but only marginally. Reduce the maximum distance to 200 miles, and surface modes become feasible alternatives. Therefore highway modes—regular route buses, private truckers, private or company automobiles or vans, and LTL general commodity truckers—compete in this market. In 1985, bus companies and surface couriers like Purolator Courier often limited weights substantially below 150 lbs. As a result, they excluded themselves from the heavier weight shipments, e.g., above 70 lbs. AMTRAK, another market competitor that is more flexible in accepting larger packages, provides train-station to train-station service. Scheduled combination airlines focus heavily on same day services in both the less than 400-miles and more than 400-mile markets; their speciality is "next flight out" services. Other competitors in both the short- and long-distance small package segments are air freight forwarders, all-cargo airlines, charter airlines, and general aviation.

less than 700 miles

Next Day Service.   Next day service for small packages, usually meaning delivery the next working day following the day of pick-up, is a highly

FIGURE 19.5.
Competition for small package shipments.

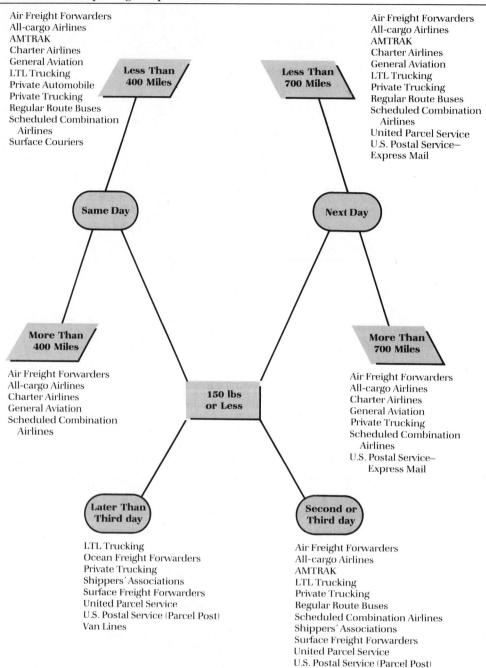

Air Freight Forwarders
All-cargo Airlines
AMTRAK
Charter Airlines
General Aviation
LTL Trucking
Private Automobile
Private Trucking
Regular Route Buses
Scheduled Combination
  Airlines
Surface Couriers

Less Than 400 Miles

Air Freight Forwarders
All-cargo Airlines
AMTRAK
Charter Airlines
General Aviation
LTL Trucking
Private Trucking
Regular Route Buses
Scheduled Combination
  Airlines
United Parcel Service
U.S. Postal Service–
  Express Mail

Less Than 700 Miles

Same Day

Next Day

More Than 400 Miles

Air Freight Forwarders
All-cargo Airlines
Charter Airlines
General Aviation
Scheduled Combination
  Airlines

150 lbs or Less

More Than 700 Miles

Air Freight Forwarders
All-cargo Airlines
Charter Airlines
General Aviation
Private Trucking
Scheduled Combination
  Airlines
U.S. Postal Service–
  Express Mail

Later Than Third day

Second or Third day

LTL Trucking
Ocean Freight Forwarders
Private Trucking
Shippers' Associations
Surface Freight Forwarders
United Parcel Service
U.S. Postal Service (Parcel Post)
Van Lines

Air Freight Forwarders
All-cargo Airlines
AMTRAK
LTL Trucking
Private Trucking
Regular Route Buses
Scheduled Combination Airlines
Shippers' Associations
Surface Freight Forwarders
United Parcel Service
U.S. Postal Service (Parcel Post)

competitive market. With 24 hours or more available, surface carriers become a greater market factor, and today it is not an uncommon occurrence to see an LTL trucker promising reliable next day service in routes under 700 miles.[2] As Fig. 19.5 shows, the list of competitors in the next day (less than 700-mile) market is similar to the group in the less than 400-miles same day segment. Deleted are surface couriers; although some firms may compete in the market, many, such as Purolator Courier, emphasize fast short-haul service. Also deleted are private automobiles, since it is not practical to drive long distances in 24 hours, and rarely is it necessary. Added were United Parcel Service (UPS) and the U.S. Postal Service's Express Mail. UPS, using its trucking fleet, delivers packages weighing up to 70 lbs. overnight in markets up to 400-miles long.[3] Also handling shipments up to 70 lbs., Express Mail overnight service transported 36.8 million packages in 1983 to points located anywhere in the continental United States.[4] Strong competitors in the next day small shipment market, regardless of distance, are all-cargo airlines and air freight forwarders.

Other market factors in all distance ranges are charter airlines, general aviation, and private trucking (up to 1200 miles)—all modes used less frequently on a routine basis, but often used to accommodate emergency small package shipments. With trucking, small shipment service can be expensive; equipment underutilization due to excess capacity is the major problem. To some extent, scheduled combination airlines compete for overnight traffic, but with flight schedules' catering to passenger preferences for daylight departures, night lift (i.e., after-dark flights), and thus overnight service, is limited.

more than 700 miles

At distances beyond 700 miles, surface competitors drop out of the small package next day market, with the exception of private trucking, which continues to offer the flexibility for meeting emergency shipper needs. Longer haul overnight traffic is essentially left to the for-hire air carriers and forwarders listed in Fig. 19.5. Speed is the deciding factor.

Second- or Third-Day Service.   Extending the delivery timeframe to between 48 and 72 hours again alters the small package competitive field. Emerging as strong market forces are UPS, which carried 1.9 billion packages in 1984,[5] and parcel post, a service of the U.S. Postal Service that handled 163 million parcel post packages in 1983.[6] As speed becomes less of a decision variable in modal and carrier selection, surface transportation becomes more important. LTL trucking companies, private truckers, shippers' associations who use for-hire trucker or railroad TOFC services,[7] and surface freight forwarders who also use trucking and railroad services all have time to build consolidated loads of small shipments. Cost economies are then partially redistributed through rate savings to shippers. Similarly, scheduled combination airlines are better able to sell belly-container space as small shipments are combined into consolidations of 1000 lbs. or more.

Lesser competitors are AMTRAK, regular route buses, all-cargo airlines, and air freight forwarders. The former two can take shipments across the country, but their shorter haul services are more appealing; they can be fast over short distances. Since air carriers' main distinguishing attribute is speed, the latter two lose their competitive advantage if minimum transit time is not a key shipper objective.

Later Than Third-Day Services. If shippers accept even longer transit times, air carriers fade from the picture and surface modes take charge. Distance and rates are important factors. Shippers understand and accept that transcontinental trucking services can take five days with terminal and other stops, such as for meals or rest for the drivers. Lower rates offered by carriers who hold shipments longer than normal at origin points are also attractive to many customers. Increased time gives shippers' associations, surface freight forwarders, ocean freight forwarders, and LTL general commodity trucking companies time to consolidate loads to hold prices down. UPS and the U.S. Postal Service are two other competitors who are efficient at building full trailer loads of small shipments. Another group includes van lines. Since deregulation, many household goods moving companies have been soliciting and hauling high-valued fragile shipments, such as computer equipment (see Chapter 13). Van lines, too, try to consolidate shipments.

intramodal competition

Quite often the stiffest competition a carrier faces is from other companies within the same mode (e.g., competition between two regular route general commodity trucking companies) and not from intermodal competition. This situation is true for the 150 lbs. or less market, as well as for other transportation-competitive markets.

Competition for General Commodity Traffic

The transportation market for general commodity shipments weighing more than 150 lbs. can also be segmented by time sensitivity. Figure 19.6 divides the market by the general terms *time-sensitive* and *less time-sensitive* to define market competitors.

Time-Sensitive General Commodity Traffic. With general commodity shipments larger than 150 lbs., carrier imposed weight restrictions, measurement (shipment size) restrictions, or both remove many potential competitors, such as regular route buses, surface couriers, UPS, and the U.S. Postal Service from the market. Air freight forwarders, all-cargo airlines, charter airlines, general aviation, and scheduled combination airlines remain in the market, provided they accept shipments larger than 150 lbs. In the shorter haul markets and as shipment sizes increase toward 45,000-lb. loads, trucking companies become important market factors. Contract truckers, irregular route common carriers, and private carriers can make excellent time. The same is true for regular route common carrier (LTL) trucking companies and van lines hauling full loads on a door-to-door basis. In addition, some trucking companies differentiate their LTL services by providing frequent departures and fast transit times; these companies dispatch vehicles regardless of load factors. In recent years, railroad piggyback service has developed rap-

FIGURE 19.6.
Competition for general commodity traffic.

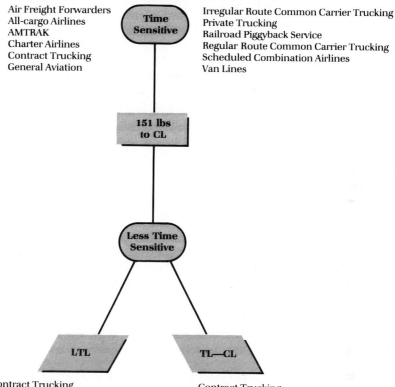

Air Freight Forwarders
All-cargo Airlines
AMTRAK
Charter Airlines
Contract Trucking
General Aviation

Time Sensitive

Irregular Route Common Carrier Trucking
Private Trucking
Railroad Piggyback Service
Regular Route Common Carrier Trucking
Scheduled Combination Airlines
Van Lines

151 lbs to CL

Less Time Sensitive

LTL

Contract Trucking
Irregular Route Common Carrier
    Trucking
Pool Consolidators and
    Distributors
Private Trucking
Property Brokers
Regular Route Common
    Carrier Trucking
Shippers' Associations
Surface Freight Forwarders

TL—CL

Contract Trucking
General Cargo Ocean Shipping
Gray Area Trucking
Irregular Route Common
    Carrier Trucking
Private Trucking
Property Brokers
Railroad Boxcar Service
Railroad Piggyback Service
Regular Route Common Carrier
    Trucking
Shippers' Agents
Surface Freight Forwarders
Van Lines

idly. Acting as wholesalers selling flat-car space to shippers' agents, shippers' associations, shippers' agricultural cooperatives, and surface forwarders (i.e., intermediaries that, according to the Association of American Railroads, were supplying 80% of the railroad industry's piggyback traffic in 1983[8]), railroad TOFC operators can offer some fast long-haul service.

           Less Time-Sensitive General Commodity Traffic.   If speed is not
LTL paramount, the competition in the general commodity market changes. Regular route common carrier (LTL) truckers dominate the LTL segment—anything less than truckload or carload volume shipments. Their competitors include shippers' associations and surface freight forwarders; by consolidating shipments, they often deny traffic to LTL truckers. Pool consolidators and distributors represent a growing market force in shipments approximating 5000 lbs. In addition, contract truckers and irregular route common carrier truckers—providing transportation services for pool consolidators and distributors, property brokers, and shippers' associations, or supplying LTL services to large corporations—have gained more than a toehold in this market segment. Private trucking is also important.

           When shipment volumes reach truckload (TL) or carload (CL) proportions,
TL-CL the competition again changes. Trucking dominates this segment of the general commodity traffic market as well. Leading competitors are contract truckers, irregular route common carrier truckers, and private truckers; all are truckload specialists. Two other trucking industry factors are regular route common carrier truckers and gray area truckers (i.e., truckers illegally hauling regulated general commodity traffic without having the proper operating certificate or permit). Van lines are also involved in TL movements of general cargo. All six of these trucking sectors offer door-to-door service from consignor's dock to consignee's door. Property brokers, acting as intermediaries between TL shippers and TL carriers, also enter the competitive picture, because they can give freight either to a carrier or to one of the carrier's competitors. Other groups, such as shippers' agents and surface freight forwarders, feed railroad piggyback carriers. Piggyback service gives railroads the means to compete for 40,000-lb–45,000-lb. (TL) loads. If shipments exceed these weights, railroad boxcar service or general cargo (i.e., ocean) shippers are market suppliers.

Domestic Intercity Passenger Competition

Similar to the case of general commodity traffic, the domestic intercity passenger business can be divided into time-sensitive and less time-sensitive segments. As Fig. 19.7 shows, these segments can then be split into subgroups according to trip distance. The short-haul segment in Fig. 19.7 covers intercity trips as long as 400 miles. The medium-haul segment covers trips from 401 to 1500 miles, and domestic trips longer than 1500 miles fall into the long-haul category.

FIGURE 19.7.
Intercity passenger competition.

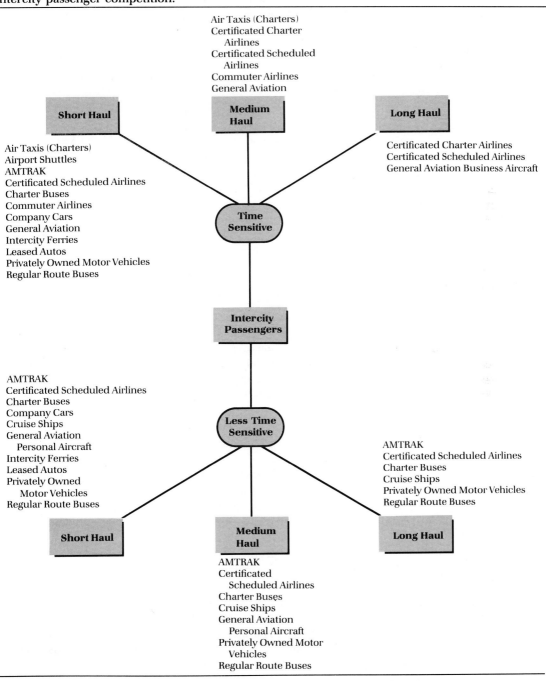

Air Taxis (Charters)
Certificated Charter
    Airlines
Certificated Scheduled
    Airlines
Commuter Airlines
General Aviation

Short Haul

Medium Haul

Long Haul

Air Taxis (Charters)
Airport Shuttles
AMTRAK
Certificated Scheduled Airlines
Charter Buses
Commuter Airlines
Company Cars
General Aviation
Intercity Ferries
Leased Autos
Privately Owned Motor Vehicles
Regular Route Buses

Certificated Charter Airlines
Certificated Scheduled Airlines
General Aviation Business Aircraft

Time Sensitive

Intercity Passengers

AMTRAK
Certificated Scheduled Airlines
Charter Buses
Company Cars
Cruise Ships
General Aviation
    Personal Aircraft
Intercity Ferries
Leased Autos
Privately Owned
    Motor Vehicles
Regular Route Buses

Less Time Sensitive

AMTRAK
Certificated Scheduled Airlines
Charter Buses
Cruise Ships
Privately Owned Motor Vehicles
Regular Route Buses

Short Haul

Medium Haul

Long Haul

AMTRAK
Certificated
    Scheduled Airlines
Charter Buses
Cruise Ships
General Aviation
    Personal Aircraft
Privately Owned Motor
    Vehicles
Regular Route Buses

Short-Haul Time-Sensitive Travel Market. Figure 19.7 shows many competitors in the short-haul time sensitive market. Privately owned motor vehicles (POMVs), such as cars, trucks, vans, motorcycles, and recreational vehicles, clearly dominate this transportation sector. They are convenient, flexible, and capable of moving individuals or small groups up to 400 miles in a day. However, they primarily compete for travelers journeying less than 100 miles; at distances under 50 miles, few competitors can match POMV door-to-door speeds. A second competitor is company-owned cars. A third competitor is leased automobiles, which are used in conjunction with airlines, AMTRAK, or other for-hire passenger modes.

Airport shuttles, commuter airlines, regular route buses, charter buses, and intercity ferries also compete for passengers going less than 100 miles. Airport shuttle services by van, bus, or limousine vehicles compete with POMVs and commuter airlines in feeding passengers to airports. Most regular route bus passengers travel less than 100 miles. In nonstop or limited stop service, buses can be quite fast over short hauls. Intercity ferries can be speed-competitive with other surface modes if the latter are forced to follow much longer routes to their destinations (e.g., driving around Lake Michigan versus crossing it by ferry).

As short-haul distances increase from 100 to 400 miles, AMTRAK emerges as a stronger competitor. Most AMTRAK passengers travel less than 200 miles, yet in places like the Northeast corridor, AMTRAK's door-to-door speed is competitive with air transportation. Train service from CBD to CBD minimizes access and egress time for city patrons. For trips from 100 to 400 miles, the speed of small airplane air transportation offered by commuter airlines and air taxis (i.e., charters) becomes more attractive, as does general aviation. Moreover, at distances from 150 to 400 miles, certificated scheduled airlines (i.e., jet aircraft operators) become the chief competitor of POMVs. Two of the airline industry's busiest markets are between Boston and New York and between New York and Washington, D.C.—markets of about 200 miles each.

Medium-Haul Time-Sensitive Travel Market. When speed—such as a matter of hours or, at most, a working day—is important over medium-haul distances, the surface modes essentially drop from the competitive scene in the domestic intercity passenger market. The medium-haul market is dominated by certificated scheduled airlines. Although there are exceptions to the 400-mile cap set on time-sensitive POMV travel (some drivers still attempt day trips over 400 miles), POMVs cannot compete with the speed of airplanes at such distances. The primary competition in this segment is intramodal air transportation: certificated scheduled airlines, commuter airlines, general aviation including business and personal aircraft, air taxis, and certificated charter airlines catering to group travel.

Long-Haul Time-Sensitive Travel Market. At distances beyond 1500 miles where speed is critical, small airplane operators such as commuter airlines, air taxis, and general aviation personal aircraft drop out as serious competitors. Certificated scheduled airlines remain as the primary market force, followed to a lesser degree by certificated charter airlines and general aviation business aircraft. The latter offers a capability of serving smaller airports with more direct, and therefore faster, transit times.

Less Time-Sensitive Short-Haul Travel Market. When speed is less a factor in modal and carrier selection, surface modes become stronger competitors in domestic intercity passenger transportation. POMVs again dominate the short-haul market, but regular route buses and AMTRAK provide attractive passenger alternatives. Company cars and leased automobiles remain in the picture. By losing their chief advantage of speed, however, air taxis and commuter airlines are not serious competitors in this market. Nevertheless, many people use certificated scheduled airlines not for speed, but for reasons such as value or more service for the money, lower prices compared to what some surface modes charge, and the love of flying. Many other passengers choose modes to sightsee or relax—to enjoy the transportation experience. Thus charter buses, cruise ships, general aviation personal aircraft, intercity ferries, AMTRAK, and POMVs are appealing short-haul passenger transportation offerings.

Less Time-Sensitive Medium-Haul Travel Market. Many medium-haul, as well as long-haul, passengers want slower speeds, circuitous routings, and the right to leave the vehicle and explore the country. AMTRAK, charter buses, general aviation personal aircraft, cruise ships, and POMVs meet this need quite well. The great flexibility of the POMV makes it the leading competitor in this market. Regular route buses and certificated scheduled airlines also draw riders because of low fares. As previously noted in Chapter 17, for individuals and couples, discount air fares can be less expensive than POMV costs. Many tourists, furthermore, fly to take advantage of enticing air transportation, rental car, and lodging price savings packages.

Less Time-Sensitive Long-Haul Travel Market. Long-haul competition is not much different from medium-haul competition in the domestic intercity passenger market, except that surface mode travelers need more time. This situation can be a problem. It is one thing to plot out a leisurely two-week roundtrip to a point some 1000 miles away; it is another to cross the United States from coast to coast, and then return home. Vacation time constraints and costs, such as for lodging and food, reduce the attractiveness of POMV travel over long distances. Certificated scheduled airline service, therefore, assumes a prominent role in this market. For those with plenty of time, such as senior citizens, AMTRAK and charter bus services—particularly combined with quality hotel/motel accommodations at stop-off points—compete well in this market. For those who can afford it, long-haul ocean cruises are enticing. Other people, looking for low prices, find regular route bus services and discount air fare services attractive opportunities.

SUMMARY

Deregulation has intensified the need for carriers to understand the competitive environment in which they struggle for profitability. A business climate once characterized by a considerable degree of protectionism has been turned upside down by entry and pricing freedoms. The influx of new firms into market niches once dominated by established common carriers, as well as counterthrusts by established carriers who have seized opportunities to penetrate once-forbidden market territories, has created a number of questions needing swift management answers.

These answers may be found in competitive theory, practice, and strategy. Today it is not sufficient merely to be good at carrier operations. Carrier managers need a firm grasp of economics and marketing—essential tools in mastering the competitive environment. The era of price competition has entered the transportation field, and carrier managers must comprehend and use cost, demand, and pricing and service concepts and strategies to their advantage. It is a time to focus on new opportunities and competitive threats both inside and outside transportation.

In the past, too much emphasis was placed on short-term carrier goals, such as maintaining the company's market share. Not enough attention was given to long-term corporate profitability. But this emphasis must change, because the future depends on the ability of carrier managers to locate profitable market niches. Price competition has given low-cost carriers an advantage in attracting discount-oriented customers. Service competition provides high-cost carriers an avenue for differentiating the market and selling better services at badly needed higher level yields. Carriers must find whatever it takes to gain the competitive edge and, more important, to keep it.

STUDY QUESTIONS

1. How does traffic density affect carrier costs?
2. Discuss intramodal diversion as a carrier strategy for attracting primary demand.
3. How can carrier management use the knowledge of "service factors influencing passenger modal and carrier choices" to its advantage?
4. In what ways do less regulated carriers have a competitive advantage over more regulated carriers?

5. Why do few surface carriers attempt to participate in the same day, more than 400-mile small package shipment market?
6. When should a carrier consider a market penetration pricing strategy?
7. Who primarily competes for general commodity shipments weighing 40,000 lbs–45,000 lbs.?
8. In what intercity passenger markets are POMVs important competitors, and why?

ENDNOTES

1. See Donald V. Harper, *Transportation in America: Users, Carriers, Government*, 2d ed. (Englewood-Cliffs, N.J.: Prentice-Hall, Inc., 1982), pp. 164–166, for a more comprehensive review of pricing in an oligopoly.

2. "Mason Dixon Guarantees Tomorrow," a promotional sale handout of Mason Dixon Lines trucking company, n.d.

3. Dave Russ, "How to Manage Your Small Package Express Costs," *Handling and Shipping Management,* June 1983, p. 38.

4. U.S. Postal Service, *Comprehensive Statement on Postal Operations: 1983* (Washington, D.C.: U.S. Postal Service, 1984), p. 22.

5. United Parcel Service of America, Inc., 10-K Disclosure, SEC File No. 0-4714, year ended December 31, 1984, Washington, D.C., p. 18.

6. U.S. Postal Service, *Comprehensive Statement,* p. 22.

7. Terance A. Brown, "Shippers' Associations: Operations, Trends, and Comparative Prices," *Transportation Journal* 21, No. 1 (Fall 1981):54.

8. Office of Transportation Analysis, Interstate Commerce Commission, *Staff Report No. 9, Highlights of Activity in the Property Motor Carrier Industry* (Washington, D.C.: ICC, 1983), p. 14.

ADDITIONAL READINGS

"ABA Meets in Coronado: The 54th Annual Meeting of the American Bus Association Examined New Marketing Strategies. . . . " *Metropolitan,* November/December 1983, p. 30.

Barks, Joe. "What LTL Shippers Really Want." *Distribution,* June 1982, pp. 49–52.

Beier, Frederick J. "Electric Utilities and the Movement of Coal." *Transportation Journal* 21, no. 4 (Summer 1982):15–24.

Blyskal, Jeff. "Attack of the Invisible Giant (Purolator Courier)." *Forbes,* 20 June 1983, pp. 40–41.

Brimelow, Peter. "Looking Ahead: Where Those Hybrid Haulers Are Headed." *Fortune,* 19 March 1984, pp. 114–116.

Chow, Garland, and Poist, Richard F. "The Measurement of Quality and Service and the Transportation Purchase Decision." *The Logistics and Transportation Review* 20, no. 1 (1984):25–43.

Cowan, Robert A. *Teleconferencing: Maximizing Human Potential.* Reston, Va.: Reston Publishing Company, 1984.

Cross, Thomas B. "Teleconferencing Can Reduce Need to Travel." *The Office,* April 1982, p. 100.

Cunningham, Wayne H. J. "Freight Modal Choice and Competition in Transportation: A Critique and Categorization of Analysis Techniques." *Transportation Journal* 21, no. 4 (Summer 1982):66–75.

Daley, James H. "Holding Companies, Common Carriers, and Public Policy." *Transportation Journal* 17, no. 2 (Winter 1979):67–73.

Davis, Frank W.; Cunningham, Lawrence W.; Wishart, Allington P.; and Wood, Wallace R. "Diversification in Major U.S. Transportation Firms." Transportation Research Forum. *Proceedings of Twentieth Annual Meeting.* Oxford, Ind.: Richard B. Cross Company, 1979, pp. 221–232.

Dentzer, Susan, and Wang, Penelope. "An Excess of Express." *Newsweek,* 9 January 1984, p. 73.

Dillion, Thomas F. "Selecting the Right Small Package Service." *Purchasing,* 29 April 1982, pp. 88–89.

Drozdowski, Ted E. "Get Ready for Surprises in Small Packages." *Purchasing,* 8 March 1984, pp. 60–61.

——. "The Story of the Trucking Services Buy." *Purchasing,* 23 February 1984, pp. 70–71.

——. "Transportation: Deregulation Spurs Rigorous Competition." *Purchasing,* 29 September 1983, p. 55.

Feldman, Joan M. "Telecommunications: A Threat to Airlines or a New Opportunity?" *Air Transport World,* June 1981, p. 18.

Graham, Kenneth R. "Rail-Based Holding Companies: A View of Some Indicators of Strategy, Management Change, and Financial Performance." *Transportation Journal* 19, no. 4 (Summer 1980):73–77.

Grayson, Alan. "Disaggregate Model of Mode Choice in Intercity Travel." Published as Part of Transportation Research Board. *Transportation System Analysis,* Transportation Research Record 835. Washington, D.C.: National Academy of Sciences, 1981, pp. 36–42.

Harper, Donald V. *Transportation in America: Users, Carriers, Government.* 2d ed. Englewood-Cliffs, N.J.: Prentice-Hall, Inc., 1982, Chapters 7–9.

Harrington, Lisa H. "Carrier-Selection Criteria Change with the Times." *Traffic Management,* September 1983, pp. 59–60.

Horn, Kevin. "Pricing of Rail Intermodal Service: A Case Study of Institutional Myopia." *Transportation Journal* 20, no. 4 (Summer 1981):63–77.

Ippolito, Richard A. "Estimating Airline Demand with Quality of Service Variables." *Journal of Transport Economics and Policy* 15, no. 1 (January 1981):7–15.

Kahn, Fritz R. "Intermodalism—a Non-Issue." *Traffic World,* 25 April 1983, pp. 52–54.

Lanconi, Richard A., and Coyle, Michael P. "A Comparison of Two Methods for Measuring Motor Carrier Market Potential." *Transportation Journal* 22, no. 1 (Fall 1982):63–74.

Lieb, Robert C. "Intermodal Ownership: The Perspective of Railroad Chief Executives." *Transportation Journal* 21, no. 3 (Spring 1982):70–75.

MCD: American Motor Carrier Directory. Atlanta: American Motor Carrier Directory, 1984.

Nupp, Byron. "Trends and Choices for Intercity Passenger Transportation in an Era of Resource Stringency—A Problem Posed." *Transportation Journal* 19, no. 4 (Summer 1980):48–52.

Stock, James R., and LaLonde, Bernard J. "The Transportation Mode Decision Revisited." *Transportation Journal* 17, no. 2 (Winter 1977):51–59.

Talley, Wayne Kenneth. *Introduction to Transportation.* Cincinnati, Ohio: South-Western Publishing Company, 1983, Chapter 2.

TSDG: Time-Sensitive Delivery Guide. Atlanta: Time-Sensitive Delivery Guide, Inc., 1984. (The Dictionary of Document and Small Package Express Services.)

"Use of Strategic Marketing Plans by Truckers Is Workshop Subject." *Traffic World,* 15 November 1982, pp. 34–37.

Voorhees, Roy, D., and Coppett, John. "New Competition for the Airlines." *Transportation Journal* 20, no. 4 (Summer 1981):78–85.

Waid, Michael. "The New U.S. Postal Service on the Move." *Air Cargo World,* February 1983, pp. 28–29.

"What the Customer Wants." *Railway Age,* September 1983, pp. 69–70.

THIS CONCLUDING PART OF THE TEXT IDENTIFIES some of the greatest challenges facing U.S. transportation in the future. Of course, these problems and challenges are not the only obstacles that must be overcome to maintain transportation services, or more idealistically, to improve services to better accommodate passengers and shippers. Chapter 20 merely tries to establish the constant need to improve transportation decision making and stimulate thinking about the future of transportation. In effect, Part 9 continues a major theme first expressed in Chapter 1 of the text: To optimize transportation efficiency, people must first understand what transportation does for this country, what it can do for their employers, and what it can do for them, individually. However, they should never take it for granted, because there is a continual need for improvement.

9

Future of Transportation

20

Transportation's Greatest Challenges

The United States was built on a transportation foundation. Without water transportation, Christopher Columbus would not have made his great discovery; without railroads, the West might never have been settled; and without air and highway transportation, the lifestyles of U.S. citizens would be vastly different. Still, as admirable as transportation's contributions have been, now is not the time to concentrate on historical accomplishments. The present and the future are at stake, and huge transportation problems must be overcome. The United States is at a crossroads, and all the talent and hard work of its people will be needed to move the country forward.

THE CAPITAL REINVESTMENT CHALLENGE

Can U.S. citizens assume that future generations will have the same or greater mobility than they have had? The answer is "no," unless the United States realizes its fullest transportation potential. Capital reinvestment is critical to the outcome. Can the United States, through a combination of private sector investments and public sector aid, modernize and expand its present transportation service capabilities? The task is monumental.

Growth Forecasts

passenger-mile forecast

On June 25, 1979, the National Transportation Policy Study Commission (NTPSC), a congressionally appointed panel of transportation experts, issued its final report, *National Transportation Policies Through the Year 2000*.[1] One

553

ton-mile forecast

of the NTPSC's functions was to forecast changes in transportation demand as measured in passenger-miles and ton-miles. The results, as presented in Table 20.1, are startling. Acording to the low-growth scenario, national passenger-mile traffic was projected to jump 61.5% between 1975 and 2000, but it could potentially jump as much as 92.3% under the high-growth scenario. The NTPSC growth scenarios were determined from values assigned to 18 selected socio-economic factors, such as projected population changes, labor force size changes, population migration, economic growth, and resource (i.e., raw material) development. An even bigger obstacle, if the NTPSC's estimates are accurate, is meeting the increased demand for handling ton-mile traffic. As Table 20.1 shows, growth was forecasted at between 66.7% and 220.8% between 1975 and 2000.

Tables 20.2 and 20.3, which focus on intercity movements, explain where much of the increased traffic volumes are projected to develop. Only the medium-growth scenario will be described here to avoid the more extreme estimates.

intercity passenger-mile projections

The NTPSC contends that travel growth will primarily occur in the automobile, including personal trucks and vans, and aviation sectors. As Table 20.2 shows, the former will see an absolute gain of 707 billion passenger-miles between 1975 and 2000, and the latter will experience the most dramatic percentage growth, 219%. The NTPSC concluded that U.S. intercity passenger travel will continue to be dominated by the automobile but that airlines will gain market share. Simultaneously, the NTPSC projected little growth for buses and railroads (AMTRAK). Consequently, these modes will be challenged to become more competitive with automobiles and airplanes.

intercity ton-mile projections

If the NTPSC's findings are accurate for intercity ton-mile projections (Table 20.3), railroads and water carriers will benefit from substantial traffic gains. Large increases in coal traffic, to be carried mainly by the railroads,

TABLE 20.1. Forecasts of traffic growth between 1975 and 2000

	Trillions of Passenger–Miles		
Scenario	1975	2000	Percentage Change
Low-growth	2.6	4.2	61.5%
Medium-growth	2.6	4.6	76.9
High-growth	2.6	5.0	92.3

	Trillions of Ton-Miles		
Scenario	1975	2000	Percentage Change
Low-growth	2.4	4.0	66.7%
Medium-growth	2.4	6.3	162.5
High-growth	2.4	7.7	220.8

Source: National Transportation Policy Study Commission, *National Transportation Policies Through the Year 2000 (Final Report)* (Washington, D.C.: U.S. Government Printing Office, 25 June 1979), p. 154.

TABLE 20.2. Forecasts of intercity passenger–mile traffic by mode between 1975 and 2000 (Medium-growth scenario)

Mode	Billions of Passenger–Miles			Percentage Change
	1975	2000	Increase	
Air carriers	148	472	324	219%
Automobiles	1,123	1,830	707	63
Buses	25	31	6	24
Railroads	5	6	1	17
TOTAL	1,301	2,339	1,038	80%

Source: National Transportation Policy Study Commission, *National Transportation Policies Through the Year 2000 (Final Report)* (Washington, D.C.: U.S. Government Printing Office, 25 June 1979), p. 159.

and crude oil traffic, carried mainly by water carriage, are the primary causes.[2] The prediction of increased trucking traffic (878 billion ton-miles) is based on the NTPSC's view that highway carriers will slightly increase their market share from 21% to 22% between 1975 and 2000.[3] Thus most trucking growth is explained by the growth in aggregate transportation demand; that is, as total transportation ton-miles grow, truck traffic will keep pace.

capital investment needs forecast

The question, ultimately, is money. NTPSC growth projections (Tables 20.2 and 20.3) assume that the U.S. transportation industry will be equipped to handle rising demand. However, by the NTPSC's own estimate in its medium-growth scenario, improvements in plant and equipment will cost $4.211 trillion by the year 2000 (see Table 20.4). Assuming, as the NTPSC did, that the government would supply $1.243 trillion, the private sector would be expected to invest $2.968 trillion.[4] But this goal might not be realized, since carrier profitability has been inadequate in recent years.

TABLE 20.3. Forecasts of intercity ton–mile traffic by mode between 1975 and 2000 (Medium-growth scenario)

Mode	Billions of Ton–Miles			Percentage Change
	1975	2000	Increase	
Railroads	673	1,983	1,310	195%
Trucking	488	1,366	878	180
Water carriers	428	1,433	1,005	235
Oil pipelines	437	1,062	625	143
Gas pipelines	312	356	44	14
Air cargo carriers	4	10	6	150
TOTAL	2,342	6,210	3,868	165%

Source: National Transportation Policy Study Commission, *National Transportation Policies Through the Year 2000 (Final Report)* (Washington, D.C.: U.S. Government Printing Office, 25 June 1979), p. 417.

TABLE 20.4. Forecasts of transportation capital investment needs between 1975 and 2000 (Millions of 1975 dollars; medium growth scenario)	
Item	**Dollars Needed (in Millions)**
Highways	$900,446
Autos	1,829,067
For-hire trucks	109,498
Private trucks	559,028
Intercity buses	2,103
School buses	4,641
Railroads	230,304
Ports, harbors, & facilities	22,225
International marine equipment	19,348
Domestic marine equipment	24,560
Private boats	33,451
Oil pipelines	25,368
Gas pipelines	50,328
Airports	34,641
Airways	8,046
Domestic air carriers	90,086
International air carriers	59,596
General aviation	41,342
Local public transit	166,724
TOTAL	$4,210,802

Source: National Transportation Policy Study Commission, *National Transportation Policies Through the Year 2000 (Final Report)* (Washington, D.C.: U.S. Government Printing Office, 25 June 1979), p. 172.

IMPROVING PROFITABILITY

The period since 1979 has been difficult for most modes and carriers. Table 14.10 in Chapter 14 described industry losses of $1.4 billion in the airline industry between 1980 and 1982 (a 1980 loss of $222 million, a 1981 loss of $455 million, and a 1982 loss of $733 million). Chapter 11 discussed how returns on equity of the 100 largest ICC-regulated trucking companies dropped from 17% in 1978 to 5.4% in 1983, as well as mentioning that 1993 intercity trucking companies failed since mid-1980.[5] Intercity regular route bus carriers were also shown to be experiencing financial problems, as noted by losses at 5 of the largest 10 companies in 1983 (see Table 11.7 in Chapter 11). Other evidence of modal difficulties includes depressed inland water carrier traffic and prices, thousands of idled barges, and more than 20% of the river and canal work force laid off (see Chapter 8).

distribution
of earnings

The only hope for full-scale modernization and expansion of the U.S. transportation system is improved income levels and a more sound distribution of earnings among dividends, employee earnings (e.g., salaries, wages, and benefits), taxes, and reinvestment capital. Reinvestment capital needs considerably more attention, since steady capital injections are essential to maintaining and improving transportation efficiency.

better management
and
personal sacrifice

Realizing this goal is a challenge. In all probability it will not happen without better management and much personal sacrifice. In general, investors must delay some of their demands for dividends, and labor and management must lower their personal salary, wage, and benefit expectations. More effort should be devoted to measures ensuring the long-term future of each company. Specifically, carriers need to be more cost-control oriented during periods of prosperity, for that is the time when capital can best be accumulated and reinvested. In addition, companies must also broaden their strategies to meet the opportunities and risks faced both within and beyond the present transportation environment.

Managing During Prosperity

The railroad industry can illustrate the need for sound management during prosperity. With the possible exception of the small package express and courier service sectors of the air-cargo industry, the railroad industry benefited the most of any mode in the deregulated period. Although Class I railroad returns on net investment were anything but spectacular (averaging 4.06% in the five-year 1980–1984 period), net railway operating income was more impressive, averaging $1.6 billion per year during the same time.[6] The railroads used this time of increasing prosperity to reinvest an average of $3.0 billion annually in capital expenditures such as for equipment and rights-of-way improvements—a positive trend.[7] However, this industry could have done more. Records show that in 1982 the railroad industry assumed the distinction of having the highest wage and fringe benefit costs per worker of all the modes ($37,474), compared with $36,712 for the second-place airline industry. In 1983, the railroad industry widened its lead as average worker costs jumped to $41,310, compared to the second-place airline figure of $38,951. Between 1980 and 1983, railroad wage-salary levels increased 34%, compared with only 17% for the trucking/warehousing industries.[8]

present and
future impact

Thus in labor costs, the railroad industry's competitive position in 1986 was actually weaker than that of the trucking industry. The railroad industry, which is trying to regain general commodity traffic market share, has an opportuniy to do so with improved TOFC services; however, the carriers might be severely handicapped by excessive labor costs that must be reflected in freight rates. In 1984 shippers both opposed railroad price increases and pressured Congress to reduce railroad pricing freedoms under the Staggers Rail Act of 1980.[9] Shippers want railroads to correct antiquated labor practices such as crew consist rules, as well as to stop asking customers to pay for carrier inefficiencies and cost excesses.

need to manage better

Carriers recognize these problems and know they must find answers,[10] because the trucking industry, which has developed better cost controls and has increased productivity since deregulation, is eager to retain general commodity traffic. If railroads intend to be successful in the long run, they must manage labor costs better during this period of prosperity. The key to the future is outperforming the competition on a service and price basis, which necessitates significant internal improvements in cost controls, productivity, operations, and marketing.

Broadening the Company Focus

Broadening the company focus is another key to long-term profitability. For the most part, and particularly until the late 1970s, transportation executives have been too myopic. They have characterized themselves as transportation specialists first and businesspeople second. This characterization must change, and the transition is well underway. In the deregulated environment, firms can gain entry into other modes of transportation; in fact, the railroads in particular have been entering trucking, aviation, and water transportation. There is also considerable freedom to move into specialized sectors of a given mode; for example, a contract trucker can obtain ICC common carrier authority. A third option is diversification into businesses totally unrelated to transportation; for example, real estate, hotel management, food services, or oil exploration. Just as carriers can enter other sectors, however, new firms can now be expected to enter previously protected transportation sectors. Carriers must seize opportunities before others beat them at their own game.

finding business opportunities

How can senior transportation managers find new business opportunities and stay informed about sources of new competition? They must tune their senses to the environment. In particular, they must become better readers. *Traffic World,* the *Wall Street Journal,* and *Business Week* are three publications that can keep transportation managers informed, but hundreds of other published sources are also available (see Appendix A, *List of Transportation and Logistics Library Sources*). Attitudes must also change. Ignorance is no excuse in today's deregulated market; education is the key.

DEVELOPING FUTURE TRANSPORTATION AND LOGISTICS LEADERS

The task of managing in the transportation and logistics field is not becoming easier. There is tremendous pressure on today's managers to reduce costs, improve productivity, find and hold market niches, raise yields, and make better investment decisions; furthermore, the tension level is likely to increase in the future. Today there is far less patience and tolerance of errors. The field of transportation and logistics is filled with opportunities and risks primarily because of increased competition. Therefore one major challenge faced by the industry is to develop a supply of intelligent, thinking, far-sighted, skilled decision makers to move transportation and logistics and the country into the twenty-first century. These future managers will be asked to make choices more quickly than is necessary at present.

The Corporate Challenge

recruiting

Corporate leaders must share with educators the challenge of developing future transportation and logistics executives. No matter how qualified and motivated college graduates are, they need help to mature into outstanding decision makers and leaders. What chance does a firm have of improving management talent if it takes a lackadaisical approach to recruiting? Too many transportation and logistics organizations settle for less than the best recruits available. Present transportation and logistics managers must start thinking like coaches and ask: What are our plans for this recruit? Where do we place this person to use his or her talents but at the same time prepare him or her for bigger plans in future years? How can we teach junior managers to be the best they can be? How do we keep them motivated so that they do not transfer to other companies?

training, motivating, and keeping talent

The future of transportation and logistics management depends on training, motivating, and keeping the best talent available. Perhaps the biggest challenge will be retaining superior young management talent—proven achievers. Someone good enough to stay is good enough to leave and take jobs with other firms that also recognize outstanding leadership potential. Senior management must try to promote proven, productive managers ahead of less-productive employees. If those who have earned the right to advance on the basis of merit are buried in a seniority-entrenched promotional system, companies will lose them. It happens daily, and it threatens many companies' futures.

ADVANCING TECHNOLOGY

Technology presents another major challenge to transportation. The industry has been engulfed by the computer age, which on the one hand enables managers to make extremely complex decisions in far less time and with far greater confidence. On the other hand, computers are replacing clerks and forcing most managers to become comfortable with, and skilled at, using these machines.

forcing operational changes

Technological changes have also altered the way carriers perform their operations. A leading example is the introduction by United States Lines in 1984 of 4400 TEU container ships, such as the one shown in Fig. 20.1. These ships have 76% more capacity than the previous largest vessels in service (for a comparison, see Fig. 9.2), and their size has forced United States Lines to

FIGURE 20.1.

Photo of *American New York,* which represents the state of the art in containership construction. (Photo reprinted courtesy of Georgia Ports Authority)

follow a load-center approach. Thus its ships serve fewer ports (i.e., load centers) and rely on surface transportation (e.g. railroad, highway, and water transportation) modes to deliver containers to and from load centers. One question raised by this new technology is whether competitors like Sea-Land and American President Lines will feel compelled to match the United States Lines' initiative, purchase similar ships, and try to gain big-ship economies of scale. Another question is whether demand can keep pace with rising supply. Will new technology trigger an excess capacity problem?

opportunities
and risks

Technology provides still other opportunities and risks. For example, longer, wider, and heavier trucks offer the promise of greater labor productivity—more ton-miles carried per driver. However, the desire to accomplish this productivity goal can force truckers to replace, prematurely, their currently owned, yet not fully depreciated, equipment, such as replacing present 45-ft trailers with 48-ft trailers. Railroads, too, have decisions to make, since two new 48-ft trailers are too long to fit on a piggyback flatcar. New technology tempts carriers to invest heavily. In the airline mode, the introductions of the Boeing-757, Boeing-767, and Airbus A-310 aircraft are good examples. These aircraft are more fuel efficient than older airplanes, such as the Boeing-727 and require only a two-person, versus a three person, cockpit crew,[11] yet decisions to borrow heavily to acquire them can produce serious financial problems as in the Eastern Airlines case.

MAGLEV and
financial impediments

Some startling transportation developments are on the horizon. A good example is high-speed magnetically levitated trains (MAGLEV). As Chapter 7 explained, before the year 2000, MAGLEV passenger trains may move people at average speeds of 200 mph. MAGLEV, however, epitomizes a common problem in bringing engineering accomplishments into operational reality. The problem is not so much engineering feasibility as potential profitability. In Japan, MAGLEV progress has been stymied by investor reluctance.[12] In Florida, four companies submitted conceptual plans in 1984 for a 295-mile

Miami–Orlando–Tampa MAGLEV system, but Florida supports high-speed rail technology only if it is privately financed.[13]

Future Technology

oil substitute

Who knows what marvelous transportation or transportation-related inventions lie ahead? For example, two South Carolina men claim they have invented a process for extracting an oil-substitute organic fuel from a waste-product of current agricultural processes. The fuel reportedly is neither a methane-type gas nor alcohol, but a liquid that allegedly is the energy equivalent of gasoline and can be substituted for gasoline, diesel fuel, or jet fuel. Furthermore, the inventors claim that there is no need to alter automobile engines or modify carburetors to use it.[14] Another inventor claims he has developed a compound that will yield nearly indestructible automobile tires. Called alphalon, the compound combines rubber and polytetrafluoroethylene (PTFE)—the principal ingredient in Teflon, a DuPont Company trademark—into a material that lasts up to 10 times longer than normal rubber because it resists wear from heat and friction.[15]

nearly indestructible tires

14,000 mph subway

More astounding than the above assertions is a statement by Professor Frank P. Davidson, head of the Massachusetts Institute of Technology's Macro-Engineering Group. According to Davidson, engineers have the expertise to build a subway capable of moving vehicles at 14,000 mph. The proposed technology would use electromagnetism within a vacuum to propel vehicles, such as from New York to Los Angeles via Dallas (2450 miles), in 21 minutes.[16]

hindrances to technological progress

Time will tell whether any of these inventions become available to the U.S. public, but each has the potential to alter transportation in a significant way. Many obstacles remain for their inventors, however. If the technology is feasible, is the U.S. economy ready for a petroleum substitute? How will oil interests react to oil substitutes that would, in all probability, diminish the value of black gold? Will the U.S. government push technological advancements such as the oil substitute, or will developments be significantly impeded by procedural or patent delays? Many existing firms do not welcome technology that will diminish their sales or make their products less attractive. Railroads primarily oppose coal slurry pipelines because they are a business threat. Airlines, in all probability, will oppose MAGLEV technology. The government should take whatever measures are necessary to further transportation technological advancements. Politics and self-interests cannot be allowed to stop meaningful progress. Investors and the public must be given the right to decide what is most efficient and what makes the most economic sense.

THE GOVERNMENTAL CHALLENGE

The future of transportation will also be linked quite closely to government actions. As noted in Chapter 4, the NTPSC identified 64 federal agencies administering nearly 1000 policies and programs affecting transportation.[17] This level of involvement is not likely to change; transportation is too important to this country. However, since the government's role in transportation needs to be improved, the following suggestions are offered:

need for an NTP

1. The government needs to remove as many conflicting policies and jurisdictional disputes as possible. The United States still has no singular national transportation policy (NTP). In its absence, there is far too much parochialism as interest groups staunchly defend and try to satisfy their particular wants. This country needs a simple, straightforward policy to define its transportation priorities. As politically unpopular as the creation of an NTP might be, establishing one is long overdue.

avoidance of unnecessary interference

2. According to the NTPSC, "When the transportation system is used to pursue nontransportation goals, [the government should] do so in a cost-effective manner."[18] National goals like energy conservation and regional development too often result in transportation waste. The government should make every effort to avoid unnecessary interference in the transportation marketplace. A good example is the 55-mph limit, which caused over-the-road truck driver costs to increase by nearly $4000 per driver per year. Because Teamster over-the-road drivers were, and still are, paid at a fixed amount based on miles driven per day, and because the law limits driving time to 10 hours per day, slower speeds reduced daily miles driven, and thereby lowered productivity. Consequently, trucking management agreed to higher labor mileage rates, which raised carrier operating costs and increased rates to shippers.

allowing capitalism to work

3. Let capitalism work. Unless compelled by urgent national priorities, government should not rescue financially troubled carriers. The prospect of governmental relief gives owners, management, and labor too many excuses for not making tough but necessary corrective decisions. Let the efficient prosper and the inefficient improve or fail. The government should become involved when carriers or customers are unfairly abused by unscrupulous competitors, however.

avoidance of frequent rule changes

4. Regulatory rules should be defined and left unchanged for numerous years. Continuously revising economic regulations creates an environment of confusion and indecision. Carriers need time to adjust to regulations or freedoms created by deregulation to reposition their efforts and make wise reinvestment choices. Major regulatory changes should be made only when absolutely necessary.

need for a healthy economy

5. The transportation industry needs a healthy economy. Federal policies are primarily responsible for recessions, periods of inflation, unemployment, and so forth. Given the growing complexity of world economics, one major challenge faced by the government is trying to keep the U.S. economy sound. The transportation industry, as a derived-demand business, needs a long period of economic prosperity.

OTHER CHALLENGES

The following questions, which challenge suppliers and users of transportation services, require answers if the U.S. transportation system is to make future headway.

1. When will the carnage on U.S. highways end, or at least be minimized? When will individuals assume greater responsibility for highway safety?

2. Can truckers and railroad carriers substantially simplify their rate structures? Is pricing really that complex, or are carriers and users unwilling to break from traditional pricing practices?

3. Can the U.S. transportation industry and its freight-shipping customers change from a domestically oriented industry to an expanded international sphere of influence?

4. What will become of the transportation common carrier? In the more deregulated environment in which revenues, costs, and profits on single shipments have acquired greater importance, what will happen to a carrier's sense of commitment to small-shipper, small-shipment, and small-town transportation needs?

5. Who will serve the rural passengers previously served by regular route intercity bus carriers?

6. Will the United States have a commercial maritime fleet capable of meeting the logistical needs of the armed services in a prolonged military confrontation?

7. What is the solution to our congested urban streets? What can be done to make public mass transportation more attractive to automobile users, yet efficient from a taxpayer cost perspective?

8. Can carriers live and operate responsibly enough in a freer marketplace to avoid creating a public outcry for a return to greater economic regulation?

9. How can the transportation and logistics industry improve its public image? Will the public appreciate the benefits of transportation and logistics?

SUMMARY

The future of the United States, like its past, will closely parallel the development of transportation. Can the transportation industry meet the needs of a growing nation? Will future generations have the same mobility and cargo-hauling capabilities that this generation is experiencing, and will transportation services improve? The U.S. transportation system faces many challenges, and there are no guarantees.

To succeed, determination, hard work, self-sacrifice, and understanding are necessary. In the 1970s and 1980s, U.S. transportation and logistics managers and workers have been severely tested by rising fuel prices and supply problems, a deep recession, near-record inflation, deregulation, and the rising tide of foreign competition. However, there is room for optimism. Although the U.S. automobile industry bent, it rebounded with improved product quality, better cost controls, and improved productivity. Truckers and airlines—many on the brink of financial disaster—were forced to manage better, and most did. In short, the transportation industry, like many other sectors of the U.S. economy, is seeing that its future rests on its ability to compete, and it is making progress toward that objective.

Still, there is room for improvement. Transportation profits must be increased and reinvested, leadership talent must be improved and retained, new technology must be encouraged rather than opposed, and the government must give capitalism a greater chance to work. The future of transportation offers much risk, but also many opportunities. If the United States wants to move forward, transportation will carry it there.

STUDY QUESTIONS

1. According to the NTPSC's medium-growth scenario, how will the automobile and aviation modes' intercity roles change by 2000?

2. According to Table 20.3, what two modes of transportation are forecast to grow the fastest between 1975 and 2000 in ton-miles hauled and percentage changes?

3. Why is it important that government refrain from frequent transportation economic regulatory changes?

4. Why should senior transportation executives today work more diligently in recruiting, developing, and retaining talented junior managers?

5. Why is it so important to the future of the United States that transportation profitability be improved?

6. How does the railroad industry illustrate the need for sound management during periods of prosperity?

7. What impedes the development of new transportation technology?

8. Why should transportation carriers consider broadening their company business focus?

ENDNOTES

1. National Transportation Policy Study Commission, *National Transportation Policies Through the Year 2000 (Final Report)* (Washington, D.C.: U.S. Government Printing Office, 25 June 1979) (hereafter cited as *National Transportation Policy Study*).

2. Ibid., p. 160.

3. Ibid., p. 418.

4. Ibid., p. 173.

5. (a) Office of Policy and Analysis, Interstate Commerce Commission, *The Effect of Regulatory Reform on the Trucking Industry: Structure, Conduct and Performance, Preliminary Report* (Washington, D.C.: ICC, 1981), p. 89; (b) Bureau of Accounts, Interstate Commerce Commission, *Class I Motor Carriers of Property Selected Earnings Data* (Washington, D.C.: ICC, 1983), p. 1; and (c) information supplied by Brinkley Garner, Office of Transportation Analysis, Interstate Commerce Commission, by phone on 21 April 1986.

6. Association of American Railroads, *Railroad Facts 1985 Edition* (Washington, D.C.: Association of American Railroads, August 1985), pp. 17–18.

7. Ibid., p. 19.

8. "Rails Replace Airlines in Top Spot in Employee Earnings-Fringe Levels," *Traffic World*, 24 September 1984, p. 78.

9. (a) "Shippers Not Too Hopeful of Negotiated Settlement in Dispute with Rails," *Traffic World*, 17 September 1984, pp. 9–10; (b) Don Byrne, "Rail Shippers Go Public on Gripes over ICC's Handling of Deregulation," *Traffic World*, 17 September 1984, pp. 18–19; (c) "Commission Opens Inquiry for Reaction of Industry on Staggers Act Handling," *Traffic World*, 17 September 1984, p. 40; and (d) Don Byrne, "Senate Drafting Language Forcing ICC to Consider Rail Shippers' Rights," *Traffic World*, 27 February 1984, pp. 25–26.

10. (a) Don Byrne, "Rail Management Seeking Showdown on Work Rules in This Year's Talks," *Traffic World*, 13 August 1984, pp. 20–21; and

(b) "Rail Management Makes Offer on 1984 Re-opening of Rail Labor Contracts," *Traffic World*, 30 January 1984, p. 73.

11. William M. Carley, "Pan Am to Buy or Lease 28 Jets Made by Airbus," *Wall Street Journal*, 14 September 1984, pp. 3, 18.

12. Stephen Kreider Yoder, "Magnetic-Train Saga Indicates Japan's Distrust of Its Home-Grown Technology," *Wall Street Journal*, 20 September 1984, p. 34.

13. "High-speed Train Plans Are Submitted to Florida," *Engineering News Record*, 12 January 1984, pp. 35, 37.

14. Bob Deans, "Fuels Revolution Brewing? Two Say Substance Taken from Plants Runs Auto Engines," *The Atlanta Constitution*, 31 August 1984, pp. 1C, 7C.

15. Hall Lancaster, "Inventor Develops Compound He Claims Will Yield Nearly Indestructible Car Tires," *Wall Street Journal*, 20 November 1984, p. 33.

16. Associated Press, "High-Speed Subway Demonstrated—In Theory," *The Atlanta Constitution*, 26 April 1984, p. 8A.

17. *National Transportation Policy Study*, p. 43.

18. Ibid., p. 249.

ADDITIONAL READINGS

Berkman, Herman G. "Some Perspectives on Transportation in the Next Decade." *Traffic Quarterly* 34, no. 1 (January 1980): 143–154.

Bess, David. "Transportation Curricula: Too Domestic?" *Transportation Journal* 18, no. 4 (Summer 1979):72–76.

Bruce, Harry J. "Needed: 'Innovative Mindset and Multimodal Perspective.'" *Railway Age*, 12 July 1984, pp. 34–35.

"Business Will Keep Labor in Line: Recession-Scarred Unions Lack Leverage in 1984's Bargaining." *Business Week*, 26 December 1983, pp. 20–21.

Butler, Robert M. "Majority of States Still Regulate Surface Transportation Companies." *Traffic World*, 20 February 1984, pp. 25–27.

Cavinato, Joseph L., and Kogon, Gary B. "Improving Top Management's View of Traffic." *Traffic World*, 1 August 1983, pp. 85–87.

Coyle, John J.; Bardi, Edward J.; and Cavinato, Joseph L. *Transportation*. St. Paul, Minn.: West Publishing Company, 1982, Chapter 23, "The Future of Transportation."

Federal Highway Administration and the Urban Mass Transportation Administration, U.S. Department of Transportation. *Microcomputers in Transportation: Software and Source Book*. Washington, D.C.: U.S. D.O.T., September 1983.

Jennrich, John H. "Transportation 2000: How America Will Move Its People and Products." *Nation's Business*, November 1979, pp. 35–36.

Koutsopoulos, K. C. "Determining Transportation Needs." *Traffic Quarterly* 34, no. 3 (July 1980):397–412.

Metz, Tim. "Goodman Systems and Its Auto-Fuel Device Find Road to Market Difficult to Traverse." *Wall Street Journal*, 23 June 1981, p. 35.

National Council of Physical Distribution Management. *Transportation Strategies for the Eighties*. Oak Brook, Ill.: NCPDM, 1982.

Pedersen, Neil J.; Schofer, Joseph L.; and Schulz, David F. "An Evolving Image of Long-Range Transportation Planning." *Traffic Quarterly* 33, no. 3 (July 1979):443–457.

Prouty, L. Fletcher. "Transportation at the Crossroads." *Transportation Quarterly* 35, no. 3 (July 1981):385–399.

Roberts, Paul O. *Transport Tomorrow: A National Priority*. Vol. 1: *Transportation: Forces of Change*. Washington, D.C.: National Chamber Foundation, 1981.

———. *Transport Tomorrow: A National Priority*. Vol. 2: *A Prescription for Effective Transportation Policies*. Washington, D.C.: National Chamber Foundation, 1981.

Sampson, Roy J.; Farris, Martin, T; and Shrock, David L. *Domestic Transportation: Practice, Theory, and Policy*. 5th ed. Boston: Houghton Mifflin Company, 1985, Chapter 29, "The Future of Domestic Transportation."

Stephenson, Frederick J. "Facing Up To Change." *Transportation Worldwide: The (Delta Nu Alpha) Alphian*, Summer 1984, pp. 11–12.

Talley, Wayne Kenneth. *Introduction to Transportation*. Cincinnati, Ohio: South-Western Publishing Company, 1983, Chapter 20, "U.S. Transportation and the Future."

Tower, Raymond C. "America's Economic Future: Lessons From the Marketplace." *Vital Speeches of the Day*, 1 December 1983, pp. 104–109.

U.S. Department of Transportation. *National Transportation Trends & Choices (To the Year 2000).* Washington, D.C.: U.S. Government Printing Office, 12 January 1977.

Urban Mass Transportation Administration and Federal Highway Administration, U.S. Department of Transportation. *Microcomputers in Transportation: Getting Started in Microcomputers, Vol. 1, Selected Readings.* Washington, D.C.: U.S. D.O.T., 1979.

Williams Jr., Ernest W. "The National Transportation Policy Study Commission and Its Final Report: A Review." *Transportation Journal* 19, no. 3 (Spring 1980):5–19.

Wood, Donald F., and Johnson, James C. *Contemporary Transportation.* 2d ed. Tulsa, Okla: PennWell Publishing Company, 1982, Chapter 15, "Future Issues and Prospects."

A

List of Transportation and Logistics Library Sources

What follows is a selection of 126 valuable library sources for serious students of transportation and logistics management (T & LM). Prepared by Arnold Balk, Business and Economics Librarian at the University of Georgia, Appendix A represents a small but highly regarded portion of the T & LM resources available in the University of Georgia Library. Appendix A lists topics alphabetically (see *Contents,* below) and, within each topic, alphabetically lists source items by title. The objectives, in choosing these particular sources, are to present a balanced offering covering a broad assortment of 23 T & LM topics and provide depth through multiple, quality sources under each topic. For more complete University of Georgia Library listings, contact Arnold Balk, Business and Economics Librarian, University of Georgia Libraries, Athens, Georgia 30602 (Telephone number: 404–542–0681). Ask for Resource List No. 6, *Periodicals for Transportation and Allied Fields* and/or Resource List No. 4, *U.S. Transportation Information Sources for Advanced Business Students.*

Another purpose in including this list of library resources is to challenge T & LM students to use these outstanding library materials. By researching, reading, and studying these sources, students, as well as T & LM career professionals, can further their knowledge of the field, stay current, and gain a competitive edge. This list is a practical extension of the text and offers a valuable supplement to classroom learning or on-the-job training.

Note: The author is deeply indebted to Arnold Balk, Business and Economics Librarian at the University of Georgia, for preparing this appendix and for his untiring efforts to advance transportation and logistics management education.

Contents

AIR TRANSPORTATION

AIR CARGO WORLD

The shipper's source

Giving to the executives in manufacturing and forwarding the feature stories and news articles they need in a highly competitive world of air freight shipping.

Communication Channels, Inc.

AIR CARRIER FINANCIAL STATISTICS

Income statement data and balance sheet data are provided for the various carrier groups: majors, nationals, large regionals, and medium regionals.

U.S. Department of Transportation

AIR CARRIER TRAFFIC STATISTICS

Lists data for scheduled and nonscheduled services, such as revenue passenger-miles, available seat-miles, revenue ton-miles, overall performance factors, departures, and so forth.

U.S. Department of Transportation

AIR TRANSPORT WORLD

The magazine of world airline management

One of the most widely read publications in the aviation world. Carries authoritative features and special reports from some of the top people in their fields. Each issue

provides facts and figures, operating data, and commuter statistics.

Penton/IPC

AIRLINE EXECUTIVE

Serving international airline management

Each issue has regular features, such as: "Financial News, International Dataline, New Products, U.S. Airline Statistics, World Airline Statistics, etc."

Communication Channels, Inc.

AVIATION WEEK AND SPACE TECHNOLOGY

Serves all aerospace market sectors worldwide, including military, government, commercial air transportation, and corporate aviation. Editorial coverage is excellent and includes the latest developments, news items, current affairs, and industry trends.

McGraw-Hill, Inc.

INTERAVIA

Aerospace review

Covering all aspects of civil aviation, the aerospace industry, and technology, including avionics, and presenting new developments and products on a worldwide basis. Each issue is devoted also to a special feature extensively researched to provide indepth coverage on topical subjects. *Interavia* is synonymous with international aviation.

Interavia, S. A.

JOURNAL OF AIR LAW AND COMMERCE

Scholarly publication focusing exclusively on the legal and economic issues affecting aviation and space.

Southern Methodist University School of Law

WORLD AVIATION DIRECTORY

The aviation/aerospace industry's standard reference including the World Helicopter Directory.

Ziff-Davis Publishing Company

BIBLIOGRAPHIC INFORMATION

CLM. SUPPLEMENT TO BIBLIOGRAPHY ON LOGISTICS MANAGEMENT (formerly NCPDM. SUPPLEMENT TO BIBLIOGRAPHY ON PHYSICAL DISTRIBUTION MANAGEMENT)

Provides managerially oriented overview of the current distribution literature.

Council on Logistics Management

THE DIRECTORY OF DIRECTORIES

An annotated guide to business and industrial directories, professional and scientific rosters, and other lists and guides of all kinds.

Updated periodically by *Directory Information Service.*

Information Enterprises, 1983

ENCYCLOPEDIA OF BUSINESS INFORMATION SOURCES

A detailed listing of primary subjects of interest to managerial personnel, with a record of sourcebooks, periodicals, organizations, directories, handbooks, bibliographies, on-line data bases, and other sources of information on each topic.

Gale Research Company, 1983

STATISTICS SOURCES

A subject guide to data on industrial, business, social, educational, financial, and other topics for the United States and internationally.

Gale Research Company, 1983

TRANSGUIDE

A guide to sources of freight transportation information, covering all modes of transportation: air, ocean, inland, water, truck, and rail.

Reebie Associates
The Associates, 1980

BIOGRAPHIC INFORMATION

THE OFFICIAL DIRECTORY OF INDUSTRIAL AND COMMERCIAL TRAFFIC EXECUTIVES

The "Who's Who" of the industrial/commercial traffic profession, covering the executives in U.S. and Canadian firms.

Traffic Service Corporation

THE POCKET LIST OF RAILROAD OFFICIALS

Covering railroads of North, Central, and South America; Australia; Japan; and the Philippines. Lists names, titles, addresses, and phone numbers of officials of railroads, railroad-operated truck lines, major transit systems, and associated industry and government bodies.

National Railway Publishing Company

REFERENCE BOOK OF CORPORATE MANAGEMENTS

It is the "Executives Who's Who" of the top U.S. companies, providing brief biographical information about top executives. A two-volume reference book of corporate managements and America's corporate leaders.

Dun & Bradstreet Corporation

STANDARD & POOR'S REGISTER OF CORPO-
RATIONS, DIRECTORS, AND EXECUTIVES

Volume 2: Provides brief biographies for
about 70,000 individuals serving as officers,
directors, trustees, partners, etc.; arranged
alphabetically.

Standard & Poor's Corporation

CORPORATE PERFORMANCE

CARRIER REPORTS

A quarterly publication designed to report
the financial experience of the nation's leading carriers. The carriers reported are generally those with annual operating revenues of $2 million or more. The fourth
quarter issue reports the cumulative annual
experience of each carrier, excluding the air
carriers. The following carriers are included: airlines, bus lines, railroads, and
truck lines.

Carrier Reports

DISCLOSURE (ANNUAL COMPANY REPORTS): 10K REQUIRED SEC FILING FORMS

The official annual business and financial
report that must be filed by most companies.

Part I: The Financial section, must be filed
within 90 days of company's fiscal
year-end.

Part II: Supporting data, containing information normally required in a
proxy statement, must be filed
within 120 days of fiscal year-end
if a proxy is not filed separately in
that period.

Disclosure, Inc.

DISCLOSURE (ANNUAL REPORT TO SHARE-HOLDERS): ARS NONREQUIRED SEC FILING FORMS

The document that most major companies
use to communicate directly with their
shareholders. Often provides nonfinancial
details of the business that are not reported
elsewhere, including forecasts of future
programs and plans.

Disclosure, Inc.

THE MEDIA GENERAL FINANCIAL WEEKLY

Presenting current, vital financial facts for
all common issues traded on the New York
Stock Exchange, the American Stock Exchange, and for 840 NASDAQ/Over-the-
Counter issues. Further providing news and
commentary, stocks by industry tables, industry summary, market summary, and so
forth.

Media General Financial Services, Inc.

MOODY'S INVESTORS SERVICE. MOODY'S TRANSPORTATION MANUAL

Providing comprehensive descriptions of almost every type of domestic transportation
company and enterprise—more than 1000,
including the following: air; rail; bus lines;
barge and steamship lines; oil pipelines;
tunnel, bridge, and canal companies; trucking; tank car companies; and automobile
and truck leasing and rental companies. Updated by: *Moody's Transportation News Reports*

Dun & Bradstreet Company

VALUE LINE INVESTMENT SURVEY

Part 1:   Summary & Index
Showing the current ratings of
1700 stocks for future relative price
performance and safety; also estimated yields, earnings, dividends,
and price-to-earnings data.

Part 2:   Selection & Opinion
Detailed analysis of an especially
recommended stock plus a wealth
of investment background included. Value Line Composite Average of more than 1700 stocks.

Part 3:   Ratings & Reports
Full-page analysis of about 130
stocks. During the course of every
13 weeks, new full-page reports are
issued on all 1700 stocks, replacing
and updating the previous reports.

For Transportation see the following:
Air Transport
Maritime
Railroad
Railroad Equipment

Railroad/Resources
Trucking/Transportation Lease

Arnold Bernhard & Company, Inc.

WALL STREET TRANSCRIPT

"The Information Center for Business and Finance—The Clearing House for Future Corporate Changes."

Each week publishing in full: reports, stud-

ies and comments from leading brokers from across the country; company studies; transportation industry surveys; chart and technical analyses; top management reports to Security Analysts Societies; and in-depth interviews with high performance money managers, registered representatives, and research directors.

Wall Street Transcript Corporation

CURRENT AWARENESS—
MULTIMODAL

BARRON'S

National business and financial weekly.

Content includes composite market quotations for each of the major stock exchanges in North America; each issue also contains lengthy articles delving into companies and/or industries offering possible investment opportunities.

Dow Jones & Company

JOURNAL OF COMMERCE AND COMMERCIAL

America's oldest business newspaper. It is a transportation paper, as well as a commodity paper, and the source for current information on banking, international trade, insurance, labor relations, services, petroleum, and so forth.

Twin Coast Newspapers Inc.

TRAFFIC WORLD

The weekly newsmagazine of transportation management.

It chronicles the news events and regulatory actions in the field of freight and passenger transportation, covering all modes of transportation—motor, rail, air, water, pipeline, container, and so forth. The working tool for the traffic and transportation profession.

Traffic Service Corporation

WALL STREET JOURNAL

The daily newspaper of the business and financial world; providing the reader with general, business, and financial news in both capsule and expanded form, as well as daily quotations from many financial exchanges.

Dow Jones & Company

DICTIONARIES

AVIATION & SPACE DICTIONARY

Provides detailed, informative, and accurate definitions of major aerospace and aviation terms.

Aero Publishers, Inc., 1980

FAIRPLAY BOOK OF SHIPPING ABBREVIATIONS

The author lists more than 3000 shipping terms, abbreviations, code names, symbols, and company names.

Kapoor, Peter
Fairplay Publications Ltd., 1980

TRANSPORTATION—LOGISTICS DICTIONARY

More than 4800 terms are clearly defined. Also contains definitions of various transportation rates for all modes; abbreviations used in the industry; summaries of the revised Interstate Commerce Act, Shipping Act of 1916, and Title 49 of the Code of Federal Regulations; listing of standard codes; etc.

Cavinato, Joseph L., editor
Traffic Service Corporation, 1982

ECONOMICS

AMERICAN ENTERPRISE INSTITUTE FOR PUB-
LIC POLICY RESEARCH

EIA Economist

A monthly report that intends to clarify
current issues of economic policy in an objective manner.

American Enterprise Institute

FUTURES

The Journal of Forecasting and Planning

It spans many disciplines and draws together articles and features on social, economic, and technological forecasting. It also
gives an overview of possible developments
throughout society.

Butterworth Scientific Ltd.

THE RAND JOURNAL OF ECONOMICS

(Formerly: *The Bell Journal of Economics*)

"The purpose of *The Rand Journal of Economics,* formerly *The Bell Journal of Economics,* is to support and encourage research in the behavior of regulated
industries, the economic analysis of organizations, and more generally, applied mi-
cro-economics."

The Rand Corporation

ENERGY

NPN NATIONAL PETROLEUM NEWS

A publication for marketing management—
operations—fuel oil—tires, batteries, and
accessories automotive aftermarket

Hunter Publishing Company

PETROLEUM INTELLIGENCE WEEKLY

National and international petroleum and
energy news, trends, forecasts, etc.

Petroleum & Energy Intelligence Weekly,
Inc.

PETROLEUM SUPPLY MONTHLY

Providing descriptive articles and statistical
data on the production, importation, and
disposition of crude oil, petroleum products, and natural gas liquids in the United
States.

Energy Information Administration
U.S. Department of Energy

QUARTERLY ENERGY REVIEW. THE WORLD

A research series covering oil, coal, gas,
and other energy

Monitors the more significant global trends
and assesses their likely consequences, addresses major issues and arguments of the
day, and forecasts global trends in the major energy groups on the basis of an analysis of regional trends in demand and supply.

Economist Intelligence Unit Ltd.

EXPORT/TRADE

AMERICAN IMPORT EXPORT MANAGEMENT

The leading monthly magazine for executives in international trade.

Containing news of import and export activities, current customs regulations, and
brief feature articles emphasizing maritime
and port activities.

North American Publishing Company

CUSTOM HOUSE GUIDE

A convenient, easy-to-use, one-volume library on international trade, containing answers to import/export questions.

Part 1:   Port Section
Part 2a: Alphabetical Import Commodity
           Index
Part 2b: Tariff Schedules of the United
           States

Part 3a: U.S. Customs Regulations

Part 3b: Appendix to Customs Regulations

Part 3c: Index to Customs Regulations

North American Publishing Company

EXPORT/IMPORT TRAFFIC MANAGEMENT AND FORWARDING

"This book is an attempt to explain in a comprehensive manner the diverse functions and varied services and the whole range of ocean traffic management which forwarders have developed over more than a century, a mechanism for keeping abreast of changing foreign and domestic governmental restrictions, rules and regulations applicable in different countries, ports and on different trade routes and by providing a complete documentation service to facilitate and coordinate the movement of goods in international commerce."

Murr, Alfred
Cornell Maritime Press, Inc., 1979

THE EXPORTER

A monthly management review of export operations, markets, training & world trade.

Trade Data Reports Inc.

TOP BULLETIN

Trade opportunities program

Contains timely information on export opportunities for U.S. firms.

U.S. Department of Commerce

HIGHWAY TRANSPORTATION

AUTOMOTIVE NEWS

The weekly newspaper of the industry. Each year the last April issue has a special section—"Almanac Issue," which contains useful statistics on U.S. car and truck registrations and production; Canadian production, prices, etc.; dealer statistics; directory of companies; etc.

Crain Automotive Group, Inc.

CHILTON'S CCJ

Commercial carrier journal

A publication for managers of private fleets and for-hire trucking companies.

Chilton Company

FLEET OWNER

A publication catering to the fleetmen who are either involved in private carriage or in the for-hire trucking business.

McGraw-Hill, Inc.

MOTOR TREND

The complete automotive magazine for a motoring world.

Petersen Publishing Company

MVMA MOTOR VEHICLE FACTS AND FIGURES

One of the most comprehensive compilations of motor vehicle data providing information on passenger cars, motor trucks, motor buses, production, registrations, use, owners, and economic trends. Data and charts help readers focus on future trends and understand historical patterns.

Motor Vehicle Manufacturers Association of the United States, Inc.

TRANSPORT TOPICS

National newspaper of the trucking industry

The latest trucking industry news, events, and issues.

American Trucking Associations Inc.

TRINC'S BLUE BOOK OF THE TRUCKING INDUSTRY

Vital information about the largest trucking firms in the United States

Balance sheet data

Revenues

Expenses

Equipment

Manpower data

Ton-miles

Intercity statistics

Trinc Transportation Consultants

WARD'S AUTOMOTIVE YEARBOOK

Automotive industry's standard reference, covering trends, production, supplies, sales, registrations, imports, recreational vehicles, material usage, Canadian statistics, etc.

Ward's Communications, Inc.

INDEXING SERVICES

BUSINESS PERIODICALS INDEX

A cumulative index to approximately 300 English language periodicals covering the various phases and fields of business; appropriate for general public and undergraduate usage.

H. W. Wilson Company

CURRENT LITERATURE IN TRAFFIC AND TRANSPORTATION

An annotated bibliography on traffic and transportation. Items are gathered from a wide range of domestic and international journals, trade magazines, and special interest research reports and published sources. The bibliography is classified by transportation mode and also includes sections on freight commodities, industrial distribution, travel, and urban transportation.

Northwestern University, Transportation Center

PREDICASTS F & S INDEX UNITED STATES

Providing comprehensive coverage of U.S. business activity. An excellent index that makes information accessible through standard industrial classification (SIC) codes and corporate names.

Predicasts, Inc.

PUBLIC AFFAIRS INFORMATION SERVICE BULLETIN (PAIS)

A useful index to publications covering economic and social conditions, public administration, and international relations printed in English throughout the world. About 1400 periodicals are scanned regularly for articles within the scope of PAIS.

PAIS, Inc.

INDUSTRY PERFORMANCE

ALMANAC OF BUSINESS AND INDUSTRIAL FINANCIAL RATIOS

Profiles corporate performance for each industry in reporting operating and financial information.

Prentice-Hall, Inc.

INDUSTRY NORMS AND KEY BUSINESS RATIOS

Dun & Bradstreet Company

STANDARD & POOR'S INDUSTRY SURVEYS

Providing continuous economic and investment analysis of 65 leading U.S. industries and approximately 1500 of their constituent companies, published in 33 surveys. For each industry grouping, an Annual Basic Survey and three Current Surveys are published during the course of the year. Indus-

try groups covered are from aerospace to utilities–gas. A unique, comprehensive, and timely source in evaluating comparative industry performance and competitive analysis vital to the decision-making process.

Standard & Poor's Corporation

U.S. INDUSTRIAL OUTLOOK . . .

It contains basic information about business in America. Short profiles of the nation's manufacturing and nonmanufacturing industries are provided, which include some statistics on recent trends, developments in domestic and overseas markets, technological advances, and a five-year outlook.

U.S. Department of Commerce

LAWS AND REGULATIONS

CODE OF FEDERAL REGULATIONS (CFR)

A cumulation of both executive agency regulations issued within each year and pre-

viously issued regulations that are still in effect. Arranged into 50 sections, each representing a broad subject area, and fully indexed. Standards or guidelines considered to be regulations because they are mandated by federal legislation are also included.

U.S. General Services Administration

FEDERAL CARRIERS REPORTER (CCH)

Federal regulation of motor carriers, water carriers, and freight forwarders.

In four volumes covering the complex rules and regulations governing this technical area of law in full text, including: ICC, Department of Transportation, court decisions, etc.

Vol. 1:   Index–Lists–Guides
Vol. 2:   State Regulations
           Motor Carriers, Freight Forwarders
           Water Carriers, Related Laws, and Regulations
Vol. 2a: State Regulations
           Department of Transportation, Forms
           General Orders and Administrative Rulings
Vol. 3:   Court Cases
           Commission Decisions
           Court Decisions
           Case Tables
           Citation Table
           Topical Index to Decisions

Commerce Clearing House, Inc.

FEDERAL REGISTER

Publishing proposed and final federal agency rules and regulations; updating the *Code of Federal Regulations.* The Register is, in a sense, also a calendar for notices of hearings, public meetings, and submission deadline dates. Furthermore, it publishes the President's proclamations and executive orders.

U.S. Government Printing Office

NATIONAL ASSOCIATION OF REGULATORY UTILITY COMMISSIONERS. BULLETIN

Reporting on important regulatory agency and court decisions and other significant events affecting the regulation of electric, gas, telephone, telegraph, water, and sewer utilities, CATV systems, and air, motor, rail, and water carriers. It also reports the status of congressional legislation of regulatory interest. The Bulletin includes periodically a NARUC committee list and a membership list of the agencies showing addresses and telephone numbers of commissioners and key staff personnel and abbreviated biographies of the commissioners.

NARUC

TRANSPORT (DE) REGULATION REPORT

Offering advice, advance alerts, ideas, interpretations, and explanations for the transportation executives who must make major distribution decisions based on new and upcoming regulatory changes.

Cahners Publishing Company

TRANSPORTATION LAW JOURNAL

A major professional publication for the field of transportation law intended for the practicing bar and academic community; published in cooperation with the Motor Carrier Lawyers Association.

University of Denver College of Law

UNITED STATES CODE (USC)

Stating the laws presently in effect.

U.S. Government Printing Office

U.S. CODE CONGRESSIONAL AND ADMINISTRATIVE NEWS

Provides the text of federal laws, arranged by Public Law number, as well as legislative history, proclamations, executive orders, and reorganization plans.

West Publishing Company

LOGISTICS (DISTRIBUTION)

BLANDING'S PRACTICAL PHYSICAL DISTRIBUTION. A HANDBOOK FOR PLANNING AND OPERATIONS

The subject matter of this book is essen-

tially the management science of physical distribution management beyond traffic and transportation management, but management science applied to day-to-day operations in a working distribution department.

Blanding, Warren
Traffic Service Corporation, 1978

CHILTON'S DISTRIBUTION

For traffic and transportation decision makers

Covering all aspects of physical distribution management.

Chilton Company

CLM ANNUAL MEETING

These proceedings report on the theory and understanding of the physical distribution process and the art and science of managing physical distribution systems.

Council of Logistics Management (formerly the National Council of Physical Distribution Management)

HANDLING & SHIPPING MANAGEMENT

The physical distribution magazine

Covering procurement and distribution of goods, transportation, warehousing, site location, inventory control, handling systems, intermodalism, protective packaging, etc.

Penton/IPC, Inc.

INTERNATIONAL JOURNAL OF PHYSICAL DISTRIBUTION & MATERIALS MANAGEMENT

Providing reports of current developments, facilitating the interchange of information among business planners and researchers on a worldwide basis, and offering a platform for new thinking on the problems and techniques of physical distribution and materials management.

MCB University Press Ltd.

JOURNAL OF BUSINESS LOGISTICS

Providing a forum for current research, opinion, and identification of trends in the logistics area.

Council of Logistics Management (formerly the National Council of Physical Distribution Management)

JOURNAL OF PURCHASING AND MATERIALS MANAGEMENT

Articles may present concepts from business, statistics, economics, engineering, behavioral science, or any discipline that contributes to the advancement of knowledge in business or government purchasing, materials management, or related areas.

National Association of Purchasing Management, Inc.

MCD WAREHOUSING/DISTRIBUTION DIRECTORY

Also known as *National Distribution Directory,* listing local cartage, short haul carriers, warehousing, and allied distribution services by state, city, and firm name.

Guide Service, Inc.

TRAFFIC MANAGEMENT

For transportation/distribution managers

Focuses on the transportation concerns of cargo shippers.

Cahners Publishing Company

PIPELINES

NATURAL GAS MONTHLY

Monthly and annual data and information at the state and national level on the supply and disposition of natural gas; also providing information on the activities of the major interstate pipeline companies.

Energy Information Administration
U.S. Department of Energy

OIL & GAS JOURNAL

Providing current oil and gas news, reporting on new technology, and publishing comprehensive industrial statistics; furthermore, each issue features special reports/reviews.

PennWell Publishing Company

PIPELINE

Covering management, operations, engineering, and gas distribution news.

Oildom Publishing Company

PIPELINE & GAS JOURNAL

Energy construction, transportation and distribution

An outstanding publication providing information about international pipeline and gas utility design, construction and operation, transportation, and distribution.

Harcourt, Brace Jovanovich Publications

PIPES AND PIPELINE INTERNATIONAL
. . . with Pipeline Report.

Covering pipeline engineering and construction; industrial pipework; pipe, hose, tube, and all ancillary equipment, and their utilization in every industry; and up-to-date news from the pipeline industry worldwide.

Scientific Surveys Ltd.

RAILROADS

IRJ

International Railway Journal and Rapid Transit Review.

Simmons-Boardman Publishing Company

MODERN RAILROADS

Serving railroads, rail transit, and intermodal transportation.

Enright/Reilly Publishing Company

MODERN RAILWAYS

A British railroad magazine with international coverage.

Ian Allan Ltd.

THE OFFICIAL RAILWAY GUIDE

North America freight service edition

Provides U.S., Canadian, and Mexican rail freight schedules, mileages, connections, and other facilities; system maps; personnel listings; TOFC information; a station index, with line and schedule cross references; and a late news digest.

National Railway Publishing Company

RAILWAY AGE

An international journal catering to the railroad, rail transit, and freight traffic sectors. Regular features include industry and market outlook, market indicators, world report, revenues, and expenses, and so forth.

Simmons-Boardman Publishing Company.

U.S. RAIL NEWS

Providing information and factual reports from Capitol Hill, government regulatory agencies, industry, and research organizations; wherever rail transportation developments are in the making.

Business Publishers, Inc.

YEARBOOK OF RAILROAD FACTS

Presents a summary of railroad operations for past and prior years for the United States as a whole and for the three regional districts to which railroads are assigned for statistical purposes.

Association of American Railroads.

RESEARCH

JOURNAL OF TRANSPORT ECONOMICS AND POLICY

Publishing academic and scholarly articles.

London School of Economics and Political Science

THE JOURNAL OF TRANSPORT HISTORY

The world's only academic journal for the study of transport as an element of economic and social history.

Manchester University Press

THE LOGISTICS AND TRANSPORTATION REVIEW

The only university-based journal in North America dealing specifically with the following:

Issues in transportation policy.
Research dealing in transportation and logistics.
Managerial problems and how transport can be made more efficient.

Quantitative solutions to transport problems.

University of British Columbia

TRANSPORTATION JOURNAL

Devoted to the publication of scholarly articles that will contribute to clear understanding of the management of transportation and stimulate interest in critical appraisals of practices and techniques of transportation and related fields.

American Society of Transportation and Logistics, Inc.

TRANSPORTATION PRACTITIONERS' JOURNAL (formerly ICC PRACTITIONERS' JOURNAL)

Devoted to promotion of the proper administration of the Interstate Commerce Act and related Acts; in the transportation field, one of the most important journals publishing scholarly articles.

Association of Transportation Practitioners

TRANSPORTATION QUARTERLY

An independent journal for better transportation

Always endeavoring to present scholarly articles on a broad range of relevant transportation subjects—without bias—discussing theory, modal treatment, policy issues, and other facets of the transportation world.

ENO Foundation of Transportation, Inc.

TRANSPORTATION RESEARCH FORUM. PROCEEDINGS

Providing a common meeting ground for the discussion of current issues and research applicable to economic, management, public policy, and broad technological problems involving the entire range of disciplines relevant to transportation and all forms of transport.

Transportation Research Forum

TRANSPORTATION RESEARCH RECORD

Consisting of collections of papers on given subjects that were prepared for presentation at the Transportation Research Board Annual Meeting.

Transportation Research Board
National Academy of Sciences

SAFETY

ACCIDENT ANALYSIS AND PREVENTION

Providing wide coverage of the general areas relating to accidental injury and damage and may deal with medical, legal, educational, behavioral, theoretical, or empirical aspects of transportation accidents, as well as accidents at other sites.

Pergamon Press, Inc.

HIGHWAY SAFETY LITERATURE

A publication financially supported by the National Highway Traffic Safety Administration of the U.S. Department of Trans-

portation providing access to technical papers, conference proceedings, journal articles, and research reports dealing with highway and nonrail mass transit safety.

Transportation Research Board
National Academy of Sciences

NATIONAL SAFETY NEWS

An official publication of a nongovernmental, nonprofit, public service organization, dealing with occupational safety and health.

National Safety Council

STATISTICAL INFORMATION

AMERICAN STATISTICS INDEX (ASI)

A comprehensive guide and index to the statistical publications of the U.S. Government. Arranged in two parts:

Abstract section—provides full descriptions of the content of each agency's statistical publications.

Index section—arranged by subject and name, by geographic category by title, and by report number.

Congressional Information Service

NATIONAL TRANSPORTATION STATISTICS

A comprehensive report bringing together related national transportation and energy statistics from a wide variety of government and private sources. Selective data cover the period of 10 years.

U.S. Department of Transportation

STANDARD & POOR'S STATISTICAL SERVICE

One of the most comprehensive collections of statistical information on business, containing more than 1000 important statistical series divided into a Security Price Index

Record Section, followed by 11 subsections on Business and Financial Basic Statistics, plus the monthly update on Current Statistics.

Standard & Poor's Corporation

STATISTICAL ABSTRACT OF THE UNITED STATES

Contains a wide range of current and historical statistics from federal, international, and private agencies on a wide variety of subjects, most of them at the national level; however, key international indicators are also covered. Contains text, tables, and graphic charts. It is the "National Data Book and Guide to Sources."

U.S. Department of Commerce

TRAVEL

JAX FAX

Travel marketing magazine

Jet Airtransport Exchange, Inc.

JOURNAL OF TRAVEL RESEARCH

A quarterly publication of the Travel and Tourism Research Association.

Business Research Division
Graduate School of Business Administration
University of Colorado

TRAVEL MARKET YEARBOOK

The yearbook of travel facts, figures, and trends

The industry's most complete, definitive

source for thousands of travel facts and statistics.

Ziff-Davis Publishing Company

TRAVEL WEEKLY

The national newspaper of the travel industry

Providing travel agent news and promotional advertisements and covering current news and events in the travel industry, such as the following: airline fare increases, strike information, management change information, regulatory changes affecting the travel industry, etc.

Ziff-Davis Publishing Company, Inc.

U.S. CONGRESSIONAL INFORMATION

CIS ANNUAL

Abstracting congressional publications and legislative histories and indexing congressional publications and public laws. It covers the working papers of the U.S. Congress, including hearings, prints, documents, reports, and special publications.

Congressional Information Service

CONGRESSIONAL INDEX (CCH)

Covering Congressional activities each week while Congress is in session and six weeks after it adjourns to facilitate anyone who needs to follow the federal legislative record as it unfolds. Quick contact is provided by topic, author, and bill number for pending bills and resolutions, and their progress is reported from introduction to final disposition.

Commerce Clearing House, Inc.

CQ WEEKLY REPORTS

Summarizes the Congressional and political activities for the current week in Congress. For the full year, see *Congressional Quarterly Almanac*.

Congressional Quarterly, Inc.

MONTHLY CATALOG OF U.S. GOVERNMENT PUBLICATIONS

Monthly listing of Government Printing Office publications.

U.S. Government Printing Office

URBAN MASS TRANSPORTATION

JOURNAL OF ADVANCED TRANSPORTATION

A publication concerned with high speed transportation; sponsored by the Advanced Transit Association.

Institute of Transportation

MASS TRANSIT

The international magazine on transportation in cities.

Mass Transit

METRO

Metropolitan: Mass transit leader since 1904.

Bobit Publishing Company

URBAN TRANSPORT NEWS

Bi-weekly business newsletter published in the nation's capitol.

Complete coverage of federal, state, and local urban transportation activities.

Robert M. Loebelson

WATER

FAIRPLAY INTERNATIONAL SHIPPING WEEKLY

One of the major authoritative publications that covers every phase of the maritime industry and operations.

Fairplay Publications Ltd.

LLOYD'S REGISTER OF SHIPPING. REGISTER OF SHIPS

Contains the names, classes, and general information concerning the ships classified by Lloyd's, with a gross tonnage of 100 and above. (3 volumes)

Lloyd's Register of Shipping

LLOYD'S REGISTER OF SHIPPING. REGISTER OF SHIPS SUBSIDIARY SECTIONS

Covering ship-borne barges, mooring buoys, miscellaneous, pontoons, air cushion vehicles, docking installations, liquefied gas carriers, refrigerated cargo installations, refrigerated stores, and container terminals classed with Lloyd's Register.

Lloyd's Register of Shipping

LLOYD'S REGISTER OF SHIPPING. STATISTICAL TABLES

Provides data on the merchant fleets of the world, such as size, age, population, tonnage, draught, classification, and so forth.

Lloyd's Register of Shipping

LLOYD'S SHIPPING ECONOMIST

Presents a regular and reliable picture of more than a million shipping movements a year, analyzed by area, fleet by fleet. From examination of data on port movements it gives historical trends and current patterns of imports and exports. It analyzes merchant fleets by type, flag, and size; also covers new buildings, world orders, sales and purchases, shipping casualties, and critical international shipping news. An outstanding information source.

Lloyd's of London Press Ltd.

THE MARITIME REVIEW AND INTERMODAL TRANSPORT NEWS

The weekly comprehensive newsletter reporting in condensed format the latest events and developments in the maritime industry worldwide.

DeLong Publishing Company, Inc.

PORTS AND HARBORS

Provides international maritime information about new port developments, issues affecting port and harbor management, etc.

The International Association of Ports and Harbors

SEATRADE

An international journal and world digest of maritime news, trends, policies, and trade.

Seatrade Publications Ltd.

SHIPPING STATISTICS YEARBOOK

Worldwide coverage of facts and figures about shipping, shipbuilding, seaports, and sea-borne trade. Updated by *Institute fur Seeverkehrewirtschaft. Shipping Statistics.*

Institute of Shipping Economics

WWS/WORLD PORTS

Official magazine of the American Association of Port Authorities, Inc.; U.S. & Canadian National Committees of the International Cargo Handling Co-ordination Association; and the Foreign Commerce Club of New York, Inc., providing news, events, and technological and management information pertaining to the ports and worldwide shipping. Each issue also presents a special feature on a segment of the industry and service.

World Wide Shipping Guide, Inc.

B

List of Transportation and Logistics Organizations

NONGOVERNMENT ORGANIZATIONS

ADVANCED TRANSIT ASSOCIATION
1200 18th Street, N.W., Suite 610
Washington, DC 20036
202-659-1251
World-wide membership open to individuals concerned with transit development, operations, finance, and service. The Advanced Transit Association's objective is improvement of transit for low-density metropolitan areas. It seeks to promote, through transit issue conferences and publications, better public understanding of critical factors affecting the development and deployment of highly cost-effective and service-effective transit for such areas.

AIR FREIGHT ASSOCIATION OF AMERICA
1710 Rhode Island Ave., N.W.
Washington, DC 20036
202-293-1030
Firms engaged in domestic and international air freight forwarding and direct air carriers engaged in cargo transportation. Formerly the Air Freight Forwarders Association of America.

Note: The author is indebted to Kathy Faust Bunnell, Kathy Newman Kardoes, and Steve Richmond for their contributions in assembling the material in this Appendix.

AIR TRAFFIC CONFERENCE OF AMERICA
1709 New York Avenue, N.W.
Washington, DC 20006
202-626-4000
The Air Traffic Conference of America, a division of the Air Transport Association of America, establishes industry standards through intercarrier agreements in the form of resolutions, for the handling of passenger services.

AIR TRANSPORT ASSOCIATION OF AMERICA
1709 New York Ave., N.W.
Washington, DC 20006
202-626-4000
The Air Transport Association of America (ATA of A) is the trade and service organization of U.S. scheduled airlines. Of all activities performed by the ATA of A, safety is foremost. Other objectives include the improvement of passenger and cargo traffic procedures, economic and technical research, and action on legislation affecting the industry.

AMERICAN ASSOCIATION OF BICYCLE IMPORTERS, INC.
Office of the President
200 Fifth Avenue
Suite 1057
New York, NY 10010
The American Association of Bicycle Importers is a voluntary association of businesses whose principal purpose and occupation is the importation of bicycles and/or bicycle components. Government trade actions and regulatory actions have been the principal areas of involvement. There are no paid employees, and all work performed is voluntary on the part of the members.

AMERICAN BUS ASSOCIATION
1025 Connecticut Avenue, N.W., Suite 308
Washington, DC 20036
202-293-5890
The American Bus Association is the national organization of the intercity bus industry. The Association handles legislative and regulatory matters, primarily at the federal level. It also promotes safety and provides aid in marketing, public relations, and other areas of interest to both the operator and travel industry segments of its membership.

AMERICAN HELICOPTER SOCIETY INTERNATIONAL
217 N. Washington St.
Alexandria, VA 22314
703-684-6777
The American Helicopter Society (AHS) is a professional association incorporated in 1943 for the advancement of vertical flight technology and its useful application. The Society's membership represents all segments of the helicop-

ter industry, including manufacturers and suppliers, civil and commercial operators, government and certifying agencies, the military, and academia. In addition to an extensive publications program, the focal point of the AHS is the Annual Forum and Technology Display each May.

AMERICAN MOVERS CONFERENCE
2200 Mill Road
Alexandria, VA 22314
703-838-1930
The American Movers Conference is the household goods moving industry's national trade association representing 1200 moving companies and an underlying membership of more than 8000 movers worldwide.

AMERICAN PACKAGE EXPRESS CARRIERS ASSOCIATION
2200 Mill Road
Alexandria, VA 22314
703-838-1887
Affiliated with the Film, Air, and Package Carriers Conference, which provides administrative support. Members are messenger courier companies and carriers of small packages.

AMERICAN PRODUCTION AND INVENTORY CONTROL SOCIETY (APICS)
500 W. Annandale Road
Falls Church, VA 22046
703-237-8344
Technical society of production and inventory control management personnel engaged in scientific and practical methods to determine optimum inventories.

AMERICAN PUBLIC TRANSIT ASSOCIATION
1225 Connecticut Ave., N.W.
Suite 200
Washington, DC 20036
202-828-2800
The American Public Transit Association is a nonprofit trade association that represents the public interest in providing safe, efficient, and economical transit services to all people and strives to improve such services in a manner enhancing the quality of life.

AMERICAN SHORT LINE RAILROAD ASSOCIATION
2000 Massachusetts Ave., N.W.
Washington, DC 20036
202-785-2250
The American Short Line Railroad Association is a nonprofit trade association representing small railroads in matters of common interest before federal agencies, the Congress, and the courts. Founded in 1913, its 1983 membership included 265 railroads and 130 associates (nonrailroads with relationships to the industry).

AMERICAN SOCIETY OF TRANSPORTATION AND LOGISTICS
P.O. Box 33095
Louisville, KY 40232
502-451-8150
The purposes of the American Society of Transportation and Logistics are to establish, promote, and maintain high standards of knowledge and professional training, as well as to serve as a source of guidance for the fields of traffic, transportation, logistics, and physical distribution management, and to serve the industry by fostering professional accomplishments. Publishes *The Transportation Journal.*

AMERICAN TRUCKING ASSOCIATIONS
2200 Mill Road
Alexandria, VA 22314
703-838-1800
Federation of 50 state trucking associations, the District of Columbia Association, and 13 national conferences of truckers that handles in general all forms of trucking industry concerns.

AMERICAN WATERWAYS OPERATORS, INC.
1600 Wilson Blvd., Suite 1000
Arlington, VA 22209
703-841-9300
The American Waterways Operators, Inc. is the national trade association representing the barge and towing industry, as well as shipyards, terminals, and related service companies. AWO promotes the interests of its members by working with the U.S. Congress and federal agencies having regulatory and other responsibilities affecting the industry.

ASSOCIATION OF AMERICAN RAILROADS
50 F Street, N.W.
Washington, DC 20001
202-639-2550
The AAR is the joint agency for its members—railroads that account for 94% of rail mileage, 98% of rail traffic, and 92% of rail labor. It acts in all matters that require cooperative handling so that the railroads can function as a national system.

ASSOCIATION OF OIL PIPE LINES
Suite 1205
1725 K Street, N.W.
Washington, DC 20006
202-331-8228
The Association of Oil Pipe Lines gathers and disseminates information to its members through meetings, publications, and periodic reports. The Association also monitors legislation and economic regulatory matters concerning the industry and, when appropriate, testifies before Congress and regulatory agencies.

ASSOCIATION OF TRANSPORTATION PRACTITIONERS
1211 Connecticut Ave., N.W.
Suite 310
Washington, DC 20036
202-466-2080
A professional association whose object is to promote the proper administration of the Interstate Commerce Act and related acts; to uphold the honor of transportation law practice; to cooperate in fostering increased educational opportunities and maintaining high standards of professional conduct; and to encourage cordial discourse among transportation practitioners. Publishes the *Transportation Practitioners Journal* (formerly the *ICC Practitioners' Journal*).

COUNCIL OF LOGISTICS MANAGEMENT (formerly, THE NATIONAL COUNCIL ON PHYSICAL DISTRIBUTION MANAGEMENT)
2803 Butterfield Rd.
Suite 380
Oak Brook, IL 60521
312-655-0985
CLM is a nonprofit organization of business personnel who are interested in improving their logistics management skills. It works with private industry, various organizations, and institutions to further the development of the logistics concept. It does this development through a continuing program of formal activities and informal discussions designed to (1) develop the theory and understanding of the logistics process, (2) promote the art and science of managing logistics systems, and (3) foster professional dialogue and development in the field.

CRUISE LINES INTERNATIONAL ASSOCIATION
17 Battery Place
Suite 631
New York, NY 10004
212-425-7400
The purpose of the CLIA is to provide training for the travel agent community and promotion to both travel agents and consumers on the concept and value of cruise vacations.

DELTA NU ALPHA TRANSPORTATION FRATERNITY, INC.
14508 John Humphrey Drive
Orland Park, IL 60462
305-894-0384
DNA's purpose is to promote the furtherance of traffic and transportation knowledge and to promote the exchange of ideas among the membership.

DISTRIBUTORS AND CONSOLIDATORS OF AMERICA, INC.
1528 W. 9th Street
Kansas City, MO 64101
816-221-9260

DACA was formed 10 years ago as a national cooperative sales organization to better serve all shippers in every regional center of the United States and Canada, as well as in every facet of transportation, including warehousing and the consolidation and distribution of goods in both intrastate and interstate commerce.

ENO FOUNDATION FOR TRANSPORTATION, INC.
P.O. Box 2055
Westport, CT 06880
203-227-4852
Eno Foundation was established by William Phelps Eno in 1921. Its purpose is to help to improve transportation in all its aspects through the conduct and encouragement of appropriate research and educational activities, and through the publication and distribution of information pertaining to transportation planning, design, operation, and regulation. Publishes *Transportation Quarterly.*

FEDERATION OF AMERICAN CONTROLLED SHIPPING
Suite 3400
50 Broadway
New York, NY 10004
212-344-1483
The Federation of American Controlled Shipping (FACS) represents U.S. companies that control more than 43 million deadweight tons of Liberian and Panamanian tankers, bulk carriers, and specialized vessels. FACS is concerned with worldwide shipping policies and practices as they affect FACS ships, other shipping organizations, labor matters, ship operations, maritime safety, and pollution prevention.

GENERAL AVIATION MANUFACTURERS ASSOCIATION
1400 K Street, N.W., Suite 801
Washington, DC 20005
202-393-1500
The General Aviation Manufacturers Association (GAMA) is a national trade association headquartered in Washington, DC, which represents 35 U.S. manufacturers of general aviation aircraft, engines, avionics, and related items. It fosters and advances the general welfare, safety, interests, and activities of general aviation.

HAZARDOUS MATERIALS ADVISORY COUNCIL
1012 Fourteenth St., N.W.
Suite 907
Washington, DC 20005
202-783-7460
The Hazardous Materials Advisory Council (HMAC) is the only national, non-profit, membership organization representing collectively shippers, carriers of modes, container manufacturers, emergency response and waste clean-up

companies, and shipper, carrier, and container manufacturer associations. HMAC is devoted to promoting safety in domestic and international transportation and handling of hazardous materials, substances, and waste.

HOUSEHOLD GOODS CARRIERS' BUREAU
1611 Duke St.
Alexandria, VA 22314
703-683-7410

The HGCB is a nonprofit organization whose purpose is the education of those engaged in transporting household goods by means of motor vehicles on matters affecting rates, tariffs, and regulatory laws and the mutual improvement and advancement of those engaged in this transportation function. The Bureau publishes tariffs and statistics for its members for the transportation of household goods in interstate and foreign commerce.

INDEPENDENT TRUCKERS ASSOCIATION
P.O. Box 54078
Los Angeles, CA 90054
213-938-7825

The purpose of the Independent Truckers Association (ITA) is to focus primary attention on federal laws affecting trucking, primarily the independent trucker segment. One avenue of pressure by the ITA's nationwide members is through letter-writing campaigns. The ITA claims to be the oldest and largest and only truly nationwide association of independent truckers, which started in 1962.

INLAND RIVERS, PORTS AND TERMINALS, INC.
P.O. Box 863 Central Station
St. Louis, MO 63188
314-241-7354

I.R.P.T. is a nonprofit corporation organized and chartered in 1974 under the laws of the State of Missouri. It claims to be the only nationwide organization dedicated solely to the interests of the ports and terminals located on the inland shallow draft navigable waterways of the United States.

INSTITUTE OF TRANSPORTATION ENGINEERS
525 School Street, S.W., Suite 410
Washington, DC 20024
202-554-8050

The purpose of the Institute is to enable engineers and other professionals with knowledge and competence in transportation and traffic engineering to contribute individually and collectively toward meeting human needs for mobility and safety and to promote professional development of members, by the support and encouragement of education, stimulation of research, development of public awareness, exchange of professional information, and maintenance of a central point of reference and action.

INTERMODAL TRANSPORTATION ASSOCIATION
6410 Kenilworth Ave.
Suite 108
Riverdale, MD 20737
301-864-2661
The purpose and objectives of the Intermodal Transportation Association are to foster and promote the interchange of transportation equipment between the modes of transportation and the leasing industry, to foster and support legislation and administrative rulings concerning intermodal transportation, and to promote standardization of practices and procedures within the intermodal community.

INTERNATIONAL AIR TRANSPORT ASSOCIATION
IATA Building
2000 Peel St.
Montreal, Quebec
CANADA H3A 2R4
The International Air Transport Association (IATA) provides a forum for air transport enterprises engaged either directly or indirectly in international air transport service. IATA's major purpose is to ensure that all airline traffic anywhere moves with the greatest possible speed, safety, convenience, and efficiency, and with the utmost economy.

INTERNATIONAL COUNCIL OF AIRCRAFT OWNER AND PILOT ASSOCIATIONS
421 Aviation Way
Frederick, MD 21701
301-695-2220
The International Council of Aircraft Owner and Pilot Associations is a nonprofit federation of autonomous nongovernmental national general aviation organizations. Its primary objective is to facilitate the movement of general aviation aircraft internationally for peaceful purposes. Its member organizations represent approximately 300,000 pilots and aircraft owners.

INTERNATIONAL FEDERATION OF FREIGHT FORWARDERS ASSOCIATION
P.O. Box 177
CH—8026 Zurich, Switzerland
FIATA, the International Federation of Freight Forwarders Association, aims at the improvement of the quality of freight forwarders' services in all countries. A standard training program, seminars for vocational training staff, glossaries, and technical publications contribute to world-wide harmonization of the forwarding profession.

INTERNATIONAL SNOWMOBILE INDUSTRY ASSOCIATION
3975 University Dr.
Suite 310
Fairfax, VA 22030
703-273-9606

The International Snowmobile Industry Association (ISIA) is a trade association composed of regular members who are manufacturers of snowmobiles, plus associate members who are suppliers of accessories and parts. ISIA is committed to informing those both inside and outside the industry on all matters pertaining to snowmobiling.

MOTHERS AGAINST DRUNK DRIVING
669 Airport Freeway, Suite 310
Hurst, TX 76053
214-254-0111
MADD's purpose for existence is to aid the victims of drunk driving crashes, to aid families of such victims, to increase public awareness of the problem of drinking or drugged drivers, and to otherwise reduce the number of injuries or deaths due to drinking or drugged drivers.

MOTOR VEHICLE MANUFACTURERS ASSOCIATION OF THE UNITED STATES
300 New Center Building
Detroit, MI 48202
313-872-4311
The Motor Vehicle Manufacturers Association of the United States, Inc. is the trade association for the U.S. car, truck, and bus makers. MVMA's nine member companies produce more than 99% of all domestically built motor vehicles. Among MVMA's activities are research projects, economic studies, collections of historical facts and figures, legal analyses, and statistical compilations. Information from these activities is communicated to legislators, government officials, educators, news media, and the public.

NASSTRAC
1750 Pennsylvania Avenue, N.W.
Suite 1116
Washington, DC 20006
202-393-5505
NASSTRAC is a national association of approximately 300 companies who are shippers dedicated to saving money on less-than-truckload (LTL) shipments. The Association produces direct savings through shipper services, seminars/workshops, and TIPS on how to save money and also engages in litigation on behalf of LTL shippers to protect their interests.

NATIONAL AIR TRANSPORTATION ASSOCIATION
4226 King St.
Alexandria, VA 22303
703-845-9000
The National Air Transportation Association exists to promote the economic and professional health of the fixed base operator, air taxi, and commuter airline industry. The Association works to provide its member companies with

effective national representation; to maintain timely, accurate communications with member companies; to advance the professional skills of individuals in member companies and thus promote their financial growth; and to identify and offer needed economic benefits to member companies.

NATIONAL ASSOCIATION OF PURCHASING MANAGEMENT (NAPM)
P.O. Box 418
496 Kinder Kamack Rd.
Oradell, NJ 07649
201-967-8585
This Association includes purchasing managers and buyers for industrial, commercial, and utility firms, educational institutions, and government agencies. Issues reports on market conditions and trends, disseminates information on procurement, and works to develop more efficient purchasing methods.

NATIONAL ASSOCIATION OF RAILROAD PASSENGERS
236 Massachusetts Ave., N.E.
Suite 603
Washington, DC 20002
202-546-1550
NARP, a nonprofit, nonpartisan consumer organization, works for improving the quality and quantity of rail passenger service in the United States, especially AMTRAK; increased public awareness of benefits of such service; equitable public policies toward all modes of transportation; and a national transportation policy that recognizes the importance of passenger trains.

NATIONAL ASSOCIATION OF REGULATORY UTILITY COMMISSIONERS
1102 Interstate Commerce Commission Building
Constitution Avenue and Twelfth Street, N.W.
P.O. Box 684
Washington, DC 20044
202-898-2200
The National Association of Regulatory Utility Commissioners (NARUC) is a quasi-governmental nonprofit organization composed of governmental agencies engaged in the regulation of public utilities and carriers. Its primary mission is to serve the consumer interest by seeking to improve the quality and effectiveness of public regulation in America.

NATIONAL ASSOCIATION OF SPECIALIZED CARRIERS, INC.
P.O. Box 1228
390 Roswell St.
Marietta, GA 30061
404-428-4433
The National Association of Specialized Carriers, Inc. acts as a research, commercial, and trade organization for motor vehicle common carriers. The association makes recommendations concerning rates, charges, and rules.

NATIONAL AVIATION CLUB
1745 Jefferson Davis Highway
Suite 308
Arlington, VA 22202
703-521-1991
The objectives of the club will be the development and advancement of aviation and the maintenance on a nonprofit basis of a common meeting place in
the national capitol where, with a minimum of formality, representatives of
all phases of aviation and aerospace may come to know each other. The club
will from time to time provide suitable recognition and due honor to individuals and organizations who have contributed to the advancement of aviation
and aerospace.

NATIONAL DEFENSE TRANSPORTATION ASSOCIATION
727 N. Washington St., Suite 200
Alexandria, VA 22314–1976
703-836-3303
NDTA represents 10,000 transportation professionals from all modes of the
industry, from the Armed Forces, and from government. Located in 10 countries, NDTA chapters are actively working for the Association's objectives in
more than 75 communities and key transportation hubs throughout the world.
Objective is a strong defense undergirded by a healthy, adequate transportation industry.

NATIONAL INDUSTRIAL TRANSPORTATION LEAGUE
Suite 410
1090 Vermont Avenue, N.W.
Washington, DC 20005
202-842-3870
The National Industrial Transportation League, an association based in Washington, DC, represents the nation's shippers and receivers. It is the major ad-
vocate for business and industry on federal transportation matters and is dedicated to assisting industry professionals in improving productivity and
effectiveness in their transportation operations.

NATIONAL MARITIME COUNCIL
1748 N. Street, N.W.
Washington, DC 20036
202-785-3754
The council is a nonprofit trade association headquartered in Washington, DC,
representing maritime labor, U.S.–flag liner carriers, and approximately 200
shippers. The NMC serves as a forum for discussing maritime issues of mutual
concern to these three groups and seeking consensus for the common good
of all NMC members. The council has committed itself to promoting a competitive U.S.–flag merchant fleet, creating more maritime jobs for U.S. citizens,
and expanding U.S. international commerce.

NATIONAL SAFETY COUNCIL
444 North Michigan Avenue
Chicago, IL 60611
312-527-4800
The National Safety Council is a nongovernmental, membership, public service organization devoted solely to saving lives, time, and money through the prevention of accidents and occupational illnesses. More than 12,000 businesses, public agencies, schools, and private individuals are members. This membership represents a work force of 30 million people.

NORTH AMERICAN TRACKLESS TROLLEY ASSOCIATION
2125 Bashford Manor Lane
Louisville, KY 40218
502-459-5261
NATTA is a nonprofit group established to document current events relative to the trolleybus in North America, and to a lesser degree current events worldwide on the trolleybus. When time and space in its newsletter, *Trolley Coach News,* are available, NATTA also reports news on other forms of electrically propelled urban transit such as AGT, People Movers, Streetcars/LRV, and Battery buses.

PIPE LINE CONTRACTORS ASSOCIATION
4100 First City Center
1700 Pacific Ave.
Dallas, TX 75201
214-969-2700
The Pipe Line Contractors Association is a national trade association concerned with maintaining high standards in the pipe line contracting business, promoting cooperative relations among contractors and those they deal with, encouraging efficiency, correcting unfair business practices, and fostering employee safety.

PRIVATE TRUCK COUNCIL OF AMERICA, INC.
2022 P Street, N.W.
Washington, DC 20036
202-785-4900
The Private Truck Council of America, Inc. is a nonprofit national association representing companies that operate trucks in furtherance of a primary commercial enterprise other than for-hire transportation. Among its purposes are the fostering and promotion of safe and economic use of transportation by industry in private motor vehicles and the cooperation with other organizations and groups having similar objectives.

RAILWAY PROGRESS INSTITUTE
700 N. Fairfax St.
Alexandria, VA 22314
703-836-2332

The Railway Progress Institute, the national association of the railway and rail rapid transit equipment and supply industry, serves as the lobbying and public relations arm of that industry. RPI was organized to study cooperatively matters of interest to the railway supply industry and to promote the welfare of the railroad industry.

RECREATION VEHICLE INDUSTRY ASSOCIATION
1896 Preston White Drive
Box 2999
Reston, VA 22090
703-620-6003
RVIA is the national association for manufacturers and component parts suppliers of motor homes, travel trailers, truck campers, folding camper trailers, park trailers, and van conversions. It provides all elements of the industry with a single, active base from which to communicate with legislators, various federal and state government departments and agencies, the financial community, allied industries, the media, and the general public.

REGIONAL AIRLINE ASSOCIATION
Suite 700
1101 Connecticut Ave., N.W.
Washington, DC 20036
202-857-1170
Formed in 1968 from the merger of the Association of Commuter Airlines and the National Air Taxi Conference. Assumed its present name in 1981. Represents regional or commuter operations; those airlines whose planes carry 60 or fewer passengers. Members consist of more than 100 carriers and their associates and affiliates. Sponsors the Commuter Airline Political Action Committee.

REGIONAL AND DISTRIBUTION CARRIERS CONFERENCE, INC.
2200 Mill Road
Alexandria, VA 22314
703-838-1990
The objectives of this motor carrier conference are as follows: to foster and promote the interests of its members; to encourage and advance the spirit of unity and friendship among its members; to secure freedom from unjust or unlawful exactions; to acquire, preserve, and disseminate valuable business information; and to do anything necessary that may be recognized as proper and lawful objectives.

SHIPBUILDERS COUNCIL OF AMERICA
1110 Vermont Avenue, N.W.
Washington, DC 20005
202-775-9060
Originated in 1920, the Shipbuilders Council of America is a voluntary, non-

profit, national trade association composed of principal domestic shipbuilders, ship repairers, and providers of shipyard equipment and services. The council's primary purpose is to promote the maintenance of a sound, privately owned, commercially operated shipbuilding and ship repairing industry in the United States.

SHIPPERS NATIONAL FREIGHT CLAIM COUNCIL, INC.
120 Main Street (Box Z)
Huntington, NY 11743
516-549-8984
The Shippers National Freight Claim Council, Inc., is a nonprofit, tax-exempt association whose principal objectives are to improve freight claims practices, procedures, and governmental regulations of such matters.

SLURRY TECHNOLOGY ASSOCIATION
Suite 300
1800 Connecticut Avenue, N.W.
Washington, DC 20009
202-332-5751
STA committees and staff work with other organizations to advance slurry transportation industry objectives and interests, including establishment of codes and standards, enactment of laws and regulations, and development of positive public policy and attitudes.

SOARING SOCIETY OF AMERICA
Box 66071
Los Angeles, CA 90066
213-390-4447
The Soaring Society of America acts as a central information source for people interested in familiarizing themselves with the sport of gliding. Membership in the society provides many special services and benefits, including the informative monthly publication, *Soaring*, and professional representation and liaison with governmental agencies to preserve airspace rights and flying privileges for soaring pilots.

SOUTHERN SHIPPER AND MOTOR CARRIER COUNCIL
P.O. Box 7219, Station C
Atlanta, GA 30357
404-898-2260
The Southern Shipper and Motor Carrier Council's purpose is to promote adequate transportation by motor common carriers to, from, and within the southern region; to interchange ideas and disseminate information concerning transportation matters; to develop and promote more efficient and economical motor common carrier transportation; and to promote cordial relations between shippers and motor common carriers.

TRANSPORTATION CLUBS INTERNATIONAL
1040 Woodcock Road
Orlando, FL 32803
305-894-8312
Transportation Clubs International (TCI) is a more than a half-century-old non-profit association comprised of hundreds of affiliated men's and women's Traffic and Transportation Clubs in the United States, Canada, and Mexico. TCI has as its primary objective the forceful articulation of the vital role played by transportation and distribution in the economic structure. A second objective, equally important, is to provide meaningful and practical assistance to each affiliated club, at the local level, as these organizations strive to implement their individual goals.

TRANSPORTATION DATA COORDINATING COMMITTEE
Suite 712
1101 17th Street, N.W.
Washington, DC 20036–4775
202-293-5514
The mission of TDCC is oriented toward the productivity improvement of business systems through the application of computer/communications technology, using the latest business data standards and message formatting techniques. Its role is that of a coordinator among product and service groups that seek the capability to substitute electronic transmission for paper documentation transactions.

TRANSPORTATION INSTITUTE
923 15th Street, N.W.
Washington, DC 20005
202-347-2590
Founded in 1968, the Transportation Institute is a nonprofit organization composed of 174 companies engaged in commercial maritime activity. The Institute disseminates information to the public and promotes better communication among shipping management, labor, government, and the media. It conducts research and educational programs on a broad range of waterborne transportation issues.

TRANSPORTATION RESEARCH BOARD
National Research Council
2101 Constitution Avenue, N.W.
Washington, DC 20418
The purpose of the Board is to advance knowledge of the nature and performance of transportation systems through the stimulation of research and dissemination of information. The scope of the Board's activities covers all factors pertinent to transportation systems: planning, design, construction, operation,

maintenance, safety, economics, financing, administration, law, and interactions with social and natural environments.

TRANSPORTATION RESEARCH FORUM
1133 15th St., N.W.
Suite 620
Washington, DC 20005
202-293-5910
The Transportation Research Forum is a joint endeavor of interested people in academic life, government service, business logistics, and the various modes of transportation. Its purpose is to provide a forum for the discussion of ideas and research techniques applicable to economic, management, and public policy problems involving transportation.

TRAVEL INDUSTRY ASSOCIATION OF AMERICA
1899 L Street, N.W.
Suite 600
Washington, DC 20036
202-293-1433
The Travel Industry Association of America's objectives are to promote and facilitate travel to and within the United States, to promote a wider understanding of travel as a major U.S. industry, to encourage reciprocal travel between nations and oppose any restrictions on such travel, and to represent the travel industry in issues before the federal government.

WATERWAYS FREIGHT BUREAU
11720 Briggs Court
Fairfax, VA 22030
703-385-8877
A ratemaking organization established under the Interstate Commerce Act to regulate barge traffic on the Mississippi River and Gulf Intercoastal Waterway Systems.

WOMEN'S TRANSPORTATION SEMINAR
Box 7753
Ben Franklin Station
Washington, DC 20044
703-256-5258
A professional society of women in transportation founded at the Union Station in Washington, DC, as a means of personal advancement and professional recognition.

GOVERNMENTAL AGENCIES/ORGANIZATIONS/OFFICES

ARMY CORPS OF ENGINEERS
Department of the Army
The Pentagon
Washington, DC 20310
202-693-6456

DEPARTMENT OF COMMERCE
14th Street Between Constitution Avenue and E. St., N.W.
Washington, DC 20230
202-377-2000

DEPARTMENT OF ENERGY
James Forrestal Building
1000 Independence Avenue, S.W.
Washington, DC 20585
202-252-5000

DEPARTMENT OF TRANSPORTATION
400 7th Street, S.W.
Washington, DC 20590
202-366-4000

FEDERAL AVIATION ADMINISTRATION
800 Independence Ave., S.W.
Washington, DC 20591
202-366-4000

FEDERAL ENERGY REGULATORY COMMISSION
825 N. Capitol Street, N.E.
Washington, DC
202-357-5200

FEDERAL HIGHWAY ADMINISTRATION
400 7th Street, S.W.
Washington, DC 20590
202-426-0677

FEDERAL MARITIME COMMISSION
1100 L Street, N.W.
Washington, DC 20573
202-523-5707

NOTE: For functions of governmental agencies/organizations/offices, see Chapter 4 of the text.

FEDERAL RAILROAD ADMINISTRATION
400 7th Street, S.W.
Washington, DC 20590
202-426-0881

INTERSTATE COMMERCE COMMISSION
12th Street and Constitution Avenue, N.W.
Washington, DC 20423
202-377-2000

MARITIME ADMINISTRATION
400 7th Street, S.W.
Washington, DC 20590
202-426-5812

NATIONAL HIGHWAY TRAFFIC SAFETY ADMINISTRATION
400 7th Street, S.W.
Washington, DC 20590
202-426-1828

OFFICE OF THE PRESIDENT
1600 Pennsylvania Avenue, N.W.
Washington, D.C. 20500
202-456-1414

SAINT LAWRENCE SEAWAY DEVELOPMENT CORPORATION
800 Independence Avenue, S.W.
Washington, DC 20591
202-426-3574

U.S. HOUSE OF REPRESENTATIVES
AVIATION SUBCOMMITTEE
The Capitol
Washington, DC 20515
202-225-9161

U.S. HOUSE OF REPRESENTATIVES
PUBLIC WORKS AND TRANSPORTATION COMMITTEE
The Capitol
Washington, DC 20515
202-225-4472

U.S. HOUSE OF REPRESENTATIVES
SURFACE TRANSPORTATION SUBCOMMITTEE
The Capitol
Washington, DC 20515
202-225-4472

U.S. SENATE
AVIATION SUBCOMMITTEE
The Capitol
.`shington, DC 20510
202-224-4852

U.S. SENATE
COMMERCE, SCIENCE, AND TRANSPORTATION COMMITTEE
The Capitol
Washington, DC 20510
202-224-5115

U.S. SENATE
MERCHANT MARINE SUBCOMMITTEE
The Capitol
Washington, DC 20510
202-224-4852

U.S. SENATE
SURFACE TRANSPORTATION SUBCOMMITTEE
The Capitol
Washington, DC 20510
202-224-4852

U.S. TRAVEL AND TOURISM ADMINISTRATION
Department of Commerce
Washington, DC 20230
202-377-3811

URBAN MASS TRANSPORTATION ADMINISTRATION
400 7th Street, S.W.
Washington, DC 20590
202-426-4043

Glossary

Acquisition The purchase of one firm by another

Aggregate demand The total demand for transportation services by all modes of transportation

Agricultural cooperative A form of shippers' association catering to agricultural (farming) interests that consolidates small shipments for its members to gain volume rate savings

Air freight forwarder An intermediary that solicits shipments and tenders consolidated loads to airlines

Air taxi operator An exempt air carrier flying people, property, or mail or any combination of these items and operating no aircraft with more than 60 passenger seats or carrying more than 18,000 lbs. of payload

Air traffic hub A city or Standard Metropolitan Statistical Area generating a high level of airline passenger traffic

Aircraft broker An intermediary who arranges a sale of an airplane between an aircraft owner and a buyer

Airways The airspace used by air carriers to connect origin and destination airports

All-cargo aircraft Airplanes that contain no passenger seats and configured for maximum cargo payloads (weight or cubic capacity); also called freighters

All-cargo carrier An airline that hauls either property only or both property and mail

AMTRAK The National Railroad Passenger Corporation that runs the country's intercity passenger train service

Arbitrary A form of additional pay for transportation workers, such as "lonesome" pay for a railroad engineer who operates a train without a fireman

Articulated train A train whose cars are permanently, or almost always, attached to one another; usually the truck that holds the two axles is positioned between two cars with one axle under the rear of the first car and the other under the front of the second car

Attrition The process whereby employees retire, resign, or die, and their positions are not refilled

Backhaul The portion of a transportation trip that returns carrier equipment to the origin point; the secondary haul

---

Note: Although there are other acceptable definitions for many of these terms, this glossary contains generally accepted definitions.

Bareboat charter   A ship lease that turns over the ship and full responsibility for its operation to the charterer (the person desiring the ship's use)

Barge (river)   A nonself-propelled shallow draft vessel

Bilateral air transport agreement   A document whose terms are sanctioned by two nations

Bill of lading   A shipping document that acts as a contract, a receipt, and evidence of title (ownership)

Binding arbitration   A process whereby labor–management disputes are given over to arbitrators (outside specialists) so that impasses can be resolved

Block time   The period from the moment an airplane's blocks (wedges placed before and behind the wheels to prevent movement) are removed until they are once again placed around the wheels at destination

Breakbulk freighter   A vessel carrying loose, noncontainerized cargo, such as boxes of manufactured goods or pallet loads

Breakbulk trucking terminal   A facility that receives loads from local, other breakbulk, and relay terminals and sorts the cargo for shipment to further points

Bridge line   A carrier that links two linehaul carriers

Broker (trucking)   An intermediary who tries to match trucking companies desiring traffic with shippers needing trucking services

Budget   A predetermined spending target

Cabotage   A policy that requires that domestic waterborne commerce be hauled in U.S.–owned, U.S.–registered, U.S.–built, and U.S.–crewed vessels

Capital   Money invested in assets such as equipment, facilities, and inventory; also, the sum of stock and long-term debt

Capital budgeting   The process of deciding what capital (fixed asset) projects to fund

Capital grants   Subsidies in the form of free land, equipment, or facilities or cash to acquire the same; subsidies for fixed assets

Capital intensive strategy   Plans calling for an investment in fixed assets versus a commitment to labor; the substitution of machines for labor

Capitalism   An economic system in which private citizens seek to earn profits as rewards for risking their money in business investments

Car pooling   Putting multiple riders in an automobile

Cargo preference rules   Rules that favor ships registered in a country for moving traffic to, from, or between ports in that country

Carrier   A supplier of transportation services, i.e., an operator in one of the five modes

Cash throw   After-tax income plus depreciation

Certificate of public convenience and necessity   A document given to a common carrier that gives it the right to provide and sell transportation services

Certificated airline   A Section 401 or Section 418 air carrier holding a federal certificate of public convenience and necessity authorizing operations of large aircraft

Charter airline   A nonscheduled airline (supplemental carrier) that keys aircraft departures to full plane loads of passengers or cargo

Charter bus services   Special trip (nonregular route) bus services planned by someone other than a bus line (e.g., by a travel agent, broker, school, or team)

Charter party   A contract between a shipowner and a charterer (the customer)

Circuitous route   An indirect path that adds extra miles to the journey

Civil aviation   Nonpublic (nongovernment) private sector airplane operations

Class 1 bus carrier   An intercity bus company with annual revenues of $3 million or more

Class I railroad   A carrier with annual sales in 1984 exceeding $87.3 million

Class rate   A shipping charge determined from ratings, rate base numbers, and weight and available for every item shipped by common carrier railroad or trucking companies

Classification   A book of rules, ratings, and regulations

Classification yard   A railroad facility where railroad cars are blocked (sorted) into groups going to common destinations

Coal slurry pipeline   A pipeline that transports pulverized coal suspended in a liquid

Coastwise trade   Waterborne commerce within the Atlantic, Gulf of Mexico, and Pacific coasts, as well as trade between the Great Lakes, Atlantic, and Gulf of Mexico coasts

COLA   An automatic cost-of-living allowance pegging pay increases to changes in the Consumer Price Index

Collective ratemaking   The situation in which a group of carriers meet, discuss, and vote on rates

Collier   A coal-hauling ship

Combination carrier   An air carrier that hauls people, baggage, cargo, and mail or people and any combination of the three commodities

Combinations   Mergers and acquisitions

Commercial aviation   The for-hire civil aviation industry

Commercial zone   An ICC-defined geographic area that contains most of a city's industrial/commercial economic activities

Commodity rate   A special rate on a specific commodity between specific points, often in only one direction

Common carrier   A for-hire carrier that promises to serve the general public and that needs to obtain a certificate of public convenience and necessity requiring that it charge reasonable rates, avoid undue or unjust discrimination, serve the public, and deliver the goods

Common costs   Variable or fixed expenses that result when various forms of traffic benefit from the same company expenditures

Common law   A legal finding long accepted as correct and whose origin comes from decisions by judges rather than from written statutes

Commuter airline   A scheduled Part 298 aircraft operator that hauls passengers and cargo at the rate of at least five round trips per week on at least one route between two or more points and according to published flight schedules

Commuter railroad   Urban passenger train service over "main-line" type railroad rights-of-way and using locomotive-hauled or self-propelled railroad passenger cars

Conference (shipping)   A group of liner (common carrier) operators who are exempt from U.S. antitrust laws and who meet, discuss, and agree on rates and other trade matters

Consequential damages   Costs related not to physical loss or damage to a shipped item but to external consequences due to problems with the shipment (e.g., missing a contract bidding deadline because the envelope carrying the bid was temporarily delayed in transit)

Consignee   The person receiving a shipment at the destination

Consignor   The person doing the shipping at the origin point

Consolidation (financial)   A merger of two or more corporations by dissolving old corporations and creating a single new one

Consolidation (traffic)   The collection of small units into volume shipments

Construction differential subsidy (CDS)   Grants that used to pay for up to 50% of the cost of a ship purchased from a domestic shipyard

Containership   A ship that carries large boxes (truck trailers without the chassis) loaded with cargo

Contract carriage   Transport services available to a user who agrees to terms specified in a legal agreement (contract) between the carrier and shipper

Contract motor carrier of property   A person who provides motor vehicle transportation for compensation under continuing agreements with one or more people by assigning motor vehicles for a continuing period of time for his or her customers' exclusive use or providing equipment designed to meet the distinct needs of such people.

Contract operators   Owner-operators and fleet operators (individuals who own more than one truck and hire drivers) who as lessors lease their rigs and drivers to trucking companies such as heavy haulers

Cost of service pricing   A theory that sets prices at levels covering variable costs, a proportionate and fair share of the firm's fixed costs, and a reasonable profit margin; synonyms are cost-based pricing or fully distributed cost pricing

Crew consist   The names and job descriptions of the members of a train crew

Crude oil pipeline   An oil pipeline hauling unrefined petroleum

Cruise line   A shipping company that operates floating resort hotels voyaging to scenic ports of call

Cryogenic tank   A highly insulated storage facility designed to prevent heat exchange and vaporization (a thermal tank)

Cube out   A situation in which a vehicle's cubic (space) capacity is totally used

Customshouse broker   A businessperson who helps shippers clear the regulation, paperwork, and taxing barriers of importing countries

De facto deregulation   A lessening of the economic regulations by commissioners who take great liberty in interpreting their powers; deregulation of transportation modes prior to the passage of deregulation laws

Deadhead   An empty backhaul; shuttling an empty vehicle to a point where a load is available

Deadweight ton (DWT)   A metric ton of cargo, fuel, water and/or supplies that can be loaded on a ship

Demand-activated transportation   Unscheduled services provided in ways that honor the customized needs of users, e.g., taxi service, charter services, and contract carriage

Demurrage   A charge levied by a railroad on a shipper for holding railroad cars beyond an acceptable loading or unloading time

Depreciation   A way of retaining earnings in a firm to set aside resources for the eventual day when obsolete or worn out assets must be replaced

Deregulation   See "regulatory reform"

Derived demand   A term referring to the fact that the demand (need) for transportation services is based on the need for goods or other services (e.g., New York residents want fresh oranges creating a demand for railroad transportation to deliver the fruit); transportation as a means to an end and not the end itself

Detention   Charges levied by truckers on shippers who unnecessarily delay equipment during loading or unloading

Differentiated product or service   A unique, not-easily-substituted-for item that may be able to command higher prices than competing products or services

Diversification   The control of a nontransportation company by a carrier or vice versa

Domestic air transportation   Interstate, overseas, or intrastate air commerce

Domestic transportation   A movement in which both the origin and destination are points in the United States or in its territories

Door-to-door speed   Total time from the origin point (a home, business, institution, etc.) to destination including transportation time frames and time for access to and egress from transportation facilities (e.g., to and from an airport)

Double locking   An inland waterway term meaning the splitting of an integrated tow into two groups of barges to pass through a lock

Double-bottom rig   A truck tractor pulling two trailers

Draft (draught)   A measure of the extent that a vessel can be loaded before its keel risks striking bottom or the vessel becomes dangerously low in the water; the vertical distance from the water's surface to the lowest point on a vessel

Dry bulk ship   A vessel that carries unpackaged dry cargo (like grain) in its holds (storage compartments)

Dry bulk trade   The business of hauling grain, minerals, and other high volume dry solids by ship

Dual authority   The right of a federally regulated trucking company to be both a common carrier and a contract carrier

Dunnage   Wood or other materials used to prevent cargo from shifting in a vehicle

Economic regulation   Rules governing carrier entry, expansion, abandonment, exit, rates, mergers, accounting practices, and ownership rights

Economies of scale   The reduction in long-run average costs as the size (scale) of the company increases

Egress   The act of leaving a place; departing from a location

Embargo   A denial of entry or departure of freight, particularly in foreign trade, and usually because of complicated circumstances such as an act of war

Eminent domain   The government-granted power to a carrier that enables it to obtain property rights-of-way by buying property or by acquiring easements despite land-owner opposition

End-to-end merger   A merger in which transportation carriers' networks connect at common points, but these carriers formerly did not compete extensively against one another

Enplaned airline revenue passenger   A paying passenger boarding certificated major, national, and regional air carriers' aircraft, including originating, stopover, and transfer passengers

Exception rate   A discount from a class rate and usually in effect because of unusual competition or the need of a carrier to retain or attract traffic volume

Excess capacity   Unused carrier cubic or weight-hauling capabilities

Exempt carrier   One that is free from economic regulation

FEU   A 40-ft-long-equivalent container unit usually measuring 8 ft high by 8 ft wide

Fixed costs   Costs that do not vary with the level of traffic (output)

Flag-of-convenience registry   Registration of a ship in a nation other than in the owner's country and for the purposes of flexibility and/or economic benefits; registry in a country whose ports an owner may never or seldom send ships to

Flat rate   A uniform charge that does not vary for longer or shorter distances

Fleeting operations   The separation of inland waterway barges from integrated tows, collection of individual barges for common destinations, and the reattachment to other integrated tows

For-hire carrier   A transportation company that is paid by a user for its services

Foreign air commerce   Flights connecting the United States, its territories, or possessions with places outside the United States, its territories, or its possessions; or flights connecting two non-U.S. points

Foreign airline   Air carriage by non-U.S. citizens whose aircraft are registered in another country

Free time   Time provided at no charge to a shipper for the purpose of loading or unloading a carrier's vehicle

Freight-all-kinds A pricing scheme in which the carrier charges a shipper for a container movement regardless of the mix of commodities contained therein

Freighter A multipurpose general cargo ship or an all-cargo aircraft

Full accessibility A federal policy directed at ensuring that elderly and handicapped people can effectively use public mass transit

Fully distributed cost pricing (See "cost of service pricing")

Funds management A financial analysis tool concerned with cash inflows and cash outflows that businesses use to collect quickly sums due and pay bills slowly so that cash can be accumulated for short-term investments

Furlough A term describing the laying off of workers

Gateway airport An airport from which international airlines depart to foreign countries or that serves flights arriving from other nations

Gathering line A pipeline that collects oil from wells and feeds the larger volume trunk lines

General aviation Personal and corporate not-for-hire air transportation

General cargo Manufactured and packaged goods, as opposed to unpackaged liquid bulk or dry bulk items

General commodities Nonspecialized commodities hauled by truckers such as boxed, bagged, or containerized items; items suitable for haulage in vans (covered trailers)

General rate increase An across-the-board percentage price markup on generally all commodities carried and by all carriers

Geographic specialization The process by which a region does what it does best

Grade crossing A point at which a road crosses railroad tracks at the same grade elevation

Grandfather rights Permission for a carrier to continue performing transportation operations that it had done before new rules were passed denying to other firms the right to do the same thing

Gross register ton (GRT) A measure of total capacity of a ship, minus the motor compartment, fuel tanks, crew's quarters, etc., with a GRT equal to 100 cubic feet

High-density seating The act of placing more seats on each aircraft

Holding company An organization usually created for tax and other financial reasons that sets up a hierarchy of control over a number of subsidiaries in or outside of transportation

Household goods agent A local moving company that books shipments and provides local pick-up and/or delivery service of personal property and that acts on behalf of an interstate moving company

Hub airport A classification of an airport on the basis of its enplaned passengers as a percentage of the national total, e.g., a large hub airport enplanes 1.00% or more

Hub and spoke operation Utilization of an airport as a central collector and dispatcher of traffic emanating from several radial feeder routes that reach out to short-haul and other passenger markets

Human resource management The recruiting, training, assigning, motivating, and managing of people

Independent action The right of a rate bureau member to ignore the decision of the rate bureau and pursue its own course of action to change a rate

Independent oil shipper People shipping oil in pipelines they do not own

Independent shipping company A water carrier that offers regularly scheduled regular route service, but is not a member of a shipping conference.

Independent shipowner Someone who owns and charters ships

Indirect air carrier An air freight forwarder or a shippers' association

Industry concentration The extent that an industry is dominated by the largest firms

Inland waterways Navigable rivers and canals capable of handling commerce

Intercity transportation A movement between one city and another city

Intercoastal trade Shipments in interstate commerce of the United States moving between ports on different U.S. coasts by way of the Panama Canal

Intercorporate hauling The right of one subsidiary of a firm to haul by truck on a compensated basis freight owned by any 100%-owned corporate family member

Interline Through services whereby passengers or cargo are transferred between two or more carriers

Intermodal competition Competition between

different modes, such as between a railroad and a water carrier

Intermodal movement A transportation movement that involves two or more modes (such as a piggyback movement)

Intermodal ownership The combination of two or more transport firms of different modes under one company's control

Intermodal ship A vessel that carries vehicles of other modes, such as truck trailers, containers, and barges

International air commerce Flights carrying passengers and/or cargo between different nations

International freight forwarder A company that solicits freight, consolidates shipments, and arranges for landside and ocean-going transportation for shippers

International transportation Movements in which either the origin or destination is in the United States or in its territories and possessions and the other point is in another country or both points are outside the United States or its territories and possessions

Interplanetary space transportation A movement through space between earth and other planets

Interstate transportation Movement from one state to another (Washington, D.C. is treated like a state)

Intramodal combination The merger of two or more companies of a single mode or the acquisition of one company in a mode by another of the same mode

Intramodal competition Competition between firms in the same mode, e.g., railroad versus railroad

Intraplanetary space transportation A movement in space around the earth

Intrastate transportation A movement between two points in the same state

Inventory carrying costs The costs of capital, property taxes, cargo insurance, product deterioration, obsolescence, and damage or loss resulting from holding goods

Inventory control The management of raw materials, parts, and finished products

Inventory ordering costs Clerical costs, supplies, order transmission charges, and overhead costs associated with processing a shipment order request

Irregular route common carrier A trucking company with broad operating authority not fixing services to specific, required routes; an example is authority to serve any point in Ohio connecting with any point in Iowa

Job security contract provisions Terms in union contracts designed to protect workers from becoming unemployed

Joint rate A single price for a movement by two or more carriers

Knot A nautical mile (6076 ft) per hour or the equivalent of about 1.15 miles per hour

Labor-intensive strategy A strategy favoring people, rather than machines

Laker A vessel that carries iron ore and other dry bulk minerals in the Great Lakes trade

Land-bridge An intermodal movement across the contiguous United States with a former and subsequent ocean shipment

Large regional carrier A certificated airline with annual revenues in the range of $10 million to $99,999,999

Large-scale production Production that encourages long production runs and creates economies of scale

LASH ship A vessel carrying nonself-propelled barges

Leadership Accomplishing tasks done through people

Leisure transportation vehicles Boats, aircraft, motorcycles, RVs, snowmobiles, bicycles, and pickup trucks used for recreational purposes

Leveraged carrier One with high debt

Lightering The process by which a deep-draft vessel has some of its cargo taken off in deep water to permit the vessel's entry into a port

Light rail system A rapid transit system using streetcar-type mass transit vehicles that operate on rails on city streets or on exclusive rights-of-way (e.g., in a subway tunnel)

Linehaul operation The long distance portion of transportation haulage

Linehaul railroad A railroad that hauls freight over long distances

Liner A regularly scheduled ship serving designated ports along a defined trade route system

Liquefied natural gas (LNG) ship A vessel that hauls natural gas in a liquefied state at 260 degrees below zero Fahrenheit

Liquidity A company's ability to meet current obligations due in less than one year

Load factor (airline passenger business) The ratio of revenue passenger-miles to available seat-miles

Local passenger bus services Regular route short-haul intercity bus services feeding commuters from outlying communities to larger urban centers

Local roads Streets used primarily for access to homes and land

Local service airline The former CAB designated short-haul, regional carriers that fed passengers to the trunk airlines

Local trucking terminal Usually a small facility that fills the roles of soliciting, collecting, and disbursing shipments and serves nearby customers

Lock A device that raises or lowers vessels from one water elevation (pool) to another

Logistics (physical distribution) The coordination of the physical movement aspects of a firm's operations so that a flow of raw materials, parts, and finished goods is achieved in such a way that total costs are minimized for the levels of service desired

Long ton A weight of 2240 lbs.

Long-term capital lease A long-term debt arrangement used to finance transportation equipment

Loop line A parallel pipeline constructed over the same right-of-way as an existing pipeline

Loss and damage Costs incurred when cargo cannot be found or is harmed while under the responsibility of a carrier

LTL A less-than-truckload shipment tendered to a general commodity trucker; either a small shipment, which does not fill a truck, or a shipment of not enough weight to qualify for a truckload (TL) quantify (usually set at about 10,000 lbs.) rate discount

Lumper An individual who loads or unloads trailers for a fee at warehouses, terminals, ports, and other facilities (like a produce market)

Maglev trains Magnetic levitation trains that float above the guideway suspended by electromagnets and that eventually could haul passengers at more than 300 miles per hour

Major carrier (airlines) A certificated airline with annual revenues of more than $1 billion

Management information system (MIS) The use of computers and electronic data processing to manage vital company communications and records

Manifest A list of passengers or shipments in a transport vehicle

Marine terminal A facility where water vessels take on and discharge cargo

Maritime trades Commerce conducted by ships on the high seas

Market competition Competition between two carriers serving the same origin but different destinations

Market dominance A situation in which a railroad (or, for that matter, a firm in another mode) serves a market absent in effective intramodal, intermodal, or other forms of competition

Market lane The route between one origin and one destination

Market penetration A pricing strategy that uses low prices to try to increase market and company demand and that is used frequently to convince customers to try a carrier's services for the first time

Market share The percentage of aggregate or modal demand or sales achieved by a company

Market skimming A pricing strategy in which carriers introduce services at high prices to attract enough demand to realize high short-term profits

Market target A consumer or industrial segment of high potential to which carrier marketers decide they will try to sell services

Marketing channels All those units, such as wholesalers, retailers, and customers, that act as an infrastructure to distribute goods from producer to consumer

Marketing concept The idea that says marketers need to ask what the customer wants and then try to satisfy those needs

Marketing mix A plan that takes into account product (services), price, promotion, and place (origin-destination network) considerations

Mass production The process by which goods are produced in long production runs and in high volume

Materials handling The management and control of all the equipment designed to aid warehouse workers in moving inventories within a single facility or between adjacent or nearby buildings

Materials management The collection of logistical efforts leading up to the point when a company's finished product is completed

Medium regional carrier A certificated airline either (1) with operating revenues of less than $10 million or (2) exclusively operating aircraft either with 60 seats or less or carrying no more than 18,000 lbs. of payload

Merchant marine Commercial vessels operating on the high seas

Merger A combination (consolidation) of two or more firms

Metric ton A weight of 2205 lbs.

Minimum tender The smallest shipment size that an oil pipeline will transport

Modal split market share The percentage of the market controlled by each mode

Mode One of the five homogeneous groups of carriers (railroads, water carriers, pipelines, highway carriers, or air carriers)

Monopolistic competition   A market structure in which there are many sellers and buyers, services are differentiated, and a price change by one carrier is not likely to have a major effect on prices of other competitors

Mothballed ship   An inactive ship in storage

Multiple ownership stock company   An oil pipeline that is built, owned, and operated by two or more parties but which acts as a single common carrier

National carrier   A certificated airline with annual revenues between $100 million and $1 billion

Net worth   The owners' wealth as measured by assets less liabilities

Network   The points (places) and routes served by a carrier

No-frills air service   Limited services at discount prices; basic air transportation without the normal level of preflight, inflight, and postflight services

Noncontiguous water shipment   A domestic ocean movement connecting a contiguous United States (48 states and Washington, D.C.) port with a port in Alaska, Hawaii, or any U.S. territory (noncontiguous points) or a movement between noncontiguous U.S. ports

Nondifferentiated product   An undistinguished item that is not likely to generate brand loyalty or command higher prices as it is easily substituted for

Noneconomic regulation   Carrier rules pertaining to such areas as safety, labor, operating, and environmental matters

Nonvessel operating common carrier (NVOCC)   A carrier that provides ocean shipping services without operating ships by performing pick-up and delivery services, container stuffing, export documentation, and cargo liability protection

OBO ship   A multipurpose vessel that can haul *ore*, other dry *bulk* cargo, and *oil*

Off-peak period   A nonbusy (low-demand) timeframe

Oligopoly   A market structure in which competition is limited to a few sellers and a small number of customers and in which a price or service change by one firm forces other carriers to respond

Operating deficit   A loss resulting when operating expenses exceed operating revenues

Operating differential subsidy (ODS)   Grants that cover differences between the costs of operating a U.S. flag vessel and the estimated costs of operating vessels under foreign registry

Operating expenses   The costs of handling traffic and generating operating revenues

Operating income   Operating revenues less operating expenses

Operating ratio   The ratio of operating expenses (before interest and taxes) to operating revenues

Operating revenues   Total money received by a carrier from transportation services and from operations incidental thereto; primarily, dollars paid by the system's users

Operating subsidies   Grants to cover deficits between operating revenues and operating expenses

Operations   The area of carrier management responsible for the physical movement of passengers and cargo

Opportunity costs   Alternative investment opportunities bypassed in favor of chosen projects

Order bill of lading   A bill of lading in which ownership of commercial cargo can change during transit

Order processing   The sum of all activities from the moment someone initiates a request for inventory through the receipt of the goods by the order initiator

Overseas air commerce   Any flight connecting a point in a state or the District of Columbia and a U.S. territory or possession, or, a flight between a U.S. territory or possession and another U.S. territory or possession

Owner-operator   A trucking operation in which the truck driver and truck owner are the same person

Part 298 airline   An exempt air taxi or commuter airline

Passenger-mile   One person traveling one mile, i.e., the product of people multiplied by the miles they travel

Passive restraint systems   Automatic seatbelts or airbags that require no human effort to engage them

Peak period   A busy (high demand) time frame

Per diem   A fee levied on railroads who use cars owned by other railroads

Permit   A document given to a contract motor carrier providing a license to operate

Physical distribution management   (See "logistics")

Piggyback   Trailers on railroad flat cars (TOFC) or containers on railroad flat cars (COFC)

Place utility Benefits derived when people or cargo arrive at the location they need to go to

Pool consolidators and distributors Agents who pick-up a series of pooled shipments, consolidate them, arrange for (or provide) linehaul services, and distribute goods at destination; their shipments generally are at least 5,000 lbs., but less than 10,000 lbs.

Pooling The allocation among carriers of traffic, revenues, profits, and other business items

Port A collection of marine terminals

Port authority A state or local governmental unit that plans, owns, and operates water terminals and other port facilities

Predatory pricing Rates or fares below variable costs that are interpreted to mean a company is trying to drive the competition out of business

Present value analysis A technique used to appraise capital acquisition opportunities that puts future cash inflows and outflows in today's money terms

Price competition The struggle to obtain a customer's business through an advantageous freight rate or passenger fare

Price elasticity of demand A measure of how price changes alter the quantity of services demanded and revenues, assuming all other variables are held constant

Primary demand Untapped potential

Primary highways The part of the Federal Aid Highway System comprised of rural arterials and their urban extensions into and through cities, including interstate highways

Private carrier A carrier that provides transportation services to the firm that owns or leases the vehicles and at no charge

Private transportation vehicle A conveyance, such as an automobile, used by the owner for his or her personal use or to provide not-for-hire (free) transportation for others

Procurement Responsibilities involved in locating and purchasing raw materials, parts, and components needed for production and consumption

Production scheduling Deciding which plants will produce what items in what quantities and at which points in time

Productivity Output per unit of input

Product pipeline An oil pipeline carrying refined (processed) oil

Profit center A subunit of a company held accountable for its management decisions and treated almost as though it were an independent company

Profitability The determination of the income levels of the firm

Property broker An intermediary involved in the general commodity sector of trucking trying to link together shippers and common or contract trucking carriers

Proration A procedure in which owners of an oil pipeline reduce their shipments to apportion space for independent oil shippers

Protective packaging Activities concerned with delivering goods to their destination in the same condition they departed the origin point, meeting required transportation packaging specifications, and controlling packaging costs

Public aircraft operations Not-for-hire government aircraft

Public sector transit Urban mass passenger transportation systems owned and/or operated by government units

Public warehouse A facility in which shippers can pay a warehouse operator to store their inventories and from which the inventories of several customers are eventually distributed; a for-hire facility versus a private warehouse used exclusively for the owner's inventories

Pup A term meaning one trailer of a double-bottom trucking rig

Purchased transportation The use of owner-operator or leased trucking equipment and drivers

Pure competition A market structure characterized by large numbers of sellers and buyers, virtually no industry concentration, virtually no service differentiation, total freedom for carriers to enter and exit markets, and perfect information

Pure monopoly A market structure in which there is no substitute for a carrier's services and no real threat from new carrier competition

Rapid transit Heavy rail or light rail urban mass transportation vehicles

Rate A charge per unit weight (such as 100 lbs.) per distance

Rate bureau An organization whose members are carriers and that hears, discusses, and votes on rate proposals and/or publishes tariffs

Rating A number that combines a group of commodities into a homogeneous class for pricing purposes

Ratio analysis The computation of company financial and traffic measures that can then be compared to norms, such as industry standards

Regular route common carrier A trucking company that follows a planned trip itinerary over fixed routes via predetermined stops

Regular route intercity bus service Passenger service characterized by fixed routes connecting urban centers that follow published schedules and published fares

Regulatory reform Refers to a lessening of federal transportation economic regulation (also called deregulation or reregulation)

Relay trucking terminal A facility used to expedite (receive and dispatch quickly) cargo movements and comply with driver rest requirements

Released value rates Discount prices offered to shippers who accept lower liability coverage

Reliability Ability of a carrier to meet its schedule; on-time performance

Reorder point The signal when to initiate stock replenishment orders

Reregulation (See "regulatory reform")

Restricted airline passenger discount fare A lower price than the regular fare but available only on certain flights and under certain conditions

Revenue split The division of sales dollars by the types of commodities hauled or by market segments

Revenues Gross sales dollars

Rights-of-way The path over which transportation vehicles move between origin and destination

Roll-on/roll-off (Ro-Ro) ship A vessel that can lower ramps to permit wheeled and mobile cargo to be driven aboard

Rule of ratemaking In general terms, a policy that says regulatory commissions (boards) should take into account, when setting rate levels, the earnings necessary for a carrier to provide adequate transportation

Sales Revenues collected from units of output sold

Scheduled operations Transport services following predetermined, announced departure times and planned arrival times

SEABEE ship A vessel that hauls nonself-propelled barges

Section 401 airline A certificated scheduled or charter carrier

Section 406 airline subsidy program A subsidy program paying airlines to serve small airport communities

Section 418 airline A certificated all-cargo airline

Section 419 airline subsidy program A program designed to guarantee essential air services

Segmenting Dividing the market into homogeneous groups of potential buyers

Selective pricing strategy Tactics whereby price changes are made in a limited number of markets, rather than across the board to all customers

Ship agency A shore-based organization that handles the needs of a ship in port, such as arranging for bunkering (fuel), supplies, and stevedore gangs and that solicits cargo on behalf of a ship operator

Ship broker An intermediary who works with shipowners and shippers in arranging charter parties

Shipper A transportation user who has cargo shipments to transport

Shippers' agent A person authorized to transact business for, and in the name of, the shipper, such as in the arrangement of transportation services

Shippers' association An intermediary that pools small shipments of its members only and tenders consolidated shipments to carriers; its purpose is to gain rate reductions from larger shipments

Short-line railroad A railroad with few miles of track that is a terminal and switching railroad, a bridge line, or an originating and/or terminating railroad

Short ton A weight of 2000 lbs.

Side-by-side merger The combination of parallel transportation carrier systems serving common points, the result of which could lead to a possibly substantial reduction in competition

Siding A piece of railroad track (1) auxiliary to the main lines of rights-of-way and that is used to let trains pass or (2) a track used to reach customer loading/unloading docks

Single-line rate A charge for local (one-carrier) service

Solvency Leverage or debt service, i.e., a company's ability to repay principal and interest payments on long-term loans

Special bus service Nonregular route bus services planned and sold by bus companies, such as a tour to a ski resort promoted by a bus company

Special commodity trucking Trucking requiring customized equipment and operations to meet unique customer needs

Statutory law Laws enacted by legislatures, i.e., bills passed by Congress and signed into law

Stockout A situation in which the number of units of an item ordered exceeds the number of units available in inventory

Straight bill of lading A bill of lading in which ownership of commercial cargo is not subject to change during transit

Strike A work-stoppage tactic used by labor to bargain for management concessions

Subsidy A cash grant or other financial aid that is not repaid by the beneficiary

Superlakers Landlocked ore boats too long to enter the Welland Canal locks and exit the Great Lakes; ships trapped in the Great Lakes by their size

Supertanker A large oil-carrying ship of 100,000 deadweight tons or more

Surface freight forwarder An intermediary who collects and consolidates small shipments to common destinations and tenders the consolidations to railroads, truckers, and water carriers (surface modes)

Take-or-pay contract An agreement signed by a natural gas transmission line and a gas producer obligating the former to accept a specified volume of natural gas or pay for a percentage of the gas whether the gas is delivered or not

Tanker A liquid bulk ship whose cargo is loaded directly into a ship's storage tanks (holds)

Tanker trade The business of hauling oil and other liquids by ship

Tapering rate A transportation charge that increases with distance but at a decreasing rate

Tariff A publication containing shipping charges (rates)

Tender The number of barrels of oil being shipped through an oil pipeline; the shipment size

Terminal and switching railroad A short-line railroad that tends to serve metropolitan areas transferring cars between connecting railroads and providing car pick-up and delivery service to shippers

Terminal manager The person responsible for the collection and distribution of passengers or cargo

TEU A 20-ft-long equivalent container unit typically 8 ft high by 8 ft wide

Throughput agreement A contract that obligates multiple ownership pipeline owners either to use or pay for a portion of an oil pipeline's capacity

Time charter A contract that secures the lease of a ship for a period of time, usually a year or more, but the responsibility for operating the ship remains with the ship owner

Time utility Benefits derived when people and cargo reach destinations when they need to be there

TL (truck load) Can mean either a full vehicle or in terms of rates, usually 10,000 lbs. or more of cargo

Ton-mile One ton of cargo moved one mile, i.e., the product of tons multiplied by the miles they are transported

Total cost concept The idea that logistical decisions that provide equal service levels should favor the option that minimizes the sum of all logistical costs and not be based on cost reductions in one area alone, such as lower transportation charges

Tow The combination of barges and towboats secured together in an integrated unit to act as a single vessel

Towboat A flat-bowed self-propelled vessel that is positioned behind barges and secured, and which then pushes an integrated tow forward

Tracing Locating shipments and obtaining shipment status information

Trackage agreement Rights whereby one railroad is allowed to operate trains over another railroad's rights-of-way for a fee or shared costs

Tractor-trailer A truck cab hooked to a separate trailer by a fifth wheel (a round hook-up unit)

Traffic The volumes of passengers and cargo transported

Traffic density The volumes of cargo or passengers moved between any two points

Traffic lane A route linking each origin and destination, e.g., between New York and Chicago

Traffic management The logistics function responsible for transportation decisions of the firm

Tramp ship An unscheduled ship plying the seas with supply and demand dictating ports, routes, and rates (a nonregular route carrier)

Transit authority A board of directors supervising a general manager of a public urban mass transportation system

Transit dependents People, such as handicapped, aged, or young persons, who must rely on for-hire urban mass transportation

Transit independents People able to provide their own urban transportation (e.g., car drivers)

Transmission line A large-diameter natural gas pipeline

Transportation The movement of people and cargo

Travel agent Someone who books and sells passenger tickets for a carrier and in return receives a commission from the carrier

Trunk airline The former CAB name for a large long-haul scheduled domestic air carrier

Trunk pipeline A large-diameter, long-haul pipeline

Tugboat A small, powerful vessel with a high pointed bow designed to pull barges and/or position ocean-going ships in harbors

Twin-trailer rig A truck tractor pulling two trailers

Two-tiered pay structure A situation in which newly hired employees are paid less than senior workers doing the same job

ULCC An ultra large crude (oil) carrier of 320,000 DWT or more

Undivided interest multiple ownership company An oil pipeline built, owned, and operated by two or more parties but whose owners act like competitors among themselves when trying to sell excess pipeline capacity

Unit train A dedicated set of locomotives and cars typically hauling one commodity from one origin to one destination bypassing freight yards

U.S. air carrier Any citizen of the United States who engages in air transportation and registers aircraft in the United States

U.S. flag ship A vessel registered in the United States and flying the U.S. flag (Stars and Stripes)

Unrestricted airline service Low-fare service not burdened by requirements specifying advanced ticket purchases, stays of a minimum number of days, round trip bookings, and/or departures on specified dates

Urban sprawl The exodus of city dwellers and businesses to the suburbs

Urban transportation A movement between any two points in a metropolitan area or in a particular city

User A passenger or cargo shipper

User charge A tax levied against those people or modes who directly benefit from a transportation system, such as a gasoline tax paid by automobile operators using the highway system

Value of service pricing A theory that sets prices according to what the traffic will bear; synonym—differential pricing

Van line A household goods agency system company that uses agents to book shipments

Van pooling Usually a company-backed program for picking up and transporting workers in a company-owned vehicle

Variable costs Costs that change with the level of output

VLCC A very large crude (oil) carrier (ship) of 160,000 DWT to less than 320,000 DWT

Voyage charter A one-trip, port-to-port ship contract, often called a spot lease

Weighting out Reaching the legal or safe maximum weight capacity of a vehicle

Wide-bodied aircraft An airplane capable of accommodating seven or more seats side-by-side

Work rules Labor contract provisions such as limits on the length of the work day, restrictions against the use of part-time labor, or craft jurisdictional rules (that specify which workers are allowed to perform what job tasks)

Working capital Current assets minus current liabilities

Yard A railroad facility where cars are received from inbound trains and local customers, classified (sorted), and dispatched as part of outbound trains

Yield Revenues per unit of output sold, such as cents per ton-mile or cents per passenger-mile

Zone of reasonableness A range of prices within which a carrier can independently set prices without prior regulatory commission approval

Index